TOTAL
AUTO
BODY
REPAIR

TOTAL AUTO BODY REPAIR

Second Edition

L. C. RHONE
H. DAVID YATES

Bobbs-Merrill Educational Publishing
Indianapolis

Copyright © 1983, 1976 by The Bobbs–Merrill Company, Inc.
Printed in the United States of America
All rights reserved. No part of this book shall be reproduced or transmitted in any
form or by any means, electronic or mechanical, including photocopying, recording,
or by any information or retrieval system, without written permission from the
Publisher:
The Bobbs–Merrill Company, Inc.
4300 West 62nd Street
Indianapolis, Indiana 46268
Second Edition
Second Printing—1984

Text and Cover Designer: Mike Benoit
Acquisitions Editor: Bob Palma, Greg Michael
Copy Editor: Jack Klasey
Production Editor: Sara Bernhardt

Library of Congress Cataloging in Publication Data

Rhone, L. C.
    Total auto body repair.

    Includes index.
    1. Automobiles—Bodies—Maintenance and repair.
I. Yates, H. David (Horace David), 1943-
II. Title.
TL255.R48 1983   629.2′6′0288   82-14782
ISBN 0-672-97967-5

Table of Contents

Preface

Total Auto Body Repair, Second Edition, has been extensively revised to make it one of the most comprehensive texts available on auto body repair and refinishing. It may be used as either a text or a reference book and will be a useful tool for schools, professional body shops, and individuals doing work on their own cars.

All areas of auto body and refinishing work are covered in this book, including techniques used in working with materials introduced since the First Edition was published in 1976. Included are complete discussions of major and minor metal straightening, filling, welding, brazing, and heat-shrinking. Repair of aluminum, galvanized metal, plastic, and fiberglass panels and body parts is well covered. Units on auto glass and trim work provide useful information in these important areas. Also included are comprehensive discussions of body panel adjustment and rust damage repair.

A very detailed section of the book is devoted to automotive refinishing. Paints, paint products, surface preparation, and painting techniques are covered, along with common paint problems and suggested solutions. Safety practices are emphasized throughout the book.

Body shop management is discussed in a three-unit section of this book. Such subjects as estimating, insurance work, shop management, and personnel are included to provide a genuine insight into the body shop as a business operation. Body shop tools and materials are thoroughly discussed and illustrated to introduce students to this vital area of knowledge.

Total Auto Body Repair, Second Edition, is arranged in seven sections, which contain a total of 28 units of material. If desired, sections may be used individually in an order that will match a given instructor's sequence of presenting various areas of body repair and refinishing. Taken in order and as a whole, however, this book provides a logical learning sequence for all areas of contemporary auto body shop operation and activity.

Acknowledgments

The information in *Total Auto Body Repair*, Second Edition, represents an effort to present the most complete text available concerning all aspects of auto body repair. The firms and individuals listed below contributed valuable time and materials for this text. The authors and the publisher sincerely appreciate their assistance.

Acme Automotive Finishes
American Optical Company
Autobody and The Reconditioned Car
Automatic Data Processing, Collision Estimating Services Division
Automotive Trades Division, 3M Company
Automotive Equipment Division, Lenco, Inc.
Automotive Systems Division, Chief Industries, Inc.
Bear Division of Applied Power Industries, Inc.
Binks Manufacturing Company
Blackhawk Division, Applied Power Industries, Inc.
Buske Industries, Inc.
Channellock, Inc.
Chrysler Motors Corporation
Clark, Mr. Howe K., Jr.
Customer Service Division, Ford Motor Company
DeVilbiss Company
Ditzler Automotive Finishes Division, PPG Industries, Inc.
Econo-Booth Industries, Inc.
Eutectic Corporation
Fibre Glass-Evercoat Co., Inc.
Fisher Body Division, General Motors Corporation
Grabber Manufacturing Company
Guy–Chart Sales, Inc.

Hand Tools Division, Litton Industrial Products, Inc.
Harris Calorific Division, Emerson Electric Company
Hobart Brothers Company
Hubbard, Mr. John M.
Hutchins Manufacturing Company
Ingersoll–Rand Company
Kansas Jack, Inc.
Lincoln Electric Company
Mac Tools, Inc.
Marson Corporation
The Martin–Senour Company
Mitchell Manuals, Inc.
National Automobile Dealers Used Car Guide Company
The Norton Company
Nevin, Mr. E. C.
Oatey Company
PPG Industries, Inc.
Plymouth Products Corporation
Prostripe Division, Spartan Plastics, Inc.
Pulmosan Safety Equipment Corporation
Refinish Division, DuPont Company
Reynolds Metals Company
Rinshed–Mason Products Division, Inmont Corporation
Road & Track Magazine
Seelye, Inc.
Snap-On Tools Corporation
Stanley Tools
Systematics, Inc.
Tech-Cor, Inc.
Tru-Way Company
The Unican Corporation
Union Carbide Canada, Ltd.
Victor Equipment Company

Section I

The Body Shop as a Modern Business

The Auto Body Shop Business

There are several types of auto body shops. Many are one department of a new-car dealership's service center, as shown in Figure 1-1. "Independent" body shops (Figs.1-2 and 1-3) come in a variety of sizes. Generally, the items needed for a successful body shop operation are the same for a new-car dealer's service center as they are for an independently owned shop.

The three main topics of this unit are: the shop's location, the building design, and the equipment that the shop owner should provide. These topics are discussed in detail to provide a better understanding of the body shop as a modern business.

LOCATING A BODY SHOP

There are several important reasons for considering the shop's location. The location should provide for good advertising, should be at least *near* an area where many late model cars are in use, and should provide room for automobile storage and parking. Future expansion should be considered, and the location should be one where the rent rates and taxes are reasonable.

Locating for Advertising

Of prime importance is a building that can be easily seen. This will allow signs, lights, and other advertisements to be seen by people who are passing by. Always keep the approach area neat and clean, both inside and out, as shown in Figure 1-4. Customers do not like to stop at a shop that is dirty and cluttered.

By giving attention to the building's appearance and location, these properties become the shop's own advertisement.

Fig. 1-1. *Body shops are often one department of a new-car dealership.*

Fig. 1-2. *A large independent body shop.*

3

Fig. 1-3. *A smaller independent body shop.*

Fig. 1-4. *An attractive shop with an easily identified entrance is a good advertisement for the business.*

Fig. 1-5. *The shop should have a parking area that allows room for future building expansion.*

Location for Vehicle Supply

A second consideration is the number and type of vehicles in the area. No one can operate a profitable body shop business without vehicles on which to work. Few body repair workers like to work on jalopies, since there is usually less profit and harder work involved in repairing these automobiles. Owners of many older-model cars will not spend the money needed to keep them in first-class condition.

For these reasons, a location in which people own good, late-model cars is necessary to operate a profitable, modern body shop.

Locating for Storage, Parking, and Expansion

The building lot should be big enough to provide space for storing wrecked vehicles. It should also provide plenty of parking space for both workers and customers.

When looking for a location, keep in mind that the building and lot should have plenty of room for easy expansion at a later date. A good parking lot with area for future expansion is shown in Figure 1-5. If a business is to grow, it must have room to expand. It is better to have the room from the beginning than to try to buy or add more later.

Locating for Rent and Taxes

The shop should be in an area where the rent and taxes are low enough that the owner can pay these bills and still make a reasonable profit. The final decision on location must strike a balance between advertising, customer access, rent, and tax rates. To run a shop successfully, the rent normally should not exceed 5 percent of the shop's net income. (Net income is clear profit after all the expenses have been paid.)

DESIGNING A BODY SHOP

Some main factors to be considered in modern body shop design include the floor plan, storage area, door and floor design, arrangement of equipment, and paint booth location.

Each of these points is important for efficient, well-organized work flow and for creating a good impression on the customer.

Floor Plan

Figure 1-6 shows a floor plan for a fairly large body shop with a volume business. Here, as many as eight or more paint jobs per day could be completed. Note that in this shop, the spray booth and drying enclosure are both in one area but are used as separate units.

This basic floor plan allows for maximum shop efficiency. The vehicles are first moved into the metal-working stalls (where metal is straightened) for the basic body work. They are then moved to the area where they will be prepared for painting. Here, time must be allowed for water and solvents to dry off the prepared surface. The vehicle is then ready to enter the spray booth and be painted.

After the vehicle is painted, it is moved from the spray booth to the drying enclosure. Here, the drying

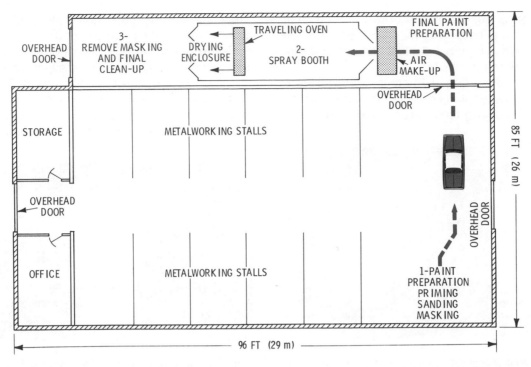

Fig. 1-6. *This floor plan shows a typical large body shop with metal-working stalls 12 × 24 ft (3.7 × 7.3 m) in size.*

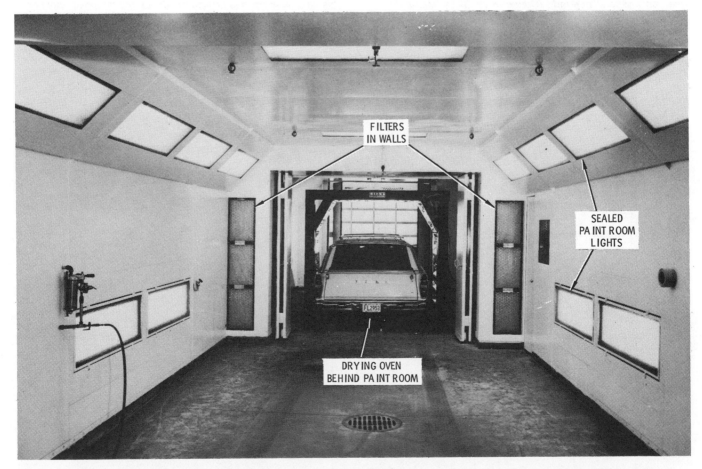

Fig. 1-7. *A drying oven separate from the paint booth allows a shop to increase the number of refinishing jobs handled in a day. (Courtesy of Binks Manufacturing Company)*

(heating) oven is put into action to fast-dry the paint. This drying oven is necessary for high-speed painting. The oven shown in Figure 1-7 might be used in a shop with a large-volume business.

The traveling oven (Fig. 1-8) moves back and forth over the vehicle then shuts off when the drying time is completed. The drying time is controlled by a pre-set timer. The oven is more thoroughly explained and pictured in the painting equipment unit.

Figure 1-9 shows a suggested layout for a smaller, independent body shop. This might be known as an average "two- or three-person" shop. The vehicle is first moved into the metal-working area to basically repair the damaged metal. Then, it is moved to the sanding and taping area for paint preparation. Glass

Fig. 1-8. *This type of drying oven operates on a track and moves slowly over the stationary car. It can be programmed to provide heat only where needed. (Courtesy of Binks Manufacturing Company)*

Fig. 1-10. *In the paint preparation area, masking is done to protect the glass, chrome, and other vehicle parts that will not be painted. This car has just been moved into the paint booth from the preparation area. (Courtesy of Binks Manufacturing Company)*

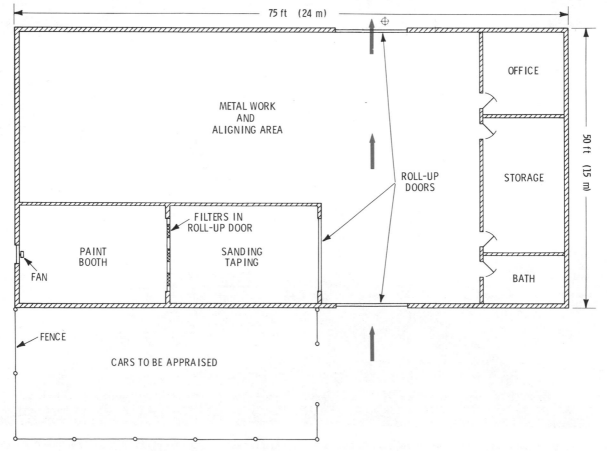

Fig. 1-9. *This floor plan shows a typical facility for a two- or three-person operation.*

and chrome parts should be taped with masking tape and paper (Fig. 1-10), so that they will not be painted. The vehicle is then moved into the paint booth.

Building Condition

Questions to be asked about the building's condition include: Are the building and floor area *large enough* to handle the expected volume of business? Is the ceiling *high enough* for raising automobiles so that they may be inspected and worked on from below?

Are there community laws about *air pollution* (paint mist, evaporating solvents) that the building cannot be equipped to satisfy? Laws in some locations require that paint mist be filtered before the paint booth fan blows it into the street or alley.

Is the building electrically *wired* for all the tools and equipment that will be needed? Does the building have skylights or windows that allow natural sunlight into the building, or will the building need artificial lighting? Will local zoning and building codes allow operation of a body repair shop at this location?

Storage

Wrecked vehicles require waiting time for appraisal and estimates of the repair cost. For this reason, there must be a place at the shop for wrecked car storage until the insurance company or owner can make adjustments. Insurance appraisers are not likely to pull a wrecked vehicle from the shop or to send it to a shop that does not have enough storage room.

If the shop is located in a city's business district, a large enough building to store several wrecked vehicles will cost a good deal of money. An extra fenced-in lot, such as the one shown in Figure 1-11, is very helpful for the storage of wrecked vehicles.

Storage costs money. Some insurance companies or car owners will not pay storage costs. This fact should be kept in mind and discussed with the car owner or insurance company beforehand.

Fig. 1-12. *Large roll-up doors are needed to provide good access to the body shop.*

Shop Doors

Having enough proper-sized doors is very important for efficient shop work. Damaged cars often have to be towed into the shop. Therefore, it is necessary to have a wide door for entrance and another one for exit. For easy access, the doors should be about 14 ft (feet) [4.2 m (meters)] high and 14 ft (4.2 m) wide.

Figures 1-2 and 1-4 show body shop doors of good size. The door pictured in Figure 1-12 is a good example of a large roll-up door used in a typical shop.

Fig. 1-11. *A body shop must have a fenced-in area to store damaged cars awaiting estimates or the arrival of parts.*

Fig. 1-13. *A smooth concrete floor will help promote clean shop conditions and make it easier to move equipment around.*

Fig. 1-14. *The area where cars are washed must be provided with a floor drain to carry away the water and dirt. (Courtesy of Binks Manufacturing Company)*

FLOOR DRAIN

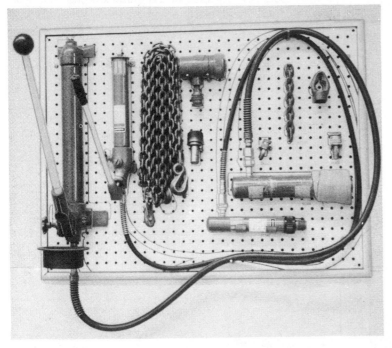

Fig. 1-15. *Good equipment that is neatly displayed will make a favorable impression on customers.*

Floor

The building should have a good, solid concrete floor (Fig. 1-13). Concrete is preferred because it is strong. Most floor jacks have small rollers that work best on smooth concrete floors. Concrete is also strong enough to support the weight of a car on jack stands.

Several drains must be installed in the floor, so that the shop can be washed down with water. Also, cars need to be washed both before and after repair, so the drain is needed to keep the shop floor dry (Fig. 1-14).

Shop Equipment Arrangement

There are two main ideas to keep in mind when planning or looking over the shop arrangement. The first of these is *convenience*. The equipment must be located where it is needed and where most of the workers can get to it easily.

The second is *advertising*. A neat display of good tools and body shop equipment is one of the best ways to advertise. Power tools, panel straighteners, wheel alignment machines, and other tools should all be located where they can be seen by the customer. This display shows the customer that the shop has the tools necessary to do high-quality work. A good arrangement of equipment is also a sign of orderly working conditions (Fig. 1-15).

Paint Booth Design

Body shops should have a paint booth if they want to do high-quality finishing work. Some shops may need more inside ventilation to remove the paint spray dust. Both the paint booth and the shop itself will be health hazards if they are not properly ventilated.

The booth should be placed in one corner of the shop (Figs.1-6 and 1-9) so that it is as far as possible from the dust of the sanding and grinding machines. Old paint, metal, and plastic dust from grinders and sanders can penetrate paint booth filters. The filters should allow only clean air to get into the booth. If dust gets through the filters, it can cause trouble by getting into the wet paint.

All paint booths need a ventilator fan to move the paint spray dust from the booth to the outside (Figs. 1-16 and 1-17). An air separator–regulator (Fig. 1-18) is needed in the paint booth. It provides the spray gun with the correct supply of clean air. A good fan, good filters, and good separator–regulator are needed in a paint booth for high-quality work.

Fast Turn-out Paint Booth. Figure 1-19 shows one of the best designs in paint booths. It allows the shop to paint several vehicles in one day. This booth is self-heated and minimizes dust problems. It has fluorescent lighting and plenty of air filters.

There are many less expensive paint booth designs that are built inside a body shop. These may be made with all types of building material, such as wood or concrete blocks. They may be grouped together as average turn-out paint booths.

Fig. 1-17. *A paint booth exhaust fan, viewed from the outside. A screen should be placed in front of the fan blades for safety. (Courtesy of DeVilbiss Company)*

Fig. 1-18. *The air transformer (separator–regulator) is a vital part of the shop's air supply system. (Courtesy of Binks Manufacturing Company)*

Fig. 1-16. *A paint booth exhaust fan, viewed from the inside. (Courtesy of DeVilbiss Company)*

Fig. **1-19.** *This large, self-contained paint booth is a type that would be found in high-volume body and refinishing shops. (Courtesy of Binks Manufacturing Company)*

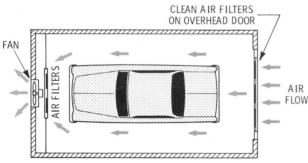

Fig. 1-20. *A typical air-drying paint booth.*

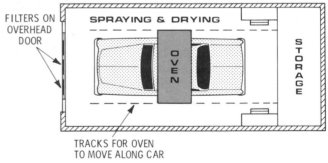

Fig. 1-21. *A typical small paint booth used for both paint spraying and drying.*

Average Turn-out Paint Booths. Figures 1-20 and 1-21 show floor plans of the two different types of average turn-out paint booths.

In an *air-drying* paint booth (Fig. 1-20), the ventilation fan pulls fresh, filtered air over the vehicle. This air movement causes the paint solvents to evaporate until the vehicle is dry.

In the *oven-drying* paint booth shown in Figure 1-21, the paint is heated with an oven on roller tracks. This causes the paint solvents to evaporate faster than in the air-drying booth.

The Downdraft Paint Booth. The DeVilbiss Company recently began marketing a new type of auto-refinishing spray booth, which it says will deliver "factory-quality" painting capabilities.

The new refinishing system uses downdraft air flow and a multistage air-filtering system to eliminate virtually all airborne dust and dirt.

As shown in Figure 1-22, the downward air flow creates an envelope of air around the car being painted. Overspray is drawn through a grating in the floor, which contains paint-arrestor filters. With the downward movement of air, overspray is drawn away from the breathing zone of the painter, for a healthier, more comfortable working environment. An integral part of the new DeVilbiss booth is the air replacement unit. This unit draws in outside air, filters it, and heats it (when needed). The conditioned air is delivered to the spray booth through a ceiling plenum (enclosed space) and filter media.

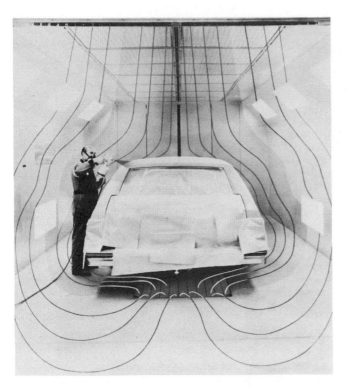

Fig. 1-22. *In this new paint booth design, air is supplied from the top and pulled down past the car to an exhaust system in the floor. (Courtesy of DeVilbiss Company)*

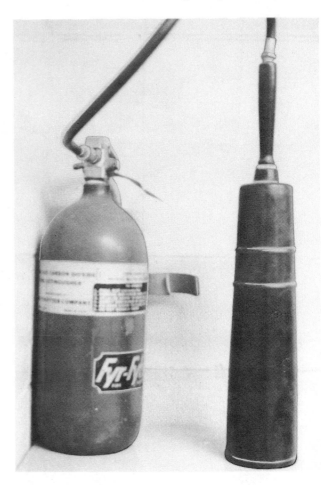

Fig. 1-23. *Good fire extinguishers are a necessity in the body shop.*

The booth is 24 ft (7.3 m) long, 14 ft (4.2 m) wide, and 9 ft (2.7 m) high. It is available with a solid back or as a drive-through model. Ten fluorescent lights and an observation window are standard features.

EQUIPPING A BODY SHOP

There are basic pieces of equipment needed by any body repair shop. The shop owner is expected to provide equipment such as fire extinguishers, air compressors, frame-straightening equipment, and other large or expensive items.

In this section, typical equipment needed for a well-equipped shop is discussed. In each case, use of the equipment is covered briefly. Later units discuss the equipment and its use more thoroughly.

It is very difficult to estimate closely the true cost of completely equipping a new body shop. However, a smaller shop could be reasonably well equipped for about $50,000. Of course, this depends on the type and size of the shop.

It *is* necessary, of course, to have the proper tools and equipment; however, it is wise to buy only what is needed to do a first-class job. Additional tools may be an unwise use of the shop's money.

It is also important to know when to *subcontract* or "farm out" certain work. Sending out such work as badly bent frames or wheels are typical examples of subcontracting. The equipment necessary to do these jobs is expensive. Unless a shop is very large, it is usually cheaper to subcontract such jobs to a shop that specializes in that type of work.

Fire Extinguisher

There is always a danger of fire in an auto body repair shop. For this reason, the shop should have several fire extinguishers on hand.

Most auto body replacement panels are welded or brazed into place. These operations create heat and may involve a hot, open flame. Both heat and flame are definite fire hazards. Also, flammable materials such as paint and cleaning solvents are used in an auto body shop. These are possible fire hazards. Figure 1-23 shows a typical shop fire extinguisher.

Air Compressor

An air compressor is a machine that places air under pressure and squeezes it into a smaller volume. When

Fig. 1-24. *A typical body shop air compressor. Compressed air is used to operate various tools, as well as the spray guns for painting.*

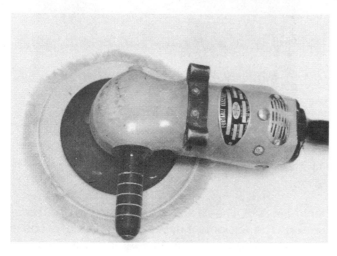

Fig. 1-25. *Polishers like this one are used in paint refinishing.*

Fig. 1-26. *The shop should have a bench grinder for sharpening tools and for other uses. (Courtesy of Snap-On Tools)*

the air is released, its expansion may be used as a source of power for shop equipment.

A common air compressor is shown in Figure 1-24. It supplies the air needed to operate many of the tools in the shop. Paint guns, jacks, power wrenches, power chisels, and many other tools may use compressed air for power.

Polisher

A polisher is used to apply rubbing compound, polish, and some waxes to the paint of the automobile. A typical polisher is shown in Figure 1-25.

Bench Grinder

The electric bench grinder has many uses in the shop. It is often used to smooth rough edges on metal and to sharpen or reshape tools. Safety goggles must always be worn when using the bench grinder. A typical shop bench grinder is shown in Figure 1-26. Sometimes, a wire brush wheel is mounted on one end of the grinder.

Vise

The shop vise is usually mounted firmly on a work bench, as can be seen in Figure 1-27. The shop vise is a useful piece of equipment. It is used to clamp and hold objects together for welding or for other types of work.

Work Bench

The work bench is usually used to work on smaller parts that have been removed from the car. By using

Fig. 1-27. *A shop vise is usually bolted to one corner of a sturdy workbench.*

the bench, the parts can be held at waist level, high enough to be easily worked on.

A typical work bench is strong, stable, and made of steel. This is very important if the bench is to be used to mount a vise, as is done in Figure 1-27. A shelf beneath the bench can be used to store smaller tools such as a tap and die set or electric drills.

Shop Bench

The shop bench is used as a seat while working on hard-to-reach panels that need straightening. This allows the employee to work comfortably, without having to stoop down to an awkward position on the floor.

The shop bench may also be used as a table for parts that have been removed from the automobile. A shop bench is shown in Figure 1-28.

Fig. 1-28. *To work on the roof of a car, a shop bench may be used as a platform. The edge of the bench should be padded with carpeting or similar material to prevent marring the paint on the side of the car.*

Fig. 1-29. *A floor jack is used to raise the car for inspection of the underside. Sturdy jack stands should be positioned to support the car before any work is done beneath it. (Courtesy of Mac Tools)*

Floor Jack

The floor jack (Fig. 1-29) is one of the most useful pieces of shop equipment. The jack must be used only to *lift* the vehicle so that safety stands can be put in place to hold the car up. Then, wheels can be removed or the worker can get underneath the car to check or repair damage.

Wrecking Equipment

Wrecking equipment, commonly called a *wrecker*, is a special truck used to safely move damaged vehicles from one place to another. A wrecker truck has *winches* to raise the damaged vehicle from either the front or rear. A common wrecker and equipment are shown in Figure 1-30.

Power Jack

Power jacks and attachments are used to line up panels and frames that are out of alignment resulting from impact or normal wear. Figure 1-31 shows a power jack and attachments that would be used to repair serious body or frame damage.

DOLLY WHEELS FOR
CARS BADLY WRECKED

HOLMES 500

SLING

24 HR
SERVICE

Fig. 1-30. *Usually, only large body shops operate their own wreckers ("tow trucks"). Smaller shops usually depend on independent towing services or "farm out" such work to other garages.*

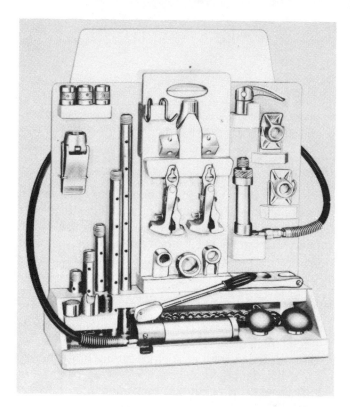

Fig. 1-31. *A good power jack and a wide assortment of jack attachments must be part of the shop's basic equipment. (Courtesy of Snap-On Tools)*

Frame Straightener

There are many basic types of frame straighteners. Smaller units are often bought by low-volume body shops. A larger shop would usually install a large, permanent frame straightener.

Frame straighteners are used to align and straighten frames that are out of alignment because of collision damage. A portable frame straightener is shown in Figure 1-32. In Figure 1-33, a power post frame straightener is shown attached to a vehicle frame.

Oxy-acetylene Welder

An oxy-acetylene welder is a very necessary tool in the auto body shop. The oxy-acetylene welder is used for heating, shrinking, welding, leading, brazing, and soldering metal (Fig. 1-34).

Arc Welder

An arc welder may be needed by many body shops, especially those that do a good deal of frame damage repair. The arc welder is able to weld thick metal (such as the car frame) quickly. It does so with less heat loss and distortion than welding done with oxy-acetylene.

A typical body shop arc welder unit is shown in Figure 1-35. This unit can weld with up to 225 amperes, which is enough current for almost every shop need.

Panel Spotter

The panel spotter in Figure 1-36 is used for panel replacement and for patching rust-out areas. The panel spotter allows fast repair work on thin metal and prevents metal warpage.

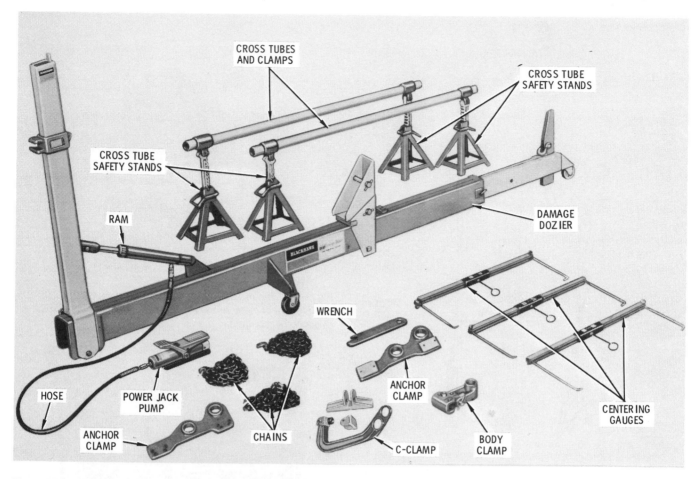

Fig. 1-32. *A typical medium-sized portable frame straightener. (Courtesy of Blackhawk Division, Applied Power Industries)*

Fig. 1-33. *Power post frame straighteners are popular with smaller shops. (Courtesy of Kansas Jack, Inc.)*

Metallic Inert Gas (MIG) Welder

The wire MIG welder is an arc welder that uses argon gas as a shield to keep out foreign matter and can weld almost any metal. It is used widely on today's high-strength steel auto bodies and also can be used on aluminum panels. This welder can be used on all parts of the vehicle. A welder of this type is shown in Figure 1-37.

Creeper

A creeper is a tool that allows the worker to roll around under the car. The four rollers on a creeper automatically move in whatever direction the creeper is pushed.

Figure 1-38 shows a worker rolling under a car for a better look at the body damage underneath. Because a creeper rolls so easily, it must not be left lying flat on the floor. If someone steps on it, the creeper can roll away causing a bad fall.

Safety Stands

Safety (jack) stands are used to support the car safely after it has been jacked up. They allow the worker to move around under the vehicle without danger.

To use jack stands properly, the vehicle is first jacked up. Then, the stands are placed in position under the

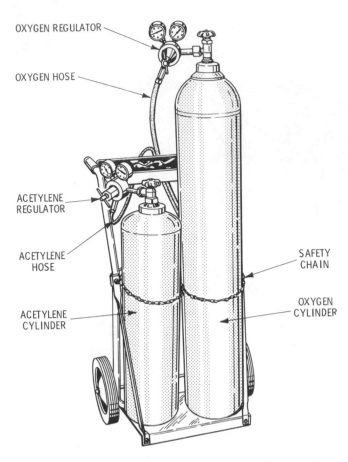

OXYGEN REGULATOR

OXYGEN HOSE

ACETYLENE REGULATOR

ACETYLENE HOSE

ACETYLENE CYLINDER

SAFETY CHAIN

OXYGEN CYLINDER

Fig. 1-34. *One of the most frequently used tools in the body shop is the oxy-acetylene welder.*

Fig. 1-35. *An arc welder is often used for work on thick metal, such as auto frames. (Courtesy of Lincoln Electric Company)*

Fig. 1-36. *The resistance spot welder, or "panel spotter," is often used for sheet metal repairs. (Courtesy of Automotive Equipment Division, Lenco, Inc.)*

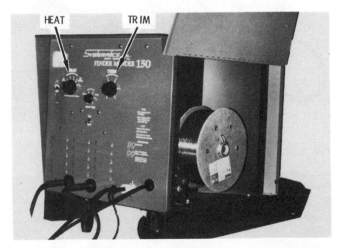

HEAT   TRIM

Fig. 1-37. *The MIG (metallic inert gas) welder is used to repair lightweight, high-strength steel or aluminum panels found on newer cars. (Courtesy of Systematics, Inc.)*

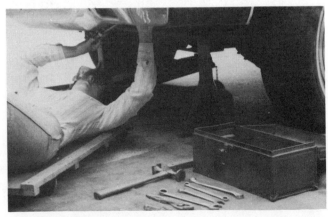

Fig. 1-38. *Body workers use a creeper like this one to move around easily beneath the car. Note the safety jack stand that supports the car.*

vehicle (Fig. 1-39). These help keep the car from falling if the jack should slip or leak down, or if the vehicle loses its balance on the jack.

The jack should be taken out from under the vehicle after it has been safely placed on the jack stands. This allows the jack to be used for other work, and the car is properly supported on the stands.

Other Shop Tools

There are many other tools and items of equipment that the shop owner must furnish. Some of these are discussed in the unit on power tools. Other are discussed in their own units.

EQUIPPING THE OFFICE

To run any body shop, a separate office area is needed. This allows the owner or manager to have a place to conduct all business activities. Usually, the office is away from the shop area, so that it can be cleaner than the shop.

The office usually has file cabinets, a desk and chair, an adding machine, a typewriter, and other small items. Larger office equipment may be purchased as the shop's business grows.

File Cabinets

The center for business records is almost always a file cabinet (Fig. 1-40). The cabinet should contain one folder for each customer, creditor, manufacturer, or other

business contact. The folder contents are arranged in order of their dates. Folders are always filed alphabetically. Cardboard guides may be used to divide the folders in each of the file drawers.

Estimates made on customers' cars are usually good for 30 days. The estimates should be kept on file for that time. This is one of the important uses of the file cabinet and necessary to a good office system.

Desk and Chair

The size or style and number of desks depends on the size of shop business. A small business needs only one desk, while a large business could use two or more. A desk that is not easily damaged, such as the

Fig. 1-40. *A filing cabinet for records and a good filing system are important for a successful body shop operation.*

Fig. 1-39. *Safety jack stands should be placed as shown before working beneath a vehicle. Working under a car supported only by a floor jack is unsafe. (Courtesy of Blackhawk Division, Applied Power Industries)*

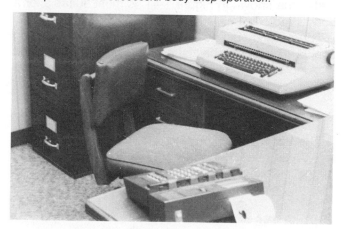

Fig. 1-41. *An office desk and chair are useful when completing estimates and doing other shop paperwork.*

Fig. 1-42. *Estimates and bills can be completed more quickly and accurately with an adding machine.*

Fig. 1-43. *A typewriter is not a "must" for a body shop, but it will help the shop make a better impression on customers and suppliers.*

metal one shown in Figure 1-41, is most suitable for a body shop office.

The desk should be large enough for ample working space. The desk chair should be comfortable when working at the desk and also may be used with the typewriter.

Adding Machine

The adding machine (Fig. 1-42) is a very important tool in the office of a body shop. It is used for totaling the estimates on damaged vehicles, for billing, and for banking, payroll, and similar work.

Typewriter

The typewriter is not a necessity, especially in a small office. However, neatly typed business letters, billings,

Fig. 1-44. *The telephone is important for everyday business activities in the body shop.*

and other correspondence create a good impression for the business (Fig.1-43).

Telephone

An auto body shop needs to make many telephone calls, both local and long distance. A large shop should employ an efficient person who is familiar with the business and can handle all the shop's telephone calls (Fig. 1-44). A person with a pleasant voice and the ability to provide intelligent answers can help establish a new shop's business.

Fig. 1-45. *The latest manufacturers' literature, estimating guides, and other references should be available in the shop's office for efficient use.*

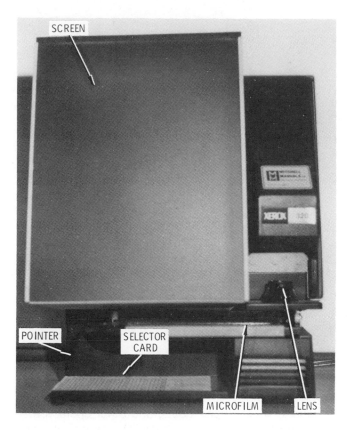

Fig. 1-46. *A typical microfilm estimator.*

Fig. 1-47. *A computer estimating system.*

This machine is used with a viewing (film) card. The card contains the name, model, and make of the vehicle. It is projected on the viewing screen. An exploded view of panels, numbers of parts, and labor time in hours also are included on the card (Fig. 1-46).

The cards are easy to use and read. The microfilm estimator is discussed in more detail in the unit on estimates.

Office Library

All offices will need a small auto body library. This should include damage report price manuals, textbooks, paint color guide manuals, service manuals from the automobile manufacturing companies, and other literature. Figure 1-45 shows a small library that is typical of many auto body repair shops.

Microfilm Estimator

Many body shops use a microfilm viewer for estimating the cost of damaged parts of the vehicle.

Computer Estimating

A computer system for estimating is used in some parts of the country. A large body shop or a department of a large car dealer can subscribe for a telephone line connected directly to a central computer. This allows the shop estimator to check the damaged parts on a special form. This information is placed in a computer terminal directly connected to the central computer.

A printed estimate is returned by the computer in minutes with correct totals and part numbers to use for ordering the parts. Figure 1-47 shows a typewriterlike computer terminal being used.

Unit 2

Estimating and Insurance

A successful auto body shop must make estimates of the cost to repair the damage on different vehicles. Estimates will range from major wrecks to small dents. Repainting jobs must also be estimated.

If possible, have only *one* person in the shop make all the estimates. This person should know how to *sell* all the body shop's many services to private car owners. Also, the estimator will have insurance appraisers (adjusters) to deal with. The appraiser is the insurance company's representative who estimates damage and authorizes payment.

The estimate is a *cost* value of the damage done and, also, the price needed to repair the damaged vehicle. The completed estimate is an itemized list that shows the cost of repairing the damage on the vehicle. A typical estimate is shown in Figure 2-1.

The estimate is sometimes called a *damage appraisal* by the insurance company. By either name, the estimate or appraisal becomes a *commitment* by both the shop's estimator and the insurance company or customer.

This chapter explains the correct method to use when making an estimate. Included are the estimate costs involved, the problems often encountered, the importance of determining the type of insurance claim (if insurance is involved), and who will pay for the vehicle's repair.

ESTIMATING IN GENERAL

Actually, an estimator makes *two* estimates. The *first* estimate is only a *visual* estimate. The estimator walks around the damaged car and generally looks it over, making mental notes (Fig. 2-2).

The *second* estimate is the actual written estimate. This report lists each item and operation needed for repair. It includes parts, labor, refinishing, body shop materials, *sublet* repair costs, and other costs, if any. Sublet repair refers to work that will be sent or charged to another shop.

The shop estimator in Figure 2-3 is working on the *written* estimate. The estimate may show the cost of five or more items: parts, labor, sublet repairs, materials, and refinishing. At least two copies of the estimate should be made. One copy should be filed in the body shop office and the other copy given to the person who asked for the estimate. This may be the car owner or the insurance company representative.

An *insurance report* (the insurance company's copy of the estimate) becomes a firm bid for doing the work during a certain length of time. Usually, it is a good idea to keep an insurance report on file for 30 days.

In some parts of the country, the estimate is called a *damage report*. This is simply a different word for the estimate. The term "damage report" may be used because customers often associate the word "free" with the word "estimate." Body shops in most locations can no longer afford to make free estimates.

In many parts of the country, a damage report will still be free *if* the shop making the report is allowed to repair the vehicle. However, if an insurance company or a car owner simply wants to know how much the repair will cost, the charge for the damage report must reflect the extent of the collision. The extent of the collision, of course, determines the amount of paperwork needed.

POPE'S BODY SHOP
205 North Claxton

ESTIMATE OF REPAIRS

SHEET _1_ OF _1_ SHEETS

NAME _Brenda Joyce_ DATE _8/10/81_

ADDRESS _683 N. Main - City_ PHONE _658-4463_

INSURED BY _City Insurance Co._ ADJUSTER _Jim Brown_ PHONE _658-3666_

BELOW IS OUR ESTIMATE TO REPAIR YOUR _1981 Ford L.T.D._

MODEL	LICENSE NO.	MOTOR NO.	SERIAL NO.	MILEAGE
1981 Ford	32C 178	658671	456572783	7,678.9

Repair/Replace	PARTS NECESSARY AND ESTIMATE OF LABOR REQUIRED	LABOR HRS.	PARTS NUMBER	AMOUNT		LABOR COST ESTIMATE	
V	Face Bar w/ guard	1.8	EOAZ17757A	167	85	36	00
V	Pad - impact (center)	.3	ECAZ17C829A	13	60	6	00
V	Pad - impact (outer)	.2	EOAZ17K833A	11	55	4	00
V	Grill	.2	E1AZ17B968C		NC	4	00
V	Re-inforcement (aluminum)	NC	EOAZ17A792B	184	30	—	—
V	Absorber - impact	.3	EOAZ17754A	59	50	6	00
V	Repair left fender inner panel						
V	Repair left front fender panel (outer)	2.5				50	00
	Paint material	2.2		36	00	44	00

| | | | | 7.5 | | | |

INSURANCE Customer PAYS $ 100.00

INSURANCE CO. PAYS $ 546 44

R.O. NUMBER #6812

SIGNED _John Jacobs_ (owner)

BY —

AUTHORIZATION FOR REPAIRS
You are hereby authorized to make the above specified repairs.

SIGNED _City Insurance Co - Roger_ DATE _8/10/81_

DIXIE PRINTING CO.,

The above is an estimate based on our inspection and does not cover any additional parts or labor which may be required after the work has been opened up. Occasionally after the work has started damaged or broken parts are discovered which are not evident on the first inspection.

TOTALS	472 80	150 00
WRECKER & TOWING		— —
TAX 5%	23 64	
TOTAL MATL. AND TAX	→	496 44
GRAND TOTAL		646 44

Fig. 2-1. *A typical damage estimate itemizes needed parts and repairs and includes the cost of parts, materials, and labor.*

Fig. 2-2. *The first step in estimating is a thorough inspection of the vehicle to determine the location and amount of damage.*

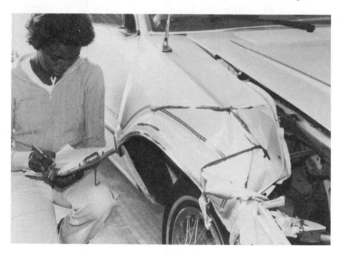

Fig. 2-3. *The second step is a careful, item-by-item listing of all parts and work needed to repair the damage.*

THE WRITTEN ESTIMATE

Writing the estimate is serious business. The estimator must be able to tell the customer whether the extent of the damage *and* the cost of repair will justify the car's being repaired. The estimator should know what the value of the vehicle was *before* the accident. Of course, the car will have to be repaired to the condition it was in before the accident.

Analyzing the Damage

A thorough examination is important before writing the actual estimate. The estimator must analyze what happened and how much the vehicle was damaged. In Figure 2-2, the estimator is making such an analysis.

The estimator must study the damage *thoroughly* to determine how serious it is, *before* making the written estimate. This time is well spent, because it helps keep the estimator from overlooking hidden damage.

38 CHEVROLET 1981

Av'g. Trd-in	Ins. Sym.	BODY TYPE	Model	Fact. A.D.P.	Ship. Wgt.	Av'g. Loan	Av'g. Retail
1981		**CITATION-AT-PS-AC-Continued**					
75		Add Deluxe Exterior				75	100
		Add Sport Equipment		$1588			
75		Add AM/FM Stereo				75	100
125		Add AM/FM Stereo/Tape		212		125	150
75		Add Power Door Locks				75	100
75		Add Power Windows				75	100
50		Add Rear Window Defogger				50	75
50		Add Luggage Rack				50	75
75		Add Speed Control				75	100
50		Add Tilt Steering Wheel				50	75
75		Add Wire Wheel Covers				75	100
250		Deduct Manual Trans.				225	250
100		Deduct Conventional Steering				100	100
350		Deduct W/out Air Conditioning				325	350
1981 MALIBU-AT-PS-AC						**Start Sept. 1980**	
MALIBU-V6		Veh. Ident.:()G1()(Model)K()B()100001 Up.					
5550	7	Sedan 4D Sport	T69	$6814	3028	5000	6425
5650	7	Coupe 2D Sport	T27	6731	3037	5100	6525
5825	7	Station Wagon 2S	T35	7030	3201	5250	6700
MALIBU CLASSIC-V6		Veh. Ident.:()G1()(Model)K()B()100001 Up.					
5800	7	Sedan 4D Sport	W69	$7196	3059	5225	6675
5900	7	Coupe 2D Sport	W27	7074	3065	5325	6775
6075	7	Coupe 2D Landau	W27/Z03	7345		5475	6950
6125	7	Station Wagon 2S	W35	7317	3222	5525	7025
MALIBU-V8		Veh. Ident.:()G1()(Model)()()B()100001 Up.					
5475	7	Sedan 4D Sport	T69	$6864	3194	4950	6350
5575	7	Coupe 2D Sport	T27	6781	3199	5025	6450
5750	7	Station Wagon 2S	T35	7080	3369	5175	6625
MALIBU CLASSIC-V8		Veh. Ident.:()G1()(Model)()()B()100001 Up.					
5725	7	Sedan 4D Sport	W69	$7246	3225	5175	6600
5825	7	Coupe 2D Sport	W27	7124	3227	5250	6700
6000	7	Coupe 2D Landau	W27/Z03	7395		5400	6875
6050	7	Station Wagon 2S	W35	7367	3390	5450	6925
100		Add Vinyl Roof				100	125
100		Add AM/FM Stereo		$178		100	125
150		Add AM/FM Stereo/Tape				150	200
225		Add AM/FM Stereo/CB		490		225	300
50		Add Luggage Rack				50	75
250		Add Estate Equipment		287		225	325
100		Add Power Windows				100	125
100		Add Power Seats		183		100	125
125		Add Wire Wheel Covers				125	150
75		Add Tilt Steering Wheel				75	100
75		Add Speed Control				75	100
75		Add Rear Window Defogger				75	100
75		Add Power Door Locks				75	100
325		Deduct Manual Trans.				300	325
450		Deduct W/out Air Conditioning				425	450
1981 CAMARO-AT-PS-AC						**Start Sept. 1980**	
CAMARO-V6		Veh. Ident.:()G1()(Model)K()B()100001 Up.					
6175	8	Sport Coupe 2D	P87	$6906	3222	5575	7075
6750	8	Berlinetta Coupe 2D	S87	7810	3275	6075	7650

DEDUCT FOR RECONDITIONING
1982 APRIL 1982   H

Fig. 2-4. *Average prices for automobiles, with varying values resulting from equipment options, are listed in booklets published by trade organizations. This page is from a popular used-car guide book. (Courtesy of National Automobile Dealers Used Car Guide Co.)*

Determining the Car's Value

An estimator may spend valuable time estimating the cost of collision repair, *then* find that the repair cost exceeds the value of the vehicle. To avoid this problem, the estimator needs to know about how much money the car is worth. This helps decide whether the car is declared a *total loss* (often simply called a "total"). Whether a wrecked car is declared a "total" must be determined by comparing *three* cash values:

Market Value. The *first* cash value to consider is the *market value*. This is the car's average *wholesale* price. Wholesale price is the price that a car dealer would pay for the car. This might be the price paid at an automobile auction or the money allowed for a car taken as a trade-in.

Of course, if a dealer is to make a profit, the car must be sold at a price *higher* than the wholesale price. The dealer often determines the *retail* price by referring to published booklets listing car values (Fig. 2-4). The publishers of the booklets make surveys to find average retail prices. These booklets are used by body shop estimators and insurance adjusters to determine the car's market value.

Repair Cost. The *second* cash value to consider is the repair cost. This is the total cost of the repair job, as listed on the estimate. It includes such items as towing fees, storage fees, paint work, labor, parts, and sublet work.

Salvage Value. The *third* cash value to consider is salvage value. Even when a car is "totally" wrecked, some parts can still be used. In many cases, these include the drive shaft, engine, transmission, and body parts not damaged in the wreck (Fig. 2-5). These usable parts have a cash value, since they can still be sold as used parts. A badly wrecked automobile still has some cash value, even though it may look worthless.

The salvage value, of course, is nowhere near what the car's market value was before the accident. For example, if the wrecked car's market value, in good condition, was $1,000, it might have a *salvage* value of only $200. If the repair cost plus the salvage value is *more* than the wholesale market price, the car will probably be declared a total loss (totaled).

Writing a very detailed estimate on a "totaled" car would be a waste of time. The experienced shop owner or estimator should immediately consider that possibility when estimating collision claims, to determine if the car is worth repairing.

Obtaining Preliminary Information

A first step in making the estimate is to obtain the *preliminary* information. This will include items such as who owns the car, who will pay the bill, whether the car is to be repaired all over or spot-repaired, and whether new or used parts are to be installed. Next, the estimator must determine whether the car is worth repairing, as discussed above. The estimator can then begin writing the estimate.

Estimating the Costs

When writing an estimate, start at one panel and estimate the cost of parts, labor, and refinishing on that panel. Go from the outside of the car inward on each damaged panel (Fig. 2-6). Be certain to include the *full amount* of the damage. Move to the next panel, and estimate it in the same manner. Continue all the way around the car including the top and the frame, if necessary. Note any mechanical repairs needed, such as suspension or brake damage.

Frame Damage. Figures 2-7 and 2-8 show an example

Fig. 2-5. *Even a badly damaged car still has a number of usable parts. The total value of these parts is the "salvage value" of the car.*

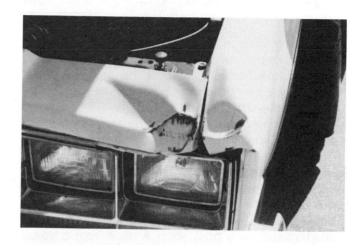

Fig. 2-6. *Estimates must include each damaged part and any damage to adjoining parts.*

Fig. 2-7. *The possiblity of frame damage must be considered and checked in most cases. Frame damage to this car is quite likely.*

of frame damage. When estimating frame damage, first identify the damaged area (for example, "left side rail, center section"). To estimate frame damage correctly, list the *name* and *location* of each section of the frame that is damaged. Estimating frame damage is more thoroughly discussed later in this unit.

Fig. 2-8. *The extent of the frame damage can be determined more accurately after other damaged parts have been removed.*

The labor charge for frame repair work is usually estimated by the complexity of the hook-up required to straighten the frame, instead of the hours involved. This is because of the shop's heavy financial investment in frame-straightening machinery.

It must be decided how the frame repair charge will be made. Either the type of hook-up needed or the labor time that will be spent on the work should be estimated. This will have to be done while visually inspecting the damaged areas.

Parts Prices. The parts prices for the estimate are taken from a collision parts manual. This manual is a very important tool for a body shop. A page from a typical manual is shown in Figure 2-9. For accurate estimates, never guess or take someone's word about prices of parts.

To simplify the estimate, the cost of refinishing material needed (paint, primer, filler) is included in the *parts* column. This is done since both material and parts are subject to sales tax in most states.

Unseen Damage. Before completing the estimate, always take a second look at the damaged vehicle. Be sure that you have included *all* the damage.

Sometimes, of course, there may be damage that cannot or will not be seen until the car is taken apart. In these cases, the parts that *might* be damaged are listed on the estimate. Then the words "left open" are written in place of the parts and labor prices. This tells the car owner or insurance company that the shop will not know how much it will cost to fix these parts until the car is taken apart and checked.

For example, note the heavy side damage to the car in Figure 2-10. Because of this impact, the transmission, driveshaft, or differential may have been damaged. Those parts would then be listed on the estimate and the words "left open" written in the price column.

Finishing Up. When the estimate is finished, the important points to double-check are:

1. *Write down* the vehicle owner's *name*.
2. Determine *who* will be responsible for *paying the bill*.
3. Find out if there is a *deductible* clause on an insurance claim estimate. Many collision insurance policies have such a clause. When this is the case, the customer pays the first $50, $100, or $200 and the insurance company pays the rest of the bill. Be sure that the customer knows about this.
4. Determine if the car is *worth* repairing. That is, whether the total repair cost plus the salvage value is less than the wholesale value of the car.
5. Remember that some damage cannot be seen. Be sure to use the term "left open" on those areas.
6. Carefully check all the part numbers and the addition on the estimate to be sure that they are correct.

COLLISION PARTS MANUALS

Collision *parts manuals* are also known as "collision *estimators*" or "collision *damage manuals*." They are available from several different book companies. These manuals are very valuable sources of information. A good body shop *must* have these on hand to make accurate estimates.

An estimator must know how to use the collision parts manual to find the *price* of the new parts and amount of *time* needed to install the parts. Of course, the estimator must allow more labor time if it is necessary to align an opening after the damaged panel has been removed.

Body and Parts Information

The collision parts manual begins with drawings used to identify the model and make of the complete car. Figure 2-11 shows a typical *model identification page*. This gives the estimator the model *number* of the car.

The model and make identification pages are followed by identification of almost every part of the car, from the front bumper to the back bumper. Each part is shown with pictures of the assemblies. A list follows the pictures, showing the part numbers, hours needed to install, and the retail price of the part. Figure 2-12 is a typical manual page.

Labor Conversion Table

On the manual pages, the labor figures are given only in *time* not *cost*. This is because labor charges per hour are different from one shop to another.

COUGAR XR7 1980-82

FRONT DOOR CONT'D
W/AIR VENT CONT'D
¶Serviced Only w/Division Bar
Plate, Rear View Mirror

15	Outer	EOSZ 17B693A-B	7.55
16	Inner	E1SZ 17K709A-B	2.40
17	Regulator, Vent	D8BZ 5423402-3B	14.50
	Handle, Vent Reg	D9BZ 5423334A	2.25

DOOR GLASS
W/O AIR VENT

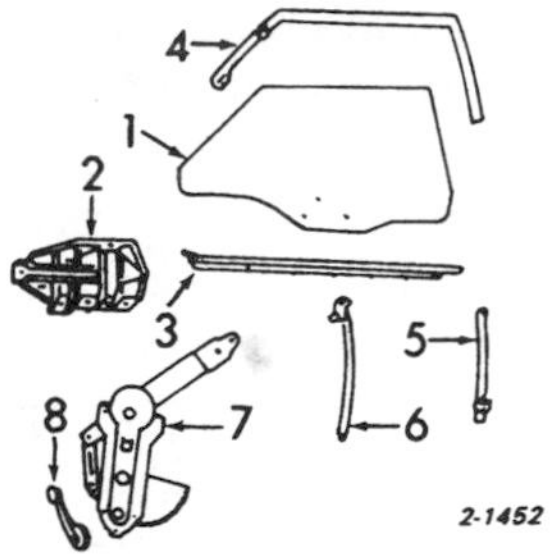

2-1452

1	Glass			
	exc	Clear	EOSZ 6621410-1A	1.2 155.50
		NAGS	C D6012-3	155.50
		Tinted	EOSZ 6621410-1B	161.05
		NAGS	T D6012-3	161.05
	w/Sail Mirror	Clear	EOSZ 6621410-1C	1.2 136.30
		NAGS	C D6010-1	136.30
		Tinted	EOSZ 6621410-1D	147.85
		NAGS	T D6010-1	147.85
2	Bracket, Channel	to 4-81	E1SZ 6623288-9A	12.95
		fm 4-81	E1SZ 6623288-9A	12.95
3	Weatherstrip, Belt			
	Outer	R except	E1SZ 6621452A	8.20
		w/Mirror	EOSZ 6621452B	4.95
		L	EOSZ 6621453B	4.95
	Inner		E1SZ 6621456-7A	7.20
4	Run, Upper			
	w/o Sail Mirror	to 11-79	EOSZ 6621596A-7B	14.50
		11-79 to 11-80 R	E1SZ 6621596B	14.50
		L	EOSZ 6621597B	14.50
		fm 11-80 R	E1SZ 6621596B	14.50
		L	EOSZ 6621597B	14.50
	w/Sail Mirror	to 11-80	EOSZ 6621596C	14.50
		fm 11-80	E1SZ 6621596C	14.50
5	Retainer, Run	R	EOSZ 66222A00A	9.05
		L	EOSZ 66222A01A	9.05
6	Run, Front	80	D8BZ 5421546A	9.50
		81-82	E1SZ 6621546A	7.90
7	Regulator	Manual	EOSZ 6623200-1A #.9	39.55
		Power	EOSZ 6623208-9A#1.0	82.50
	# Exc w/Glass Rem - Man.5, Pwr .6			
8	Handle, Reg		EOSZ 6623342A	9.30
	Motor, Regulator	R	D3AZ 5723395A	102.65
		L	D8TZ 9823394A	104.55

ROOF

Refinish Roof Panel		3.5
R&R Headliner		2.5
Add to Roof Panel R&R		
w/Vinyl Cover		5.0

SHEET METAL
Panel Roof

Use w/o Sun Roof		EOSZ 6650202A	18.0 153.15
Use w/Sun Roof	80	E1SZ 6650202A	20.0 254.35
	81-82	E1SZ 6650202A	20.0 254.35
Reinforcement, Roof			
	80	EOSZ 6650222A	11.60
	81-82	E1SZ 6650222A	16.50
Moulding, Inside Garnish(a)			
Side	R/L	EOSZ 6651752B	5.65
(a)Paint to Match			
Rail, Roof Side			
Front Outer		E1SZ 6651186-7A	1.5 21.80
Center	R	EOSZ 66513A74A	1.5 17.60
	L	EOSZ 66513A75A	1.5 17.60
Rear Inner		EOSZ 6651212-3A	1.5 31.00
Frame, Back Window		EOSZ 6642220A	2.5 10.55

CONT'D

ROOF CONT'D
MOULDINGS & TRIM
W/O CARRIAGE ROOF

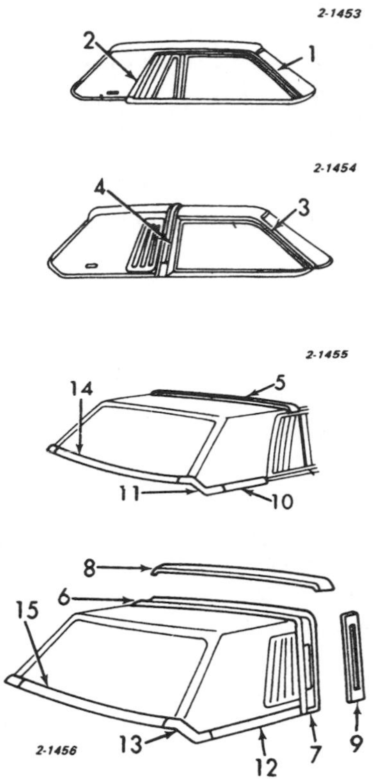

2-1453

2-1454

2-1455

2-1456

Moulding, Drip Finish
w/o Luxury Option

1	Front	except to 9-79 R	EOSZ 6651726E	.2	21.70
		L	E1SZ 6651727A	.2	19.60
		fm 9-79	EOSZ 6651726-7E	.2	21.70
		Decor Opt 80	EOSZ 6651726-7C	.2	19.60
		81-82 to 6-81	E1SZ 6651726-7D	.2	19.60
		fm 6-81	E1SZ 6651726-7G	.2	19.60
2	Rear	except	EOSZ 6651728-9A		3.80
		Decor Opt to 6-81	EOWY 6651728-9AA		7.90
		fm 6-81	E1WY 6651728-9CA		16.25
	w/Luxury Option				
3	Front		EOSZ 6651726-7D	.3	19.60
4	Rear		EOSZ 6651728-9E		5.55
	Moulding or Panel, Roof				
5	Except(a)	R	EOWY 66517A02AA	.3	6.90
		L	EOWY 66517A03AA	.3	6.90
	w/Luxury/Decor Option				
6	Panel(a)	Upper	EOSZ 6650448AA	.3	44.85
7	Panel	Side	EOSZ 6650448-9A		28.35
8	Insert(a)	Upper	EOSZ 6650448B	.2	48.05
9		Side R	EOSZ 66517C98AA	.2	12.05
		L	EOSZ 66517C99AA	.2	12.05
	(a)Order by Color				
	Moulding, Side Belt				
	w/o Luxury/Decor Opt				
10	Front	exc R	EOWY 66423A18A		6.50
		L	EOWY 66423A19A		6.50
		(a) R	EOSZ 66423A18HA		17.50
		L	EOSZ 66423A19HA		17.50
11	Rear	exc R	EOWY 66423A18B		9.85
		L	EOWY 66423A19B		9.85
		(a) R	EOWY 66423A18AA		17.50
		L	EOWY 66423A19AA		17.50
	w/Luxury/Decor Opt				
12	Front(b)	R	EOSZ 66423A18CA		6.95
		L	EOSZ 66423A19CA		6.95
13	Rear(b)	R	EOWY 66423A18FA	.3	7.95
		L	EOWY 66423A19FA	.3	7.95
	(a)Use w/Wide Door Belt Mldg & Order by Color				
	(b)Order by Color				
	Moulding, Back Belt				
14	w/o Luxury/Decor Opt				

CONT'D

ROOF CONT'D
W/O CARRIAGE ROOF CONT'D

	Bright	EOWY 66423A20A	12.50
	Black(a)	EOWY 66423A20BA	14.60
15	w/Luxury/Decor Opt		
	Black(a)	EOWY 66423A20BA	14.60
	Ornament, Side	R EOWY 66517A57AA	3.95
		L EOWY 66517A56AA	3.95
	Lamp Assy, Coach		
	To 5-81	EOSZ 15B437A-B	23.15
	Fm 5-81	E1SZ 15B437A-B	23.15
	Cover, Vinyl(a)	80 EOWY 6653700A2S	# 262.55
		81-82 E1WY 6653700A3A	# 262.55
	(a)Order by Color		
	#7.5 - Does Not Incl R&R Any Glass		

MOULDINGS & TRIM
W/CARRIAGE ROOF

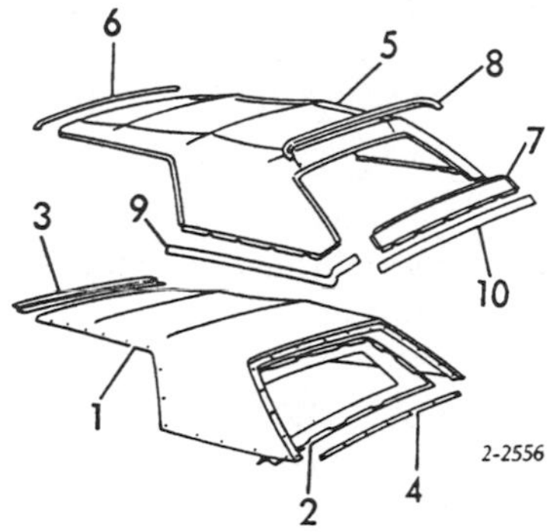

2-2556

1	Panel, Outside Trim	E1SZ 6653790A	852.15
2	Moulding, Garnish		
	See Back Window		
	Retainer, Outside Panel		
3	Front	EOLY 66537A48A	31.90
4	Rear	E1SZ 66537A06A	9.70
5	Cover, Outside	Blue(a) E1SZ 6652700A8B	730.00
6	Seal, Header	Blue(a) E1SZ 6603045A8B	59.95
7	Cover, Rear Lower		
	Blue(a)	E1SZ 6652788A8B	112.80
8	Moulding, Rear Upper		
	Blue(a)	E1LY 66517A62AB	45.45
	Moulding, Belt		
	Side	R E1SZ 66423A18C	40.60
		L E1SZ 66423A19C	40.60
	Lower	E1SZ 66423A20C	76.60
	(a)Order by Color		

SUN ROOF

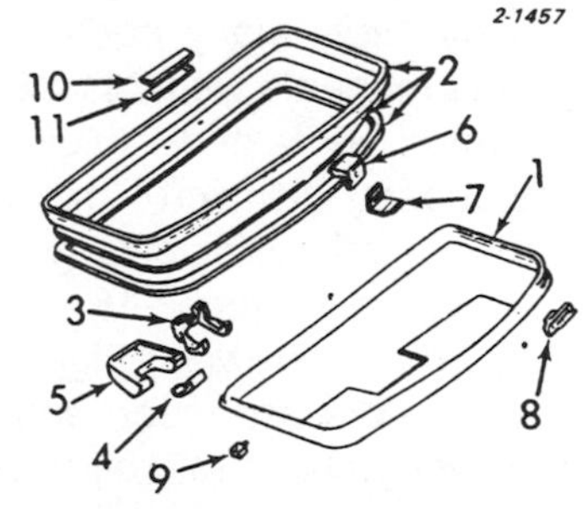

2-1457

1	Housing¶ - NSS		
	Weatherstrip, Housing¶		
	To 11-19-79	EOSZ 6651346B	20.85
	Fm 11-19-79	EOSZ 6651346B	20.85
	¶Included in Roof Panel		
2	Glass w/WStrip	EOSZ 6650054A	346.80
		NAGS R6014	281.45
	Weatherstrip, Glass	EOSZ 66502C50B	37.75
3	Bracket, Handle	80-81 E1FZ 61502M70A	6.05
		82 D8RZ 64502M70A	14.05
	Lever, Lifter	80-81 R D9ZZ 66502M85A	11.40
		L D9ZZ 66502M86A	11.40

CONT'D

Fig. 2-9. *A page from a typical collision parts manual. Such manuals show the cost of each part and the time needed to replace it. (Courtesy of Mitchell Manuals, Inc.)*

Fig. 2-10. *An example of a vehicle with severe collision damage.*

When the estimate is written, all the labor should be put down in *hours*. Then, the hours can be multiplied by the shop's charge per hour to get the *total* labor cost for the entire estimate.

To save the estimator time, each manual contains a *labor conversion table*. In the table, the labor charge is computed from 0.1 to 40 hours. Labor rates from $10 per hour to $50 per hour may be used in some manuals (Figs. 2-13 and 2-14).

Using the Table. As shown in Figure 2-13, if the shop's labor rate is $29 per hour, and if the labor total is 4.2 hours, the charge for labor is $121.80. The table provides quick, accurate results when figuring labor charges, and it saves the time of multiplying or using a calculator.

MICROFILM ESTIMATORS

The auto body teacher in Figure 2-15 is explaining a *microfilm estimator*. Many body shops are replacing collision parts manuals with this machine and its films. The information contained in collision parts manuals can be purchased on microfilm, and the film can be "shown" on the microfilm estimator. A microfilm estimator is shown in Figure 2-16, while one of the thin microfilm "cards" is shown in Figure 2-17.

These estimators are much easier to use than the thicker, bulkier manuals. Microfilm estimators speed up the estimating work on a damaged vehicle. They can cut the time involved by as much as 50 percent.

When the damage involves only a few parts, the microfilm estimator can be used to price the job while the customer looks on. The customer can see how much the parts cost and the labor time needed to install them.

Basically, a microfilm estimator is a film projector. The picture on the microfilm is magnified and projected onto the machine's lighted screen. The microfilm estimator uses a 4 × 6 in. [10.1 × 15.2 cm (centimeters)]

microfilm *card* and a 4 × 8 in. (10.1 × 20.2 cm) picture *selection card*. Each microfilm card contains about 100 pictures of body parts (Fig. 2-17). Figures 2-18 through 2-23 show how to use a microfilm estimator.

COMPUTER ESTIMATES

The cumbersome part of the estimating process has always been looking up all the parts and writing them out on the estimate, being careful to copy the part numbers correctly. A new computerized estimating system is now available. The estimator uses a worksheet with drawings of the proper make of vehicle, as shown in Figure 2-24.

The estimator decides which part is needed and checks the appropriate box. The illustration on the worksheet helps the estimator visualize the damage better and make a more accurate estimate. Current part numbers and prices are automatically supplied by the computer. This system calculates labor dollars (using hourly rates supplied by the estimator), discounts or other adjustments, local taxes, and totals. The completed estimate is computer printed for clarity.

The procedure to use when estimating a damaged vehicle is shown in Figures 2-25 to 2-29.

TYPICAL ESTIMATES

Figure 2-30 shows an example of an outer door panel (sometimes called a "skin"), which must be replaced. The inner door panel is also damaged, so additional labor is needed to straighten it. The estimate for this repair would be written as shown in Figure 2-31.

The price of the outer door panel and installation time is obtained from the collision parts manual. The price for aligning the inner door panel must be estimated. Collision parts manuals cannot tell the time needed to straighten such damage, because it depends on the seriousness of the wreck. This time must be determined by the estimator, based on experience with similar repairs.

When estimating vehicles that have not been in an accident, but have normal wear damage (such as rust-out), the estimator must be careful of areas that have been damaged for long periods of time. These can be very time consuming to fix thoroughly. Figure 2-32 shows a completed damage report (estimate) for the car in Figure 2-33. This is an example of the way in which an estimator or insurance adjuster might write an estimate for such damage.

A vehicle with heavy damage to the right side is shown in Figure 2-34. Figures 2-35 through 2-37 show the correct way to examine the damage before and during the writing of the estimate.

MODEL IDENTIFICATION

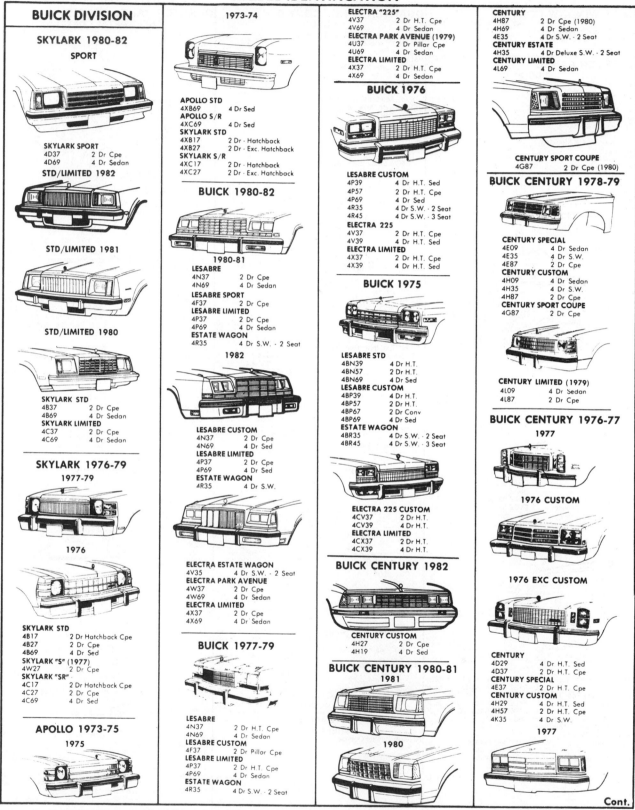

BUICK DIVISION

SKYLARK 1980-82
SPORT

SKYLARK SPORT
4D37   2 Dr Cpe
4D69   4 Dr Sedan

STD/LIMITED 1982

STD/LIMITED 1981

STD/LIMITED 1980

SKYLARK STD
4B37   2 Dr Cpe
4B69   4 Dr Sedan
SKYLARK LIMITED
4C37   2 Dr Cpe
4C69   4 Dr Sedan

SKYLARK 1976-79
1977-79

1976

SKYLARK STD
4B17   2 Dr Hatchback Cpe
4B27   2 Dr Cpe
4B69   4 Dr Sed
SKYLARK "S" (1977)
4W27   2 Dr Cpe
SKYLARK "SR"
4C17   2 Dr Hatchback Cpe
4C27   2 Dr Cpe
4C69   4 Dr Sed

APOLLO 1973-75
1975

1973-74

APOLLO STD
4XB69   4 Dr Sed
APOLLO S/R
4XC69   4 Dr Sed
SKYLARK STD
4XB17   2 Dr - Hatchback
4XB27   2 Dr - Exc. Hatchback
SKYLARK S/R
4XC17   2 Dr - Hatchback
4XC27   2 Dr - Exc. Hatchback

BUICK 1980-82

1980-81
LESABRE
4N37   2 Dr Cpe
4N69   4 Dr Sedan
LESABRE SPORT
4F37   2 Dr Cpe
LESABRE LIMITED
4P37   2 Dr Cpe
4P69   4 Dr Sedan
ESTATE WAGON
4R35   4 Dr S.W. - 2 Seat

1982

LESABRE CUSTOM
4N37   2 Dr Cpe
4N69   4 Dr Sed
LESABRE LIMITED
4P37   2 Dr Cpe
4P69   4 Dr Sed
ESTATE WAGON
4R35   4 Dr S.W.

ELECTRA ESTATE WAGON
4V35   4 Dr S.W. - 2 Seat
ELECTRA PARK AVENUE
4W37   2 Dr Cpe
4W69   4 Dr Sedan
ELECTRA LIMITED
4X37   2 Dr Cpe
4X69   4 Dr Sedan

BUICK 1977-79

LESABRE
4N37   2 Dr H.T. Cpe
4N69   4 Dr Sedan
LESABRE CUSTOM
4F37   2 Dr Pillar Cpe
LESABRE LIMITED
4P37   2 Dr H.T. Cpe
4P69   4 Dr Sedan
ESTATE WAGON
4R35   4 Dr S.W. - 2 Seat

ELECTRA "225"
4V37   2 Dr H.T. Cpe
4V69   4 Dr Sedan
ELECTRA PARK AVENUE (1979)
4U37   2 Dr Pillar Cpe
4U69   4 Dr Sedan
ELECTRA LIMITED
4X37   2 Dr H.T. Cpe
4X69   4 Dr Sedan

BUICK 1976

LESABRE CUSTOM
4P39   4 Dr H.T. Sed
4P57   2 Dr H.T. Cpe
4P69   4 Dr Sed
4R35   4 Dr S.W. - 2 Seat
4R45   4 Dr S.W. - 3 Seat
ELECTRA 225
4V37   2 Dr H.T. Cpe
4V39   4 Dr H.T. Sed
ELECTRA LIMITED
4X37   2 Dr H.T. Cpe
4X39   4 Dr H.T. Sed

BUICK 1975

LESABRE STD
4BN39   4 Dr H.T.
4BN57   2 Dr H.T.
4BN69   4 Dr Sed
LESABRE CUSTOM
4BP39   4 Dr H.T.
4BP57   2 Dr H.T.
4BP67   2 Dr Conv
4BP69   4 Dr Sed
ESTATE WAGON
4BR35   4 Dr S.W. - 2 Seat
4BR45   4 Dr S.W. - 3 Seat

ELECTRA 225 CUSTOM
4CV37   2 Dr H.T.
4CV39   4 Dr H.T.
ELECTRA LIMITED
4CX37   2 Dr H.T.
4CX39   4 Dr H.T.

BUICK CENTURY 1982

CENTURY CUSTOM
4H27   2 Dr Cpe
4H19   4 Dr Sed

BUICK CENTURY 1980-81
1981

1980

CENTURY
4H87   2 Dr Cpe (1980)
4H69   4 Dr Sedan
4E35   4 Dr S.W. - 2 Seat
CENTURY ESTATE
4H35   4 Dr Deluxe S.W. - 2 Seat
CENTURY LIMITED
4L69   4 Dr Sedan

CENTURY SPORT COUPE
4G87   2 Dr Cpe (1980)

BUICK CENTURY 1978-79

CENTURY SPECIAL
4E09   4 Dr Sedan
4E35   4 Dr S.W.
4E87   2 Dr Cpe
CENTURY CUSTOM
4H09   4 Dr Sedan
4H35   4 Dr S.W.
4H87   2 Dr Cpe
CENTURY SPORT COUPE
4G87   2 Dr Cpe

CENTURY LIMITED (1979)
4L09   4 Dr Sedan
4L87   2 Dr Cpe

BUICK CENTURY 1976-77
1977

1976 CUSTOM

1976 EXC CUSTOM

CENTURY
4D29   4 Dr H.T. Sed
4D37   2 Dr H.T. Cpe
CENTURY SPECIAL
4E37   2 Dr H.T. Cpe
CENTURY CUSTOM
4H29   4 Dr H.T. Sed
4H57   2 Dr H.T. Cpe
4K35   4 Dr S.W.
1977

Cont.

Fig. 2-11. *A model identification page from a collision parts manual. Because of parts differences, it is important to identify the exact model of the damaged car. (Courtesy of Mitchell Manuals, Inc.)*

BACK WINDOW CONT'D

Black¶	E14Y 5442404AA		17.90

¶Order by Color
Moulding, Inside Garnish
Paint to Match   E1DZ 5442410A   6.00

QUARTER PANEL
2 DOOR
SHEET METAL

Refinish Quarter Outside		3.0
Add For Pillar		.5
R&I Rear Seat & Quarter Trim		.8
Add to Quarter R&R		
To Drill For & Install		
One Moulding		.3
Each Additional Moulding		.2
w/Vinyl Roof		1.0
R&R Quarter Outer Panel		
w/Roof Removed		
Right		12.0
Left		11.0
Lower Section¶		
Right		12.5
Left		11.5
¶Cut Below Back Glass		

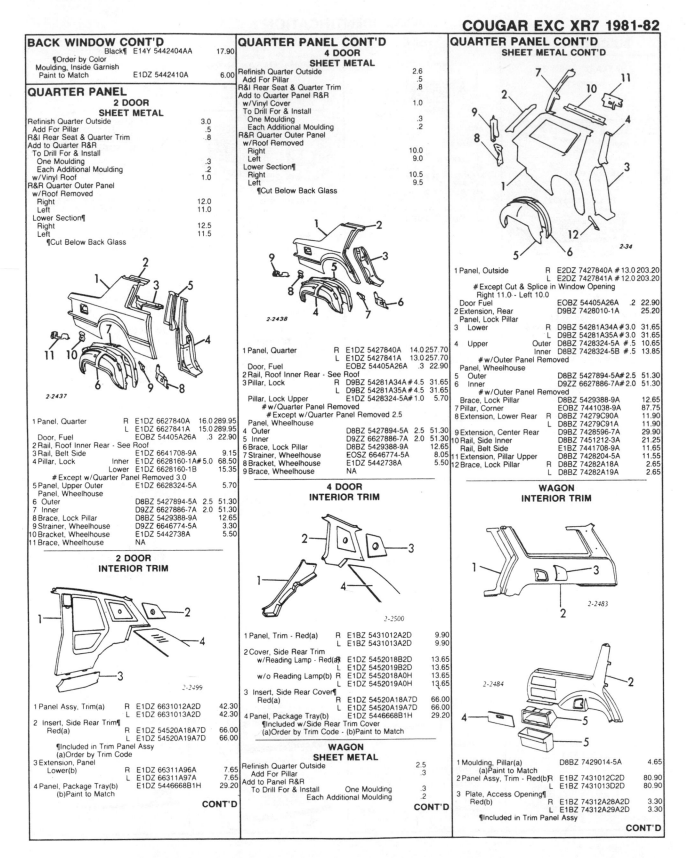

2-2437

1 Panel, Quarter	R	E1DZ 6627840A	16.0	289.95
	L	E1DZ 6627841A	15.0	289.95
Door, Fuel		EOBZ 54405A26A	.3	22.90
2 Rail, Roof Inner Rear - See Roof				
3 Rail, Belt Side		E1DZ 6641708-9A		9.15
4 Pillar, Lock	Inner	E1DZ 6628160-1A#	5.0	68.50
	Lower	E1DZ 6628160-1B		15.35
# Except w/Quarter Panel Removed 3.0				
5 Panel, Upper Outer		E1DZ 6628324-5A		5.70
Panel, Wheelhouse				
6 Outer		D8BZ 5427894-5A	2.5	51.30
7 Inner		D9ZZ 6627886-7A	2.0	51.30
8 Brace, Lock Pillar		D8BZ 5429388-9A		12.65
9 Strainer, Wheelhouse		D9ZZ 6646774-5A		3.30
10 Bracket, Wheelhouse		E1DZ 5442738A		5.50
11 Brace, Wheelhouse		NA		

2 DOOR
INTERIOR TRIM

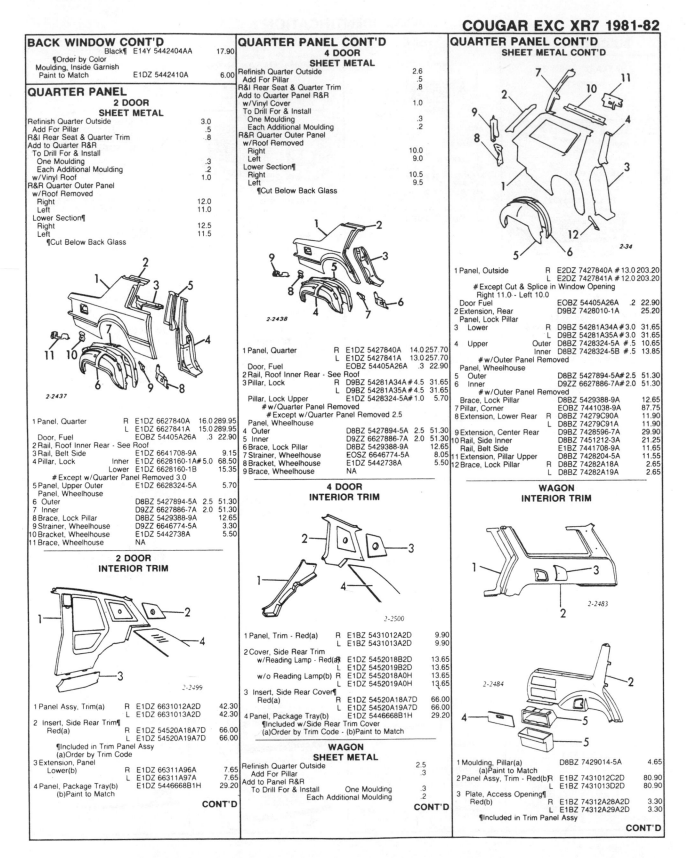

2-2499

1 Panel Assy, Trim(a)	R	E1DZ 6631012A2D		42.30
	L	E1DZ 6631013A2D		42.30
2 Insert, Side Rear Trim¶				
Red(a)	R	E1DZ 54520A18A7D		66.00
	L	E1DZ 54520A19A7D		66.00
¶Included in Trim Panel Assy				
(a)Order by Trim Code				
3 Extension, Panel				
Lower(b)	R	E1DZ 66311A96A		7.65
	L	E1DZ 66311A97A		7.65
4 Panel, Package Tray(b)		E1DZ 5446668B1H		29.20
(b)Paint to Match				

CONT'D

QUARTER PANEL CONT'D
4 DOOR
SHEET METAL

Refinish Quarter Outside		2.6
Add For Pillar		.5
R&I Rear Seat & Quarter Trim		.8
Add to Quarter Panel R&R		
w/Vinyl Cover		1.0
To Drill For & Install		
One Moulding		.3
Each Additional Moulding		.2
R&R Quarter Outer Panel		
w/Roof Removed		
Right		10.0
Left		9.0
Lower Section¶		
Right		10.5
Left		9.5
¶Cut Below Back Glass		

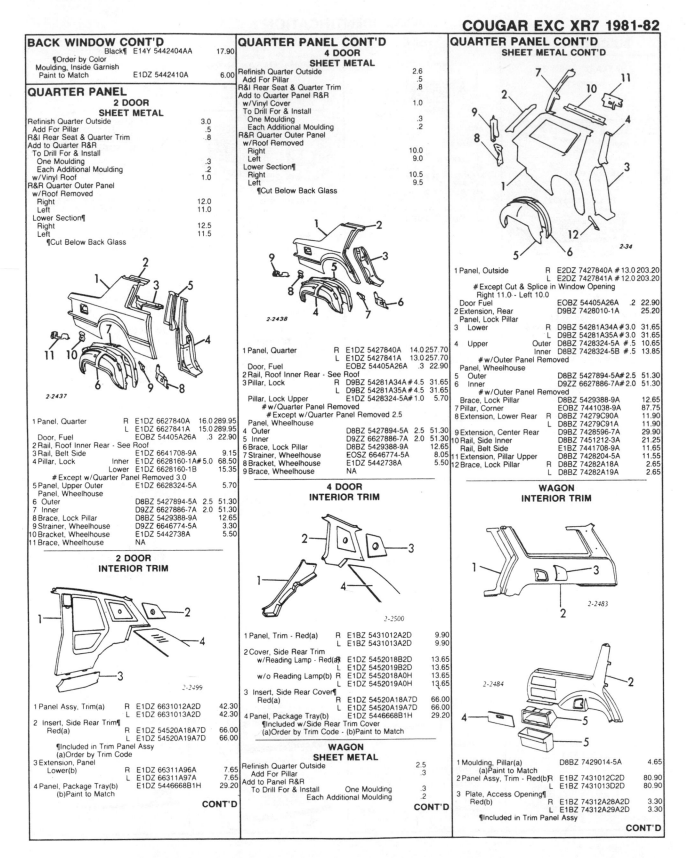

2-2438

1 Panel, Quarter	R	E1DZ 5427840A	14.0	257.70
	L	E1DZ 5427841A	13.0	257.70
Door, Fuel		EOBZ 54405A26A	.3	22.90
2 Rail, Roof Inner Rear - See Roof				
3 Pillar, Lock	R	D9BZ 54281A34A#	4.5	31.65
	L	D9BZ 54281A35A#	4.5	31.65
Pillar, Lock Upper		E1DZ 5428324-5A#	1.0	5.70
# w/Quarter Panel Removed				
# Except w/Quarter Panel Removed 2.5				
Panel, Wheelhouse				
4 Outer		D8BZ 5427894-5A	2.5	51.30
5 Inner		D9ZZ 6627886-7A	2.0	51.30
6 Brace, Lock Pillar		D8BZ 5429388-9A		12.65
7 Strainer, Wheelhouse		EOSZ 6646774-5A		8.05
8 Bracket, Wheelhouse		E1DZ 5442738A		5.50
9 Brace, Wheelhouse		NA		

4 DOOR
INTERIOR TRIM

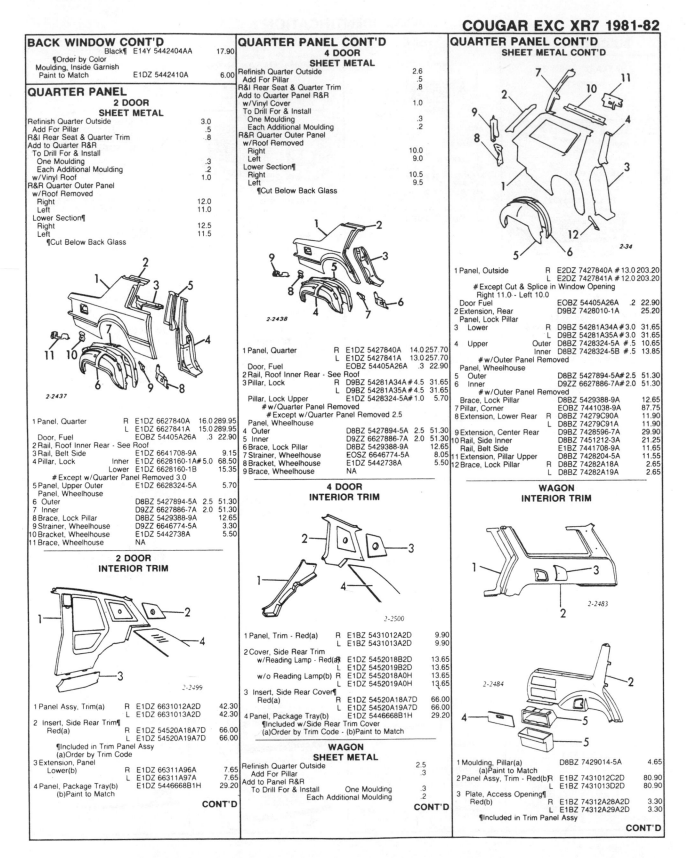

2-2500

1 Panel, Trim - Red(a)	R	E1BZ 5431012A2D		9.90
	L	E1BZ 5431013A2D		9.90
2 Cover, Side Rear Trim				
w/Reading Lamp - Red(a)	R	E1DZ 5452018B2D		13.65
	L	E1DZ 5452019B2D		13.65
w/o Reading Lamp(b)	R	E1DZ 5452018A0H		13.65
	L	E1DZ 5452019A0H		13.65
3 Insert, Side Rear Cover¶				
Red(a)	R	E1DZ 54520A18A7D		66.00
	L	E1DZ 54520A19A7D		66.00
4 Panel, Package Tray(b)		E1DZ 5446668B1H		29.20
¶Included w/Side Rear Trim Cover				
(a)Order by Trim Code - (b)Paint to Match				

WAGON
SHEET METAL

Refinish Quarter Outside		2.5
Add For Pillar		.3
Add to Panel R&R		
To Drill For & Install	One Moulding	.3
	Each Additional Moulding	.2

CONT'D

QUARTER PANEL CONT'D
SHEET METAL CONT'D

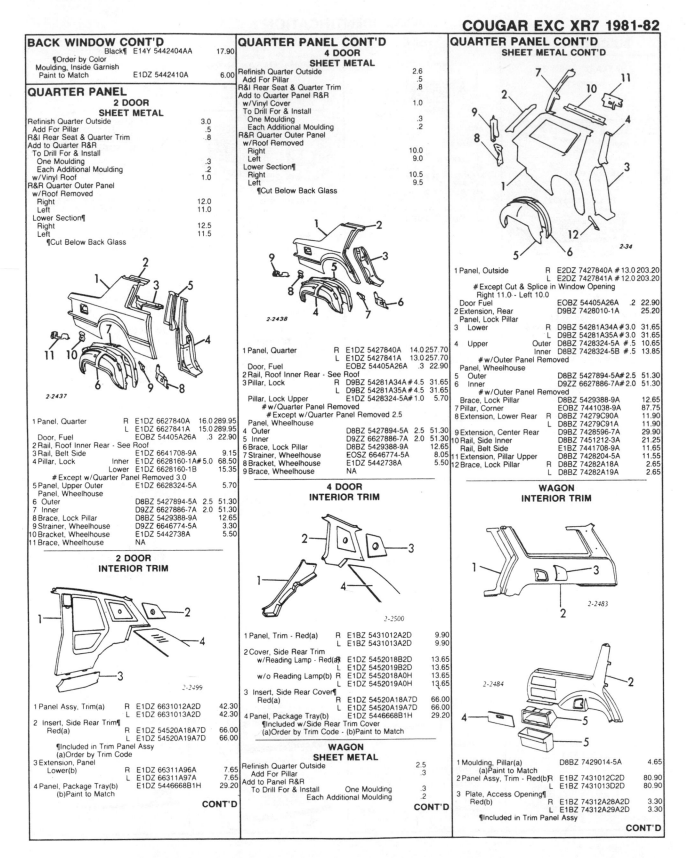

2-34

1 Panel, Outside	R	E2DZ 7427840A #	13.0	203.20
	L	E2DZ 7427841A #	12.0	203.20
# Except Cut & Splice in Window Opening				
Right 11.0 - Left 10.0				
Door Fuel		EOBZ 54405A26A	.2	22.90
2 Extension, Rear		D9BZ 7428010-1A		25.20
Panel, Lock Pillar				
3 Lower	R	D9BZ 54281A34A#	3.0	31.65
	L	D9BZ 54281A35A#	3.0	31.65
4 Upper	Outer	D8BZ 7428324-5A #	.5	10.65
	Inner	D8BZ 7428324-5B #	.5	13.85
# w/Outer Panel Removed				
Panel, Wheelhouse				
5 Outer		D8BZ 5427894-5A#	2.5	51.30
6 Inner		D9ZZ 6627886-7A#	2.0	51.30
# w/Outer Panel Removed				
Brace, Lock Pillar		D8BZ 5429388-9A		12.65
7 Pillar, Corner		EOBZ 7441038-9A		87.75
8 Extension, Lower Rear	R	D8BZ 74279C90A		11.90
	L	D8BZ 74279C91A		11.90
9 Extension, Center Rear		D9BZ 7428596-7A		29.90
10 Rail, Side Inner		D8BZ 7451212-3A		21.25
Rail, Belt Side		E1BZ 7441708-9A		11.65
11 Extension, Pillar Upper		D8BZ 7428204-5A		11.55
12 Brace, Lock Pillar	R	D8BZ 74282A18A		2.65
	L	D8BZ 74282A19A		2.65

WAGON
INTERIOR TRIM

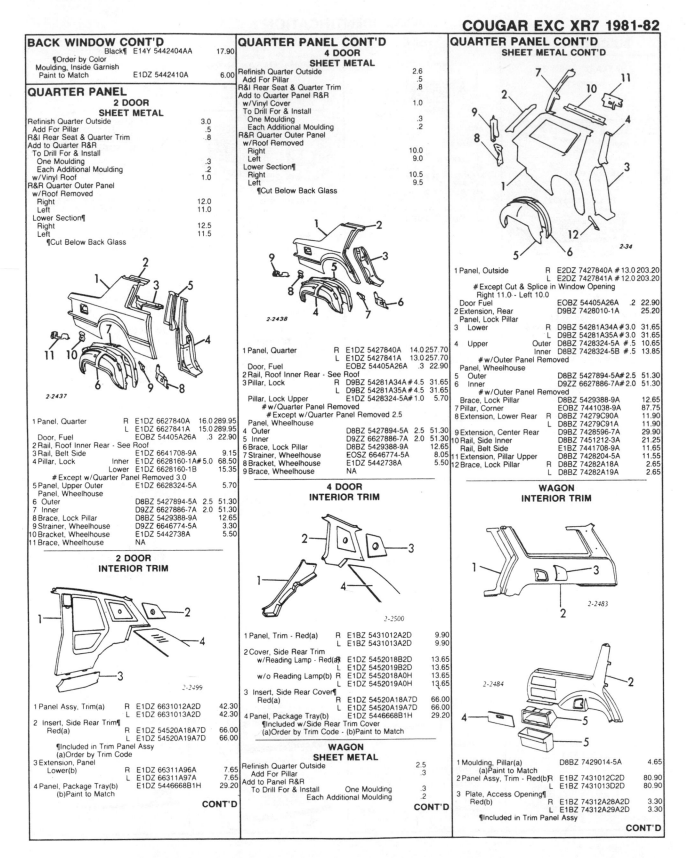

2-2483

2-2484

1 Moulding, Pillar(a)		D8BZ 7429014-5A		4.65
(a)Paint to Match				
2 Panel Assy, Trim - Red(b)	R	E1BZ 7431012C2D		80.90
	L	E1BZ 7431013D2D		80.90
3 Plate, Access Opening¶				
Red(b)	R	E1BZ 74312A28A2D		3.30
	L	E1BZ 74312A29A2D		3.30
¶Included in Trim Panel Assy				

CONT'D

Fig. 2-12. *An accurate estimate depends on being able to use the collision parts manual. The part number is listed, along with its price and the installation time. (Courtesy of Mitchell Manuals, Inc.)*

CONVERSION TABLE
Labor Times to Dollars

FOR DOLLAR RATES ENDING WITH 50 CENTS, ADD THIS COLUMN TO YOUR RATE COLUMN.

Time	$10	$11	$12	$13	$14	$15	$16	$17	$18	$19	$20	.50	$21	$22	$23	$24	$25	$26	$27	$28	$29	$30
0.1	1.00	1.10	1.20	1.30	1.40	1.50	1.60	1.70	1.80	1.90	2.00	.05	2.10	2.20	2.30	2.40	2.50	2.60	2.70	2.80	2.90	3.00
0.2	2.00	2.20	2.40	2.60	2.80	3.00	3.20	3.40	3.60	3.80	4.00	.10	4.20	4.40	4.60	4.80	5.00	5.20	5.40	5.60	5.80	6.00
0.3	3.00	3.30	3.60	3.90	4.20	4.50	4.80	5.10	5.40	5.70	6.00	.15	6.30	6.60	6.90	7.20	7.50	7.80	8.10	8.40	8.70	9.00
0.4	4.00	4.40	4.80	5.20	5.60	6.00	6.40	6.80	7.20	7.60	8.00	.20	8.40	8.80	9.20	9.60	10.00	10.40	10.80	11.20	11.60	12.00
0.5	5.00	5.50	6.00	6.50	7.00	7.50	8.00	8.50	9.00	9.50	10.00	.25	10.50	11.00	11.50	12.00	12.50	13.00	13.50	14.00	14.50	15.00
0.6	6.00	6.60	7.20	7.80	8.40	9.00	9.60	10.20	10.80	11.40	12.00	.30	12.60	13.20	13.80	14.40	15.00	15.60	16.20	16.80	17.40	18.00
0.7	7.00	7.70	8.40	9.10	9.80	10.50	11.20	11.90	12.60	13.30	14.00	.35	14.70	15.40	16.10	16.80	17.50	18.20	18.90	19.60	20.30	21.00
0.8	8.00	8.80	9.60	10.40	11.20	12.00	12.80	13.60	14.40	15.20	16.00	.40	16.80	17.60	18.40	19.20	20.00	20.80	21.60	22.40	23.20	24.00
0.9	9.00	9.90	10.80	11.70	12.60	13.50	14.40	15.30	16.20	17.10	18.00	.45	18.90	19.80	20.70	21.60	22.50	23.40	24.30	25.20	26.10	27.00
1.0	10.00	11.00	12.00	13.00	14.00	15.00	16.00	17.00	18.00	19.00	20.00	.50	21.00	22.00	23.00	24.00	25.00	26.00	27.00	28.00	29.00	30.00
1.1	11.00	12.10	13.20	14.30	15.40	16.50	17.60	18.70	19.80	20.90	22.00	.55	23.10	24.20	25.30	26.40	27.50	28.60	29.70	30.80	31.90	33.00
1.2	12.00	13.20	14.40	15.60	16.80	18.00	19.20	20.40	21.60	22.80	24.00	.60	25.20	26.40	27.60	28.80	30.00	31.20	32.40	33.60	34.80	36.00
1.3	13.00	14.30	15.60	16.90	18.20	19.50	20.80	22.10	23.40	24.70	26.00	.65	27.30	28.60	29.90	31.20	32.50	33.80	35.10	36.40	37.70	39.00
1.4	14.00	15.40	16.80	18.20	19.60	21.00	22.40	23.80	25.20	26.60	28.00	.70	29.40	30.80	32.20	33.60	35.00	36.40	37.80	39.20	40.60	42.00
1.5	15.00	16.50	18.00	19.50	21.00	22.50	24.00	25.50	27.00	28.50	30.00	.75	31.50	33.00	34.50	36.00	37.50	39.00	40.50	42.00	43.50	45.00
1.6	16.00	17.60	19.20	20.80	22.40	24.00	25.60	27.20	28.80	30.40	32.00	.80	33.60	35.20	36.80	38.40	40.00	41.60	43.20	44.80	46.40	48.00
1.7	17.00	18.70	20.40	22.10	23.80	25.50	27.20	28.90	30.60	32.30	34.00	.85	35.70	37.40	39.10	40.80	42.50	44.20	45.90	47.60	49.30	51.00
1.8	18.00	19.80	21.60	23.40	25.20	27.00	28.80	30.60	32.40	34.20	36.00	.90	37.80	39.60	41.40	43.20	45.00	46.80	48.60	50.40	52.20	54.00
1.9	19.00	20.90	22.80	24.70	26.60	28.50	30.40	32.30	34.20	36.10	38.00	.95	39.90	41.80	43.70	45.60	47.50	49.40	51.30	53.20	55.10	57.00
2.0	20.00	22.00	24.00	26.00	28.00	30.00	32.00	34.00	36.00	38.00	40.00	1.00	42.00	44.00	46.00	48.00	50.00	52.00	54.00	56.00	58.00	60.00
2.1	21.00	23.10	25.20	27.30	29.40	31.50	33.60	35.70	37.80	39.90	42.00	1.05	44.10	46.20	48.30	50.40	52.50	54.60	56.70	58.80	60.90	63.00
2.2	22.00	24.20	26.40	28.60	30.80	33.00	35.20	37.40	39.60	41.80	44.00	1.10	46.20	48.40	50.60	52.80	55.00	57.20	59.40	61.60	63.80	66.00
2.3	23.00	25.30	27.60	29.90	32.20	34.50	36.80	39.10	41.40	43.70	46.00	1.15	48.30	50.60	52.90	55.20	57.50	59.80	62.10	64.40	66.70	69.00
2.4	24.00	26.40	28.80	31.20	33.60	36.00	38.40	40.80	43.20	45.60	48.00	1.20	50.40	52.80	55.20	57.60	60.00	62.40	64.80	67.20	69.60	72.00
2.5	25.00	27.50	30.00	32.50	35.00	37.50	40.00	42.50	45.00	47.50	50.00	1.25	52.50	55.00	57.50	60.00	62.50	65.00	67.50	70.00	72.50	75.00
2.6	26.00	28.60	31.20	33.80	36.40	39.00	41.60	44.20	46.80	49.40	52.00	1.30	54.60	57.20	59.80	62.40	65.00	67.60	70.20	72.80	75.40	78.00
2.7	27.00	29.70	32.40	35.10	37.80	40.50	43.20	45.90	48.60	51.30	54.00	1.35	56.70	59.40	62.10	64.80	67.50	70.20	72.90	75.60	78.30	81.00
2.8	28.00	30.80	33.60	36.40	39.20	42.00	44.80	47.60	50.40	53.20	56.00	1.40	58.80	61.60	64.40	67.20	70.00	72.80	75.60	78.40	81.20	84.00
2.9	29.00	31.90	34.80	37.70	40.60	43.50	46.40	49.30	52.20	55.10	58.00	1.45	60.90	63.80	66.70	69.60	72.50	75.40	78.30	81.20	84.10	87.00
3.0	30.00	33.00	36.00	39.00	42.00	45.00	48.00	51.00	54.00	57.00	60.00	1.50	63.00	66.00	69.00	72.00	75.00	78.00	81.00	84.00	87.00	90.00
3.1	31.00	34.10	37.20	40.30	43.40	46.50	49.60	52.70	55.80	58.90	62.00	1.55	65.10	68.20	71.30	74.40	77.50	80.60	83.70	86.80	89.90	93.00
3.2	32.00	35.20	38.40	41.60	44.80	48.00	51.20	54.40	57.60	60.80	64.00	1.60	67.20	70.40	73.60	76.80	80.00	83.20	86.40	89.60	92.80	96.00
3.3	33.00	36.30	39.60	42.90	46.20	49.50	52.80	56.10	59.40	62.70	66.00	1.65	69.30	72.60	75.90	79.20	82.50	85.80	89.10	92.40	95.70	99.00
3.4	34.00	37.40	40.80	44.20	47.60	51.00	54.40	57.80	61.20	64.60	68.00	1.70	71.40	74.80	78.20	81.60	85.00	88.40	91.80	95.20	98.60	102.00
3.5	35.00	38.50	42.00	45.50	49.00	52.50	56.00	59.50	63.00	66.50	70.00	1.75	73.50	77.00	80.50	84.00	87.50	91.00	94.50	98.00	101.50	105.00
3.6	36.00	39.60	43.20	46.80	50.40	54.00	57.60	61.20	64.80	68.40	72.00	1.80	75.60	79.20	82.80	86.40	90.00	93.60	97.20	100.80	104.40	108.00
3.7	37.00	40.70	44.40	48.10	51.80	55.50	59.20	62.90	66.60	70.30	74.00	1.85	77.70	81.40	85.10	88.80	92.50	96.20	99.90	103.60	107.30	111.00
3.8	38.00	41.80	45.60	49.40	53.20	57.00	60.80	64.60	68.40	72.20	76.00	1.90	79.80	83.60	87.40	91.20	95.00	98.80	102.60	106.40	110.20	114.00
3.9	39.00	42.90	46.80	50.70	54.60	58.50	62.40	66.30	70.20	74.10	78.00	1.95	81.90	85.80	89.70	93.60	97.50	101.40	105.30	109.20	113.10	117.00
4.0	40.00	44.00	48.00	52.00	56.00	60.00	64.00	68.00	72.00	76.00	80.00	2.00	84.00	88.00	92.00	96.00	100.00	104.00	108.00	112.00	116.00	120.00
4.1	41.00	45.10	49.20	53.30	57.40	61.50	65.60	69.70	73.80	77.90	82.00	2.05	86.10	90.20	94.30	98.40	102.50	106.60	110.70	114.80	118.90	123.00
4.2	42.00	46.20	50.40	54.60	58.80	63.00	67.20	71.40	75.60	79.80	84.00	2.10	88.20	92.40	96.60	100.80	105.00	109.20	113.40	117.60	121.80	126.00
4.3	43.00	47.30	51.60	55.90	60.20	64.50	68.80	73.10	77.40	81.70	86.00	2.15	90.30	94.60	98.90	103.20	107.50	111.80	116.10	120.40	124.70	129.00
4.4	44.00	48.40	52.80	57.20	61.60	66.00	70.40	74.80	79.20	83.60	88.00	2.20	92.40	96.80	101.20	105.60	110.00	114.40	118.80	123.20	127.60	132.00
4.5	45.00	49.50	54.00	58.50	63.00	67.50	72.00	76.50	81.00	85.50	90.00	2.25	94.50	99.00	103.50	108.00	112.50	117.00	121.50	126.00	130.50	135.00
4.6	46.00	50.60	55.20	59.80	64.40	69.00	73.60	78.20	82.80	87.40	92.00	2.30	96.60	101.20	105.80	110.40	115.00	119.60	124.20	128.80	133.40	138.00
4.7	47.00	51.70	56.40	61.10	65.80	70.50	75.20	79.90	84.60	89.30	94.00	2.35	98.70	103.40	108.10	112.80	117.50	122.20	126.90	131.60	136.30	141.00
4.8	48.00	52.80	57.60	62.40	67.20	72.00	76.80	81.60	86.40	91.20	96.00	2.40	100.80	105.60	110.40	115.20	120.00	124.80	129.60	134.40	139.20	144.00
4.9	49.00	53.90	58.80	63.70	68.60	73.50	78.40	83.30	88.20	93.10	98.00	2.45	102.90	107.80	112.70	117.60	122.50	127.40	132.30	137.20	142.10	147.00
5.0	50.00	55.00	60.00	65.00	70.00	75.00	80.00	85.00	90.00	95.00	100.00	2.50	105.00	110.00	115.00	120.00	125.00	130.00	135.00	140.00	145.00	150.00
5.1	51.00	56.10	61.20	66.30	71.40	76.50	81.60	86.70	91.80	96.90	102.00	2.55	107.10	112.20	117.30	122.40	127.50	132.60	137.70	142.80	147.90	153.00
5.2	52.00	57.20	62.40	67.60	72.80	78.00	83.20	88.40	93.60	98.80	104.00	2.60	109.20	114.40	119.60	124.80	130.00	135.20	140.40	145.60	150.80	156.00
5.3	53.00	58.30	63.60	68.90	74.20	79.50	84.80	90.10	95.40	100.70	106.00	2.65	111.30	116.60	121.90	127.20	132.50	137.80	143.10	148.40	153.70	159.00
5.4	54.00	59.40	64.80	70.20	75.60	81.00	86.40	91.80	97.20	102.60	108.00	2.70	113.40	118.80	124.20	129.60	135.00	140.40	145.80	151.20	156.60	162.00
5.5	55.00	60.50	66.00	71.50	77.00	82.50	88.00	93.50	99.00	104.50	110.00	2.75	115.50	121.00	126.50	132.00	137.50	143.00	148.50	154.00	159.50	165.00
5.6	56.00	61.60	67.20	72.80	78.40	84.00	89.60	95.20	100.80	106.40	112.00	2.80	117.60	123.20	128.80	134.40	140.00	145.60	151.20	156.80	162.40	168.00
5.7	57.00	62.70	68.40	74.10	79.80	85.50	91.20	96.90	102.60	108.30	114.00	2.85	119.70	125.40	131.10	136.80	142.50	148.20	153.90	159.60	165.30	171.00
5.8	58.00	63.80	69.60	75.40	81.20	87.00	92.80	98.60	104.40	110.20	116.00	2.90	121.80	127.60	133.40	139.20	145.00	150.80	156.60	162.40	168.20	174.00
5.9	59.00	64.90	70.80	76.70	82.60	88.50	94.40	100.30	106.20	112.10	118.00	2.95	123.90	129.80	135.70	141.60	147.50	153.40	159.30	165.20	171.10	177.00

Fig. 2-13. *A labor conversion table allows the estimator to determine labor charges quickly. This chart is for shorter jobs at lower hourly rates. (Courtesy of Mitchell Manuals, Inc.)*

CONVERSION TABLE
Labor Times to Dollars

FOR DOLLAR RATES ENDING WITH 50 CENTS, ADD THIS COLUMN TO YOUR RATE COLUMN.

Time	$31	$32	$33	$34	$35	$36	$37	$38	$39	$40	.50	$41	$42	$43	$44	$45	$46	$47	$48	$49	$50
6.0	186.00	192.00	198.00	204.00	210.00	216.00	222.00	228.00	234.00	240.00	3.00	246.00	252.00	258.00	264.00	270.00	276.00	282.00	288.00	294.00	300.00
6.1	189.10	195.20	201.30	207.40	213.50	219.60	225.70	231.80	237.90	244.00	3.05	250.10	256.20	262.30	268.40	274.50	280.60	286.70	292.80	298.90	305.00
6.2	192.20	198.40	204.60	210.80	217.00	223.20	229.40	235.60	241.80	248.00	3.10	254.20	260.40	266.60	272.80	279.00	285.20	291.40	297.60	303.80	310.00
6.3	195.30	201.60	207.90	214.20	220.50	226.80	233.10	239.40	245.70	252.00	3.15	258.30	264.60	270.90	277.20	283.50	289.80	296.10	302.40	308.70	315.00
6.4	198.40	204.80	211.20	217.60	224.00	230.40	236.80	243.20	249.60	256.00	3.20	262.40	268.80	275.20	281.60	288.00	294.40	300.80	307.20	313.60	320.00
6.5	201.50	208.00	214.50	221.00	227.50	234.00	240.50	247.00	253.50	260.00	3.25	266.50	273.00	279.50	286.00	292.50	299.00	305.50	312.00	318.50	325.00
6.6	204.60	211.20	217.80	224.40	231.00	237.60	244.20	250.80	257.40	264.00	3.30	270.60	277.20	283.80	290.40	297.00	303.60	310.20	316.80	323.40	330.00
6.7	207.70	214.40	221.10	227.80	234.50	241.20	247.90	254.60	261.30	268.00	3.35	274.70	281.40	288.10	294.80	301.50	308.20	314.90	321.60	328.30	335.00
6.8	210.80	217.60	224.40	231.20	238.00	244.80	251.60	258.40	265.20	272.00	3.40	278.80	285.60	292.40	299.20	306.00	312.80	319.60	326.40	333.20	340.00
6.9	213.90	220.80	227.70	234.60	241.50	248.40	255.30	262.20	269.10	276.00	3.45	282.90	289.80	296.70	303.60	310.50	317.40	324.30	331.20	338.10	345.00
7.0	217.00	224.00	231.00	238.00	245.00	252.00	259.00	266.00	273.00	280.00	3.50	287.00	294.00	301.00	308.00	315.00	322.00	329.00	336.00	343.00	350.00
7.1	220.10	227.20	234.30	241.40	248.50	255.60	262.70	269.80	276.90	284.00	3.55	291.10	298.20	305.30	312.40	319.50	326.60	333.70	340.80	347.90	355.00
7.2	223.20	230.40	237.60	244.80	252.00	259.20	266.40	273.60	280.80	288.00	3.60	295.20	302.40	309.60	316.80	324.00	331.20	338.40	345.60	352.80	360.00
7.3	226.30	233.60	240.90	248.20	255.50	262.80	270.10	277.40	284.70	292.00	3.65	299.30	306.60	313.90	321.20	328.50	335.80	343.10	350.40	357.70	365.00
7.4	229.40	236.80	244.20	251.60	259.00	266.40	273.80	281.20	288.60	296.00	3.70	303.40	310.80	318.20	325.60	333.00	340.40	347.80	355.20	362.60	370.00
7.5	232.50	240.00	247.50	255.00	262.50	270.00	277.50	285.00	292.50	300.00	3.75	307.50	315.00	322.50	330.00	337.50	345.00	352.50	360.00	367.50	375.00
7.6	235.60	243.20	250.80	258.40	266.00	273.60	281.20	288.80	296.40	304.00	3.80	311.60	319.20	326.80	334.40	342.00	349.60	357.20	364.80	372.40	380.00
7.7	238.70	246.40	254.10	261.80	269.50	277.20	284.90	292.60	300.30	308.00	3.85	315.70	323.40	331.10	338.80	346.50	354.20	361.90	369.60	377.30	385.00
7.8	241.80	249.60	257.40	265.20	273.00	280.80	288.60	296.40	304.20	312.00	3.90	319.80	327.60	335.40	343.20	351.00	358.80	366.60	374.40	382.20	390.00
7.9	244.90	252.80	260.70	268.60	276.50	284.40	292.30	300.20	308.10	316.00	3.95	323.90	331.80	339.70	347.60	355.50	363.40	371.30	379.20	387.10	395.00
8.0	248.00	256.00	264.00	272.00	280.00	288.00	296.00	304.00	312.00	320.00	4.00	328.00	336.00	344.00	352.00	360.00	368.00	376.00	384.00	392.00	400.00
8.1	251.10	259.20	267.30	275.40	283.50	291.60	299.70	307.80	315.90	324.00	4.05	332.10	340.20	348.30	356.40	364.50	372.60	380.70	388.80	396.90	405.00
8.2	254.20	262.40	270.60	278.80	287.00	295.20	303.40	311.60	319.80	328.00	4.10	336.20	344.40	352.60	360.80	369.00	377.20	385.40	393.60	401.80	410.00
8.3	257.30	265.60	273.90	282.20	290.50	298.80	307.10	315.40	323.70	332.00	4.15	340.30	348.60	356.90	365.20	373.50	381.80	390.10	398.40	406.70	415.00
8.4	260.40	268.80	277.20	285.60	294.00	302.40	310.80	319.20	327.60	336.00	4.20	344.40	352.80	361.20	369.60	378.00	386.40	394.80	403.20	411.60	420.00
8.5	263.50	272.00	280.50	289.00	297.50	306.00	314.50	323.00	331.50	340.00	4.25	348.50	357.00	365.50	374.00	382.50	391.00	399.50	408.00	416.50	425.00
8.6	266.60	275.20	283.80	292.40	301.00	309.60	318.20	326.80	335.40	344.00	4.30	352.60	361.20	369.80	378.40	387.00	395.60	404.20	412.80	421.40	430.00
8.7	269.70	278.40	287.10	295.80	304.50	313.20	321.90	330.60	339.30	348.00	4.35	356.70	365.40	374.10	382.80	391.50	400.20	408.90	417.60	426.30	435.00
8.8	272.80	281.60	290.40	299.20	308.00	316.80	325.60	334.40	343.20	352.00	4.40	360.80	369.60	378.40	387.20	396.00	404.80	413.60	422.40	431.20	440.00
8.9	275.90	284.80	293.70	302.60	311.50	320.40	329.30	338.20	347.10	356.00	4.45	364.90	373.80	382.70	391.60	400.50	409.40	418.30	427.20	436.10	445.00
9.0	279.00	288.00	297.00	306.00	315.00	324.00	333.00	342.00	351.00	360.00	4.50	369.00	378.00	387.00	396.00	405.00	414.00	423.00	432.00	441.00	450.00
9.1	282.10	291.20	300.30	309.40	318.50	327.60	336.70	345.80	354.90	364.00	4.55	373.10	382.20	391.30	400.40	409.50	418.60	427.70	436.80	445.90	455.00
9.2	285.20	294.40	303.60	312.80	322.00	331.20	340.40	349.60	358.80	368.00	4.60	377.20	386.40	395.60	404.80	414.00	423.20	432.40	441.60	450.80	460.00
9.3	288.30	297.60	306.90	316.20	325.50	334.80	344.10	353.40	362.70	372.00	4.65	381.30	390.60	399.90	409.20	418.50	427.80	437.10	446.40	455.70	465.00
9.4	291.40	300.80	310.20	319.60	329.00	338.40	347.80	357.20	366.60	376.00	4.70	385.40	394.80	404.20	413.60	423.00	432.40	441.80	451.20	460.60	470.00
9.5	294.50	304.00	313.50	323.00	332.50	342.00	351.50	361.00	370.50	380.00	4.75	389.50	399.00	408.50	418.00	427.50	437.00	446.50	456.00	465.50	475.00
9.6	297.60	307.20	316.80	326.40	336.00	345.60	355.20	364.80	374.40	384.00	4.80	393.60	403.20	412.80	422.40	432.00	441.60	451.20	460.80	470.40	480.00
9.7	300.70	310.40	320.10	329.80	339.50	349.20	358.90	368.60	378.30	388.00	4.85	397.70	407.40	417.10	426.80	436.50	446.20	455.90	465.60	475.30	485.00
9.8	303.80	313.60	323.40	333.20	343.00	352.80	362.60	372.40	382.20	392.00	4.90	401.80	411.60	421.40	431.20	441.00	450.80	460.60	470.40	480.20	490.00
9.9	306.90	316.80	326.70	336.60	346.50	356.40	366.30	376.20	386.10	396.00	4.95	405.90	415.80	425.70	435.60	445.50	455.40	465.30	475.20	485.10	495.00
10.0	310.00	320.00	330.00	340.00	350.00	360.00	370.00	380.00	390.00	400.00	5.00	410.00	420.00	430.00	440.00	450.00	460.00	470.00	480.00	490.00	500.00
10.5	325.50	336.00	346.50	357.00	367.50	378.00	388.50	399.00	409.50	420.00	5.25	430.50	441.00	451.50	462.00	472.50	483.00	493.50	504.00	514.50	525.00
11.0	341.00	352.00	363.00	374.00	385.00	396.00	407.00	418.00	429.00	440.00	5.50	451.00	462.00	473.00	484.00	495.00	506.00	517.00	528.00	539.00	550.00
11.5	356.50	368.00	379.50	391.00	402.50	414.00	425.50	437.00	448.50	460.00	5.75	471.50	483.00	494.50	506.00	517.50	529.00	540.50	552.00	563.50	575.00
12.0	372.00	384.00	396.00	408.00	420.00	432.00	444.00	456.00	468.00	480.00	6.00	492.00	504.00	516.00	528.00	540.00	552.00	564.00	576.00	588.00	600.00
12.5	387.50	400.00	412.50	425.00	437.50	450.00	462.50	475.00	487.50	500.00	6.25	512.50	525.00	537.50	550.00	562.50	575.00	587.50	600.00	612.50	625.00
13.0	403.00	416.00	429.00	442.00	455.00	468.00	481.00	494.00	507.00	520.00	6.50	533.00	546.00	559.00	572.00	585.00	598.00	611.00	624.00	637.00	650.00
13.5	418.50	432.00	445.50	459.00	472.50	486.00	499.50	513.00	526.50	540.00	6.75	553.50	567.00	580.50	594.00	607.50	621.00	634.50	648.00	661.50	675.00
14.0	434.00	448.00	462.00	476.00	490.00	504.00	518.00	532.00	546.00	560.00	7.00	574.00	588.00	602.00	616.00	630.00	644.00	658.00	672.00	686.00	700.00
14.5	449.50	464.00	478.50	493.00	507.50	522.00	536.50	551.00	565.50	580.00	7.25	594.50	609.00	623.50	638.00	652.50	667.00	681.50	696.00	710.50	725.00
15.0	465.00	480.00	495.00	510.00	525.00	540.00	555.00	570.00	585.00	600.00	7.50	615.00	630.00	645.00	660.00	675.00	690.00	705.00	720.00	735.00	750.00
15.5	480.50	496.00	511.50	527.00	542.50	558.00	573.50	589.00	604.50	620.00	7.75	635.50	651.00	666.50	682.00	697.50	713.00	728.50	744.00	759.50	775.00
16.0	496.00	512.00	528.00	544.00	560.00	576.00	592.00	608.00	624.00	640.00	8.00	656.00	672.00	688.00	704.00	720.00	736.00	752.00	768.00	784.00	800.00
16.5	511.50	528.00	544.50	561.00	577.50	594.00	610.50	627.00	643.50	660.00	8.25	676.50	693.00	709.50	726.00	742.50	759.00	775.50	792.00	808.50	825.00
17.0	527.00	544.00	561.00	578.00	595.00	612.00	629.00	646.00	663.00	680.00	8.50	697.00	714.00	731.00	748.00	765.00	782.00	799.00	816.00	833.00	850.00
17.5	542.50	560.00	577.50	595.00	612.50	630.00	647.50	665.00	682.50	700.00	8.75	717.50	735.00	752.50	770.00	787.50	805.00	822.50	840.00	857.50	875.00
18.0	558.00	576.00	594.00	612.00	630.00	648.00	666.00	684.00	702.00	720.00	9.00	738.00	756.00	774.00	792.00	810.00	828.00	846.00	864.00	882.00	900.00
18.5	573.50	592.00	610.50	629.00	647.50	666.00	684.50	703.00	721.50	740.00	9.25	758.50	777.00	795.50	814.00	832.50	851.00	869.50	888.00	906.50	925.00
19.0	589.00	608.00	627.00	646.00	665.00	684.00	703.00	722.00	741.00	760.00	9.50	779.00	798.00	817.00	836.00	855.00	874.00	893.00	912.00	931.00	950.00
19.5	604.50	624.00	643.50	663.00	682.50	702.00	721.50	741.00	760.50	780.00	9.75	799.50	819.00	838.50	858.00	877.50	897.00	916.50	936.00	955.50	975.00

Fig. 2-14. *This labor conversion chart is used for longer jobs at higher hourly rates. (Courtesy of Mitchell Manuals, Inc.)*

Fig. 2-15. *An instructor explains the microfilm estimator to an auto body class.*

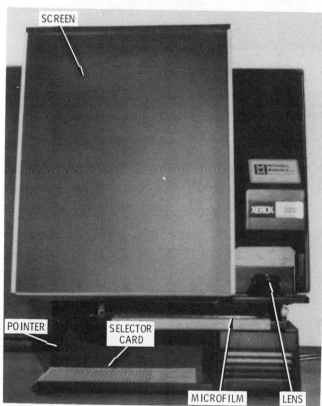

Fig. 2-16. *The major parts of a typical microfilm estimator.*

Time Limit on the Estimate

Usually, the repair price quoted on an estimate is good for only 30 days. This time limit is set for several reasons. In 30 days, for example, the damaged area may rust and deteriorate further, making it cost more to repair.

Other factors can also cause a change in repair costs after 30 days. The prices of parts and labor rates may change, and some used parts may no longer be available.

The 30 day limit should be stated on the estimate sheet, as shown at the bottom of the sample estimates in this unit.

A Small Car Damage Estimate

When estimating cost of repairs on a small unitized body car or any other vehicle, closely inspect and report all damage. Reopening an estimate is frowned upon by insurance companies and customers, unless an item is questionable and "left open" on the estimate (such as a differential, which cannot be seen readily).

The vehicle in Figure 2-38 has been hit hard on the left side, causing severe damage to the front end, hood, door, grille, bumper, and fender panels. A step-by-step procedure is necessary to keep from missing any damage. Starting at the left front, the first damage to estimate is the fender. The fender panel is so severely damaged that it must be replaced. The fender moldings are missing and have to be replaced. The fender skirt, the complete fender pan side, and the left MacPherson strut shock also must be replaced.

The next damage estimated was the bumper and grille panels (Fig. 2-39). Parts needing replacement are the bumper face bar, the left bumper cushion im-

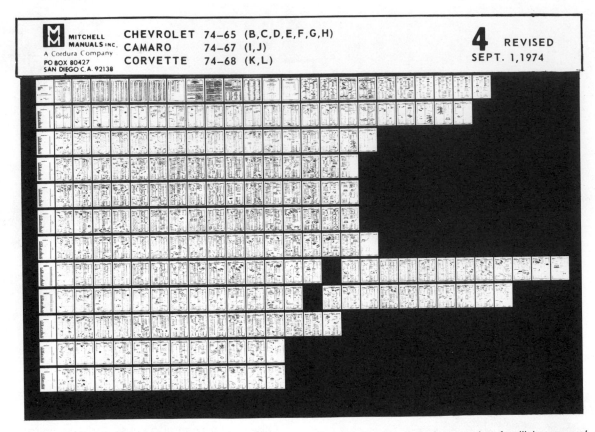

| MITCHELL MANUALS INC. A Cordura Company PO BOX 80427 SAN DIEGO C.A. 92138 | CHEVROLET 74–65 (B,C,D,E,F,G,H) CAMARO 74–67 (I,J) CORVETTE 74–68 (K,L) | **4** REVISED SEPT. 1,1974 |

Fig. 2-17. Microfilm cards, *also known as* microfiche cards, *contain many tiny photographs of collision manual pages. (Courtesy of Mitchell Manuals, Inc.)*

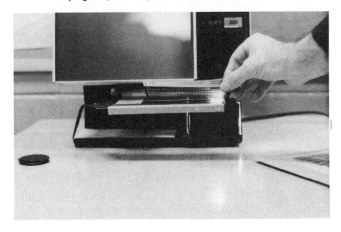

Fig. 2-18. *The first step in using a microfilm estimator is to select the proper film card and place it in the film holder.*

Fig. 2-19. *To find the proper image on the microfilm card,* a picture selection card *is used.*

pact, the energy absorber, the grille, the radiator support, and the bar upper tie (Fig. 2-40).

On the front end, replacement items include the fan, water pump, shroud, light capsule assembly, headlight door, and radiator core (Fig. 2-41). As shown in Figure 2-42, the hood and the left hood hinge must be replaced, as must the windshield and sealant. Two wheel covers are missing and have to be replaced.

Repair Items. The left door, shown in Figure 2-43, has to be repaired. The windshield post and the shroud panel (Fig. 2-44) also have to be repaired. The right door and fender (Fig. 2-45) must be aligned. Frame alignment is necessary to remove sidesway and sag. The front end and the MacPherson strut also must be aligned. The front end panels must be refinished. Figure 2-46 shows how the estimate is written for this car.

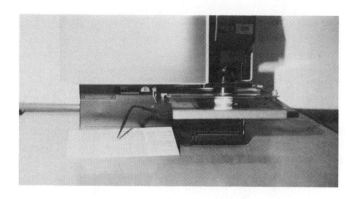

Fig. 2-20. *The picture selection card is slid onto a platform beneath the pointer.*

Fig. 2-21. *The pointer and picture selection card in working position.*

Courtesy Estimate

When making a visual estimate, determine if the vehicle is repairable, or if it must be considered "totaled" (damaged beyond repair).

Figures 2-47 through 2-51 show a car that a visual estimate indicates is "totaled." The damage shown would exceed the cost of the vehicle when the salvage value

Fig. 2-23. *On the microfilm estimator's screen, the image of the collision manual page is larger than the page of an actual printed manual. This makes it easier to read.*

OFF   **MITCHELL MANUALS MICROFICHE SYSTEM**   ON

← Move carrier LEFT   Move carrier RIGHT →

A	27	26	25	24	23	22	A	20	19	18	17	A	15	14	13	12	A	10	9	8	7	A	5	4	3	2	A
B							B					B					B					B					B
C	27	26	25	24	23	22	C	20	19	18	17	C	15	14	13	12	C	10	9	8	7	C	5	4	3	2	C
D							D					D					D					D					D
E	27	26	25	24	23	22	E	20	29	18	17	E	15	14	13	12	E	10	9	8	7	E	5	4	3	2	E
F							F					F					F					F					F
G	27	26	25	24	23	22	G	20	19	18	17	G	15	14	13	12	G	10	9	8	7	G	5	4	3	2	G
H							H					H					H					H					H
I	27	26	25	24	23	22	I	20	19	18	17	I	15	14	13	12	I	10	9	8	7	I	5	4	3	2	I
J							J					J					J					J					J
K	27	26	25	24	23	22	K	20	19	18	17	K	15	14	13	12	K	10	9	8	7	K	5	4	3	2	K
L							L					L					L					L					L

OPERATING INSTRUCTIONS

LOAD FILM

1. Pull carrier forward to open.
2. Place film to rear right hand side of carrier.
3. Push carrier in to operate.

VARI-OPTICS

1. To increase image size, loosen Vari-Optic lock on rear of reader. Move Vari-Optic handle toward the rear of the reader until the desired magnification is attained. Tighten Vari-Optic lock.
2. To decrease magnification, reverse procedure.

TO FOCUS

Applying slight downward pressure, rotate ring on top of the lens until projected image is sharp.

Fig. 2-22. *A picture selection card. (Courtesy of Mitchell Manuals, Inc.)*

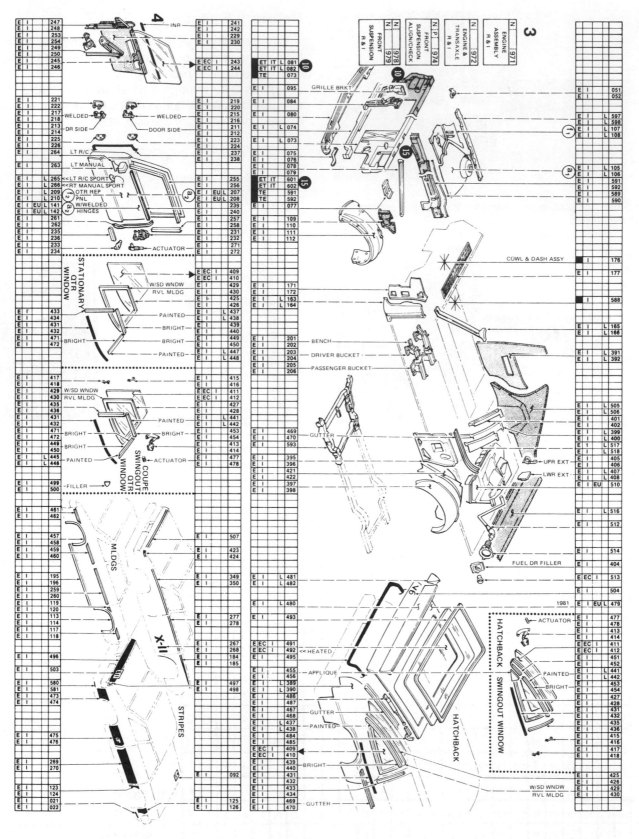

Fig. 2-24. *The basic tool used for computer-estimating systems is a printed form like this one. Pictures and numbers are used to identify each damaged part. The estimator checks off each damaged part on the sheet as he or she examines the vehicle. (Courtesy of Automatic Data Processing, Collision Services Division)*

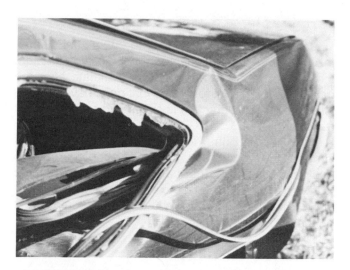

Fig. 2-25. *A portion of a damaged vehicle on which computer estimating will be done.*

Fig. 2-26. *The estimator carefully examines the damage, marking each part to be replaced on a worksheet like the one shown in Figure 2-24.*

Fig. 2-27. *Information from the worksheet is entered in the computer system with a typewriterlike terminal.*

is added to the repair cost. Such an estimate is made for a customer or insurance company and is called a "courtesy estimate."

Frame Damage Estimate

Frame damage often is estimated differently from panel damage, because the frame repair work may be

Fig. 2-28. *The computer contains a large amount of information on parts for every make and model of car. The information is often displayed on a screen as it is entered, allowing the operator to check entries for accuracy.*

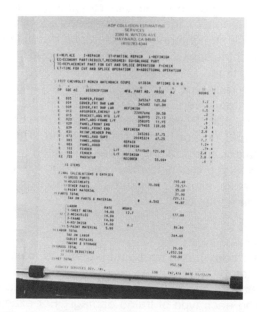

Fig. 2-29. *The computer prints out a complete estimate, including the cost of all parts and the time needed to install them. Since the shop's hourly labor charges are also entered, the printed estimate includes labor costs for the entire job, as well. (Courtesy of Automatic Data Processing, Collision Services Division)*

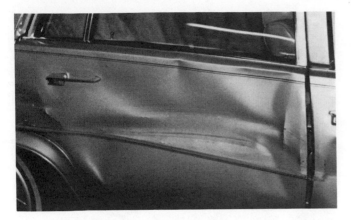

Fig. 2-30. *An example of collision damage that requires replacement of the outer door panel (skin).*

priced by the number of hook-ups. Each place where a chain, clamp, or jack is placed on the frame to pull, push, or hold is called a *hook-up*. The price may vary from shop to shop and from city to city. It depends on the type of frame equipment the shop owner has for the shop's volume of business. The technical skill needed to make the hook-ups and the space available in the shop are also factors in figuring the flat rate for frame repairs. In any case, the charge would still be based on the number of hook-ups.

A small body shop may have a *portable* frame straightener, like the one shown in Figure 2-52. If so, the shop may charge less than would a larger shop. The larger shop may be equipped with a large *rack-type* frame straightener, as in Figure 2-53. Generally speaking, a portable unit can straighten almost any type of frame damage that can be handled with a rack-type frame straightener. The difference is that the portable machine can usually straighten only *one* damaged area at a time.

A large rack-type machine, on the other hand, is able to straighten several damaged areas at the same time, with one pull. Portable machines are usually much slower and do not have as much power. This is because a portable straightener has only one power jack. The rack-type machine may have up to six or eight power jacks, allowing hook-ups for six to eight pulls to be made at one time.

Hourly Frame Rate

Some body-frame shops may prefer to make frame estimates by the *hour*, as for other work. This type of estimate is priced by the hours of labor to be spent repairing each type of frame damage. For example, a frame that has *mash* damage (Fig. 2-54) would be estimated at so many hours for this type damage. (The different types of frame damage are explained later in the book.)

Farming Out

If a body shop does not have a frame straightener, the frame damage is "left open" on the estimate. Then, the cost of repair is added to the estimate *after* the frame has been sent to a shop that *does* have a frame straightener. This practice is called *subcontracting*, or "farming out."

When this is done, the frame shop bills the body shop for the work. Often, the frame shop charges the body shop less than normal retail labor price for the work. Then, the body shop can charge the retail labor price. This allows the body shop to make a small profit on the frame repair also.

PARTS AVAILABILITY

Most body shop jobs need new or good used parts to complete damage repairs. Small parts (moldings and light housings) or large parts (complete fenders) may be damaged beyond repair. When this happens, replacement parts must be found to repair the vehicle properly.

New Parts

When working on cars less than about 5 years old, it is usually easier to repair the car with all new parts. New parts are usually still available from the manufacturer. They can also be more easily installed, when compared to used parts.

New parts, of course, generally cost more money. For this reason, the car owner or insurance adjuster may want the car to be repaired with used parts.

Used Parts

Used parts from wrecking companies (salvage yards) are sometimes used to repair damage. In this way, the good parts on a "total" wreck may be salvaged to repair another car. The value of those good used parts still on the car is what gives the car its *salvage value*, discussed above.

Salvage Yard Operations. When used parts are purchased, they are usually removed from the wrecked vehicle *by* the salvage yard. Many times, the yard will also deliver the parts to the body shop.

Figure 2-55 shows a group of "totaled" vehicles in a salvage yard. Larger salvage yards often remove the good parts and bail up the remainder of the wreck as good business procedure. For example, if the wrecks in Figure 2-55 were allowed to sit as they are, valuable storage space would be used to store parts that are worthless.

Figures 2-56 and 2-57 show used parts being properly stored in a large salvage yard. Note that space is

BILL'S PAINT & BODY SHOP
Corner 9th And Cumming Street
Phone 493-7950

ESTIMATE OF REPAIRS			
OWNER *John Doe* PHONE *4958772*			
ADDRESS *Forest Road, City*			
INSURANCE CO. *City Insurance Co.* PHONE *473-8692*			

Date	*10/2/82*
Est. No.	*2284*
Year Make	*1980 Cadillac*
Model	*Sedan Deville*
Serial No.	*—*
Mileage	*27,338*
License	*QWZ 224*

Replace	Repair	DESCRIPTION OF JOB — ESTIMATE OF PARTS AND LABOR REQUIRED	Paint Cost Estimate		Parts Cost Estimate		Labor Cost Estimate	
✓		Outer door panel			82	50	110	00
	✓	Inner door panel					44	00
		Paint and Material	60	50				
		Refinishing repair					32	00

The above is an estimate based on our inspection and does not cover additional parts or labor which may be required after the work has been opened up. Occasionally after work has started worn parts are discovered which are not evident on first inspection. Because of this the above prices are not guaranteed.

ESTIMATED BY *Tom Savage*   ESTIMATE APPROVED BY *Jerry Carter*

AUTHORIZED AND ACCEPTED

DATE *Oct. 6, 1982*

BY OWNER OR AGENT *Billy Ashberry*

TOTAL LABOR	186	00
TOTAL PARTS	82	50
TOTAL PAINT	60	50
TAX @ 5%	7	15
SUBLET REPAIRS	–	–
TOTAL COST	336	15

Fig. 2-31. *An estimate for work needed to repair the damage shown in Figure 2-30.*

Fig. 2-32. *A completed estimate for repair and replacement work on the damage shown in Figure 2-33.*

saved by storing the parts on neat racks where they cannot be easily damaged.

Using Salvaged Parts. The body shop manager should be careful when deciding to order used parts. When making estimates on late-model vehicles, it is a good idea to write up the estimate using only the prices for *new* parts.

Many customers may not want repairs to be made with used parts. The insurance adjuster may ask for used parts if the insurance company is paying for the job. However, the repair worker must remember that the customer is looking to the body shop for a good-looking repair on the vehicle.

When used parts are purchased from a salvage yard, there is always a chance that the parts have been previously damaged and then repaired. For this reason, the body shop manager must be sure that the parts are in usable condition. The used parts should be inspected carefully before they are installed on the customer's vehicle.

One reason that the wrecking company exists, of course, is to sell used parts for repairs. This resource should not be overlooked when repairing older vehicles. The damage on these cars often can be repaired in less time if used parts are available. Sometimes, new parts may not be available for older models. In such a case, used parts *must* be located and installed.

Rechromed Bumpers

Many wrecks require replacement of the bumper or face bar. On a vehicle less than 2 years old, the bumper is usually replaced with a new chrome bumper bar. However, when a vehicle is several years old, a re-chromed bumper bar is often used.

A rechromed bumper is a damaged bumper that has been sent to a rechroming company for repairing. A new chrome plating is put on the front side of the old bumper bar. The chemical process is much like chrome plating a new bumper face bar by the original manufacturer.

A rechromed bumper costs less than a new bumper. The rechroming service gets damaged bumper face bars to rechrome from body shops. The body shop trades the damaged bumper bar removed from the vehicle in exchange for the rechromed bumper.

Rechromed bumpers usually *look* as good and shiny as new when installed. However, the chrome may later begin to peel off. If this happens within a certain length of time, the body shop owner can often get the re-chroming shop to replace the peeling bumper, since it was defective.

However, there is still the question of who pays the *labor charge* to install the replacement bumper. The body shop manager or estimator should look ahead. *Before* the rechromed bumper is installed, it should be understood that the customer or the insurance company must pay for additional labor to put on a second rechromed bumper, if the first one should fail. The shop owner cannot afford to provide free labor for such an installation.

Additional Parts Costs

There are other costs to be considered when the estimate is being written. Are new parts available at the local dealership? Will the parts have to be ordered by the dealer? Who pays the freight charges, if there are any? The shop owner cannot afford to pay for freight or long-distance telephone calls while looking for parts.

Often, there is a new-car dealership in the community, from which the parts can be obtained. In other cases, the local salvage yard may have the parts. An important concern is how much time is needed to get the parts to the shop and who will deliver them or pick them up.

INSURANCE

Many auto body repairs are paid for, at least in part, by an insurance company. When an insurance claim (payment) is involved, the entire business of body repair becomes more complicated. This is because there are now *three* people involved: the body shop *estimator or owner*, the *car owner*, and the *insurance adjuster*.

ESTIMATE OF
REPAIR COST

Phone: 493-3527

J. M. Jackson Buick-Cadillac Co.

NAME	ADDRESS	PHONE	DATE
Troy Khone	196 Forest Road	491-9773	6-20-81

YEAR	MAKE	MODEL	LICENSE No.	SPEEDOMETER	MTR. No.
1980	Cad	Sedan Deville	674-467	22558	SER. No.

INSURANCE CARRIER	ADJUSTER	PHONE	CAR LOCATED AT
City Insurance Co.	Mark Yates	836-0209	Spring Hill

	OPERATIONS	PART NO.	PARTS	LABOR
1	Headlight bezel (door) R.S.	1610802	14 00	—
1	Head light Halogen	1619622	31 50	—
1	Side parking light assy.	913242	35 00	—
1	Side parking bezel	1609 50	6 80	4 50
1	Header panel	1609 346	79 25	37 50
1	Header panel moulding	1610074	10 45	—
1	Retainer filler	1610405	2 85	—
1	Right front fender	3516533	295 00	39 00
1	Right front fender (wheelhousing) moulding	1608563	17 70	4 50
1	Right front fender wheelhousing	1609563	61 00	7 50
1	Right front fender moulding (lower)	3634346	13 90	3 00
1	Radio Antenna, Motor with C.B.	2201415	137 00	—
1	Right front door	20130343	346 00	75 00
1	Remote Control Mirror	20096532	48 25	22 50
1	Right front door side Moulding (blue)	9635225	18 10	3 00
1	Right front door belt Moulding	20010026	3 75	6 00
1	Right rear door	20113469	395 00	61 50
1	Right rear door side Moulding (blue)	9635314	16 80	3 00
2	Right rear and front edge moulding @ 6.25	1606986 1606984	12 50	6 00
	Repair Right quarter panel	—		90 00
1	Quarter panel side Moulding	9635368	32 25	3 00
1	Aim headlight	—		9 00
	Align front end	—		25 50
	Refinish all damaged panels and strips	—		120 00
	ESTIMATE GOOD FOR 30 DAYS			

INSURED PAYS $100.00 INS. CO. PAYS $2175.90 R. O. No. _____

INS. CHECK PAYABLE TO Jackson Buick-Cadillac Co.

THE ABOVE IS AN ESTIMATE, BASED ON OUR INSPECTION, AND DOES NOT COVER ADDITIONAL PARTS AND LABOR WHICH MAY BE REQUIRED AFTER THE WORK HAS BEEN OPENED UP. OCCASIONALLY, AFTER WORK HAS STARTED, WORN, BROKEN OR DAMAGED PARTS ARE DISCOVERED WHICH ARE NOT EVIDENT ON FIRST INSPECTION. QUOTATIONS ON PARTS AND LABOR ARE CURRENT AND SUBJECT TO CHANGE

EST. MADE BY _____

TOTALS	1606 10	526 50
WRECKER SERVICE		
TAX 5%	83 31	
PAINT & MTL.	60 00	
TOTAL OF ESTIMATE		2275 91

AUTHORIZATION FOR REPAIR. YOU ARE HEREBY AUTHORIZED TO MAKE THE ABOVE SPECIFIED REPAIRS TO THE CAR DESCRIBED HEREIN

SIGNED City Insurance Company   DATE 7/2/81

Fig. 2-33. *The right side of this car has been heavily damaged in a sideswipe collision.*

Fig. 2-34. *Careful inspection of all damaged areas must be done when making an estimate. This car has considerable damage along the right side.*

Fig. 2-35. *Damage includes the light, fender, and bumper.*

Fig. 2-36. *The right front door is damaged and molding is missing.*

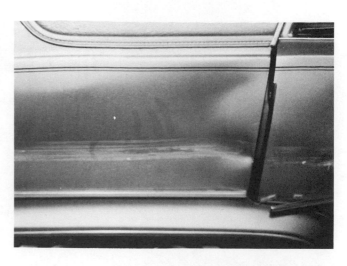

Fig. 2-37. *There is also damage to the right rear quarter panel.*

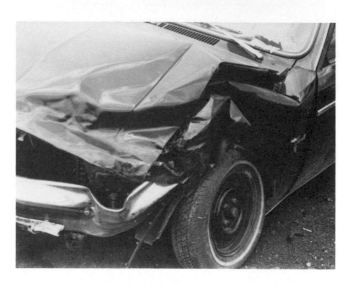

Fig. 2-38. *This small car has severe damage to the left front area.*

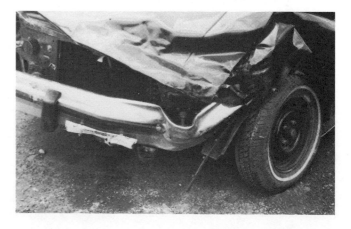

Fig. 2-39. *The bumper bar and energy absorber unit have been damaged.*

Fig. 2-40. *With the hood removed, damage to the radiator support, fender, and suspension strut system can be seen.*

Fig. 2-41. *Damage to the radiator core is severe.*

Fig. 2-42. *The hood, hood hinges, windshield, and door have sustained damage.*

Fig. 2-43. *The door damage is more clearly visible from this angle.*

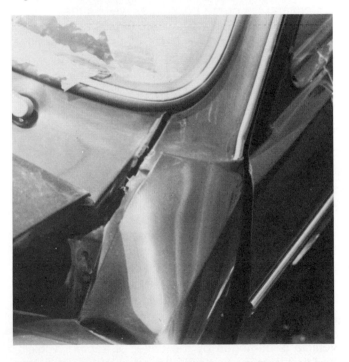

Fig. 2-44. *A closer view of the damage to the windshield, windshield post, and adjoining areas.*

Types of Insurance Claims

To complete the estimate, the estimator needs to know the type of insurance claim involved. The estimator must know the different types of insurance claim or repair situations. The estimator also needs to know

Fig. 2-45. *On the right-hand side of the vehicle, the door and fender alignment has been affected by the collision.*

how to deal with both insurance adjusters *and* customers about insurance matters. The estimator should understand his or her position as well as the rights of both the insurance company and the car owner.

There is no difference in the cost of the repair, whether or not the job is covered by insurance. However, the written estimate should list *which* of the four following situations is involved. Employees, shop owners, and estimators must know about these four situations.

1. No-insurance jobs.
2. Third-party claims.
3. First-party claims.
4. No-fault insurance claims.

No-insurance Jobs. If the customer does not have insurance (or does not want to use insurance), the estimator deals with him or her directly. Then, of course, the estimator has to *sell* the job to get the work into the shop. The customer who is not using insurance pays the total charge directly to the body shop. A good example of a *no-insurance* situation would be an overall paint job on a car 5 or 6 years old.

Third-party Claims. A third-party claim occurs when a vehicle is damaged by the driver of another vehicle, and that damage is clearly the other driver's fault. In a third-party claim, the driver at fault may have *liability* insurance. Liability insurance pays for the damage that the driver causes, whether to someone else's car or other property.

The driver at fault *cannot* have his or her own vehicle repaired by the liability insurance he or she carries. Liability insurance *only* covers damage to *another person's* property.

The owner who is *not* at fault should not have to pay the cost of repairing his or her car. That cost should be paid by the driver at fault, or by that driver's liability insurance. Of course, the body shop manager must not get involved with the matter of who is at fault. The shop owner must see to it that the bill has been paid before the repaired car is returned, regardless of who is at fault.

First-party Claims. A first-party insurance claim involves one of two kinds of coverage: *collision* or *comprehensive.* Collision insurance is coverage that will pay for fixing a car no matter who is at fault. If the car owner runs into a tree, the collison coverage pays for fixing the car, even though it was his or her fault. Most people have both *liability* insurance (in case they *damage someone else's* vehicle) and *collision* insurance (in case they damage *their own* vehicles).

Comprehensive coverage pays for damage to the car resulting from vandalism, fire, theft, hail storms, or causes other than collision.

Sometimes, both collision and comprehensive insurance policies have a *deductible* clause. This clause states that the owner must pay the first $50, $100, or $200 (or another amount) of the repair cost on each claim. The insurance company then pays the remainder.

No-fault Claims. A type of insurance that is becoming more common is *no-fault insurance.* No-fault insurance is different from most insurance plans. Most insurance plans require that the party who *is* at fault pay for the injury and damage caused to the party who *is not* at fault.

Basically, no-fault insurance allows the person to collect payment for the loss from her or his own insurance company, no matter who is at fault. The major feature of no-fault insurance is that it often eliminates lawsuits between the motorists and insurance companies involved.

The advantages of no-fault insurance should include the following:

1. Prompt payment of all claims.
2. Payment for reasonable loss, but not *over-payment.*
3. Benefits for persons who would not have been paid for their loss in the past.
4. Equalizing and lowering the cost of automobile insurance.

Many states are adopting no-fault insurance laws. This is a result of both the insurance industry and the public recognizing the flaws of normal liability insurance, as discussed below.

Administrative delays and court costs have often made liability insurance unable to provide prompt payment for the growing number of people injured and cars

LEGAL PART
OF
ESTIMATION

Covington Appraisal Service

Nº 1253

Telephone 205-493-3709

OWNER: Lari Jean	DATE 9-21-81	ID# 6C47S5Q1001
APPRAISED FOR City Insurance		APPRAISER Jroy Wayne
MAKE Chevette	YEAR 1980	BODY STYLE 2 door	LIC. BZL 558	MILES 12,860

Repair	Replace		PARTS	LABOR HRS	SUBLET
	✓	Left fender panel	108 00	2	
	✓	" " Molding Center	13 50	2	
	✓	" " wheel housing molding	8 55	2	
	✓	" " inner fender skirt and pan	102 95	8 3	
	✓	" strut shock replaced and aligned	19 95	1 5	
	✓	Bumper bar and cushion	142 05	1 1	
	✓	Energy absorber 2 @ 35.15	70 30	1 2	
	✓	Radiator support	32 50	3	
	✓	Grill with emblem	50 90	3	
	✓	Radiator core.	116 00	7	
	✓	Fan	11 55	N C	
	✓	Water pump	19 90	1.5	
	✓	Left headlight (completed)	33 70	.3	
	✓	Hood panel	186 00	1 2	
	✓	" hinge	4 65	N C.	
	✓	" molding	11 10	2	
	✓	Rocker molding	18 50	3	
	✓	Windshield	192 00	1 2	
	✓	Two wheel covers @ 34.25	68 50	N C	
✓		Left door and alignment		4 5	
✓		Windshield post and shroud		3	
✓		Straighten frame and align front end @ 30.⁰⁰ 8 hrs			240 00
✓		Align right door and fender		2	
✓		Refinish panels repaired	75 00	8 5	
		Transmition, differential and motor left open			

SIGNATURE BELOW GUARANTEES REPAIRS AS ESTIMATED WHEN AUTHORIZED BY OWNER 1285 60   43.9   240 00

REPAIR SHOP	ACCEPTED BY		
City Repair Shop David Eric	LABOR 43 9 HRS @ $ 20⁰⁰ PER HOUR	$ 878	00
	NET ITEMS	$	
ESTIMATION GOOD FOR 30 DAYS	PARTS LESS — % $	$ 1285	60
	STATE TAX @ 6%	$ 77	14
THIS IS NOT AN AUTHORIZATION FOR REPAIRS	TOTAL	$ 2480	74

Fig. 2-46.   *This completed estimate is for the damage shown in Figures 2-38 through 2-45.*

Fig. 2-47. *The front-end damage to this vehicle is severe enough to require replacement of the entire front-end assembly. Such an assembly includes the hood, two fenders, header panel, grille, front bumper, radiator core, fan shroud, and air-conditioning condenser.*

Fig. 2-48. *Also damaged in the collision were the roof panel, the molding, and the windshield.*

Fig. 2-49. *Damage to the rear of the car includes the right rear quarter panel, quarter-panel extension, molding, and rear bumper.*

Fig. 2-50. *At the left rear, damage to the quarter panel, the molding, and the trunk lid can be seen.*

Fig. 2-51. *There is also damage to the left front door and the mirror. The cost of repairing the car, with all the damage, would exceed its value. Thus, it would be declared a "total," which means that it is wrecked beyond economical repair.*

Fig. 2-52. *A typical small, portable frame straightener in use. (Courtesy of Guy–Chart Systems)*

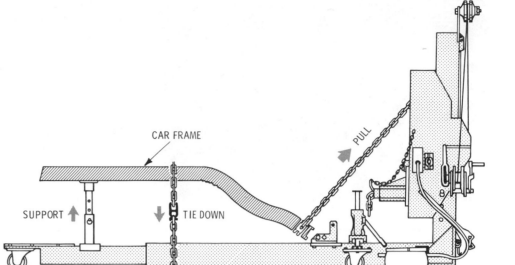

CAR FRAME

PULL

SUPPORT ↑   ↓ TIE DOWN

Fig. 2-53. *A large, permanently installed frame straightener. (Courtesy of Automotive Systems Division, Chief Industries)*

Fig. 2-54. *This rack-type frame straightener is hooked up to correct mash damage to the rear part of the frame. (Courtesy of Bear Division, Applied Power Industries)*

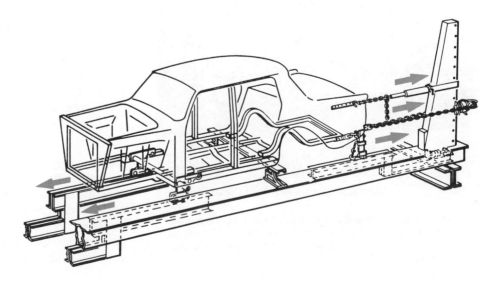

Fig. 2-55. *Wrecked vehicles awaiting dismantling in a salvage yard. Usable parts will be salvaged and stored for later sale.*

Fig. 2-56. *An assortment of good used doors at a salvage yard.*

Fig. 2-57. *Used front-end assemblies, known as "doghouses," are stored on racks at a salvage yard. Note that some have damaged parts that would have to be replaced before they could be used on a vehicle.*

damaged in automobile accidents. Regular liability insurance uses about 58 percent of the money paid in for legal and court costs. This leaves only 42 percent of the money to compensate injured people and repair their cars. Also, in many cases, settling injury claims may take 3 years or longer.

No-fault insurance plans promise to speed up payment for both injuries and repairs. Claims should be settled more quickly, allowing the vehicle to be repaired almost immediately.

Dealing with Insurance Claims

As mentioned above, several parties are involved when dealing with insurance claims: the insurance adjuster, the customer, and the body shop estimator or manager. The body shop employee must be able to deal with each person fairly, yet charge a reasonable price and make a fair profit. The employee should not be subjected to threats by an insurance adjuster, nor should the worker attack the insurance adjuster's viewpoint.

These ideas are explained in the following sections concerning the repair shop's responsibility for the customer's vehicle, the legal rights of the customer, and the way to treat the customer and the insurance adjuster with fairness and honesty.

Repair Shop Responsibility. The vehicle's owner is a customer and deserves a first-class repair job, no matter who is paying for the repair. The estimator should always be fair to the shop, to the customer, and to the insurance company. Above all, the employee and the shop should not be ashamed to make a profit, since that is why the shop is in business. The established labor rate for that area of the country should be used.

When making out the estimate, keep the following in mind:

1. Know the value of the vehicle. Be sure that the cost of repair plus the salvage value does not exceed the vehicle's value.
2. Know the availability of parts.
3. Remember that the vehicle owner is, first of all, a customer.
4. Be sure that there is a clear understanding of who is going to pay the bill and that the bill must be paid in full before the repaired car is released.

Insurance adjusters, too, are customers. However, they may not be interested in the quality of the repair, as long as the insured party is satisfied. The employee must be aware of the insurance adjuster who is inexperienced or who is *only* trying to save the insurance company money without caring about the customer or shop owner. Of course, the adjuster's job is to save the insurance company's money, so a *compromise* may be needed. Illegal procedures and threats, however, should not be tolerated by the body shop estimator or manager.

Estimator's Position. The question of who is right and who is wrong is a job for a lawyer, not the estimator. There is no need to argue or take sides with either a customer or an insurance company. In other words, let the customer and insurance company know that the shop's interest is in repairing the vehicle to pre-accident condition and in collecting a reasonable price for the repair. *All* of the costs of repairing the vehicle must be paid completely. In the end, the vehicle's owner is responsible for paying the bills in full.

The Customer's Legal Rights. The vehicle owner is the body shop's customer. This customer has a right to have the shop of his choice check the repairs on the vehicle, regardless of where it is repaired. (The insurance adjuster may want the car to be moved to another shop for repair.) The insurance adjuster may be notified by the customer that his or her repair worker will inspect the vehicle after the damage has been repaired, no matter where the work is done. The repairs, then, have to meet with everyone's approval before the vehicle is returned to the customer.

If the car is taken out of the shop in which the customer wanted it to be repaired, the owner may demand from the insurance company that there be a time limit to repair the damage. After a reasonable period, the owner may demand that the insurance company provide a rental car of equal or better value and condition while the vehicle is being repaired.

Fairness and Honesty. To be sure of making an estimate that is fair and honest to all concerned, complete the itemized estimate *before* the insurance adjuster arrives. Whether an insurance adjuster is involved or not, the shop's main interest should be in giving the customer a good job at a fair price.

For this reason, keep the following items in mind when writing the estimate:

1. Can the parts on the car be repaired satisfactorily, or will they have to be replaced?
2. Are satisfactory used parts available, or will new parts have to be used?
3. Will the customer accept used parts or the repair of the old parts?
4. Will the insurance company pay for new parts, if the customer *wants* new parts?
5. Will the insurance company pay for new or used parts if the adjuster feels that the old parts can be repaired?

When dealing with insurance adjusters, remember that they, too, are trying to earn a living. Treat them courteously, but be firm and correct. If the adjuster knows that a certain shop has a good reputation for doing quality work at a fair price, the adjuster will usually trust that shop. Then, the shop will have little trouble collecting the full and fair price for the repair work.

There should be a mutual understanding among the adjuster, the owner, and the body shop. When writing estimates and discussing work and prices, remember that there are usually three main concerns: the *body shop's concern*, the *vehicle owner's concern*, and the *insurance company's concern*. Usually, if everyone is reasonable and considerate, the vehicle can be repaired correctly and quickly and at a fair price. In the end, this is in everyone's best interest.

Unit 3

Body Shop Jobs and Personnel

There are a number of different jobs in an auto body repair shop. For example, every shop has an *owner*, such as the car dealer standing in front of his shop in Figure 3-1. In a smaller independent shop, the owner usually works on cars as well as runs the shop.

Another important person is the shop *manager* or *supervisor*. In very large shops, the manager and the supervisor may be two different people. In most shops, however, the manager and the supervisor are the same person. Figure 3-2 shows a shop supervisor directing a car into a working stall.

Other workers in the body shop include the *metal workers*, who actually straighten and fill the metal parts of the car body. Figure 3-3 shows a young worker finishing a metal repair before primer paint is applied. The shop supervisor is giving some pointers on the job. In Figure 3-4, a student is learning metal work from an experienced body repair worker. When younger workers are employed to learn the trade, they are called *apprentices*.

Specialty workers may be employed in the body shop. Examples include *painters* and *frame technicians*. These workers specialize in only one type of work, such as painting or frame straightening.

SHOP OWNER

The owner, of course, must be concerned with who runs the auto body shop. Sometimes, after a few years of experience, a worker may ask the owner about becoming the shop manager. Or, the worker may think about opening a shop. In any case, *all* workers should have some knowledge of the shop owner's responsibilities.

The average independent body shop may be small compared to the *service shop* of a large auto dealership (Fig. 3-5). The owner of a large new-car dealership usually has a service *manager* or *supervisor* to oversee all the service departments. Each department in turn, has its own supervisor.

The shop owner must be concerned with all areas of work in the shop. In smaller shops, the owner also acts as manager. He or she must understand the work of

Fig. 3-1. *Every body shop has an owner. Some new-car dealerships include a body shop as part of the total operation. (Courtesy of Grabber Manufacturing Company)*

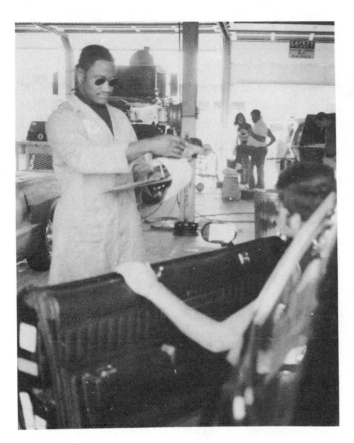

Fig. 3-2. *The shop* manager *or supervisor is one of the busiest people in the operation.*

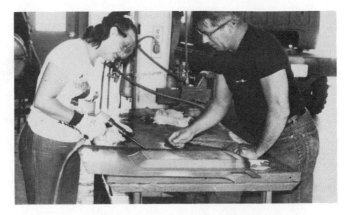

Fig. 3-3. *One responsibility of the body shop supervisor is to help teach new workers their duties.*

Fig. 3-4. *Apprentices learn the body shop trade from more experienced workers.*

Fig. 3-5. *In a large operation, such as this body shop division of a new-car dealership, the owner often hires a manager to run the day-to-day activities.*

the shop supervisor, the work of the body repair people, and all the other work done in the shop and the office. Either the shop owner or the manager is in charge of hiring and firing employees. The owner or manager also has to decide on promotions or raises for employees. For all these reasons, the manager must know about training new workers, the employment outlook, wage scales, and other areas of body shop operation.

In addition, the shop owner or the manager must understand and supervise the office work. He or she must also be concerned with safety in the shop, since this is management's responsibility to the workers.

SHOP MANAGER

The job of managing any business is a highly skilled position. A body shop is not an easy business to operate. Keeping a body shop clean, for example, is a large problem. However, it *is* an important job, since many people would not want their vehicles repaired in a dirty shop. A shop that is dirty and cluttered will lose business in the long run.

A good display of tools and equipment is important. The manager must be sure that employees keep the tools properly stored, as in Figure 3-6. Good lighting

for work areas and for the customer waiting area should be another concern of the shop manager. Comfortable conditions help the customer feel appreciated and indicate that the shop wants the work.

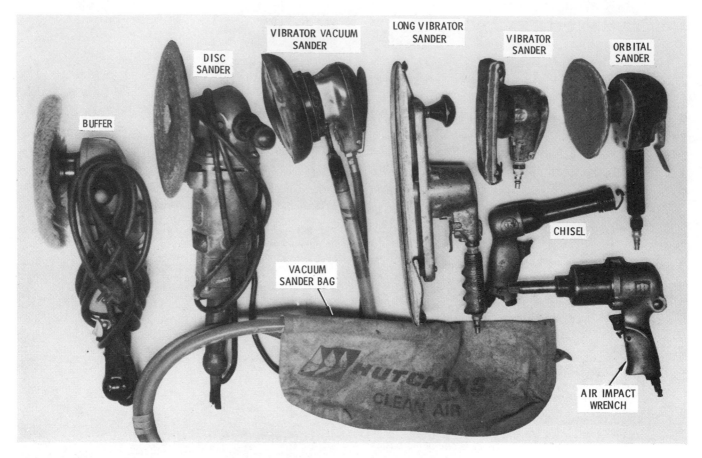

Fig. 3-6. *A display of clean, good-quality tools will make a good impression on the shop's customers.*

Fig. 3-7. *The body shop manager should show the customer that the shop has the equipment needed to do the work efficiently and correctly. Equipment such as this bench system for alignment work will make a good impression. (Courtesy of Blackhawk Division, Applied Power Industries)*

During the working day, the manager receives customers' wrecked vehicles and decides into which work stall or area the vehicle is to be taken. The manager also informs customers when their vehicles are repaired and schedules work throughout the shop. Usually, the manager also orders parts needed for vehicle repair. In a few large shops, an office worker may do this job.

Selling Repair Jobs

Collision repair is only one part of the auto body repair business. Painting, glass replacement, upholstery repair, vinyl top work, and other jobs are also profitable parts of the business. This noncollision work is normally not covered by insurance. So, the shop manager will have to "sell" the customer these jobs.

Whenever a car enters the shop, a good manager will point out any visible damage to the customer. Then, the manager can give the customer a price and recommendation for repairs. The manager should explain what needs to be done and make the customer feel comfortable in the shop. Customers want to feel that their vehicles are in good hands. Because of this, a good manager takes customers through the shop and shows what kind of work the shop does.

There are several jobs that the shop manager must be able to do to sell work successfully. These jobs include pricing work while the customer waits, providing interesting displays of the shop's work, and emphasizing the quality of a newly refinished car.

Pricing Work While the Customer Waits. This is a difficult job. If the customer is in a hurry, the manager may overlook some damage, which will make the estimate lower that it should be. On the other hand, a customer always wants the best job possible for the money. Pricing work while the customer waits must be done carefully and courteously.

Providing Work Displays. The shop manager should have some of the shop's quality work on display. Items such as cars being worked on (Fig. 3-7), pictures of wrecks before and after repairs, and a visible supply of quality material (name brand products, as in Fig. 3-8) are all valuable. If a customer comes in for a minor repair, the displays may make it easier for the shop manager to sell the customer on more complete repairs. The customer may decide to let the shop work on all areas of the car needing attention, rather than repairing one simple damaged place.

Selling the Refinish Job. Most customers take pride in their automobiles. A customer can be shown that a completely refinished car is more valuable and looks better than one that has been only partly repainted.

Figure 3-9 shows a newly repainted car. This car was first brought in for only collision damage. Then, the customer was shown how little extra it would cost to have the car completely repainted at the same time. If possible, a completely refinished car may be on display to demonstrate the shop's quality work.

Identifying Needed Work. A good shop manager takes a customer around the vehicle and points out all areas that should be repaired. This gets the customer personally involved in the process of increasing the vehicle's value. The customer can see the need for the other small repairs. Usually, the customers are not surprised at the total repair cost if all the areas needing work are pointed out beforehand.

Fig. 3-8. *Brand-name products will help to make a good impression, especially if they are stored and used in an orderly, clean working area. (Courtesy of Rinshed–Mason Products Division, Inmont Corporation)*

Fig. 3-9. *When this car was brought into the shop for collision repair, the owner agreed to an overall paint job. The refinishing enhanced the car's appearance and value.*

Pricing Repair Jobs

One of the shop manager's most important tasks is *estimating* (pricing repair jobs). The shop manager must know good estimating and insurance practices to do this job correctly.

Usually, the cost of parts is the same for each section of the country. The hourly *labor* rate charged is usually the same for all the cities in a certain area of the country. For successful operation, the manager must charge enough to make a fair profit on each vehicle repaired.

Using Shop Manuals

Automobile companies print *shop manuals* each year showing the different makes and models of their vehicles (Figs. 3-10 and 3-11). These give important information about body styles and parts. Both managers and repair workers must know how to use the shop manuals.

Types of Information. Shop manuals usually give several different types of information. They are good reference books for both the body repair worker and the shop manager. Information may include:
1. Instructions on how to use the manual.
2. Model names (Dart, Impala) and numbers.
3. Body style names (two-door hardtop, station wagon) and numbers.
4. Parts identification names (Fig. 3-12).
5. Parts identification numbers (Fig. 3-12).

Also included may be information on installing parts such as lock cylinders, door windows, windshields, and window regulators. The manuals also tell about the types of paint the manufacturer used at the factory, the types of paints to use when refinishing, and the problems the shop might have when refinishing. The shop

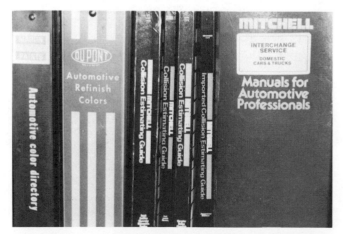

Fig. 3-10. *Manuals such as these are referred to constantly by the body shop manager and estimators. Parts manuals must be up-to-date to reflect current prices, if estimates are to be accurate.*

manual also includes information on how to cut keys for vehicle locks.

Buying Shop Manuals. New-car shop manuals are available to all body shops. The manager should write to the manufacturing company about buying manuals for more popular models.

Using Paint Manuals

The manager and the shop's painter must also know how to use the *paint manual*. For accurate repaint work, the automobile has a body identification *plate* (Fig. 3-13). This plate gives all the information needed to identify the car body and the paint used on it by the manufacturer.

The plate may be located on either the *door jamb* (driver door opening) or on the *cowl* (below the windshield under the hood). Figure 3-14 shows a typical identification plate on the cowl.

The plate gives the year model of the car and the car's paint code letter or number, as circled in Figure 3-13. The code letter or number can be looked up in the paint manual (Fig. 3-15). A color *chip* (sample) of the paint used on the vehicle also is shown. Use of the paint manual and identification plate is thoroughly discussed in the section on automotive painting.

BODY MECHANIC

The automobile body repair mechanic is a skilled metal worker who repairs motor vehicles that are damaged either by collision or by deterioration (such as rust).

A body repair mechanic's work provides great variety. Each vehicle repair presents a different problem, since no two vehicles are damaged in exactly the same way. A good auto body mechanic must have a broad knowledge of vehicle construction and repair techniques and be able to put that knowledge to work on each repair job.

Most body mechanics find their work challenging. They take pride in being able to restore badly damaged automobiles. Body mechanics are expected to be able to repair all types of vehicles. Most body repair work is done on automobiles and small trucks, buses, or truck trailers.

Typical Work

A good, all-around body mechanic must know how to use many tools. The body shop employee needs to use *power tools* such as the disc grinder (Fig. 3-16) and the featheredging sander (Fig. 3-17). A good knowledge of basic *hand tools* is needed, as is the ability to use *special auto body tools*. These include

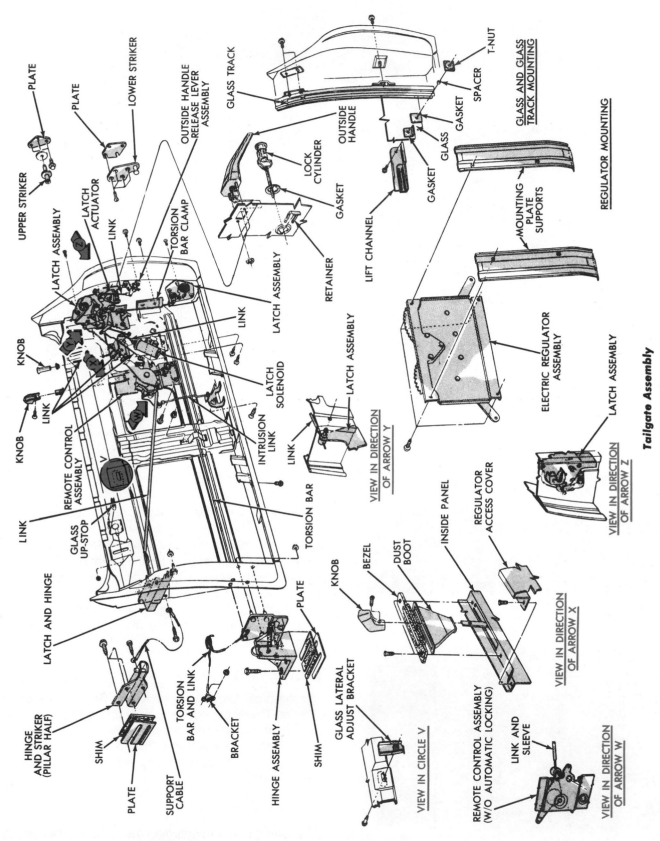

Fig. 3-11. *The manager and the shop's repair workers may have to refer to shop manuals to learn about assemblies such as the station wagon tailgate shown on this page. (Courtesy of Chrysler Corporation)*

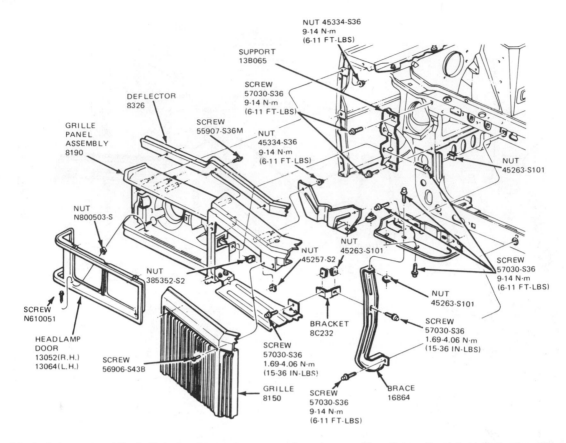

NUT 45334-S36
9-14 N·m
(6-11 FT-LBS)

SUPPORT
13B065

SCREW
57030-S36
9-14 N·m
(6-11 FT-LBS)

DEFLECTOR
8326

SCREW
55907-S36M

NUT
45334-S36
9-14 N·m
(6-11 FT-LBS)

GRILLE
PANEL
ASSEMBLY
8190

NUT
45263-S101

NUT
N800503-S

NUT
45263-S101

NUT
45257-S2

SCREW
57030-S36
9-14 N·m
(6-11 FT-LBS)

NUT
385352-S2

NUT
45263-S101

SCREW
N610051

HEADLAMP
DOOR
13052(R.H.)
13064(L.H.)

SCREW
56906-S43B

SCREW
57030-S36
1.69-4.06 N·m
(15-36 IN-LBS)

BRACKET
8C232

SCREW
57030-S36
1.69-4.06 N·m
(15-36 IN-LBS)

GRILLE
8150

SCREW
57030-S36
9-14 N·m
(6-11 FT-LBS)

BRACE
16864

Fig. 3-12. *A typical shop manual illustration, showing part names and part numbers and how the parts relate to each other. (Courtesy of Customer Service Division, Ford Motor Company)*

Fig. 3-13. *The paint code, circled in this illustration, may be found on the vehicle's body identification plate.*

Fig. 3-14. *This body identification plate is located on the car's cowl.*

the pick hammer (Fig. 3-18) and the slide hammer (Fig. 3-19).

Skilled body mechanics know how to do jobs such as the glass replacement job shown in Figure 3-20. Good mechanics also know how to do oxy-acetylene welding, brazing, and heat treating. Figure 3-21 shows oxy-acetylene welding being done. Also, a working knowledge of automotive painting is helpful. The more a body mechanic knows about *all* types of work done in the shop, the greater are his or her chances for promotion and higher pay.

SPECIALIST

Large body shops may have one or more specialty workers. These are body repair people who have extra training or experience in one area. Usually, they do most of the work needed in that area. There are two main types of specialty employees: *frame technicians* and *painters*.

Frame Technician

Repairing and straightening frames is a skilled job in the body shop. A person who works only on frames is called a *frame technician* and usually deals only with

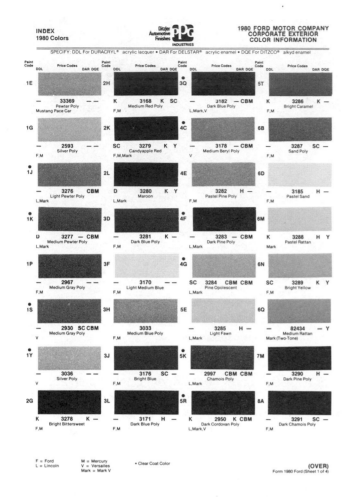

Fig. 3-15. *Paint codes and color chips are shown on this typical page from an automotive paint manual. (Courtesy of Ditzler Automotive Finishes Division, PPG Industries, Inc.)*

Fig. 3-17. *A repair worker must know how to use a featheredging sander for smaller areas and finer work.*

Fig. 3-16. *A large disc grinder is often used by the body worker.*

serious wrecks. The job of the frame technician is to see that the car's frame is straight, so that the other parts fit correctly and the car can be driven properly.

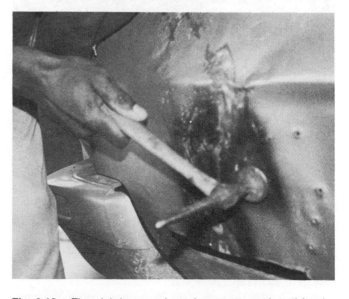

Fig. 3-18. *The pick hammer is an important repair tool for the skilled body worker.*

Fig. 3-19. *The slide hammer is used to pull out large creases in body sheet metal.*

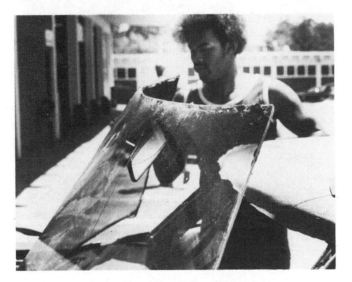

Fig. 3-20. *A repair worker must have a basic knowledge of auto glass installation.*

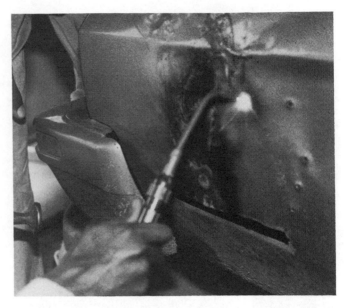

Fig. 3-21. *Using the oxy-acetylene torch for welding, brazing, and cutting is a basic repair skill.*

rubber/plastic body front panel is being painted. This may need different products and techniques to be painted properly, compared to sheet metal. The shop painter must keep up-to-date on new products and techniques.

In Figure 3-24, a painter is applying a thin paint stripe (*pin stripe*) to the car. All of the painter's jobs require a good deal of knowledge about paint products and how to mix them (Fig. 3-25). The painter also must know how to compound a new finish properly to full lustre, as is being done in Figure 3-26.

QUALIFICATIONS FOR AUTO BODY REPAIR WORK

Young people who are interested in auto body shop work should be in good physical condition and should have good eye–hand coordination. Although a high school diploma may not always be a requirement for getting an entry-level job, it is an advantage to have one. Many employers believe that the diploma shows that a person is able to "finish a job." Some high schools, of course, offer courses in body repair. These may be taken for credit toward graduation.

Learning About Auto Body Work

Auto body repair can be learned through on-the-job training or a formal apprenticeship program.
On-the-job Training. Most auto body workers learn the trade while working full-time or part-time in a body shop. This is called *on-the-job training*. Before making repairs by themselves, new employees receive instruc-

The frame technician in Figure 3-22 is straightening out a small bend in the frame behind the left front wheel. If this is not done correctly, the car's front wheels cannot be properly aligned.

Painter

A good painter is always a very valuable employee in any body shop. The painter applies the final work done to the car. This is the work that the customer sees first when the car is picked up. If the paint looks good and matches well, the customer is more likely to be satisfied with all the other work. Skilled auto painters are usually in high demand.

Today's painter is faced with an even more challenging job than in the past. In Figure 3-23, for example, a

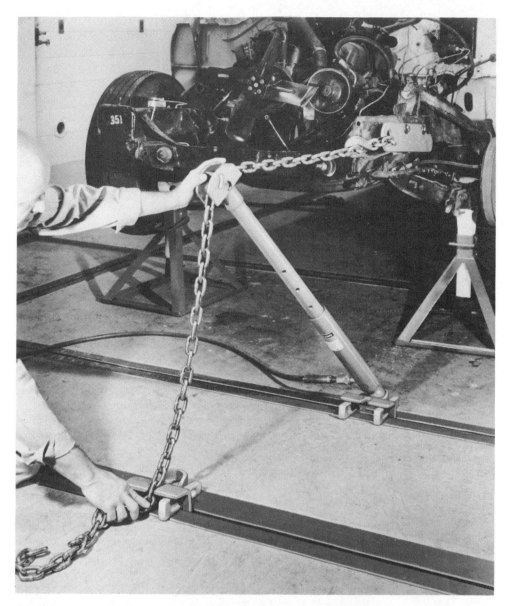

Fig. 3-22. *The frame mechanic is a specialist with a serious and important job on the body shop staff. (Courtesy of Blackhawk Division, Applied Power Industries)*

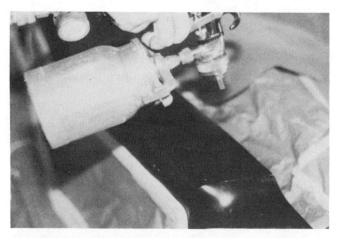

Fig. 3-23. *New materials, such as plastic and rubber used for body parts, make it necessary for the auto body worker to keep up-to-date on techniques for repair and painting.*

Fig. 3-24. *A good painter must be able to do pinstriping work, as well as basic panel painting.*

tion from an experienced technician or from the shop's manager or owner. The new employee can then learn which parts are to be repaired and which are to be

Fig. 3-25. *Paint products must be mixed properly, in clean equipment, if the final paint job is to be attractive and durable. Note the safety glasses worn by this worker to protect against paint and chemical droplets.*

Fig. 3-26. *Compounding with a polisher is an important step in achieving a high-quality lacquer finish.*

Fig. 3-27. *An experienced painter shows an apprentice how to adjust air line pressure to the spray gun.*

Fig. 3-28. *A new body worker installs a fender under the guidance of an experienced body mechanic.*

replaced. The new worker also learns to estimate how much time different repairs should take.

Learning on-the-job has many advantages. However, the new worker must be careful to watch and listen to the more experienced employee from whom he or she is learning. For example, the new worker in Figure 3-27 is paying close attention as the shop's painter adjusts the paint gun air line pressure before painting. In Figure 3-28, a young worker is being shown how to reinstall a repaired fender.

The on-the-job training program is also called the *helper apprenticeship program.* Experienced technicians are assisted by helpers who are in *apprenticeship training.* An *apprentice* is a person who is learning a trade by working at it.

Helpers begin by working with body technicians on such jobs as removing damaged parts, installing repaired parts, and sanding repaired surfaces before painting. Then, they gradually learn how to remove small dents and make minor repairs. After some time, they can progress to more difficult jobs.

Generally, about 3 to 4 years of apprenticeship training is needed before a helper becomes a fully qualified auto body technician.

Formal Apprenticeship Program. Most auto body workers pick up the skills of the trade informally, as on-the-job apprenticeship helpers. However, many training authorities recommend that the learner complete a *formal* apprenticeship program in a vocational/trade school, high school, or junior college. A formal program is generally the best way to learn the auto body trade and work into the auto body business.

Formal programs include *both* on-the-job training *and* related classroom work. By taking the courses offered in these programs, students can learn both basic and advanced work in auto body repair. At the same time, credit is being earned toward a diploma. This type of program is a definite advantage for students who want to go into the auto body repair business after graduating from school. It provides career training while in school, and it is conducted by persons who have been trained to teach.

The vocational school program is the quickest way to become a body repair mechanic. Usually, it requires about 1 to 2 years to complete, instead of the 3 or 4 years of the "helper" on-the-job program.

Keeping Up-to-Date

Auto body repair is one of the most challenging jobs in the auto industry. The automobile industry is constantly making changes and advances on newer automobiles, creating the need for more education. Because of this, body repair workers must continue learning new skills and techniques. A well-trained repair mechanic keeps up with changes and new ideas. Even after finishing an informal on-the-job program or a formal vocational school, a repair technician will need to return to some type of learning program from time to time. Often, major companies offer free or low-cost training sessions for body repair mechanics using their products. Good technicians realize the need for this extra training and normally take advantage of it.

ADVANTAGES OF BODY SHOP WORK

There are several advantages to making a living as an auto body repair technician. One of the main advantages is that almost all the work is done inside, out of the weather. Also, most body work is done in the daytime, leaving evenings and weekends free. The demand for *good* auto body repair mechanics is usually high. It is *very* high in some parts of the country.

Many employers provide holiday and vacation pay. Others may pay additional benefits such as life, health, and accident insurance. Some employers also contribute to retirement plans.

Body repair technicians in some shops are furnished with uniforms like the one worn by the shop manager in Figure 3-2. These are usually rented, and the cleaning is usually paid for by the shop owner. They are furnished free of charge to the body repair worker.

Employment Outlook

Auto body repair technicians usually have a choice of good jobs in every section of the country. About half of the country's technicians work in the eight states with the largest number of automobiles: California, New York, Pennsylvania, Ohio, Texas, Illinois, Michigan, and New Jersey. Also, these states usually offer the highest average wages.

The need for auto body repair workers is expected to increase in the future. Thousands of new job openings will become available each year. Jobs will also open up as some technicians retire or transfer to other lines of work.

The number of workers needed is expected to increase *mainly* because of the growing number of motor vehicles damaged in traffic accidents. As the number of motor vehicles in use grows, the total number of wrecks is expected to continue increasing. Improved highways, driver training courses, added safety features, and stricter law enforcement may slow down the *rate* of increase, but the total number of wrecks will probably continue to rise.

The need for more workers as a result of the rising number of accidents may be somewhat offset, however, by the increasing efficiency of body repair practices. Such practices as replacing (rather than repairing) damaged parts and using plastics to fill dents, plus the use of improved tools, will allow body repair workers to complete repair jobs in less time. In the long run, this benefits both the body repair worker and the consumer.

Pay Scales

When deciding how much to charge for labor, the shops in a given area often work together to set the hourly rate for their city or county. Insurance companies may help determine the hourly rate by stating the maximum that they will pay. The National Automobile Dealers Association (NADA) may be asked to help determine the hourly rate to be charged in a certain area.

Once shop owners or managers know how much can be charged for labor, they can decide how much to pay the technicians working for them. The worker will be paid less than the rate charged, because the body shop has to make a profit. The owner also must pay for large tools, the building, insurance, and utilities (lights, heat, and water).

Generally speaking, body repair employees work from 37 ½ to 48 hours per week, depending on the job and

Fig. 3-29. *An office worker must know how to take accurate notes.*

Fig. 3-30. *For accuracy, an adding machine should be used whenever estimates or statements are being prepared. The adding machine also is used when checking bills and preparing bank deposits.*

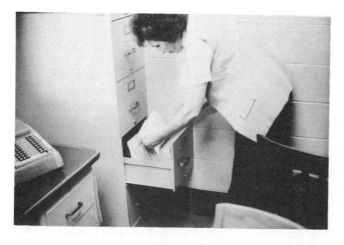

Fig. 3-31. *Estimates and other paperwork must be filed in a way that allows easy reference when necessary. Filing is an important part of the office worker's job.*

location of the shop. There are three basic ways in which a body repair worker may be paid:

1. Straight commission (percentage).
2. Salary plus small commission.
3. Straight salary or wage.

Straight Commission. Some shops pay workers a *straight commission*. Using this method, the worker is paid a *percentage* of the total labor cost charged to the customer on each completed repair job. The commission is usually about 50 percent. The repair worker's earnings depend on how much work is assigned and how fast it is completed.

Salary Plus Small Commission. Some repair workers are paid a weekly salary plus a smaller commission on each job completed. In this arrangement, the worker is getting paid something even if the shop is empty. Of course, the worker wants to finish as many jobs as possible to earn the extra commission.

Wage or Straight Salary. Body repair workers employed by trucking companies, taxi firms, bus lines, and other organizations that repair their own vehicles are usually paid an hourly rate (wage). On the other hand, they may be paid a straight salary (a set amount per week no matter how many hours are worked).

BODY SHOP OFFICE WORKERS

Another interesting area to consider in the auto body shop is working in the shop *office*. Effective office workers must use common sense and clear thinking. The office routine is adapted to the needs of the shop and its workers.

Fig. 3-32. *In larger shops, one office worker may be assigned to do all the parts ordering. Such orders are usually placed by telephone.*

An office worker may be called upon to make clear notes (Fig. 3-29); check bills, money, and bank statements (Fig. 3-30); and file estimates, letters, and receipts (Fig. 3-31).

Ordering Parts

One of the important jobs in a body shop is ordering, receiving, and paying for the parts, tools, and equipment needed by the shop to do business. In some cases, this may be done by the shop manager or owner. In larger shops, an office worker often has this responsibility.

Ordering parts begins by telephoning the parts store, new-car dealer, or salvage yard. When the call is made (Fig. 3-32), the parts should be clearly listed for the order taker. If possible, parts numbers from the collision manuals should be used.

Receiving Parts

Most parts houses operate a delivery truck (Fig. 3-33) to deliver ordered parts to body shops and other customers.

When the parts are delivered, they are brought to the shop's office. The bill for the parts is presented to the office worker or owner (Fig. 3-34). The items on the bill should be compared with the items in the box, to be sure that everything listed has been delivered.

Paying for the Parts

When the parts are received and checked against the bill, they may be paid for by charging them to the shop's account or by writing a check.

Charging Parts to an Account. When using this method, the body shop has an account with the parts store. The office worker or manager signs at the bottom of the bill when parts are delivered. Then, the shop is charged

Fig. 3-33. *Most parts stores and salvage yards have their own delivery trucks to bring orders to the body shop.*

for *all* the signed bills at the end of each month. This saves the trouble of paying for each order as it is delivered. The signature on the bill, of course, indicates that the shop *did* receive the parts.

Paying by Check. This method is used to pay the parts store driver for each parts order as it is delivered. A

Fig. 3-34. *When parts are delivered, the driver will present a bill to the manager or office worker.*

Fig. 3-35. *In many cases, shops prefer to pay for parts when they are received. The driver will accept the shop's check and mark the bill "paid." One copy of the bill is kept for the shop's files.*

Fig. 3-36. *Paying for parts and materials by check will allow the shop to keep an accurate record of expenses.*

check is given to the driver when the bill is presented (Fig. 3-35). The driver should always be paid with a check, rather than with cash. The check serves as the body shop's proof of having paid the bill.

When the driver arrives with the parts and the bill, the items are checked to be sure that everything has been delivered. Then, a check can be written for the amount of the bill. Note that in Figure 3-36 the check *number* and *amount* are entered on the check *register* to the left of the check itself. The driver should write "PAID" and the check number on the bill before turning the bill over to the shop.

Charging Parts to a Job

The office worker should make sure that all the parts and materials bought are charged to the proper vehicle. The charge on the vehicle repair will be the *retail* price, giving the shop a fair and reasonable profit.

Types of Office Workers

Small body shops may not have a regular office worker. In these cases, the owner or manager takes care of day-to-day office work. The owner then usually hires an accountant or bookkeeper to figure the books each month. The accountant may keep books for several other small businesses too.

A larger body shop may have a full-time bookkeeper and office worker. A very large shop may have two or more full-time office workers. One of these would usually be a full-time bookkeeper.

Bookkeeper. Every small business, and especially a body shop, needs a full- or part-time *bookkeeper*. The bookkeeper knows simple tax and accounting laws and when certain taxes are due. The bookkeeper knows what reports need to be made and when they are due. A set of properly kept books tell the owner exactly what the shop's profit or loss is for a certain period of time. In a small business, the bookkeeper can help make the system very simple.

One important task of the bookkeeper is keeping the *bank account* up-to-date. Handling the bank account involves:

1. Making deposits.
2. Writing checks and paying bills.
3. Checking bank statements.

When *making deposits*, all deposit slips for putting money in the bank are made in *duplicate*. One copy is for the bank teller, the other is kept on file in the body shop office. Deposits should be entered on the *stub* of the checkbook (Fig. 3-36).

When *paying bills*, all bills should be paid as soon as possible, and always by check. If payment is made in cash, a receipt for the cash *must* be received and kept.

When *checking the bank statement*, the bookkeeper looks at checks written by the body shop that have been returned from the bank. Each check is then compared with its stub in the checkbook. The deposits entered on the checkbook stubs should also be compared with the deposits listed on the bank statement. The bank statement and the checkbook must agree in all respects. If not, all entries must be double-checked carefully until the error is found.

Section
II

Body-working
Tools

Hand Tools

A body repair worker often uses tools to remove and replace damaged parts on automobiles. Some tools are used to tighten and loosen the nuts or bolts that hold the parts in place. Other tools are used to hold parts for cutting, welding, or other work. Figures 4-1 through 4-4 show a repair worker using different tools to remove a deck lid. Tools that may be used to remove the deck lid are shown in Figure 4-5.

Each type of hand tool is usually used for only one or two different jobs. Because of this, different tools are made for many different jobs. Generally, a tool should not be used for a job if another tool could do the job more easily or more safely.

Most body repair workers have a "feel" for their own tools. For this reason, a fellow worker's tools may not feel as comfortable to a worker as would one of his or her own tools.

Good body repair workers do not abuse their tools by using them incorrectly. Tools should always be kept clean and properly stored. Most hand tools will last for years if they are of good quality and if they are taken care of properly. Of course, a worker must expect to replace worn-out tools before they become dangerous to use. Tools that are no longer used should be sold or stored out of the way.

An auto body repair worker is normally expected to supply his or her own basic hand tools. Figure 4-6 shows a good selection of personal hand tools. An experienced technician may have this complete set, while a new worker (Fig. 4-7) would have fewer tools. Most schools recommend that graduates who are entering auto body work have a complete set of both hand tools and air tools. These tools are the worker's personal

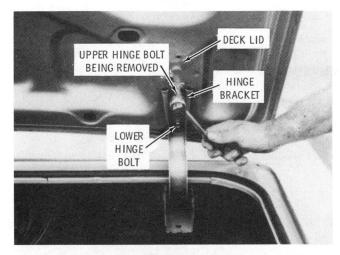

Fig. 4-1. *Using a* socket *and* ratchet handle *to remove a deck lid bolt.*

Fig. 4-2. *Using a* socket, extension, *and* ratchet handle *to remove a deck lid bolt.*

Fig. 4-3. *Using a* box-end wrench *to remove a deck lid bolt.*

Fig. 4-4. *Using an* open-end wrench *to remove a deck lid bolt.*

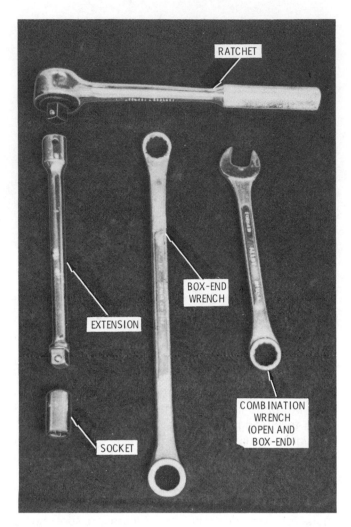

Fig. 4-5. *Any one of these basic hand tools, as shown in Figures 4-1 through 4-4, can be used for a simple job such as removing a deck lid bolt.*

property and are taken from one place of employment to another if the worker changes jobs.

The shop owner is expected to furnish larger or more expensive tools. These include tools such as the vise, post and body jacks, tap and die set, wheel (lug) wrench, and other items that are too large or expensive for each individual employee to furnish. In Figure 4-8, a body repair worker is using a post jack to straighten a damaged door.

PERSONAL TOOLS

A good body repair worker owns many different hand tools. These tools are from several basic groups, such as wrenches, screwdrivers, or pliers. Within each group, there may be different types of tools, such as *open-end* wrenches, *box-end* wrenches, or *combination* wrenches. In each group are tools of various sizes and shapes. A new worker will need a number of different types of tools from each basic group.

Wrenches

A wrench is used to grip and turn the head on a nut or bolt. The word "wrench" means to *twist* or *turn*. There are many different types of wrenches.

The overall *length* of a wrench depends on the size of the nut or bolt on which it will be used (Fig. 4-9). Longer wrenches have larger openings on their ends.

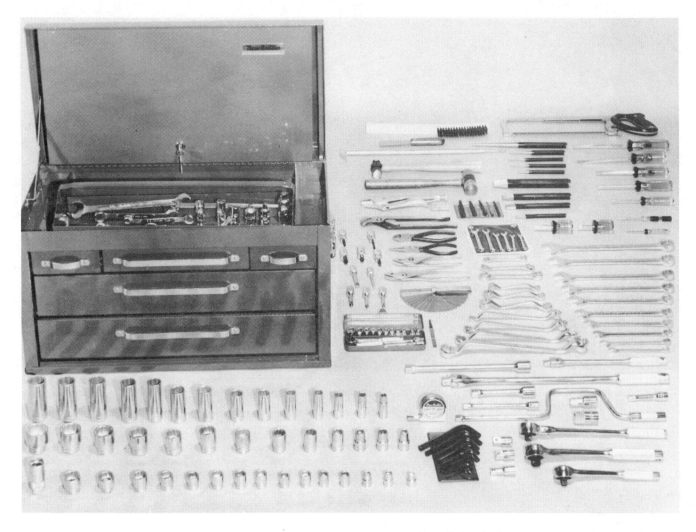

Fig. 4-6. *A complete set of personal tools. (Courtesy of Hand Tools Division, Litton Industries)*

The extra length gives the worker more *leverage* on larger nuts or bolts, which are usually harder to turn and need to be tightened more when installed.

Wrench Size. The *size* of any wrench is the width of the opening on one end of the wrench. For example, an open-end wrench with a 9/16 in. (14 mm) opening will fit snugly on a 9/16 in. (14 mm) nut or bolt head.

Actually a wrench size will always have to be just slightly larger than the nut or bolt head, because it would not fit if it were *exactly* the same size as the head. Many vehicles have both customary and metric fasteners. Metric nuts and bolts are marked for the worker's identification with *blue paint*. The blue color is for *identification* and is temporary.

Metric fasteners must be replaced with metric fasteners, since they are not interchangeable with customary fasteners.

Table 1 shows the metric equivalents of fractions of an inch (1 inch is 25.4 millimeters). Conversion factors for customary to metric units are given in Table 2.

Fig. 4-7. *All body workers are expected to provide their own hand tools.*

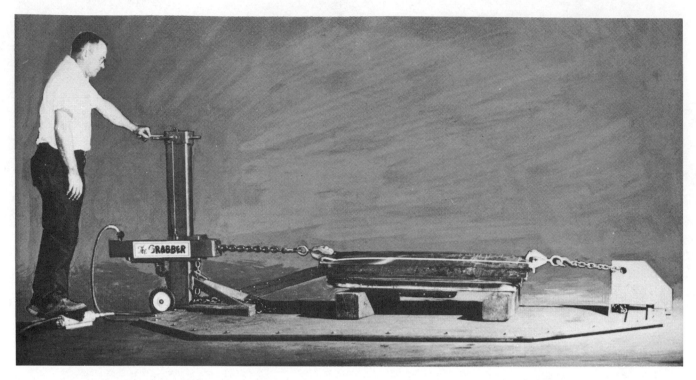

Fig. 4-8. *Larger or more expensive tools, such as the post jack being used to straighten a door in this illustration, are provided by the shop itself. (Courtesy of Grabber Manufacturing Company)*

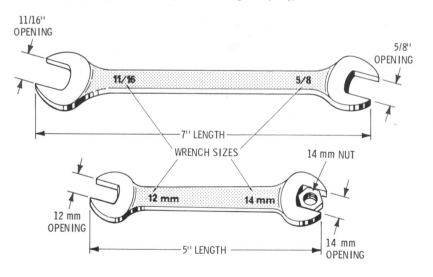

Fig. 4-9. *The size of a wrench, in either conventional or metric terms, is the size of the nut or bolt it will grasp properly.*

Open-end Wrench. A full set of open-end wrenches will be found in the tool boxes of all good repair workers. These tools are called *open-end* wrenches because they are open at *both* ends, as shown in Figure 4-9. Open-end wrenches will fit both square head (four-corner) and hex-head (six-corner) nuts or bolts.

The main jobs for open-end wrenches include holding a nut or bolt for disassembly. Figure 4-10 shows how an open-end wrench holds a common bolt.

The main advantage of an open-end wrench is that it can be used where a wrench cannot be lowered over the top of a nut, such as a nut on a long shaft. The main *disadvantage* of an open-end wrench is that it grips only *two* points of the nut or bolt head. If too much pressure is applied, the wrench may "round off" the corners on the nut or bolt. This will damage the nut or bolt head. If the wrench slips, the worker's hands may be injured.

Most sets of open-end wrenches include sizes from 7/16 in. through 1 in. Metric sets often include sizes from 6 mm to 19 mm. Special larger or smaller sizes may be purchased for the times when they are needed.

Table 1

Metric Equivalents of Fractions

Fractions— in.	Metric— mm	Fractions— in.	Metric— mm	Fractions— in.	Metric— mm
1/64	0.4	23/64	9.1	11/16	17.5
1/32	0.8	3/8	9.5	45/64	17.9
3/64	1.2	25/64	9.9	23/32	18.3
1/16	1.6	13/32	10.3	47/64	18.7
5/64	2.0	27/64	10.7	3/4	19.0
3/32	2.4	7/16	11.1	49/64	19.4
7/64	2.8	29/64	11.5	25/32	19.8
1/8	3.2	15/32	11.9	51/64	20.2
9/64	3.6	31/64	12.3	13/16	20.6
5/32	4.0	1/2	12.7	53/64	21.0
11/64	4.4	33/64	13.1	27/32	21.4
3/16	4.8	17/32	13.4	55/64	21.8
13/64	5.2	35/64	13.9	7/8	22.2
7/32	5.6	9/16	14.3	57/64	22.6
15/64	6.0	37/64	14.7	29/32	23.0
1/4	6.4	19/32	15.1	59/64	23.4
17/64	6.7	39/64	15.5	15/16	23.8
9/32	7.1	5/8	15.9	61/64	24.2
19/64	7.5	41/64	16.3	31/32	24.6
5/16	7.9	21/32	16.7	63/64	25.0
21/64	8.3	43/64	17.1	1	25.4
11/32	8.7				

The number of wrenches in a complete set ranges from 6 to 15, depending on the cost of the set. Figure 4-11 shows several different sets of open-end wrenches.

A new body repair worker should include a set of *metric-size* wrenches when purchasing tools. These will be used to work on newer cars and on foreign makes. Metric-size and customary-size wrenches are *not* interchangeable. For example, a 1/2 in. wrench will not fit snugly enough on a 12 mm bolt head. It will tend to "round off" the corners. See Table 2 for a comparison of metric and customary socket sizes.

Box-end Wrench. These wrenches are very common to the auto repair trade. *Box-end wrenches* are named for their boxed (enclosed) ends. These ends enclose a nut or bolt head, as shown in Figure 4-12.

Box-end wrenches have either 6-point or 12-point openings on the ends. *Points* are the number of openings into which the nut or bolt may go. Note that in Figure 4-13, only 6 of the 12 points are being used to grip the bolt head. The 12-point box-end wrench is easier to use because of the 12 positions in which it may be placed on the nut. Note the 12-point wrenches in Figure 4-14A, B, and E.

Box-end wrenches also come in 8-point and 6-point styles. The 8-point wrenches are not too popular, because they fit only square-head bolts and nuts. The 6-point style has the strongest grip, because its sides are larger and stronger. They allow less chance of slipping off or rounding the nut. Figures 4-15 shows several box-end wrench sets.

Table 2

Customary to Metric Conversion

Multiply	by	To Find Number of
Length		
inch (in.)	25.4000	millimeters (mm)
inch (in.)	2.5400	centimeters (cm)
foot (ft)	0.3048	meters (m)
yard (yd)	0.9144	meters (m)
mile (mi)	1.6093	kilometers (km)
Volume		
quart (qt)	0.9464	liters (L)
gallon (gal.)	3.7854	liters (L)
Mass		
pound (lb)	0.4536	kilograms (kg)
ton (long)	1016.0000	kilograms (kg)
ton (short)	907.1848	kilograms (kg)
Pressure		
pounds per square inch (psi)	6.895	kilopascal (kPa)
Temperature		
degrees Fahrenheit(F)	(°F × 32)/1.8	degrees celsius(°C)

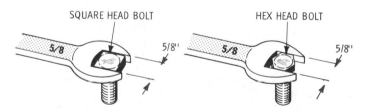

Fig. 4-10. *An open-end wrench grasps any two sides of the nut or bolt.*

The ends of the wrench are offset (the head is lower than the handle). In this way, the worker's hand is *above* the surface or any object that might be in the way as the nut or bolt is turned. Note that the wrenches in Figure 4-14 are not offset by the same amount.

The main advantage of a box-end wrench is that it has complete contact with all 6 points on the bolt head. This *completely* surrounds and grips the bolt head or nut, allowing less chance of the wrench slipping. With all 6 points of contact, the box-end wrench will not easily cut off the corners of the bolt head or nut. This makes the box-end wrench the safest wrench to use.

The main *disadvantage* of a box-end wrench is that there must be room for the end to go *over* the top of the bolt head or nut. Also, the wrench will have to be

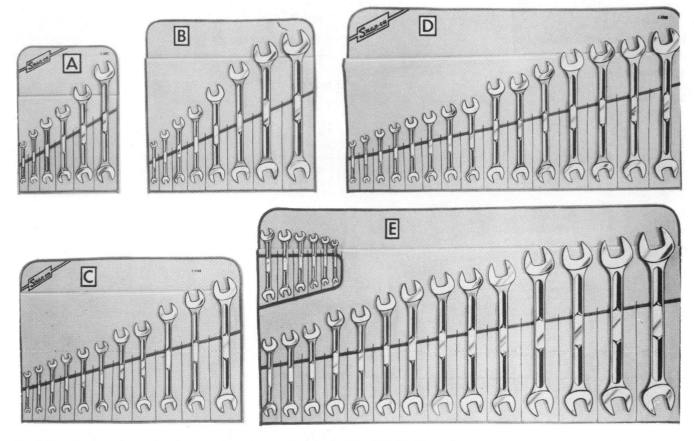

Fig. 4-11. *Open-end wrench sets in a variety of sizes. (Courtesy of Snap-On Tools)*

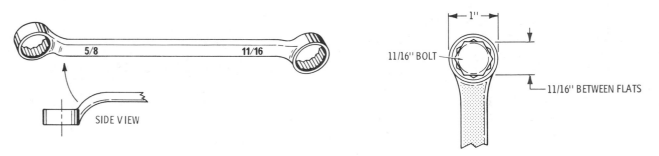

Fig. 4-12. *The box-end wrench usually has a different size opening on each end.*

Fig. 4-13. *The size of the box-end wrench is measured across the flats.*

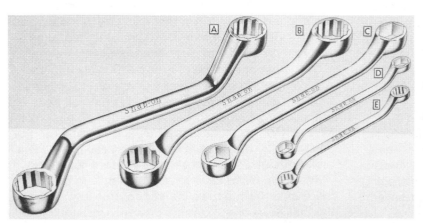

Fig. 4-14. *Box-end wrenches are available in 12-point (A,B,E) or 6-point (C,D) styles. (Courtesy of Snap-On Tools)*

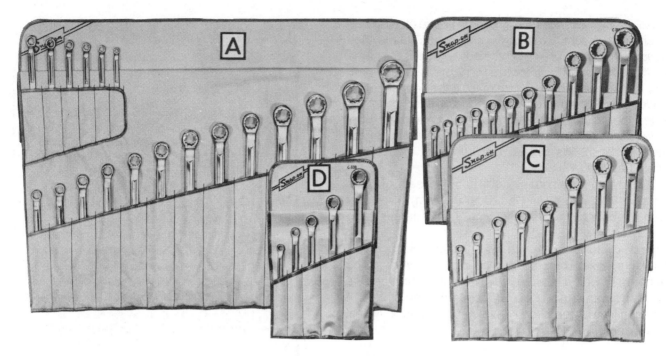

Fig. 4-15. *Several sets of 12-point box-end wrenches. (Courtesy of Snap-On Tools)*

lifted off the nut or bolt and put into a new position each time a pull is made.

Box-end wrenches come in sets of from 6 to 15 wrenches (Fig. 4-15). The more common sets include sizes from 7/16 in. to 1 in. or metric sizes from 6 mm to 19 mm. Box-end wrenches can also be purchased in smaller or larger sizes, as necessary.

Combination Wrench. These wrenches have an *open end* on one end of the wrench and a *box end* on the other end (Fig. 4-16). Therefore, these tools are known as *combination* wrenches. Either end of the wrench fits the *same size* bolt head or nut.

Combination wrenches are used for the same purposes as open-end and box-end wrenches and can be bought in the same sizes. A combination wrench *set* is usually bought in addition to sets of open-end and box-end wrenches. Combination wrenches should not be bought in place of open-end and box-end wrenches, because more than one wrench of the same size may be needed when holding a bolt and removing a nut of the same size.

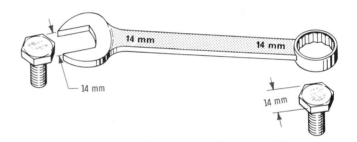

Fig. 4-16. *The combination wrench has one box-end and one open-end. Both ends are the same size.*

Adjustable Wrench. This tool has a screw that allows the open end of the wrench to be adjusted for different sizes of nuts or bolts (Fig. 4-17). An *adjustable wrench* can be adjusted from a fully closed to a wide-open position. Generally, *longer* adjustable wrenches will open wider than will shorter wrenches. A 4 in. (10 cm) wrench, for example, may have a maximum opening of about ½ in. (13 mm). A 15 in. (33 cm) adjustable, though, might have a maximum opening of 1 ¾ in. (5 cm).

Fig. 4-17. *The adjustable wrench has a movable jaw to change the size of the opening. (Courtesy of Channellock, Inc.)*

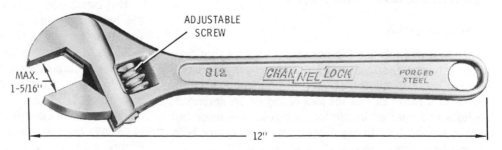

Adjustable wrenches are handy because they can easily fit different sizes of nuts or bolts. This is their main *advantage*. Their main *disadvantage* is the same as that of open-end wrenches: only *two* points of contact on the nut or bolt. This can allow the wrench to slip under heavy pressure. Also, as the wrench becomes worn, the adjusting screw is less able to hold the movable jaw in correct alignment. For these reasons, adjustable wrenches should *not* be used when other wrenches are available.

Adjustable wrenches usually come in sets of three lengths: 6, 8, and 12 in. (15, 20, and 30 cm). They may also be bought individually. Smaller and larger sizes are available.

Pipe Wrench. This tool, like the adjustable wrench, has movable jaws. The pipe wrench also has very strong gripping power. It is used mainly on pipes and gets its name from this use. Pipe wrenches can be bought in many different lengths. Figure 4-18 shows a typical pipe wrench.

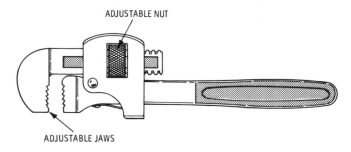

ADJUSTABLE NUT

ADJUSTABLE JAWS

Fig. 4-18. *The pipe wrench, like the adjustable wrench, has a movable jaw. The teeth on the jaws allow it to grip and turn round objects.*

Pipe wrenches have an advantage over open-end and box-end wrenches because they can grip and hold round objects, such as pipes or *studs* (screws without heads). They are useful for several smaller jobs in a body shop, so a body repair worker may want to keep an average-size [10 in. (25 cm)] wrench in the tool box.

Hex and Torx® Wrenches. Figures 4-19 and 4-20 show a group of wrenches that are used the same way and for the same purpose as the hex and Torx® screwdrivers (see below). These are usually called "L" and "T" wrenches, because of their shapes.

Socket Wrench

A socket wrench set is a collection of tools that may be *interchanged* (substituted for each other). The basic parts of the set are the *sockets* themselves. They fit over a bolt head or nut for loosening or tightening it. Sockets are shaped inside like a box-end wrench but have a closed top. In the closed top is a square hole into which a handle may be placed (Fig. 4-21).

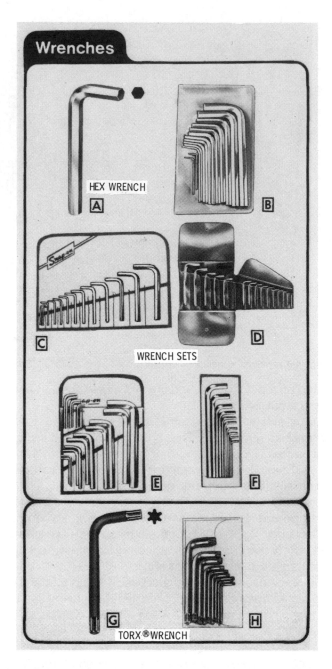

Wrenches

HEX WRENCH
A
B

WRENCH SETS
C
D

E
F

G
H

TORX®WRENCH

Fig. 4-19. *Hex (Allen) and Torx® wrench sets are used with their matching fasteners. Torx® fasteners are frequently used in late-model cars. (Courtesy of Snap-On Tools)*

The basic socket wrench is made up of two parts: the handle and the socket. The handle is made to fit the several sizes of sockets that make up a set. Figure 4-22 shows how the handle lug fits in a socket. Notice that the square *drive lug* on the handle and the square hole in the socket are the same size (in this case, ½ in.).

The part of a socket that fits over the nut or bolt head is usually not the same size as the drive. As shown in Figure 4-21, *this* part of the socket is 9/16 in. (14 mm)

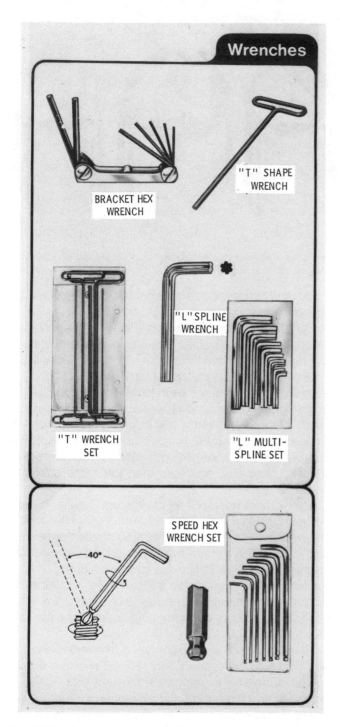

Fig. 4-20. *Some variations of the hex (Allen) wrench. (Courtesy of Snap-On Tools)*

note that the hole is quite deep. This helps keep the socket from easily slipping off the nut or bolt head.

Socket Size. The *size* of a socket is the same as the nut or bolt size on which it is used. A ½ in. (13 mm) socket fits a ½ in. (13 mm) bolt head or nut; a 9/16 in. (14 mm) socket fits a 9/16 in. (14 mm) bolt head or nut and so on. Table 3 shows the metric equivalent of customary socket sizes.

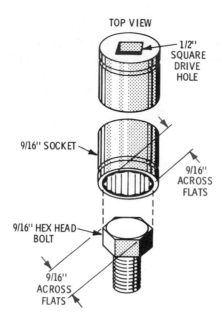

Fig. 4-21. *The size of a socket is the size of the nut or bolt it will fit correctly. Sockets are available in both conventional and metric sizes. A body worker should have both.*

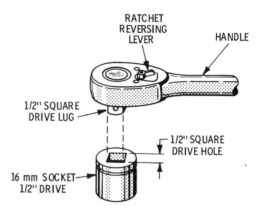

Fig. 4-22. *The basic socket wrench is made up of a socket and one of the several forms of drive handle. They both must be the same drive size.*

Drive Sizes. The handle shown in Figure 4-23A has what is known as a ½ in. *drive size.* The drive size is the *width* of the square peg or square hole on socket tools. The handle in Figure 4-23B has a 3/8 in. drive. These are the two most common drive sizes used in auto body work.

Other drive sizes include ¼, ¾, and 1 in. The small ¼ in. drive socket set is used for work on small parts or interior trim. The larger ¾ and 1 in. drive sets are usually used only by truck and heavy equipment mechanics.

Socket Points. The socket itself is a small, round cylinder. The *inside* of the small cylinder is made with 6, 8, or 12 *points*, as shown in Figure 4-24.

Table 3

Comparison of Customary and Metric Sockets

Customary Socket Size—in.	Metric Socket Size—mm
1/8	4
3/16	5
1/4	6
5/16	8
3/8	10
7/16	11
1/2	13
9/16	14
5/8	16
11/16	17
3/4	19
13/16	20
7/8	22
15/16	24
1	25

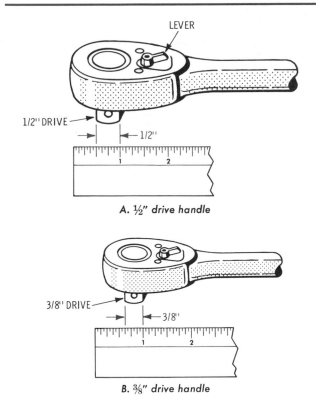

Fig. 4-23. *The* drive *size is the width of the square peg on the handle and its matching hole in the socket.*

The three sockets in Figure 4-24 will all fit the same size bolt head or nut. However, the 8-point socket will fit only a square-head nut or bolt, whereas the 6- or 12-point sockets will fit only 6-sided (hex-head) nuts or bolts.

Sockets can be bought in almost any size and in many different shapes. They are available in both customary and metric sizes. Special sockets have been

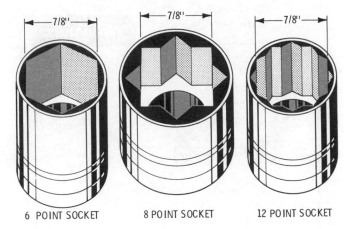

Fig. 4-24. *The number of "points" in a socket is the number of notches cut into its wall.*

made and are available for special jobs. Figure 4-25 shows several common sets of sockets.

Socket Depth. Many sockets are longer (deeper) than others of the same size. This allows the socket to fit down over a long bolt to reach a nut, as in Figure 4-26. These long sockets are called *deep-well* sockets.

Deep-well sockets are used for removing spark plugs, many bumper bolts, and other nuts or bolts in hard-to-reach places. The extra depth gives the socket the clearance necessary to remove or tighten the nut. For normal work, standard-depth (shorter) sockets are sturdier. They also cost less than the same size in a deep-well socket.

A socket set has sockets of different *depths*, as can be seen in Figures 4-25, 4-26, and 4-27. The depths may range from 7/8 in. (22.2 mm) in smaller drive sets to 3 1/4 in. (82.5 mm) in the larger drive sets. Sockets also can be bought in special, longer lengths.

Socket Tools. Most socket sets include a number of tools or attachments. Generally, these tools are used either to hold or to extend the usefulness of the sockets themselves.

There are several different types of handles used to hold and turn the sockets. Figure 4-28 shows a simple socket handle. The handle is the tool that allows a worker to turn the socket, thereby turning the bolt head or nut. This particular handle gives leverage in removing nuts by "breaking over" so that the drive lug is at an angle to the handle. For this reason, this handle is sometimes known as a *breaker bar*. Another common name for this handle is a *power handle*.

The *speed handle*, shown in Figure 4-29, is used for quick work. This tool speeds up the work of removing and replacing bolts and nuts that are out in the open. By using this tool with both hands, a worker may spin nuts on and off in a hurry.

The *ratchet handles* shown in Figure 4-30B, C, D, and E are time-saving tools. They are the most com-

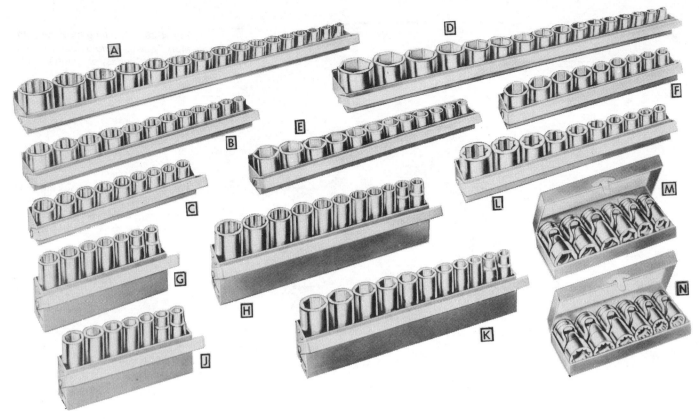

Fig. 4-25. *A number of common socket sets. (Courtesy of Snap- On Tools)*

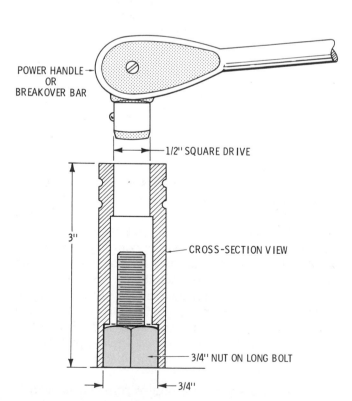

POWER HANDLE OR BREAKOVER BAR

1/2'' SQUARE DRIVE

CROSS-SECTION VIEW

3''

3/4'' NUT ON LONG BOLT

3/4''

Fig. 4-26. *A deep-well socket is used to reach and remove a nut that is far down on the bolt threads.*

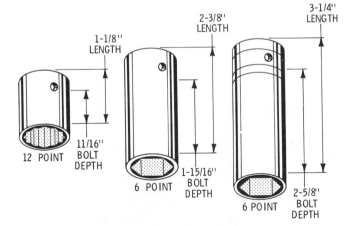

3-1/4'' LENGTH

2-3/8'' LENGTH

1-1/8'' LENGTH

12 POINT

11/16'' BOLT DEPTH

6 POINT

1-15/16'' BOLT DEPTH

6 POINT

2-5/8'' BOLT DEPTH

Fig. 4-27. *The same size socket for example, 1 in. (2.5 cm) can be purchased in various depths.*

monly used socket tools. The handle drive rests on a ratchet wheel, allowing it to back up without taking the socket off the nut. By flipping a small lever on the back of the ratchet, the ratchet direction may be reversed. The ratchet is a strong, useful, and handy socket tool. With proper care, it can last many years.

The *ratchet adapter* (Fig. 4-30) is a converter. That is, it can be put on any socket handle that is not ratcheted. These handles would then be converted to ratchet handles, able to move back and forth without being lifted off the nut and put back for each turn.

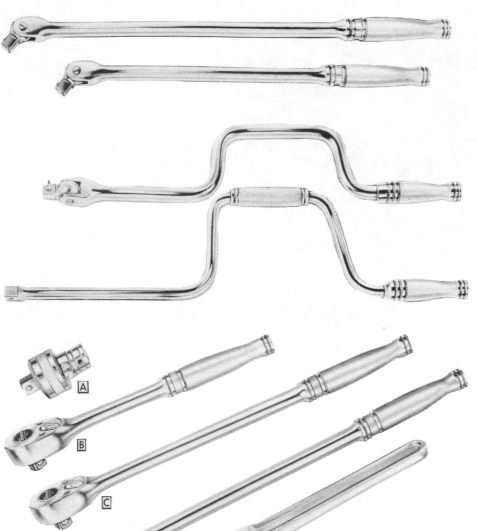

Fig. 4-28. *Two lengths of the common "power handle" used to turn sockets. (Courtesy of Snap-On Tools)*

Fig. 4-29. *Speed handles are used to quickly remove or tighten nuts or bolts with a socket. (Courtesy of Snap-On Tools)*

Fig. 4-30. *Varieties of ratchet handles used with sockets. (Courtesy of Snap-On Tools)*

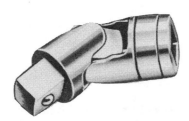

Fig. 4-31. *A universal joint allows use of a socket in hard-to-reach places. (Courtesy of Snap-On Tools)*

A *universal joint* (Fig. 4-31) is one of the biggest time-savers that can be purchased. This handy tool can be placed on the end of a handle or extension to work *around* parts of the car that are in the way. It allows the mechanic to reach nuts or bolts that have to be removed at an angle, as in Figure 4-32.

A simple *extension* (Fig. 4-33) is used between other socket tools. Its main purpose is to extend the *length* of the handle. Extensions come in many lengths, usually from 1 to 36 in. (2.5 to 91 cm). The extension allows the socket to be placed in holes, between parts, or in other places that could not normally be reached. A ratchet or other handle may be placed on one end and a socket fastened on the other.

A simpler socket tool handle is a *slide bar*, or "T-handle" (Fig. 4-34). This tool is used to turn the socket from both sides, allowing the worker to push with one hand while pulling with the other. The bar may be slid all the way to one end, allowing it to be used as a regular handle.

Figure 4-35 shows a group of *screwdriver attachments* that are very useful in a body shop. Figure 4-35A shows a hex-head (or Allen-head) screwdriver attachment; B is a short Phillips® screwdriver attachment; C is a short standard screwdriver attachment; D is a new type of screwdriver called Pozidriv® that provides a tighter, more positive connection between the driver and the screw; E is a special tool known as a *clutch-head* screwdriver attachment; F is a carburetor screwdriver attachment; G is tri-wing socket attachment; H is a double square socket attachment; I is a Torx® screwdriver attachment made for use on tamper-proof fasteners for late-model automobiles; J is a double square socket attachment; K is a standard screwdriver attachment; L is the Torx® driver set. These sockets allow a handle to be used for extra leverage on a stubborn screw.

CAUTION: These attachments are for *hand* operation only. They should not be used with air tools.

Common Socket Sets

Figure 4-36 shows several socket sets with attachments. The most complete set includes a short extension, a ratchet, a slide bar, a breaker bar, a long extension, a plastic handle, a universal joint, and several sockets.

Socket sets usually can be purchased in any of the four common drive sizes: ¼, ⅜, ½, or ¾ in.

Quarter-inch Drive Set. The ¼ in. drive set, also known as the "midget set," is the smallest set made. These sets usually have sockets to fit the smallest nuts used on auto bodies, up to about ½ in. (13 mm). Good ¼ in. drive sets include a ratchet handle, a universal joint, and several extensions.

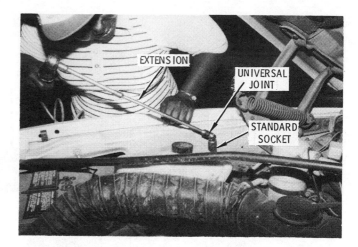

Fig. 4-32. *A universal joint and extension can be used to tighten or loosen bolts in areas where access is difficult. When an extension is used with an air tool, care must be exercised. A low speed should be used to prevent damage to the tool or bolt head or potential injury to the user.*

Fig. 4-33. *A typical socket extension.*

Fig. 4-34. *A slide bar, or T-handle, may be used when enough room is available to turn it.*

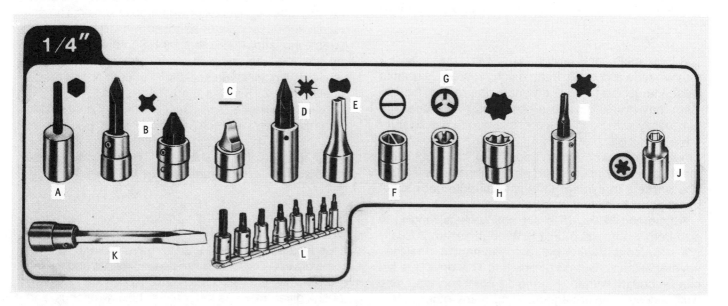

Fig. 4-35. *A variety of special socket accessories for various uses. They are identified in the text. (Courtesy of Snap-On Tools)*

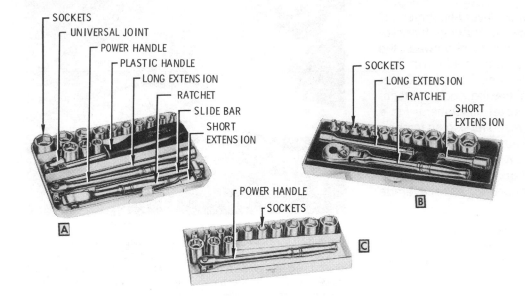

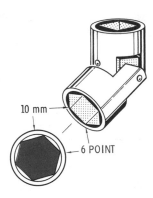

Fig. 4-37. *The* flexocket *combines the socket with a universal joint.*

Fig. 4-36. *A beginning body repair worker should have at least one small socket set. Several varieties are shown here. (Courtesy of Snap-On Tools)*

A ¼ in. drive set is limited to use with small, easy-to-remove nuts and bolts. If too much pressure is used to loosen larger-sized bolts and nuts, the ratchet mechanism may break. If such a bolt head or nut does not turn easily with ¼ in. drive socket tools, use a larger drive socket set.

Three-eighths-inch Set. A good ⅜ in. drive set is the most commonly used set in an auto body repair shop. The sockets in this set fit almost all auto body sheet metal panel bolts and nuts.

A common ⅜ in. drive set has sockets ranging in size from ⅜ through ¾ in. (10 through 19 mm). Usually are included a breaker bar, a speed handle, a ratchet, several extensions, and a slide bar. This drive size set can be bought with 6-, 8-, and 12-point sockets. Deep well sockets, universal joints, and many other accessories may be included.

Flexockets (Fig. 4-37) are usually available only in ⅜ in. drive. These very handy and special sockets are used in the same way as are universal joints. A universal joint is a *drive* attachment, whereas the flexocket is a *socket* attachment. Flexockets are usually available in the same sizes as standard sockets. However, ⅜ in. drive flexockets are limited to nuts and bolts of sizes up to ¾ in. (19 mm).

Half-inch Drive Set. This is a sturdier set than the ⅜-in. drive. It is used for heavy work such as removing bumpers, front suspension parts, and other heavy jobs.

Half-inch drive sets usually include socket sizes from 7/16 to 1 ¼ in. (11 to 32 mm). These sizes make the set very useful for heavier automobile repair. The set usually includes several handles, a slide bar, several extensions, and a universal joint. Sometimes, flexockets are available in ½ in. drive. Half-inch drive sets usually will not include sockets to fit nuts or bolt heads smaller than 7/16 in. (11 mm).

Three-quarter-inch Drive Set. This heavy-duty socket set is not often used for auto body work. Because of this, it is not practical for each body repair worker in the shop to purchase such a set. This set is discussed in the section on tools furnished by the shop.

Screwdrivers

Body repair workers usually have several sets of *screwdrivers*. These tools are used to loosen and tighten screws. They are called screwdrivers because they drive (push) different kinds of screws. Like wrenches and most other tools, they come in many sizes and designs.

Each type and size of screwdriver is made for a certain type and size of screw. A screwdriver's *size* is the length of the *blade* or shank. A group of common round-shank screwdrivers is shown in Figure 4-38. The smallest of these screwdrivers (the stubby) is a 1 ½ in. (38.1 mm) size because its shank is 1 ½ in. (38.1 mm) long. The largest of the round-shank screwdrivers pictured is an 8 in. (20.3 cm) size. Its blade is 8 in. (20.3 cm) long.

Standard-tip Screwdriver. A common screwdriver used in almost all auto repair work is a *standard-tip*, shown in Figures 4-38 and 4-39. Standard-tip screwdrivers may range in size from as short as a 1 ½ in. (38.1 mm) blade to a 20 or 24 in. (50.8 or 61.0 cm) blade (shank).

A set of standard-tip screwdrivers that a new body repair worker should choose is the type with *insulated* handles. These will help prevent electrical shock if the tool accidentally comes in contact with the vehicle's battery or electrical wiring. Many new body repair workers begin with a set of six standard-tip screwdrivers, then add more later.

The main advantage of standard-tip screwdrivers is that they fit all slotted screws: sheet metal screws, wood screws, self-tapping screws, and many others. If used properly, the standard tip screwdriver is safe. The disadvantage of this tool is that it may be used incorrectly as a chisel. Also, some workers do not keep standard-tip screwdrivers properly sharpened.

Phillips® Screwdriver. This type of screwdriver is very common to auto body repair. Sets usually include four to six screwdrivers, in length from 4 to 8 in. (10.1 to 20.3 cm). Figure 4-40 shows a typical set of Phillips® screwdrivers.

Phillips® screwdrivers are used many times a day in an auto body shop. This is because Phillips-head screws are widely used on modern automobile bodies. The main advantage of a Phillips-head screw is the screw's appearance. A Phillips-head screw is generally better looking than a standard screw.

The tip of Phillips® screwdriver meets *four* surfaces in the screw head, as shown in Figure 4-41. When enough pressure is applied, this helps make the screw back off or tighten more easily. As with standard-tip screwdrivers, the handle should be insulated to help prevent electrical shock.

Disadvantages of Phillips® screwdrivers include the fact that they can only be used on Phillips-head screws. Also, Phillips® screwdrivers tend to wear out more quickly than other screwdrivers. Sometimes, a Phillips® screwdriver wears out quickly because it has been used as a punch. This is an incorrect and unsafe way to use such a screwdriver.

Clutch-type Screwdriver. This unusual screwdriver is also known as a *clutch head*. Like a Phillips® screw-

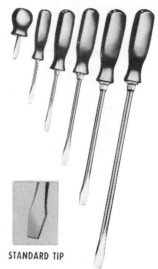

Fig. 4-38. *The body repair worker needs a good selection of standard (straight) tip screwdrivers. These have a round shank. (Courtesy of Snap-On Tools)*

STANDARD TIP

Fig. 4-39. *Some workers prefer screwdrivers with a square shank, such as the ones shown here. (Courtesy of Snap-On Tools)*

STANDARD TIP

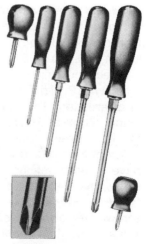

Fig. 4-40. *Phillips® screwdrivers are a necessary part of the body worker's tool kit. Phillips-head screws are often used to fasten interior trim parts. (Courtesy of Snap-On Tools)*

PHILLIPS TIP

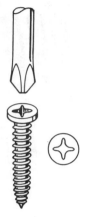

Fig. 4-41. *The Phillips® screwdriver has four "teeth" that fit into the recess in the head of the Phillips screw.*

driver, the clutch-type also has four sides for applying pressure (Fig. 4-42). They come in lengths from 4 to 8 in. (10.1 to 20.3 cm).

Clutch-type screwdrivers have limited use because not many vehicles use this type of screw. They are found most frequently on General Motors trucks.

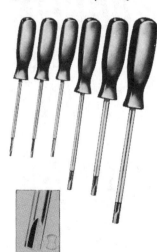

CLUTCH-TYPE TIP

Fig. 4-42. *Clutch-type screwdriver tips fit into a special recess on clutch-head screws. (Courtesy of Snap-On Tools)*

Reed and Prince Screwdriver. The screwdriver shown in Figure 4-43 is a *Reed and Prince* screwdriver. This type of screwdriver is normally sold in lengths from 4 to 8 in. (10.1 to 20.3 cm).

Reed and Prince screwdrivers should not be confused with Phillips® screwdrivers. There is a good deal of difference in the screw slots and in the screwdriver points. Look at Figures 4-40 and 4-44, and compare the tips closely. Note that each screwdriver tip fits a different type of screw. Reed and Prince screwdrivers have a more definitely pointed tip, whereas Phillips® screwdrivers are more blunt.

Pozidriv® Screwdriver. This tool is called a *Pozidriv®* screwdriver because of its positive action and grip. It looks somewhat like the Phillips® screwdriver, but it provides a tighter grip and more positive connection

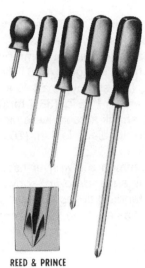

REED & PRINCE

Fig. 4-43. *Reed and Prince screwdrivers are similar to Phillips® screwdrivers, but they have more sharply pointed tips. (Courtesy of Snap-On Tools)*

Fig. 4-44. *The Reed and Prince screwdriver matches the recess in the head of a Reed and Prince screw.*

between the driver and the screw (Fig. 4-45). This tool is made in several forms, such as the screwdriver for use with a socket set, as shown in Figure 4-35.

Torx® Screwdriver. The *Torx®* screwdriver is designed for use on the Torx® fasteners rapidly becoming commonplace in the automobile industry (Fig. 4-46).

Tape Measure

One tool that is frequently used in the body shop is the *tape measure*, also known as a *steel tape*. A steel tape (Fig. 4-47) is used to make measurements when cutting or aligning damaged panels or when aligning frames.

Punch and Chisel Set

Many times, auto body technicians must cut or punch holes in metal panels or other parts. At other times, holes need to be aligned to assemble body parts. These jobs are done with tools from a good *punch and chisel set*. Several typical sets are shown in Figure 4-48.

Punches. These tools have round points. *Punches* come in sizes from about 4 to 20 in. (10.1 to 50.8 cm) long, depending on the use for which they were designed. Some of the more standard punch sizes are shown in Figure 4-48.

Some punch sets include a measuring gauge and a holder. The measuring gauge is used to measure the *angle* on the punch tip. The holder is used to hold the punch or chisel while it is being driven with a hammer. This lessens the possibility of injury to the technician while using the punch.

During metal-straightening work, the punch may be used to raise small dents that would be hard to reach with a pick hammer. Another use for the tool is to punch holes in panels for sheet metal screws or for pulling out dents. Finally, punches are used to align holes by pulling them to the same spot. This allows bolts to be inserted, holding the panels together and in alignment.

Chisels. The main use for these tools is to *cut* metal. Several chisel sets are shown in Figure 4-48.

A good, sharp chisel will cut easily and smoothly, making clean cuts on metal parts. The main use for a chisel is to cut metal when removing a panel. Other common uses include breaking weld joints and cutting off screws, rivets, or rusted parts.

Chisels come in many sizes, from about 4 to 18 in. (10.1 to 45.7 cm) long, and in many different shapes. Most chisel and punch sets also include a measuring gauge and holder.

Pliers

Pliers come in many different sizes and shapes. All body repair workers need good *pliers* for gripping, cutting, holding, and many other jobs in the shop. Figure 4-49 through 4-57 show some of the many different kinds of pliers.

POSIDRIV ®

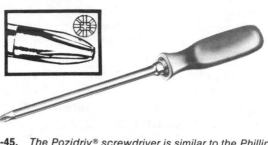

Fig. 4-45. *The Pozidriv® screwdriver is similar to the Phillips® in shape, but it has a tip that is more blunt. Pozidriv® screwdrivers may be identified by their red-colored handles. (Courtesy of Snap-On Tools)*

TORX ®

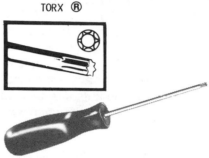

Fig. 4-46. *The Torx® screwdriver is used with fasteners that have been adopted by many auto manufacturers. (Courtesy of Snap-On Tools)*

Fig. 4-47. *A steel tape measure is useful for many body shop jobs. (Courtesy of Snap-On Tools)*

Fig. 4-48. *A variety of punch and chisel sets. (Courtesy of Snap-On Tools)*

PUNCHES CHISELS PUNCH MEASURING GAUGE PUNCH HOLDER

Interlocking-grip Pliers. These pliers (Fig. 4-49) have a tight gripping action. *Interlocking-grip* pliers have long handles, allowing the worker a strong grip on the tool and the object in the tool's jaws. They are basically used for holding and turning large nuts, bolts, and round pieces. These pliers are also known as *Channellock®* pliers. Older auto mechanics may refer to these as "water pump" pliers, because they were used to tighten water pump seals on older-model cars.

Below the jaws of this tool are several interlocking channels, from which the tool gets its name. These allow the pliers to fit both large and small parts by changing channels (and, therefore, the jaw size). They have the advantage of being fast and easy to use. Since the jaws are offset, they can reach many hard-to-get-to places. These pliers usually come in sizes from about 6 to 14 in. (15.2 to 35.6 cm) long. A *disadvantage* is that these pliers have a tendency to round off the corners of bolts and nuts. For this reason, they should not be used for such work when wrenches are available.

Combination Pliers. These are the most common pliers. *Combination* pliers are so named because they have both *notched* and *flat* jaws (Fig. 4-50). These jaws allow the pliers to grip either round or flat work. These pliers are the most frequently used, general-purpose pliers in the tool box. They have long handles to allow good leverage and a movable center bolt to change the jaw size. Combination pliers usually come in lengths from 6 in. (15.2 cm) on up.

Many combination pliers also can be used to cut wire. For this reason, combination pliers may some-times be referred to as *wire pliers*. The wire cutter is under the gripping jaws and above the adjusting bolt in the center of the pliers.

Midget Pliers. These pliers get their name from the fact that they are very small. *Midget pliers* (Fig. 4-51) are used for very close work in limited space. This would include work on switches, gauges, and other instrument panel work.

Like the combination pliers, midget pliers have a movable center bolt to adjust the jaws. They also have fairly long handles for good leverage. The main disadvantage of midget pliers is that they are small and must not be used with too much force. If there is room enough, it is better to use larger pliers.

Battery Pliers. These special pliers, shown in Figure 4-52, are very useful. The long handles on *battery pliers* give a body worker good leverage on nuts or bolts. Basically, battery pliers are used to remove the nut on battery cable bolts. Battery acid may have caused the nut to corrode so that it can no longer be removed with a wrench.

Battery pliers usually come in only one or two sizes, from about 6 to 10 in. (15.2 to 25.4 cm) long. A disadvantage of battery pliers is that they are not adjustable. They only fit a few sizes of nuts and bolts.

Lineman Pliers. These special pliers, shown in Figure 4-53, are used more in electrical work than in auto body work. *Lineman pliers* are most likely to be used by an electrician or a power lineman.

These pliers also have a wire-cutting edge. They can easily strip the insulation off electrical wires and usually have insulated handle grips to help guard against electrical shock. A disadvantage of these pliers is that their best work is done on electrical equipment.

Locking-jaw Pliers. Pliers like those shown in Figure 4-54 through 4-57 are widely used in the auto body repair trade. These pliers have a spring-type mechanism to lock the jaws in position. When *locking-jaw* pliers are closed on an object, they continue to hold firmly *after* they are released; this explains their name. These pliers are available in various lengths from 6 to 12 in. (15.2 to 30.5 cm). Special models also are available and are discussed later.

Standard locking-jaw pliers are useful for many types of work. They have double-action lock jaws, will grip almost any shape, and normally will not slip. These pliers will work in close quarters and at any angle. They are often used as a substitute for a vise, a clamp, or a pipe wrench. Standard locking-jaw pliers have either straight jaws (Fig. 4-54) or curved jaws (Fig. 4-55).

Special locking-jaw pliers are available to hold panels together for brazing or welding. Shown in Figure 4-56, these pliers allow both hands to be free for welding or brazing. The special "reach over" top jaw can fit over

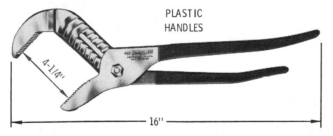

Fig. 4-49. *Interlocking-grip pliers have a wide range of adjustment. (Courtesy of Channellock, Inc.)*

Fig. 4-50. *Simple combination pliers. (Courtesy of Channellock, Inc.)*

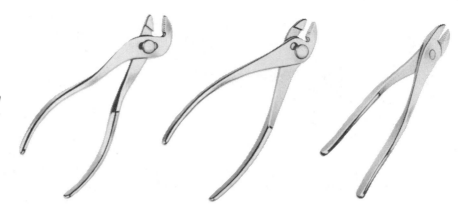

Fig. 4-51. *Midget pliers are useful when working with small parts or in restricted spaces. (Courtesy of Snap-On Tools)*

Fig. 4-52. *Battery pliers are used to remove clamps from battery terminals. (Courtesy of Channellock, Inc.)*

the top of seams or panel flanges, making the tool more useful.

The *bending tool*, shown in Figure 4-57, is another special locking-jaw plier. This tool has wide jaws that make it ideal for the bending and shaping that is needed during sheet metal work. These tools are also useful for upholstery work, because the material can be pulled and stretched without damage.

Brushes and Scrapers

In a body shop, *brushes* (Fig. 4-58) are used for cleaning off rust and old paint. Qualities of a good brush include stiffness, durability, and long life. The group of brushes in Figure 4-58 includes wire brushes and bristle (hair) brushes.

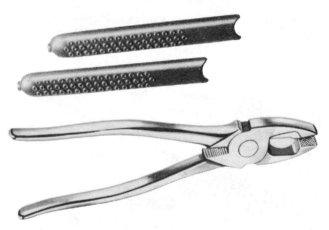

Fig. 4-53. *Lineman's pliers are most often used by electricians, but they are useful for some body shop jobs. (Courtesy of Snap-On Tools)*

Fig. 4-54. *Locking-jaw pliers, like this straight-jaw type, are very useful tools for holding parts together or for obtaining a very firm grip on a part. (Courtesy of Channellock, Inc.)*

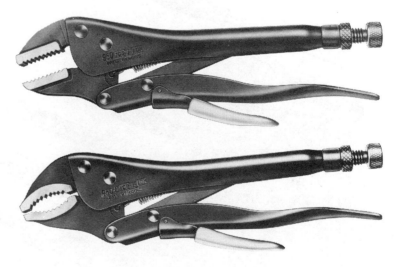

Fig. 4-55. *Curved-jaw pliers of the locking type are useful for gripping round objects. (Courtesy of Channellock, Inc.)*

Fig. 4-56. *These special locking-jaw pliers are used to hold panels together for welding or brazing. (Courtesy of Snap-On Tools)*

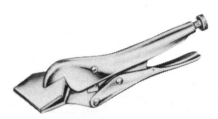

Fig. 4-57. *The wide, flat jaws of these locking-jaw pliers make them useful for bending sheet metal. (Courtesy of Snap-On Tools)*

The main uses of *scrapers* in a body shop are to remove paint and cements. Figure 4-59 shows scrapers commonly used in the auto body trade. Wide scrapers are sometimes used to spread plastic or other resin-base materials.

Scratch Awl

Similar to an ice pick, but stronger, is the *scratch awl* (Fig. 4-60). In a modern body shop, this is a much used tool. Scratch awls are used to scratch (mark) metal for cutting, drilling, or fastening. They also are used to pierce holes in thin metal instead of a drill. The awl is much faster than a drill for rough holes. Awls are made with a sharp point that can pierce metal easily. For heavier jobs, an awl can be *driven* through metal with a light tap from a hammer. Like all cutting tools, awls must be kept sharp to be safe and effective.

Fig. 4-60. *The scratch awl is used to scratch lines on metal and to punch holes. (Courtesy of Snap-On Tools)*

Fig. 4-58. *To clean rust and other debris from body parts, brushes like these are used. (Courtesy of Snap-On Tools)*

Fig. 4-59. *Scrapers are useful for removing paint and cements from body parts. (Courtesy of Snap-On Tools)*

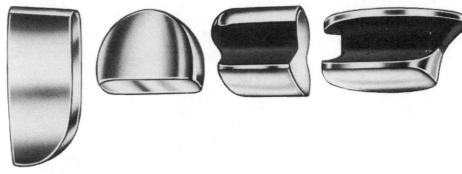

Fig. 4-61. *Types of body dollies include, from left: toe, heel, general purpose, and anvil. (Courtesy of Snap-On Tools)*

Fig. 4-62. *Pry bars. (Courtesy of Snap-On Tools)*

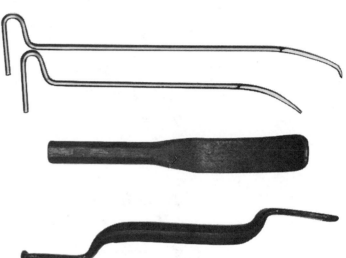

Dolly Block

These small, heavy metal blocks are basic auto body tools. *Dolly blocks*, often called "dollies," are small, simple tools. Each block has many curves and angles (Fig. 4-61). Different dolly blocks are easy to identify by their shapes, such as (left to right in Fig. 4-61) toe, heel, general-purpose, and anvil.

Dollies are mainly used *under* damaged areas. When choosing a dolly for a given job, select one that fits the shape of the panel *before* the panel was damaged. Then, use a hammer on the side of the metal opposite the dolly block. Light hammering will align and "rough out" the damaged metal. A dolly may also be used by itself to bump up low spots.

While a hammer would be used to bump *down* high crowns (outward dents), dolly blocks would be used *beneath* the panel to force the panel *up*, toward its original curve or contour. For the most part, dollies are used as back-up tools for hammers. Dollies come in many sizes and shapes. A set of the four most common dollies is usually enough for a beginning body repair worker.

Pry Bars

Another common metal-working tool is a *pry bar* or "pick tool" (Fig. 4-62). These tools are available in different lengths (sizes) and shapes. Most tool companies offer them as part of a set of body tools. Or, of course, they may be purchased separately as needed.

When repairing doors, the bar may be slipped (or punched) through drain holes along the bottom edge of the door. If the holes are not near the damage, other holes may be made. Then, small dents and creases in the outside door panel can be pried out from the inside, sometimes without removing trim or window parts.

Fig. 4-63. *Spoons are used for a number of body shop jobs.*

Body Spoons

The most common use of a *body spoon* is to reach hard-to-get-at places such as the insides of doors, deck (trunk) lids, and hoods. Like pick tools (pry bars), body spoons are used when the repair worker cannot get to an area with a hammer or dolly. Two common body spoons are shown in Figure 4-63. Spoons come in many sizes and shapes.

Body spoons also may be used to pick up low spots when there is not enough room to use a hammer. They can be used as alignment tools in hard-to-reach places. When they are used this way, the visible end is bumped with a hammer to align an inside panel.

Spring hammering is also done with a body spoon. The spoon is placed against a crown or ridge near a dent or gouge (Fig. 4-64). Then the spoon is hammered to flatten the high ridge down evenly to its proper position.

Hammers

Good *hammers* are vital tools in an auto body repair shop. A group of body shop hammers is shown in Figure 4-65. Some hammers are used for aligning or

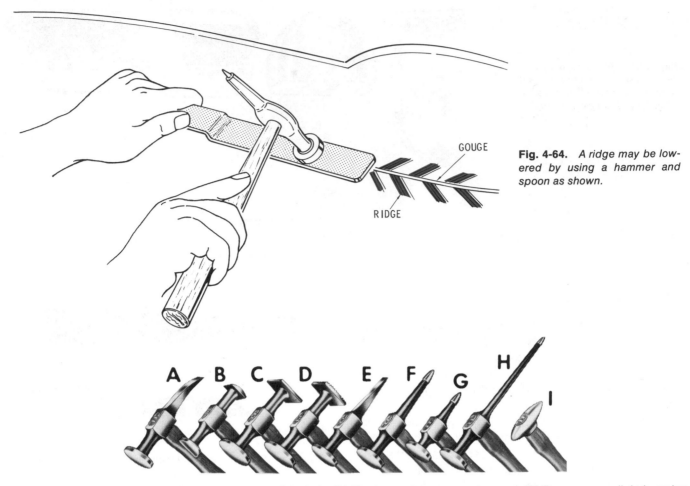

Fig. 4-64. *A ridge may be lowered by using a hammer and spoon as shown.*

Fig. 4-65. *Common hammers used in body shop work include: (A) Short curved cross-peen hammer. (B) Reverse curve light bumping hammer. (C) Wide-face shrinking hammer. (D) Shrinking hammer. (E) Wide-nose cross-peen hammer. (F) Long low-spot pick hammer. (G) Picking and dinging hammer. (H) Long picking hammer. (I) Short head pick hammer. (Courtesy of Snap-On Tools)*

roughing out damaged metal. Other hammers are used for shaping and smoothing the metal after it has been roughed out.

The *size* of a hammer is the *weight* of the hammer *head*. The length or weight of the hammer handle has nothing to do with the hammer's *size*. For example, a 16 oz [453.6 g (gram)] ball peen hammer has a head that weighs 16 oz (453.6 g) *before* the handle is installed.

There are special hammers that do not have metal heads. Instead, they have rubber or plastic heads. These are used when the part being worked on would be damaged by a metal head. Several basic types of body shop hammers are discussed below.

Ball Peen Hammer. This is a general-purpose hammer. The *ball peen* hammer is also called the "shop hammer" (Fig. 4-66). It may be used to rough out metal or to drive punches and chisels.

Ball peen hammers come in several sizes. The 40 and 30 oz (1134.1 and 850.6 g) sizes are most commonly used in a body shop. They have a flat, finished face on one end and a round face on the other end.

Fig. 4-66. *Ball peen hammer.*

Plastic-tip Hammer. This hammer is used for work on parts that might have their finish damaged by a metal hammer head. *Plastic-tip* hammers are used more often on mechanical parts than on body parts. The tough plastic tip will withstand a good deal of pounding without seriously marring the face. Many better hammers have plastic tips that are easily replaced when necessary (Fig. 4-67).

Soft-face Hammer. This hammer usually has tips of hard *leather* (Fig. 4-68). Soft-face hammers are used for working metal parts such as chrome trim without mars or damage. They may be used on parts that are more delicate than those on which a plastic-tip hammer would be used. The replaceable leather tips on better soft-face hammers are designed to resist chipping, flaking, and mushrooming (spreading out on the face).

Brass-face Hammer. This special hammer (Fig. 4-69) has faces of soft *brass*. A *brass-face* hammer is especially suited for driving mechanical parts that should not be scarred during installation. In body shop work, this would be especially true for parts involved in front suspension and alignment.

Pick Hammers. These are some of a body worker's most used hammers. *Pick* hammers have a flat, smooth face on one end and a sharp point on the opposite end. In body work, a pick hammer has three main jobs:

1. The smooth face is used to work down high spots.
2. The smooth face is used to work metal down on the dolly (Fig. 4-70).
3. The sharp, pointed end is used to pick up small dents (Fig. 4-70).

When using a pick hammer, be careful. The sharp, pointed end can build up a great deal of pressure and may damage the metal if not used carefully. Use only light, small blows, and then only on small dents. Pick hammers can easily punch holes in the body sheet metal.

When the damage has been roughed out to the correct *general* contour, the process known as hammering and dollying begins. A dolly is placed under the damaged area and the hammer's smooth face is used to work down the high spots, as in Figure 4-70.

A pick hammer should *not* be used to strike heavy blows. Instead, the hammer should be held *loosely* in one hand. Then, as it lightly strikes the metal, the hammer will automatically spring back into position for another blow, as in Figure 4-71. The metal's "spring" makes the hammer bounce back, off the surface being worked. The body repair worker must guide the hammer's direction as it springs back.

Then, using the dolly, the low place is bumped on the underside. This brings the low place up and smooths out the damaged area. The dolly brings the metal *up*. The pick hammer works the high places *down*. Together, they work as shown in Figures 4-70 and 4-71.

The *sharp* end of the pick hammer is used to lift up tiny low spots left by the dolly *underneath* the surface. Here, the dolly is held on the *outside* of the panel, over the dent. It backs up the sharp end of the hammer, as shown in Figure 4-72. This keeps the metal from coming too far upward.

Slide Hammer. The newest member of the hammer family is the *slide* hammer, also known as the "snatch hammer." A typical slide hammer is shown in Figure

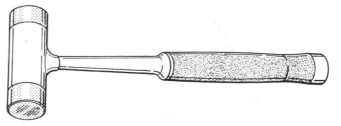

Fig. 4-67. *Plastic-tip hammer.*

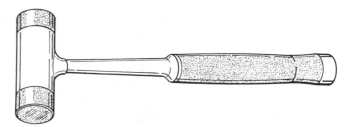

Fig. 4-68. *Soft-face hammer.*

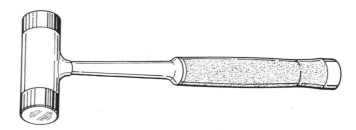

Fig. 4-69. *Brass-face hammer.*

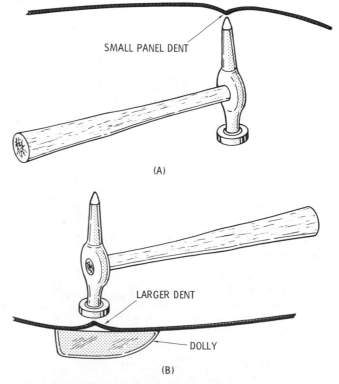

SMALL PANEL DENT

(A)

LARGER DENT

DOLLY

(B)

Fig. 4-70. *Common uses for a pick hammer.*

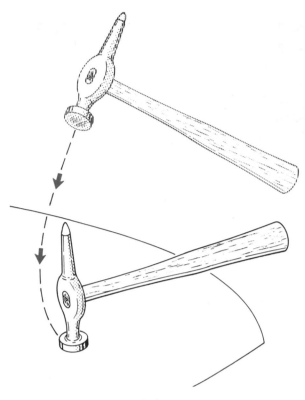

Fig. 4-71. *The* spring *of the sheet metal will rebound the hammer for the next blow.*

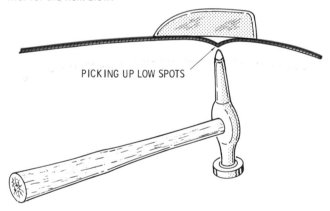

PICKING UP LOW SPOTS

Fig. 4-72. *Using the sharp point of the hammer to "pick up" small dents in sheet metal.*

4-73. This tool is one of the more popular hammers in a body shop.

A slide hammer is used in a way opposite that in which a pick hammer is used. With a slide hammer, the metal is *pulled* up instead of being *bumped* up. This most often must be done on newer types of body construction, such as cars with unitized bodies. These construction methods do not allow as much room for body workers to get underneath or behind the panels.

To repair panels with a slide hammer, a hole is first punched or drilled in the metal. (An awl or drill may be used to make the hole.) Then, a large sheet metal screw is threaded into the hole. A screw-holding attachment is placed on the end of the slide hammer, as in Figure 4-73. Attachments are made to fit almost any size metal screw. Pulling on the screw will then pull out on the metal. This will allow the body worker to pull the metal back into position, as shown in Figure 4-74.

Fig. 4-74. *Both the slide hammer and the pick hammer can be used to pull out and level a long gouge in a panel.*

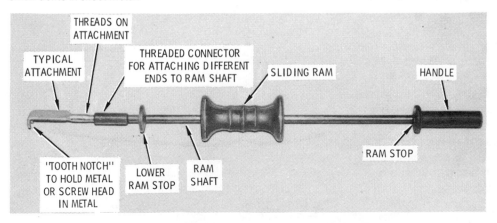

THREADS ON ATTACHMENT

TYPICAL ATTACHMENT

THREADED CONNECTOR FOR ATTACHING DIFFERENT ENDS TO RAM SHAFT

SLIDING RAM

HANDLE

"TOOTH NOTCH" TO HOLD METAL OR SCREW HEAD IN METAL

LOWER RAM STOP

RAM SHAFT

RAM STOP

Fig. 4-73. *Parts of the slide hammer. (Courtesy of Snap-On Tools)*

Actually, there are *two* methods by which the slide hammer may hold onto the sheet metal screw. These are shown in Figure 4-75. In the *first* method, the slide hammer attachment has a slot that fits under the screw head. With this attachment, the screw is first threaded into the damaged panel. Then, the slide hammer is used to pull outward on the screw and, therefore, pull out the metal.

In the *second* method, the sheet metal screw is actually *attached* to the slide hammer. This is shown, cutaway, in Figure 4-75. The sheetmetal screw is first put in position on the end of the slide hammer body. A "tooth" on the body end keeps the screw from turning. Then, a screw-holding *sleeve attachment* is screwed over the sheet metal screw threads onto the end of the slide hammer body. This attachment surrounds the screw head and holds it tightly on the end (and the tooth) of the slide hammer body.

While either method will work, the second method (Fig. 4-75) has a disadvantage. The screw must be installed on the slide hammer *before* being screwed into the damaged panel. Then, the slide hammer becomes a large screwdriver, to turn the screw into the damaged panel before pulling (Fig. 4-74).

After the metal has been pulled back into place, the damaged area is levelled. Usually, polyester plastic body filler is used to fill the screw holes and low places. Plastic may be used because the body panel's back side cannot be easily reached for hammering and dollying.

Pull rods. Pull rods, like the slide hammer, are actually "hammers used in reverse." They are used to pull instead of push (Fig. 4-76).

Pull rods are used for shallower dents than are the heavier slide hammers. Usually, one pull rod is used at a time, as in Figure 4-77. A hole must be drilled or

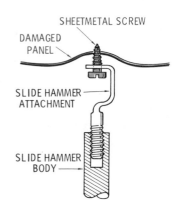

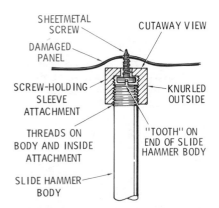

Fig. 4-75. *A sheet metal screw is used to attach the slide hammer to the panel.*

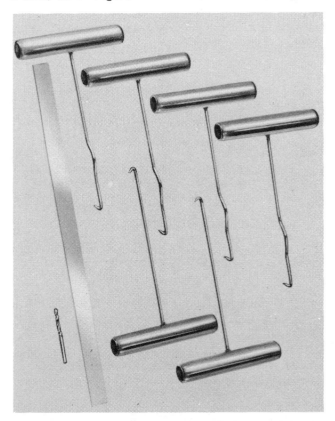

Fig. 4-76. *A pull rod tool kit includes a drill bit, a straight edge, and several pull rods. (Courtesy of Snap-On Tools)*

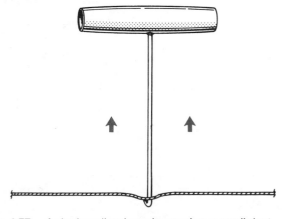

Fig. 4-77. *A single pull rod can be used on a small dent.*

punched in the metal to use a pull rod. Later, the hole will have to be filled with body solder or plastic.

An advantage of pull rods is that several can be used at the same time, as in Figures 4-78 and 4-79. To do this, several holes should be drilled or punched in large damaged areas. Pull rods can then be placed in the holes and a large section of damage pulled out at one time. To repair creases more easily, the high crown around the outer edge of the low place can be worked down with a pick hammer while the rods are pulled. This is being done in Figure 4-79. Pulling and hammering helps the metal to straighten back to its original position.

Whenever pull rods are used, a straight edge like the one shown in Figure 4-76 may be used to see if the metal contour is correct. If necessary, the metal may be worked down or pulled up to level. Generally, pull rods are used for only light work.

Files

For many years, metal *body files* have been used by the repair worker to smooth metal. Figures 4-80 and 4-81 illustrate major body files. The different types of body files are used for different contours (slopes) on metal body panels.

Reveal File. This is the smallest file used in body repair work (Fig. 4-80). *Reveal files* are used to file in tightly rounded places, such as around windshields, backlights (rear windows) and wheel openings. Blades for reveal files can be purchased in almost any *shape*. However, the blades and the holders are all the same length.

When a reveal file is used, the cutting is done on the pulling stroke. If the file is pushed, it may bounce, producing a rough cut. Properly used, however, reveal files can help a worker produce good, very detailed results.

Body File. This tool is also known as a metal file or metal body file (Fig. 4-81). *Body files* are used to work

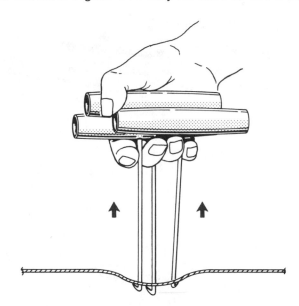

Fig. 4-78. *For larger dents, several pull rods may be used.*

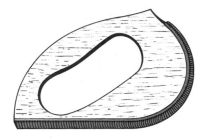

Fig. 4-80. *A small reveal file has a curved shape.*

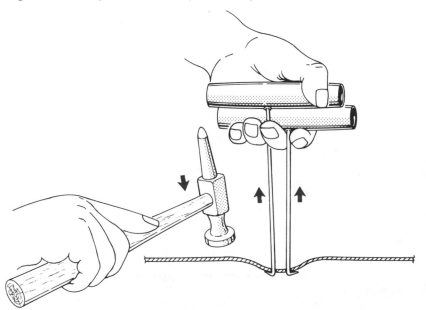

Fig. 4-79. *A picking hammer may be used to work down a raised area around a crease at the same time that pull rods are used on the crease itself.*

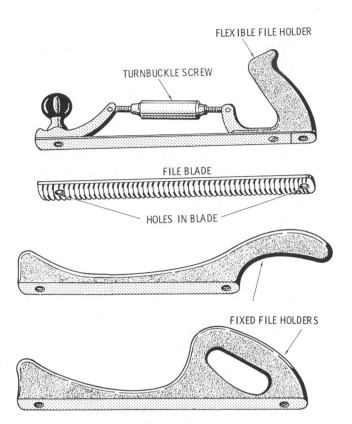

Fig. 4-81. *Holders for body files are available in several shapes.*

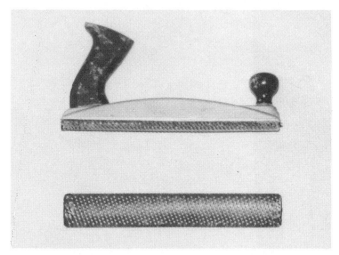

Fig. 4-82. *The* Surform *file is used with a holder. (Courtesy of Stanley Tools)*

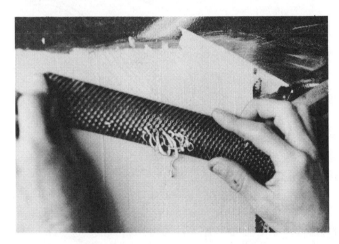

Fig. 4-83. *Semi-cured plastic filler may be grated with the* Surform *tool.*

down very small high places after the damaged area has been aligned and dollied to almost exactly the right contour. The file cuts the high spots off the metal. Then, a pick hammer and dolly may be used again to raise the low spots, making the metal smooth.

Blades for a body file come in three basic shapes: curved, round, and straight. Straight-shaped files can be *flexed* to fit the contour of the metal when using a holder with a turnbuckle screw (Fig. 4-81). By rotating the turnbuckle right or left, the holding plate of the file holder can be flexed. This forces the file to flex as well. Flexible file holders may be used for filing both concave (curved in) and convex (curved out) metal. The turnbuckle may also be adjusted for straight cutting.

Surform File. This special file has many nicknames, such as cheese grater, cabbage grater, cabbage cutter, grating file, etc. All of these names refer to the *Surform* file tool shown in Figure 4-82. *Surform* is the name given to the tool by its inventor, the Stanley Tool Company. The name comes from two words *sur*face and *form*.

In body shop work, this tool is used to grate plastic body filler when the filler becomes semi-hard (Fig. 4-83). The *Surform* tool speeds up body work done with plastic filler because the plastic may be partly worked down with the tool before it is completely cured. This reduces waiting time, because the plastic can be worked sooner after it is applied. After using the tool,

the surface is smoother than when the plastic was first applied. When the plastic has completely cured, it can then be sanded smooth with a fine *speed* file, discussed below.

The *Surform* tool cannot be used effectively on fully cured (hardened) plastic. Cured plastic will quickly wear the cutting edge off the blade. When the plastic is fully hardened, it may be sanded with a speed file and then prepared for refinishing.

Speed File. This tool is used to hold strips of sandpaper *flat* for smooth, even surface preparation. For this reason, the tool is sometimes known as a "flat boy." A typical *speed file* is shown in Figure 4-84.

Normally, a speed file is used *after* the *Surform* tool has been used. The tool is first wrapped with sandpaper and then used to smooth the plastic filler further.

These tools are usually made of wood, with a hard fiber backing plate to hold the sandpaper flat. Speed files are about 17 in. (43 cm) long and 2 ¾ in. (7 cm)

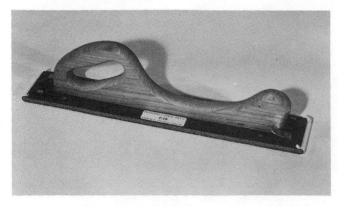

Fig. 4-84. *Strips of sandpaper are used with the speed file or "flat boy." (Courtesy of Hutchins Manufacturing Company)*

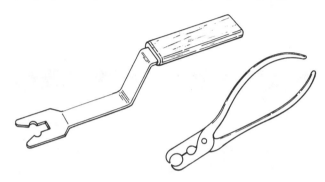

Fig. 4-85. *Two types of door handle tools.*

Fig. 4-86. *The upholstery tool is used for interior trim work.*

Fig. 4-87. *Panel cutters. (Courtesy of Snap-On Tools)*

Fig. 4-88. *Metal cutters, sometimes known as "aviation snips," are available with straight jaws or with jaws curved to the left or right. (Courtesy of Snap-On Tools)*

Fig. 4-89. *Tin snips. (Courtesy of Snap-On Tools)*

wide. First #40 and then #80 sandpapers are used to smooth the plastic for final preparation. The advantages of a speed file are that it is fairly *long*, increasing sanding speed, and *flat*, allowing surfaces such as doors and hoods to be sanded without waves or uneven areas.

Door Handle Tool

This tool is used by repair technicians for interior door trim work. The *door handle tool* is used to remove the inside door and window handles or cranks. Door handle tools are also known as "clip tools" or "clip pullers" (Fig. 4-85).

Door and window regulator handles are usually held in place by wire spring clips shaped like horseshoes. These clips fit over the window regulator or door handle shaft inside the door. The clips hold the handle to the shaft, forcing it to press up against the door panel upholstery for a good fit. Some door handle tools *pull* out the clip, whereas others *push* out the clip. This tool is needed to work on automobile doors properly.

Upholstery Tool

This tool (Fig. 4-86) is most often used in a trim (upholstery) shop. Auto body workers doing trim work will find an *upholstery tool* to be very useful.

The tool is used to remove the trim pad (upholstery) on door and quarter panels inside the car. The fork end of the tool is offset to allow the worker to pry upward, removing upholstery tacks, nails, and spring clips that hold the trim in place. These clips are very different from door handle clips.

Metal Snips

Many times, panels or metal pieces must be trimmed or fitted in a body shop. The main purpose of *metal snips* (Figs. 4-87 through 4-89) is to cut *thin* metal. Body workers may use the snips to cut metal into new shapes for patching holes from damage or rust-out. There are several types of snips available. Most body workers own at least one pair of metal snips.

Panel Cutters. These special snips (Fig. 4-87) may be used to cut either straight or curved lines on existing *panels* of the car. They cut through body steel easily and leave a clean, sharp edge on the metal. The sharp edge is very important when a section of panel is being removed and another being installed in its place.

Metal Cutters. These cutters are used for hard metals, such as stainless steel. *Metal cutters* (also known as "aviation snips") have a narrow body that allows the cut metal to pass freely over the snips. The blades have *serrated* (slightly toothed) edges for easy cutting. Metal cutters are shown in Figure 4-88.

Tin Snips. These snips are among the more common cutting tools in use. *Tin snips* can cut straight, circular, or irregular shapes. The blades are shaped to draw the metal into the jaws. The jaws have great leverage for easy cutting into heavy steel. Figure 4-89 shows a typical set of tin snips.

Eye Protection

For safety on the job, workers must keep their eyes protected at all times. Either safety or welding goggles *must* be used when working with certain hand tools, all power tools, or welding equipment. Goggles may be purchased in many different styles and shapes. Some are held in place by frame horns that fit behind the ears; others have elastic bands that fit around the head.

Safety Goggles. Clear goggles (Fig. 4-90) are used on jobs that do not involve welding or heat. These *safety goggles* are lightweight and are made with a wide clear plastic rim for wearing comfort. They have a wide, distortion-free field of vision. They are used to protect the eyes from flying particles, such as those from a grinder, sanders, or hammers and chisels.

Welding Goggles. These goggles (Fig. 4-91) are used when welding, brazing, and cutting with an oxy-acetylene torch. The dark lenses in *welding goggles* protect eyes from *both* harmful particles and harmful rays of bright light.

Fig. 4-90. *Clear safety glasses are used for sanding, painting, and other body shop jobs that do not involve the use of welding equipment.*

Fig. 4-91. *Shaded goggles are used for welding or cutting with an oxy-acetylene torch. A full face shield is usually used for arc-welding work.*

Lenses for welding goggles may be bought in several shades. The lightest lenses are number 1. The darkest lenses normally used for oxy-acetylene work are number 8. The final choice of lens depends on the type of work being done. Normal oxy-acetylene *welding* and *brazing* requires a number 4 or 5 lens, whereas oxy-acetylene *cutting* normally requires a number 5 or 6 lens. Usually, a number 5 lens is sufficient for oxy-acetylene work in a body shop.

Rivet Gun

This handy tool is used to fasten two pieces of metal together when only *one* side of the joint is *accessible* (able to be reached). The *rivet gun* (Fig. 4-92) is also known as a "riveter" or a "pop-rivet gun." The rivets used with this tool are the small metal pins shown in Figure 4-93.

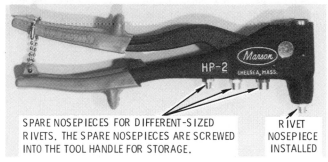

SPARE NOSEPIECES FOR DIFFERENT-SIZED RIVETS. THE SPARE NOSEPIECES ARE SCREWED INTO THE TOOL HANDLE FOR STORAGE.

RIVET NOSEPIECE INSTALLED

Fig. 4-92. *The pop-rivet gun has several nosepieces for use with different rivet sizes. (Courtesy of Marson Corporation)*

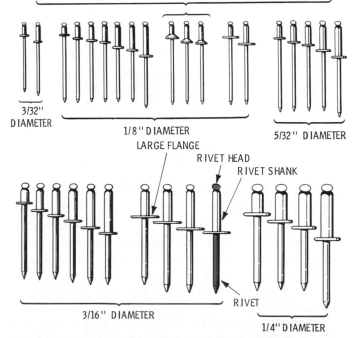

COUNTERSUNK RIVETS FOR JOBS THAT REQUIRE A FLUSH SURFACE. D-120 DRILL MAKES HOLE AND COUNTERSINKS IN ONE OPERATION.

3/32" DIAMETER

1/8" DIAMETER

5/32" DIAMETER

LARGE FLANGE

RIVET HEAD

RIVET SHANK

RIVET

3/16" DIAMETER

1/4" DIAMETER

Fig. 4-93. *Rivets of many different sizes are available for use with the pop-rivet gun. (Courtesy of Marson Corporation)*

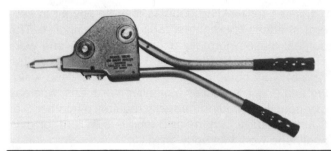

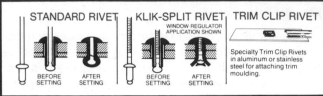

Fig. 4-94. *For heavy-duty riveting jobs, a larger riveting tool and rivets up to 1/4 in. (6.4 mm) in diameter may be used. The long handles provide extra leverage and reach. (Courtesy of Marson Corporation)*

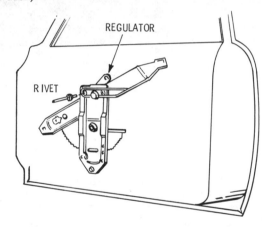

Fig. 4-95. *A rivet may be used to secure a window glass regulator.*

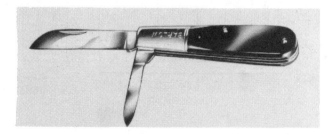

Fig. 4-96. *The pocket knife is a tool with many body shop uses. (Courtesy of Snap-On Tools)*

To use the riveter, a hole is first drilled through *both* pieces of metal to be joined. The hole must be 0.005 in. (0.13 mm) larger than the size of the rivet being used. It must go completely through both pieces along the joint's edge.

When the hole has been drilled, the proper size *rivet* (Fig. 4-93) and the proper size *nosepiece* for that rivet (Fig. 4-92) must be selected. A different nosepiece is used for each *diameter* of rivet. Finally, the rivet is inserted point first into the rivet gun. The blunt, ball-shaped end of the rivet sticks out of the nosepiece.

The blunt end of the rivet is placed in the hole through the joint. The rivet gun then pulls the rivet *through* the long shank. The rivet head forces the shank to spread out on the *underside* of the joint. Thus, the two pieces of metal are firmly held together. The rivet gun then breaks the rivet off on the outside, at the circular shoulder.

Heavy-duty Riveter

A *heavy-duty riveter* is shown in Figure 4-94. This riveter is much larger and stronger than the "pop-rivet gun" in Figure 4-92. The long handle and long nose allow it to reach hard-to-get-at places, such as inside the vehicle doors. It is very useful when working with glass regulators like the one shown in Figure 4-95. It is also used on door handles and glass stops on many automobiles and trucks. This riveter easily sets 3/16 to 1/4 in. (4.8 to 6.4 mm) blind rivets.

Pocket Knife

Most body technicians keep a good *pocket knife* available. This tool is helpful for a number of jobs when repair work is being done. It is especially useful for cutting masking tape, cleaning in close places, and removing excess plastic filler from body seams and joints. Figure 4-96 shows a typical pocket knife.

Tool Chest

A strong tool box, or tool *chest* is very important, since repair workers must have their tools with them during working hours. A portable tool box is very desirable because the box can be moved around easily to different jobs. A tool box will be stocked with all the hand tools that are needed in day-to-day jobs. Figure 4-97A shows a hand-carried portable tool chest. Figure 4-97B shows a cabinet-type chest with the hand-carried portable chest on top of it.

Sometimes, a repair worker may want more tools than can be carried around easily. For those who want to buy more tools than are ordinarily used, two tool boxes or chests might be needed. Of course, a new body repair worker should keep in mind that it is usually not a good idea to purchase seldom used tools. These may be furnished by the shop owner.

SHOP TOOLS

The shop owner is usually expected to furnish special, expensive, or heavy tools used by all the workers in the shop. The exact selection of these tools may vary from shop to shop. They usually include large vises, thread-cutting tools, cleaning and washing supplies, and other tools for very heavy work. Tools furnished by the shop are usually stored in a supply room. In larger shops, these tools may be checked out as needed to do special jobs. In smaller shops, they may simply be left in one area for use by all the employees.

Generally, repair workers can expect the shop owner to provide the following tools:

1. Shop vise.
2. Tap and die set.
3. Auto washing materials.
4. Rim (lug) wrench.
5. ¾ in. drive socket set.
6. Heavy shop *equipment*, discussed later.

Vise

This tool (Fig. 4-98) is for most general automotive service work where pieces need to be held for working. The usual shop vise is medium duty and has serrated (saw-cut) metal jaws for a firm grip on the material being held. Most have a swivel base so that the vise and jaws may be turned. The vise is usually bolted to a heavy table and used by all the employees in the shop.

Tap and Die Set

This tool is used to make threads for nuts and bolts to be used as fasteners. A tap and die set may also be used to repair damaged threads on nuts, bolts, or *studs* (threaded fasteners, which are a part of a larger body piece). The good-quality *tap and die set* shown in Figure 4-99 may be used for most of the tap and die needs in a body shop. This set can straighten or make threads on nuts, bolts, and parts with diameters as large as ½ in. (12.7 mm).

A. Portable, hand-carried tool chest.

B. Cabinet-type tool chest on rollers, with a portable unit on top.

Fig. 4-97. *For clean, protected storage of hand tools, a sturdy steel tool box or chest should be purchased. (Courtesy of Snap-On Tools)*

Fig. 4-98. *A medium-duty bench vise.*

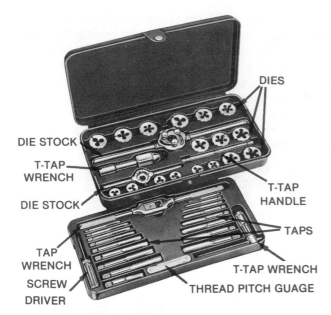

Fig. 4-99.   *A tap and die set. (Courtesy of Snap-On Tools)*

Fig. 4-100.   *An auto body washing brush.*

Fig. 4-101.   *Using a washing brush on an automobile.*

Washing Materials

Vehicles must be *washed* both before and after their repair. To do this correctly, body *washing materials* are

Fig. 4-102.   *A washing mitt is often used in cleaning cars.*

Fig. 4-103.   *The auto washing mitt.*

needed. These are normally provided by the shop. The person hired to wash cars may not have any tools of his or her own at the shop.

An auto body *washing brush*, shown in Figure 4-100, is used for fast, thorough cleaning of vehicles. Good brushes are filled with long, soft nylon and horse-hair bristles. Plenty of soap and water must be used when washing cars with a washing brush (Fig. 4-101).

Figure 4-102 shows a worker using a *washing mitt*. Washing mitts are made of different materials. The good, soft mitt shown in Figure 4-103 is a shag, cloth type. Washing mitts can get into closer places than can a brush. This would include areas around door handles or bumper ends.

Rim Wrench

These tools are most often used to remove wheel lugs (nuts or bolts holding the wheels in place). Four-way *rim (lug) wrenches* have the four most often used sizes of hex openings for wheel lugs (Fig. 4-104). The cross shank of the wrench is usually about ⅝ in. (15.9 mm) in diameter for extra strength. The hex sockets are fairly deep for long bolts.

Three-quarter-inch Drive Socket Set

A ¾ in. drive socket set is used for very heavy shop work. Individual body repair workers will usually *not* have enough uses for this set to buy one. However, many shop owners will want to have this large set on hand for use during some frame work and heavy jobs such as work on large trucks.

Most of these sets come with socket sizes of ¾ through 2 ⅜ in. (19.0 through 60.3 mm). The set usually includes a strong power handle (breaker bar), ratchet, and several extensions. This set is too heavy for daily use in the shop. Its use is limited to very large bolts and nuts. Because the sets are rugged, they can take a good deal of punishment.

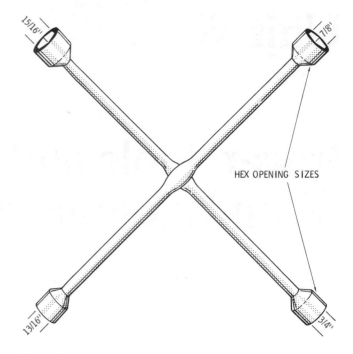

Fig. 4-104. *A rim (lug) wrench.*

Unit 5

Power Tools and Shop Equipment

To operate profitably, an auto body shop must have a number of power tools and other pieces of shop equipment. These include the jacks, wrenches, drills, spray painters, sanders, and other types of power tools and equipment in use every day. Although power tools are necessary for top working speed, it *is* possible for a shop to operate without them. However, jobs will be turned out much more slowly without power tools.

Figure 5-1 shows a typical group of hand-held shop power tools. These tools use either *air* or *electricity* as

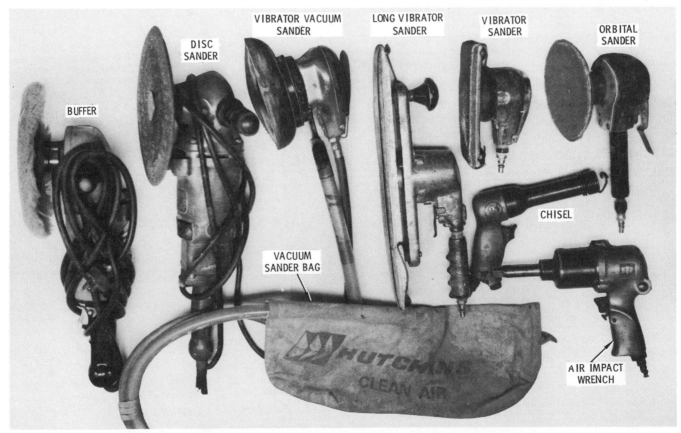

Fig. 5-1. *A typical selection of hand-held power tools.*

a source of power. The *air*-powered tools are also known as *pneumatic tools*. They are powered with compressed air.

The main reason that power tools are used is to increase working *speed*, to enable the shop to finish jobs quicker. Most auto body repair jobs, of course, are "sold" by contract bid. Therefore, the *time* involved is one of the main factors on the cost estimate. Labor costs when no power tools will be used are usually *higher* because it will take *longer* to do the same job. If a shop wants to compete favorably for new business, purchasing power tools will be one of the shop's best investments.

Power tools and good shop equipment *are* expensive. However, most shop owners find that they pay for themselves and return more profit in a short time. The tools and equipment discussed in this unit include power jacks, air-powered tools, and electric-powered tools.

POWER JACKS

Several different types of jacks are used in an auto body shop. Some are used for raising or lowering vehicles, or for moving a vehicle when it cannot be driven. When a vehicle has been raised with a *power jack*, it must be placed on safety (jack) stands (Fig. 5-2).

Elsewhere in the shop, repair workers will use *body jacks* for aligning panels. Body jacks are smaller than large power jacks and are used for lighter work. Body jacks are available with many different accessories (Fig. 5-3). These accessories, plus the jack's small size, allow it to do many different types of work.

Another type of jack is the *frame and panel straightener*. This large tool may be either stationary or portable. It has many attachments that are used for good leverage while bending or pulling. Figure 5-4 shows a typical *stationary* frame and panel straightener. Note that the jack part of this tool is much larger than other jacks.

Figure 5-5 shows one company's line of jacks and a few of the areas on a vehicle where each of them might be used.

Hydraulic is the word used to describe how a power jack develops its power. *Hydraulic* means that the jack uses an oillike liquid (hydraulic fluid) to develop pressure for pushing or pulling.

On simple jacks, the worker pumps on a handle to build up the fluid pressure. On *power* jacks, however, a small motor develops the pressure needed to force the hydraulic fluid into the jack.

Power jacks, therefore, are known as either "electricity over hydraulic" or "air over hydraulic." *Air* or *electricity* over hydraulic means that either an air-powered or an electric-powered motor is used to force the hydraulic fluid into the jack cylinder. The jack cylinder then causes the jack to operate when a button is pushed or a lever is turned. In Figure 5-2, for example, note

Fig. 5-2. *Using a power jack to raise a car for frame-straightening work. (Courtesy of Blackhawk Division, Applied Power Industries)*

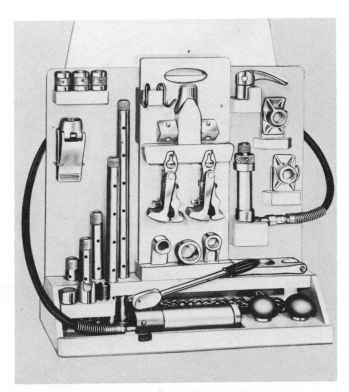

Fig. 5-3. *A body jack with many attachments. (Courtesy of Snap-On Tools)*

Fig. 5-4. *Stationary frame and panel straightener. (Courtesy of Blackhawk Division, Applied Power Industries)*

that only thumb pressure is being used on the hydraulic jack lever to raise the car.

Frame and Panel Straighteners

Frame and panel straighteners, also known as frame and panel *pullers* or *jacks*, are usually the largest and most expensive power tools in a body shop. There are many sizes of frame and panel pullers. However, all of them are either *portable* (Fig. 5-6) or *stationary* (Fig. 5-7).

Most frame and panel straighteners are *portable*. They have many attachments for pulling, pushing, or holding a panel to straighten or align the metal. Portable units are usually lower in cost than are stationary units. However, they cannot make as many pulls at one time as can the stationary units. Figure 5-8 shows a portable frame and panel jack with attachments. Figure 5-9 shows how the jack ram parts are assembled for various jobs.

Stationary frame straighteners can pull and push in several directions at one time, as in Figure 5-7. This is done by multiple hook-ups. The frame straightener is attached to several different points on the vehicle at the same time, allowing more than one pull to be made.

The main *disadvantage* of a stationary frame straightener is its cost. It often is considered too expen-

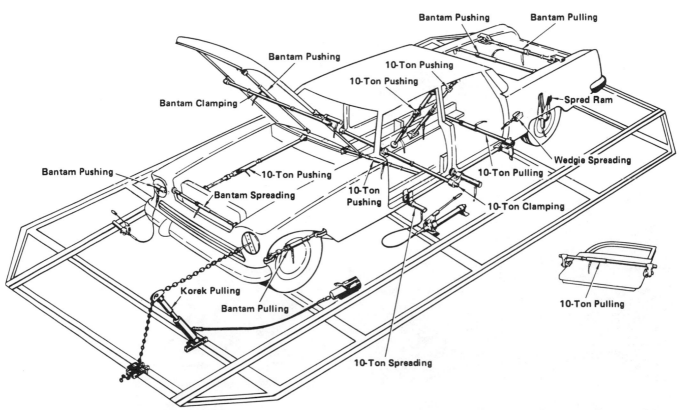

Fig. 5-5. *Power jacks may be used with different attachments at various points on the vehicle. (Courtesy of Blackhawk Division, Applied Power Industries)*

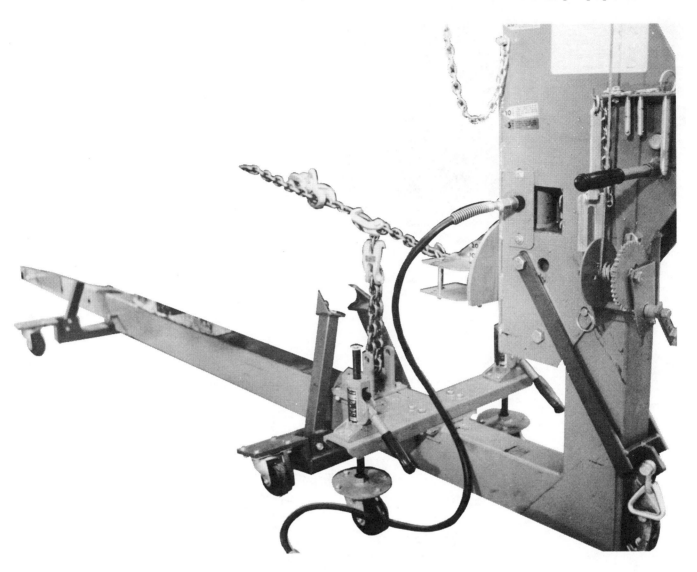

Fig. 5-6. *Portable frame straighteners are easily moved around the shop. (Courtesy of Guy–Chart Systems)*

sive for shops that do not specialize in frame straightening. This is the reason that most shops use only a *portable* frame straightener, even though the portable can usually make only one push or pull at a time.

Hook-ups. Repair workers must understand how to make *hook-ups* for repairing frame or body damage with a frame and panel straightener. Figure 5-10 shows how the one straightener is hooked up to pull and align the front section of a vehicle's frame. In Figure 5-11 the frame and panel straightener is being used to align a damaged quarter panel. More information on frame and panel hook-ups is given in later units.

Body Jacks

Body jacks may be used with a frame straightener, or they may be used by themselves. Hydraulic body jacks are often used power tools in body shops today.

Although a jack is a simple tool, a body worker must have some knowledge of how it works.

As a useful source of power, a body jack can be used for an almost unlimited number of jobs. The basic jack and several jack tools (Fig. 5-12) may be hooked up to a number of different attachments (Fig. 5-13). They can then be used to push or pull to align body panels. The assembled tool can be made long or short. Power can be applied to either end or both ends of the jack at the same time.

No matter how many accessories the jack has, the *basic* body jack itself normally has three major parts: (1) the *pump*; (2) the *hose*; and (3) the *ram*.

Pump. Figure 5-14 shows the *pump* section of a body jack. The pump acts as a power source for the jack assembly. It is also a reservoir for the hydraulic fluid that is pumped through the hydraulic hose into the ram.

Hydraulic pressure is applied to the ram section by

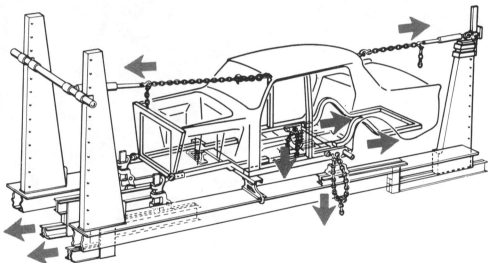

Fig. 5-7. *A stationary frame straightener is fastened to the shop floor. It can make a number of pulls at one time. (Courtesy of Guy–Chart Systems)*

operating the pump handle. This causes the fluid to pass through the hose *from* the pump reservoir *to* the ram section.

A small valve at the end of the pump is used to control the flow of the hydraulic fluid in or out of the pump. This is known as a *fluid control valve*. To allow fluid to go out to the ram section, the valve must be turned fully *clockwise*.

To *release* the pressure and allow the fluid to return to the pump reservoir, the fluid valve must be turned *counterclockwise*. When this is done, most body jack rams will pull back automatically. If the ram does not return automatically, the pump handle must be raised and lowered to help the ram section move inward.

Hose. Figure 5-15 shows a body jack *hose*. The hose is made of strong, reinforced rubber. It must be de-

signed to transmit the powerful hydraulic fluid force *from* the pump *to* the ram.

When assembling a body jack, one end of the hose is first attached to the *pump* section. The other end of the hose is then attached to the *ram* section. The hose is attached at either end by screwing a connecting *nut* onto the threaded hose connection *fitting*.

Ram. Figure 5-16 shows a jack *ram*. The ram part of the jack is the section that does the actual work. It may be set up in almost any position. (See Fig. 5-5 for examples.) Depending on design, the ram may pull or push by making itself longer when hydraulic fluid is pumped into it.

Ram Attachments. Most of the attachments shown in Figure 5-3 can be joined directly to the ram section. Figure 5-9 shows how major attachments may be as-

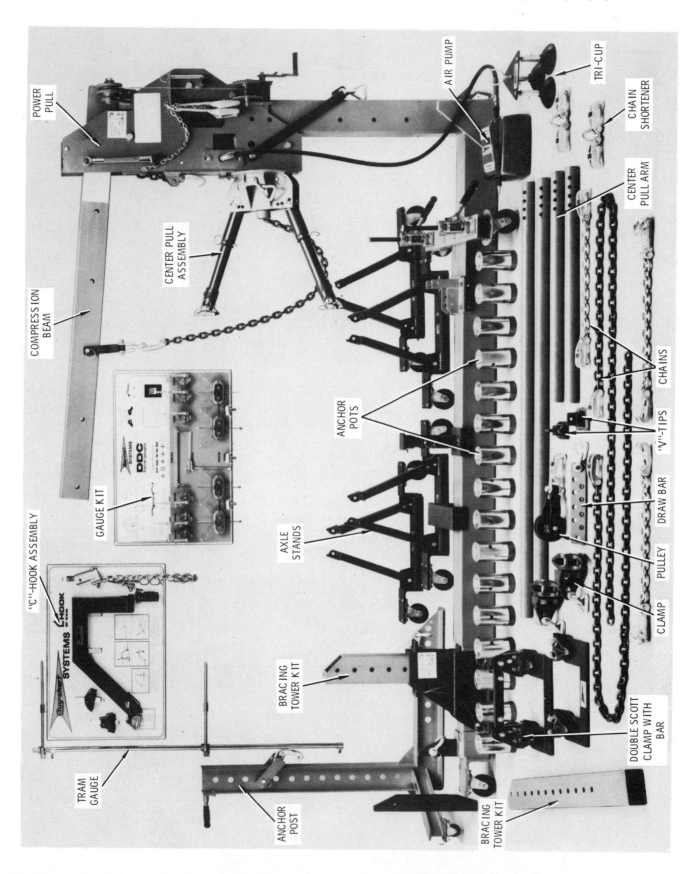

Fig. 5-8. *A complete portable frame straightener system has many attachments. (Courtesy of Guy-Chart Systems)*

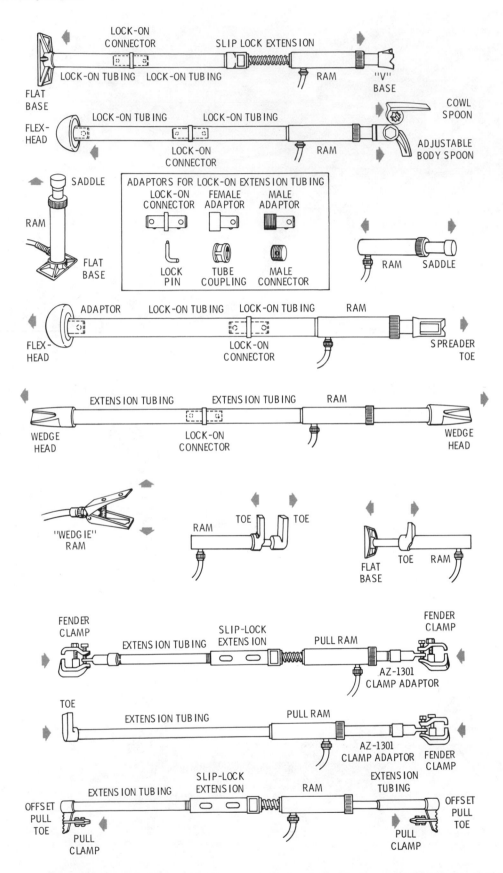

Fig. 5-9. *Different ways of assembling the jack ram and attachments for various jobs. (Courtesy of Guy–Chart Systems)*

Fig. 5-10. *Making a hook-up for a front pull on a stationary frame straightener. (Courtesy of Blackhawk Division, Applied Power Industries)*

sembled onto the ram section. Some attachments are used to hold the ram at an angle on the frame straightener or on a panel. Other attachments are used to clamp and hold body panels for pushing or pulling. Still others are used to straighten or align body panel structure parts.

Special ram attachments are available to fit almost any contour on an automobile body or structure. Use of body jack and jack attachments will be fully discussed in later units.

Floor Jacks

Often, vehicles need to be *elevated* (raised off the floor) so that certain areas can be seen or reached. Hydraulic *floor jacks* are designed for these jobs (Figs. 5-17 and 5-18). They can be used under bumpers or major suspension parts, or under frame or unitized body side rails. (These are located behind the rocker panel on the vehicle's side, as shown in Fig. 5-17.) Floor jacks have wheels so that the vehicle can be moved while on the jack and so that the jack may be easily

Fig. 5-11. *A portable straightener hooked up to pull on a quarter panel. (Courtesy of Guy–Chart Systems)*

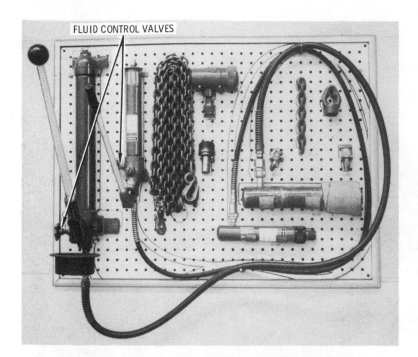

Fig. 5-12. *Basic body jack parts.*

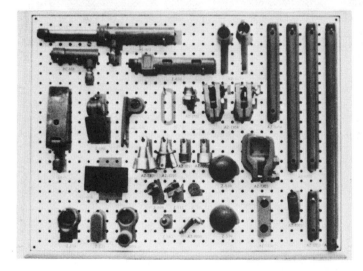

Fig. 5-13. *Special attachments used with the body jack.*

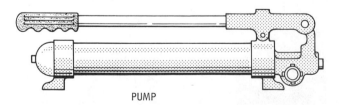

PUMP

Fig. 5-14. *Body jack pump.*

moved about the shop. After raising a vehicle, always put safety stands under the car before working on it.

Manual Floor Jack. Most repair shops have at least one *manual* floor jack, as in Figure 5-17. These jacks have a hydraulic pump that is operated by moving the jack handle up and down. When the jack handle is raised to its highest position, the hydraulic piston moves to the back of the fluid chamber. Then, when the jack handle is pushed down, the piston forces the fluid forward in the jack cylinder. This moves the jack *pad* up a few inches, thus raising the vehicle. Pumping is continued until the vehicle is raised.

Air Floor Jack. An *air* floor jack is usually designed to raise vehicles by placing the jack under the bumper or the front portion of the frame. Then, the vehicle may be raised to the desired height. Like the manual floor jack in Figure 5-17, this jack is sometimes used under the frame rail or unitized body reinforcing rail behind the rocker panel on the vehicle's side.

Air floor jacks are usually *pneumatic*, which means that the jack is operated with *compressed air*. The compressed air is controlled by a valve on the jack. When the air valve lever is moved in one direction, it forces air into the hydraulic cylinder. The force of the air pressure is then used to raise the vehicle. Note the air valve lever on the top of the jack in Figure 5-18. When the lever is moved in the opposite direction, the jack lowers the vehicle to the floor by releasing the air pressure in the hydraulic cylinder.

AIR SUPPLY EQUIPMENT

Air-powered tools and equipment used in an auto body repair shop need a good supply of clean, dry *compressed air*. The *air compressor* is an important piece of shop equipment for this reason. The air is compressed and stored, under great pressure, in a storage tank (Fig. 5-19).

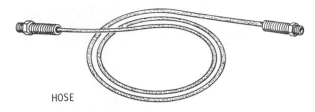

Fig. 5-15. *Body jack hose.*

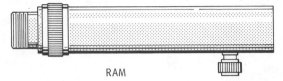

Fig. 5-16. *Body jack ram.*

Fig. 5-17. *A manually operated hydraulic floor jack.*

Fig. 5-18. *An air-operated hydraulic floor jack. (Courtesy of Blackhawk Division, Applied Power Industries)*

Compressed air is then piped from the storage tank to one or more *separator–regulators* in the shop. Here, the air is cleaned, and the pressure is regulated for the air-powered tool being used. Finally, the air is transferred by a rubber hose *from* the separator–regulator *to* the tools and equipment, as in Figure 5-20.

Fig. 5-19. *A typical air compressor.*

The shop owner and all employees must know something about air compressors, especially how to care for them. For this reason, air supply equipment is discussed in greater detail in another unit of this book.

AIR-POWERED TOOLS

Air-powered tools use *compressed air* as a power source. The compressed air is supplied from the air compressor through pipes and the separator–regulator. Common air-powered tools include paint *spray guns* (Fig. 5-21), air *wrenches* (Fig. 5-22), air *chisels* (Fig. 5-23), air *sanders* (Fig. 5-24), and air *drills*.

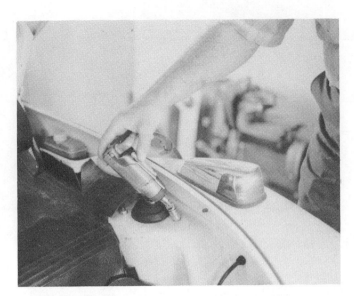

Fig. 5-22. *A ⅜ in. drive, air-powered impact wrench.*

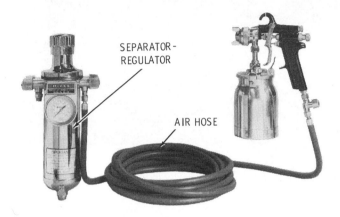

Fig. 5-20. *An air separator–regulator, hose, and spray gun. (Courtesy of Binks Manufacturing Company)*

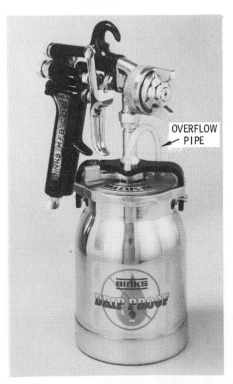

Fig. 5-21. *A suction-type spray gun with an overflow pipe. (Courtesy of Binks Manufacturing Company)*

Fig. 5-23. *An air chisel with several attachments.*

Paint spray guns are used for almost all the shop's refinishing work. Air wrenches are used to loosen and tighten bolts and nuts quickly. Air chisels are used to cut flanges or punch sheet metal parts. Repaired metal or plastic filler surfaces are sanded by using air-powered sanders. Holes may be drilled for repair work by using an air drill.

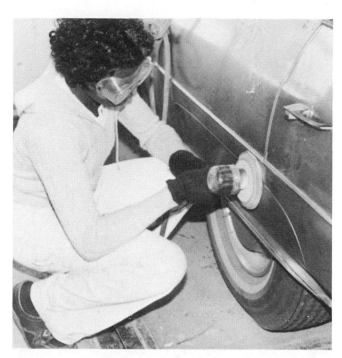

Fig. 5-24. *An air sander.*

Paint Spray Gun

Probably the most used of the air-powered tools in many body shops is the *paint spray gun*. It is one of the most efficient air-powered tools. Paint spray guns are used in almost all body repair shops, since most shops do refinishing work.

There are *two* basic types of spray guns. They are the *pressure pot* type, shown in Figure 5-25, and the *suction cup* type, shown earlier in Figure 5-21. The suction cup type is the easier gun to move from one place to another. Therefore, suction cup spray guns are used in most auto body repair shops.

Because paint spray guns are air-powered tools, they need a good supply of clean, dry air. The air is first piped from the air compressor to the separator–regulator. Next, a flexible, reinforced rubber hose takes the air pressure *from* the separator–regulator, *to* the spray gun, as was shown in Figure 5-20. One-quart (0.9 L) capacity, suction cup spray guns are the type used in most repair shops. These guns need a hose with an *inside* diameter of ⁵⁄₁₆ in. (7.9 mm). The hose is usually about 50 ft (15.2 m) long.

Suction cup paint guns are portable, easy to handle, lightweight, and durable. Good guns will last for many years if they receive proper care. Use of the paint spray gun is discussed in another unit.

Air Impact Wrench

One important tool for quick work is an *impact wrench*. This tool uses an impact (pounding) motion to loosen

or tighten nuts or bolts. Impact wrenches may be powered with an electric motor or an air-powered motor. The most common impact wrenches used in a body shop are the *air* impact wrenches.

These wrenches can be bought in different sizes, just as any other socket-holding tool (Figs. 5-26 and 5-27). Air impact wrenches have different sets of sockets for each drive size. A ⅜ in. drive wrench might have sockets ranging in size from ⅜ to ¾ in. (10 to 19 mm). A ½ inch drive wrench might have socket sizes from ⁷⁄₁₆ to 1 ¼ in. (11 to 32 mm).

Air impact wrenches may be equipped with universal joints, deep sockets, extensions, or other accessories used to make them more useful. In Figure 5-28, for example, the body worker is using an extension and a universal joint with a ⅜ in. (10 mm) drive air impact wrench.

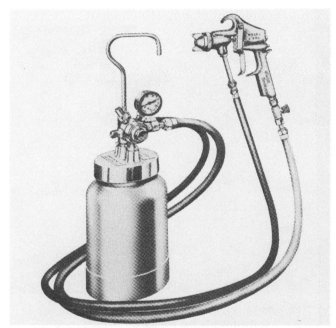

Fig. 5-25. *A pressure pot spray gun. (Courtesy of Refinish Division, DuPont Company)*

Fig. 5-26. *A small, ⅜ in. drive air impact wrench.*

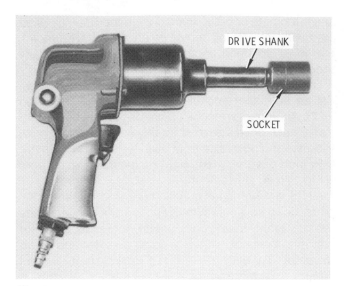

Fig. 5-27. *A larger, ½ in. drive air impact wrench.*

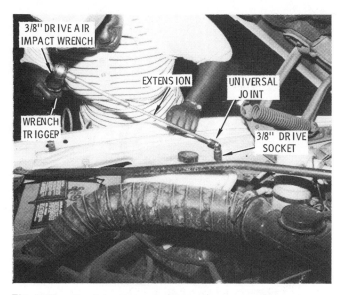

Fig. 5-28. *An air impact wrench can be used with accessories to reach into restricted places. For safety, the wrench should be used at low speed when a long extension is attached, as in this illustration.*

Good air impact wrenches are built for durability and high-speed work. When fasteners (nuts and bolts) are located in hard-to-reach places, there may not be enough room to use an air wrench. In these cases, it is necessary to use hand tools. Generally, impact wrenches are limited to use on wheels, bumpers, and other places where there is plenty of room.

Air Chisel

Figure 5-29 shows an air-powered *chisel* and replaceable chisel attachments. An air chisel is used for many different cutting and punching jobs in a body shop. Removing damaged panels and trimming re-

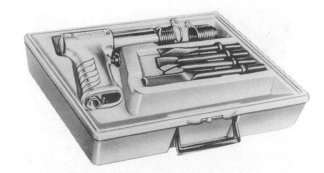

Fig. 5-29. *An air-powered chisel and attachments. (Courtesy of Snap-On Tools)*

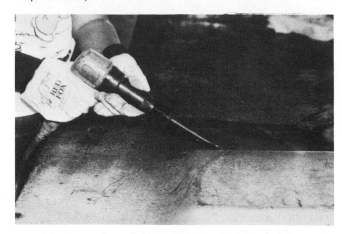

Fig. 5-30. *Using an air chisel to trim a replacement panel.*

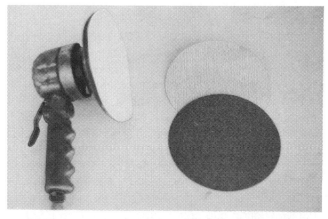

Fig. 5-31. *An air-powered disc sander and sanding discs.*

placement panels to the proper size are two common jobs (Fig. 5-30). Power chisels are also used to make a fast, smooth job of cutting spot welds for sheet metal repair. An air chisel also may be used to make patches for repairing holes in panels and fenders.

Disc Sander

A common air-powered body shop tool is a *disc sander* (Fig. 5-31). This tool uses compressed air to rotate a disc. Different types of sandpaper are cemented to the disc backing plate, which revolves with a clockwise motion. The disc backing plate and sanding discs can be bought in large or small sizes. Two of the different sizes and types of sanding discs are shown with the sander in Figure 5-31.

Good disc sanders are rugged tools. Light in weight and easily handled, they may be found in any well-equipped body repair shop. They are used for lightly sanding smaller areas of damaged surfaces. This prepares the surface for final hand sanding. With finer grit sanding discs, this tool is used for *featheredging* a broken (scratched) finish. For this reason, the disc sander is often known as a *featheredger*.

Orbital Sanders

Another common air-powered sander is an *orbital sander*. These sanders come in several sizes. Figure 5-32 shows two different sizes of orbital sanders that are available. These sanders are sometimes called *oscillating* or *vibrator* sanders. In some body shops, the smaller sander is known as a "jitterbug."

By whatever name, this tool's main job is to level old paint or plastic filler quickly and evenly for a smooth, *even* finish. Usually, 80-grit sandpaper is first used on the sander. When only the rough 80-grit sandpaper is used, the metal must be heavily primed after sanding. However, good 120-grit sandpapers are available to be used after the 80-grit sandpaper has broken down the rough surface. When the finer paper is used, the metal does not have to be as heavily primed.

Vacuum Sanders. Figures 5-33 and 5-34 show special types of sanders known as *vacuum sanders*. These vacuum sanders are the same tool and do the same jobs as do regular orbital sanders.

On *vacuum* sanders, however, a special vacuum cleaner and bag are added to the tool. When the sander is used, the sanding dust is collected in the vacuum bag. This cuts down on the dust and dirt in the air and helps the shop turn out better, "cleaner" paint jobs. Also, the workers in the shop do not have to breathe the sanding dust. This is a very important feature, especially for the worker operating the sander, and in shops that do not have a large dust collector.

Tube-type Sandpaper

Round tube-type production sandpaper is used for shaping and sanding contours. These abrasive tubes are 1 ½ in. (3.8 cm) in diameter and 18 in. (45.7 cm) long. They can be purchased in 36, 40, and 80 grit and can be cut any length with a hack saw. Figure 5-35 shows a 40-grit tube being used on a lower door panel.

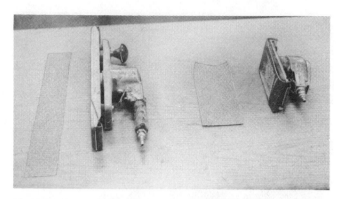

Fig. 5-32. *Two basic sizes of orbital sanders.*

Fig. 5-33. *An orbital sander equipped with a vacuum system to capture sanding dust. (Courtesy of Hutchins Manufacturing Company)*

Fig. 5-34. *A smaller vacuum-equipped sander. (Courtesy of Hutchins Manufacturing Company)*

Fig. 5-35. *Tube-type production sandpaper in 40-grit size. (Courtesy of Automotive Trades Division, 3M Company)*

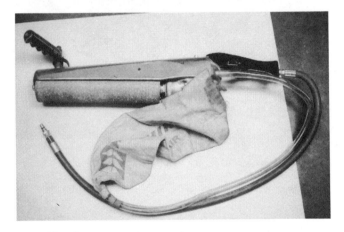

Fig. 5-36. *A common rotary sander.*

Fig. 5-37. *An air-powered drill.*

Rotary Sander

A final type of air-powered sander is a *rotary sander*, shown in Figure 5-36. This sander is usually used to

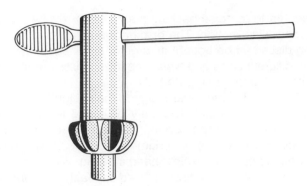

Fig. 5-38. *A drill chuck key, used to tighten bits or other attachments firmly in the drill chuck.*

Fig. 5-39. *Typical drill bit sets. (Courtesy of Snap-On Tools)*

work down plastic filler. Regular 8 ½ × 11 in. (21.5 × 27.9 mm) sheet sandpaper may be mounted on the round cylinder of the sander. Usually, only a coarse (60- or 80-grit) sandpaper is used, since rotary sanders are most often used for rough sanding. A surface on which a rotary sander is used will need additional work and priming to smooth the sanding scratches.

Air Drill

Figure 5-37 shows an *air drill*. This tool does the same jobs as an electric drill but uses compressed air for power instead of electricity. An air drill is used to bore holes in metal panels being repaired. On the end of the drill is a *chuck* that holds the drill bit firmly in place.

Chuck Key. The chuck *key* is a small tool used to loosen or tighten the drill *chuck*. This is done when installing or removing a drill bit from the chuck. Figure 5-38 shows a drill chuck key.

Drill Bits. Figure 5-39 shows several sets of drill *bits*. Drill bits are usually available in sizes of from 1/32 in. to 1 in. and in equivalent metric sizes. If a hole larger than 1 in. (2.5 cm) needs to be drilled, a hole cutter should be used. These are sometimes known as *hole saws*. Two hole cutters are shown in Figure 5-40.

Fig. 5-40. *Hole cutters (hole saws) are used to cut holes larger than 1 in. (25.4 mm) in diameter through sheet metal. (Courtesy of Ingersoll–Rand Company)*

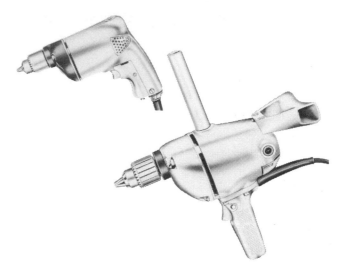

Fig. 5-42. *Two examples of electric-powered drills. (Courtesy of Snap-On Tools)*

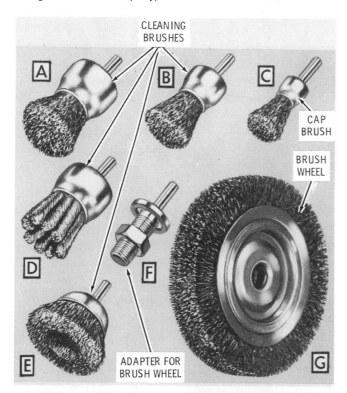

Fig. 5-41. *Common brushes and attachments used with both air-powered and electric drills. (Courtesy of Snap-On Tools)*

Drill Brushes. Either air or electric drills may be used to clean away rust and paint. Wire brush attachments are available for these jobs. Figure 5-41 shows some of the more common wire brushes and attachments that may be used on a power drill.

ELECTRIC TOOLS

Impact wrenches, sanders, and drills can also be powered by *electric* motors, instead of compressed air.

Fig. 5-43. *Using an electric disc sander. (Courtesy of Automotive Trades Division, 3M Company)*

For example, Figure 5-42 shows two common *electric drills*. Figure 5-43 shows an *electric disc sander* being used. These electric tools are almost the same tools and do the same jobs as air-powered tools. However, they use electricity as a power source.

Some tools are normally available with only electric power. These include bench grinders, vacuum cleaners, paint shakers, polishing machines (polishers), and drill presses. These "electric only" tools are described below.

Bench Grinder

Figure 5-44 shows a shop *bench grinder*. This electric power tool is usually bolted to one of the shop's work benches. It may be used to sharpen (or "dress") tools such as drill bits, screwdriver blades, and chisels. Often, a wire brush wheel will be attached to one end of the grinder. Bench grinders can be purchased in several different sizes.

Vacuum Cleaner

All paint and body shops need a vacuum cleaner, such as the one in Figure 5-45. A vacuum cleaner should be one of the first tools used when a vehicle is to be refinished. The vehicle should be thoroughly vacuumed and washed *before* it is prepared for painting. This will help reduce the chance of dirt getting into the paint job.

Vacuum cleaners may be purchased in a number of sizes. Most paint and body shops have a cleaner with

a 1 or 2 horsepower motor and a 20 or 30 gal. (75.7 or 113.6 L) dust tank. Good vacuum cleaners have a 10 to 12 ft (3.0 to 3.7 m) hose. Many attachments are available for cleaning hard-to-reach areas inside vehicle interiors or trunks.

Paint Shakers

For good paint work, it is very important that the paint be properly and completely *mixed*. While the shop's painter might do this by stirring the paint, stirring is a very time-consuming job. The mixing job will be done

Fig. 5-46. *A large, two-can paint shaker. (Courtesy of Ditzler Automotive Finishes Division, PPG Industries, Inc.)*

Fig. 5-44. *A bench grinder. (Courtesy of Snap-On Tools)*

Fig. 5-45. *To maintain a clean shop, a large vacuum cleaner is a good investment.*

Fig. 5-47. *A smaller, one-can paint shaker.*

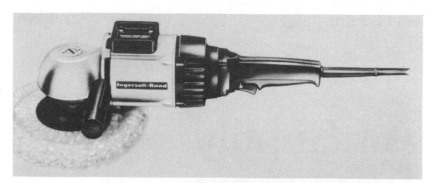

Fig. 5-48. *An electric polisher, which requires considerable practice to use correctly. (Courtesy of Ingersoll–Rand Company)*

better and faster if the shop has a good *paint shaker*.

Many newer vehicles are painted at the factory with *metallic* paint topcoats. These paints actually contain tiny particles of metal. These particles are flakes of aluminum that are heavier than the paint itself. They quickly settle to the bottom of the can. For this reason, metallic paint requires very thorough stirring or mixing.

The paint shaker in Figure 5-46 is a large model. This type may be used by businesses such as parts houses selling a large volume of paint, as well as by large body shops. The smaller shaker in Figure 5-47 is the "one-can" type used by most body shops. Paint shakers are designed to hold and shake the entire closed can of paint.

Polishing Machine

This tool is also known as a *polisher* (Fig. 5-48). By either name, a polishing machine or polisher is used to "buff up" the topcoat of paint. The tool is used on old paint to restore the luster (shine). It is *also* used to "cut" new lacquer paint with rubbing compound to bring up the paint's correct color and luster. In Figure 5-49, a painter is compounding new lacquer paint. New *enamel* paint, however, must not be compounded or it will ruin the finish. Polyurethane and acrylic enamels can be compounded if catalyst is added.

Drill Press

An electric drill that is permanently mounted in a rigid frame with a platform for drilling is known as a *drill press*. Drill presses are used in larger body shops for many drilling jobs, such as making holes in thin sheet metal repair pieces. These tools are built so that the electric motor and the drill are held on top of a pipelike stand (Fig. 5-50). A square-shaped platform is attached to the stand, and it may be adjusted up or down. The platform is used to hold and support the material being drilled.

Fig. 5-49. *Machine-compounding a new lacquer finish.*

Fig. 5-50. *Larger shops may be equipped with a drill press.*

Unit 6

Air Supply Equipment

All auto body shops must have a good supply of clean and dry *compressed air*. This can be provided by an air compressor large enough to supply several pieces of equipment at the same time. Figure 6-1 shows a typical air compressor as might be used in a smaller shop. Many body shops have more than one air compressor. In Figure 6-2 is a gang of three air compres-

Fig. 6-1. *A medium-sized (5 horsepower) air compressor is adequate for the needs of a smaller body shop. (Courtesy of Ingersoll–Rand Company)*

sors. Such a setup would be required in a large body shop.

The compressed air must be cleaned and then delivered to the air-powered tools throughout the shop. From the air compressor, *air lines* run to different work stations. Air lines are steel pipes used to transport the compressed air. A simple air line is shown in Figure 6-3.

When the air has been piped to the work stations, it must be cleaned and its pressure regulated before it passes through flexible hoses to the air tools. This is done with air supply equipment known as *separator–regulators*. High-pressure air goes in the separator–regulator directly from the air line. Figure 6-4 shows a typical separator–regulator with couplings for the hoses.

Finally, *air hoses* take the air to the air-powered tools. Air hoses must be strong, reinforced, and flexible. Figure 6-5 shows an air hose from separator–regulator being connected to a paint gun. Quick-change fittings are being used; these are discussed later in the unit.

One way to test for an ample air supply in the shop is to leave the paint gun hose open, releasing compressed air. If the compressor builds up enough pressure to shut off even though the paint hose is open, there will be enough compressed air to operate an average-size body shop. The average shop will need a 7 to 10 ton (7 to 10 horsepower) compressor to furnish enough air.

USES OF AIR

Air is a mixture of oxygen, nitrogen, and other gases. Body repair workers use air for much of the work done in an auto body shop. Oxy-acetylene welding, for instance, uses oxygen that is found in the air. Auto body

Fig. 6-2. *A large body shop might have an extensive air supply system like this one. (Courtesy of Binks Manufacturing Company)*

repair shops have many tools that require air for power, cleaning, or applying paint.

HOW AIR IS COMPRESSED

The air compressor draws air in and packs (compresses) it into a small volume. The compressor does this by first pulling the air into the compressor unit, and then forcing it into the storage tank. Figures 6-6 and 6-7 show the air compressor unit and the storage tank.

The compressed air in the tank is stored under very great pressure. It is held in the storage tank until an air outlet in the shop is opened to let the air escape.

Air Compressor Parts

As shown in Figure 6-8, a shop air compressor has three main parts:

1. The motor.
2. The compressor unit.
3. The storage tank.

Most compressor setups have a shut-off valve on the air line system (Fig. 6-9). The valve is used to shut off the air supply to the shop's air line system. This holds the air in the storage tank, allowing air line repairs to be made.

Compressor Motor. The air compressor's *motor* may be either electric or gasoline powered. Most repair shops use a compressor with an *electric* motor (Fig. 6-10). The compressor motor rotates the compressor pulley and flywheel through a "V-belt" drive (Fig. 6-11).

When the motor turns the flywheel, it rotates the crankshaft, which then moves the compressor unit's pistons.

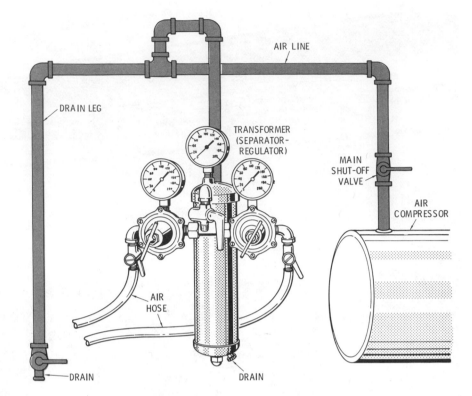

Fig. 6-3. *A simple air line system.*

Fig. 6-4. *A smaller separator–regulator.*

Fig. 6-5. *Air hoses are used to connect spray guns to the separator–regulator.*

Fig. 6-6. *The air compressor pump compresses or "squeezes" air to increase its pressure. The fins on the cylinders help dissipate heat.*

Fig. 6-7. *After being compressed, air is stored in a strong steel tank under pressure.*

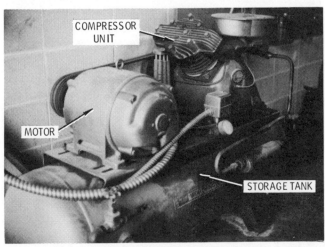

Fig. 6-8. *The three basic parts of an air compressor.*

Fig. 6-9. *A shut-off valve allows all the air to the shop to be shut off if repairs are needed in the air line system.*

Fig. 6-10. *A typical electric motor used to power a medium-sized air compressor.*

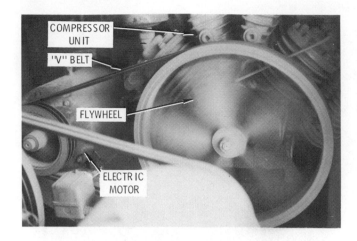

Fig. 6-11. *A "V" belt is used to transmit power from the motor to the compressor flywheel.*

Fig. 6-13. *Level of the compressor oil can be checked through a gauge window.*

Compressor Unit. The basic part of an air compressor is the compressor unit itself (Fig. 6-12).

In the compressor unit, a piston is attached to the crankshaft. When running, the piston is pulled *down* in the compressor cylinder by the crankshaft. At the same time, an air inlet check valve opens and allows air from the air cleaner to enter the cylinder.

Then, as the crankshaft revolves, the piston is pushed back *up* in the cylinder. The air intake check valve closes, trapping the air in the cylinder.

The compressed air leaves the cylinder through an air *exhaust* valve. It goes through a short pipe into the storage tank. A check valve keeps the air from coming back out of the storage tank and into the compressor unit.

Most body shop compressor units have two or more pistons that are attached to the same crankshaft. If the air is pumped from one cylinder into the next cylinder and *then* into the storage tank, the compressor is known as a *two-stage* air compressor. In a single-stage unit, both cylinders pump air directly into the storage tank.

Compressor Lubrication. An air compressor unit has a number of moving parts. The crankshaft, pistons, connecting rods, and other moving parts must be lubricated. This is the job of the compressor unit's *lubricating*

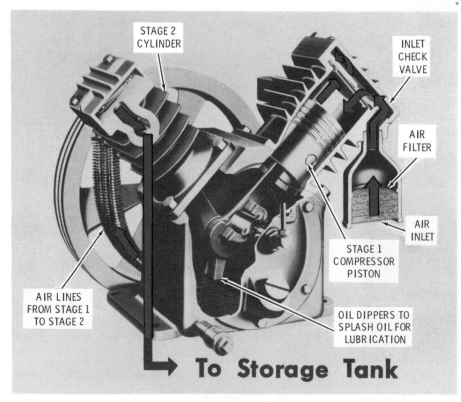

Fig. 6-12. *This cutaway view shows route of the air as it is compressed. In this two-stage compressor, air is compressed in the first cylinder, then further compressed in the second cylinder. (Courtesy of Ingersoll–Rand Company)*

system. The lubricating system usually consists of dippers on the connecting rods (Fig. 6-12). As the crankshaft turns, these dip into the oil and splash it onto the parts inside the units.

The unit must have the correct amount of oil in it for long compressor life. For this reason, compressor units may have an oil level gauge (Fig. 6-13). The oil level on the glass should be on the **FULL** mark. If not, oil should be added. Not all compressor units have such a sight glass. Some have a plug to be removed (Fig. 6-14) and others have an auto engine-type oil dipstick.

Generally, SAE 20 or SAE 30 motor oil should be used in the compressor unit. Most compressors have a tag on them describing what oil to use. Oil is added by removing the oil cap and pouring the oil into the opening. Figure 6-14 shows the oil cap on one compressor.

Storage Tank. The *storage tank* holds the highly compressed air until it is needed. The storage tank on an average body shop air compressor holds from 60 to 80 gal. (227.1 to 302.8 L).

Most storage tanks have a pressure *gauge* like the one shown in Figure 6-15. An average body shop needs about 150 psi (*pounds per square inch*) of pressure [1034 kPa (kilopascals)] to operate air tools and equipment.

Also on the compressor tank is an automatic electric *switch box* (Fig. 6-15). As air is drawn from the tank, the air pressure drops. When the pressure drops to a pre-set level, the automatic switch starts the compressor's motor. This builds up pressure in the tank to replace the air that was used. When the air pressure is built up enough, the switch turns the electric motor off. This on–off procedure goes on automatically, day after day. This ensures that the compressor tank always has enough air for the shop.

Draining the Tank. When air is compressed, it becomes hotter. This is why air compressor units have fins on them. The fins help cool the unit.

When the hot newly compressed air arrives in the storage tank, it begins to cool. As the air cools, moisture *condenses* and forms water droplets inside the storage tank. (This is much the same as the *dew* formed on grass when water condenses out of cool night air.)

The storage tank should be drained *each day* to remove the water. The water takes up space that could be used to store compressed air. It also can cause the inside of the tank to rust and may get into air-powered tools and cause trouble. Worst of all, the water may get into the air going to a paint spray gun, causing severe painting problems. When the air compressor's water tank is drained daily, these problems are eliminated.

Compressor storage tanks usually have a drain valve like the one shown in Figure 6-16. When the drain

valve is opened, air pressure in the tank forces the water out the valve.

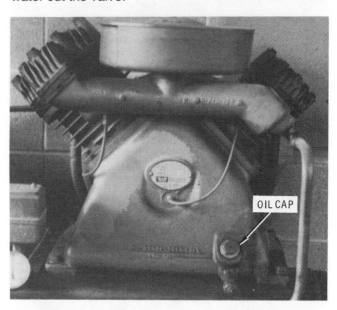

Fig. 6-14. *Oil is added to the compressor through an oil cap or pipe plug.*

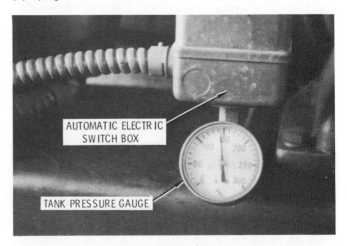

Fig. 6-15. *The automatic electric switch shuts off the compressor when a pre-determined pressure is reached in the storage tank. The gauge shows tank pressure at a given time.*

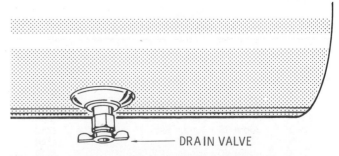

Fig. 6-16. *A drain valve is located at the bottom of the tank and should be opened daily to remove accumulated moisture.*

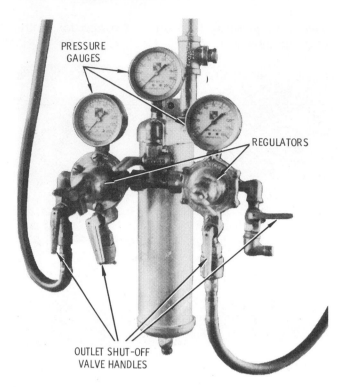

PRESSURE GAUGES

REGULATORS

OUTLET SHUT-OFF VALVE HANDLES

Fig. 6-17. *A separator–regulator with outlets for four air-operated tools or spray guns.*

AIR LINES

Figure 6-3 illustrates a system of *air lines*. Air lines are the *metal pipes* that take the air from the compressor storage tank to one or more separator–regulators. These lines are usually made of galvanized pipe to resist rust.

Air Line Moisture

The air line system should begin with a connection *above* the possible water level of the storage tank. Taking the air out *above* the possible water level will keep as much moisture out of the air lines as is possible. If the air line were attached to the *bottom* of the storage tank, water could be forced into the lines, separator–regulators, and air tools. Note that the outlet

Table 4

Recommended Air Line Diameters

Compresssor Horsepower	Main Air Line Length— ft	(m)	Recommended Main Air Line Diameter— in.	(cm)
1½–2	under 50	(under 15)	½	(1.2)
1½–2	50-200	(15-61)	¾	(2.0)
3–5	under 200	(under 61)	¾	(2.0)
3–5	200-400	(61-122)	1	(2.5)
5–10	under 400	(under 122)	1½	(3.8)
5–10	over 400	(over 122)	2	(5.0)

lines in Figure 6-3 are attached to the *top* of the main line.

The air lines will then run to any number of transformers (separator–regulators) to clean the air and regulate its pressure. The number of separator–regulators used in a shop depends on how many air-powered pieces of equipment are in use. A separator–regulator may have up to *four* different outlets for air hoses leading to equipment (Fig. 6-17). Only one separator–regulator is needed for each four pieces of equipment when this type of unit is used.

If more than one separator–regulator is used, a separate pipe must run from the main air line to each of them. The main air line and the outlet lines will either go through the center of the shop or around the shop's inside wall. Either system allows tools and equipment to be used easily in different areas of the shop.

Main Line Size

The main air line from the air compressor to the separator–regulator outlets should be larger than the air outlet lines. For example, if the main air line has a 1 ½ in. (38.1 mm) diameter, the air outlet line coming off this main line should be about ¾ in. (19.0 mm) diameter. In this way, enough pressure is left in the main line at all times no matter how many tools are connected to the air supply.

The main line should be large enough to carry all the air needed by the shop equipment being used. Also, the main line should increase in diameter as it runs longer distances from the air compressor. See the recommendations in Table 4.

Main Line Shutoff Valve

In all air supply systems, there should be a shut-off valve on the main line, close to the storage tank (Figs. 6-3 and 6-7). This valve is used to shut off the air at the storage tank.

Keeping the air shut off at the storage tank overnight ensures a full tank of air when the shop is opened each day. It also prevents the compressor from running all night should a leak develop. (Air equipment and outlets in the shop normally have very small leaks.) If the air compressor is turned on in the morning and the storage tank is empty, there will be a waiting period while the tank fills. This will be avoided if the air is turned off at the storage tank at the end of each working day.

Air Line Drain Leg

An air line *drain leg* should be used in the main air line (Fig. 6-3). As moisture collects in the main air line, air pressure forces it into the drain leg. The drain leg is usually connected near the end of the main line. This

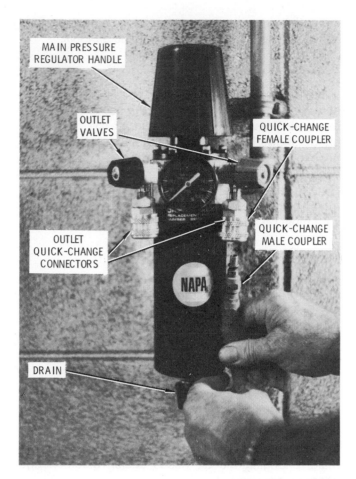

Fig. 6-18. *Parts of a typical separator–regulator with two outlets.*

allows the moisture to collect in the drain leg from all along the main system. Then, the moisture can be drained from the drain leg by *first* emptying the air tank and *then* opening the drain leg cap or valve. The drain leg helps to keep moisture from entering any of the separator–regulators in the system.

SEPARATOR–REGULATORS

Figure 6-18 shows a typical air system separator–regulator. Separator–regulators are also sometimes known as *transformers*. However, this is not exactly correct. An air *transformer* can only reduce and control the air pressure. A separator–regulator does that *and* cleans the air, as well. The transformer would be the *regulator* part of a complete separator–regulator assembly.

Ordinary compressed air from the main line may contain small amounts of oil, dirt, and water. The air separator–regulator changes this contaminated air to the cleaner air needed for shop use.

The separator–regulator actually has *two* jobs. The *first* job, discussed above, is to separate water, dirt, and oil from the air. The *second* job is to regulate the

air pressure to a constant, lower pressure. This is the same as an electrical transformer that changes a high electrical voltage to a lower voltage.

Cleaning the Air

Air pressure of about 150 to 160 psi (1034 to 1103 kPa) is built up by the air compressor and stored in the storage tank. This pressure forces the air through the main and secondary air lines and into the separator–regulator. Of course, the air pressure is still 150 to 160 psi (1034 to 1103 kPa).

As the air enters the separator–regulator, it is forced down the sides of the separator section, as shown by the arrows in Figure 6-19. The air then strikes baffling plates (*baffles*) on the sides of the baffle jacket. The baffles cause the air to be deflected (thrown) against the sides of the baffle jacket. This causes the moisture to "fall out" of the air and drip down to the bottom of the separator section. There, it can be drained through a drain plug or valve.

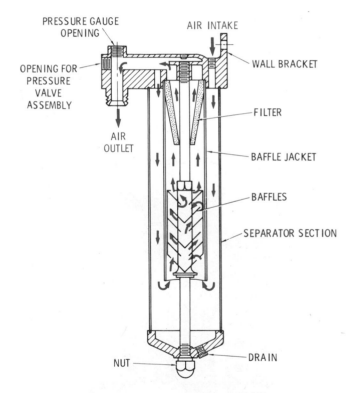

Fig. 6-19. *Air flow through the separator section of a separator–regulator.*

As the air is forced up through the baffles, it loses most of its moisture. Then, it passes through a rock-wool *filter*. This filter cleans remaining moisture, dirt, and oil from the air. Clean, dry air then enters the regulator section of the separator–regulator.

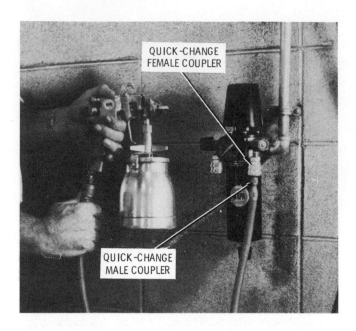

Fig. 6-20. *Parts of the quick-change adapter.*

Regulating the Air Pressure

As the clean air goes into the regulator section, it passes by a *diaphragm* that controls the air flow. The diaphragm is controlled by a regulator valve *handle* (Fig. 6-18).

As the valve handle or cap is tightened, the regulator diaphragm is pushed away from its seat. This allows more compressed air to pass through the regulator to

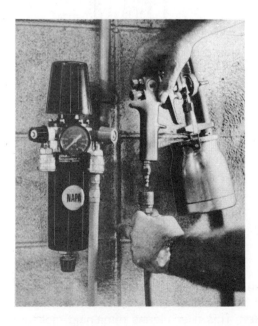

Fig. 6-21. *Connecting a spray gun to the separator–regulator with a quick-change adapter.*

the outlet air pressure gauges and the air outlets. This increases the pressure supplied to the air tools.

Pressure Gauges

Some separator–regulators have *two* types of pressure gauges, as in Figure 6-17. One gauge shows how much air pressure is in the main air line. The other gauge shows how much air pressure is going out the hose to the working tools. Once the regulator handle is used to set a certain pressure on the gauge, the diaphragm keeps the air flow *at* that pressure while the air tool is being used. For this to work correctly, the pressure must be adjusted *while the tool is turned on*.

Hose Shut-off Valves

Most separator–regulators have a hose shut-off valve at each regulated pressure outlet. This valve turns off the air supply to the hose at that valve. This reduces any air leakage from tools and equipment that are not being used. The air regulator in Figure 6-17, for example, has four outlets and four shut-off valves.

Quick-change Adapters

Many separator–regulators have the air hoses screwed directly into the regulator outlet. This is not convenient for easily changing air hoses or fittings. To make changing the air hoses easier, *quick-change* adapters are used.

Figure 6-20 shows an air hose being attached to a paint gun, using a quick-change adapter. Quick-change adapters make it easy to switch the air hose quickly from one air tool to another. By using these adapters throughout the shop, the slower process of changing air lines with a wrench is avoided.

Adapter Parts. Quick-change adapters are made in two parts: the male fitting and the female fitting (Fig. 6-18). The *female* fitting is threaded onto the separator–regulator outlet, using a wrench. It stays on the outlet all the time. A valve in the female fitting keeps the air from escaping when there is nothing attached to it.

The *male* fitting of the coupler is attached to the *air hose* and left there all the time. When the two parts are snapped together, the air can pass through the adapter, into the air hose. The hose can be connected or disconnected quickly and easily.

Attached to the *other* end of the air hose is *another* female fitting. This allows an air tool or other piece of equipment to be attached as shown in Figure 6-21. All tools and equipment that use air should have *male* adapter fittings permanently attached in the air inlet ports. Using quick-change adapters throughout the shop saves time.

AIR HOSES

To transfer air *from* the regulators *to* the tools requires very strong flexible *air hoses*.

Air hoses are made of a special rubber, heavily reinforced with fabric. They are specially coated inside to help prevent air leakage. Hoses are available in different lengths, coatings, and diameters. Air hose inside diameter should be no smaller than $5/16$ in. (7.9 mm). Although they come in many lengths, most shop air hoses are either 50 or 75 ft (15.2 to 22.9 m) long.

A special paint room hose should be used in the paint booth. Paint room hose is different from other air hoses and is made for use only with paint guns. It does not lose as much pressure between the regulator and the paint gun as regular air hoses. It is designed and made with better materials to do a more thorough job of holding the air.

Air hoses must be properly cared for and protected from cuts, oil, and grease. Shop employees should be careful not to drive cars over the air hoses. Also, hoses should not be used to pull attached air tools across the shop floor. This weakens the hose walls and connections. All air hoses should be neatly coiled for storage at the end of the working day.

Section III

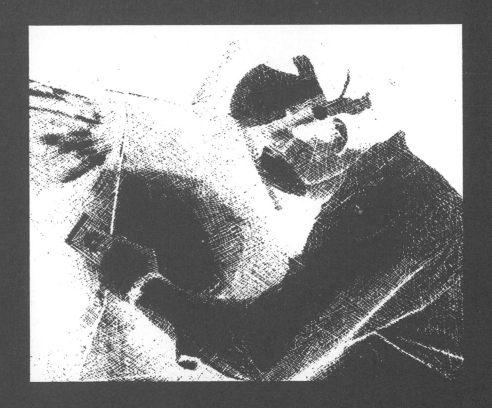

Body Shop Materials

Body Fillers

The process of completely working the metal panels to remove *all* dents and make it smooth enough for painting is very difficult. Even the best "metal worker" will need to spend a good deal of time to work out all the damage. Working out all the damage *is* possible but is often very difficult and time consuming. For this reason, it is usually easier and less costly to use a *filler* on top of the damaged metal.

The use of fillers to repair damaged panels is increasing each year. The rising rate of automobile accidents and the high cost of accident repairs are among the reasons for this trend.

Body fillers will smooth the surface to its final contour without the metal underneath having to be "perfect." This will allow the repair to be completed more easily and quickly. Also, the cost of the filler material will be much less than the additional labor cost to smooth the panel without using filler.

Body fillers also may be used to fill dents that cannot be removed with bumping hammers and dollies. Figure 7-1 shows such a dent. The panel is boxed in so that the dent cannot be easily worked from the back side. Figure 7-2 shows the back side of the damaged door panel in Figure 7-1. When panels are boxed in, as in Figures 7-1 and 7-2, they will mostly have to be worked from the outside. Figure 7-3 shows a similar situation with a panel being worked from the outside before using a filler. The demand for fuel economy is causing manufacturers to use plastic panels to make cars and trucks lighter. Thus, more repair shops are turning to plastic repair. Body fillers, except for body solder, also can be used on plastic panels.

In this unit, the proper use of plastic fillers (bondo),

fiberglass fillers, foam fillers, and body solder is covered. Fiberglass body panel repair and patching, along with the repair of soft (plastic) panels, such as bumpers, inner fenders, and other parts, also are discussed.

TYPES OF FILLERS

There are four basic types of *body fillers* in use today. The most common is *plastic* body filler, which can be used on all types of auto bodies. There are many plastic fillers on the market, such as the one in Figure 7-4.

Another common filler is *fiberglass* filler. Shown in Figure 7-5 is a fiberglass filler kit. This material may be used on either fiberglass or metal bodies.

Fig. 7-1. *A damaged door panel. Body filler will be needed to achieve a finished repair.*

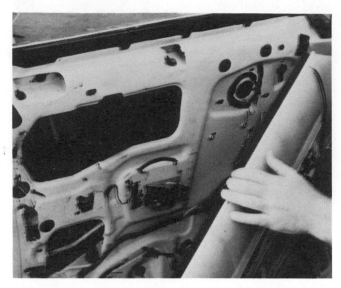

Fig. 7-2. *Access to the back of the dented area shown in Figure 7-1 is limited by the boxed-in structure of the door's back side.*

Fig. 7-3. *Dents and creases that cannot be reached from the back may be pulled out by drilling holes and using a slide hammer. Body filler will be used to achieve a smooth surface.*

Fig. 7-4. *A typical body filler material. (Courtesy of Ditzler Automotive Finishes Division, PPG Industries, Inc.)*

Fig. 7-5. *Components of a typical fiberglass repair kit. (Courtesy of Oatey Company)*

For many years, the most common filler was body *solder*. This soft metal is a mixture of lead and tin. It is applied to the panel with heat from a torch. The torch melts the solder stick and causes the metal to flow out over the body surface being repaired (Fig. 7-6). The use of body solder, often simply called "lead," requires more skill and time than does plastic filler. For this reason, and because of the increasing number of plastic panels on automobiles, plastic filler is replacing body solder in many shops. Body *solder*, of course, cannot be used on fiberglass bodies.

Foam filler is a liquid chemical action material. The foam filler is packaged in two parts. The parts are mixed together, then used as a back-up material for plastic filler.

Its primary use is to repair rust-out areas on all types of bodies. It can be used on steel, aluminum, galvanized metal, and fiberglass.

Any filler product should be mixed according to the manufacturer's recommendations. The instructions for mixing and using most products are written on the package.

Fig. 7-6. *Using body solder (body lead) to level a surface.*

PLASTIC FILLERS

Plastic fillers have become some of the most used materials in modern auto body shops. Almost all damaged metal will need some plastic to complete the repair. Good brands of plastic filler are easy to work down and hold up well during use.

The two most common types of plastic filler are *polyester* plastic and *metal* plastic (Figs. 7-7 and 7-8). Both are used widely throughout the automobile body repair trade.

Polyester plastic contains resin and magnesium silicate. The *resin* is the binder that holds the mixture in solution and binds it to the surface on which it is used. Unfortunately, resin is a gummy substance and is extremely difficult to file or sand. Therefore, the resin is mixed with magnesium silicate so that the product is easy to sand or file.

This product must be mixed with a hardener before it is used. The hardener is the curing agent, which causes a chemical reaction, drying and hardening the material. A common polyester plastic auto body filler is shown in Figure 7-4. Figure 7-7 shows another common brand with its cream hardener.

Metal plastic contains resin and ground aluminum particles, mixed together to form a paste. Before it is used, a hardener must be added to make the product cure (harden).

Metal plastic filler is sometimes referred to as *metal mender*, and often costs more than polyester plastic fillers. Metal fillers (Fig. 7-8) are often stronger than polyester fillers, which offsets the additional cost on high-quality work.

Lightweight plastic (Fig. 7-9) is mixed with microscopic glass bubbles, which makes it light and easy to work. This plastic provides a working time about 15 to 20 minutes longer than polyester plastic. Lightweight plastic uses a cream hardener for curing.

Advantages of Plastic Fillers

Generally, plastics are quick, easy to use, and have good adhesion to a clean base metal. Plastics are easy to apply and will cure fast, forming a hard finish that may be sanded and painted as if it were metal. Paint primer–surfacers adhere well to plastic, if the surface is well prepared. Plastic fillers are low in cost. When using plastic fillers, damage can be repaired fast, and the repair will last for years if properly done.

Disadvantages of Plastic Fillers

The greatest disadvantage of plastic filler is that the repair is likely to crack within a few months, if it is applied more than ¼ in. (6 mm) thick. Plastic filler will

Fig. 7-7. *A typical polyester plastic body filler and a cream hardener. (Courtesy of The Martin–Senour Company)*

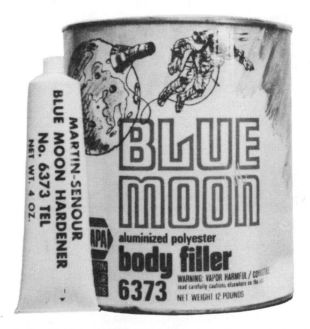

Fig. 7-8. *Aluminized plastic body filler, sometimes called* metal plastic. *The tube contains a hardener used with the filler. (Courtesy of The Martin–Senour Company)*

not adhere well to metal unless the metal surface is roughened (Fig. 7-10). The plastic needs a rough area for good holding power.

When plastic is sanded, it creates a fine dust in the repair shop. This plastic dust is a major shop problem and must be carefully controlled. Plastic dust will easily float through the air, causing breathing problems and collecting on other vehicles in the shop. Worst of all, the plastic dust may sift through paint booth filters, causing "dirty paint."

Fig. 7-9. *Microscopic glass bubbles are mixed with the plastic material to make an extra-light body filler. (Courtesy of Oatey Company)*

Fig. 7-10. *A panel that has been straightened and ground, ready for the application of body filler.*

When to Use Plastic Filler on Metal Panels

Plastic filler may be used on almost every damaged area. This includes dents, rusted-out areas, and broken edges of panels. Adaptability, wide range of use, and ease of application are the reasons for plastic filler's popularity. Plastic filler will not crack if properly applied. It may be used to level out large, *shallow* areas of damage that putty and primer–surfacer cannot fill properly.

Generally, metal panel areas that may be repaired with plastic fillers include:

1. Body sections that cannot be fully worked with tools such as a hammer and dolly.
2. Sections that cannot be completely restored to the original contour by working from the inside of the panel.

3. Panel holes or tears (after they have been properly repaired).
4. Sections weakened or damaged by rust-out (after the area has been properly repaired).
5. Areas that have been patched by welding, or over seams where entire replacement panels have been fastened.

When a metal panel cannot be bumped or aligned from its back side, the damage will then have to be repaired from the front side. To do this, the dent first must have holes made in it, using an awl or a drill.

Then, a *slide hammer* is used to pull out the dent. This was shown earlier in Figure 7-3. After pulling with the slide hammer, the surface of the damage will still be slightly rough and uneven. The holes will still be present, as well. The metal is cleaned, then plastic filler is smoothed over the damage area. The filler is shaped to the original contour of the metal.

How to Apply Plastic Filler on Metal Panels

Polyester plastic filler is widely used on sheet metal. When mixed with hardener, the product forms a thick, mudlike paste that may be easily spread over the uneven surface of a panel. The repair worker in Figure 7-11 is spreading polyester plastic on a prepared metal panel. Figure 7-12 shows the plastic spread on another panel to finish leveling a dented area. Polyester plastic is sometimes referred to by nicknames such as "mud" or "bondo."

Plastic body filler is often used to complete and smooth patch work done with other materials. It is also used to fill small damaged areas in the metal. The procedure for applying plastic filler is described below.

Preparing the Surface. To use a plastic filler successfully, *the surface area of the damage or low spot must be carefully prepared*. First, dirt and road grime must be removed, using soap and water.

After washing, the area must be cleaned with grease and wax remover. This cleans off any tar, wax, silicone, and other contaminants.

Old paint and minor surface rust is then ground off the damaged area, using a #16 grit open-coat grinding disc. This disc gives the surface the roughness the plastic must have to adhere to the metal (Fig. 7-10). The plastic needs a rough area for good holding power.

Preparing the Plastic Filler. Before mixing the material, always read carefully any instructions on the container. No two plastic filler products are exactly the same. For this reason, it is very important to follow the manufacturer's instructions for mixing and using the product correctly.

First, scoop out the amount of plastic needed for the repair, and place it on a clean, smooth mixing plate.

Fig. 7-11. *Applying body filler. A firm plastic spreader is used.*

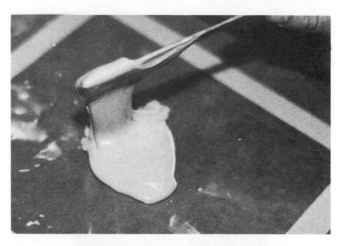

Fig. 7-13. *The plastic material can be dipped from the can with a paint-mixing paddle. A piece of glass may be used for a mixing plate.*

Fig. 7-12. *The plastic filler in place on the panel before rough grating.*

Fig. 7-14. *An air-pressure-operated dispenser for plastic filler. (Courtesy of Oatey Company)*

The plastic may be dipped out of the can with a paint paddle, as shown in Figure 7-13, or drawn from a dispenser (Figs. 7-14 and 7-15). These figures show an air-pressure plastic dispenser. The dispenser is connected to an air line that puts pressure on the can. When the handle is turned, the plastic flows out onto the plastic mixing board, as shown in Figure 7-15.

Next, the hardener is added (Fig. 7-16). For best results, buy and use the hardener recommended by the plastic's manufacturer. Add *only* the amount of hardener needed to make the plastic cure as fast as is desired. Either the can of plastic or the tube of hardener will have directions on the amount of hardener to use. If too much hardener is added, the plastic will cure before it can be applied and smoothed. It will also tend to *pinhole* as it cures.

Using the paint paddle or other stirring device, *mix* the plastic and hardener thoroughly. Stir the hardener and plastic until the mixture becomes a smooth, creamy paste that is all one color with no streaks (Fig. 7-17). The mixture must *not* be whipped. If it is, air bubbles will be mixed into the plastic. Later, when the plastic has hardened, these bubbles will cause the surface to have small *pinholes*. These will need additional filling. By stirring (instead of whipping), air will be worked out

of the plastic. Be careful not to get any hardener into the large can of plastic filler. This will cause lumps in the unused plastic.

Spreading Plastic Filler. The plastic filler must always be applied immediately after mixing. It begins curing very rapidly after it has been mixed with hardener. A plastic spreader like the one in Figure 7-18 should be used to apply a smooth, even layer of filler to the entire damaged area.

The flatter the spreader is held, the thicker the layer of plastic that will be built up on the surface. If the

Fig. 7-15. *Plastic filler is ejected onto the mixing board when the handle of the dispenser is operated. (Courtesy of Oatey Company)*

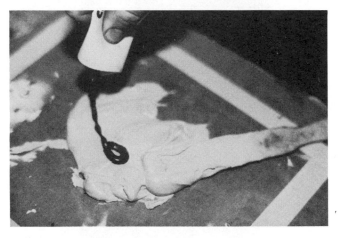

Fig. 7-16. *Hardener must be added to the plastic in the recommended proportion.*

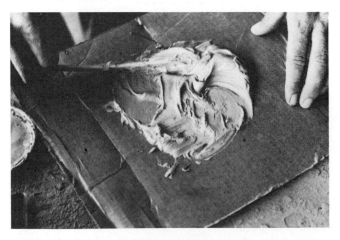

Fig. 7-17. *To avoid trapping air bubbles in the mixture, the plastic and hardener are gently stirred together.*

Fig. 7-18. *A plastic spreader is used to apply and smooth the filler.*

spreader is held more vertically, a thinner coat of plastic will be applied. Plastic should *never* be applied to a thickness greater than ¼ in. (6.4 mm). Such a thick layer of plastic is likely to crack after the repair is a few months old.

Smooth the plastic as much as possible while it is still soft. Allow the plastic to dry until it is semi-cured (beginning to harden and not sticky), before beginning to shape the repaired area to the desired contour (Fig. 7-19).

After old paint is ground away and the area filled, the bare metal must be cleaned with metal conditioner to prevent rusting. Figure 7-20 shows an area being cleaned with metal conditioner. The metal conditioner must be wiped off immediately with a clean wet rag (Fig. 7-21).

FIBERGLASS FILLERS

Figure 7-22 shows a fiberglass filler repair kit. A typical repair kit will contain a 1 qt (0.9 L) of resin, a tube of hardener, a 4 ft (1.2 m) square piece of fiberglass matting material, a mixing cup, a paddle to mix the resin and hardener, and a plastic spreader. Fiberglass

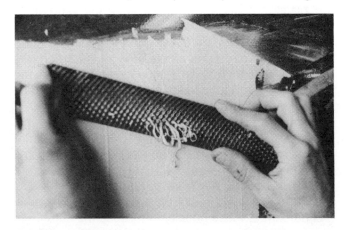

Fig. 7-19. *A Surform tool is used to grate and shape the filler as it begins to cure (harden).*

Fig. 7-20. *Applying metal conditioner to bare metal surfaces will help prevent rust from forming beneath the new finish. (Courtesy of Refinish Division, DuPont Company)*

repair kits are designed for body shop use and include written instructions.

CAUTION: Use rubber gloves and a particle mask when working with fiberglass filler. The material may cause skin or lung irritation.

Fiberglass resin and hardener are used with a reinforcing matting. The resin is a thick syrup that is mixed with hardener to become a firm binder. This mixture is spread on the fiberglass matting. This matting may be either the loosely woven, strawlike fabric shown in Figure 7-23, or the closely woven fabric shown in Figure 7-24. Both types are woven from fiberglass yarn.

The resin and hardener mixture is applied to the matting, then the matting is placed over the damage. A plastic filler made especially for use on fiberglass is spread over the matting. The *plastic* filler is easier to smooth and finish than the fiberglass filler.

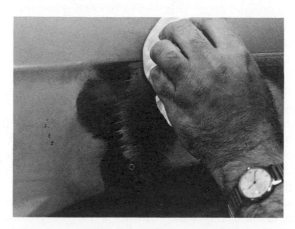

Fig. 7-21. *The metal conditioner must be wiped off the surface before it dries. (Courtesy of Refinish Division, DuPont Company)*

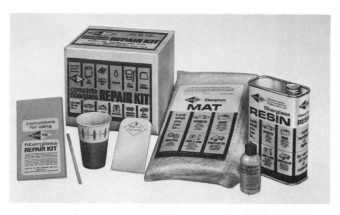

Fig. 7-22. *Parts of a typical fiberglass repair kit used for larger repairs. (Courtesy of Oatey Company)*

Fig. 7-23. *One form of fiberglass matting is loosely woven and resembles straw. It is shown here being saturated with fiberglass resin.*

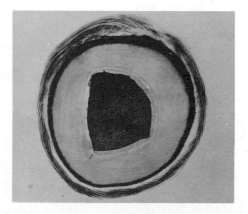

Fig. 7-24. *Another type of fiberglass matting is a more tightly woven fabric. (Courtesy of Ditzler Automotive Finishes Division, PPG Industries, Inc.)*

Advantages of Fiberglass Filler

Fiberglass filler is a quick and easy way of making many body repairs. Pound for pound, it may be built up to be stronger than steel. It will not rust or dent. Fiberglass repairs may be primed, sanded, and painted like any other type of repair.

Fig. 7-25. *A fiberglass part that has been damaged in a collision.*

Fig. 7-26. *An example of "rust-out," in which rust has eaten completely through the metal.*

Fig. 7-27. *Before rust-out repair begins, grease and other surface deposits must be removed with a pre-cleaning solvent.*

Fiberglass filler is durable and is easy to mix and apply. Filler kits can be bought in large or small sizes. They are excellent for repairing cars with complete fiberglass bodies (such as the Corvette) or the fiberglass parts on steel bodies, such as the front panel

shown in Figure 7-25. Metal bodies may also be repaired with fiberglass filler kits. If available, a kit with *epoxy* resin (rather than polyester resin) should be used for repairs on metal.

There are many auto body repair jobs that can be done with fiberglass. It may be used on tears, cracks, gouges, dents, or rust-outs. The following section outlines a step-by-step procedure for repairing a rusted-out metal body section with fiberglass filler.

In the snow belt, there is a good market for fiberglass repair work on snowmobiles. Procedures for repairing damaged snowmobile bodies are the same as those used for fiberglass automobile bodies.

Disadvantages of Fiberglass Filler

Fiberglass matting or resin may cause skin irritation. Rubber gloves and a particle mask should be used. Also, fiberglass filler is difficult to sand and work because of its gummy, varnishlike properties. Usually, it is best to use a plastic filler coat over fiberglass repair sections.

How to Use Fiberglass Filler to Repair Rust-out

Most of the sheet metal on auto bodies is thin. If this metal is exposed to the weather for a period of time, it will have rust holes eaten through it. Figure 7-26 shows this type of rust damage. Rust-out damage can be repaired with fiberglass matting and resin, as outlined below.

Cleaning and Sanding. The area to be repaired should first be cleaned with a grease and wax remover to remove the contaminants from the paint and metal (Fig. 7-27). Then, the area must be rough-sanded (ground) to remove the surface rust and expose the bare metal around the hole. Figure 7-26 shows how the surface has been ground 2 to 3 in. (50.8 to 76.2 mm) beyond the damaged area. This allows the fiberglass material to adhere to the rough metal.

Depressing the Damaged Area. A hammer is then used to tap down the damaged area so that it forms a depression. The fiberglass material will then be built up to fill the depression until the repair is even with the rest of the panel.

Cutting Fiberglass Matting. The fiberglass matting is trimmed to fit the area being repaired (Fig. 7-28). It should be cut about 2 in. (5 cm) larger than the damaged area. This allows the material to have plenty of undamaged metal on which to hold.

Mixing Fiberglass Resin. A container, usually a paper cup, is used to mix the resin for the matting. About 4 oz (113 g) of resin is needed for each square foot of fiberglass matting. The hardener is added to the resin as recommended by the kit manufacturer (Fig. 7-29). The resin and hardener are then mixed together.

Usually, about 30 drops of hardener is needed for each 4 oz (113.4 g) of resin. Manufacturers provide specific directions for mixing their products. Most use the formula of one tube of hardener to 1 qt (0.9 L) of resin.

CAUTION: Heat or flame must not be allowed near the fiberglass resin. It is highly explosive.

Applying the Matting. After the resin is mixed, place the cut piece of matting on a plastic bag or piece of plastic wrapping. The matting will not stick to the plastic when the resin has been poured or spread on it.

Lightly coat the matting by brushing on resin (Fig. 7-30). Then, apply the matting to the damaged area, with the resin-coated side against the metal. The 2 in. (50.8 mm) overlap provides the matting with plenty of metal contact.

Saturating the Matting. Using a plastic spreader, saturate the attached matting with the resin mixture. Spread the resin *evenly* over the entire matting, as is being done in Figure 7-31. A second or third layer of matting and resin can be placed over the first layer, if needed. The more layers of material that are used, the stronger the repair.

Removing Air Bubbles. Air bubbles will sometimes form under the resin or fiberglass mat. To remove bubbles, press the material with the spreader, working from the center toward the outside. The air bubbles will easily move out from under the material.

Allow the resin and matting to dry on the damaged area. After drying, the matting may be trimmed if it is too wide at any point.

Applying Plastic Filler. After the fiberglass resin filler cures (usually about 15 minutes), it may be covered with plastic filler (Fig. 7-32). Before plastic filler can be

Fig. 7-29. *Resin and hardener, in the recommended proportions, are mixed in a clean container, such as a paper cup.*

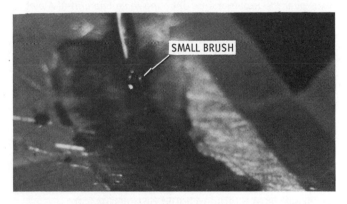

Fig. 7-30. *The resin mixture is applied to the matting with a small brush. The matting should be saturated with resin.*

applied, the gummy surface of the fiberglass resin must be removed with a cleaning solvent. Plastic filler is used over the fiberglass because it is easier to sand and smooth. Be sure to use a plastic filler specifically designed for use on fiberglass. As it hardens, the plastic filler is worked down and finished as usual. The repair of fiberglass bodies and panels is discussed in a later unit.

Fig. 7-28. *Fiberglass matting is cut about 2 in. (50.8 mm) larger than the area to be repaired. Fiberglass can cause skin irritation, so the use of gloves is recommended.*

Fig. 7-31. *The resin-saturated matting is placed over the damage and smoothed to eliminate air bubbles. Several layers may be used.*

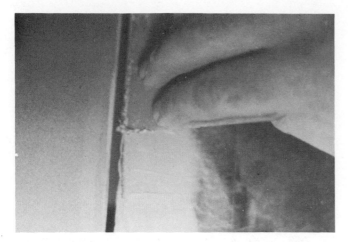

Fig. 7-32. *Plastic filler designed for use with fiberglass is applied over the repaired area once the resin has cured. A plastic spreader is used.*

BODY SOLDER

Body solder, also known as body *lead*, is a product made from *lead* and *tin*. Usually "body lead" is made in 12 in. (30.4 cm) sticks about ½ in. (12.7 mm) in diameter. The sticks weigh about ½ lb (0.22 kg) each.

Shown in Figure 7-33 is a stick of body solder. Also in Figure 7-33 is a roll of *acid core solder*. This product is used to clean a panel during the body soldering ("leading") process. *Tinning acid*, used for the same purpose, is available in liquid or powder form.

Advantages of Body Solder

Body solder is a metal material, so it makes a good filler for metal panels. It will adhere well to properly prepared steel. Body solder is hard and will not mar easily. When properly cleaned, it may be painted with regular automobile paints. Body solder does not crack,

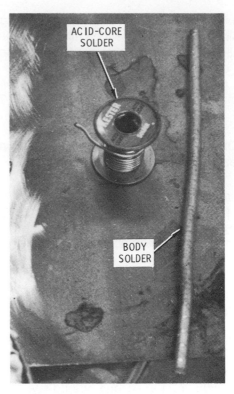

Fig. 7-33. *Body solder, in stick form, is used for premium quality repairs. Acid-core solder is used to prepare the metal surface for body solder.*

is very stable, and lasts as long as the panel itself. It is best used to repair edges or corners that will be exposed to abuse.

Disadvantages of Body Solder

Body solder is still used in some shops. However, it has generally been displaced by other materials for many types of work. For high-priced custom body work,

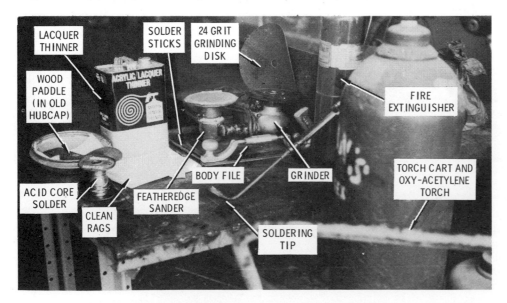

Fig. 7-34. *The tools and equipment used for body solder work.*

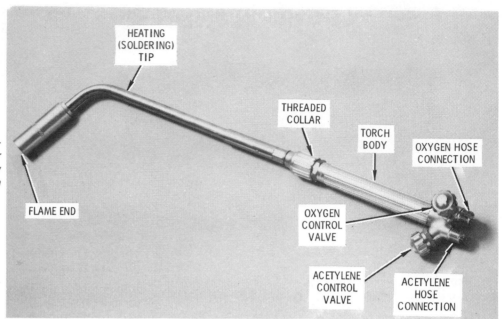

Fig. 7-35. *A soldering tip is attached to the oxy-acetylene torch for body solder application. (Courtesy of Harris Calorific Division, Emerson Electric Company)*

however, many people prefer the use of body solder as a filler. In these cases, the customer is often willing to pay the higher price of body solder work.

Body solder is expensive, and using it as a filler is slow. Fiberglass and polyester plastic are more commonly used today. Body solder is becoming obsolete. The procedures for using body solder are shown in Figures 7-34 to 7-43.

Fig. 7-36. *The damaged metal surface is prepared for body soldering by grinding with a disc grinder.*

Fig. 7-37. *Acid core solder is used to tin the metal, preparing it for body solder.*

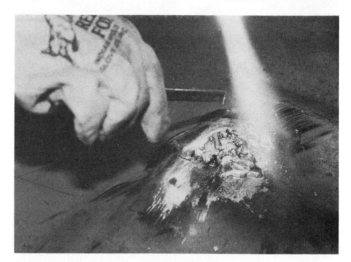

Fig. 7-38. *Both the metal surface and the acid core solder are heated with the torch.*

Fig. 7-39. *While the solder is still molten (liquid), a clean rag is used to wipe it across the metal surface.*

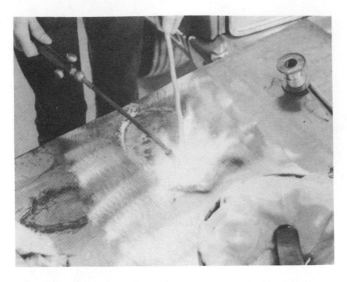

Fig. 7-40. *The torch is held at a 45° angle to the metal as the body solder stick is melted.*

Fig. 7-41. *The molten solder is spread with a wooden paddle.*

Fig. 7-42. *Once the solder has hardened, it is smoothed and leveled with a metal body file.*

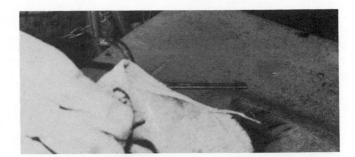

Fig. 7-43. *Lacquer thinner is wiped on the smoothed body solder surface to neutralize the acid in the tinning material.*

FOAM FILLER

Foam filler consists of two liquids that are mixed together. The mixture will expand to nine times its original volume and will fill holes easily when the damaged area is properly prepared. The mixture forms a tough, durable polyurethane foam that can be sanded in about 1 hour from the time the material is applied.

Foam filler has several uses. These include filling holes and depressed areas, deadening sound, insulating, eliminating the metal flexing known as "oil-canning" or "fluttering," and stopping wind noises. Foam can be used for reinforcement when installing "T" tops and moon roofs on a vehicle. It is also used to modify panels in custom work.

How to Mix Foam Filler

The foam filler package has "A" and "B" parts. The package is cemented together on the inside with a small adhesive strip that separates the two chemicals (Fig. 7-44). To mix the two parts, the strip of adhesive is pulled apart, as shown in Figure 7-45. The two chemicals are pressed back and forth in the package 25 to 30 times to start the chemical action (Fig. 7-46).

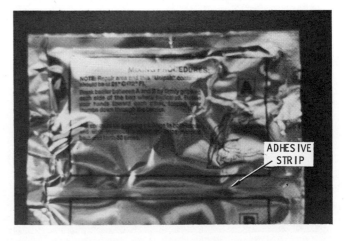

ADHESIVE STRIP

Fig. 7-44. *An adhesive strip separates the two parts of the foam filler material in the package.*

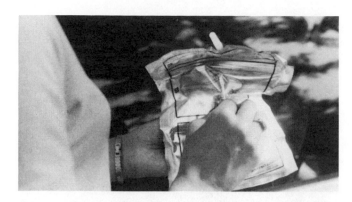

Fig. 7-45. *The sides of the package are pulled apart to loosen the adhesive strip and allow the two parts of the filler material to mix.*

Fig. 7-46. *The package is kneaded 25 to 30 times to mix the two parts of the filler material thoroughly.*

How to Use Foam Filler

Rust along the lower edge of a body panel is a common repair. The rust-out area in Figure 7-47 was repaired with foam filler. The steps used for the repair are shown in Figures 7-48 through 7-52.

Fig. 7-47. *A rust-out area that can be repaired with foam filler. (Courtesy of Automotive Trades Division, 3M Company)*

Fig. 7-48. *After cleaning with a solvent, the area is ground to remove rust and old paint. (Courtesy of Automotive Trades Division, 3M Company)*

Fig. 7-49. *Wide masking tape is applied to the outer surface of the repair area. This will hold the foam material in place until it expands and "sets up." (Courtesy of Automotive Trades Division, 3M Company)*

Fig. 7-50. *After being mixed in the package, the foam material is squeezed into the quarter panel from the inside. It will expand, filling the rust-out area and forming a base for body filler. (Courtesy of Automotive Trades Division, 3M Company)*

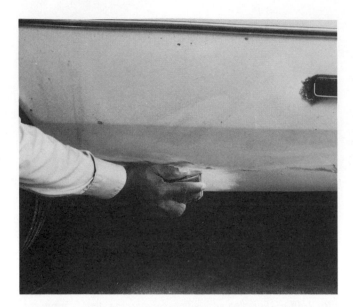

Fig. 7-51. *Once the foam filler has hardened, the masking tape is removed. A sanding block and 36-grit sandpaper are used to smooth the filler and lower it about ¼ in. (6.4 mm) below the metal surface. (Courtesy of Automotive Trades Division, 3M Company)*

Fig. 7-52. *Plastic filler is applied and smoothed over the foam material in the same way as when filling dents on sheet metal. (Courtesy of Automotive Trades Division, 3M Company)*

Body Abrasives

In body shop work, it is often necessary to remove material from a body or panel surface. This may be old paint, rust, or excess body filler. To remove such material, tools with body shop *abrasives* are used.

An *abrasive* is a substance that is used to cut material off a surface. Abrasives used in the body shop should be chosen with the same care used to choose other tools and equipment. Different types of repair jobs, and different steps on the *same* repair jobs, will require various types of abrasives.

For example, *grinding discs* (Fig. 8-1) are used to remove paint or rust from a panel to be repaired. *Sandpaper*, on the other hand, is normally used for finer jobs such as preparing the surface of bare metal or primer–surfacer (Fig. 8-2). Finally, *cutting* (rubbing) compound is used to clean old finishes and to rub out new lacquer, acrylic enamel, and urethane paints (Fig. 8-3).

GRINDING DISCS

Grinding discs are used for rough jobs, such as grinding off paint and rust. For grinding discs to perform these jobs, they must have a hard, rugged surface, or *grit*. Notice the coarse texture of the #24-grit grinding discs in Figure 8-1.

Characteristics of Grinding Discs

Almost all grinding discs are *round*. Large discs are used on a disc sander or a large body grinder. Smaller discs are used on a power drill. (Grinding discs should

Fig. 8-1. *Grinding discs. (Courtesy of The Norton Company)*

not be confused with *sandpaper* discs. Sandpaper discs have a finer, less durable grit and a softer backing material.)

Disc Sizes. Grinding discs are available in sizes from 3 to 9 in. (7.6 to 22.8 cm) in diameter. The most common discs are the 7 and 9 in. (17.7 and 22.8 cm) sizes shown in Figure 8-4. Other shapes used for grinding can be purchased or cut in the shop (Fig. 8-5). Some grinding discs have either ½ or ⅞ in. (12.7 or 22.2 mm) center holes. The center hole is used to fasten the disc and the backing plate to the grinder. This is done by using a special screw and spacer (Fig. 8-6). Other discs are not attached in this way. Instead, they are *glued* onto the backing plate.

Disc Backing Plate. Because grinding discs are thin and easily bent, they must have a *backing plate* (pad). The plate provides stiffness for the revolving disc. The

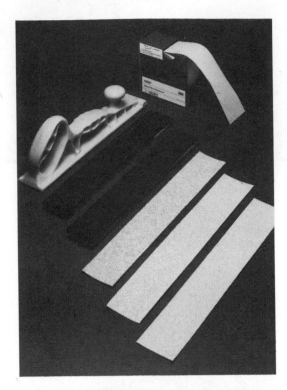

Fig. 8-2. *Sandpaper strips for use on primer–surfacer or bare metal. (Courtesy of Automotive Trades Division, 3M Company)*

Fig. 8-3. *Cutting (rubbing) compound.*

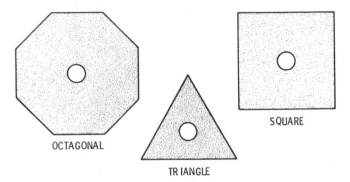

Fig. 8-4. *The two most common size grinding discs are 7 and 9 in. (17.7 and 22.8 cm) in diameter.*

OCTAGONAL

TRIANGLE

SQUARE

Fig. 8-5. *Sanding discs in square, octagon, or triangle shapes can be cut from old round discs. They are useful for sanding reverse curves and other hard-to-reach areas. Care should be exercised, since the corners of such discs can break off in use. Safety goggles should always be worn when grinding or sanding.*

plate must be the same size as the grinding disc. Figure 8-7 shows a 9 in. (22.8 cm) backing plate that would be used with a 9 in. (22.8 cm) disc.

Some small grinding discs [3 in. (7.6 cm) or smaller] have a stud on the back, as shown in Figure 8-8. The stud will fit down into the drill chuck.

Fig. 8-6. *Three different sizes of backing pads and the spacer and screw used to mount such pads. (Courtesy of Automotive Trades Division, 3M Company)*

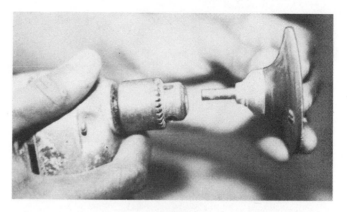

Fig. 8-8. *A backing pad with a built-in spindle that fits into the drill chuck.*

Fig. 8-7. *A 9 in. (22.9 cm) backing pad that is screwed onto the spindle of a grinder. (Courtesy of Automotive Trades Division, 3M Company)*

Other small discs are mounted on small *backing pads*. The discs themselves have a stud to fit into the backing pad, as shown in Figure 8-9.

Disc Cutter. Many repair shops buy grinding discs in only the 9 in. (22.8 cm) size. Then, after the outer edge of the disc has been worn off, a *disc cutter* is used. The disc is cut down to fit a 7 in. (17.7 cm) backing pad. This saves the cost of buying new discs for the shop's 7 in. (17.7 cm) grinders. When the 7 in. (17.7 cm) disc is worn down on the edges, it may then be cut to fit a 5 in. (12.7 cm) backing pad.

Figure 8-10 shows how a disc is trimmed with a disc cutter. The cutter is operated by turning the handle and feeding the disc around the cutter. This money-saving piece of equipment may be used to cut discs for most sizes of backing plates.

Fig. 8-9. *A small sanding disc that snaps into the backing pad shown in Figure 8-8.*

Manufacture of Grinding Discs

Grinding discs are made by attaching a rough *grit* (the cutting material) to a glue-covered *backing*. The grit must first be *sized*, and then bonded to the backing by one of several processes.

The cutting part of a disc is the *grit*, also known as the *grain*. Both *man-made* grit and *natural* grit are used.

Man-made grits are either *aluminum oxide* or *silicon carbide*. Aluminum oxide is the most widely used grit in automobile repair work. Figure 8-11 shows an aluminum oxide "rock" before being crushed into grit.

Natural grits include emery, garnet, and flint. All of these are minerals mined from the earth. These natural minerals are very hard. They are often used for grinding very hard surfaces. Figure 8-12 shows a mound of ungraded garnet grit.

Fig. 8-10. *A disc cutter is used to trim the worn outer edge from a grinding disc. It may then be used on the next smaller-sized backing pad. (Courtesy of Plymouth Products Corp.)*

Fig. 8-11. *Aluminum oxide material before crushing. (Courtesy of The Norton Company)*

Fig. 8-12. *Natural garnet grit before grading. (Courtesy of The Norton Company)*

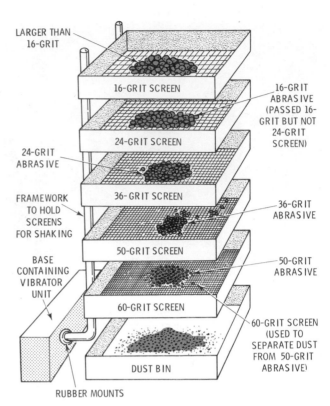

Fig. 8-13. *A set of vibrating screens is used to separate abrasive material into different grit sizes.*

Grit Sizes. There are four basic *grades* (grit sizes) used to make grinding discs: 16-grit, 24-grit, 36-grit, and 50-grit. The coarsest grade is 16-grit; 50-grit is the finest grade.

To sort the sizes of grit, a pile of crushed material is placed in the top hopper of a grading machine (Fig. 8-13). When the machine is vibrated, the grit falls through the holes in the hopper screens.

As the grit falls down through the hopper screens, each lower screen has smaller openings. The top screen, with 16 holes per square inch, will filter out any material *larger* than 16-grit. Material that is 16-grit or smaller falls to the next lower screen, which has 24 holes per square inch. Since the 16-grit size cannot pass through the 24-grit screen, the 16-grit grains collect on top of that screen. Smaller particles continue downward. This process continues until the finest grit size has been filtered out and only dust remains.

Bonding the Grit. Grit particles of a certain size are glued to a paper or fiber backing with a *bonding* agent. To do this, a coat of resin binder is first applied to the backing. Then the sized grit is applied.

Several methods are used to apply the grit. Of these, the *electrostatic* method is the most popular. In this method, shown in Figure 8-14, the grit is pulled onto the resin-covered backing by electrical forces. The electrostatic method spaces the grit evenly and *orients* (positions) it with the sharpest points of each grain upward for good cutting. This method also firmly embeds the grit into the bonding material.

After the grit is stuck to the backing, the resin is allowed to dry. Then, another coat of resin is applied to anchor the grit firmly to the backing material.

Disc Coats

The *coat* of a disc refers to how close together the pieces of grit are positioned. There are only two basic coat types: *open coat* and *closed coat*. The difference between the two is shown in Figure 8-15. Closed-coat discs are made by allowing the backing and resin to be *completely* covered with grit. Open-coat discs, on the other hand, have abrasive material covering only about 60 percent of the backing surface.

The main reason for using a *closed-coat* disc instead of an open-coat disc in the same grit size is to produce a slightly smoother cut. Since the entire surface area is covered with abrasive grit, there is less chance of the disc digging into the panel. The *open-*

coat design, however, helps to keep the disc from becoming clogged with old paint and metal.

Use of Grinding Discs

Grinding discs are normally used on a *disc grinder*. Hardback 16- and 24-grit grinding discs are most often used. A 9 in. (22.9 cm), 24-grit closed-coat disc is mounted on the grinder being used in Figure 8-16.

Grinding discs are used for removing paint, preparing metal for filler, grinding off welds, and removing rust. Figure 8-16 shows a worker using a grinding disc to prepare rough metal for filler. Note that the worker is using a safety shield and a dust mask. Such safety devices *must* be used when performing grinding operations.

A 9 in. (22.9 cm) disc should *only* be used on disc sanders that revolve at less than 4,000 rpm (revolutions per minute). A 7 in. (17.8 cm) disc should only be used on equipment that produces less than 5,500 rpm. A disc used at a higher speed than is recommended will heat up the surface of the metal being worked. This heat may cause the metal to warp, ruining the straightening work that had been done on the metal. Also, too much speed may cause the disc to break. This could cause injury to the worker using the sander.

SANDPAPER

Sandpaper is a body shop material similar to the grinding disc. This is because both discs and sandpaper have grit, cement, and backing. Some sandpapers are made to be used for either *hand* sanding, *block* sanding, or *machine* sanding. Many can be used either dry or with water (wet).

Sandpaper is manufactured in large sheets. It is then cut into smaller sheets or discs of various sizes (Fig. 8-17). The most common sandpaper disc sizes are 5, 6, and 8 in. (12.7, 15.2, and 20.3 cm). Discs are packed in boxes of 50, 100, or 200.

Sandpaper for auto body repair work is made with one of two types of grit material: *silicon carbide* or *aluminum oxide*. Sandpaper that may be used wet or dry is made of silicon carbide. Sandpaper made of aluminum oxide can be used only for *dry* sanding. Figure 8-18 shows an aluminum oxide sandpaper disc. Discs may be purchased with or without a center hole.

Grit Size

Figure 8-19 shows a mound of graded abrasive grit *before* being applied to the paper backing. As with grinding grits, sandpaper grits are "riddled" through screens to determine the grade size. The size, of course, is the sandpaper's number.

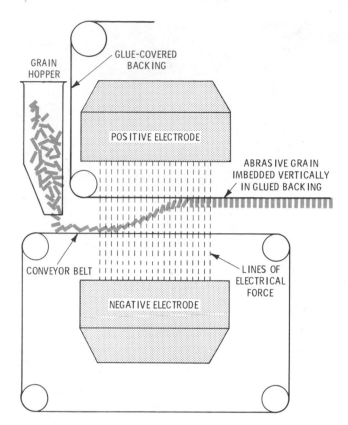

Fig. 8-14. *The electrostatic process used to attract grit particles to the resin-covered backing material. (Courtesy of The Norton Company)*

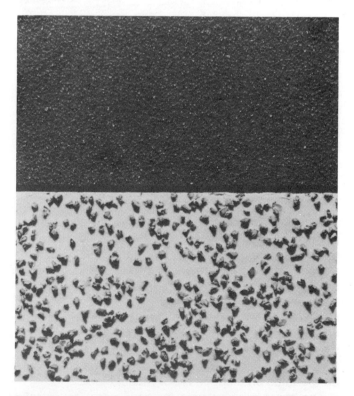

Fig. 8-15. *A closed-coat surface is shown at top; open-coat at bottom. (Courtesy of The Norton Company)*

Fig. 8-16. *A grinding disc being used to prepare a rust-out area for repair work. Note the safety shield and particle mask being worn by the worker. (Courtesy of Automotive Trades Division, 3M Company)*

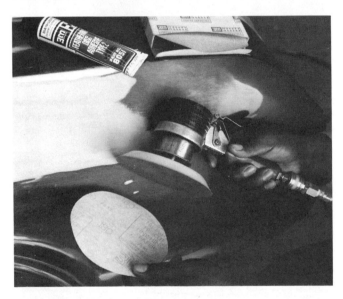

Fig. 8-17. *A silicon carbide sanding disc. It is attached to the backing plate with a special adhesive. (Courtesy of Automotive Trades Division, 3M Company)*

Fig. 8-18. *An aluminum oxide sanding disc with a center hole for mounting on a large sander. Discs are available in various sizes, with or without the center hole. (Courtesy of The Norton Company)*

Fig. 8-19. *Sandpaper grit before being glued to the backing paper. (Courtesy of The Norton Company)*

A display of several different grits of sandpaper in protective wrappers is shown in Figure 8-20. There are many different grit sizes on the market (See Table 5). Several basic grits are most often used in the auto repair business. These range from a coarse 40-grit to the finest 800-grit.

Choosing a Grit Size. The grit size to use depends largely on the job to be done. If sandpaper is being used to rough-sand plastic filler, as in Figure 8-21, then a 40- or 80-grit paper would be used. The paper would be mounted on a speed file or rubber block.

The most popular grits for final metal and plastic finishing are 150- and 220-grit (Fig. 8-22). After using one of these two grits, the repaired area must be covered with primer–surfacer. This is done to fill the sanding marks (*sandscratches*) before the finish coat is applied.

Sandpaper Backing

Sandpaper grits may be cemented to different types of *backings*. The different backings are known as the sandpaper's "weight." Different backing weights are chosen for different jobs because of their *flexibility* (how much they may be bent and twisted without breaking).

Sandpaper backings range from *A* weight to *E* weight. The weight labeling letters are shown after the grit

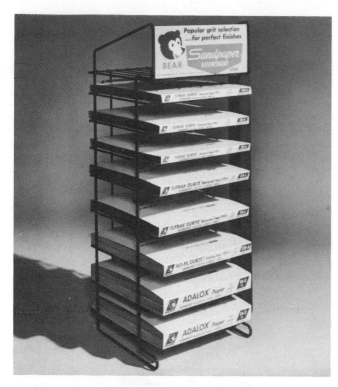

Fig. 8-20. *A sandpaper selection rack containing boxes of the most often used grit sizes of sandpaper in sheet form. (Courtesy of The Norton Company)*

Table 5

Abrasive Papers

Grit	Aluminum Oxide	Silicon Carbide	Primary Use for Auto Body Repair
Ultra Fine		800	Used for color-coat sanding. Used with water.
Very Fine		600	Used for color-coat sanding. Also for sanding the paint before polishing. Used with water.
	400	400	Used for sanding primer–
	320	320	surfacer and old paint prior
	280	280	to painting. Used as wet
	240	240	sanding paper.
	220	220	Used for dry sanding for top coat. Also can be purchased for wet sanding.
Fine	180	180	Used for final sanding of
	150	150	bare metal and smoothing old paint.
Medium	120	120	Used for smoothing old paint
	100	100	and plastic filler.
	80	80	
Coarse	60	60	Used for rough-sanding
	50	50	plastics.
	40	40	
	36	36	
Very Coarse	24	24	Used on sander or grinder
	16	16	to remove paint.

numbers on the packages. *A* weight is the most flexible and will tear most easily. If a tougher, more tear-resistant backing is needed, then *C*, *D*, or *E* weights may be used. Although they are stronger, they are also less flexible. *E* weight is usually the stiffest backing available.

The *A*, *B*, and *C* backings are most often used with finer grit papers. *D* and *E* backings, on the other hand, are more often found on coarse-grit papers.

Dry Sandpaper

Dry sandpaper is always used without water. Dry sandpaper is used for smoothing metal and plastic repairs and for sanding old finishes. For example, a worker might use an orbital sander with 80-D dry sandpaper to smooth a plastic filler repair. This step could also be done with a hard rubber sanding *block* and 80-D paper.

The cement used to hold the grit on dry sandpaper is animal glue. This glue must not be used with water because it will dissolve and allow the grit to come off the paper backing.

Although most dry sandpapers are coarse-grit, fine-grit sandpapers are available. For example, Figure 8-18 shows a dry, aluminum oxide sandpaper disc. This disc is a fine 220-grit and has a 6 in. (15.2 cm) diameter. A soft rubber backing pad like the one in Figure 8-23 is used with sandpaper discs.

Fine-grit dry sandpaper is also used in sheets. Fig-

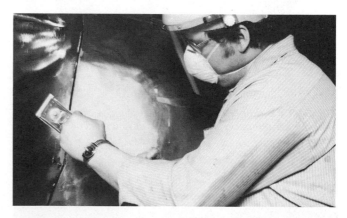

Fig. 8-21. *A body worker using sandpaper to smooth plastic body filler. (Courtesy of Automotive Trades Division, 3M Company)*

ure 8-24 shows a repair worker using dry, 220-grit sandpaper. The paper is used on a rubber sanding block to featheredge old paint and finish smoothing a plastic-filler repair. Rubber blocks can be used for either wet or dry sanding.

Wet Sandpaper

Wet sanding is usually done to a surface during final preparation before the color coat is applied. Wet

Fig. 8-22. *Sanding to a smooth surface is done with 150-grit and 220-grit sandpaper. (Courtesy of Automotive Trades Division, 3M Company)*

Fig. 8-23. *A rubber backing pad like this one should be used with dry sandpaper discs. (Courtesy of Automotive Trades Division, 3M Company)*

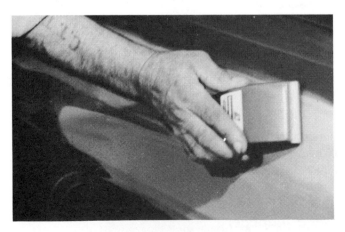

Fig. 8-24. *A sanding block and 220-grit sandpaper can be used to featheredge plastic body filler. (Courtesy of The Norton Company)*

"waterproof" sandpaper is made with silicon carbide grit and a resin binder. It is usually sold in fine grit sizes from 220 to 800.

Figure 8-25 shows a package of 220-grit waterproof sandpaper. Waterproof sandpaper is usually sold in packages of 50 sheets. Each package is known as a *sleeve* and each sheet in the sleeve is 9 × 11 in. (22.9 × 27.9 cm) in size. Normally, the sheets are cut and folded to get more use out of each sheet. A newer form of packaging is sleeves of 9 ½ × 5 ½ in. (24.1 × 14.0 cm) half sheets. These may be cut and used for the sanding block.

Waterproof sandpaper is usually used wet (Fig. 8-26). Water acts as a *lubricant* for the sandpaper. It allows the paper to sand more smoothly by floating away the sanding dust. This keeps the paper unclogged. Waterproof paper may be used without water, but this use is not recommended. Used dry, the paper is more likely to clog, resulting in a rougher surface finish.

Fig. 8-25. *Waterproof sandpaper is usually sold in "sleeves" of 50 sheets. (Courtesy of The Norton Company)*

Fig. 8-26. *In wet-sanding, water is used as a lubricant for the sandpaper. (Courtesy of Automotive Trades Division, 3M Company)*

Fig. 8-27. *Cutting (rubbing) compound is made in both hand and machine grades.*

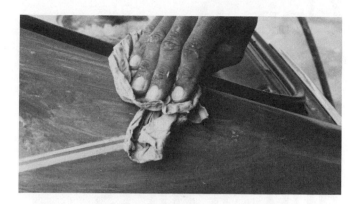

Fig. 8-28. *Compounding by hand.*

CUTTING COMPOUND

A shop-sized 1 gal (3.8 L) can of cutting compound is shown in Figure 8-27. This product may be known as *cutting* compound, *rubbing* compound, or simply *compound*. By whatever name, the product is used on the top (color) coat of a vehicle's finish. The compound will smooth and polish the topcoat by cutting off the high parts of the paint. It will also remove the dull top film on an old finish. Compound is used both on new finishes and on old finishes that have aged and become dull because of exposure to rain, sun, and chemicals.

Types of Compound

There are several different types of compound available. These are graded according to the coarseness of the abrasive in the compound. Terms such as *hand-cut*, *fast-cut*, and *polish* are used to describe the qualities of different compounds. Many are used with water. The compound and the water are mixed together before being used on the finish. Some compounds should not be used on enamel finishes. The manufacturer's recommendations and directions for the particular *line* (brand) of compounds being used should be followed closely.

How Compound Is Made. Cutting compound grit is made from *volcanic pumice*, a type of natural glass. The pumice is first ground to a fine, dustlike grit. Then, the grit is added to the compound paste.

Use of Compound

When compound is rubbed on paint, it cuts off the rough and dull top surface, leaving a smooth and glossy

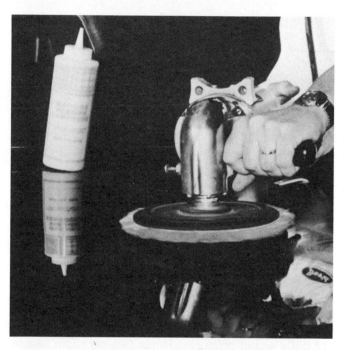

Fig. 8-29. *The high gloss on this finish is the sign of compounding by a skilled body worker. (Courtesy of Automotive Trades Division, 3M Company)*

finish. Figure 8-28 shows a worker using compound by hand. The pumice used in hand-cutting compound is coarser than that used in machine-cutting compound.

Most compounding done in a body shop is done by *machine*. A polishing machine was used to produce the glossy finish shown in Figure 8-29. Machine compounding, or *wheeling*, is a job requiring experience, practice, and talent. The step-by-step procedures for using compound are fully explained in the unit on paint rub-out and restoration.

Unit 9

Body Leaks and Sealers

An automobile body is made of many different parts and panels. It must be built to be waterproof, dustproof, and (to a degree) soundproof. Every outside panel of the body must be sealed as well as possible to keep out moisture, dust, and noise. For each space or joint between two pieces of metal, or between metal and another material such as glass, there is a special sealer. Because there are many different types of joints, different types of adhesives and sealers are used in auto body work.

This unit shows different ways to locate and correct water or dust leaks that may occur in an auto body. To *correct* leaks, a repair worker must know about different body sealer products. These include *seam sealer*, *rubber seal*, *caulking compound*, and *undercoating*.

Spot-welded panels, for example, are sealed with a soft, flexible *seam sealer*. This material will correctly seal the panel joint for many years. Figure 9-1 shows

sealer being applied along a body seam to seal it against dust and water leaks.

Rubber seal is used around door jambs and trunk lid openings where the joint will be opened and closed. *Caulking compound* is normally used to stop water leaks. The repair worker in Figure 9-2 is using caulking compound to seal a leak in the luggage compartment. Sometimes, a small leak will develop around a window glass that is otherwise satisfactory. This type of leak may often be stopped with a windshield sealer (Fig. 9-3).

Undercoating is used to seal the underside of an automobile body. In Figure 9-4, a pressurized can of undercoating is being used to spray a new underbody welded seam. This will protect the seam and seal it from water and dust leaks. Undercoating also helps to deaden road noise, making the car quieter.

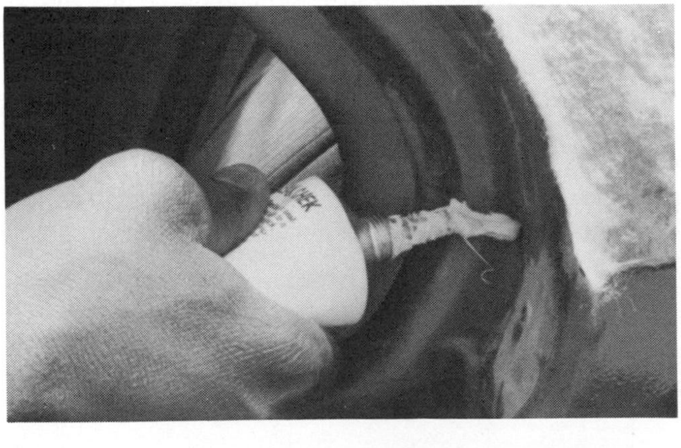

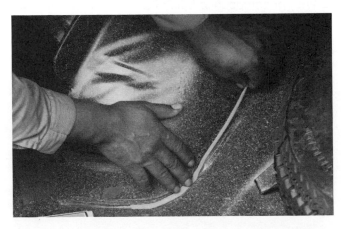

Fig. 9-1. *Using seam sealer to prevent leaks in body seams.*

Fig. 9-2. *Using caulking compound in strip form to seal a trunk leak. (Courtesy of Automotive Trades Division, 3M Company)*

BODY LEAKS

Body leaks (such as air, water, and dust) can be irritating problems for both the vehicle's owner and a service shop. Both new- and used-car dealers are generally given the responsibility of stopping any body leaks in the cars they have sold. The dealer's auto body shop or an independent shop will likely be called on to correct these problems.

Often, water or dust leaks can cause serious damage if they are not found and corrected quickly. Because of this, body workers must know where to look for these leaks and how to stop them.

LEAK TESTS

Several basic tests may be used to find body leaks. When any leak is found, it may be assumed that air, dust, or water could leak in at that point.

Testing for body leaks should be done carefully, so that none is missed. A leak cannot be stopped unless it is *first* determined exactly where it is. There are several basic tests used to find body leaks. These include the water test, chalk test, powder test, paper test, light test, and, finally, air test. More than one test may need to be used to find the source of a difficult leak.

Water Test

The water test should always begin at the *bottom* of the panel or area being tested. The water hose is then moved up the panel slowly, as shown in Figure 9-5. A gentle stream of water should be used, and only one section should be tested at a time.

When making the *water test*, have a helper check from the inside, and mark any places where even the slightest dampness comes through. The water test may be used to find water and dust leaks around the edges of doors, windows, and trunk lids.

Chalk Test

The *chalk test* is used mainly at the rubber seals around door and deck lid openings. All that is needed for this test is a stick of white chalk.

To make the test, first rub the chalk along the rubber seal, as is being done in Figure 9-6. Then close the deck lid or door. Open the door or deck lid, and check to see where the chalk has not been touched. Dust and water could enter the opening at the point.

Powder Test

The *powder test*, like the chalk test, is used along the rubber seals on door and trunk lid openings. To make this test, talcum powder (or other light powder) and a common rubber syringe are needed.

Fig. 9-3. *Windshield sealer can be used to stop small leaks around fixed glass. (Courtesy of Automotive Trades Division, 3M Company)*

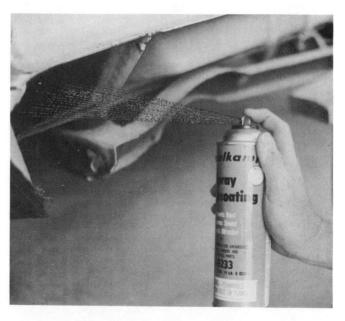

Fig. 9-4. *Sealing and protecting an underbody seam with spray undercoating.*

First, put the powder in the syringe. Close the car door or deck lid and use the syringe to pump the powder in the rubber seal area between the two metal panels (Fig. 9-7). Then, *very slowly* open the deck lid or door to avoid disturbing the powder. Look carefully to see if the powder line is broken. Anywhere that the

Fig. 9-5. *Testing for water leaks should be done with water under low pressure. A high-pressure stream of water would splash, making it more difficult to find the leak.*

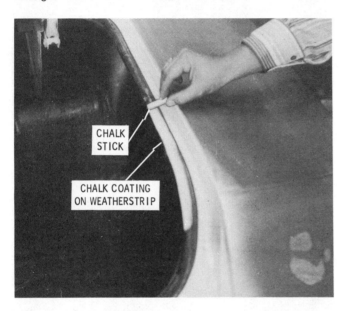

CHALK STICK

CHALK COATING ON WEATHERSTRIP

Fig. 9-6. *The chalk test can be used to locate air and water leaks around door openings.*

powder went all the way *under* or around the rubber seal, a leak is probably present.

Paper Test

The *paper test* is used to see if the rubber seal around a door, deck lid, or window is tight enough. To make the test, use a piece of paper about the size and shape of a dollar bill.

Place the paper strip against the rubber seal and hold it in place while closing the door, window, or deck lid (Fig.9-8). Then slowly pull the paper out. If the rubber seal is tight enough, the paper will have a good drag when pulled out of the closed joint. If the paper pulls out easily (or falls out), the rubber seal is not tight enough. Either the joint needs adjusting or the seal must be replaced.

Light Test

The *light test* is easy to make with a bright flashlight or shop trouble light.

First, place the light where the leak is suspected, as in Figure 9-9. Check for light on the *other* side of the area; for example, inside the trunk. Where light shows through, a leak is present, and water and dust will probably enter.

Air Test

The *air test* is also known as the "sonic test." This test, along with the paper test, is often used for checking high-speed wind noises (air leaks). Moisture and dust can enter wherever air can enter. The test is especially helpful when trying to locate small leaks around windows and doors.

To make the air test, first close the vehicle tightly. Then turn the heater blower to the "high" position. This

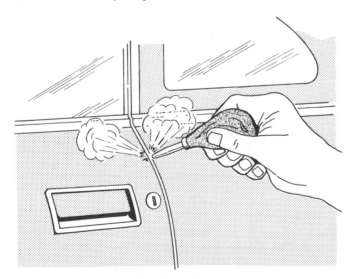

Fig. 9-7. *Powder is blown into a closed joint with a syringe to help locate leaks.*

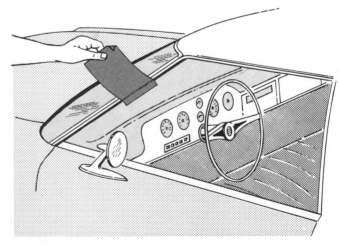

Fig. 9-8. *The* paper *test is useful in finding air leaks around windows and doors.*

will pressurize the inside of the vehicle, since air will be trying to get out. Get out of the vehicle and check for escaping air by feeling along the door and window openings. When a leak is found, mark it with masking tape or chalk. Continue checking until the entire car has been examined. Often, there is more than one leak.

An air test can be made by using masking tape. Check for air noise around window glass or doors by taping around the glass or door edges, leaving one side unmasked. Drive the vehicle and listen for the wind noise. Remove one taped edge at a time and continue driving until the area that is making the noise has been found. This also can be accomplished by taping one edge at a time and driving. When the wind noise *cannot* be heard while driving, the edge that has been taped will be the source of leaking air.

SOURCES OF BODY LEAKS

There are two major types of body leaks: *dust* and *water*. Any body *air* leak may also let in dust and water, depending on where the air leak is located.

Water and dust leaks are more common in certain body areas. Figure 9-10 shows where each type of leak happens most frequently. In the upper part of the vehicle, water leaks are more common. Dust leaks, on the other hand, are more often located in the lower section of the body.

Upper Body Leaks

Leaks that cause owners the most problems are normally in the windshield and back glass areas, around the upper doors, and around the deck lid opening. These upper parts of the vehicle are more exposed to rain, so water leaks are more likely to happen in this area.

Upper Door Glass Leaks. The various joints in the upper part of the door may leak if they are not properly fitted. Leaks may occur where the door and door glass meet or where the door glass and the roof meet. Figure 9-11 shows a typical door glass leak.

There are four major causes of water leaks above the belt line in the upper door glass area. These include:

1. Doors that are not properly fitted.
2. Sealer that does not cover the seams or joints around the nearby metal panels.
3. Space around the glass resulting from improper adjustment.
4. Damaged weather stripping.

Drip Rail Leaks. The drip rail is the *uppermost* place that is likely to leak. It is very susceptible to leaks because the roof panel and the drip rail are spot-welded together. They form a seam that is supposed to drain

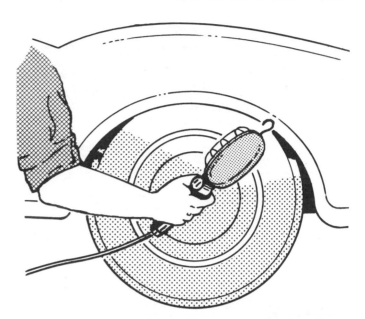

Fig. 9-9. *A trouble light outside the car can aid in finding leaks in the trunk area. Areas where light can be seen from the inside are possible leak locations.*

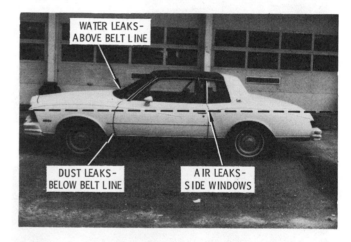

Fig. 9-10. *Areas where different types of leaks occur on the auto body.*

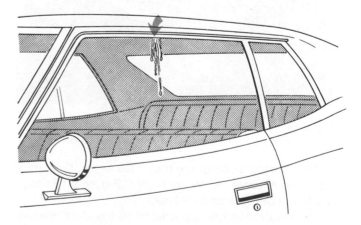

Fig. 9-11. *A typical upper door glass leak.*

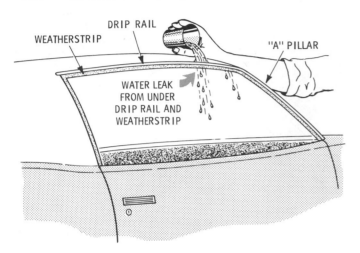

Fig. 9-12. *Testing a drip rail seam for leaks.*

Fig. 9-13. *Sealing small leaks along the drip rail.*

Fig. 9-14. *To test a windshield for leaks, always begin at the bottom, then work up along each side, then across the top.*

water from the sides of the roof. This seam, then, must be properly sealed to prevent leaks. Figure 9-12 shows a drip rail being tested for leaks.

The drip rail is usually welded to the door opening *pillow plate*. This plate is the metal body part that is above the door and is part of the door jamb. The purpose of the drip rail is to keep water that runs off the roof from dripping on passengers as they enter or leave the vehicle. It catches the water and channels it to either the front or rear of the vehicle.

The pillow plate and the drip rail are spot-welded about every ¾ in. (19.0 mm) along the sides of the roof. If there is a break anywhere in the sealer used in this seam, a leak can occur.

When moisture appears on the floor mat near the front of the front door or at the rear of the back door, a thorough check of the drip rail seam must be made. Water may leak in at the middle of the seam and travel along the pillow plate *inside* the body, yet above the door opening. This may cause the leak to appear at the front, middle, or rear door jamb post, or back in the quarter-panel area.

To seal holes along the drip rail, check closely to find the opening causing the leak. Remember, the opening may be at some distance from where the moisture appears in the car. Then, seal the opening with a clear sealer or with seam sealer the same color of the car. This will eliminate the need for repainting the area around the hole. Figure 9-13 shows a drip rail hole being sealed with seam sealer.

Stationary Glass Leaks. Most modern windshields (front glass) or backlights (rear glass) are held in place with a gumlike sealer. They usually have a finished (reveal) molding around the edge of the glass. These moldings are held in place with spring-type clips. The clips are often fastened with metal nails or sheet metal screws. Water can leak in around these fasteners if they are not properly sealed. For this reason, fasteners should be sealed with caulking compound as they are installed. The compound should be placed on the fastener *before* it is driven or screwed into place.

To check for windshield leaks, first run water along the *bottom* of the windshield (Fig. 9-14). Have a helper inside looking for leaks. If the leak does not appear, slowly run the water *up* each side of the windshield (the pillow rails) and then *across* the top of the windshield.

When a leak is found, mark the spot and finish checking the entire windshield. Go completely around the glass area, because there is often more than one leak. Finally, repair leaks as follows:

1. Place protective covers over the working areas in front of and behind the windshield.
2. Remove all the moldings and the wiper blade arms. Use a molding removal tool (Fig. 9-15), as shown in Figure 9-16.
3. Using soap and water, clean around the area where the leak is marked. Clean well beyond the leak area.

4. Trim away any old cement and sealer around the leak.
5. Reseal the complete area with windshield sealer or caulking compound.
6. Check the repair with water *before* replacing the moldings and wiper blades.
7. Replace the moldings and wiper blade arms.
8. Clean the entire work area as needed.

Lower Body Leaks

The section of the vehicle below the belt line is more subject to *dust* leaks than is the upper section. This is because the vehicle's wheels stir up dust from the road. As a vehicle moves along, it creates a *vacuum*. This vacuum helps to pull dust and water into the vehicle.

The lower sections where leaks are most frequently found include:

1. Underbody welded seams.
2. Trunk (deck lid) joints.
3. Quarter panel joints.
4. Moldings.
5. Lower door openings.

Underbody Seam Leaks. There are a number of seams in a vehicle's underbody area. Figure 9-17 shows the location of the seams on a typical vehicle.

The most common cause of underbody leaks is an open place in one of these seams. When the car is involved in a collision or an object strikes the underbody, sealer can be knocked off a seam. This may cause dust and moisture leaks at the seam. Carefully *looking* at the seams will reveal the area where sealer is missing.

To repair underbody leaks, first examine the seams carefully to locate the leak. Then, clean the area with a wire brush. When the dirt, broken sealer, and undercoat have been removed, clean the area with a solvent such as lacquer thinner. Finally, apply seam sealer with a caulking gun, then undercoat the area.

Trunk Leaks. Trunk leaks often are caused by rust-out in the area directly under the rear glass. Moisture is trapped under the reveal molding at the edge of the rear glass and stays there until the metal rusts through (Fig. 9-18). A rust hole will allow water to leak into the trunk. When moisture or dust appear in the trunk of a vehicle, climb into the trunk. Check the area along the bottom of the rear window. If water or dust is entering, rust or dust will appear on the *underside* of the panel.

There are several other places where dust and water may leak into the trunk. Leaks may occur around the taillights, the wheel housing *flanges* (where the inside wheel housing panel and the quarter panel meet), the rubber deck lid seals, and any molding screws or clip holes. Figure 9-19 shows several of these likely trunk

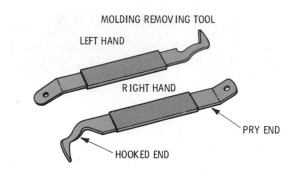

Fig. 9-15. *Window molding removal tools.*

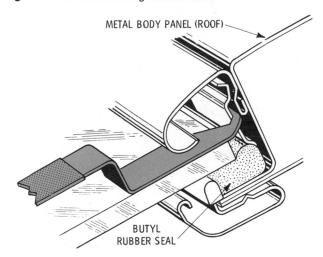

Fig. 9-16. *Using a window molding removal tool.*

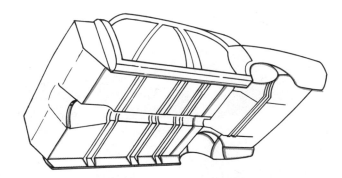

Fig. 9-17. *Locations of typical underbody seams.*

leak locations. A twisted rubber seal, which could cause a leak in the trunk, is shown in Figure 9-20. This could be easily repaired by cementing the seal in place with trim or rubber cement.

Quarter-panel Joint Leaks. Quarter-panel leaks are usually found in one of two places:

1. At the seam where the quarter panel and wheel housing panel meet.
2. At the lower seam where the quarter panel and floor pan are welded together.

Figure 9-21 shows a repair worker testing for leaks at the seam where the quarter panel and floor pan are

Fig. 9-18. *When water is trapped under the molding around fixed glass (Top), rust-out can occur beneath the molding (Bottom). This allows water to leak into the trunk.*

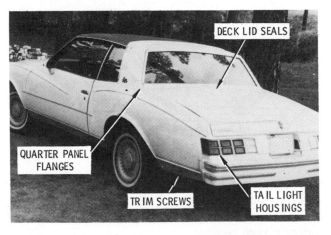

Fig. 9-19. *Areas where water or dust may leak into the trunk.*

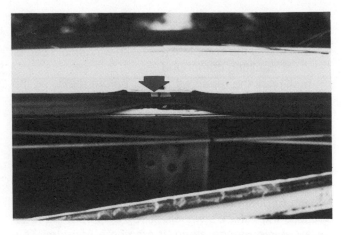

Fig. 9-20. *A twisted rubber trunk seal can allow water to leak in.*

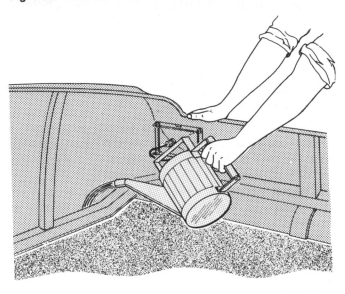

Fig. 9-21. *To test for leaks at the quarter-panel bottom seam, water may be poured into the seam. A small amount of leakage (allowing water to drain out) is acceptable. Sealer should be applied if leakage seems excessive. (Courtesy of Customer Service Division, Ford Motor Company)*

welded together. To stop leaks in this area, clean and reseal the joint with seam sealer and undercoat.

Molding Leaks. Almost all vehicles have some moldings attached with some type of clip. If the *holes* that the clip fasteners go through are not properly sealed with caulking compound, water and dust may enter the car body.

To repair molding leaks, reseal the clip fastener screw hole with sealer (Fig. 9-22).

Door Opening Leaks. There are many places around a door where water and dust may leak into the vehicle. To check for leaks at a door opening, use the water test shown in Figure 9-5. Start at the bottom of the door, then work up each side. Finally, check the top edge of the door. Check the window glass as well as the door. Have a helper inside the vehicle looking for any water leaks. When a leak appears, mark the spot and continue checking the entire door.

Check the rubber seal (weatherstrip) to see if it is cracked, cut, worn, or twisted anywhere near the leak. If it is twisted or sagging, it should be cemented with weatherstrip adhesive (Fig. 9-23). If the weatherstrip is damaged, replace the entire piece with new material.

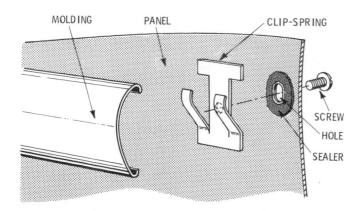

MOLDING PANEL CLIP-SPRING SCREW HOLE SEALER

Fig. 9-22. *When screws are used to install molding clips, sealer should be applied around the screw holes to prevent leaks.*

Fig. 9-23. *To repair an upper door leak, loose molding may be cemented to the door frame.*

If repairing the weatherstrip does not stop the leak, the door or window must be realigned. This type of repair is discussed in the units on body panel aligning and on glass work.

Undercoating. Undercoating sealer is a thick, black, oily material. It is usually applied on only the *outside* of the underbody. It is used to seal parts such as wheel housings, flooring, frame, and outside of the gas tank. Undercoating is useful because it provides insulation that helps keep out moisture and noise. It also helps seal seam joints on the underbody parts.

To undercoat a vehicle or replace parts properly, the material must be applied *evenly*. The undercoat must be a high-quality product that will stay flexible and not crack over long periods of time. Undercoat should be applied to places on the underbody where repairs were made or seam sealer was applied to repair a leak. An aerosol can of undercoat is the easiest method for undercoating these small repair areas.

Undercoating is also used during certain replacement panel work. For example, when a quarter panel is replaced, the underside of the panel and the wheel housing should be given a thorough undercoating. Welding joints on replacement panels should be sealed

Fig. 9-24. *When a door skin has been replaced, the inside of the new panel should be undercoated to help deaden noise and prevent rust.*

with undercoating after seam sealer has been applied. This will help prevent rust and deaden road noises.

Replacement door panels (Fig. 9-24) are sprayed on the inside with undercoat. This is done so that the door will close with a secure "thunk" and sound tight.

Section IV

Using Heat to Work Metal

Oxy-acetylene Welding Equipment

Many times, auto body repairs will need *heat* to be completed. Heat will be needed to soften a metal for welding, bending, and many other jobs. To supply the high heat needed for these jobs, *welding equipment* is used.

The type of welding most often done in an auto body shop is *oxy-acetylene* welding. This welding process creates heat from an *acetylene* flame burning in pure *oxygen*. A typical oxy-acetylene welding outfit is shown in Figure 10-1. Common tasks using the oxy-acetylene equipment include welding or brazing two pieces of thin sheet metal (Fig. 10-2) and cutting a metal panel for a patch repair (Fig. 10-3).

The compressed oxygen and acetylene gases used for the oxy-acetylene process are stored in tall, round tanks called *cylinders*. The gases are held under great pressure in the tanks, the hoses, and other parts of the system. Oxy-acetylene welding equipment is designed to contain these high-pressure gases so that they can be used safely under controlled conditions.

Even though welding equipment today is very safe, repair workers *must* keep in mind that very high heat and very hot flames will be present during *any* oxy-acetylene welding process. There is always the possibility of gas leaks when setting up and using oxy-acetylene equipment. The combination of heat, flames, and leaks is dangerous and can cause an explosion or a fire. For this reason, workers should be especially careful when checking the connections of welding equipment and at all times when the equipment is in use. A fire extinguisher (Fig. 10-4) should be "standard equipment" on or near every welding cart.

This unit describes the different pieces of equipment needed for oxy-acetylene welding and cutting. Also discussed is how the equipment should be set up for safe operation. Later units discuss the correct procedures for using the equipment.

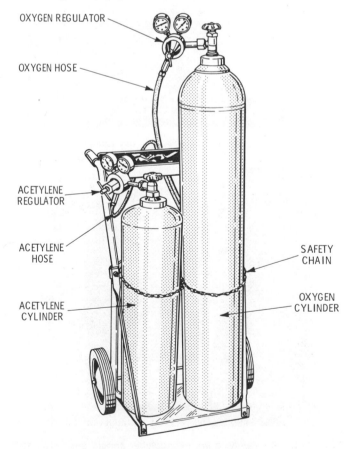

OXYGEN REGULATOR

OXYGEN HOSE

ACETYLENE REGULATOR

ACETYLENE HOSE

ACETYLENE CYLINDER

SAFETY CHAIN

OXYGEN CYLINDER

Fig. 10-1. *A typical oxy-acetylene welding outfit.*

Figure 10-5 shows the major parts of a basic oxy-acetylene welding outfit:

1. The oxygen and acetylene cylinders.
2. The portable carrier cart.

Fig. 10-2. *Brazing thin sheet metal parts with an oxy-acetylene torch.*

Fig. 10-3. *Cutting a body panel with an oxy-acetylene torch.*

Fig. 10-4. *For safety, a fire extinguisher should always be attached to the welding cart.*

3. The regulators.
4. The hoses.
5. The torch blowpipe and tip.

These major parts must be examined and set up carefully, observing *all* safety precautions, before the equipment may be used. The following sections explain the *function* of each major part, any *accessory equipment* used with the part and the correct *procedure* to set up the equipment using each of the parts.

GAS CYLINDERS

Figure 10-6 shows a typical *oxygen* cylinder. When the cylinder is full, the walls may be holding a pressure of over 2,000 psi (13 790 kPa). Oxygen cylinders are made of thick, high-carbon steel conforming to a government standard. Oxygen cylinders are painted either yellow or green for easy identification.

Figure 10-7 pictures a typical *acetylene* cylinder. This cylinder must be especially designed to store a liquid known as *acetone*. The liquid acetone absorbs acetylene gas.

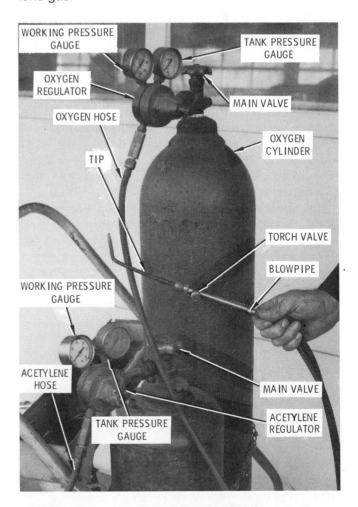

Fig. 10-5. *Parts of the basic oxy-acetylene welding outfit.*

The acetylene gas pressure inside the cylinder may be as high as 250 psi (1 724 kPa). Acetylene cylinders are not hollow, as are oxygen cylinders. Instead, they are filled with *porous* materials such as asbestos or charcoal in a wet, cementlike mixture. When manufactured, the cylinder is *baked* with the material inside. This baking causes the material to form a porous, spongelike mass. Liquid acetone is then added to the cylinder.

When acetylene cylinders are filled, the acetone absorbs the acetylene gas and keeps it stable. This helps prevent any high-pressure pockets of acetylene from forming. Acetylene cylinders should always be stored upright to help avoid any unequal distribution.

Acetylene cylinders have one or more *safety valves* on the ends. One is usually near the main valve (Figs. 10-8 and 10-9). These valves are installed in case fire, upset, or other trouble should cause the pressure inside the cylinder to go too high. In that case, the valves will automatically open to release the gas.

Acetylene cylinders are usually painted either red or black. Black is the more common color. Both oxygen and acetylene cylinders should be firmly chained or otherwise attached to a portable carrier cart when they are to be moved.

Valve Protection Caps

Both oxygen and acetylene cylinders are made with safety caps to protect the valves when the cylinders are stored or shipped. These caps (Figs. 10-6, 10-7, and 10-8) will help protect the valve from breakage if the cylinder falls over. Valve protection caps must not

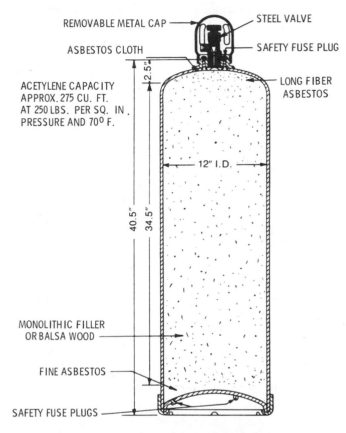

Fig. 10-8. *Cutaway view of an acetylene cylinder.*

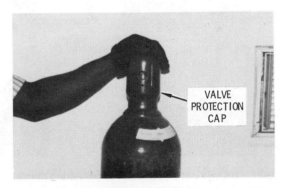

Fig. 10-6. *A valve protection cap installed on an oxygen cylinder.*

Fig. 10-7. *A valve protection cap installed on an acetylene cylinder.*

Fig. 10-9. *A safety valve (fuse plug) on an acetylene cylinder.*

be removed before the cylinder is safely chained to a portable carrier cart. Figure 10-10 shows a worker unscrewing a cap before attaching a regulator.

Carrier Cart

An oxy-acetylene outfit mounted on, and chained to, a carrier cart is shown in Figure 10-1. The carrier cart is a type of two-wheel *truck*. The cart is used to move the cylinders, welding equipment, and tools from place to place in the shop.

A typical cart is made up of a metal frame, a safety chain, two wheels, and an axle for the wheels. A safety chain (Fig. 10-11) is used to hold the cylinders securely on the cart. The chain must be fastened *all* the time by slots, hooks, or nuts and bolts. In Figure 10-12, a worker is chaining a replacement cylinder to the welding cart.

Changing Cylinders

When a cylinder on the cart is empty, it must be replaced. To do this, first be sure to fasten a valve protection cap on the cylinder. Then, move the empty cylinder from the cart.

To move the replacement cylinder to the cart, tip it so that it is on edge, as in Figure 10-13. Then, carefully roll the cylinder to the welding cart. Finally, chain the cylinder to the cart frame.

Caution must always be used when moving a cylinder. Sudden movements might cause a spark that could ignite the gas from a leaking acetylene cylinder. Sudden pressure release (such as from a broken-off valve) can turn the oxygen cylinder into an uncontrolled missile. With so much pressure in an oxygen cylinder, it can break through concrete walls if the valve is broken

off. Severe injury or death could be caused by such a situation.

Clearing the Cylinder Valve

After the cylinder has been installed on the welding cart and securely held with the chain, the cap may be removed. To remove the cap, simply unscrew it in a counter-clockwise direction.

The cylinder valve then may be "cracked" to blow out any dust or dirt in the valve opening and threads where the regulator will be attached. Dirt or other foreign matter might get into the regulator and later cause serious damage or trouble. To "crack" the valve, grasp the cylinder valve handle, as is being done in Figure 10-14. Quickly open and close the valve. After clearing the valve openings, the regulators may be attached.

Fig. 10-11. *Slots are often provided as anchoring points for the safety chains on a welding cart.*

Fig. 10-10. *Removing the valve protection cap from an oxygen cylinder.*

Fig. 10-12. *Chaining a replacement tank to the cart.*

REGULATORS

Figures 10-15 and 10-16 show the *regulators* used in oxy-acetylene welding. One regulator (Fig. 10-15) is used for the *oxygen* cylinder gas. A different regulator (Fig. 10-16) is used for the acetylene cylinder gas. Oxygen regulators may be color-coded *green* for easy identification. Acetylene regulators are often color-coded *red*.

Regulators control the *pressure* of the gases leaving the cylinders and going through the hoses to the welding torch. As the regulator adjusting handle is turned (Fig. 10-17), the *outlet* pressure gauge will show the pressure of the gas leaving the regulator.

The regulator *inlet* pressure gauges (Fig. 10-15 and 10-16) register how much total gas pressure still re-

Fig. 10-14. *"Cracking" the cylinder valve to blow out dust.*

Fig. 10-13. *Cylinders should be carefully rolled from place to place.*

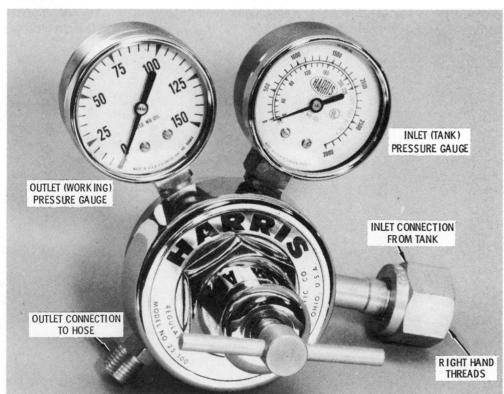

Fig. 10-15. *An oxygen regulator and gauges. Note that the inlet connector has right-hand threads. (Courtesy of Harris Calorific Division, Emerson Electric Company)*

OUTLET (WORKING) PRESSURE GAUGE

INLET (TANK) PRESSURE GAUGE

INLET CONNECTION FROM TANK

OUTLET CONNECTION TO HOSE

RIGHT HAND THREADS

mains in the tank. Whenever the tank valve is opened, gas pressure will pass through the valve to the regulator. The regulator inlet pressure gauge will report how much gas is left in the tank.

Installing Regulators

Each regulator is designed for use with either the oxygen or the acetylene tank. They are *not* interchangeable. The threads on the regulator connections and the cylinder outlets are designed so that the regulators cannot be accidentally connected to the wrong cylinder. This is standard for all manufacturers of welding equipment.

Oxygen Regulator. The threads on the connecting nut of an *oxygen* regulator are *right-hand* threads. These threads will fit the right-hand threads on the oxygen cylinder's outlet valve. Figure 10-18 shows how to install and tighten the oxygen regulator. Use an open-end wrench, and tighten the nut *clockwise*. Before the nut is completely tight, turn the regulator assembly so that the gauges are easy to read. Then, tighten the nut to a snug fit.

Acetylene Regulator. The threads on the acetylene regulator nut and the acetylene cylinder valve are *left-hand* or "reverse" threads. For additional identification, *notches* are cut into the nut on an acetylene regulator, as shown in Figure 10-16. The acetylene regulator should be connected, positioned, and tightened in the same way as the oxygen valve, using an open-end wrench. However, the acetylene connections must be tightened with a *counter-clockwise* motion.

Caution: No part of an oxy-acetylene outfit should ever be lubricated. Do not use oil or grease to lubricate regulator connection threads. These products could become highly explosive when combined with pure oxygen. This could cause an explosion when the torch is in use.

Flash Guards

Because oxygen and acetylene are dangerous gases in the presence of flame, *flash guards* are used (Fig. 10-19). Flash guards are installed between the regulators and the hoses to keep a flame from entering the cylinder. This safety feature should be used on all oxy-acetylene welding units. Figure 10-20 shows how the flash guard is placed between the hose and regulator. In Figure 10-21, the hose is being tightened on the flash guard.

HOSES

After the regulators are attached, the *hoses* may then be connected. First, attach the *green* hose to the *oxygen* cylinder, and tighten the connection snugly with an open-end wrench (Fig. 10-21). Then, attach the other end of the green oxygen hose to the welding blowpipe and tighten it. The red acetylene hose is attached to the regulator and the torch body in the same way. Remember that the acetylene hose connections and threads are left hand, or "reverse." Finally, check both the oxygen and acetylene connections at the blowpipe to be certain that they are tight (Fig. 10-22).

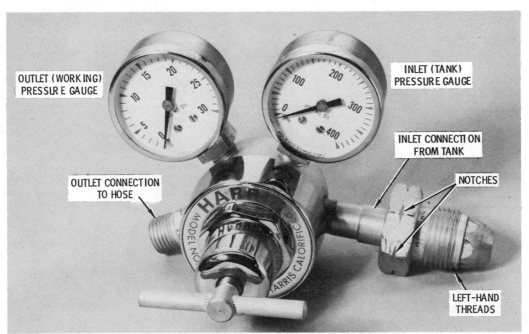

OUTLET (WORKING) PRESSURE GAUGE

INLET (TANK) PRESSURE GAUGE

OUTLET CONNECTION TO HOSE

INLET CONNECTION FROM TANK

NOTCHES

LEFT-HAND THREADS

Fig. 10-16. *An acetylene regulator and gauges. Note that the inlet connector has left-hand threads and is notched for easy identification. (Courtesy of Harris Calorific Division, Emerson Electric Company)*

Fig. 10-17. *Turning the adjusting handle to regulate gas pressure from the tank to the hose and torch.*

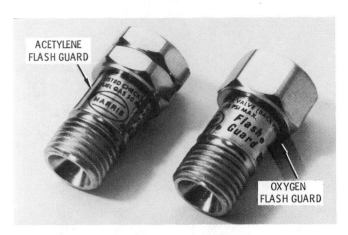

Fig. 10-19. *Flash guards, installed between the hoses and the regulators, are important safety features. (Courtesy of Harris Calorific Division, Emerson Electric Company)*

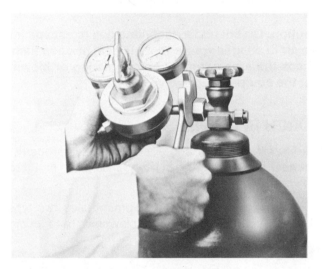

Fig. 10-18. *Installing the oxygen regulator. A special wrench is used. (Courtesy of Victor Equipment Company)*

Fig. 10-20. *Attaching the oxygen hose to the regulator outlet.*

Purging the Hoses

After the regulators and hoses are connected, the hoses must be purged (cleaned out). To do this, the tank valves and regulators are opened briefly to clear any dirt out of the regulators and hoses. Both the oxygen and acetylene assemblies are purged in the same way.

To purge the assemblies properly, follow these directions separately for each cylinder:

1. Loosen the regulator pressure valve. Turn the valve handle *counter-clockwise* until it is loose and easy to turn. This helps protect the regulator from possible damage when the cylinder valve is opened.

Fig. 10-21. *Tightening the oxygen hose connection.*

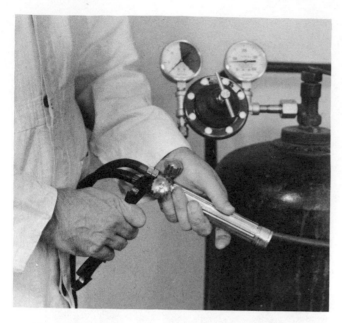

Fig. 10-22. *Attaching the oxygen and acetylene hoses to the torch blowpipe. (Courtesy of Harris Calorific Division, Emerson Electric Company)*

2. Open the cylinder valve (Fig. 10-23). This allows the gas to leave the cylinder and enter the regulator. The cylinder pressure gauge will rise, indicating how much gas is in the tank. Open the *oxygen* cylinder valve *all the way*, but open the *acetylene* cylinder valve only *one-half* turn.

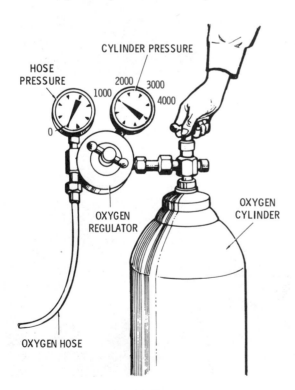

Fig. 10-23. *Opening the cylinder valve to purge the hose.*

3. With the cylinder valve opened, *tighten* the regulator pressure valve. Turn the valve handle *clockwise* until gas begins coming out of the hose.
4. When gas comes out of the hose, turn the *torch valve* off. This will shut off the gas flow from the end of the torch or blowpipe.
5. There now will be gas pressure throughout the system. Use a mixture of soapy water over all the regulator and hose connections to check for leaks (Fig. 10-24). Leaks will cause bubbles in the soapy solution. Tighten any connections that leak. If no leaks are found, reopen the torch valves.
6. Turn off the gas at the *cylinder* valve. This will cause gas to stop flowing through the regulator and hose.
7. Repeat Step 1. Should any gas leak from the cylinder valve, this will prevent it from flowing through the regulator and hose.

Caution: Do not allow acetylene gas to escape into the air in an area where there is heat or open flame. Check the area carefully before testing or blowing out the equipment.

TORCH BLOWPIPES

To *mix* the oxygen and acetylene gases properly, a chamber is needed. This mixing takes place in a torch *blowpipe*.

Basically, oxy-acetylene equipment uses two types of torch blowpipes: *welding* blowpipes and *cutting*

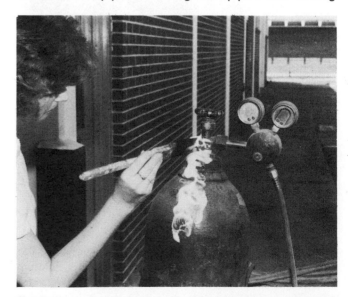

Fig. 10-24. *Using a soapy mixture and paintbrush to test connections for gas leaks.*

Fig. 10-25. *A typical welding torch assembly. (Courtesy of Harris Calorific Division, Emerson Electric Company)*

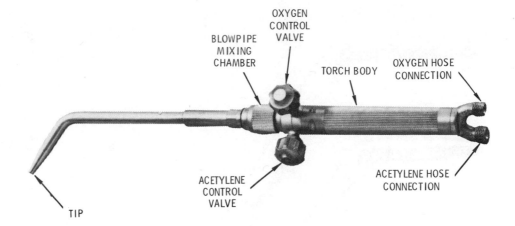

Fig. 10-26. *A typical cutting torch assembly. (Courtesy of Harris Calorific Division, Emerson Electric Company)*

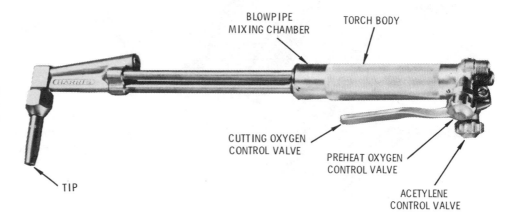

blowpipes. Figures 10-25 and 10-26 show these two pieces of equipment. Welding torch blowpipes and tips are used for welding metal parts. Cutting torch blowpipes and tips are used to cut metal.

Torch blowpipes are made of copper, special steels, or aluminum. They are lightweight and often have ridged handles to keep them from turning in the worker's hand.

Torch Blowpipe Parts

Both torch blowpipes have three main parts: the oxygen and acetylene control valves, the mixing chamber, and the tip. A *cutting* torch also will have a cutting oxygen control valve.

The *control valves* are used to meter the amounts of oxygen and acetylene that go into the blowpipe's *mixing chamber*. The gases mix in the chamber and exit the torch at the *tip* where they are burned in a high-temperature flame.

Either type of torch blowpipe may be used with various tips. Figures 10-27 and 10-28 show two typical *tip sets*. Detailed information on using the tips is given in later units.

Installing the Torch Blowpipes

Each torch blowpipe has two threaded inlets where the hoses are attached, as shown in Figure 10-25. The *oxygen* hose fits the inlet with "normal" *right-hand* threads. The *acetylene* hose fits the inlet with "reverse" *left-hand* threads. Some torches have the letters "oxy" and "act" stamped or cast near the inlets. Other models may have the inlet connections color-coded green for oxygen and red for acetylene.

To install the torch blowpipe assemblies, tighten hoses into the correct inlets. Use an open-end wrench to tighten the connections snugly. The oxygen hose connection must be tightened *clockwise* and the acetylene connection, *counter-clockwise*.

WELDING TIPS

When a new oxy-acetylene outfit is purchased, there are usually several tips included. These include *welding tips* and *cutting tips*. Cutting tips may be used with either a cutting attachment (Fig. 10-29) or a standard cutting torch (Fig. 10-26). Torch tips and cutting attachments should be screwed onto the torch blowpipe *hand-tight only*.

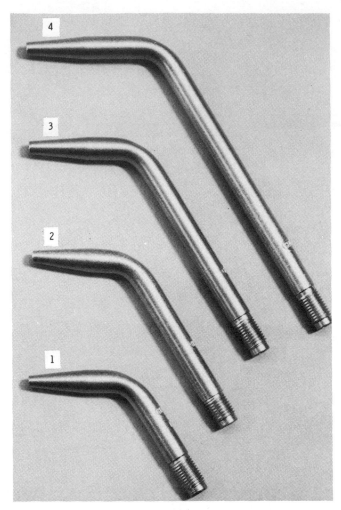

Fig. 10-27. *Some typical welding tips. The numbers indicate sizes. (Courtesy of Harris Calorific Division, Emerson Electric Company)*

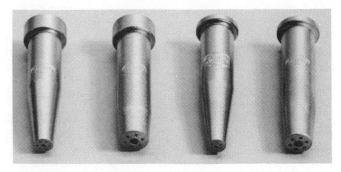

Fig. 10-28. *Typical cutting torch tips. (Courtesy of Harris Calorific Division, Emerson Electric Company)*

Fig. 10-29. *A cutting attachment which can be uséd to replace the welding tip on an oxy-acetylene torch body. (Courtesy of Harris Calorific Division, Emerson Electric Company)*

WELDING ACCESSORIES

To weld or cut metal safely and successfully, several *accessories* are needed. These include the tools used to light and clean the torch properly (Fig. 10-30). Additional tools and accessories are needed to use the equipment safely and reduce the chance of injury. These include welding goggles and gloves.

Torch Lighter

Figure 10-30 shows a torch *lighter* or *striker*. This striker uses *flints* that may be replaced as they wear down. The flints create the spark for lighting the torch. The lighter has a *cup* under the striker bar. This cup traps acetylene when the torch acetylene valve is opened (Fig. 10-31). Squeezing the striker handle causes a spark, lighting the acetylene gas.

Caution: Matches and cigarette lighters should not be used to light an oxy-acetylene torch. If the torch is lit with these open flames, the worker's hands can be burned. Also, an open flame may travel up the blowpipe, causing an explosion at the shut-off valves. This will damage the O-ring seals, allowing the torch to become leaky and unsafe.

Tip Size

Welding tips used for work in a body shop are sized #1 through #8. The tips normally used for welding thinner body sheet metal are #1, #2, and #3.

The smaller the tip number, the smaller the opening, or *orifice*. The size of the orifice determines the size of the welding flame and the amount of heat that the flame produces.

Table 6 shows how the thickness of the metal being welded determines the tip size and the gas pressures needed. Metal thickness may be identified by its *gauge number*. The *larger* the gauge number, the *thinner* the metal. For example, a 16-gauge metal is about 1/16 in. (1.6 mm) thick; 28-gauge metal is about 1/64 in. (0.4 mm) thick. The gas pressures in the table show the oxygen and acetylene regulator pressures needed at the torch.

Table 6

Oxygen and Acetylene Pressures for Different Welding Jobs

Tip No.	Thickness of Metal— In.	(mm)	Thickness of Metal— gauge	Oxygen & Acetylene Pressure[1,2]— psi	(kPa)	Acetylene Flow[2]— cfh	(L/min)	Oxygen Flow[2]— cfh	(L/min)
00	1/64	(0.3)	28	1	(6.9)	0.1	(0.005)	0.1	(0.005)
0	1/32	(0.7)	22	1	(6.9)	0.4	(0.189)	0.4	(0.189)
1	1/16	(1.5)	16	1	(6.9)	1	(0.472)	1.1	(0.519)
2	3/32	(2.3)	13	2	(15.8)	2	(0.943)	2.2	(1.037)
3	1/8	(3.1)	11	3	(20.7)	8	(3.771)	8.8	(4.149)
4	3/16	(4.7)		4	(27.6)	17	(8.014)	18	(8.486)
5	1/4	(6.3)		5	(34.5)	25	(11.786)	27	(12.729)
6	5/16	(7.9)		6	(41.4)	34	(16.029)	37	(17.443)
7	3/8	(9.5)		7	(48.3)	43	(20.271)	47	(22.157)
8	1/2	(12.7)		8	(55.2)	52	(24.514)	57	(26.871)
9	5/8	(15.8)		9	(62.1)	59	(27.814)	64	(30.171)
10	3/4	(19.0)		10	(68.9)	67	(31.586)	73	(34.414)

[1]*Pressures and consumptions are approximately correct for both separable tips with appropriate mixers and for tip-mixer assemblies.*
[2]*Gas pressures should be increased slightly for hose lengths greater than 25 ft (7.6 m).*
Courtesy of Canadian Liquid Air

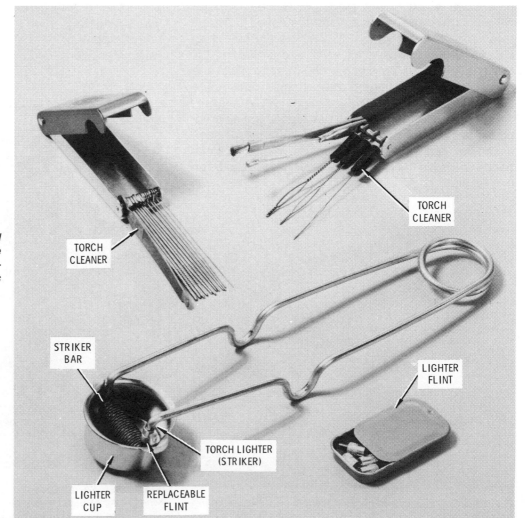

Fig. 10-30. *Accessories used for lighting and cleaning the torch. (Courtesy of Harris Calorific Division, Emerson Electric Company)*

TORCH CLEANER

TORCH CLEANER

STRIKER BAR

LIGHTER FLINT

TORCH LIGHTER (STRIKER)

LIGHTER CUP

REPLACEABLE FLINT

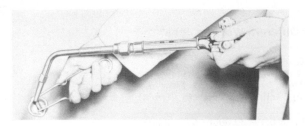

Fig. 10-31. *Opening the acetylene valve to fill the striker cap with acetylene gas. (Courtesy of Victor Equipment Company)*

Tip Cleaners

Tip cleaners are used when a welding tip becomes clogged with dirt or soot. This causes a poor welding flame. Most sets of tip cleaners have a file to smooth and shape worn or damaged welding tips. Two sets of slightly different tip cleaners and a file are shown in Figure 10-30.

Some tip cleaners have a grooved surface, whereas others are made of two pieces of twisted wire. Tip cleaners are moved in and out of the orifice to scrape away soot or dirt (Fig. 10-32). The *correct size* of tip cleaner should be used for each size of welding tip. Using a too small tip cleaner could fail to clean the orifice properly. Too large a cleaner could damage the tip.

Frequent use of tip cleaners is a good safety practice. If a tip becomes partly blocked by dirt or soot, *flashback* can occur. This happens when the flame backs up *inside* the torch or tip. A dangerous explosion can result.

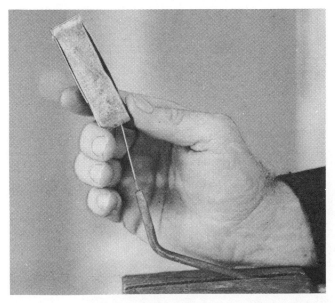

Fig. 10-32. *Cleaning a torch tip. Cleaners must be used carefully and inserted straight into the tip to prevent damage.*

Safety Equipment

Safety is a very important consideration when welding or cutting. Safety precautions must always be followed when setting up a welding torch. Leaks, for example, can be a special problem around the acetylene regulator connections and hoses.

Safety equipment must always be used during welding and cutting. *Safety goggles* and *leather gloves* (Fig. 10-33) protect a worker using the torch. Torch *lighters*, discussed above, provide a safe method to light the torch. Tip *cleaners*, also discussed earlier, keep the torch tip clean and free of dirt or soot. Finally, a good *fire extinguisher* will help control any trouble that might happen while using the torch.

Safety Goggles. Tinted *safety goggles*, like those being used in Figure 10-33, must always be used when either welding or cutting. This is because the torch gives off ultraviolet rays that can cause eye damage.

Gloves. Leather *gloves* should be used when working with a torch, especially during cutting. Sparks from molten metal can cause serious burns. Gloves will help prevent these. Also, gloves will help prevent burns should you accidentally touch hot metal after welding or cutting. Properly using safety equipment helps prevent welding accidents and injuries.

Fig. 10-33. *Welding goggles and gloves should always be worn when using oxy-acetylene equipment. (Courtesy of Harris Calorific Division, Emerson Electric Company)*

Oxy-acetylene Welding and Cutting

Welding is the process of joining two pieces of metal by applying heat and, sometimes, pressure. A welding job on a mild steel panel is being done in Figure 11-1. Oxy-acetylene welding is also known as *gas welding*, and, in some areas, *torch welding*. Oxy-acetylene welding equipment may be moved from place to place easily and, because of its flexible hoses, can be used in almost any position.

Oxy-acetylene equipment may be used to weld, heat, or cut metal. Figure 11-1 shows a welder using an oxy-acetylene torch to *weld* two pieces of metal, whereas Figure 11-2 shows a torch being used to *cut* metal. The main purpose of an oxy-acetylene welder in a *body* shop is to weld and cut *thin* sheet metal. These are jobs that cannot be easily done with an *arc* welder. Oxy-acetylene welding equipment is economical and safe and does a good job on most metals. Its simplicity makes it easy to learn to use.

OXY-ACETYLENE WELDING PRINCIPLES

Auto body repair workers must be good welders of thin sheet metal. Welding heat will melt thin sheet metal fast [a neutral flame has a temperature of 5900°F (3260°C) at the torch tip]. If this heat is not carefully controlled, the metal will warp and cause extra work for the mechanic. Generally, it is harder to control the heat and keep the metal from warping on *low-crown* metal (panels with low or slight curves) than on *high-crown* metal. Door panels, quarter panels, and lower fender parts may be problem-causing, low-crown sheet metal areas. When welding on these panels, warpage will be harder to control.

When oxy-acetylene welding, the *thickness* of the

metal being welded must be taken into account. The metal thickness will partly determine the tip and filler

Fig. 11-1. *Using an oxy-acetylene torch to weld metal.*

Fig. 11-2. *Using a cutting torch on mild steel. (Courtesy of Victor Equipment Company)*

rod sizes needed. The gas pressures needed are also determined by the thickness of the metal.

Most body shop welding is done on thin metal, so the torch welding tip and welding rod must be small. A #00, #0, #1, #2, or #3 tip is used for most auto body panel repair. Figure 11-3 shows several sizes of welding tips, and Figure 11-4 shows an ⅛ in. (3.2 mm) welding rod. For most auto body work, the welding rod sizes used are ¹⁄₁₆ to ⅛ in. (1.6 to 3.2 mm) in diameter. Tip and gas pressure recommendations for common metal thicknesses were shown in Table 6.

Generally, the gauges on the oxygen and acetylene regulators should be adjusted to read the same pressures during common welding jobs. The regulator pressure is set by turning the valve handle. Most of the light sheet metal welding in a body shop may be done with 5 psi (34.5 kPa) from each regulator.

There are exceptions to all rules. Welding is a skill that is handed down from one person to another or is learned by "trial and error." Not all good welders will use the same tip size and regulator pressures on the same thickness of metal. However, most better welders (or those trained in technical schools) will often use the recommendations shown in Table 6.

Lighting the Torch

The correct procedure for lighting the torch should always be followed. "Shortcut" methods may be unsafe and should never be used. Setting up and lighting the torch will be quick, easy, and *safe* if the following directions are used.

First, be sure the equipment is set up properly, as shown in Figure 11-5. Then, select and install the proper tip for the metal thickness being used. Finally, open the oxygen and acetylene cylinder valves, and set the correct pressure readings on the regulator gauges.

Welding Goggles. Be sure to put on *welding goggles* before lighting the torch. Place the goggles on your forehead, so they may be easily pulled down over your eyes after the torch is lit. Goggles must *always* be worn when welding is being done.

With goggles in place, open the torch acetylene valve from ⅛ to ¼ turn (Fig. 11-6). Then, hold the torch tip in the striker. Make a spark by squeezing the striker (Fig. 11-7). Be sure to use a friction lighter (striker) to light the torch, *not* a match or cigarette lighter. Lighting the torch can be dangerous if the proper tool is not used.

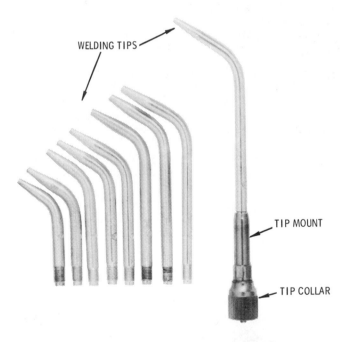

WELDING TIPS

TIP MOUNT

TIP COLLAR

Fig. 11-3. *Different welding tips are needed for different jobs. (Courtesy of Harris Calorific Division, Emerson Electric Company)*

Fig. 11-4. *A common ⅛ in. (3.2 mm) welding rod.*

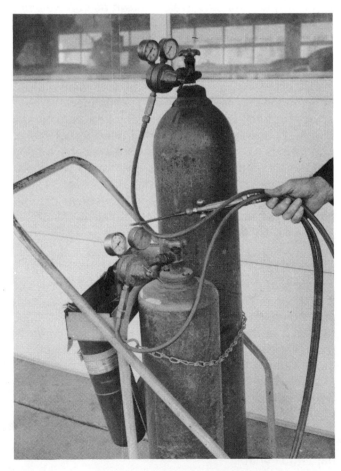

Fig. 11-5. *A properly set-up welding outfit, ready for use.*

The acetylene will burn with a bright, bushy-orange flame. This flame *looks* violent but actually is not hot enough for welding. To adjust this flame properly, open the acetylene valve slightly until the flame "jumps" off the end of the tip (Fig.11-8), leaving an air gap. Then, *close* the acetylene valve slightly until the flame *just returns* to the tip.

Next, *slowly* open the oxygen valve until the acetylene flame starts to "calm down," becoming smaller *and* hotter (Fig.11-9). Finally, the orange acetylene flame will become part of the sharply defined, intense blue inner cone of the *neutral flame* (Fig.11-10).

Flame Properties

A *neutral* oxy-acetylene welding flame may be used on almost all types of metal. It should not be used, however, for bright metal parts such as door handles, aluminum trim, or chrome bumpers. Because of the neutral flame's wide use, one of the more important steps in welding is correctly adjusting the control valves for such a flame.

Neutral Flame. The *neutral* flame gets its name from the fact that it does *not* change the chemical composition of the metal being melted. That is, it does not add either carbon or oxygen to the molten metal.

With the neutral flame, the *form* of the metal is changed from a solid to a liquid, but the chemical makeup stays the same. The correct amounts of oxygen and acetylene are being burned in the neutral flame, so there is no "extra" carbon (acetylene) or oxygen to enter the molten metal.

A correctly adjusted neutral flame will cause the metal to melt quickly, so that the pieces may be properly welded together. When the flame is too cool (has too much acetylene), it will put unburned carbon into the

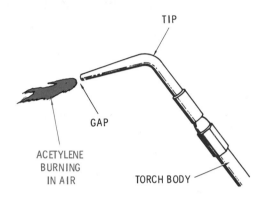

Fig. 11-8. *Opening the acetylene control valve too far will cause the flame to "jump off" the torch tip.*

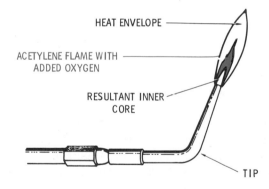

Fig. 11-9. *As oxygen is added, the orange acetylene flame will begin to disappear into the bright blue inner cone of the oxy-acetylene flame.*

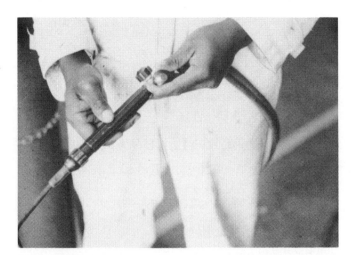

Fig. 11-6. *Open the acetylene control valve slightly before lighting the torch.*

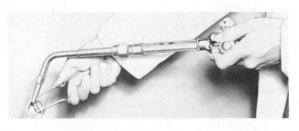

Fig. 11-7. *Squeeze the striker to light the pure acetylene. (Courtesy of Victor Equipment Company)*

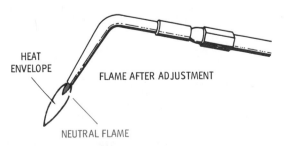

Fig. 11-10. *As the oxygen valve is opened further, the acetylene flame completely disappears into the blue inner cone. This is a neutral flame.*

molten metal. When this happens, the metal is *carbonized* (sometimes called *carburized*), and the pieces will not weld together properly. On the other hand, if there is too much *oxygen* in the flame, it will "oxidize" the metal. This may cause the weld to crack in the center, because the weld metal will be too hard when it cools.

The *length* of the neutral flame's inner cone is measured and known as **X** length. For this reason, it is known as an **X** flame. The **X** neutral flame is easily identified. It does not have any acetylene feather on the inner cone. It also has a smooth, round head on its inner cone and is fairly quiet (when compared with the hissing sound of the oxidizing flame discussed later).

Other torch flames can be measured by comparing them with the neutral flame. An *oxidizing* flame is present when more oxygen is added to a neutral flame, and the inner cone becomes pointed and shorter (Fig. 11-11). An oxidizing flame is shorter than a neutral flame and produces a hissing sound.

When *acetylene* is added to a neutral flame, it becomes a *carbonizing* flame. A carbonizing flame is present when a flame "feather" appears between the cone and the outer flame, as in Figure 11-9. This feather indicates that excess acetylene is causing too much carbon in the flame. The feather is two to three times as long (**2X** or **3X**) as the inner cone.

Oxidizing Flame. Figure 11-11 shows an *oxidizing flame*. This is not a good welding flame. An oxidizing flame has too much oxygen, causing chemical changes as excess oxygen is added to the molten metal. This excess oxygen causes the metal to boil, flame, and spark, making welding dangerous and difficult. An oxidizing flame has a violent hissing sound.

An oxidizing flame weakens the weld area by oxidizing the edges of the metal being welded. Welding with an oxidizing flame often leaves a hairline crack in the metal when the weld cools. Sometimes, a close inspection with a magnifying glass will show the small crack.

An oxidizing flame *does* have some good uses. For example, an oxidizing flame may be used to cut the thin metal. This saves the time needed to change to a cutting tip. However, this type of flame is not recommended for cutting thick metal or for a long cutting job.

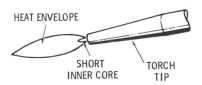

Fig. 11-11. *An oxidizing flame has a shorter inner cone than a neutral flame and produces a hissing sound.*

Carbonizing Flame. Figure 11-9 shows what a *carbonizing* flame looks like. This flame is also known as a *carburizing* flame or a *reducing* flame. It is produced when there is too much acetylene in the mixture. The acetylene deposits excess carbon in the melted metal. This type of flame makes welding difficult because it is not as hot as is a neutral flame. This flame will not melt the metal as easily.

A carbonizing flame *is* used for some oxy-acetylene jobs. When brazing or soldering, for example, a slightly carbonizing flame may be used. A flame with a feather one or two times (**1X** or **2X**) longer than the neutral cone is used when *brazing* depending on the thickness of the metal. Soldering is often done with a flame feather three times (**3X**) as long as the neutral flame cone.

Safety Review

When the torch has been properly set up and safely started, it may be used for practice welding. Practicing oxy-acetylene welding will be safe if these six basic safety rules are followed:

1. The connections of a welding outfit must never be lubricated.
2. The acetylene valve must always be turned *on first* and *off last*.
3. Welding must be done in an area free of fire or smoke.
4. Welding or torch work must be done with *goggles* for eye protection.
5. The torch should always be turned off immediately after use.
6. When welding is finished, the cylinder valves must be closed.

BASIC OXY-ACETYLENE WELDING

After lighting the torch, the first step in any welding operation is to make a puddle of molten metal. Then, the torch may be used to melt puddles of molten metal across a piece of flat steel. This is known as *running the bead*. This most basic type of welding practice is being done in Figure 11-12.

When running the bead has been done successfully, welding *rod* can be added to the puddle for further practice. Welding rod gives the bead the buildup necessary for a strong weld. Figure 11-13 shows the torch and rod positions necessary for practicing welding with a welding rod.

Often, practice panels need to be *tack-welded* before practice (Fig.11-14). This is done *first* so that the practice pieces will remain in place while the bead is run.

Practice Flame. A *neutral flame* always must be used when practice welding, either with or without welding rod. A neutral flame will help keep the molten metal from popping and throwing hot metal during practice. During practice, the *tip* should be held in a position where the hot metal will not block it (Fig.11-13).

Bead Running

The easiest oxy-acetylene welding technique to practice is *bead running*. The first step toward bead running is to be able to make and recognize a molten metal *puddle*. The puddle is formed when the torch flame has melted the metal. Then, you must *guide* the puddle in the direction in which the metal is to be welded or the bead is to be run.

To form a puddle, hold the neutral flame *cone* about 1/16 to 1/4 in. (1.6 to 6.4 mm) from the metal until the metal melts into a bright orange puddle.

Then, use a circular tip motion, and slowly move along the panel to melt new metal. This will form beads of solid metal as the torch passes by, as shown in Figure 11-12. This movement causes the molten metal to "run" in a straight line of beads and is, therefore, known as bead running.

Adding Welding Rod. A very important part of bead running is adding *welding rod* to the bead. To do this, first form a puddle of molten metal. Then, move the torch tip in a circular pattern over the puddle while slowly adding and melting filler rod. Tilt the torch back to about 45° above the metal. The rod should be held in the opposite direction at about the same angle (Fig. 11-15). Oxy-acetylene welding can be done without a rod, but this may leave low and weak places in the bead.

Welding Two Pieces. When practice welding *two* pieces of metal, a space is left between the two pieces about as wide as the filler rod being used (Fig. 11-16). For example, if a 1/16 in. (1.6 mm) rod is being used, there

should be a 1/16 in. (1.6 mm) space between the two pieces of metal.

Problems. If the torch pops and cracks even though the flame is neutral, *both* the oxygen and the acetylene valves should be opened more. The flame is too cool, causing trouble when trying to melt the metal. When this happens, you may be tempted to push the cone too far into the molten metal. This will cause a pop, throwing molten metal out of the weld in a small explosion. This condition can cause a serious torch problem known as *flashback*.

A *flashback* happens when the flame "backs up" into the mixing chamber of the torch. The flame actually begins to burn *inside* the torch, instead of at the tip. This is very dangerous. When a flashback occurs, the torch must be shut off *immediately*. This will keep the tip from getting too hot. Tips are made of brass and quickly become very hot. Also, it will keep the flame from backing up into the hoses and possibly causing a serious explosion.

Torch Movement

When simple *bead running* with a filler rod has been mastered, additional practice will include different welding jobs and more experience in *torch movement*. When the metal has been melted and a puddle formed, for example, move the torch from side to side approximately 1/8 in. (3.2 mm) at a time to weld thin body sheet

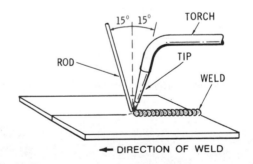

Fig. 11-13. *Using a welding rod and torch for practice.*

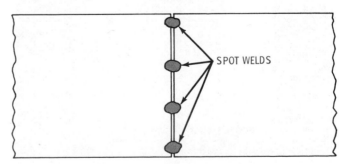

Fig. 11-14. *Tack welding may be used to hold the practice pieces in position.*

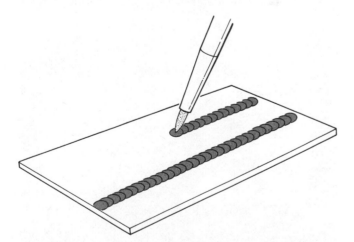

Fig. 11-12. Running the bead *is the first, and easiest, form of welding practice.*

metal. Make the flame curve around the end of the weld and filler rod as it goes from side to side, in a shape like the letter **C**. While moving the flame from side to side, move forward along the weld line very slowly. Be sure that the *sides* of the weld bead overlap the sides of the panels being welded.

Some welders move the torch in a circular motion, rather than in the side-to-side, C-shape motion. The circular motion is also a good technique. Practice both methods of torch movement to determine the one that is best for you. If a method is comfortable and you are able to make good welds with it, then it is a good method to use.

Welding With Filler Rod

To practice fusing (welding two pieces of metal together), have all the needed equipment and materials nearby, including the correct welding rod. Then, position and properly space the pieces of metal. Tack-weld the pieces to prevent them from spreading apart while welding. Space the "tacks" about 1 in. (25.4 mm) apart.

With the pieces positioned and tacked, start welding from the left side. Bring the torch almost straight down on the end of the joint, heating the metal to form a

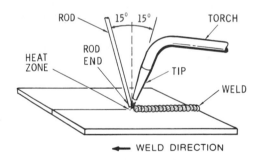

Fig. 11-15. *Adding filler metal from the welding rod to the molten metal puddle.*

Fig. 11-16. *When welding thicker metals, the pieces should be spaced the width of the welding rod apart.*

puddle. As the puddle begins to form, tilt the torch back in the weld direction about 45° (Fig. 11-13). Hold the tip about ¹⁄₁₆ to ¼ in. (1.6 to 6.4 mm) away from the work just after forming the puddle.

Place the filler rod at the *front* edge of the puddle at about a 45° angle to the metal. Keep the flame in a position so that the puddle remains hot. The molten metal at the front edge of the puddle can be used to melt the filler rod.

Move the torch tip and filler rod back and forth so that the molten puddle and filler rod build up a weld bead down the joint. Remember to move the torch tip in a slightly curved, C-shape motion. Of course, the torch must be moved backward slightly, and the filler rod must be moved a little each time the tip goes across the molten puddle. The filler rod must be moved down as it melts into the joint.

Puddle Control. To control the heat so that the molten metal does not melt down *through* the panel, raise or lower the tip as needed. When the metal in the puddle gets too hot, raise the tip.

The puddle heat also is controlled by the *angle* at which the tip is tilted. Tilt the torch *backward* (toward the metal) to keep the hot metal from melting holes in the panel. Tilting the torch backward also helps keep the puddle molten.

After a practice welding job is completed, check the *back* side of the weld to make sure of good penetration. Figure 11-17 shows the back side of a partially completed weld. Notice that there is an open area in the joint where the weld is yet to be made.

Fig. 11-17. *A partially completed weld, seen from the back side.*

Welding Without Filler Rod

Two pieces of metal may also be welded together *without* using a filler rod. A weld made without filler rod can be neat, clean, solid, and strong. Welding without a rod can be as easy as welding with a rod. To do this, first position the two pieces of metal. Overlap the edges on which the weld will be made (Fig.11-18). The overlap should be at least the width of a welding rod, since the overlapped area takes the place of the rod.

After overlapping the two pieces, tack-weld them in position. (If you are left handed, it will probably be easier to work from right to left.) When forming a puddle for the tack welding, aim the torch more toward the bottom piece of metal, as in Figure 11-18. This is done because the wide bottom piece of metal is harder to melt than is the edge of the top piece. Thus, the torch should be aimed to equalize the melting time needed for both pieces of metal.

Procedure. When making a weld without rod, hold the neutral flame about 1/16 to 1/4 in. (1.6 to 6.4 mm) from the joint to form *most* of the puddle on the bottom piece. Hold the torch at approximately the angle shown in Figure 11-18. When the puddle forms, move the torch back and forth across the edge of the top piece of metal to fuse it with the molten lower piece. Keep in mind that the thin edge of the upper piece will melt more quickly than the thicker surface of the lower piece. For this reason, the torch must be pointed at the lower piece during most of this weld.

WELDING POSITIONS

Auto body repair workers must be able to weld metal in several *positions*. The four basic positions include: *flat*, *horizontal*, *vertical*, and *overhead*. When you have mastered the processes of bead running and simple welds, you will have little problem welding in the different positions.

Flat Weld

A *flat* weld is made whenever the torch tip is pointed *downward* during welding (Fig.11-13). Flat welding is almost always used when a panel is being repaired *off* the vehicle. Flat welding is usually the easiest position to learn.

Horizontal Weld

The *horizontal* position is the one that will be used more on the *side* of an auto body. Some horizontal welding must be done during almost all panel replacements. The torch and rod are pointed *up*, to control the puddle and keep it from running down (Fig. 11-19).

Vertical Weld

Figure11-20 shows how *vertical* welding is done up and down on a panel. Nearly all panel installations, especially on the sides of a vehicle, will require *some* vertical welding. Although this type of weld is not difficult to make, it does require slightly different techniques. First, welding is normally done from the bottom to the top. Second, the torch and filler rod are held closer together, with the torch on the bottom. See Figure 11-20 for the angles to be used when welding in the *vertical* position.

Overhead Weld

Making good welds in the *overhead* position (Fig. 11-21) is one of the hardest welding jobs to do. The area being welded is often in a difficult place to reach. A danger during overhead welding is that *burns* can be suffered as a result of sparks or molten metal dripping from the weld puddle. For this reason, always position yourself to *one side* of the immediate weld puddle. Notice the correct angles for the torch tip and filler rod in Figure 11-22.

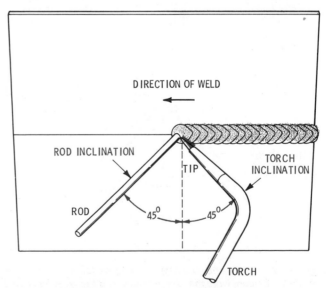

Fig. 11-19. *Torch and welding rod angles used for welding in the* horizontal *position.*

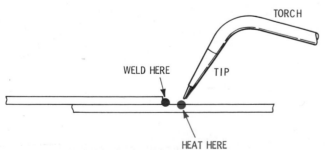

Fig. 11-18. *Directing the heat of the flame toward the larger area of the base metal will help metal melt evenly along the joint.*

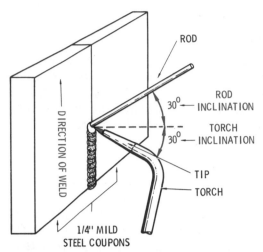

Fig. 11-20. *Torch and rod angles for welding in the* vertical *position.*

Fig. 11-21. *An example of* overhead *welding.*

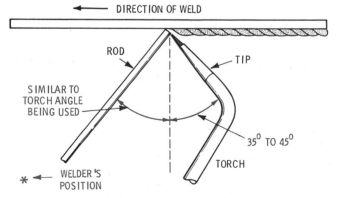

Fig. 11-22. *Torch and welding rod angles for welding in the overhead position. Note that the person doing the welding should not stand directly below the weld, since sparks or drops of molten metal could cause burns.*

TYPES OF WELD JOINTS

When two pieces of metal are to be welded together, they must first be positioned next to each other. *How* they are positioned determines the type of *weld joint* that will result.

There are five basic types of weld joints. They are shown in Figures 11-23 through 11-28. The joints are listed below.

1. Butt welds.
2. Lap welds.
3. Edge welds.
4. Tee welds.
5. Corner welds.

Auto body repair workers must know how to weld the type of joint needed for a specific job. Usually, body replacement panels are made to be fastened in place with one type of welded joint. Replacement panels sometimes are made with an offset flange that requires a special weld.

Butt Weld

A *butt weld* joint is made by placing two pieces of metal side by side, with or without a gap. A typical *butt joint* is shown in Figure 11-23. Most holes or tears in body panels are butt welded.

Whenever metal cracks are being repaired, a butt weld is normally used. To do this, the two sides of the tear or crack are aligned and then butt welded. When butt welds are made, the bead should be built up as little as possible. The outside edges of the bead should be melted back into the sides of pieces being welded. The back side of the completed weld should be checked, if possible, to make sure of complete weld penetration.

Lap Weld

A *lap weld* joint is made when two pieces of metal overlap each other, as in Figure 11-24. A lap weld is often used on outer replacement panels.

To make a lap weld, first tack-weld the two pieces of metal. Then, run the weld bead along both sides of the

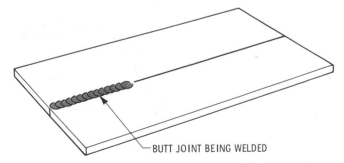

Fig. 11-23. *Butt weld joint.*

lap to complete the weld. When welded on both sides, a lap weld joint is stronger than a butt weld joint. The greater strength is a result of the *two* welds.

Edge Weld

Figure 11-25 shows how two pieces of metal are positioned for making an *edge weld* joint. This type of weld makes a fairly strong weld. The two L-shaped flanges often make the edge weld stronger than a butt weld.

This type of weld is also known as a "flange weld." It is used often during auto body manufacturing, where it is known as a *pinch weld.* At the factory, the two flanges are pinched together with the points of an electric *spot welder.* This makes a spot weld at the pinch, joining the flanges (Fig.11-26).

Tee Weld

Tee weld joints are not often used in auto body repair. Figure 11-27 shows how the two pieces of metal are positioned. The end of one piece is placed against the side of another piece. This joint can be very strong if it is welded on both sides of the tee.

When making a tee weld joint, there is more metal area to be heated by the flame. This extra metal area absorbs much of the flame's heat. To make up for this heat loss, use a tip one size larger than normally would be used for that thickness of metal. The torch should be positioned evenly between the two panels and held *up* to provide a slight amount of extra heat on the bottom panel.

Corner Weld

A *corner weld* joint is made when two pieces of metal are positioned at right angles to each other and welded on the intersecting edge of the pieces. Figure 11-28 shows how two pieces of metal would be positioned for this type of weld joint. This type of weld is often done without using a filler rod.

Corner weld joints are fairly easy to make. However, the torch flame must be handled carefully so as not to overheat the edge where the panels intersect. If this

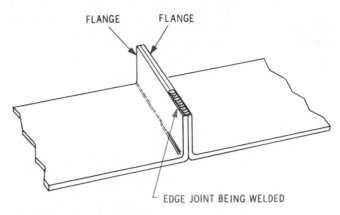

Fig. 11-25. *Edge weld joint.*

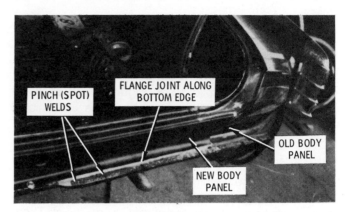

Fig. 11-26. *A body panel that has been welded along the flange. (Courtesy of Automotive Equipment Division, Lenco, Inc.)*

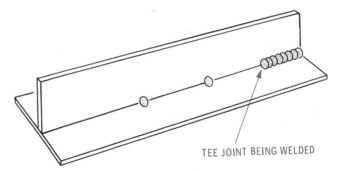

Fig. 11-27. *Tee weld joint.*

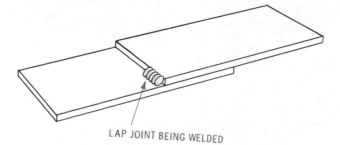

Fig. 11-24. *Lap weld joint.*

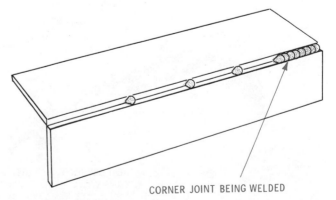

Fig. 11-28. *Corner weld joint.*

edge becomes too hot, the puddle will burn through the metal and will drip through to the underside of the joint. To avoid this problem, raise the flame slightly when moving back and forth over the edge.

OXY-ACETYLENE CUTTING PRINCIPLES

Some type of oxy-acetylene *cutting* has been done ever since the welding torch was first invented. The earliest cutting torches were no more than a pipe clamped along the side of a normal welding tip. When the metal became hot enough to melt, more oxygen would be added through this outside pipe. This extra oxygen would then cause a hole to be burned in the metal.

Although cutting torches or cutting attachments are still used to supply extra oxygen to the flame, their design has advanced along with all other welding tools. Figure 11-2 shows a welder using a modern cutting attachment to cut mild steel. Figure 11-29 shows a cutting attachment and the torch blowpipe with which it would be used.

Setting Up for Cutting

Setting up the welding equipment for cutting is similar to setting up for welding. The cylinders, regulators, hoses, and torch body are all set up as usual. There are two major changes, as noted below.

First, a *cutting attachment* must be fastened to the torch instead of a welding tip. The cutting attachment should be positioned so that the cutting oxygen valve handle is *between* the torch oxygen and acetylene valves.

Second, the oxygen regulator must be adjusted to 25 psi (172 kPa) for the type of cutting done in a body shop. This extra oxygen pressure is needed because a good deal of oxygen will be released when the cutting oxygen lever is depressed. Adjust the oxygen regulator with the *torch* oxygen valve and the *cutting* oxygen valve all the way *open*. (When the torch oxygen valve is opened, no oxygen will escape unless *either* the preheat oxygen valve *or* the *cutting* oxygen valve is opened.)

Safety Checks. After setting up the equipment for cutting, remember to make *all* the usual safety checks. Use soapy water to test for leaks, as discussed earlier. Check to be sure that the cutting equipment, and the metal to be cut, are away from any oil, grease, paint, or other flammable materials.

At all times, be sure to notice the direction in which the cutting torch is being pointed. When cutting near a vehicle's *gas tank*, remove the tank, and place it a safe distance from the cutting area. Also note where the torch *hoses* are. A serious fire could start if the hoses are cut by sparks or metal from the cutting job. A cutting torch must be used with extreme caution, since the flame and sparks are hotter than those of a welding torch.

When cutting, always wear *dark* tinted safety goggles to prevent eye injury. Figures 11-30 and 11-31 show the types of safety goggles that would work well for protection from cutting rays. Also, double-check to be sure that there is a *fire extinguisher* in the work area. Note the extinguisher on the back of the welding outfit shown in Figure 11-5.

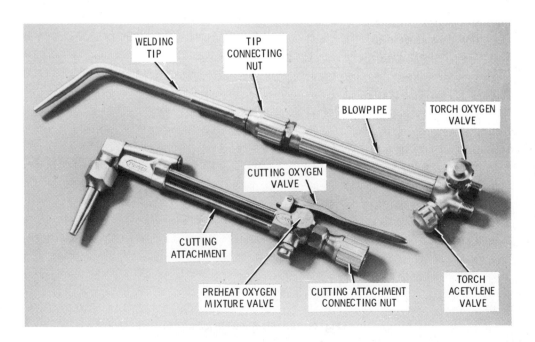

Fig. 11-29. *A welding torch with welding tip and a cutting attachment for use with the same torch. (Courtesy of Harris Calorific Division, Emerson Electric Company)*

Final Preparation. If *unpainted* metal is to be cut, obtain some soapstone. This is used for marking the direction in which the cut will be made. Soapstone marks will show up easily on bare steel, as in Figure 11-32. Either a scratch awl (Fig.11-33) or a soapstone may be used for marking the cut line on *painted* metal.

Before beginning the cutting operation, position the metal at a convenient working height. This could be on a metal table or on metal stands. Then, draw a cut line on the metal in the direction to be cut. Double-check to be certain that any flammables and hoses are safely out of the way.

Lighting the Cutting Torch

When all the equipment is set up in the cutting area, the torch is ready to be lit. To light the torch, follow these steps *in order.* Refer to Figure 11-34 as needed.

1. Open the torch oxygen valve all the way.
2. Depress the cutting oxygen lever to release oxygen. With the lever depressed, check to see that the outlet gauge pressure on the oxygen regulator is 25 psi (172 kPa). Adjust the regulator if necessary.
3. Release the cutting oxygen lever.
4. Open the torch acetylene valve about 1/6 turn.
5. Use the striker to light the acetylene at the cutting tip.
6. Open the torch acetylene valve until the acetylene flame "jumps" from the tip (Fig.11-35).
7. Close the acetylene valve until the flame just returns to the tip.
8. Open the *preheat oxygen valve* on the side of the cutting attachment (Fig.11-34) to form neutral flames with the acetylene.
9. Adjust the *torch acetylene valve* as required to get good, long neutral preheat flames. The preheat flames will be made up of *several* neutral cones. If any cones are shorter or look different, shut off the torch and clean the preheat holes in the cutting tip after the torch has cooled.
10. When the preheat flames have been adjusted to be neutral flames, press down on the *oxygen cutting lever* to be certain that the extra oxygen is coming out of the tip.

Fig. 11-30. *Typical welding goggles. (Courtesy of American Optical Company)*

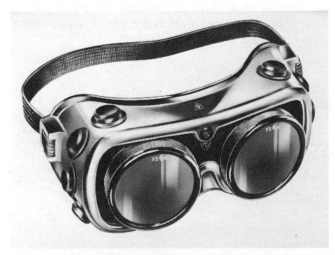

Fig. 11-31. *Welding goggles for use over eyeglasses. (Courtesy of American Optical Company)*

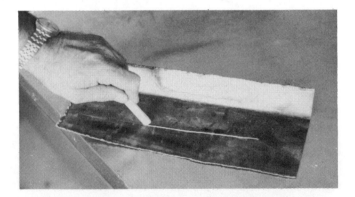

Fig. 11-32. *Marking a cutting line on bare metal with a piece of soapstone.*

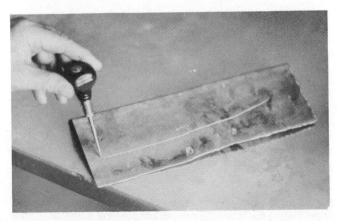

Fig. 11-33. *Marking a cutting line on painted metal with a scratch awl.*

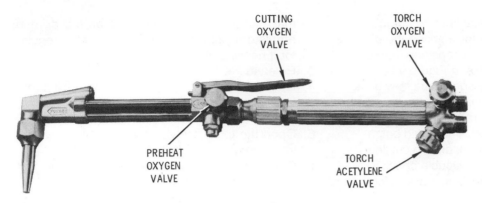

CUTTING OXYGEN VALVE

TORCH OXYGEN VALVE

PREHEAT OXYGEN VALVE

TORCH ACETYLENE VALVE

Fig. 11-34. *A torch with a cutting attachment connected to it. (Courtesy of Harris Calorific Division, Emerson Electric Company)*

Preheating

The end of a cutting tip has a number of small holes that surround a larger center hole (Fig.11-36). During operation, each of these outside holes will have an oxy-acetylene neutral preheating flame. The larger inside hole, however, is used *only* for the *cutting oxygen* after the metal has been preheated. When preheating the metal, the cutting oxygen control handle is not used.

The first step is to *preheat* the area to be cut. Place the neutral flame at the edge of the metal *on* the cut line marked earlier. Preheat a point on the edge of the

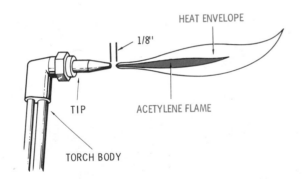

HEAT ENVELOPE

1/8"

TIP

ACETYLENE FLAME

TORCH BODY

Fig. 11-35. *To adjust the pre-heat flame, turn the acetylene control knob until the flame "jumps off" the tip, then close the valve sufficiently to bring the flame back to the tip.*

Fig. 11-36. *Neutral pre-heat flames come from the outside holes of the cutting tip. When the oxygen control level is operated, pure cutting oxygen flows from the center hole. (Courtesy of Union Carbide Canada, Ltd.)*

metal until it becomes cherry red and just begins to melt, as shown in Figure 11-37.

Cutting

After preheating the starting point, the metal may then be cut with the cutting oxygen. To do this, the control handle is depressed to supply the extra burst of oxygen needed. This oxygen leaves the tip through the center hole.

To actually make the cut, push down the cutting oxygen handle, as is being done in Figure 11-2. Then, *slowly* move the torch along the line to be cut, holding the neutral preheat flames just above the metal surface. Move the torch only as fast as a clean, distinct cut can be made. This will take practice. *Flashback*, discussed earlier, usually is not a problem while cutting. If flashback occurs, however, first close the oxygen valve, then the acetylene valve.

Shut Down

Whether a welding tip or a cutting attachment is being used, the torch must be shut down when work is complete. With either a cutting attachment or a welding tip, the torch is shut down in basically the same way. A cutting attachment, however, has an extra oxygen valve to be turned off.

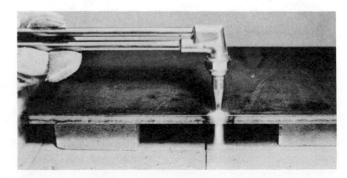

Fig. 11-37. *The metal to be cut is heated to a bright cherry red, using only a pre-heating flame. (Courtesy of Victor Equipment Company)*

Below is the correct procedure to follow to shut down the torch safely. If the torch is being shut down for a few minutes, only the first two steps need be done. However, all six steps must be done when the torch will be shut down overnight or for several hours.

1. Close the torch acetylene valve.
2. Close the torch oxygen valve. On the *cutting* attachment, close the preheat oxygen valve.
3. Close the acetylene cylinder valve.
4. Close the oxygen cylinder valve.
5. Release the pressure against the regulator valves by turning the regulator handles counter-clockwise.
6. Open both the acetylene and oxygen torch valves to let the remaining pressure off the regulator gauges.

ALUMINUM WELDING

Aluminum has been used for automobile panels for many years. European cars were the first to use aluminum sheet metal panels. These panels, when torn or cracked, can be welded.

Thin sheet aluminum can be welded with the oxy-acetylene torch. The metal and the aluminum filler rod must be approximately the same temperature for the filler rod to bond to the aluminum. If they are not, the filler will roll off the surface of the metal. Joints are created by surface bonding.

Pure aluminum melts at 1218°F (659°C). Filler rods must melt at or below this temperature. Welding aluminum is much like welding sheet steel. Steel is a ferrous metal; that is, it contains iron. Aluminum is nonferrous; therefore, it *cannot* be welded with a steel rod. Aluminum must be welded with an aluminum rod.

To practice welding thin aluminum, these basic steps should be followed:

1. Lay a piece of aluminum on two firebricks.
2. Use a wire brush to clean the surface, as shown in Figure 11-38.
3. Figure 11-39 shows a collection of aluminum welding rods and fluxes. Different rods are used according to thickness of the aluminum metal. Some rods are *flux-cored* and others are *flux-coated* for the purpose of cleaning and adhesion.
4. Light an oxy-acetylene torch, and use a carbonizing flame (very little oxygen) to blacken the area with soot, as shown in Figure 11-40.
5. Start heating the aluminum, holding the tip of the torch 4 to 6 in. (10.2 to 15.2 cm) away from the metal. Heat until the soot begins to disappear, as shown in Figure 11-41.
6. When the soot has disappeared, the aluminum is ready for the welding rod to be used.

Caution: **Do not overheat the metal.**

7. Heat the rod, then place it in the flux (Fig. 11-42).

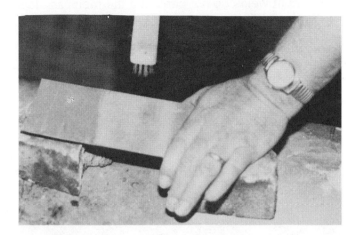

Fig. 11-38. *A wire brush is used to clean aluminum before welding.*

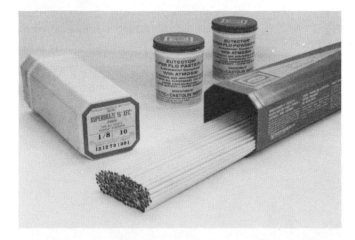

Fig. 11-39. *Welding rods and fluxes for use on aluminum. (Courtesy of Eutectic Corporation)*

Fig. 11-40. *The aluminum surface is coated with soot, using a carbonizing flame.*

8. Place the aluminum rod in the flame (Fig.11-43). The flame is never held very close to the hot metal when welding thin aluminum.

9. The aluminum rod melts on the surface of the hot metal in process similar to brazing. Aluminum welds do *not* penetrate the metal as steel does (Fig.11-44).

Welding Heavy Aluminum

Heavy aluminum is welded much like heavy steel. The torch tip for welding heavier aluminum is larger than that used for thin metal. An example of heavy aluminum metal use is the bumper bars shown in Figure 11-45. These damaged bumper bars will be repaired as orders come in for them. Figure 11-46 shows a small hole and a split that have been welded on a heavy aluminum bumper bar. The torch tip can be held closer to the metal when welding heavy aluminum.

Fig. 11-41. *The surface is then heated until the soot begins to disappear.*

Fig. 11-42. *The welding rod is heated, then dipped in the flux to coat it. (Courtesy of Eutectic Corporation)*

Fig. 11-43. *The welding rod is melted onto the surface of the aluminum. The rod and flame are held as shown.*

Fig. 11-44. *Aluminum welds do not penetrate the surface of the metal.*

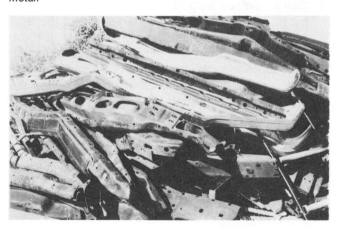

Fig. 11-45. *Aluminum bumper bars awaiting repair.*

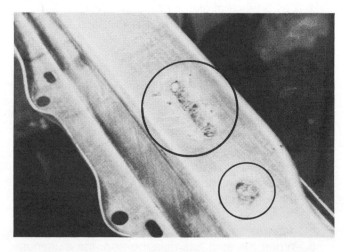

Fig. 11-46. *Welds on an aluminum bumper reinforcing bar.*

Brazing and Heat Shrinking

The oxy-acetylene processes of *brazing* and *heat shrinking* have much in common. An oxy-acetylene torch is used for both types of work. The same regulator gauge settings may be used for either process. Both processes may accurately be described as *low-temperature* welding processes. They are done without the extreme heat that must be used for welding. Whether brazing or heat shrinking, the base metal being repaired is worked *without* melting any part of it.

Oxy-acetylene *brazing* is a joining process done with brass rods. These rods are melted to form the puddle and run the bead. The panels being joined are not actually melted. Instead, they are held together by the melted brass from the rods. The melted brass does not actually go all the way through the base metal.

Oxy-acetylene *heat shrinking* is the process of shrinking stretched metal back to a smaller size by using the oxy-acetylene flame. When sheet metal is damaged, caved in, or gouged, it is often *stretched* out of shape. Figure 12-1 shows a damaged area of this type. This type of damage can be brought closer to the metal's original contour by using an oxy-acetylene flame to heat and shrink it.

BRAZING PRINCIPLES

Oxy-acetylene *brazing*, like oxy-acetylene welding, uses the heat of an oxy-acetylene flame to join together two pieces of metal. During brazing, however, a lower-melting-point metal is added to make the joint. Brazing rod melts at approximately 1600°F (871°C). Brazing is often used to replace quarter panels, door outer panels ("skins"), and other auto body panels.

During brazing, the oxy-acetylene flame first heats the base metal. Then, the brass filler rod is melted and drawn into the joint by the metal's heat. The brass seeps into the base metal's *pores*. The two pieces of metal are held together strongly when the liquid brass cools and becomes solid.

Advantages of Brazing

The main advantage of brazing is that it allows metal to be joined at a lower temperature than welding. When done properly, brazing firmly joins pieces of almost any

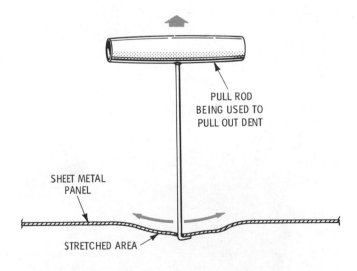

Fig. 12-1. *Metal that has been dented is usually stretched. After the dent has been pulled out, the metal usually must be shrunk back to its original area.*

189

type of metal. When panels are joined by brazing, there is less danger of the base metal's warping. This is because the joint is made at a low temperature. Thus, the panels are subjected to less heat than if they were welded.

Another advantage of brazing is that the oxy-acetylene carbonizing flame, rather than the neutral flame, is used. The carbonizing flame is slightly cooler than a neutral flame. Thus, it requires less oxygen than a neutral flame. In addition to needing less oxygen than welding, brazing is also a *faster* process. Less time is

Fig. 12-2. *Brazing rods coated with flux.*

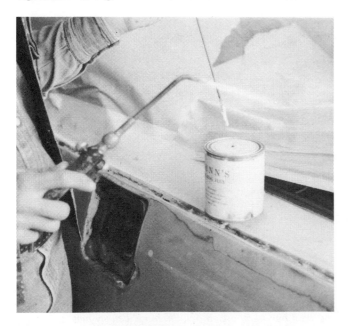

Fig. 12-3. *An uncoated brazing rod must be heated and dipped in a can of flux.*

required to get the base material up to brazing temperature than to welding temperature.

Oxy-acetylene brazing is often used for joining soft metals such as copper or brass. Extreme heat should not be used on these metals since they will melt easily. Brazing also is used to repair and join *cast iron*. Cast iron will crack easily if it is not evenly heated.

Brazing Equipment

The equipment needed for brazing is about the same as the equipment needed for welding. For brazing, an oxy-acetylene torch, brass filler rods, welding goggles, gloves, and a torch lighter are needed. The brass rods should be coated with *flux*, a cleaning agent necessary for brazing (Fig. 12-2).

If *uncoated* brass rods are used, a container of *flux* must be placed in the work area and the rod dipped in the flux before brazing. Figure 12-3 shows a container of flux and the coated and uncoated portion of a brass rod. The brass rod is heated, then pushed into the can of flux. This causes the flux to stick to the brass rod.

Brazing Tip Size

In brazing, as in welding, the thickness of the metal determines the tip and rod sizes and the regulator gauge pressures. Generally, the sizes and pressures given earlier for welding may also be used for brazing. Many body workers, however, prefer to use a tip size one number larger than would be used for *welding* metal of the same thickness.

For most oxy-acetylene brazing on outer body sheet metal, gauge pressures of 5 to 6 psi (34 to 41 kPa) may be used with 1/16 in. (1.6 mm) diameter brazing rod and a #2 or #3 welding tip. For thicker metal (unitized body subframes, for example), 1/8 in. (3.2 mm) diameter rod and a #3 or #4 tip should be used. Slightly higher gas pressures may be needed for the larger tips.

Brazing Flame

During welding, the neutral flame is used. The flame to use for *brazing*, however, is a slightly *carbonizing*, or "reducing" flame. The torch oxygen valve does not have to be opened as much for a carbonizing flame as it does for the neutral flame.

The carbonizing flame can be recognized by its flame "feather" positioned just above the inner flame cone (Fig. 12-4). The flame feather should be about one or two times longer (**1X** or **2X**) than the flame cone, depending on the thickness of the metal.

When brazing, the torch tip should be held about twice as far from the work as when welding. This is because the molten brass may be blown away by the flame if the tip is held too close. Usually, a distance of about ¼ in. (6.4 mm) is far enough from the surface for good brazing.

Brazing Rods

Two types of brass rods are used for brazing: those *coated* with flux and those *not coated* with flux. Flux-coated rods are easily identified, because they are much thicker than uncoated rods. Also, flux-coated rods may have different colors, whereas uncoated rods are brass colored (yellow-gold). Uncoated brass rods must be coated with flux when being used for brazing.

Flux. The flux, either in a can or on a rod, is very necessary for good brazing and has several purposes. Flux is used to *clean* the metal for better adhesion by the melted brass. Flux also helps prevent the brass rod from *oxidizing*. This allows the brass to flow freely onto the base metal.

BRAZING THIN METAL

Thin metal [up to ⅛ in. (3.2 mm) thick] is not normally brazed in the same way as is thicker metal. Thin metal, such as auto body sheet metal, is usually brazed as shown in Figure 12-5. It may also be brazed in a butt weld joint (Fig. 12-6). Thin metals normally can be brazed by making one pass over the joint. This pass will usually leave a layer of brass from 1⁄16 to ⅛ in. (1.6 to 3.2 mm) thick. Brazing thicker metal requires a different procedure.

Preparation

Brass will adhere properly only to metal that is *clean*. Before actually brazing, the metal to be brazed must be cleaned. Soap and water or enamel reducer may be used. The metal should be scrubbed with a wire brush. Some workers skip this step, but it *should* be done to ensure good adhesion by the brass.

If an uncoated brass rod is being used, the rod must be coated with flux each time it is used. Use the torch to heat about 1 ½ in. (38.1 mm) of the end of the rod. Push the heated end into the can of flux to pick up a coating of flux. The rod is then ready for use.

Forming the Puddle

To begin brazing, move the torch back and forth across the metal joint. Heat a short space to *just* a dull red color, *no* more. Next, position the rod at about a 45° angle to the heated metal (Fig. 12-7). Then, melt the flux-coated part of the rod onto the hot metal to form a brass puddle (Fig. 12-8).

Fig. 12-4. *The inner cone of a carbonizing flame is two or three times as long as the inner cone of a neutral flame.*

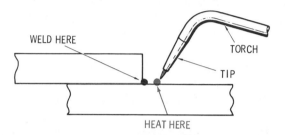

Fig. 12-5. *A lap joint is sometimes used when brazing thin metal.*

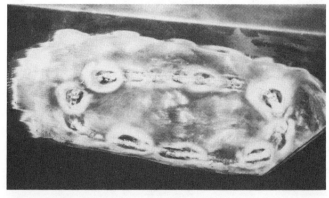

Fig. 12-6. *Bright yellow-gold filler metal is a sign of a joint that has been brazed.*

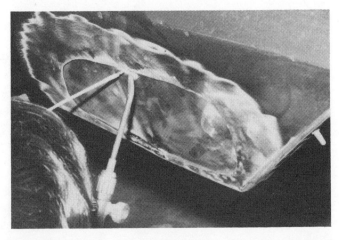

Fig. 12-7. *The correct angle for feeding a brazing rod into the joint is shown here.*

Running the Bead

Before running a brass bead along the joint, tack the panels or pieces being joined. Place the "tacks" about 1 in. (25.4 mm) apart, as in Figure 12-9. Be sure to follow the same procedure for each tack: *coat* the rod with flux (if it is uncoated), *heat* the metal, and then *melt* the rod on the hot metal. Each tack should be about ¼ in. (6.3 mm) long.

When actually running the bead, the temperature of the puddle is controlled by raising and lowering the torch tip. Normally, the torch tip is held at about a 45° angle to the metal's surface and about ¼ in. (6.3 mm) away from the puddle (Fig. 12-10). The flame heat is used to direct the puddle flow as desired. For good brazing, use the same back-and-forth torch movement as for welding.

During brazing, the puddle moves much faster than during welding. The brass bead will also spread a little wider than does a steel weld bead. If the brazing bead

is made a little higher than the two pieces being brazed, it may later be ground off level.

BRAZING THICK METAL

Metal over ⅛ in. (3.2 mm) thick, such as cast iron, requires the use of a different brazing procedure. Thick metal should not be overlapped, as is done with thin metal. Instead, thick metal edges should be ground back to a slight angle, so that they form a "V" when butted together (Fig. 12-11). This may be done with a disc grinder.

After preparing the pieces and placing them so that the "V" shape is formed, brazing may begin. The brazing procedure is almost the same as when working with thin sheet metal. When heating the metal to a dull red, be careful to not overheat the *top* edges of the "V."

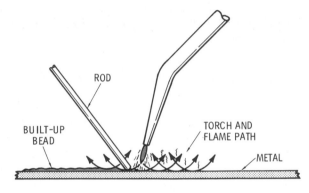

Fig. 12-10. *An up-and-down, back-and-forth movement of the torch tip is used while brazing.*

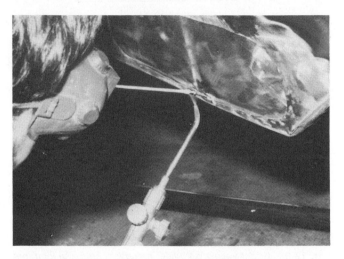

Fig. 12-8. *Forming a puddle while brazing.*

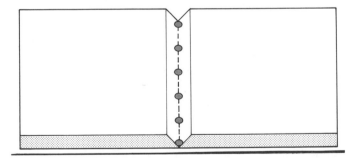

Fig. 12-11. *When thicker metal is to be joined by brazing, the edges should be ground back to form a "V" at the joint.*

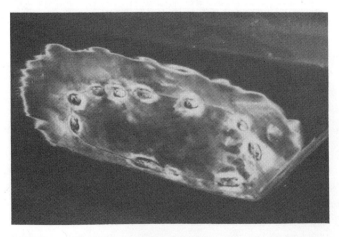

Fig. 12-9. *"Tacks" (spot-brazing) are used to hold metal in position for brazing.*

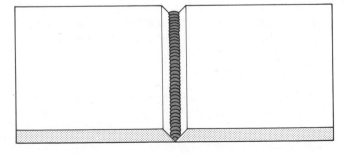

Fig. 12-12. *The first brazing pass on a thick-metal joint will be convex, as shown.*

Several passes will usually be needed, since one layer of brass is not normally enough to fill the "V." On the *first* pass, the bead should be made so that it is *convex* (humped), as in Figure 12-12. The bead of the *second* pass should almost fill the "V." It will be only slightly convex, as shown in Figure 12-13. The *third* and final pass should overfill the "V." The bead is made a little higher than the level of the base metal (Fig. 12-14).

A TYPICAL BRAZING JOB

Because it causes less heat distortion than welding, brazing is often used when replacing the thin outer sheet metal panels of automobiles. By *brazing* replacement panels in place, there is less chance that the repair will be warped. Such warping would require a good deal of additional body work before refinishing. Brazing is one of the most important skills a body repair worker may have.

A typical panel replacement done with brazing is shown in Figures 12-15 to 12-22. In this series, the severely damaged quarter panel shown in Figure 12-15 is replaced with a panel from a salvage yard (Fig. 12-16). In Figure 12-17, the car has been brought into the shop, opened up, and placed on jack stands.

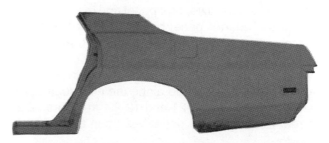

Fig. 12-16. *A used quarter panel obtained from a salvage yard to replace the damaged panel shown in Figure 12-15.*

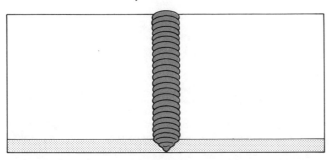

Fig. 12-13. *The second brazing pass will be only slightly convex and will almost fill the "V" joint.*

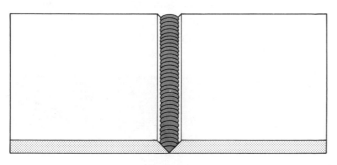

Fig. 12-14. *The final brazing pass will fill the "V" and project above the surface of the metal.*

Fig. 12-17. *The damaged car has been jacked up and placed on safety stands. As the first step in replacement of the quarter panel, the rear bumper has been removed.*

Fig. 12-15. *This quarter panel is damaged beyond economical repair. The best solution is to install a replacement panel.*

Fig. 12-18. *The used quarter panel is trimmed to fit exactly in the place of the damaged panel.*

The rear bumper has been removed for the repair. In Figure 12-18, the replacement panel has been trimmed for installation on this particular car. (When a salvage yard removes a used part, it may not be cut off the wrecked car exactly as needed for the car being repaired.)

In Figure 12-19, the damaged quarter-panel section has been cut away. This is best done with an air chisel, which will leave a clean, sharp edge for brazing. After the panel is removed, the edges must be cleaned and the weatherstripping laid aside.

The first step toward installing the replacement panel is to *spot braze* it in position. This has been done in Figure 12-20. The lower roof panel and matching upper edge of the quarter panel have had the paint ground off with a disc sander in preparation for brazing along that seam.

When the panel has been spot-brazed in position, it may be completely brazed along the new seams. This is shown in Figures 12-21 and 12-22. In Figure 12-21, the rear section of the panel has been brazed to the

car's tail piece. In Figure 12-22, the panel has been partially brazed to the lower roof panel. After brazing, the repair will have to be leveled and filled with body filler. The panel may then be refinished.

HEAT SHRINKING

Heat shrinking is an important part of repairing damaged metal. "Shrinking" will be needed when the metal has been stretched out of shape by the impact of a collision. If the metal is not "shrunk," a complete repair of the panel will be difficult. The repaired area will have a wavy appearance when the stretched metal is forced to fit the smaller original area.

All metal has a certain amount of "give." It will normally return to its original contour after a *light* blow. However, when a blow causes the metal to exceed the limits of its "give," it is stretched out of shape. This

Fig. 12-21. *A brazed joint on the rear edge of the replacement panel. The black soot is from the excess acetylene in the carbonizing flame used for brazing. The brazed joint must be cleaned and leveled before the panel is refinished.*

Fig. 12-19. *The damaged panel has been cut away.*

Fig. 12-20. *Spot-brazing is used to hold the replacement panel in position.*

Fig. 12-22. *Another example of a brazed joint. This is the point where the replacement panel is joined to the lower edge of the car roof.*

would happen, for example, when an object hits a panel and causes a deep gouge or dent. The metal will bend and stretch.

Heat Distortion

To shrink body sheet metal successfully, a repair worker must understand the effect of *heat* on metal. When *heat* is applied, it causes the metal to *expand*. Then, as the metal cools, it shrinks. This is caused by the movement of the molecules in the metal as it is heated and when it cools. The more extreme the heat, the more expansion will take place. If the metal is quickly cooled, it will contract (shrink) even more than when it cools slowly.

The effect of heat on metal can best be understood by noticing how it changes a flat piece of undamaged sheet metal. If a torch is used to heat the metal in one spot, it will first expand (Fig. 12-23). Then, as the metal cools, it will contract slightly (Fig. 12-24). As the metal is heated, its molecules expand *toward* the heat (the molecules nearest the heat are getting hotter and becoming larger than those underneath). As the metal cools, the molecules contract, reducing their size and causing the bulge to shrink.

Metal should not be shrunk with water while it is extremely hot. Wait until the metal cools to a blue-black color.

Warpage. How much expansion and contraction of metal takes place is controlled by the *amount* of heat applied and the *size* of the area heated. The *hotter* the area, the more the panel expands and contracts (warps). The *larger* the heated area, the greater the resulting warpage.

Metal that is low-crowned (has no sharp bends) or is slightly curved is easily warped by heat. If too much heat is applied, the panel will quickly become wavy and irregular in contour. Panel warpage can be controlled through practice in handling a torch while heat shrinking.

The warpage that takes place may be partially controlled by noting the *size* of the area heated and the *amount* of heat applied to that area. Also, there are several methods used to speed up the shrinking process. These include using a bumping hammer and dolly and cooling the heated area by using water-soaked rags or sponges.

Shrinking Procedure

To heat shrink metal properly, be prepared to work *quickly*. Have on hand all the materials needed before beginning to heat the metal. Materials on hand should include an oxy-acetylene torch, a fire extinguisher, a bumping hammer and dolly, and a bucket of water with rags or sponges. Usually, a #1 welding tip is used for

heat shrinking thin auto body sheet metal.

Heating the Area. To heat the stretched area properly, first bring the oxy-acetylene torch to a neutral flame. Keep the inner cone of the flame about ½ in. (12.7 mm) from the surface of the metal (Fig. 12-25). Normally, only a small area (no larger than a dime) is heated at a time. Sometimes, the damaged area may have an oblong (elongated) shape. In such cases, it is often convenient to heat only a narrow strip of the damaged area.

Heat the first spot to be shrunk to a cherry-red color, as has been done in Figure 12-25. This will cause the

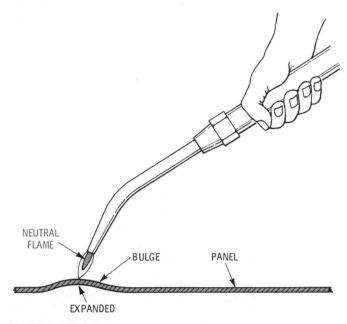

Fig. 12-23. *When a piece of flat sheet metal is heated, it will expand and bulge upward.*

Fig. 12-24. *If the metal is allowed to cool slowly, it will contract slightly.*

Fig. 12-25. *Metal to be shrunk should be heated to a cherry red color. The inner cone of the flame should be held about ½ in. (12.7 mm) from the metal surface.*

damaged area to expand outward, forming a slight bulge. Take care not to overheat the metal. Do not allow the cone to come too close to the metal, since this could burn a hole in it. After the metal is heated, use a hammer to bump down and shape it, as shown in Figure 12-26.

Using the Hammer and Dolly. A bumping hammer and dolly are often used to speed up the shrinking process after the metal has been heated. Since the heated metal is soft, it can easily be worked down into shape as it begins cooling (Fig. 12-27).

Use the open face of the bumping hammer to strike two light blows on the heated spot as soon as the metal is hot. Next, place a dolly, which is shaped similar to the original contour, on the backside of the damaged area. Flatten or shape the metal by working it against the dolly with the hammer (Fig. 12-28). Be *careful* when doing this, since the metal being worked is *hot*.

Using Water. When the damaged area cannot be reached on the back side, a hammer may be used without a dolly for some jobs. However, *water* also may be used to speed up the shrinking process. This is done by wiping a wet sponge or rags across the heated area, causing it to cool faster. Figure 12-29 shows how this is done. The amount of shrinkage is more difficult to control when water is used. Care must be taken to avoid getting burned while holding the wet sponge or rags against the hot panel.

Practice. The ability to shrink metal properly takes a good deal of *practice.* Working *quickly* is important

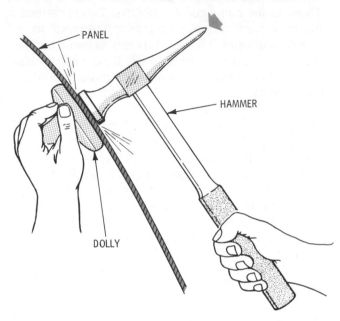

Fig. 12-28. *A dolly of the correct shape can be used behind the heated metal to obtain the desired contour.*

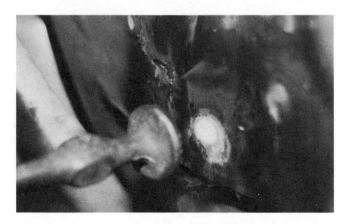

Fig. 12-26. *A hammer can be used to work down the expanded metal while it is still hot.*

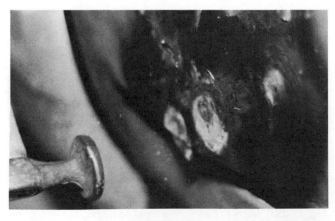

Fig. 12-27. *Since the hot metal is soft, it can be worked easily with the hammer or with a hammer and dolly.*

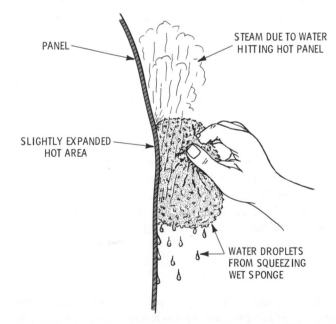

Fig. 12-29. *Greater shrinkage of the metal can be obtained by cooling it rapidly. The technique of using a wet rag or sponge is shown here. Care must be taken to avoid steam burns as the water boils away. Water should not be applied until the metal cools to a dull red.*

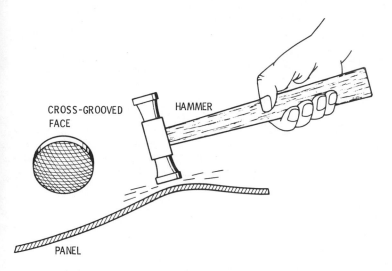

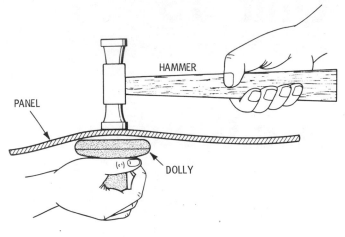

Fig. 12-30. *Care must be used when heat shrinking aluminum, since it melts at a lower temperature than steel. Once the area has been heated, it is tapped gently with a hammer that has a cross-grooved face.*

Fig. 12-31. *A hammer and dolly may be used on aluminum panels, in the same way that they are with steel. Since aluminum transmits heat more rapidly then steel, it must be "worked" more quickly after heating.*

because the metal must be worked while it is *hot* for the best results. After the metal is worked down close to its original size, it may be smoothed, filed, and filled as needed before refinishing.

SHRINKING ALUMINUM

Stretched aluminum can be shrunk in much the same way as steel. The same tools and equipment are used.

Heat shrinking is possible to some degree, but alumimum *does not* respond as well as steel. Heat applications must be kept below 1200°F (649°C) to avoid melting the metal. After the stretched metal has been prepared for shrinking, heat is applied with the torch. Be careful: Aluminum *does not* turn red when heated as steel does. The risk of melting is greater than with steel.

When shrinking aluminum, the work must be performed much faster than with steel. Aluminum is a good conductor of heat, so the heat will spread out to a larger area. This may warp the adjoining aluminum.

Figure 12-30 shows an aluminum panel that has been heated. The heated aluminum bulges upward just as steel does. Most workers will use a hammer with a cross-grooved face when tapping the hot metal.

The hammer and dolly may be used to straighten the hot aluminum (Fig. 12-31). Hot aluminum is tapped very lightly with the hammer to prevent stretching.

A wet sponge or rags may be used after the heated area has cooled partially. Quenching while too hot can shrink aluminum more quickly than it would steel. Cooling with water while the metal is too hot could cause the panel to buckle. Quenching aluminum with water should be done gradually to avoid distortion.

Unit 13

Arc Welding

Arc welding (Fig. 13-1) is a welding process that uses *electric current* as a source of power and heat. For this reason, arc welding is also known as *electric welding*. Basically, arc welding uses two cables and an *electrode* (an electric welding rod) to direct the flow of electricity, as shown in Figure 13-2.

Figure 13-3 shows an arc welding electrode. Electrodes are coated with different types of *flux* to provide the chemical cleaning and protection necessary as the

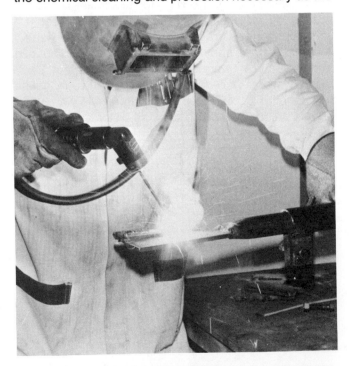

Fig. 13-1. *Arc welding is often used on thick-metal parts that must be repaired.*

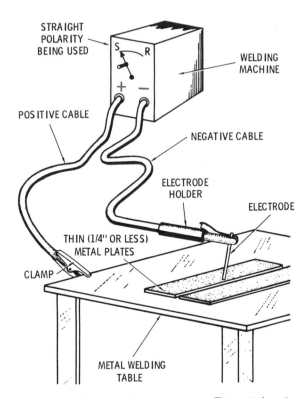

Fig. 13-2. *A typical arc welding setup. The metal part, metal welding table, and wires form a complete path (circuit) for the electric current which provides the heat for welding.*

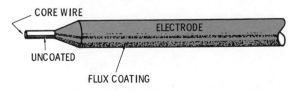

Fig. 13-3. *A typical arc welding electrode with a thick flux coating.*

198

arc makes the weld. The weld is formed at the arc (Fig. 13-4) because electricity flows through power lines to form a complete circuit. When the circuit is broken, an *arc* is formed as the electricity "jumps" the gap in the circuit. The hot arc melts and joins together the metals being welded *and* the metal that is melting from the electrode.

All arc welders work on the principle of electricity going through heavy cables and causing the weld by arcing onto the surface of the metals being welded. The electricity comes *from* the welding machine, *through* the electrode, *across* the arc, and then *through* the metal to the ground cable. It completes the circuit by returning, through the ground cable, to the welding machine. A typical machine is shown in Figure 13-5.

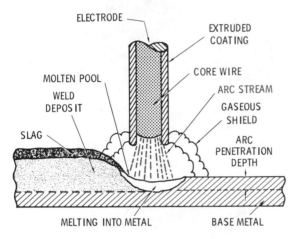

Fig. 13-4. *The welding arc.*

Fig. 13-5. *A typical arc welding machine used in body repair shops. (Courtesy of Lincoln Electric Company)*

Some of the newer electric welding machines operate in a more complicated manner, but all use the same basic principle. They all have lead (electrode) cables to provide the current to the electrode holder, and they all have a ground (work) cable to complete the circuit by returning the electricity to the machine. Figure 13-2 shows how this set up provides a path for the electricity.

Until recently, arc welding was seldom used in auto body repair shops because most thin sheet metal could be warped by the heat of a heavy current arc welding machine. However, recent developments have produced arc-welding machines that can be used to weld overlapping panels of thin sheet metal easily.

There are three basic types of electric welders that may be used in an auto body shop:

1. Conventional arc welders.
2. MIG welders (Fig. 13-6).
3. Resistance spot welders (panel spotters).
   In the body shop business, the processes of *MIG welding* and *panel spotting* are quite important. These processes are discussed in detail later in the unit. To be able to use electric welding correctly, body mechanics must know how to select the type of welding equipment and the materials needed to best complete the job.

CONVENTIONAL ARC WELDERS

There are several types of *conventional arc welders.* Most are known as *transformer machines* and may be operated from 220-volt electric power lines (Figs. 13-5, 13-7, and 13-8). On the other hand, portable *gasoline-powered* welding machines, like gasoline-powered air compressors, can be operated where there is no other electric power. These machines (Figs. 13-9 and 13-10) have an electric generator powered by a gasoline engine.

Fig. 13-6. *A MIG welder. (Courtesy of Hobart Brothers Company)*

Transformer Machines

The most common arc welders are those that operate from the shop's electric power lines. The output sizes of these *transformer machines* include 180, 225, and 250 amperes. This is the amount of current that they are able to put out (current is measured in amperes or *amps*).

Transformer welding machines operate from 220 volt electric lines. The differences between machines are the size and the maximum amperage that they are able to produce. The 180 or 225 amp machines are satisfactory for welding any guage metal found on a modern auto body or frame. Although a 250 amp welder can produce faster welds, it is more often used in industries such as construction. Much heavier metal pieces than found in an automobile are welded with 250 amp units.

Portable Machines

Portable, gasoline-powered welding machines get their name from the fact that they can be operated anywhere to which they can be moved. Basically, these machines operate like any other conventional arc welder. The difference is that they produce their own electricity from a gasoline-engine-powered generator. Figures 13-9 and 13-10 show two common portable machines. The machine in Figure 13-10 has a second control for

fine adjustment of the amperage supply. This is used to adjust the "rough" amperage selection of the first dial more carefully .

Welding Equipment

Both types of conventional welding machines use the same attachments and supplies. This equipment includes supply cables and electrode holders, ground

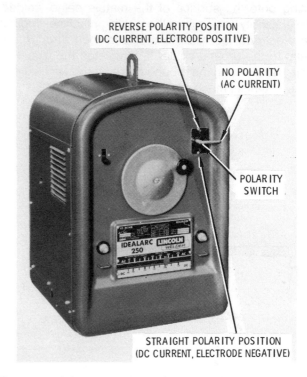

Fig. 13-8. *A fixed, 250-amp arc welder. (Courtesy of Lincoln Electric Company)*

Fig. 13-7. *A portable, 225-amp transformer arc welding machine. (Courtesy of Lincoln Electric Company)*

Fig. 13-9. *A small, gasoline-powered generator welding machine. (Courtesy of Lincoln Electric Company)*

cables and clamps, welding helmets, electrodes, and gloves (Fig. 13-11).

CAUTION: A welding helmet must always be worn while using an arc welder.

The welding arc is much brighter than an oxy-acetylene welding flame, so proper eye protection is a "must" while arc welding. Although oxy-acetylene welding can be done with a #4 or #5 shade, the lense for arc welding should be #10. Do *not* substitute one for the other. A good supply of electrodes should be kept on hand, since the electrodes burn down as they form weld metal. Electrodes should be discarded when they are burned down to a 1 to 1 ½ in. (25.4 to 38.1 mm) length.

Fig. 13-10. *A larger, gasoline-powered generator welding machine. (Courtesy of Lincoln Electric Company)*

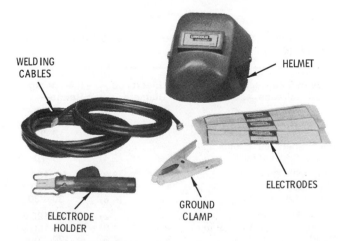

Fig. 13-11. *Equipment needed for arc welding. (Courtesy of Lincoln Electric Company)*

Types of Electrodes. There are many different kinds of electrodes. Electrode manufacturers color-code the electrodes according to several factors. These include the base metal on which the electrode should be used, the type of flux coating on the electrode, the welding position in which the electrode should be used, and other factors.

To be sure of using the right electrode for the job, read a color-coding chart. Table 7 lists the applications and color-code dots for various electrodes. These are industry standards.

Using Conventional Machines

Transformer welding machines are simple to operate. Generally, the controls include an off–on switch, a control for setting the amperage, a *polarity* selector (on DC machines), and two lead terminals. One of the terminals is used for connecting the supply (output) cable to the machine. The supply cable is also known as the *electrode* cable. The other terminal is used for connecting the ground (work) cable to the machine. The

Table 7

Popular Arc Welding Electrodes and Their Common Uses

Color Codes and Color Locations	Electrode Usage
Brown None	Mild steel. Sheet metal. Used for all positions, especially useful for general machinery repair. Most popular electrode in general use.
Orange Blue White	Nickel alloy machineable cast. Good for blocks, gear teeth, and cylinder heads. Excellent for welding steel to cast iron.
Orange None	Mild steel for cast iron. Weld cannot be machined.
None Green	Mild steel for deep penetration at high amperages in flat or horizontal positions. Excellent as a cutting rod. AWS #E-6020.
Red None Yellow	Stainless steel for unlike metals. Also used for carbon steels such as bulldozer blades, spring tooth harrows, rakes, car bumpers, etc.
Brown Yellow Red	Medium hard surface for soil-tilling farm equipment, manufacturing, and construction equipment.
Blue Blue Red	Used on road machinery, tractor treads, crusher jaws, hammer-mill hammers, and gravel-handling, and mining equipment.
None Blue	Mild steel. Deep penetration at medium amperages. All positions. Excellent for vertical and overhead welds. AWS #E-6011.
Blue Orange Green	Low-hydrogen rod for welding problem steels. AC or DC reverse. AWS #E-6028 and #7028.
Black Yellow None	Mild steel. Good for high speed flat and horizontal position welding. Iron powder flux coating.

ground cable clamps directly onto the metal being welded, so that the electricity can be returned to the machine. This completes the circuit needed for welding.

Polarity. On an automobile battery, you may have noticed that the battery connections are marked + and −, or *plus* (positive) and *minus* (negative). This is because an automobile has a direct current, or *DC*, electrical system. When an electrical system (circuit) is DC, one of the connections must be positive and the other negative.

Electricity used in a home or shop is known as *AC* or *alternating current.* Alternating current has no positive or negative connections, as long as the circuit is *complete* (has an unbroken path for the electricity to follow). Most smaller transformer welding machines, such as the one in Figure 13-7, put out only AC current, so polarity is no problem.

Larger machines, however, such as the one in Figure 13-8, have a *polarity switch.* This allows the welder to choose the polarity needed if an electrode or a certain position calls for it. These larger machines use *rectifiers* to change the incoming AC to DC for welding. These machines are more properly known as *transformer/rectifier* welding machines.

Most body shop welding may be done with AC current, using the type of welder shown in Figure 13-7. If a machine with a *polarity selector* (Fig. 13-8) is being used, the selector should be set on AC unless the electrode or job application recommends DC straight or DC reverse polarity. When a machine is set on DC *straight* polarity, the welding cable to the electrode holder must be the *negative* cable. For DC *reverse* polarity, the welding cable to the electrode holder must be the *positive* cable.

To use a conventional arc welder successfully, a worker must know how to strike an arc with the electrode and how to use the arc to make a molten puddle for welding. The same types of joints made with an oxy-acetylene welder can be made with an arc welder. However, there are slight differences when arc welding is used. For example, the metal may not be spaced in the same way, and the electrode may not be held at the same angle as would an oxy-acetylene torch. The following material explains how to use conventional arc welders correctly for body shop welding jobs.

Selecting Amperage and Electrode. To make good arc welds, the proper diameter *electrode* must be selected for the metal thickness being welded. The correct *amperage* must be used for that diameter electrode. Table 8 shows the recommended amperages and electrode diameters for common arc welding jobs in an auto body shop.

Tables 7 and 8 should be used together to determine the correct electrode number, diameter, and amperage to use for each job. When practicing, it is a good idea to start with the *lowest* recommended amperage shown in Table 8. Then, if the weld penetration or speed is not great enough, higher amperages may be used.

Setting Up. Before striking the arc, correctly connect the cables (leads) to the welding machine. Be certain that the ground cable is firmly attached either to the work or to a metal table on which the work is being done. Finally, squeeze the electrode holder (Fig. 13-11), and insert the electrode into its open jaws.

Striking the Arc. Before striking the arc, turn on the welding machine, put on the welding gloves, and *lower the welding helmet.* Then, strike the arc by scratching or touching the electrode to the metal (Figs. 13-12 and 13-13).

Once the arc is working, the electrode must be held at the correct distance from the base metal to maintain the arc. If the electrode is held too far away from the base metal, the arc will be broken. On the other hand, if the electrode is held too close, it may become welded to the work! When this happens, the electrode holder can usually be twisted to free the electrode from the work surface.

Table 8

Amperage and Electrode Specifications for Auto Body Arc Welding

Type of Metal and Thickness	Electrode Diameter—		Amperage Range—
	in.	(mm)	amps
Light Gauge Sheet Metal [outer sheet metal, etc., up to 7/64 in. (2.8 mm) thick].	1/16	(1.6)	10–30
	5/64	(2.0)	25–45
	3/32	(2.4)	40–70
Thin Mild Steel [inner body structure, etc., 7/64 to 3/16 in. (2.8 to 4.8 mm) thick].	1/8	(3.2)	50–130
	5/32	(4.0)	90–180
	3/16	(4.8)	130–230
Thick Mild Steel [frames, etc., 3/16 to 5/16 in. (4.8 to 7.9 mm) thick].	1/8	(3.2)	60–120
	5/32	(4.0)	90–160
	3/16	(4.8)	120–200
	1/4	(6.4)	190–300

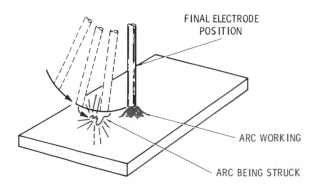

FINAL ELECTRODE POSITION

ARC WORKING

ARC BEING STRUCK

Fig. 13-12. *The "scratch" method of striking an arc is most often used when welding with AC.*

Maintaining the correct arc length will require practice. Usually, an arc length of $\frac{1}{16}$ to $\frac{1}{4}$ in. (1.6 to 6.4 mm) is used, depending on the electrode diameter (Fig. 13-14). This arc length should be maintained for the entire length of the weld. The electrode must be moved down to maintain the correct arc length as it melts into the weld (Fig. 13-15).

Running the Bead. When the arc has been struck, the molten base metal and electrode metal may be used to form a bead across the joint or work surface. Figure 13-16 shows how the electrode should be held to do this. For the arc to melt the base metal properly, the electrode should be held at an angle of about 15° back toward the direction of travel.

If you are right handed, hold the electrode holder in your right hand. Use your left hand to help steady the right. Using *both* hands on the electrode holder gives better control over the electrode movement. If you are left handed, reverse the hand positions. Hold your elbows in close to your body for added balance and control.

As the arc burns and melts the electrode, a puddle of molten metal is formed. This puddle will become solid, forming the bead, as the hot arc and melting electrode move forward along the weld line. When welding is done at the proper forward speed, the bead ridge where the puddle becomes solid will be about $\frac{3}{8}$ in. (9.5 mm) behind the arc and electrode. As you weld, *watch the puddle carefully.* Be certain that the weld

bead is forming evenly along the weld line for the speed being used.

Move the electrode at an even, steady speed while watching the weld bead solidify. Be sure to maintain the proper arc gap and electrode angle with the work. Usually, only a forward motion is needed for bead practice. Avoid moving the electrode backward, sideways, or up and down. Correctly moving the electrode forward while lowering it as it melts will provide a strong, even weld. Figure 13-17 shows examples of common weld defects. While practicing, these welds should be used for comparison. Also, notice the example of a *good* weld shown in Figure 13-17. Arc welding skill is best learned by continued *practice*. For this reason, do not become discouraged if your first few arc welds have a poor appearance. Continue practicing the basic steps until you are able to control and direct the weld properly.

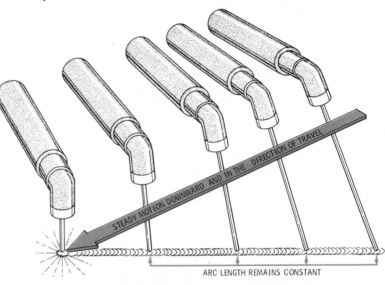

Fig. 13-15. *The electrode holder must be moved closer to the metal as the electrode melts down, so that the arc length remains constant.*

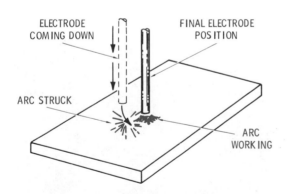

Fig. 13-13. *When welding with DC, the "tap" method is often used to strike an arc.*

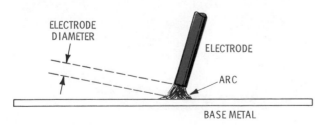

Fig. 13-14. *Once the arc is struck, the distance between the electrode and the metal should be equal to the electrode diameter.*

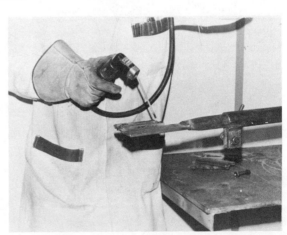

Fig. 13-16. *The electrode should be held at the angle shown for practice welding.*

Arc Weld Joints

The five basic types of joints used in arc welding are the same as those used for oxy-acetylene welding. These include the butt, lap, tee, edge, and corner weld joints discussed in the oxy-acetylene unit. When thin sheet metal is arc-welded, a lap joint is most often used.

Metal plates should first be *tack* welded to keep them from spreading apart while welding. When making a butt joint arc weld, be careful not to space the pieces too far apart. Generally, a space of about 1/16 in. (1.6 mm) should be used between *thin* sheet metal pieces, and a space of about 1/8 in. (3.2 mm) between heavier pieces. Proper spacing provides good penetration and helps avoid melting away the edges of the metal.

MIG WELDERS

The metallic inert gas (MIG) welder, also known as a wire welder, meets the needs in the auto body repair shop. It was introduced primarily for use on high-strength, low-alloy steel panels (identified by HSS or HSLA). It consists of a 150 amp power supply, a wire feeder, and a gun. This welder is mounted on a sturdy wheeled carriage, which also carries an argon gas cylinder (Fig. 13-18). The 150 amp welder has excellent arc characteristics and is suitable for all types of MIG welding. It can be used for MIG welding both steel and aluminum auto body materials. The welder generates enough heat to be used for frame work and similar jobs. A typical 150 amp MIG welder is shown in Figure 13-19.

Fig. 13-18. *The MIG welder cart has provision for the argon gas cylinder.*

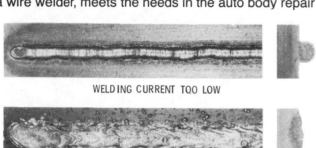

WELDING CURRENT TOO LOW

WELDING CURRENT TOO HIGH

ARC TOO LONG (VOLTAGE TOO HIGH)

WELDING SPEED TOO FAST

WELDING SPEED TOO SLOW

PROPER CURRENT VOLTAGE & SPEED

Fig. 13-17. *Samples of defective practice welds and the causes of the defects. (Courtesy of Hobart Brothers Company)*

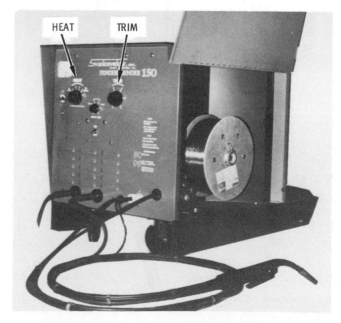

Fig. 13-19. *A spool of wire is mounted on the MIG welder. The wire serves as the electrode when welding. (Courtesy of Systematics, Inc.)*

Types of Gas

No flux is used in MIG welding, since an inert arc shielding gas keeps oxygen away from the weld site. Carbon dioxide (CO_2), argon, or mixed gas (75% argon, 25% CO_2) may be used.

The MIG welder uses a wire 0.030 in. (0.76 mm) or 0.035 in. (0.89 mm) in diameter (Fig. 13-20). This wire can be purchased through the local welding supplier. The MIG welder operates on a 200 volt AC electrical supply.

Connecting the Unit

After the 110 amp welder has been connected to the electrical outlet, it is set for welding sheet metal. The gas hose is connected to a regulator gas supply. Mixed gas (75% argon, 25% CO_2) is recommended for steel welding. The welder is being used on the sheet metal of a truck body in Figure 13-21.

On the front of the unit, the gun power cable is plugged in to the positive red socket. The ground cable is connected to the negative black socket and to the workpiece to make a reverse polarity connection.

Fig. 13-20. *This large spool of wire is mounted on the MIG welder cart. Different types of wire are used for steel and for aluminum.*

Fig. 13-21. *A MIG welder being used on sheet metal panels. (Courtesy of Hobart Brothers Company)*

The gun control cable is plugged into the receptacle on the front of the cabinet, and the gas hose is connected.

The controls on MIG welders usually include:

1. Heat range setting.
2. Wire feed control.
3. Heat range fine adjustment (trim).
4. Spot timer.

The following material outlines the procedure used to operate one type of MIG welder.

Steel Welding

For steel welding, it is best to use a triple deoxidized steel wire and mixed gas. Carbon dioxide gas is also satisfactory but gives a rougher arc and needs more careful trim adjustment.

To prepare for welding, set the *heat control* to 3. This step-type switch should not be changed while welding. The *trim knob* should be set to about mid-scale. The wire should be extended so that ⅜ to ½ in. (9.5 to 12.7 mm) is showing beyond the cup (Fig. 13-22). The gas flow is set at 12 to 15 cfh (cubic feet per hour) [339.4 to 424.3 L/h (liters per hour)].

In steel welding, the gas cup is kept ⅜ in. to ½ in. (9.5 to 12.7 mm) from the work to ensure good gas coverage and stable conditions (Fig. 13-23). The cup

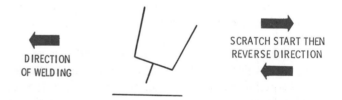

DIRECTION OF WELDING

SCRATCH START THEN REVERSE DIRECTION

Fig. 13-22. *To begin welding, the wire should extend ⅜ to ½ in. (9.5 to 12.7 mm) from the holder. (Courtesy of Systematics, Inc.)*

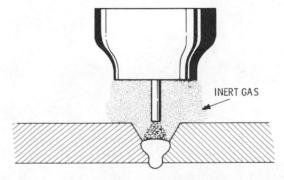

INERT GAS

Fig. 13-23. *The gas cup should be held ⅜ to ½ in. (9.5 to 12.7 mm) from the metal surface. (Courtesy of Reynolds Metals Company)*

is usually held perpendicular to the work or is slightly inclined in the direction of welding (Fig. 13-24). Travel should be with a backhand motion. The gun is usually moved in a slight side-to-side circular pattern. Welding can be done in all positions.

With your welding shield in place bring the wire in contact with the work piece and press the trigger. Welding will start (Fig. 13-25). If the heat is too high or low, stop welding. Adjust the knob up or down to get the desired heat. Adjust the *trim knob* so that a light frying sound is obtained at the arc. If the wire is stubbing into the work and making a popping sound, increase the *trim* setting. If you have a long arc with a hissing sound and drops of molten metal are falling into the puddle, reduce the trim.

Steel welding is usually done with the gun connected to the *red dot* (+) terminal of the welder. The best quality welding arcs are obtained with this connection. This connection makes the sheet hot and the wire cool. When welding on very thin material, as in auto body panel repair, this connection can be reversed. This will make the sheet metal cooler and the welding wire hotter at very low currents. Put the *ground* clamp cable on the *red dot* (+) terminal. This can normally be done only on heat setting of 1 or 2 to allow a smooth arc. This applies only to steel.

Aluminum Welding

Aluminum welding requires the use of a high-grade, H-18 or H-19 hard, *aluminum* wire of the proper composition. The use of soft, oxidized or dirty wire will cause feeding problems.

Pure argon shielding gas must be used at a flow of 25 to 30 cfh (708.3 to 849.9 L/h). An aluminum gun kit must be obtained and installed before welding. This kit consists of a nylon liner for the conduit, contact tip, tip

adapter, gas cup, and outlet bushing. When welding with *aluminum* wire, the arc is started by lightly brushing the wire to the work, *opposite* the direction you wish to travel when welding. When the arc starts, move the gun in the direction of the weld to be made. The aluminum gun is angled slightly away from the direction of welding. The gas cup is kept ½ to ⅝ in. (12.7 to 15.8 mm) above the work.

Watch the end of the welding wire to be sure that a good weld is being made (Fig. 13-26). In Figure 13-27, several MIG welders are being used to build an aluminum truck body.

RESISTANCE SPOT WELDERS

Resistance spot welders (Fig. 13-28) are special arc-welding machines used for spot welding in a body shop.

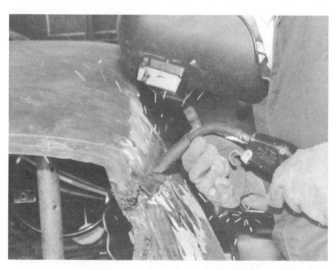

Fig. 13-25. *The wire is brought in contact with the metal and the trigger is pressed to begin welding.*

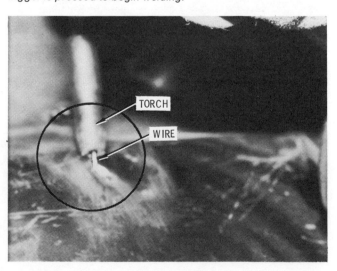

Fig. 13-26. *Watch the end of the wire to be sure that a good weld is being produced.*

Fig. 13-24. *The welding tip should be held at a right angle to the work.*

Fig. 13-27. *Several workers using MIG welders to fabricate an aluminum truck cab. (Courtesy of Hobart Brothers Company)*

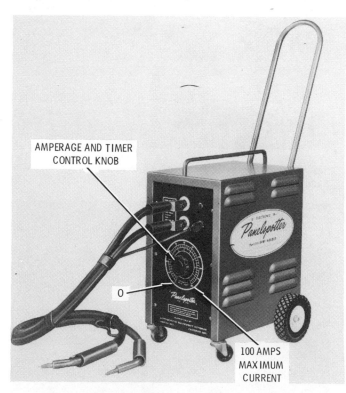

AMPERAGE AND TIMER
CONTROL KNOB

0

100 AMPS
MAXIMUM
CURRENT

Fig. 13-28. *A typical resistance spot welder (panel spotter), which makes two spot welds at one time. (Courtesy of Automotive Equipment Division, Lenco, Inc.)*

They are commonly referred to as "panel spotters." Panel spotters are used only on flange or lap joints or on two pieces of metal that are closely clamped together. An advantage of panel spotters is that they always make *two* spot welds at the same time. This allows the work to be done faster.

A typical panel spotter has an automatic timer built into the amperage control. The amperage control may be adjusted from 0 to 100 amps. Each electrical cable of the panel spotter actually does two jobs. It *first* acts as a supply cord, *then* as a return cable for the electricity. The spot welding electrodes have special tips that do not melt into the weld. Normally, they are used for several months before being replaced.

Panel Spotter Operation

To use a panel spotter, first turn the control dial to the correct amperage and time selection for the job being welded. These may vary according to the manufacturer's recommendations for the type of job being done. For this reason, *refer to the manufacturer's instructions and recommendations* for the brand of equipment being used.

Next, turn on the machine, and place the two electrode "guns" on the areas where the *two* spot welds are to be made (Fig. 13-29). Then, operate the control button on one electrode handle, turning on the current. The machine will then automatically produce two time-controlled spot welds. Examine the welds to determine if changes in time or current is needed.

Replacing a Panel

To replace the damaged panel in Figure 13-30, the panel is first marked with masking tape for cutting. Then, it is cut along the line with a power chisel. The cut is about 2 in. (5.1 cm) below the back glass at the upper part of the panel, as shown in Figure 13-31.

The area where the *new* panel will be overlapped and spot-welded must then be lightly ground with a disc sander. This is done to remove the finish down to bare metal, preparing the surface for spot welds and filler. The new panel is then positioned so that it overlaps the cut-off edge of the old panel. Finally, the panel spotter is used to spot-weld the two panels. Figure 13-32 shows the newly spotted replacement panel before being filled, leveled, and refinished.

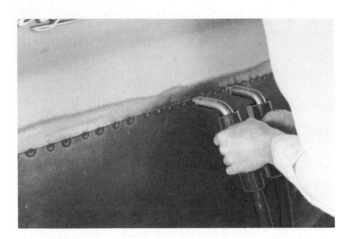

Fig. 13-29. *Positioning the electrode guns to make spot welds on a replacement panel. (Courtesy of Automotive Equipment Division, Lenco, Inc.)*

Fig. 13-30. *A buckled and badly dented quarter panel that must be replaced.*

Spot Welding Advantages

Resistance spot welders used for fastening thin sheet metal are not as likely to buckle or warp the metal as would the flame of an oxy-acetylene torch. This is because the heat from the actual weld itself is concentrated in a small area. These small electric welders are also less of a fire hazard than are oxy-acetylene welders, especially around fuel tanks and upholstery.

These machines produce fewer metal sparks and less molten metal than conventional arc or oxy-acetylene welders. The weld is time controlled, so the surrounding metal gets no hotter than is absolutely necessary.

Spot Welding Disadvantages

A major *disadvantage* of spot welding machines is that they cannot be used to fill large holes, tears, or gaps. Generally, even *conventional arc welders* should

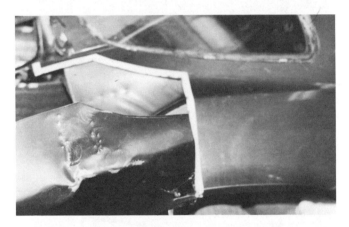

Fig. 13-31. *The damaged quarter panel has been cut away with a power chisel.*

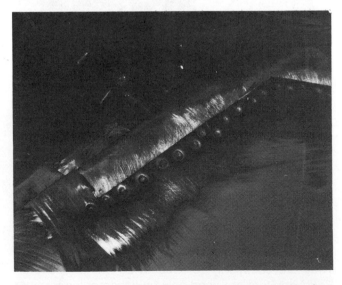

Fig. 13-32. *A new quarter panel has been spot-welded in place.*

not be used on openings more than ⅛ in. (3.2 mm) wide. This is because the high arc temperature may *burn away* the edges of a large opening, making it even larger. Care must be taken to leave an opening of *less than* ⅛ in. (3.2 mm) when two pieces of metal are to be welded electrically.

Another disadvantage is that the electrode "guns" must be held more or less *perpendicular* to the base metal for the best welds. Oxy-acetylene welders, of course, can also be used at different angles to the base metal. This allows a body worker doing oxy-acetylene welding to have more control over heating the metal and moving the torch. Finally, oxy-acetylene equipment can be used to *heat* metal without welding it.

Section V

Major Repairs

Bumper Assemblies

Since the 1920s, most automobiles have had front and rear bumpers as standard equipment. Many present-day bumpers, like the one shown in Figure 14-1, are made of bright, shiny, chrome-plated spring steel. There are also spring steel bumpers that are not chrome plated. These bumpers are simply painted (Fig.14-2).

Some of the latest bumper designs are not made of steel. Instead, they are made of a special rubber called *urethane*. This material is molded around a steel core, and the core is then attached to the car's frame. Because the urethane has no special color of its own, it may be colored the same as the car's body, or "body color." A urethane front bumper is shown on the Corvette in Figure 14-3.

The bumper is very important in auto body design and is usually an expensive item. The bumpers provide the only protection for both the front and rear panels of the vehicle.

Fig. 14-1. *A chrome-plated bumper, also known as a face bar.*

Fig. 14-2. *A painted bumper, like those often used on light trucks.*

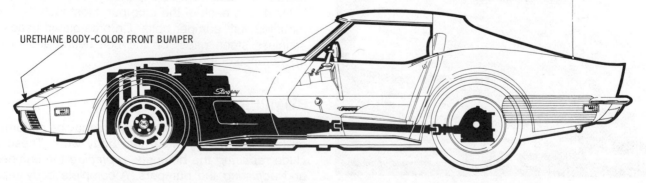

URETHANE BODY-COLOR FRONT BUMPER

Fig. 14-3. *Body-color urethane bumper covers are used on some newer cars. (Courtesy of Road & Track Magazine)*

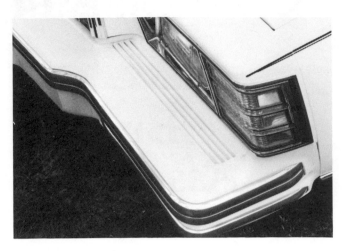

Fig. 14-4. *A front bumper that wraps around and helps protect the front fender.*

Bumpers on many vehicles also protect *side* areas. These bumpers curve around the lower parts of the front fenders (Fig.14-4) and the rear quarter panels (Fig.14-5). These extensions provide additional protection for the sides of the vehicle. Before 1972, automobiles were usually protected with a fixed bumper. Figure 14-6 shows an impact-absorbing bumper. These bumpers are used on most cars today.

BUMPER PARTS

Automobile bumpers have several basic parts: a front or rear *face bar*, *bolts*, and, sometimes, *bumper guards*. Brackets are used to attach the bumper to the energy-absorbing units of the automobile.

Face Bar

The bumper *face bar* on many cars is hard spring steel that is plated with the bright metal *chromium*.

Fig. 14-5. *A rear bumper than wraps around and helps protect the rear quarter panel.*

Some cars have a rubberlike (urethane) material covering the bumper. The front bumper is protection for the front end parts of the body. The front face bar is also an accent molding, which helps beautify the automobile.

Chrome Face Bar. Chrome-plated bumper face bars are made from the same steel for both front and rear units. Rear bumpers serve as an accent panel for the vehicle and help protect it during very minor rear-end collisions.

Soft Face Bar. Many automobiles have a soft face bar called a bumper cover. Figure 14-4 shows a urethane bumper cover. This type of bumper has two major parts, the *bumper cover* and the *support bar*.

The cover is a soft rubberlike material that is molded to fit over the support bar and conform to the contour of the vehicle. Bolt holes are molded in the cover, which is bolted onto the support bar.

The support bar is a very strong component that fits behind the cover. It is the strength of the bumper. The support bar is made of both steel and aluminum. Both box-type and channel-type support bars are made. Figure 14-7 shows a rear bumper cover support bar.

Bumper Guards

A face bar with *bumper guards* attached is shown in Figure 14-8. Bumper guards have the same job as the face bar. The main job of a bumper guard is to prevent other bumpers from riding up over the vehicle's bumper. Bumper guards are also used to accent the appearance of the face bar and the grille or panels behind the bar.

Bumper Bolts

Bolts are used to fasten *the face bars to the support bar*. These bolts normally have a square shoulder just below the head (Figs.14-9 and 14-10). This shoulder fits into the square hole in the face bar, as shown in Figure 14-10. A flat washer, lock washer, and nut hold the bolt in place from behind the frame bracket, which is located in back of the face bar. Most face bars are mounted with bumper bolts. Chrome-plated heads or stainless steel "caps" on the bolt heads add to the appearance of the face bar.

BUMPER REPAIRS

There are several operations that may be performed on bumpers during most auto body work. These include *repairing* the bumpers, *replacing* the bumpers, and *adjusting* the bumpers. A complete body repair may be criticized if the bumpers are not properly aligned and adjusted.

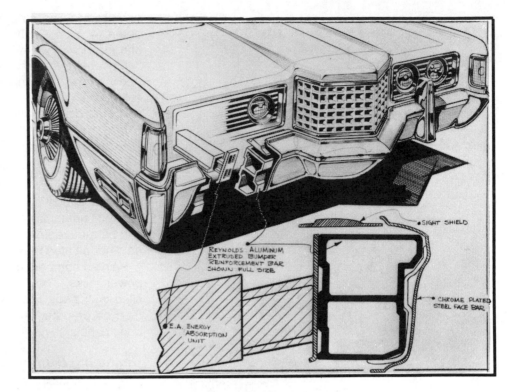

Fig. 14-6. *A typical impact-absorbing front bumper. (Courtesy of Customer Service Division, Ford Motor Company)*

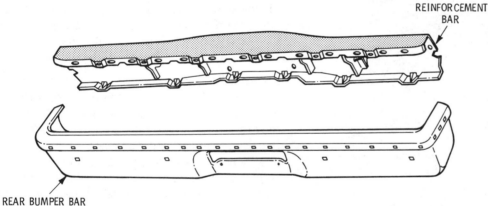

Fig. 14-7. *The face bar and reinforcement bar. (Courtesy of Customer Service Division, Ford Motor Company)*

Repairing Chrome-plated Bumpers

Most chrome-plated bumpers that are damaged cannot be repaired in a body shop. This is because a damaged chrome surface cannot be ground smooth and filled as can a painted surface.

Chrome plating is applied to a repaired (or new) metal bumper surface by an electrical process. This process is used by automobile manufacturers and in rechroming shops, but it is too complicated and expensive to be used in an average body shop. Chrome plating, therefore, is not normally done by a body repair shop.

The damaged bumpers are usually exchanged for rechromed bumpers from a rechroming shop. These shops pick up damaged chrome bumpers that can be repaired. Then, workers at the rechrome shop reshape

Fig. 14-8. *The face bar is often equipped with bumper guards.*

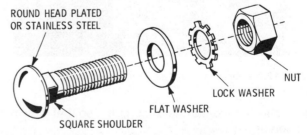

Fig. 14-9. *To hold the bumper to the mounting brackets, bumper bolts are used. The bolt has a square shoulder to prevent rotation and is used with a flat washer, a lock washer, and a nut.*

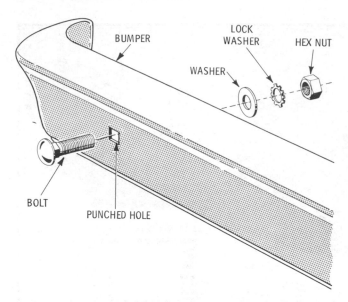

Fig. 14-10. *The square shoulder of the bolt fits a matching hole in the bumper face bar.*

Fig. 14-11. *A chrome-plated face bar that has been extensively damaged.*

Fig. 14-12. *A face bar that has been straightened, rechromed, and installed on a car.*

and rechrome the damaged bumpers so that they may be used again.

Figure 14-11 shows a damaged chrome-plated bumper face bar. Although the damage looks bad, this

bumper may be straightened, rechromed, and used again. A bumper that has been reshaped and rechromed is shown in Figure 14-12.

Most rechrome shops do not attempt to repair very badly damaged bumpers. However, many shops may splice (weld together) the good halves of two bumpers that were badly damaged on opposite ends.

Repairing Painted Bumpers

Bumper face bars that are not chrome plated may be painted with enamel paint. Painted bumpers are used on almost all *trucks*. Figure 14-2 illustrated a painted bumper from a small truck. This type of bumper can be repaired and refinished in much the same way as other painted metal parts.

Painted bumpers may be reshaped and aligned with power jacks. They can then be ground smooth and filled with body filler, as needed. The bumpers may then be prepared and repainted in the same way as body panels.

Replacing Bumpers

When a vehicle has been involved in a front-end or rear-end collision, the bumper usually must be replaced. Whether a new, rechromed, or repainted bumper is installed, the procedure is basically the same. To replace a bumper, follow the procedure outlined below.

1. For impact-absorbing bumpers, plan to remove the bumper face bar from the energy absorber. Fixed bumper mounting brackets should be removed along with the face bar.
2. Roll under the car, and disconnect any light wires or attachments running to the bumper.
3. Remove the bumper nuts and bolts. A rust penetrant may be needed to help break the bolts loose.
4. Have a helper hold the bumper as you remove the last two bolts.
5. With the helper, remove the complete bumper assembly from the car.
6. Place the bumper face down on a convenient work surface.
7. Check the bolt holes on each absorber unit. Be sure that they are not badly torn or stretched. If they are, the vehicle may have additional frame damage.
8. Set the replacement bumper next to the old bumper.
9. Transfer all undamaged parts from the old bumper to the replacement.
10. If the vehicle has bumper *guards* (Fig.14-13), be certain that they are installed correctly. First, install the rubber strip, if the guard is so equipped

(Fig. 14-14). Then, install the guard on the bumper (Fig.14-15).

11. With a helper, install the replacement bumper on the vehicle. Leave the *energy absorber* bolts (or fixed bumper mounting bracket bolts) *loose* to allow for adjustment.

12. Connect any wires running to lights in the bumper assembly.

13. Adjust the bumper for a correct, even fit.

Adjusting Bumpers

To allow the bumper to fit the contour of the car closely and correctly, it can be adjusted up, down, in, and out. This is possible because of the slotted holes in the end section of the frame to which the energy absorbers (or fixed bumper mounting brackets) are attached. These slots allow most bumpers to be adjusted as much as 1 in. (2.5 cm) up and forward or down and inward. Similar holes on the front of the energy-absorbing units allow side-to-side adjustments. The slotted holes are covered with large flat washers to hold the parts in alignment when the bolts are tightened.

To adjust a bumper, have a helper hold it in position as you tighten the bolts from beneath the car. Tighten the bolts just enough to hold the bumper in place, then roll out from under the car. Check the alignment at the corners and across the top edge of the bumper. Be certain that clearances are *equal* all the way across and around the bumper. If necessary, loosen the bolts slightly and realign the bumper.

Finally, tighten the bolts firmly. Then, check the operation of any lights in the bumper to be sure that they are working correctly.

IMPACT-ABSORBING BUMPERS

Since the early 1970s, most automobiles built in the United States have been equipped with bumpers that will withstand much more shock than will fixed bumpers. These bumper assemblies have many parts and are known as *impact-absorbing* bumpers. Impact-absorbing bumpers are able to withstand impact with a flat barrier at 5 mph (miles per hour) [8 km/h (kilometers per hour)] in the front and 2.5 mph (4 km/h) in the rear, without being damaged. They are designed to withstand these impacts without damage to the vehicle's lighting, exhaust, fuel, cooling, and hood and deck-lid latching systems. The bumpers were developed to provide better protection for both the vehicle *and* its passengers.

Impact-absorbing bumpers are able to absorb minor impacts and then return to their original position without being damaged. Because of the design requirements, new parts and new technology were needed to

Fig. 14-13. *Bumper guards can be replaced when damaged.*

Fig. 14-14. *The rubber strip on the front of the bumper guard being replaced.*

Fig. 14-15. *The reassembled bumper guard is attached to the bumper.*

produce impact-absorbing bumpers. Figure 14-16 shows a typical breakdown of an impact-absorbing bumper assembly. A basic feature of most systems is the use of energy-absorbing hydraulic cylinders to which the bumper assembly is mounted. Figure 14-17 shows a

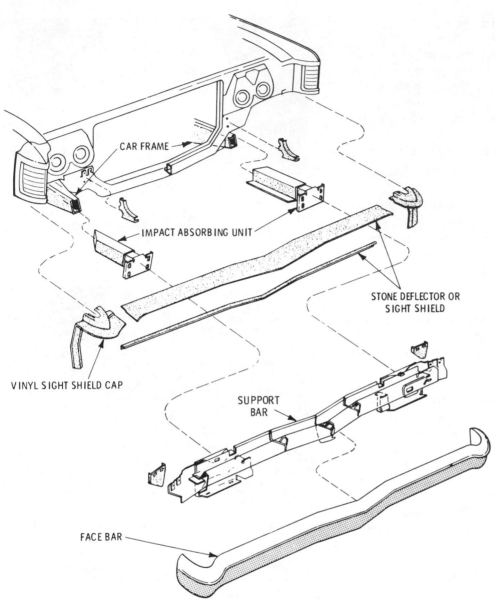

CAR FRAME

IMPACT ABSORBING UNIT

STONE DEFLECTOR OR
SIGHT SHIELD

VINYL SIGHT SHIELD CAP

SUPPORT
BAR

FACE BAR

Fig. 14-16. *A typical impact-absorbing bumper assembly. (Courtesy of Customer Service Division, Ford Motor Company)*

Fig. 14-17. *A typical impact absorber unit used with impact-absorbing bumpers. (Courtesy of Fisher Body Division, General Motors Corporation)*

typical hydraulic cylinder energy absorber unit. A different type of energy absorber is shown in Figure 14-18.

Design of the Energy Absorber

The energy absorber (Fig. 14-19) consists of two main parts, an outer cylinder and an inner cylinder containing a return spring and a piston. Inside the cylinder is a reservoir containing hydraulic fluid. The piston has a small hole (orifice) in it. As the bumper comes in contact with an object, fluid is forced through the orifice in the piston. This allows the bumper to move backward slowly. After the impact, the pressure is released on the bumper. The return spring causes the bumper

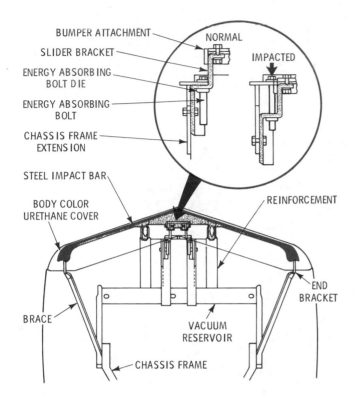

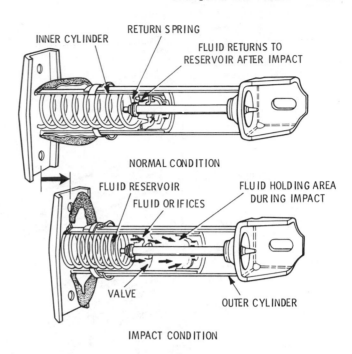

Fig. 14-19. *How an impact absorber works. (Courtesy of Chrysler Corporation)*

Fig. 14-18. *An impact-absorbing system that uses metal deformation to "soak up" an impact. In a minor collision, these parts are permanently damaged and must be replaced. (Courtesy of Fisher Body Division, General Motors Corporation)*

to return to the normal position. The fluid flows back to the reservoir.

Other Systems. Some impact-absorbing bumper systems are completely different from those used on most larger, late-model passenger cars. In the design shown in Figure 14-18, a "metal deformation" technique is used to absorb the impact. The bumper face bar *surface* is actually a "body color" urethane pad covering a steel bumper bar. The pad looks like part of the body because it is closely fitted and is the same color as the body.

After an impact at up to 5 mph (8 km/h), the urethane pad returns to its original shape with little or no *visible* evidence of the bump. However, the steel impact bar, the two energy-absorbing bolts, and the two end brackets *must* be replaced, since they will have been permanently damaged (deformed) by the impact.

This system offers lower initial cost and lighter weight. However, it is more expensive to *repair* this system because the damaged parts must be replaced after low-speed impacts.

Impact-absorbing System Bumper Parts

Impact-absorbing bumper systems usually have more parts than fixed bumpers. The impact-absorbing system parts are generally heavier, stronger, and more expensive than comparable parts of a fixed bumper system.

Face Bars and Bumper Covers. The chrome-plated steel bumper face bar has been used on the automobile for many years. Bumper covers are soft and flexible. The cover is bolted to a strong *support* bar, usually made of aluminum (Fig.14-20). The support bar is attached to the energy absorber units.

Support Bar. Impact-absorbing bumper systems have strong, heavy *support bars* just in back of the face bar. The face bar is bolted to the support, which is then bolted to the energy absorbers. Notice the heavy support bar in Figure 14-16.

A number of bumper bolts hold the face bar to the support bar. This is done because the face bar and support bar must be securely fastened together to act as one unit. Large bolts then hold the support bar to the energy absorbers (Fig.14-21).

Energy Absorbers. The support bars are attached to the energy absorbers, which fit onto the frame horns as shown in Figures 14-16 and 14-21.

Like other automotive parts, the design and shape of the energy absorbers vary from one manufacturer to another. The energy absorbers are generally either *round* (Fig.14-17) or *square* (Fig.14-21). Whether square or round, all energy absorbers do basically the same job.

When a low-speed impact occurs, the bumper assembly is pushed back *into* the energy absorbers. The units absorb the blow, so that it is not passed on to the frame of the vehicle. When pressure is released, the

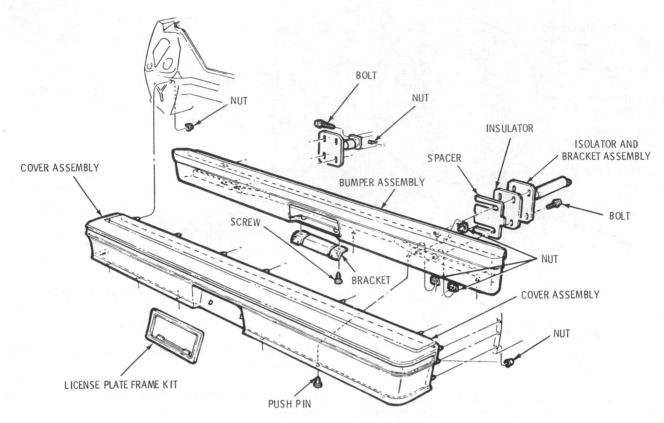

Fig. 14-20. *Components of an impact-absorbing bumper system. (Courtesy of Customer Service Division, Ford Motor Company)*

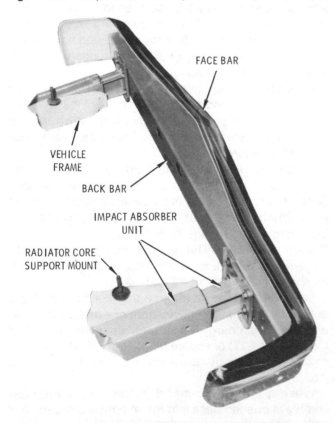

Fig. 14-21. *An assembled impact-absorbing bumper system. (Courtesy of Customer Service Division, Ford Motor Company)*

energy absorber pushes the bumper back out to its normal position. Thus, low-speed [under 5 mph (8 km/h)] impacts are absorbed without damaging the vehicle's body parts. At speeds *over* 5 mph (8 km/h), the energy absorbers and other parts of the car are likely to be permanently damaged. Body shop work will be required to repair and replace the damaged parts.

Impact-absorbing Bumper Tests

Impact-absorbing bumper systems may be *tested* to see if they are in proper working condition. Testing involves separately compressing the energy absorber on each side of the car. The absorber must be compressed at least ⅜ in. (9.5 mm). After this compression, the bumper will return to its normal position if the energy absorber is working properly.

Test Procedure. To test the impact absorber system, the vehicle's ignition must be turned off, the transmission placed in *park* and the parking brake *firmly* set. The car must be parked facing a suitable barrier. Good barriers include a pillar, a sturdy block wall, or a post. Then, place a hydraulic or mechanical jack in a horizontal position between the face bar and the barrier (Fig.14-22).

Align the jack so that it is directly in front of the energy absorber being tested. (Bumper jack slots under the bumper may be used to locate the absorbers.) Position the jack *squarely* with the bumper to avoid having it accidentally slip off.

Use the jack to apply pressure to the bumper. Compress (push in) the bumper at least ⅜ in. (9.5 mm), using a ruler to measure the travel. Release the jack pressure, and allow the bumper to return to its normal position. Repeat the test procedure on the other energy absorber on the opposite side of the bumper.

If both energy absorbers function correctly, the bumper system is able to withstand low-speed impacts. If a unit fails to return to its original position, it should be replaced. (*Driving* into a post, wall, or other barrier to perform this test is NOT recommended.)

Testing Collision Cases. A similar test may be used to check energy absorbers that have been removed from the vehicle to make repairs after a collision. In this case, the jack is again used to compress each absorber. However, *two* fixed barriers must be used. To do this, one barrier is placed behind the jack, and a second barrier is placed behind the impact absorber to hold it firmly in position.

Make the test and observe whether the unit returns to its normal length after being compressed. If it does not, the unit is damaged internally and must be replaced.

Replacing Impact-absorbing Bumpers

When an impact-absorbing bumper has been damaged in a collision, certain precautions must be taken when working on the assembly. These are necessary

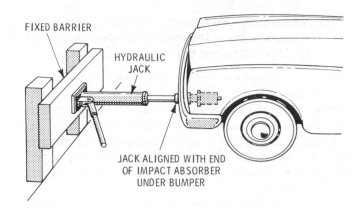

Fig. 14-22. *One method used for testing the effectiveness of an impact absorber. (Courtesy of Fisher Body Division, General Motors Corporation)*

because the absorber units are filled with either a gas or a liquid, which may be under considerable pressure. Impact absorbers can produce a large amount of force if they are bound up (stuck in a compressed position), then suddenly released.

Generally, removal and adjustment procedures for impact-absorbing bumpers and fixed bumpers are similar. However, when working on an impact-absorbing bumper system, keep the following points in mind:

1. *Do not* apply heat to the energy absorbers, either with a welding torch or other heat tools.
2. *Do not* attempt to weld or bend energy absorbers. If a unit does not work correctly, it must be replaced.

Fig. 14-23. *Slotted holes allow adjustment of the impact-absorbing bumper.*

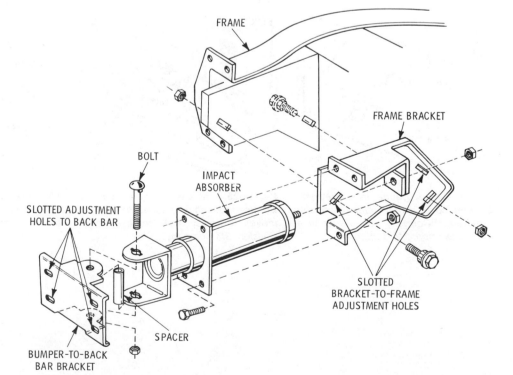

3. When only *one* energy absorber is being removed, support that end of the bumper so that it will not fall when the absorber is removed.

Bound-up Absorbers. When a vehicle with *round* energy absorbers has been involved in a bad collision, one or both absorbers may have been pushed back and bent. This causes them to stick (bind up) in the *compressed* position. Such a situation can be dangerous. If the pressure keeping the absorber compressed is suddenly released, it may shoot forward, causing injury or damage.

To handle this problem and disassemble the damaged bumper without being injured, follow these directions:

1. Wear safety goggles.
2. Stand clear of the bumper at all times.
3. Attach a chain or cable to the bumper to keep it from flying forward if the pressure is suddenly released.
4. *Relieve* the pressure in the absorber by drilling a small hole in it. This should be done at the front part of the absorber, near the bumper back bar.
5. With the pressure relieved, remove and discard the damaged impact absorber unit.

Adjusting Impact-absorbing Bumpers

Impact-absorbing bumpers must be properly *adjusted* for good fit and appearance when collision damage has been repaired. To adjust impact-absorbing bumper assemblies, slotted holes are usually provided. These are located in the rear of the support bar where it bolts to the absorber bracket and at the absorber-to-frame bracket (Fig.14-23).

Side-to-side face bar adjustments are normally made at the slotted holes in the bumper-to-back bar bracket. Up-and-down or in-and-out adjustments are usually made at the frame. The exact adjustment procedures will vary from car model to car model. Impact-absorbing bumper assemblies are quite heavy. Two helpers will probably be necessary to hold the assembly while it is being aligned and the bolts tightened.

SOFT-FACE BUMPER COVER REPAIR

Damage to soft-face bumper covers often can be repaired to look like the original finish. Damage to soft-face bumpers, such as tears, cracks, and punctures, can be repaired by following the steps shown in Figures 14-24 to 14-38.

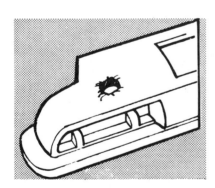

Fig. 14-24. *A gouge in a urethane bumper cover. Such damage can be repaired. (Courtesy of Automotive Trades Division, 3M Company)*

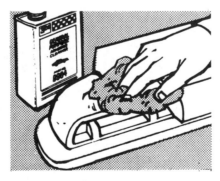

Fig. 14-25. *The area to be repaired must be cleaned with a grease and wax remover. (Courtesy of Automotive Trades Division, 3M Company)*

Fig. 14-26. *Paint is removed and the surface is roughened with a 36-grit sandpaper disc. (Courtesy of Automotive Trades Division, 3M Company)*

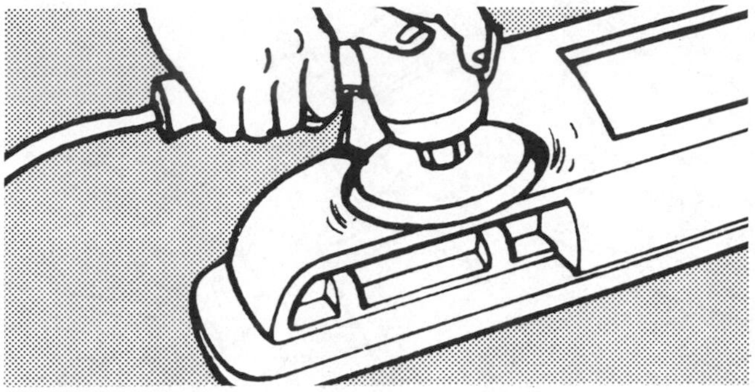

Fig. 14-27. *Paint around the repair area is featheredged. (Courtesy of Automotive Trades Division, 3M Company)*

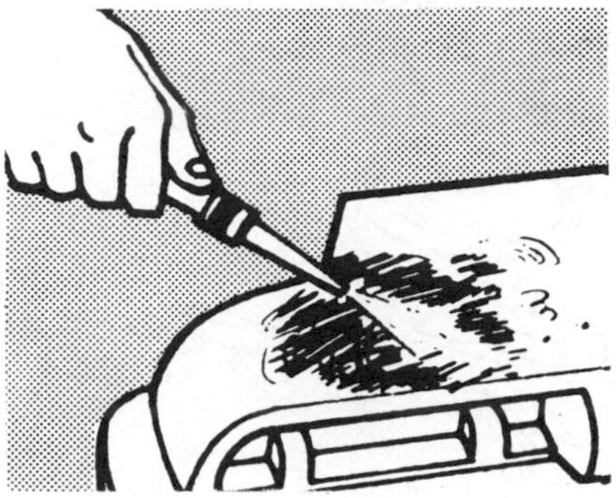

Fig. 14-28. *An air hose is used to remove loose sanding dust. (Courtesy of Automotive Trades Division, 3M Company)*

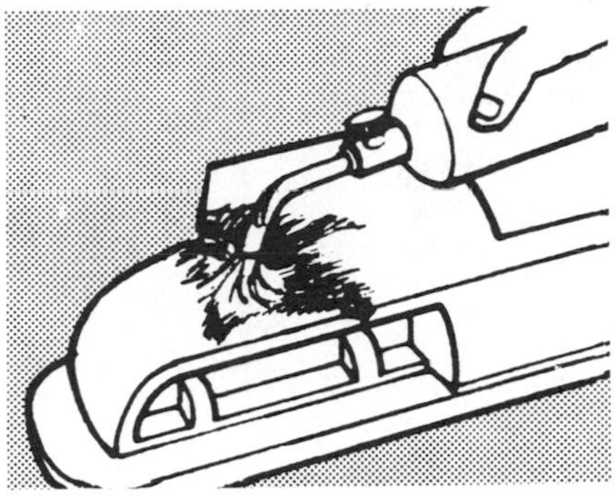

Fig. 14-29. *A torch is used to singe the repair area lightly and to prepare it for structural adhesive. (Courtesy of Automotive Trades Division, 3M Company)*

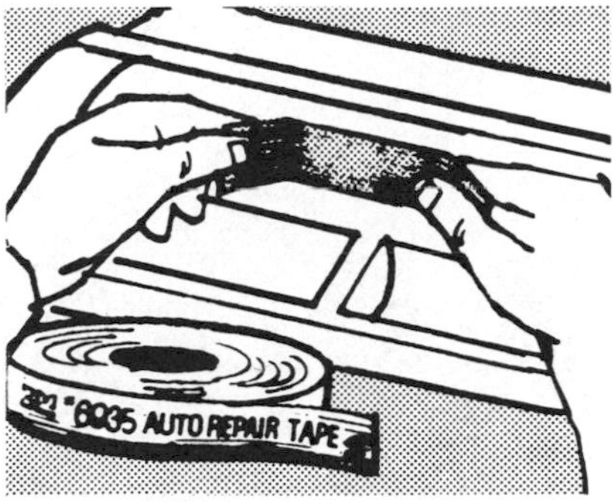

Fig. 14-30. *The underside of the repair area is cleaned with a solvent to remove wax and grease, then auto body tape is applied to form a support for the adhesive. (Courtesy of Automotive Trades Division, 3M Company)*

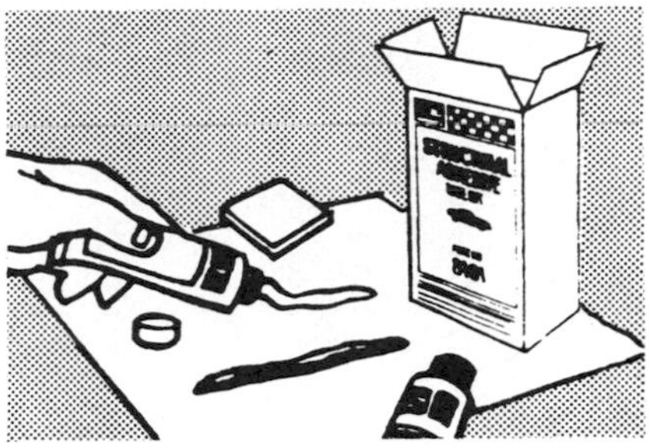

Fig. 14-31. *Structural adhesive is mixed according to the manufacturer's directions. For deep gouges and cracks, the adhesive is usually applied in two steps. Material for each step is mixed separately. (Courtesy of Automotive Trades Division, 3M Company)*

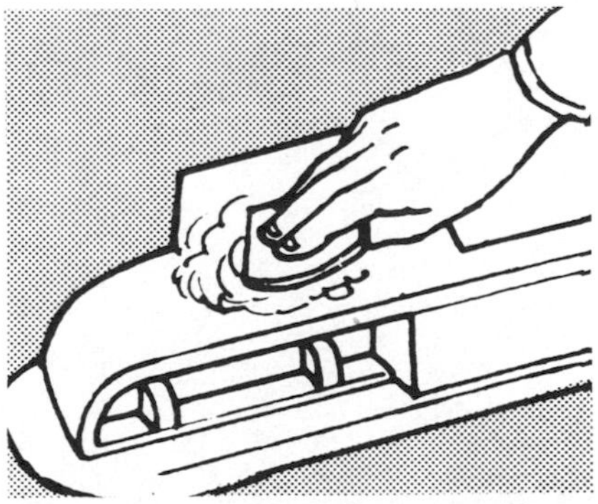

Fig. 14-32. *The adhesive is applied over the entire repair area, using a rubber squeegee. If two coats are used, the first is allowed to dry before the second is mixed and applied. (Courtesy of Automotive Trades Division, 3M Company)*

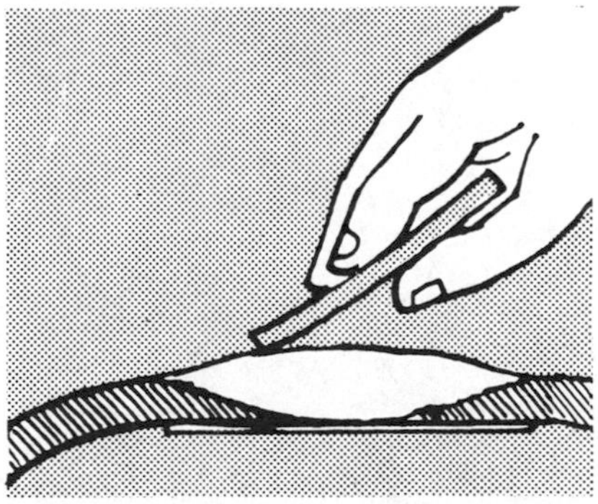

Fig. 14-33. *The adhesive is spread from the edge of the area toward the center. Body putty should* not *be used on flexible parts. (Courtesy of Automotive Trades Division, 3M Company)*

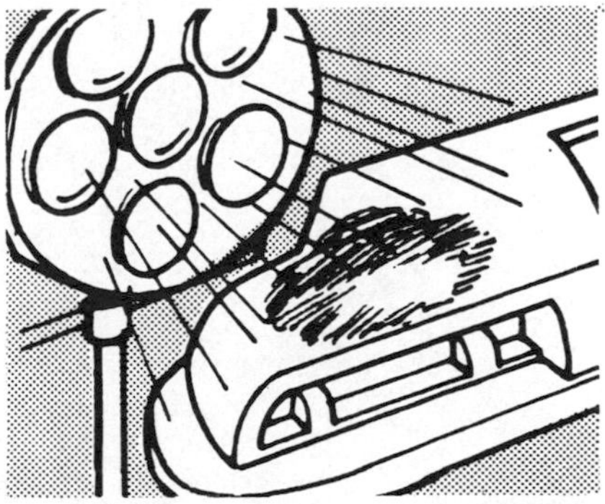

Fig. 14-34. *A heat lamp may be used to speed drying of the adhesive. (Courtesy of Automotive Trades Division, 3M Company)*

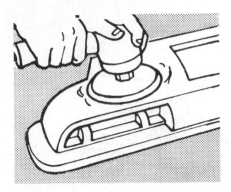

Fig. 14-35. *The dried structural adhesive is leveled with 240-grit sandpaper, then further smoothed with 320-grit paper. (Courtesy of Automotive Trades Division, 3M Company)*

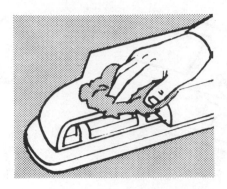

Fig. 14-36. *The repair is wiped with a clean, dry rag and then with a tack rag to remove any dust from sanding. (Courtesy of Automotive Trades Division, 3M Company)*

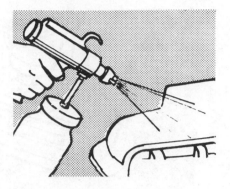

Fig. 14-37. *An elastomeric primer is applied, then sanded with wet 400-grit sandpaper when dry. Finish coats of elastomeric paint may then be sprayed on. (Courtesy of Automotive Trades Division, 3M Company)*

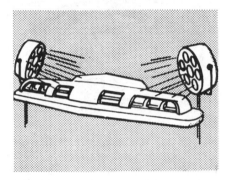

Fig. 14-38. *To speed drying of the paint, a heat lamp may be used. (Courtesy of Automotive Trades Division, 3M Company)*

Unit 15

Frame Straightening

Automobile *frames* are made in different shapes and from different types of steel. The basic job of the frame is to provide a firm and correctly aligned foundation for the vehicle. The frame must support such major parts as the engine, the front and rear suspensions, and the body. Because the frame is so important, expensive and accurate equipment (Fig. 15-1) is used to straighten a frame correctly when it becomes bent.

THE VEHICLE FRAME

All vehicles have some type of *frame* to act as the foundation. The underbody parts, such as the front and rear suspensions, must be attached to the steel beams or box sections of the frame. The vehicle's "drive train" or "running gear" also must be attached to the frame. This includes all the parts needed to turn the wheels and move the vehicle forward, such as the engine, transmission, driveshaft, and differential. The body, with its passenger compartment, is also fitted onto the frame (Fig. 15-2).

Since the body and other major parts of a vehicle are attached to it, the *frame* can be considered the most important part of the vehicle. The frame must provide the support and strength needed by the parts

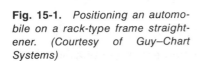

Fig. 15-1. *Positioning an automobile on a rack-type frame straightener. (Courtesy of Guy–Chart Systems)*

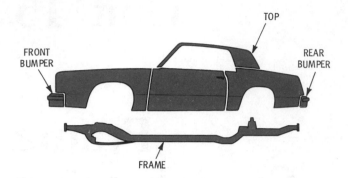

Fig. 15-2. *The auto body is built up around the vehicle frame.*

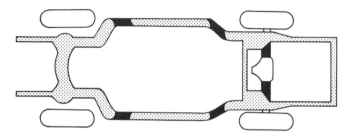

Fig. 15-3. *A conventional frame.*

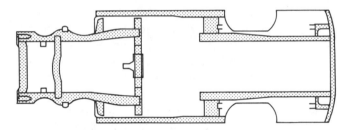

Fig. 15-4. *A common unitized body-frame design.*

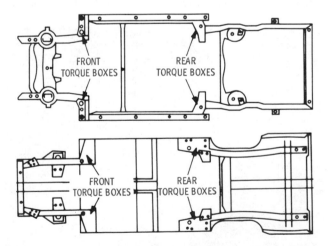

Fig. 15-5. Torque boxes *may be used with either conventional frames or unitized body-frames.*

attached to it. If the frame is designed to go around the outside of the underbody, it will form a metal barrier that acts as a safety guard for the body section of the vehicle. The frame must be strong enough to keep the

Fig. 15-6. *A typical conventional frame.*

other parts of the car in alignment. It must help them to withstand forces and twisting action involved in all types of driving and minor impacts.

Basic Frame Types

Since the early days of the automobile, there have been many design changes and developments in frame sections and frame designs. Generally, these changes have centered upon the development of *two basic types* of frames. These are known as the *conventional* frame (Fig. 15-3) and the *unitized body-frame* (Fig. 15-4).

In the conventional frame, the body is *bolted* to the frame. Unitized body-frames, however, are a body and frame designed and built as one piece.

Many late-model frame designs use *torque boxes* for a smooth ride. Figure 15-5 shows the common locations of torque boxes on these frame designs. Frames with torque boxes may be safer than frames without them. The frame's torque box areas will absorb much of the impact of a front or rear collision. The torque boxes will give, absorbing some of the impact.

Conventional Frame

A typical *conventional* frame from under a late-model vehicle is shown in Figure 15-6. This conventional frame is built of strong steel. Not all conventional frames are designed like the one in Figure 15-6. Designs used for other types of conventional frames are shown in Figure 15-7.

Conventional frames are built much like a bridge. They usually have two strong, heavy beams that run the full length of the vehicle. These are known as *side rails*. Several *crossmembers* hold the side rails in place, equally spaced from each other. There are usually four or more crossmembers (Fig.15-8).

The body and other major parts of the vehicle are normally *bolted* to the frame. Basically, the earliest conventional frame designs and the current designs are fairly similar, except for minor changes. For example, crossmembers were first joined to the side rails by being *riveted*. Today, they may be joined by being riveted, welded, or bolted in place. Note that the crossmember in Figure 15-9 is *bolted* to the side rail. The most basic change in conventional frame design, however, has been in the *shape* of the side rails and crossmembers.

Early Frame Designs. On the first conventional frame designs, the side rails were fairly simple, flat steel beams. Crossmembers were either made of flat pieces or were shaped from so-called *channel iron.*

Later Frame Designs. First, the side rail's shape was changed from a flat beam shaped to an "I-beam" shape. This was done by simply welding plates to the top and bottom of the standard flat beam (Fig.15-10).

Many side rails were then changed from an I-beam to an angle-iron shape (Fig.15-11). Later, the channel iron shape (first used for crossmembers) was adapted to side rail design. Figure 15-12 shows channel iron designs.

Current Frame Design. Finally, the side rail was changed to a *box* shape. This was done by welding two channel iron pieces together to form a box section, as in Figure 15-13. This is the type of side rail commonly used in current frame designs. The crossmembers used with this side rail have either a channel iron or box shape.

This design provides a strong, safe frame. Even though it is strong, it is also *flexible*. It may give on impact, absorbing much of the shock of a collision. This makes the vehicle safer for the passengers.

Unitized Body-frame

The newer unitized body-frame has the same purpose and does the same jobs as a conventional frame. However, the unitized body-frame *design* and *principle* are different, because the body and frame are one piece (Fig.15-14).

When unitized body-frame vehicles were first developed, the frame section was in some ways similar to that of conventional frame vehicles. The side rails extended the entire length of the vehicle, as shown in Figure 15-15. The difference was that the body floor panels were *welded* to the frame, rather than *bolted*.

The body panels and frame sections of a unitized body-frame design are *joined together* as *one unit*. The body and frame should be thought of as *one piece*, rather than as two separate parts. This is the reason for the name "unitized or unit body-frame."

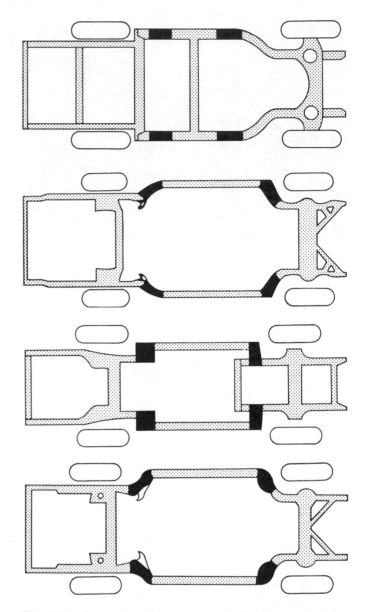

Fig. 15-7. *Conventional frames are basically the same but may differ from manufacturer to manufacturer, as shown.*

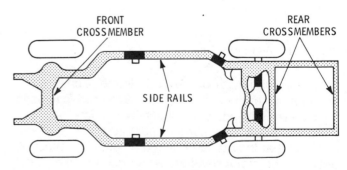

Fig. 15-8. *The basic parts of a conventional frame.*

Figure 15-16 shows how some of the later unitized body-frame designs differ from conventional frame designs. Note that these designs do not have side rails

Fig. 15-9. *A typical crossmember bolted to the side rail.*

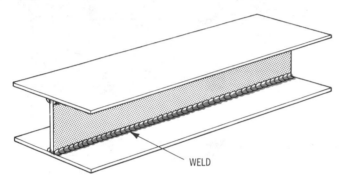

Fig. 15-10. *I-beam iron.*

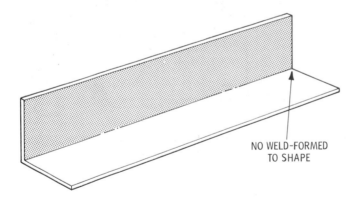

Fig. 15-11. *Angle iron.*

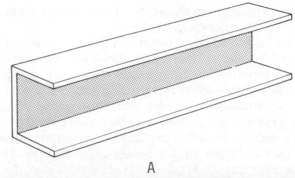

A

B

Fig. 15-12. *(A) Simple channel iron. (B) A rear frame crossmember made of channel iron.*

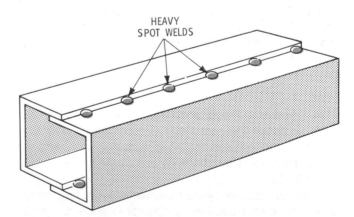

Fig. 15-13. *Two pieces of channel iron welded together to form part of the "box frame" design used for many automobile side rails.*

down the full length of the body frame. Some of the body panels are heavily built and reinforced to replace the side rail sections of a conventional frame.

An important *advantage* of unitized body-frame vehicles is that they tend to be more tightly constructed, because the major parts are all welded together. Most unitized body-frame parts are made of thinner steel than are the frame sections of conventional frame vehicles. Also, most of the frame section panels are made with a boxlike construction. This makes the body frame stronger but more flexible.

A major *disadvantage* of unitized body-frames is that when one frame section is damaged, the frame sections attached to it are usually damaged as well. This means that the shop will need more equipment to repair the unit body.

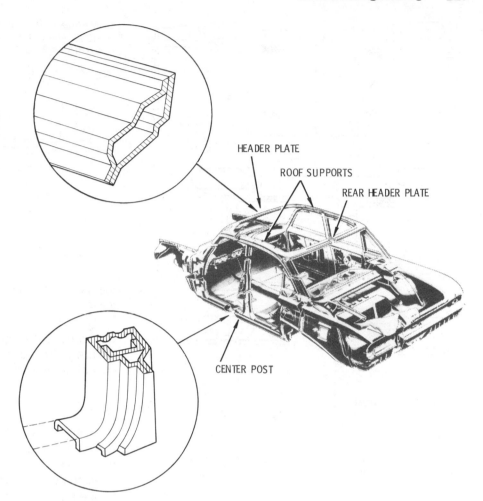

Fig. 15-14. *A unitized body-frame design. (Courtesy of* Autobody and the Reconditioned Car*)*

HEADER PLATE

ROOF SUPPORTS

REAR HEADER PLATE

CENTER POST

Floor. The *floor* part of a unitized body-frame is made of heavier metal than that of a floor designed for a conventional frame. The floor is usually made up of a strong sheet metal stamping, reinforced with several crossmembers. These crossmembers and the floor stamping are welded together. The floor section becomes several strong box sections. These boxlike sections make the floor very strong, but difficult to realign if it is seriously damaged.

The *floor* of an unitized vehicle plays a major role in the alignment of the entire unit. If the floor has been buckled or damaged in an accident, the estimator must add extra time and labor charges to align the floor structure.

Additional strength is sometimes built into the floor by welding metal strips inside the box-shaped crossmembers or side rails. These metal strips usually run from one corner of the box to the other (Fig.15-17). The name *reinforced channel* is used to describe these parts.

Stub Frame. Some unitized body-frame designs appear to have side rails extending down the full length of the vehicle, when viewed from under the hood. This

is not the case, however. Instead, this is a so-called "stub frame" design, shown in Figure 15-18. Stub frames are widely used throughout the automobile industry.

The stub frame looks like, and is built like, a conventional frame. However, this "frame" does not extend under the complete vehicle. Rather, the stub frame stops under the car at about the front seat. Several bolts hold the stub frame to the reinforced floor of the unitized body-frame.

With a stub frame design, then, the center part of the unitized body-frame has *no* side rails. The floor section

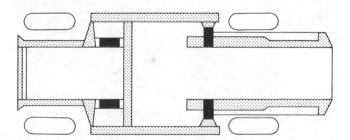

Fig. 15-15. *A unitized body-frame design with welded side rails. The dark areas are lift points.*

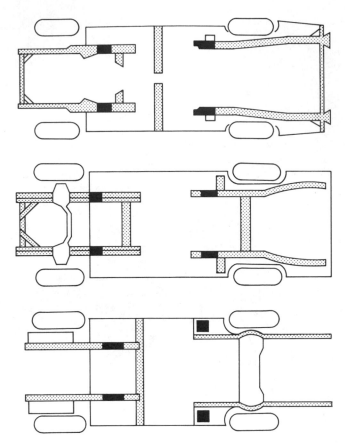

Fig. 15-16. *Several common unitized body-frame designs. The dark areas are lift points.*

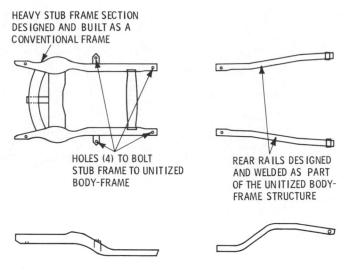

Fig. 15-18. *A stub frame is bolted to the front of a unitized body-frame.*

takes the place of the extended side rails. This makes the floor section very important, as in the case with other unitized body-frame designs.

The stub frame assembly is replaceable. When the front or side rail parts are severely damaged, they may be replaced. The floor section of the unitized body-frame also may be replaced if it is damaged so severely that realignment is impossible. However, it usu-

ally *can* be realigned. If the floor is damaged *that* severely, the car is probably "totaled." This means the cost of repair exceeds the value of the vehicle.

Torque Boxes

An important design development leading to smoother riding and longer life was the *torque box* concept. Torque boxes may be used on either conventional frames or unitized body-frames. A typical conventional frame with torque boxes is shown in Figure 15-19. A unitized body-frame design with torque boxes is illustrated in Figure 15-20.

In a torque box design, the passenger compartment is *wider* than either the front or rear frame sections. The corners of this compartment are attached to the front and rear sections of the frame or unitized body-frame with *torque boxes*. These boxes actually twist to absorb the shock of bumps or rough roads. The torque boxes also absorb much of the impact of a collision.

Torque is a twisting or turning force. The torque *boxes* allow the front and rear sections of the frame to move up and down (twist) to absorb road shocks or impacts (Fig. 15-21). This helps keep the shocks and jolts from reaching the passenger compartment, providing a smooth ride. If one wheel hits a bump, part of the shock transferred to the frame is absorbed by the torque box near that wheel. This reduces the shock transferred to the passenger compartment.

Most conventional and unitized body-frames are equipped with some type of torque box design. Torque boxes are so specialized that automotive engineers often use a computer to determine exactly where the torque boxes should be and how they should be made. If the boxes become misaligned or damaged, the ve-

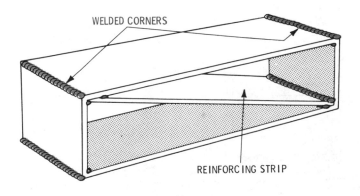

Fig. 15-17. *A reinforcing strip welded inside a box channel will make it much stronger.*

hicle's steering and riding comfort may be seriously affected.

FRAME ALIGNMENT

Automobile frames are made from strong metal. They must hold the vehicle and its parts in alignment for a long time, under many types of driving conditions.

It is very important that the frame be in correct *alignment* if the car is to handle and ride properly. Frames are designed and built with reference points for measuring and checking alignment. When a vehicle has been involved in an accident or may otherwise be misaligned, these points are used to be sure of correct alignment. Figure 15-22 shows the location of reference points used for one frame.

Frame alignment is a *very* important part of total auto body repair. If the frame is misaligned, the vehicle's body will also be misaligned. Frame misalignment will affect the appearance, the ride, and the handling of the vehicle. It also can cause greatly increased tire wear. The increased friction caused by misalignment may cause greater fuel use, since the engine must work harder to move the car. The procedures for checking and aligning frames are discussed later in this unit.

Importance Of Frame Straightening

The vehicle's tightness, panel fit, and driving accuracy depend on good frame alignment, so frame work

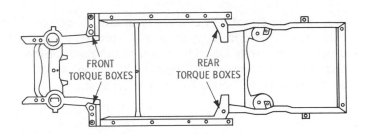

Fig. 15-19. *Torque boxes are located under the corners of the passenger compartment in a conventional frame design.*

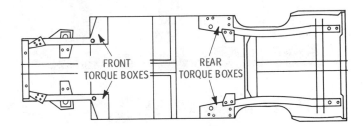

Fig. 15-20. *Torque boxes on the corners of the passenger compartment in a unitized body-frame design.*

Fig. 15-21. *Torque boxes actually allow the frame to move up and down (or twist) along with the suspension as the car moves along the road. The movement is very small and cannot be seen.*

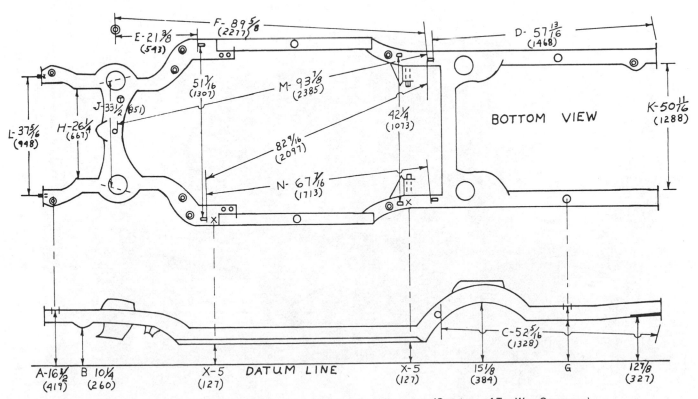

Fig. 15-22. *Measuring points on the frame, used to establish correct alignment. (Courtesy of Tru-Way Company)*

is a very important part of any larger auto body repair business. There is a good deal of profit in frame-straightening work. Considering the time saved and the customer satisfaction involved, most frame straighteners will pay for themselves in a short time.

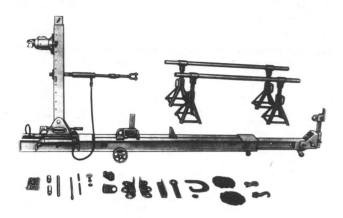

Fig. 15-23. *A portable frame straightener. (Courtesy of Bear Division, Applied Power Industries)*

Frame Technician's Job. To get the best results, a body mechanic or frame technician must know both the basic principles of frame straightening *and* how to operate the unit being used in the shop. The technician must know how to *dissect* a frame (check it by sections) for a complete and accurate appraisal of damage. He or she must be also able to estimate the *cost* of repairs. The repair technician must know how to use a *specification book.* This helps the technician see how much damage is present and how far the frame is out of alignment. Finally, this specialist must know how to gauge (measure) a frame after repair, to be sure that all the measurements are within specification.

TYPES OF FRAME STRAIGHTENING EQUIPMENT

Nearly all body shops are equipped with some type of *frame straightener.* Smaller shops normally have *portable* units priced from several hundred dollars on up, such as the one in Figure 15-23. Permanent *rack-type* straighteners, costing several thousand dollars,

Fig. 15-24. *A stationary frame straightener, which would be bolted to the shop floor. (Courtesy of Guy–Chart Systems)*

Fig. 15-25. *The bench system frame straightener is used to both diagnose and correct frame alignment problems. (Courtesy of Blackhawk Division, Applied Power Industries)*

are found in large shops or frame specialty shops. A typical rack-type straightener (Fig. 15-24) is available with many attachments.

Portable Units

Portable frame straightening units are profit-making pieces of equipment. They are especially useful in small shops that cannot afford the more expensive rack-type equipment. A main advantage of the portable unit is that it can be moved anywhere in the shop and easily stored out of the way. Portable units are light, strong, and inexpensive.

Anchor Rail Units

Heavy anchor rail-type frame straighteners are stationary and more expensive than portable units. The advantage of this type of frame straightener is *speed*. The vehicle is either pulled or driven onto the rack, and *several* hook-ups are made. This allows more than one damaged area to be pulled *at the same time*, a feature that is not available on most portable units.

Bench Systems

There are two types of bench measuring and aligning systems: the *dedicated bench system* shown in Figure 15-25, and the *universal bench system* shown in Figure 15-27. Both systems do the same job and are primarily used on compact and subcompact vehicles. ***Dedicated Bench.*** The dedicated bench system is a "pre-measured" jig that fits a vehicle frame (Fig. 15-25). The measuring towers are placed in specific spots on the underbody. The frame is out of alignment

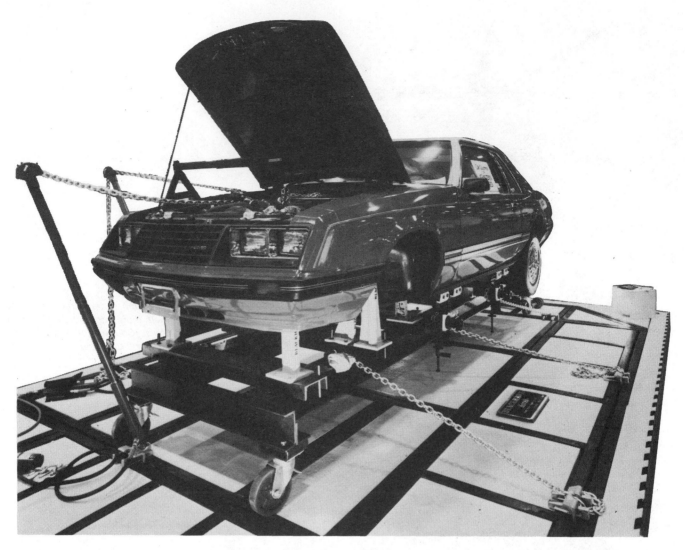

Fig. 15-26. *The bench system uses special jigs for each make and model of car. (Courtesy of Blackhawk Division, Applied Power Industries)*

Fig. 15-27. *A universal bench measuring and aligning system.*

when a tower does not match the factory specification mark on the underbody. The dedicated bench uses the undamaged portion of the frame to get an accurate measurement. It can be used on almost all unitized body-frames, and with most in-the-floor-type frame straighteners (Fig. 15-26).

Universal Bench. The universal bench is a measuring and aligning system (Fig. 15-27). The measuring towers are on the bench frame and can be used to measure from the bench frame to the vehicle frame. The correct measurements are taken from the frame specification book and measured upward (Fig. 15-28) into the factory specification holes on the frame of the vehicle.

Frame Clamp

The pinch-weld box clamp is a heavy frame used to support and align the light unitized underbody. The frame is made with strong angle or channel iron. The box sides are adjustable to fit most unitized underbodies.

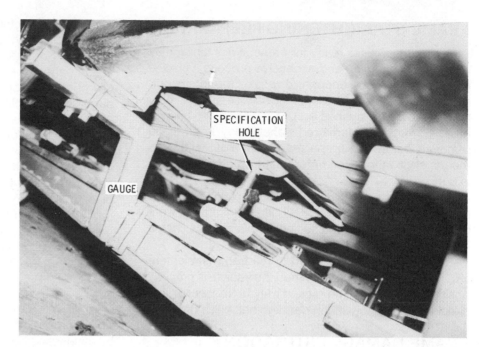

Fig. 15-28. *A universal bench gauge and a frame specification hole.*

The box corners have strong clamps that attach to the vehicle pinch-welds of the vehicle's unitized underbody. When the box clamp is securely attached to the pinch welds, the pull jack can apply pressure and align the underbody of the damaged vehicle.

Figure 15-29 shows an underbody support clamp that is used while pulling and aligning the unitized bodyframe. Some of the clamps used when alignment pulls are made are shown in Figure 15-30.

The box clamp allows front and rear end sway to be remedied easily without tearing or twisting the rocker panels. MacPherson strut tower pulls can be made as well.

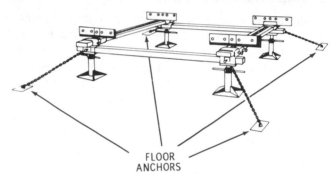

Fig. 15-29. *Adjustable channel and webbed crossbar frame support clamps used to place under a unitized body while alignment pulls are made. (Courtesy of Buske Industries, Inc.)*

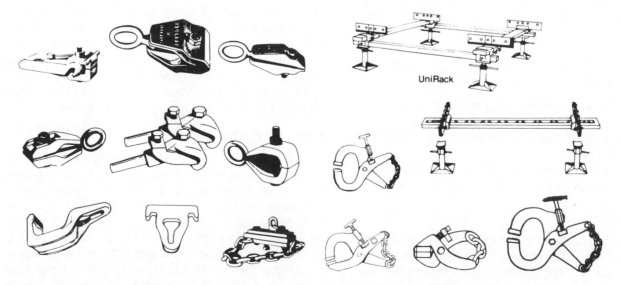

Fig. 15-30. *Clamps and other fixtures used for making hookups. (Courtesy of Buske Industries, Inc.)*

FRAME-STRAIGHTENING PREPARATION

Getting the vehicle ready for frame straightening may be a time consuming and expensive process. Vehicles in collisions serious enough to require frame straightening often cannot be driven. Because of this, they must be towed or pushed around the shop and parking area. Sometimes, damaged panels may need to be removed *before* the frame may be straightened. This means shop labor even before the frame straightening is done.

When a seriously wrecked vehicle is pulled to a shop, it is usually left in storage until all the insurance work and legal action has been settled. A daily storage charge is usually made.

Then, the vehicle is moved to the frame-straightening area or the frame rack. When the vehicle is properly positioned on the frame rack, it may be measured and checked to see how much damage has been done.

FRAME DAMAGE ESTIMATION

There are four basic steps used to straighten a frame. They must be considered when making an *estimate* of the cost to repair any frame damage. All four steps are important to correct frame straightening. Because of this, the time spent doing each step will affect the total cost of the frame repair. The steps are:

1. Diagnosis.
2. Preparation.
3. Hook-ups.
4. Checking.

Diagnosis

Making a *diagnosis* of frame damage includes using your eyes *and* the frame gauges to inspect the frame and see just how much damage has been done. This should include a complete mental diagnosis of the damage and "thinking out" the method that will be used to straighten the damage. When making this diagnosis, try to answer the following questions.

1. How many parts will need to be removed?
2. How much time will the hook-ups take?
3. Will the frame need to be welded or heated during the repair?
4. How much time will the actual pulls require?
5. How much time will the *total* frame repair take?

Preparation

To prepare yourself for the frame repair on a given job, first know and understand the type of frame on which you are working. Next, find and arrange the materials needed. Put the needed tools and alignment equipment in the frame work area. Arrange all the charts and specification books for the vehicle frame to be repaired. For example, Figure 15-31 shows a specification page for a conventional frame automobile. Figure 15-32, on the other hand, shows a specification page for a unitized body-frame automobile. Figure 15-33 shows one manufacturer's specification book and tools marketed for checking frame damage.

The next preparation step is to move the vehicle onto the frame rack. If the vehicle is badly damaged, it may have to be towed or pushed into the frame repair area or onto the alignment rack. With the vehicle in place, remove any sheet metal panels that are blocking easy access to the needed repair. In Figure 15-34, for example, most of the damaged sheet metal (the "doghouse") has been removed to allow good access.

Hook-ups

The process of repairing the frame damage is done by connecting holders, pushers, and pullers to various parts of the frame. Then, when these tools are jacked or pulled, the frame is straightened out to its original shape. Making these connections is known as *making the hook-ups*.

The hook-ups should be planned after locating the point of impact and determining what happened to the frame parts during the collision. Then, hooking-up and beginning the pulls may be done. (On a unitized body-frame, the frame and the body panels are usually pulled at the same time.) Generally, pulls apply pressure in a direction opposite that in which the area was pushed. This is being done in Figure 15-35.

Checks

A frame damage estimate must include the cost of *checking* the job to make sure that the frame is in proper alignment. This is done by checking the frame alignment specifications with those in the specification book. Another minor cost will be repainting all the frame areas where heat and chains have removed or damaged the paint. Frame (chassis) paint or undercoat may be used to repaint the damaged frame areas.

FRAME GAUGES

There are two main tools used to straighten a frame: the *frame straightener* itself and the *frame gauges*. The frame *straightener* is the unit that actually bends the frame back into position. The frame *gauges* are used to establish the frame's condition before, during, and after straightening. They are also used to help determine the location and extent of the frame damage.

To repair frame damage correctly, a technician must know about each of the different gauges and how to

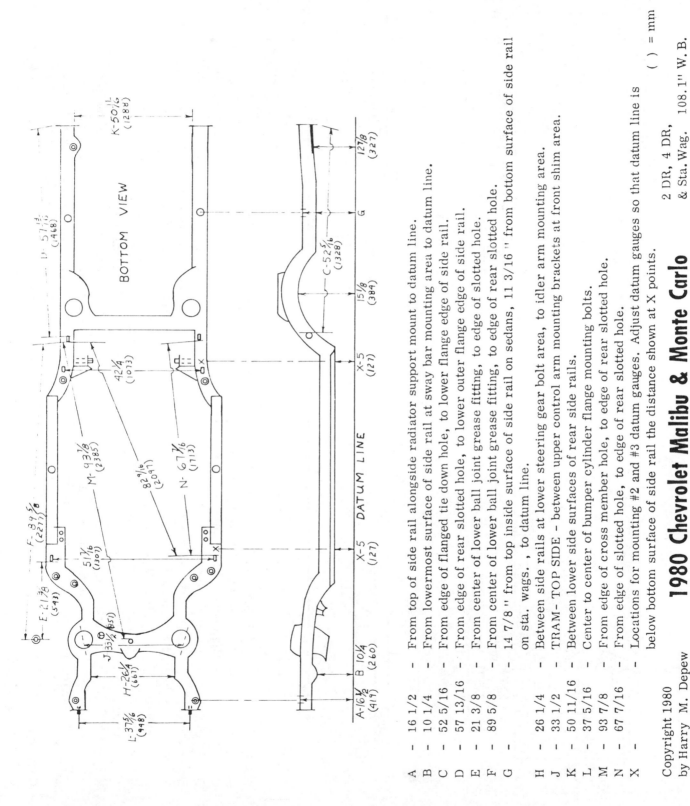

A – 16 1/2 – From top of side rail alongside radiator support mount to datum line.
B – 10 1/4 – From lowermost surface of side rail at sway bar mounting area to datum line.
C – 52 5/16 – From edge of flanged tie down hole, to lower flange edge of side rail.
D – 57 13/16 – From edge of rear slotted hole, to lower outer flange edge of side rail.
E – 21 3/8 – From center of lower ball joint grease fitting, to edge of slotted hole.
F – 89 5/8 – From center of lower ball joint grease fitting, to edge of rear slotted hole.
G – – 14 7/8 " from top inside surface of side rail on sedans, 11 3/16 " from bottom surface of side rail
on sta. wags., to datum line.
H – 26 1/4 – Between side rails at lower steering gear bolt area, to idler arm mounting area.
J – 33 1/2 – TRAM- TOP SIDE – between upper control arm mounting brackets at front shim area.
K – 50 11/16 – Between lower side surfaces of rear side rails.
L – 37 5/16 – Center to center of bumper cylinder flange mounting bolts.
M – 93 7/8 – From edge of cross member hole, to edge of rear slotted hole.
N – 67 7/16 – From edge of slotted hole, to edge of rear slotted hole.
X – – Locations for mounting #2 and #3 datum gauges. Adjust datum gauges so that datum line is
below bottom surface of side rail the distance shown at X points.

( ) = mm

2 DR, 4 DR,
& Sta. Wag.   108.1" W. B.

1980 Chevrolet Malibu & Monte Carlo

Copyright 1980
by Harry M. Depew

Fig. 15-31. *Typical frame alignment specifications for a conventional frame. (Courtesy of Tru-Way Company)*

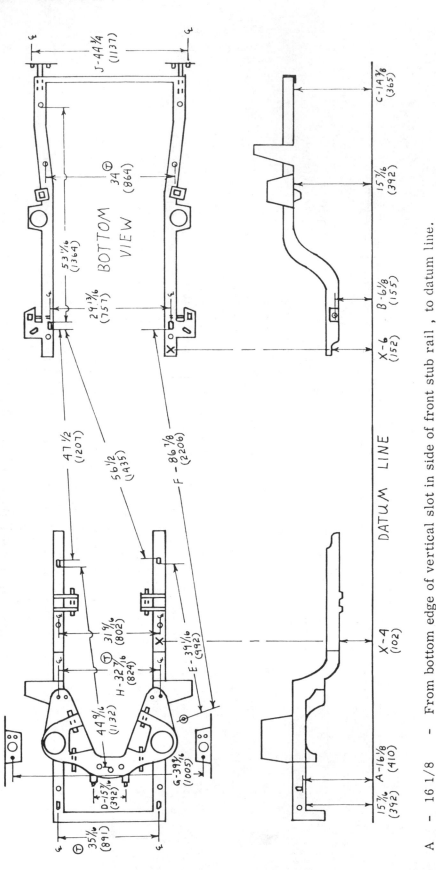

BOTTOM VIEW

DATUM LINE

1980 Ford Thunderbird

A – From bottom edge of vertical slot in side of front stub rail , to datum line.
B – From center of rear axle radius arm pin, to datum line.
C – Immediately in front of rear X member bottom flange on bottom of side rail, to datum line.
D – Center to center of steering rack mounting bolts.
E – From center of lower ball joint grease fitting, to edge of indicated slotted hole.
F – From center of lower ball joint grease fitting, to edge of indicated slotted hole.
G – TOP SIDE– From center to center of strut adjusting plate pivot bolts.
H – Center to center of X member outer mounting bolts.
J – Center to center of rear bumper cylinder lower outer mounting bolts.
X – Locations for mounting #2 and #3 datum gauges. Adjust datum gauges so that datum line is below bottom surface of side rail the distance shown at X points.

Ⓣ Dimensions require tramming with tram bar parallel to plane of frame; other dimensions are direct.

A – 16 1/8
B – 6 1/8
C – 14 3/8
D – 15 7/16
E – 39 1/16
F – 86 7/8
G – 39 9/16
H – 32 7/16
J – 44 3/4
X –

108. 4" W. B.
( )= mm

Copyright 1980
by Harry M. Depew

Fig. 15-32. *Typical frame alignment specifications for a unitized body-frame. (Courtesy of Tru-Way Company)*

use them. There are five basic types of frame gauges:

1. Bench system.
2. Self-centering.
3. Tracking.
4. Tram.
5. Laser beam.

Each gauge has a certain frame location to gauge or measure. For example, self-centering gauges (also called *centering gauges*) always gauge the frame *side rails* to see if they are *level*. The tram gauge, on the other hand, may be used to check measurements above or below an object or obstruction (such as an engine), as shown in Figure 15-36.

Bench System

The bench system is a good, accurate system. The locating fixtures can be placed in the manufacturer's specification holes of the undamaged rear area of the car that has been in a front-end collision. These holes will not be out of alignment. If the front controlling holes do not line up, the frame is out of alignment. One bench system is shown in Figure 15-25.

Using the Bench System. If the bench system is used, centering gauges are not needed. The body location fixtures are placed in the specification holes of the undamaged part of the frame. The fixture towers are set at the correct specifications. If the fixture towers do not fit in the location holes, the frame is damaged in that section.

Self-centering Gauges

Self-centering frame gauges are used to find a center line when checking to see if the frame side rails are

parallel. Each *self-centering gauge* consists of two sliding crossbars that may be adjusted for almost any frame width (Fig. 15-37). Each end of the gauge may

Fig. 15-33. *Specification books and tools used to check frame alignment. (Courtesy of Guy–Chart Systems)*

Fig. 15-34. *Often, sheet metal must be removed to give better access to damaged frame parts.*

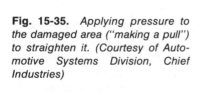

Fig. 15-35. *Applying pressure to the damaged area ("making a pull") to straighten it. (Courtesy of Automotive Systems Division, Chief Industries)*

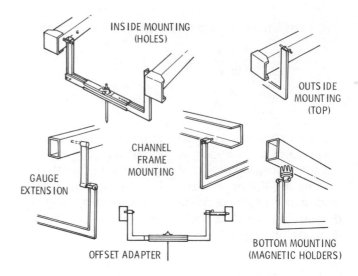

Fig. 15-39. *Various mounting and extension accessories used with self-centering frame gauges. (Courtesy of Bear Division, Applied Power Industries)*

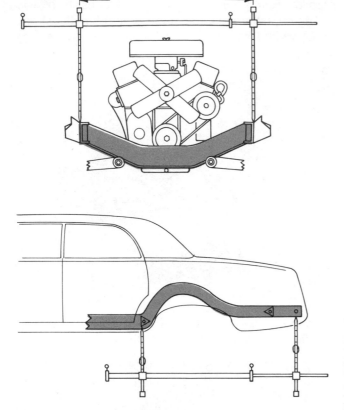

Fig. 15-36. *Using a tram gauge to measure over an obstruction. (Courtesy of Guy–Chart Systems)*

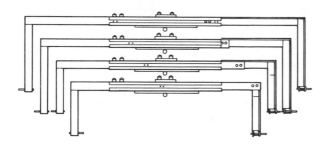

Fig. 15-37. *Self-centering frame gauges. (Courtesy of Bear Division, Applied Power Industries)*

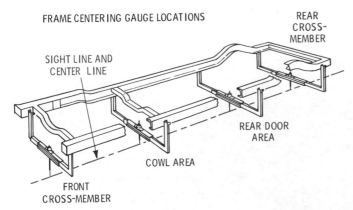

Fig. 15-38. *Typical locations in which self-centering gauges are used. (Courtesy of Bear Division, Applied Power Industries)*

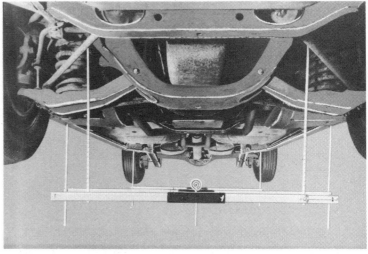

Fig. 15-40. *A "bullseye" type combination datum line and self-centering gauge. (Courtesy of Blackhawk Division, Applied Power Industries)*

have an *extension hanger* that can be adjusted to different heights and then tightened in that position to hold the gauge steady.

The pin in the center of the gauge is a *sighting pin*. The gauge is designed so that the sighting pin is kept *centered* at all times, thus the name "self-centering" gauge. When one side (leg) of the gauge is moved, the other side automatically moves the same distance in the opposite direction.

Using Self-centering Gauges. To gauge a frame with self-centering gauges correctly, at least three gauges must be used. Sometimes four gauges are used, as in Figure 15-38. Hang the gauges in the matching factory-formed holes on opposite sides of the frame. Actually, any two points where the same mark or holes can be found on either side of the frame may be used to "hang" the centering gauges. A number of attachments are available (Fig. 15-39) to hang the centering gauges. They allow the gauges to be used at points where the frame has no holes (or hard-to-reach holes) in the area to be checked.

When the gauges are in place, they are checked to see if the frame side rails are parallel and if the frame is square and level. This is done by sighting down the center pins and crossbars of the gauges to see if they line up properly.

Datum Line Gauge

The datum line gauge is combined with the self-centering gauge. When the centering pins form a bullseye *and* when all the horizontal bars are level (as in Figure 15-40), the frame datum line is correct.

Tracking Gauges

Wheel *tracking gauges* show when the front and rear wheels are in alignment with each other. Figure 15-41 shows a typical wheel tracking gauge. If the front and rear wheels are not in alignment, the vehicle will not handle properly. For example, note the wheel tracking problem resulting from the bent frames in Figure 15-42.

Using Tracking Gauges. Wheel tracking is measured by comparing the front-wheel-to-rear-wheel measurement on one side of the vehicle with the same measurement on the other side of the car (Fig. 15-42). Thumbscrews are used to tighten the tracking gauge pointers in position when one side of the vehicle is measured. Then, the gauge is moved to the other side of the vehicle to check the measurement. If the wheel tracking is correct, the dimensions will be the same on both sides.

Tram Gauges

Figure 15-43 shows one manufacturer's *tram gauge*. Basically, tram gauges are used to gauge above or below objects or obstructions (such as the engine, transmission, or differential). Tram gauges are often used to check types of frame damage that would cause frame shortness. (Specific types of damage are explained later in this unit.)

Using Tram Gauges. To use a tram gauge, place the pointers in the specified holes, according to the frame alignment charts. Use the gauge to measure from one side rail to another, or from one point to another on the same side rail. When the measurement has been made, compare it with the specification on the frame align-

WHEEL TRACKING GAUGE

Fig. 15-41. *A typical wheel-tracking gauge.*

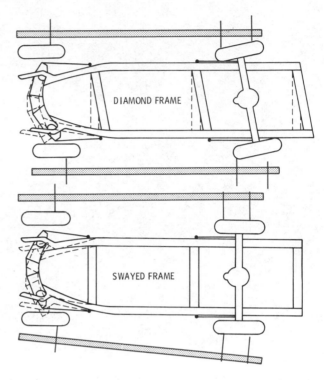

DIAMOND FRAME

SWAYED FRAME

Fig. 15-42. *Common types of frame damage may be determined by using a wheel-tracking gauge. (Courtesy of Blackhawk Division, Applied Power Industries)*

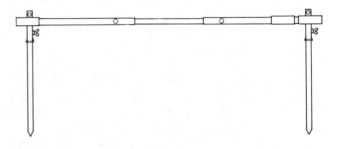

Fig. 15-43. *A tram gauge. (Courtesy of Blackhawk Division, Applied Power Industries)*

Fig. 15-44. *A laser alignment system can be used to establish alignment of many different parts of the vehicle. (Courtesy of Kansas Jack, Inc.)*

ment chart. If they do not match, the frame is damaged and must be straightened.

Laser Beam Alignment

There are several laser beam systems on the market. All use a laser light of high intensity. The light will not burn the skin or clothes.

While there are several systems on the market, the Kansas Jack Lazer Beam Aligner® system will be used to explain laser beam aligning.

The reason for using the laser beam, instead of the centering gauges and the bench system, is that it allows measuring the alignment of different parts of the vehicle. For proper handling, not only the underbody, but the *entire vehicle* must be in alignment. This requires properly restoring the vehicle strut tower location, rear axle alignment, engine cradle location, rack and pinion mounting bracket location, and other parts of the vehicle.

The Kansas Jack Lazer Beam Aligner® system (Fig. 15-44) uses a series of calibrated bars that are attached to the vehicle at various points, in much the same manner as frame-centering gauges. The laser

Fig. 15-45. *A heavy truck front end being aligned with a laser system. (Courtesy of Kansas Jack, Inc.)*

beam replaces the human eye in analyzing the damage. This system is "three-dimensional" and allows measurement of the upper body shell, roof line, and wheel alignment, as well as frame alignment. It may be used for all types of vehicles, including motor-homes, vans, and trucks (Fig. 15-45).

Figure 15-46 shows how the frame centering gauges are made three-dimensional with the Lazer Beam Aligner® system. Roof lines are no more of a problem than the floor pan. Figures 15-47 to 15-49 show some ways the system is used in measuring a vehicle. The laser beam system is strictly a *measuring* device. The pulling and correcting of a vehicle's damaged body and frame is done with other equipment.

INTRODUCTION TO FRAME STRAIGHTENING

The *basics* of frame diagnosis, straightening, and checking have not changed for more than 30 years. When analyzing frame damage, the repair technician still must determine the location and the extent of the damage before repairs can be made. This analysis is best done by mentally dividing the vehicle's frame into

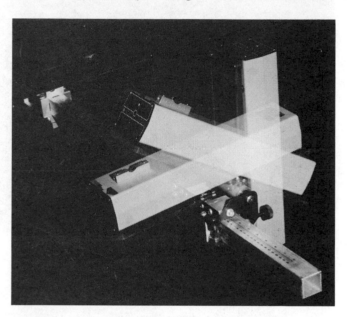

Fig. 15-47. *The laser gun is mounted on a calibrated pivot and can be aimed at targets positioned at any point on the vehicle. (Courtesy of Kansas Jack, Inc.)*

Fig. 15-46. *The frame-centering gauge is made of a three-dimensional tool with the use of a laser beam alignment system. (Courtesy of Kansas Jack, Inc.)*

Fig. 15-48. *The laser unit may be left in place while pulls are made, to identify when correct alignment is achieved. (Courtesy of Kansas Jack, Inc.)*

Fig. 15-49. *A laser alignment system can be used to align front wheels for proper camber, caster, steering axis inclination, and turning radius center steering. (Courtesy of Kansas Jack, Inc.)*

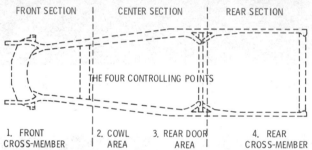

FRONT SECTION | CENTER SECTION | REAR SECTION

THE FOUR CONTROLLING POINTS

1. FRONT CROSS-MEMBER | 2. COWL AREA | 3. REAR DOOR AREA | 4. REAR CROSS-MEMBER

Fig. 15-50. *The three sections and the four controlling points of a conventional frame. (Courtesy of Bear Division, Applied Power Industries)*

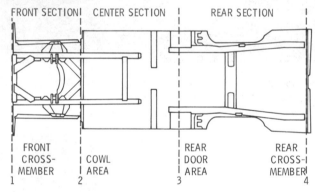

FRONT SECTION | CENTER SECTION | REAR SECTION

FRONT CROSS-MEMBER 1 | COWL AREA 2 | REAR DOOR AREA 3 | REAR CROSS-MEMBER 4

Fig. 15-51. *The three sections and the four controlling points of a unitized body-frame. (Courtesy of Bear Division, Applied Power Industries)*

three sections: front, center, and rear. These sections are shown on a conventional frame in Figure 15-50 and on a unitized body-frame in Figure 15-51. Each of these sections is bordered by what are known as *controlling points*.

Controlling Points

The controlling points on any frame structure are the areas at the front *crossmember*, *cowl*, *rear door*, and *rear crossmember*. When estimating frame damage, the technician must examine the controlling points and indicate on the appraisal sheet the section or sections that are damaged. Inspecting frame damage by examining the controlling points will help the technician avoid overlooking any damage *and* quickly identify the location and extent of the damage.

Measuring Points

A vehicle frame that provides a foundation for a good-driving vehicle must be square and level. To determine if it is square and level, there must be measuring points built into the frame and specifications provided for the distances between these points.

The measurments may be made from side rail to side rail, from a hole in a crossmember to a side rail, from one point to another on the same side rail, or any of several other points, as called for on the specifications. The frame may be measured with a steel tape or a tram gauge, depending on the measurement location. Measurements involving *holes* are always taken from the *center* of the hole unless otherwise specified.

Not all specifications can be given between two points on the frame itself. For example, each *end* of the frame must be a certain distance from the ground and from the center of the car. To provide these specifications, the vehicle's manufacturer must use two *imaginary* lines: the *center line* and the *datum line*.

Center Line. The *first* specification line is the imaginary line that runs down through the *center* of the frame from front to rear. This line determines the boundaries of the right and left sides of the frame. The center line may be seen by looking at either the top or bottom of the frame specifications. Notice the center line in the specifications shown in Figure 15-52.

Datum Line. The *second* specification line is the imaginary *datum line*. It also runs lengthwise, but is *under* the bottom of the frame. The datum line is an imaginary line *between* the frame and the shop floor. Measurements are made down *to* the datum line, as shown in Figure 15-53. Arrows on specification drawings (Fig. 15-54) show where the datum line gauges should be placed on the frame. The datum line is normally checked by using the side rail and the gauges. When the frame is straight, the datum line measurements will be correct, and the datum line will be straight. Then, the gauges may be viewed from either the front or rear of the vehicle and they will line up. All the gauges will be at the same level, *which is the datum line*.

BASIC FRAME-STRAIGHTENING JOBS

The "key" to even the most difficult frame-straightening job is to *analyze the frame damage completely in three major steps*. The first step is to locate and describe the damage on each of the three sections of the frame. This requires a good knowledge of frame and automobile construction *and* a knowledge of how to use the shop's frame equipment (Fig. 15-55) and the specification charts.

The *second* step is to *remove* all the parts that block access to the damaged sections of the frame. This has been done in Figure 15-56. Finally, the *third* step is to *make the correct hook-ups* necessary to straighten the frame.

To be able to straighten damaged frames, the body or frame technician must be able to recognize and understand the different types of frame damage. Also, there is usually a pattern to collision damage. A technician should learn the pattern and *in what order* damage is likely to happen as a vehicle is hit from the front, rear, or side. If this is learned, the technician will have little trouble repairing frame damage.

Side Rail Damage

The first major frame damage that normally happens in a collision is *side rail* damage. The three most com-

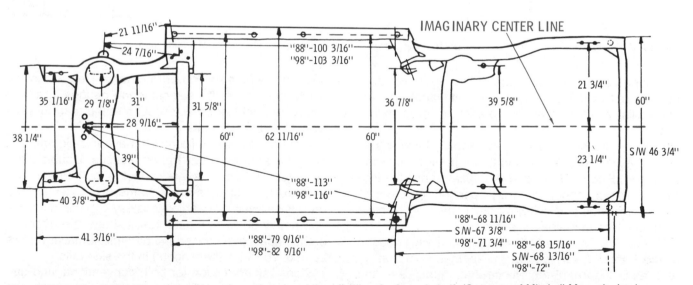

Fig. 15-52. *The center line of the frame is an imaginary line dividing the frame in half. (Courtesy of Mitchell Manuals, Inc.)*

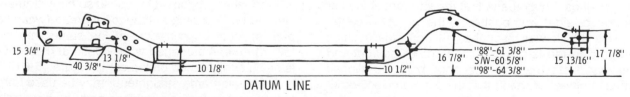

Fig. 15-53. *The datum line runs just below the frame. (Courtesy of Mitchell Manuals, Inc.)*

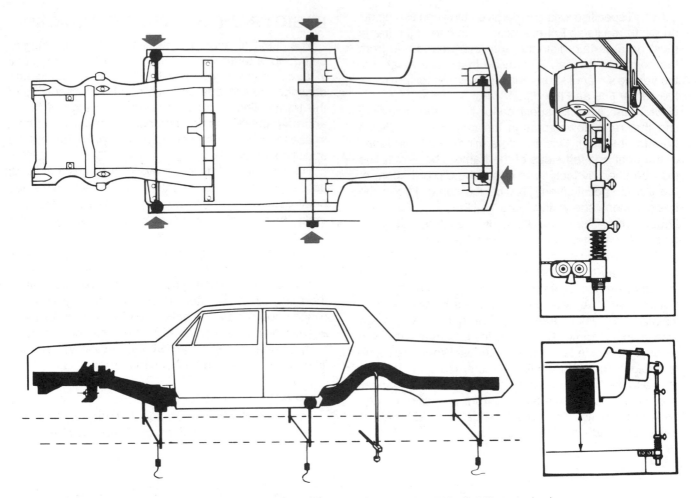

Fig. 15-54. *Datum line gauges may be mounted in the positions shown. (Courtesy of Mitchell Manuals, Inc.)*

mon types of side rail damage on the *front* section of the side rail include *sidesway*, *sag*, and *mash*. In rear-end collisions, sag is usually present only on severe wrecks.

Sidesway. Sidesway damage is normally the first side rail damage to happen during either front- or rear-end collisions. Figure 15-57 shows typical front-end side-sway. This type of damage may be found on both conventional frames and unitized body-frames, which have been involved in major accidents.

To check for sidesway, fasten self-centering gauges to the frame. Then, look at the gauges from front to rear, as in Figure 15-58. Notice that, in this case, the rings do not line up—the front ring is to one side of the two rear rings. This means that the left front of the car (the driver's side) was pushed to the left of the center line. This vehicle was hit on the right front side, pushing the frame to the left; a condition known as *front-end sidesway*. Note that the horizontal bars are aligned with each other, indicating that there is no up-and-down damage, or *sag*.

Rear sidesway, shown in Figure 15-59, is misalign-

ment in the *rear* section of the frame. Rear sidesway would appear on the self-centering gauges in a way similar to front sidesway, except that the rear bullseye would be out of alignment.

A *double* sidesway frame will have misalignment of *both* the front and rear frame sections. Double side-sway results from a severe impact in the *center* frame section. The vehicle's entire frame (front, center, and rear) is affected by double sidesway collision damage. The heavy arrow in Figure 15-60 shows the *direction* of the impact that caused the damage. Smaller arrows point out buckles (bent spots) in the side rails.

Sidesway correction for both conventional and unitized body-frame vehicles is made in the same way, with a few exceptions. On a unitized body-frame vehicle, the body panels at the *wheel areas* (*wheelhouse* panels) must be corrected at the same time as the lower frame. A damaged wheelhouse at the right front is being straightened on the car in Figure 15-61.

A portable frame straightener may be used to repair sidesway damage on a unitized body-frame, as shown in Figure 15-62. When a permanent *rack-type* frame

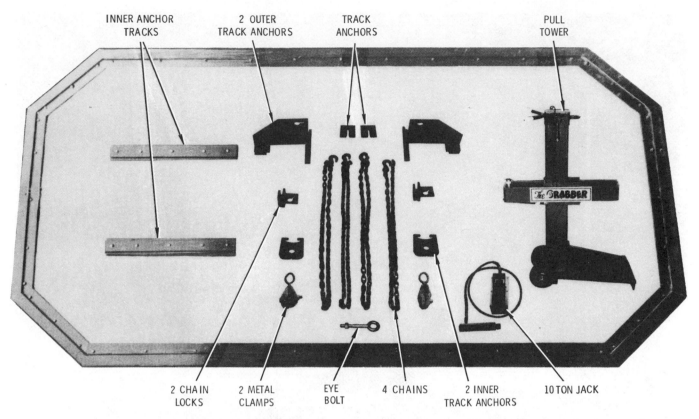

INNER ANCHOR TRACKS   2 OUTER TRACK ANCHORS   TRACK ANCHORS   PULL TOWER

2 CHAIN LOCKS   2 METAL CLAMPS   EYE BOLT   4 CHAINS   2 INNER TRACK ANCHORS   10 TON JACK

Fig. 15-55. *Equipment used with a permanent rack-type straightener. (Courtesy of Grabber Manufacturing Company)*

Fig. 15-56. *For easy access to the damaged frame, all sheet metal covering the area should be removed.*

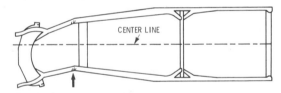

CENTER LINE

Fig. 15-57. *Sidesway at the front of the frame, caused by a front-end collision.*

straightener is used, multiple hook-ups are possible (Fig. 15-63). A rack-type straightener is being used to correct *double* sidesway in Figure 15-64.

Sag. Typical side rail *sag* may involve damage to the frame at the cowl area, as shown in Figure 15-65. Sag usually results from a heavy impact. The impact causes the front of the frame to kick up, making the side rail appear to drop at the cowl. The actual amount of side

rail buckling depends on the severity and the direction of the impact. Sag may occur on either or both sides of the car *and* on either the front or rear.

To check for sag on one side of the frame's *front* section, sight along the centering gauges from the front of the car. The sag will appear *behind* the high point of the #1 gauge (Fig. 15-66). To check the exact amount of sag, place two frame-centering gauges at the controlling points on the front section, and sight along the lower bars of the gauges, as in Figure 15-66. Here, the sag is located on the right front side, behind the high corner of the front gauge.

To check for *rear* sag, place one centering gauge at the rear door area on the frame. Then, locate the other gauge *ahead* of the mash area, near the rear axle housing (Fig. 15-67). Finally, sight along the bars of the gauges. Sag is located on the frame rail behind the high corner of the #1 gauge, shown in Figure 15-67.

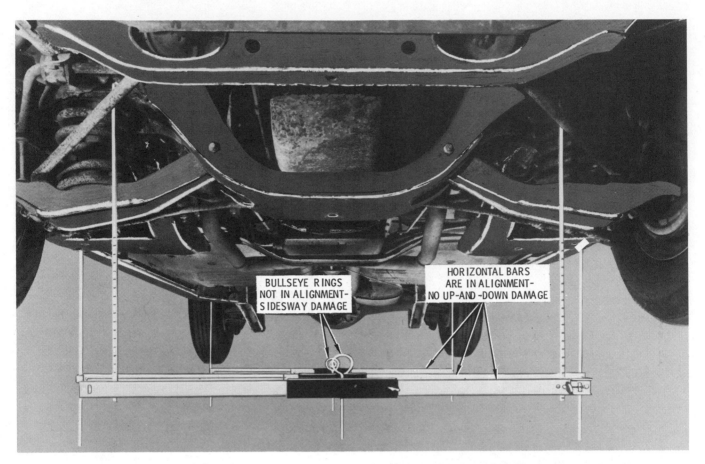

Fig. 15-58. *The gauges are in alignment, indicating no up-and-down damage, but the bullseyes are not in alignment, indicating sideway damage. (Courtesy of Blackhawk Division, Applied Power Industries)*

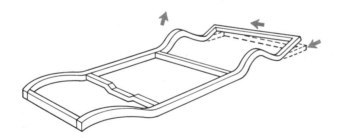

Fig. 15-59. *Rear sideway.*

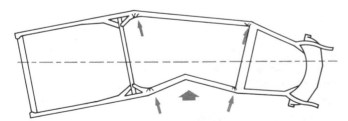

Fig. 15-60. *Double sideway on the frame's outer section.*

Fig. 15-61. *Straightening a bent wheel housing panel and structure on a unitized body-frame vehicle. (Courtesy of Grabber Manufacturing Company)*

Notice that, when checking sag, the gauges are placed in *front* of any mash and sideway damage on the frame's rear section; this will give a correct gauging of *only* the sag damage.

The most serious type of sag occurs in *both* side rails. Notice that, in Figure 15-68, the sighting pins are centered, indicating that the frame has no sideway

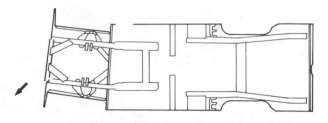

Fig. 15-62. *Using a portable frame straightener to correct sidesway damage on a unitized body-frame vehicle. (Courtesy of Bear Division, Applied Power Industries)*

Fig. 15-63. *Using multiple hookups to correct sidesway damage. (Courtesy of Blackhawk Division, Applied Power Industries)*

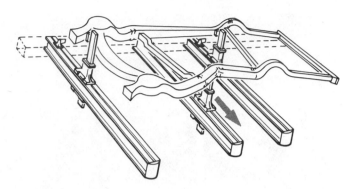

Fig. 15-64. *Correcting double sidesway on a permanent rack-type frame straightener. (Courtesy of Bear Division, Applied Power Industries)*

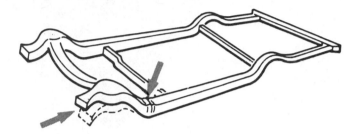

Fig. 15-65. *Sag on the left front section of the frame, due to a front-end collision. Note buckling of the frame at the cowl. (Courtesy of Bear Division, Applied Power Industries)*

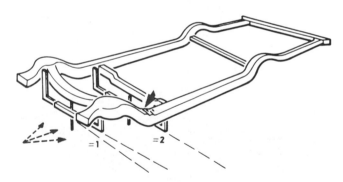

Fig. 15-66. *Gauge arrangement used to measure front sag. (Courtesy of Bear Division, Applied Power Industries)*

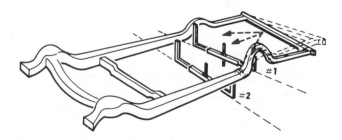

Fig. 15-67. *Gauge arrangement used to measure rear sag. (Courtesy of Bear Division, Applied Power Industries)*

damage. Although the horizontal bars are parallel to each other, the center gauge is *lower* than the other two gauges. This indicates that sag damage has occurred equally, on both side rails, in the cowl area.

The gauges in Figure 15-68 show that the #1 gauge is high *all the way across*. This means that the frame has sag on both the right and left sides. If only one side had sag, only that side of the gauge would be high. **Mash.** Side rail *mash* is a buckled area located on the underside of the side rail. If it is directly behind the front crossmember (Fig. 15-69), it is known as *front mash*.

Or, it may be located on the underside of the side rail directly over the rear axle housing. This is known as *rear mash* (Fig. 15-70).

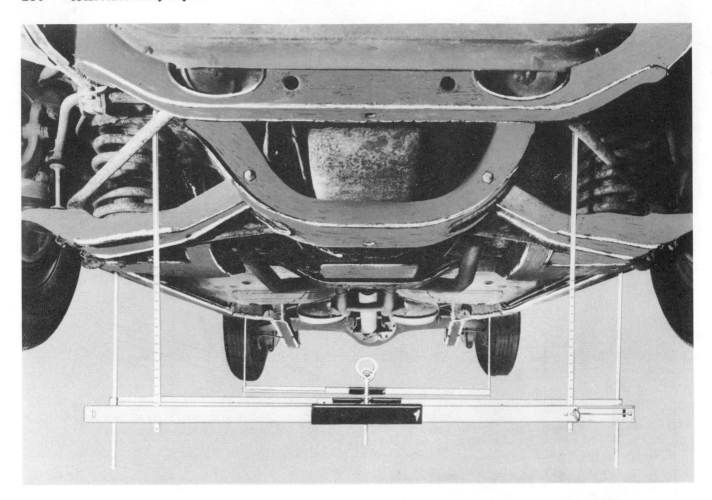

Fig. 15-68. *This gauge setup indicates sag on both front side rails. (Courtesy of Blackhawk Division, Applied Power Industries)*

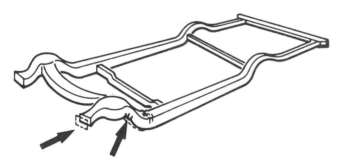

Fig. 15-69. Mash *damage on the left front side rail. (Courtesy of Bear Division, Applied Power Industries)*

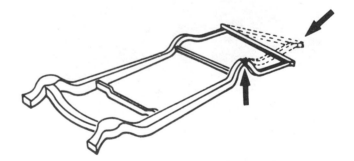

Fig. 15-70. *Mash damage on the left rear side rail. (Courtesy of Bear Division, Applied Power Industries)*

In either case, mash causes the frame side rail to become shorter. Mash results from a heavy impact on one corner (end) of the frame side rail, causing it to "mash up" and shorten.

To check for front mash, measure from a point on the side rail at the front crossmember to a point on the side rail near the cowl (Fig. 15-71). Compare the measurement to the same measurement on the opposite side rail *and* to the vehicle's frame specification chart.

To correct mash damage, either a permanent or a portable frame straightener may be used. In Figure 15-72, for example, the mechanic is hooking up for a straight mash pull on a unitized body-frame automobile, using a permanent straightener. In Figure 15-73, another type of unitized body-frame is being repaired with a portable frame straightener. Here, the top hook is pulling to correct *sag* while the bottom hook is pulling to correct *mash*. This is an example of a portable straightener being used to make two pulls at one time.

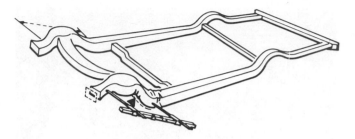

Fig. 15-71. *Gauging mash damage on the left front side rail. (Courtesy of Bear Division, Applied Power Industries)*

Diamond

Another type of frame damage is known as *diamond*. Diamond damage affects the entire frame, not just the side rails. A diamond frame usually happens as a result of a heavy impact on one corner of the vehicle. This impact is severe enough to push one side rail back, out of square with the opposite side rail, and distort the crossmembers (Fig. 15-74).

When diamond damage exists on a frame, it must be the *first* damage corrected. The diamond damage must be repaired before any work is done on sag, mash, or other frame damage.

Check for Diamond. To check for diamond damage, use a tape measure or tram gauge. Measure the center (body) section of the frame, between the cowl and rear door areas, as shown in Figures 15-75 and 15-76.

When a frame has diamond damage, the center section by itself will look like a diamond. One of the measurements will be *longer* than the other, indicating diamond damage. In Figure 15-76, a tram gauge is being used to measure between two holes on the vehicle's frame. This measurement will be compared with the measurement between the *other* two holes at the white arrows in Figure 15-76. If the measurements are not the same, the frame has diamond damage.

Correcting Diamond. During frame repairs, remember that diamond is the first damage to correct. Stretch and pull hook-ups are usually used, securing one end of the frame and pulling on the other. Diamond correction may be made with either permanent (Fig. 15-77) or portable (Fig. 15-78) frame straighteners.

Diamond has been corrected when the two diagonal measurements at the frame's center section are equal. If the frame is "diamond" by ½ in. (12.7 mm) for example, pulling one side rail only ¼ in. (6.4 mm) will make the measurements equal. As one side rail is pulled forward, the other is forced backward.

Twist

Another type of *total* frame damage is known as *twist*. This is a serious type of frame damage. In twist dam-

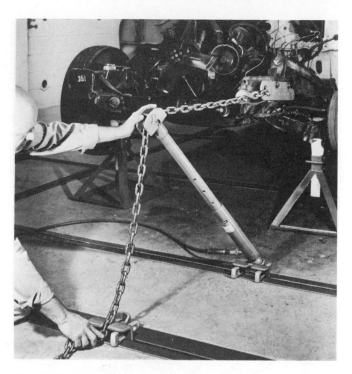

Fig. 15-72. *Using a rack-type straightener to pull out mash damage on the front of a unitized body-frame vehicle. (Courtesy of Blackhawk Division, Applied Power Industries)*

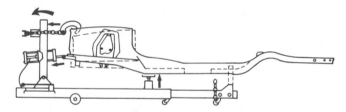

Fig. 15-73. *Using a portable frame straightener to pull out sag and mash damage at the same time. (Courtesy of Bear Division, Applied Power Industries)*

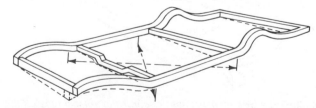

Fig. 15-74. Diamond *damage to a frame, caused by an impact on the left front corner of the vehicle.*

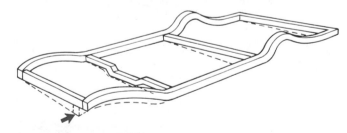

Fig. 15-75. *Making the measurements that will identify diamond damage.*

Fig. 15-76. *Using a tram gauge to check for diamond damage. (Courtesy of Blackhawk Division, Applied Power Industries)*

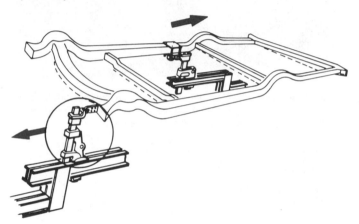

Fig. 15-77. *Correcting diamond damage with a permanent, rack-type frame straightener. (Courtesy of Bear Division, Applied Power Industries)*

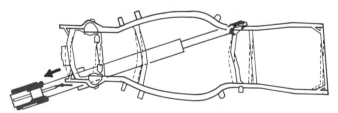

Fig. 15-78. *Correcting diamond damage with a portable frame straightener. (Courtesy of Bear Division, Applied Power Industries)*

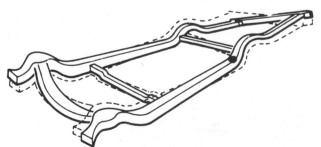

Fig. 15-79. *Twist damage can occur if the vehicle runs off the road and into a ditch. (Courtesy of Bear Division, Applied Power Industries)*

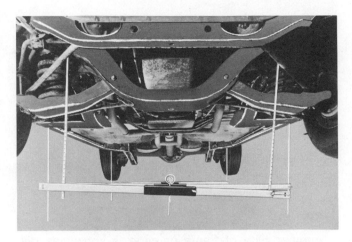

Fig. 15-80. *The bullseyes are aligned, but the horizontal bars of the gauges are not, indicating* twist *damage. (Courtesy of Blackhawk Division, Applied Power Industries)*

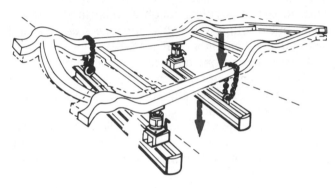

Fig. 15-81. *Using a rack-type straightener to correct twist damage. (Courtesy of Bear Division, Applied Power Industries)*

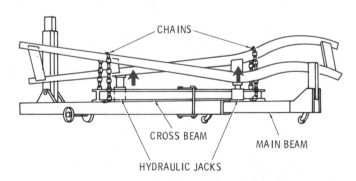

CHAINS

CROSS BEAM   MAIN BEAM

HYDRAULIC JACKS

Fig. 15-82. *Using a portable frame straightener to correct twist damage. (Courtesy of Bear Division, Applied Power Industries)*

age, the side rails are not on the same plane with each other (Fig. 15-79). This is usually caused by running into a ditch or by some other severe twisting action on the vehicle's frame and chassis parts.

Diagnosing Twist. When a frame is suspected of having twist, the vehicle may be put on the rack and the self-centering gauges fastened to the frame (Fig. 15-80). Notice that the gauge *center pins* show correct

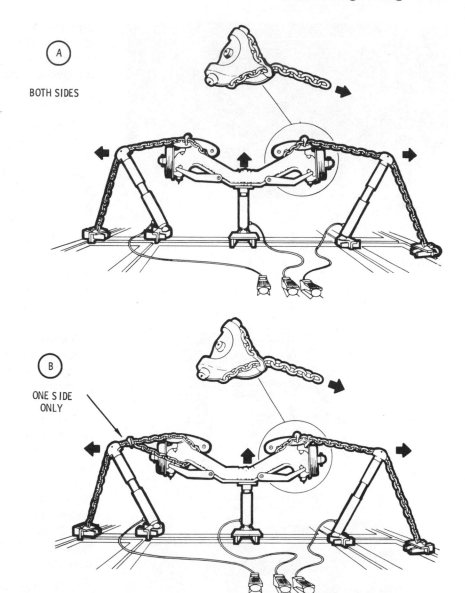

Ⓐ
BOTH SIDES

Ⓑ
ONE SIDE
ONLY

Fig. 15-83. *Correcting crossmember sag. (A) Hook-up for correcting sag at both sides. (B) Hook-up for correcting sag at one side. (Courtesy of Blackhawk Division, Applied Power Industries)*

vertical and horizontal alignment since the "bullseyes" are OK.

However, the position of the *horizontal* bars is not correct. Note that the bars are tilted; the left front and the right rear are both low. This shows that twist damage is present, since the frame is not level.

Correcting Twist. Twist has been corrected when both of the side rails are square and level. Either a permanent or a portable straightener may be used to repair twist damage. Figure 15-81 shows an example of a rack-type (permanent) frame straightener being used to correct twist.

When a *portable* frame straightener is used to correct twist damage, a heavy *crossbeam* must be used. The crossbeam is mounted *on top* of the main beam (Fig. 15-82). The crossbeam is used to help correct the twist by holding the high points of the frame with chains.

To make the repair, the frame straightener is positioned under the frame with the crossbeam in place. Then, the crossbeam is chained to the high points of the frame. Equal pressure is applied to the *low* end of each side rail by hydraulic jacks on the main beam.

Crossmember Damage

One type of serious frame damage is *crossmember damage.* This damage, especially on the front crossmember, can affect the safe handling of the vehicle by causing it to pull or wander. Although crossmember damage is rare, it must be detected and repaired if it is present.

The crossmember most often damaged in an accident is the *front* crossmember. This is because the engine is usually attached to either end of the crossmember with a *motor mount.* In a roll-over accident,

Fig. 15-84. *When the frame is correctly aligned, all bullseyes and horizontal parts of the gauges will line up. (Courtesy of Blackhawk Division, Applied Power Industries)*

Fig. 15-85. *A complete bench system and fixtures. (Courtesy of Blackhawk Division, Applied Power Industries)*

especially, the engine weight pushing and pulling on the ends of the crossmember is likely to cause damage.

Correcting Crossmember Damage. Crossmember damage may be corrected as shown in Figure 15-83. This is done by using two chains, three hydraulic jacks, and anchor rails. The chains hold the ends of the crossmember to the anchor rails, while the hydraulic jacks apply pressure to the center of the crossmember.

Check the repair with a tram gauge, and compare the measurements to the specifications on the frame dimension charts. The tram gauge can be placed either underneath or on top of the crossmember. Gauging should be done on each side of the crossmember, where it connects to the side rails. The tram gauge will be needed to measure over or under the engine.

Correct Frame Alignment

When a frame is in correct alignment, all the frame-centering gauges will line up. Notice how the centering gauges in Figure 15-84 show that the frame of this vehicle is in correct alignment. The horizontal bars are parallel to each other, indicating that the frame is level and has no twist. The round sighting pins form the correct "bullseye" target, indicating a perfect center line. The gauges show that the frame rails are in the proper position, both horizontally and vertically. The frame has no sidesway, sag, or mash. The vehicle will handle properly if all the chassis parts are also in good condition.

ALIGNMENT WITH A BENCH SYSTEM

A complete set of fixtures used for a small unitized body-frame vehicle is shown in Figure 15-85. This is a complete bench system; not all the fixtures are used on every repair. Fixture selection depends on whether the damage is in the front or the rear of the vehicle.

The fixtures do not carry the anchoring load. Chains are attached to the anchor rail, as are the jacks, which do the pulling, as shown in Figure 15-86. The bench system is used only for *measuring* and *welding*.

Proper alignment is very important on late-model vehicles, which have fully unitized body-frames. The wheel alignment is also important. The vehicle in Figure 15-87 has been involved in a front-end collision. It is typical of vehicles with lightweight unitized body-frame construction.

Analyzing the Damage

The car was hit in the right front corner. The right side rail and inner fender moved backward, causing the MacPherson strut mount to move backward as well (Fig. 15-88). The damage to the inside of the side rail, the inner fender, and the strut housing is shown in Figure 15-89.

The car is mounted on the bench using six fixtures on the undamaged part of the car. This locates the vehicle in the proper position. Figure 15-90 shows fixtures mounted to the rear section of the frame through the bumper openings. The frame of this part of the car is not damaged. Once the six fixtures are placed in position, the remaining fixtures can be placed to indicate exactly the location and degree of the damage. Figure 15-91 shows the fixtures that mount to the jacking holes in the underbody and the rear attachment of the lower control arm. These fixtures are marked with an "L" in Figure 15-92.

Fig. 15-86. *Anchor chains are attached to the rails. (Courtesy of Blackhawk Division, Applied Power Industries)*

The upper MacPherson strut mount is pushed back and up, as shown in Figure 15-93. The right lower control arm front attachment also is tipped back and up (Fig. 15-94). Now the exact location and the extent of the overall damage can be seen. How far to pull to correct the damage can be seen as well.

The Pulling Operation

Figure 15-95 shows the left bumper attachment and adjoining sheet metal. They are too high and swayed to the left.

The damaged sheet metal must be pulled and aligned to fit the fixtures before any replacement parts are installed. This will allow all replacements to fit correctly.

Figure 15-96 shows the first hook-up. The basic anchoring setup uses four chains (two on each side from the body clamps to the anchor rails). The body clamps carry the pulling force directly from the car to the rail. Figure 15-97 shows how two straight pulls are made, one to the side rail and one to the MacPherson strut tower. This hook-up restored the right side of the car to the proper length and also removed some of the sidesway.

Fig. 15-87. *A vehicle that has been involved in a front-end collision. (Courtesy of Blackhawk Division, Applied Power Industries)*

Fig. 15-88. *The MacPherson strut mount has been forced backward. (Courtesy of Blackhawk Division, Applied Power Industries)*

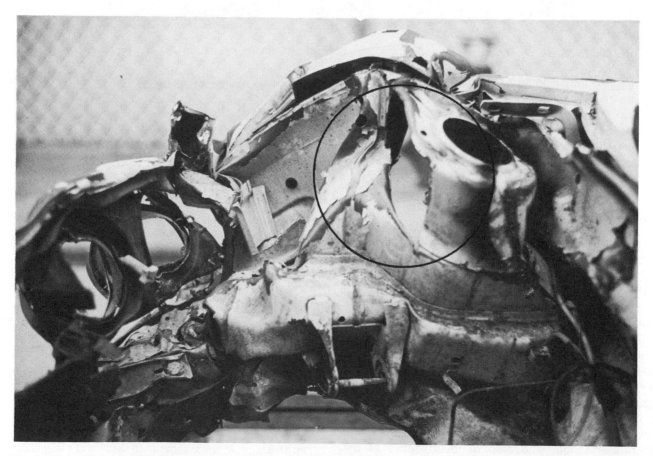

Fig. 15-89. *Damage to the side rail, inner fender, and strut housing. (Courtesy of Blackhawk Division, Applied Power Industries)*

For the second hook-up, a third chain is placed to pull sideways at the top of the apron. The lower straight pull is moved from the end of the side rail to the pinch-weld flange directly above the lower control arm attachment (Fig. 15-98). Using the three pulls together, the proper width and length on the right side is restored and the sidesway on the left side is eliminated.

Figure 15-99 shows how the MacPherson strut tower has been corrected. The fender apron has been restored to the proper location, as shown in Figure 15-100. The left front corner must be pulled down into position. This is done with the setup in Figure 15-101. The complete pulling operation is accomplished without heat. With this thin metal, heat could cause problems; hammering and dollying is more effective (Fig. 15-102). Notice that the radiator support and sheet metal parts have been removed. All the sheet metal on the cowl and firewall is being straightened with the hammer and dolly.

Fig. 15-90. *Bench fixtures mounted to the rear bumper openings. (Courtesy of Blackhawk Division, Applied Power Industries)*

Replacing Damaged Parts

One of the advantages of the bench system is that it can be used as a welding fixture for replacement of damaged parts, as shown in Figure 15-103.

The damaged parts were cut at the factory seam for easy fitting of the new parts. Figure 15-104 shows the new parts fitted to the fixtures and to the MacPherson strut. Figure 15-105 shows the new parts clamped in place and ready for welding. In Figure 15-106, the sheet metal has been replaced.

The vehicle's wheels can be aligned with the wheel aligning attachment in Figure 15-107. Figure 15-108 shows how to align a MacPherson strut housing and tower for correct front-end alignment.

Restoring A Wrecked Vehicle

The impact on the vehicle shown in Figure 15-109 was severe enough to cause damage to the entire front end. A used front-end assembly is obviously the most economical way to repair such severe sheet metal damage.

Identifying Frame Damage. The conventional frame of this vehicle is damaged extensively. In any front-end collision with a conventional frame, the first damage that occurs is almost always sidesway. The next damage to occur is sag in the cowl area. This is the result of the front end raising up and pushing the heavy motor downward. This causes the frame to sag in the cowl area. The third damage to occur is mash in the area of the front wheel, just behind the crossmember. With such an impact, the frame most likely has diamond damage as well. The vehicle shown in Figure 15-109 has all four types of damage to the frame.

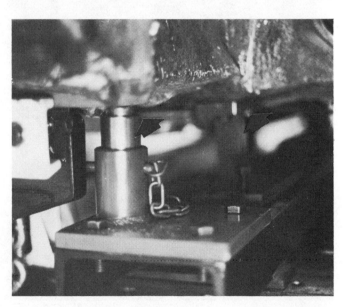

Fig. 15-91. *Fixtures, indicated by arrows, are mounted to the jacking holes of the lower control arms. (Courtesy of Blackhawk Division, Applied Power Industries)*

Aligning the Sheet Metal Before Removing. Figure 15-109 shows the damage to the grille and header plate. All the damaged sheet metal will be aligned with a power jack before being removed from the vehicle. The front-end assembly is then removed. The vehicle is placed on safety stands and tied down with chains so that it cannot move, as shown in Figure 15-110.

Gauging Frames. Four frame gauges are placed on the vehicle for a correct frame damage analysis (Fig. 15-111). This frame has sidesway, sag, mash, and "diamond." Diamond damage is detected with a tram gauge and diagonal measurements.

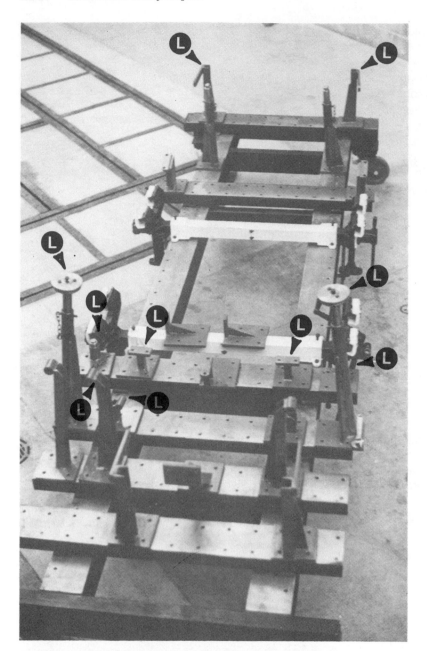

Fig. 15-92. *The fixtures used to measure and correct the damage in Figures 15-87 to 15-91 are marked with an "L." (Courtesy of Blackhawk Division, Applied Power Industries)*

Fig. 15-93. *The strut mount is pushed back and upward. (Courtesy of Blackhawk Division, Applied Power Industries)*

Correcting Diamond. To align the frame, diamond is almost always corrected first. The left front side rail is pulled forward, while a chain anchors the right side rail at the rear torque box. The right rear side rail is pulled backward, causing the rails to move back in place and square the center section of the frame (Fig. 15-112).

Correcting Sidesway. Sidesway can be corrected with the same hook-up as used for diamond. A chain on the left side at the cowl area is used for a *straight* pull to correct sidesway.

Correcting Mash. The mash damage behind the left wheel and crossmember also can be corrected with the sidesway hook-up. Heat is applied to the frame at the *mash* area, then a straight pull is made (Fig. 15-113).

Fig. 15-94. *The lower control arm is bent back and upward. (Courtesy of Blackhawk Division, Applied Power Industries)*

Fig. 15-95. *The left bumper attachment and adjoining sheet metal is too high and has been swayed to the left, as shown by the arrows. (Courtesy of Blackhawk Division, Applied Power Industries)*

Fig. 15-96. *A basic anchoring setup, using four chains. (Courtesy of Blackhawk Division, Applied Power Industries)*

Fig. 15-97. *Two straight pulls are being used to move the sheet metal forward. (Courtesy of Blackhawk Division, Applied Power Industries)*

Correcting Sag. A jack is placed under the frame side rail at the sag area. While a chain anchors the side rail, the jack pushes up on the sag area to level the frame (Fig. 15-114).

After checking with a tram gauge, it is found that the right front side rail is in alignment and the front crossmember is in tolerance but that the left side rail frame horn at the front is out of alignment. Two chains and a turnbuckle are placed on the frame at the crossmember, and the turnbuckle is tightened to hold the frame stationary in that area. A tie-down chain is placed around the right side rail at the crossmember section to hold the right side rail in place. Another chain is placed at the front section of the frame and a pull jack is attached to the left side frame rail, in order to pull the left frame horn at the front into alignment (Fig. 15-115).

Figure 15-116 shows the front-end replacement set in place. After the frame is aligned, the front end fits without any trouble. Figure 15-117 shows that the fender

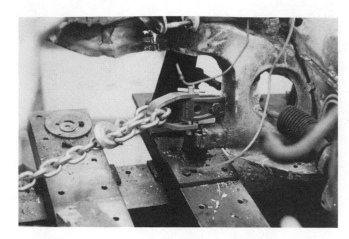

Fig. 15-98. *A pinch-weld clamp attached to the control arm. (Courtesy of Blackhawk Division, Applied Power Industries)*

Fig. 15-99. *The strut tower alignment has been corrected by pulling. (Courtesy of Blackhawk Division, Applied Power Industries)*

Fig. 15-100. *The fender apron has been restored to proper shape and position. (Courtesy of Blackhawk Division, Applied Power Industries)*

and the door are in proper alignment. The vehicle, after the refinishing was completed and the moldings were re-installed, is shown in Figure 15-118.

Fig. 15-101. *Pulling the left front corner into position. (Courtesy of Blackhawk Division, Applied Power Industries)*

Fig. 15-102. *Using a hammer and dolly to straighten sheet metal. (Courtesy of Blackhawk Division, Applied Power Industries)*

THE MACPHERSON STRUT SYSTEM

The MacPherson strut suspension system was first used widely on European cars. When American vehicles became lighter in weight, the strut system was ideal for them (Fig. 15-119). There are several variations of the strut system.

Fig. 15-103. *Spot-welding replacement parts. (Courtesy of Blackhawk Division, Applied Power Industries)*

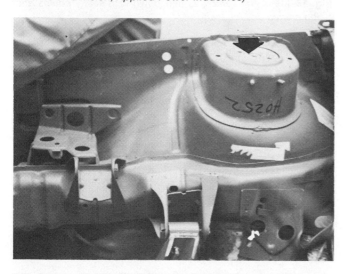

Fig. 15-104. *New parts have been installed. Arrow indicates MacPherson strut. (Courtesy of Blackhawk Division, Applied Power Industries)*

Fig. 15-105. *New parts have been clamped in place, ready for welding. (Courtesy of Blackhawk Division, Applied Power Industries)*

Fig. 15-106. *Sheet metal has been replaced. (Courtesy of Blackhawk Division, Applied Power Industries)*

Figure 15-120 shows a MacPherson strut; whereas Figure 15-121 shows the internal components of the strut. Figure 15-122 shows a conventional suspension system. Most strut systems are designed with shocks and springs. On General Motors cars, the coil spring slips over the shock and is bolted to the suspension (Fig. 15-123). The adjustment to the camber on this suspension also is shown in Figure 15-123.

The strut system usually permits little or no adjustment. Alignment is measured and set to the manufacturer's specifications. Figure 15-124 shows a strut system aligning kit. This kit was shown in use in Figure 15-108. Frame and wheel alignment is very important on the strut-equipped vehicle. Figure 15-125 shows frame components being measured to study alignment problems.

Types of MacPherson Strut Systems

There are two types of MacPherson strut assemblies on the market. In one type, the shock absorber unit can

Fig. 15-107. *Using the wheel lining gauge. (Courtesy of Automotive Systems Division, Chief Industries)*

Fig. 15-108. *Aligning the MacPherson strut housing and tower. (Courtesy of Automotive Systems Division, Chief Industries)*

Fig. 15-109. *Severe front-end damage to be corrected with repair and replacement.*

Fig. 15-110. *The vehicle is tied down with safety chains after being placed on jack stands.*

Fig. 15-111. *Using the frame gauges to analyze damage.*

Fig. 15-112. *Making a pull to square the center section of the frame.*

be replaced with a new unit; in the other, the shock absorber must be repaired or the entire strut assembly replaced.

Most American-made cars have two strut units in the front and two conventional shock absorbers in the rear. The *strut assembly* replaces the shock absorber, spring,

Fig. 15-113. *Correcting mash. The metal is heated before being pulled.*

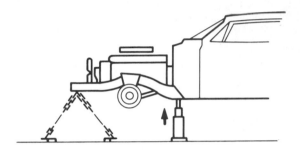

Fig. 15-114. *Using a jack and pulling to correct sag. (Courtesy of Blackhawk Division, Applied Power Industries)*

Fig. 15-115. *Straightening the frame horns.*

Fig. 15-116. *A new front end assembly ("doghouse") has been set in place on the car.*

Fig. 15-117. *The fender and front door are in correct alignment.*

Fig. 15-118. *The repaired vehicle after refinishing.*

upper ball joint, upper control arm, and (on some vehicles) the spindle of conventional suspensions. Notice the parts of the strut and how it is assembled in Figure 15-121.

MacPherson Strut Repair

Auto body repair shop workers must know how the MacPherson strut works. Compare Figure 15-120, the MacPherson strut, and Figure 15-122, the conventional suspension.

Almost all struts have a hydraulic shock absorber and a spring, much like those on conventional systems. The spring is held in place by top and bottom spring seats, as shown in Figure 15-126. The upper steering pivot on the strut replaces the upper ball joint of the conventional system.

Fig. 15-119. *MacPherson struts on a damaged vehicle. (Courtesy of Kansas Jack, Inc.)*

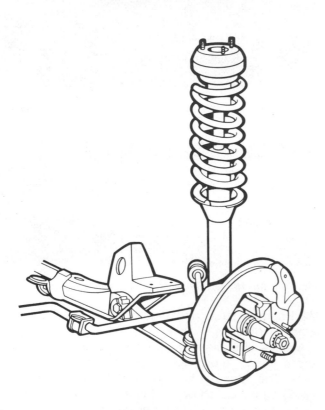

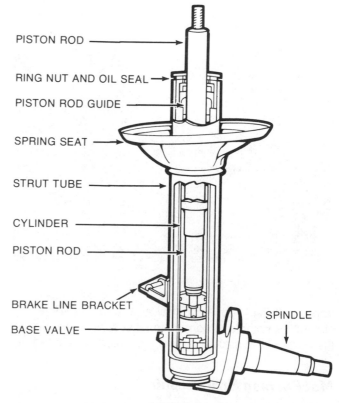

PISTON ROD

RING NUT AND OIL SEAL

PISTON ROD GUIDE

SPRING SEAT

STRUT TUBE

CYLINDER

PISTON ROD

BRAKE LINE BRACKET

BASE VALVE

SPINDLE

Fig. 15-120. *The MacPherson strut assembly. (Courtesy of Tech-Cor, Inc.)*

Fig. 15-121. *Parts of a typical MacPherson strut. (Courtesy of Tech-Cor, Inc.)*

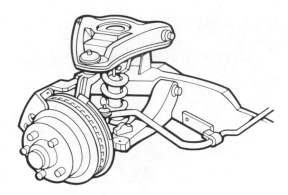

Fig. 15-122. *A conventional suspension system. (Courtesy of Tech-Cor, Inc.)*

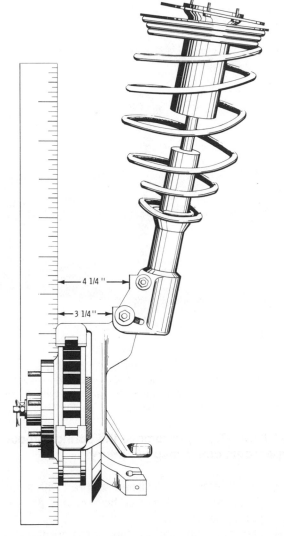

Fig. 15-123. *Camber adjustments on a strut. (Courtesy of Tech-Cor, Inc.)*

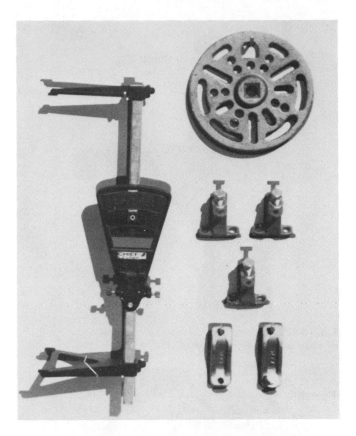

Fig. 15-124. *A universal strut suspension alignment kit. (Courtesy of Automotive Systems Division, Chief Industries)*

Fig. 15-125. *Frame components being measured to study alignment problems. (Courtesy of Tech-Cor, Inc.)*

Removing the Strut. The following procedure can be followed for removing the strut from most cars.

1. Remove the top *mount* nuts that hold the strut

in place in the engine compartment (Fig. 15-127).
2. Place the vehicle on safety stands, and remove the wheel.

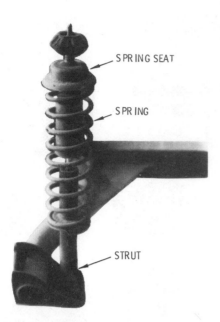

Fig. 15-126. *Spring seats at top and bottom hold the coil spring in place on a MacPherson strut.*

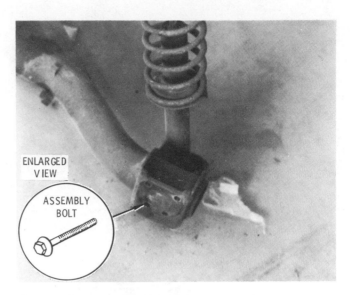

Fig. 15-128. *The strut is freed from the car at the lower end by removing assembly bolts.*

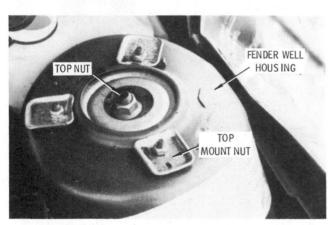

Fig. 15-127. *To repair or replace a strut, the three top mount nuts must be removed to free the assembly at the upper end. The "top nut" is not removed until the strut is off the car and ready to be disassembled.*

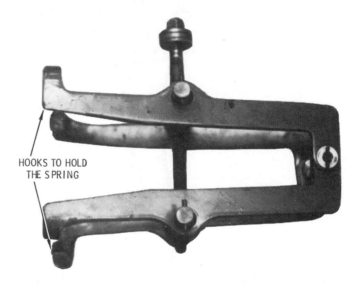

Fig. 15-129. *For safe disassembly of the MacPherson strut, a spring compressor must be used. The compressor relieves pressure on the top nut, so that it may be removed and the shock-absorbing unit repaired or replaced.*

3. Remove the brake hose clamp, and move the hose out of the way.
4. Remove the mounting bolt on the lower part of the strut (Fig. 15-128).
5. Remove the strut from the vehicle, using a pry tool if necessary.

Disassembling the Strut. The strut is disassembled by following the procedure below.

1. Place the strut in a vise, being careful not to damage the shock absorber tube. Use padding to prevent marring the tube.
2. Use a spring *compressor* (Fig. 15-129) to compress and hold the spring for removal.

CAUTION: Trying to remove the spring without the proper tools could result in injury.

3. After the spring has been secured with the compressing tool, remove the top nut and upper spring seat.
4. Remove the spring (still held in the spring compressor).
5. Inspect the unit, removing components one at a time. For ease in re-assembly, label each part as it is removed.
6. Repair or replace damaged parts.
7. To re-assemble the unit, reverse the procedure.

Major Body Repairs

The body of an automobile or small truck is made up of sections. These sections are built up from *groups* of panels that are fitted together to form the entire body assembly. The body assembly *and* the vehicle's frame make up the entire vehicle.

The major body assembly includes everything except the bumpers, window glass, trim (such as door handles and moldings), and any other moving parts. In conventional construction, the body assembly is *bolted* to the frame. In unitized body-frame construction, on the other hand, the body and frame assembly is *welded* together. The doors, front fenders, hood, deck lid, and bumpers are bolted to the body assembly.

When straightening major body structure damage, the repair must be made from the *inside to the outside*. For example, the major body assembly and its inner and outer panels cannot be properly aligned if the *frame* is not properly aligned *first*. Then, the *outer* panels cannot be correctly aligned until the *inner* panels are correctly aligned. Notice the extensive damage in Figure 16-1. The outer panel damage cannot be corrected until the inner body panels have been straightened or replaced. Even that cannot be done until the *frame* is repaired and aligned.

VEHICLE BODIES

Vehicle bodies either fit on, or form the top of, the vehicle's *frame*. There are several jobs that *any* vehicle body must be able to do. It must provide a solid foundation for the passenger seats, glass, instrument panel, doors, and all other body parts. It must protect passengers, luggage, and the engine from the weather. The

Fig. 16-1. *Both inner and outer panels will have to be repaired or replaced on this badly damaged car. (Courtesy of Automotive Systems Division, Chief Industries)*

body must be designed with ample luggage, passenger, and engine space.

Main Body Sections

All automobile bodies have three main sections. These are identified in Figure 16-2.

1. The front end assembly.
2. The passenger section.
3. The rear section.

The various sections of an auto body are often given short "nicknames" by auto body repair workers and auto body designers. For example, notice the used automobile front-end assembly, "F.E.A.," in Figure 16-3. This assembly will be used to repair an automobile that has heavy front-end damage. This assembly is sometimes called a *doghouse*, because of the way

267

it looks from the back side when it is taken off an automobile (Fig. 16-4). It is made up of the hood, front fenders and inner fenders, grille, radiator support framework, trim, and small parts.

The *passenger* section is often called the *greenhouse*, because of the large amount of *glass* it contains. This section is made up of roof panels, window glass, cowl and instrument panels, floor pan, door frames, doors, and other major parts. Usually, the center section is not replaced during a collision repair. If the damage is so bad that the center section is beyond repair, the car is undoubtedly "totaled."

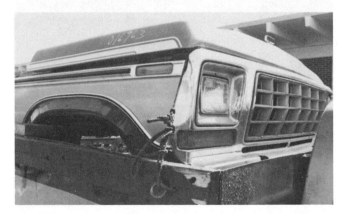

Fig. 16-2. *The automobile body is made up of three main sections.*

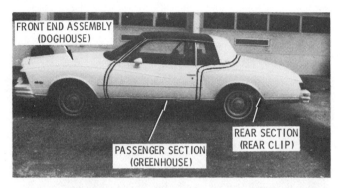

Fig. 16-3. *A used "doghouse" (front end assembly) from a salvage yard.*

Fig. 16-4. *Rear view of a "doghouse."*

Finally, the back, or *rear section*, is usually referred to as the *rear clip*. When this section is badly damaged, it cannot be unbolted and removed, as can a doghouse. The rear section must be *cut off* with a cutting torch or power chisel. When this is done, the rear section appears to have been "clipped" from the passenger section. This may be why it is known as a rear clip, or simply *clip*. This section includes the upper extension panel, deck lid, lower extension panel, quarter panels, trunk floor, and other trim and rear body parts (Fig. 16-5).

Body Types

There are two basic types of bodies, just as there are two basic types of frames. The two body types are the *conventional* body and the *unitized* body-frame. Both do the same jobs, and both have basically the same parts. However, they differ in certain design features and in the way that they are attached to the frame. The different body designs make necessary two different ways of handling the same problem, or doing the same job.

Conventional Body. In conventional body construction, the sections and parts are either bolted or welded to each other. Then, the entire assembly is bolted to the frame. In early automobiles, the body was not designed to be as strong as the rigid frame. In many recent designs, however, the body is quite strong, and the frame is less rigid and more flexible. The flexible conventional frame (often with torque boxes) is used under a strong body so that they may flex together to provide a smooth, tight ride.

Fig. 16-5. *A "rear clip," or rear section, of a vehicle. This assembly is lying on its side.*

Unitized Body-frame. The *unitized body-frame* is actually the same large assembly discussed earlier as a *frame*. In a unitized body-frame vehicle, the body and the frame are designed and built as a single piece of construction. A unitized body-frame is a reinforced shell (or welded group of boxes) to which the running gear and suspension are attached. Certain parts of the unitized body-frame support and align the running gear and suspension parts. Thus, the structure must provide support and alignment points for the vehicle.

The structural member parts of the unitized body-frame are designed to reinforce each other. Figure 16-6 shows how the *entire* body is welded together

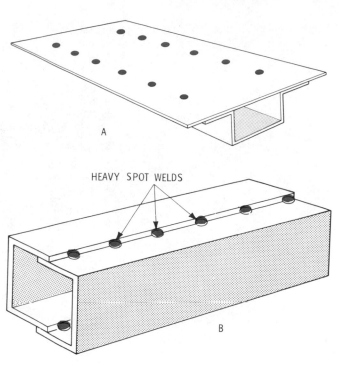

HEAVY SPOT WELDS

Fig. 16-7. *Closed box assemblies. (A) A flat plate welded to the top of an open box. (B) Two channel iron pieces spot-welded together.*

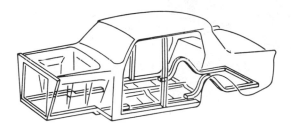

Fig. 16-6. *A common unitized body-frame. (Courtesy of Bear Division, Applied Power Industries)*

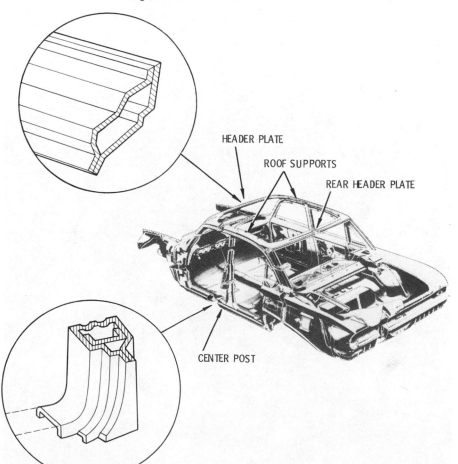

HEADER PLATE

ROOF SUPPORTS

REAR HEADER PLATE

CENTER POST

Fig. 16.8. *Some Structural members of a unitized body-frame. (Courtesy of* Autobody and The Reconditioned Car)

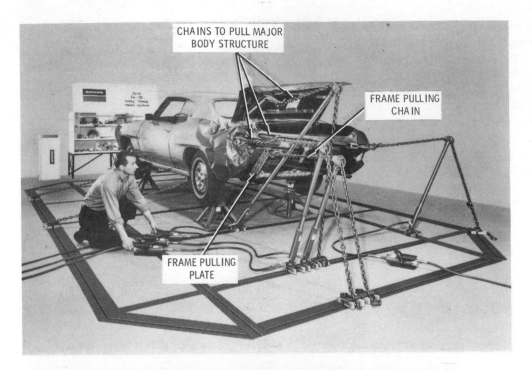

CHAINS TO PULL MAJOR BODY STRUCTURE

FRAME PULLING CHAIN

FRAME PULLING PLATE

Fig. 16-9. *Multiple pulls on a rack-type straightener can be used to straighten both major body structures and the frame at the same time. (Courtesy of Blackhawk Division, Applied Power Industries)*

Fig. 16-10. *Several pulls will be made to correct the severe frame damage on this car. (Courtesy of Blackhawk Division, Applied Power Industries)*

from several box sections. The "box" idea is particularly important in the floor section, as shown in Figure 16-7. The important sections of the unitized body have several support assemblies, which are usually sheet metal pieces spot-welded into box sections (Fig. 16-8).

BASIC ALIGNING PRINCIPLES

When an automobile is badly wrecked, there is usually some type of frame damage that must be repaired *before* the inner and outer panel damage can be successfully dealt with. For example, the car in Figure 16-9 has extensive frame damage. All types of frame damage must be repaired before body panel repair and replacement can begin.

Techniques

To repair major body damage, a body repair worker may not have to begin at the same point on every job. Since straightening tools and major wrecks vary greatly, no specific procedures can be outlined to apply to all jobs. However, the following generalizations hold true for work with the two basic types of auto construction.
Conventional Construction. When repairing major damage on a car with *conventional* construction, the frame, inner panels, and outer panels can be pulled separately, if the type of wreck and the equipment being used require it. On the other hand, they may be pulled at the *same* time by using *multiple hook-ups* (Fig. 16-9). In Figure 16-9, most of the chains are fastened to the car's frame. The "frame chain" requires more pull than the others, since the frame must be straightened just ahead of the major body parts. Also, the frame is stronger, requiring more force to straighten it.
Unitized Body-frame Construction. When repairing major damage on a car with *unitized* construction, any major parts *bolted* onto the welded structure may have

to be removed to provide access to the major structure (Fig. 16-10). They may need to be removed anyway, if they must be replaced as a result of serious damage. Such parts include doors, front fenders, hood, deck lid, and bumpers. These parts can be repaired while they are off the vehicle. If they are not too severely damaged, they can be bolted back onto the unitized body-frame after it has been straightened. They may then be repaired on the car.

Inner and Outer Panels

Usually, there is at least one *inner* panel for every outer panel. Inner panels may be made from either very strong or very thin sheet metal, depending on the job they perform. When an outer panel is badly damaged, the inner panel is normally damaged as well (Fig. 16-11). The inner panel will also require repair or replacement.

On most modern body structures, inner panels are spot-welded together wherever possible. The inner panels also may be spot-welded to the *outer* panels (Fig. 16-12). Although this makes the auto body stronger, it makes repair more difficult than if all parts were bolted together.

DAMAGED VEHICLE ALIGNMENT

Major body and frame repairs are required on the car shown in Figure 16-13. Many inner panels are badly damaged, in addition to the outer panels that can be seen easily.

Close inspection shows that all the quarter panels on the left side of the car are damaged. The outer and inner quarter panels are badly damaged. The rear floor is damaged, the frame is bent, and the roof is damaged. The bumper and many pieces of trim must be

Fig. 16-11. *When there is damage to an outer panel, the inner panel is usually damaged as well. The outer panel has been cut away to show damage to the inner panel.*

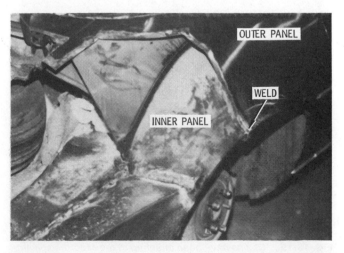

Fig. 16-12. *The inner and outer panels are often spot-welded together.*

Fig. 16-13. *The damaged vehicle shown in Figure 16-1 has been placed on a rack-type straightener for repairs. (Courtesy of Automotive Systems Division, Chief Industries)*

Fig. 16-14. *Multiple hook-ups can pull in several directions at the same time. (Courtesy of Automotive Systems Division, Chief Industries)*

Fig. 16-15. *Chains have been attached to the MacPherson strut tower and other front-end points for this pull. (Courtesy of Automotive Systems Division, Chief Industries)*

Fig. 16-16. *The center frame section being aligned. (Courtesy of Automotive Systems Division, Chief Industries)*

replaced. The alignment and repair of this car will take the knowledge of a skilled body repair worker.

Basic Hook-ups

After the vehicle has been placed on the frame-straightening unit and made safe for pulling, multiple hook-ups are used. By using three towers (front, side, and rear), pulls can be made in almost any direction. As shown in Figure 16-14, chains are hooked to the roof, windshield pillar post, quarter panel, and door post. Another chain is placed on the frame at the rear to help pull the sidesway in the center section of the frame.

The outer panels have been removed from the front, and chains have been hooked to the front end of the frame for a straight pull to help straighten the frame center section (Fig. 16-15). A chain is hooked to the strut tower, and another is hooked to the inner fender.

As shown in Figure 16-16, pinch-weld clamps have been placed on each side of the frame damage at the center section, and a jack has been positioned between them. The chain hook-ups on each end of the frame will exert a pulling force, while the jack applies "push" pressure in the sway area.

Another jack is placed to the rear of the pinch-weld clamps for extra pressure on the center sway area. Two jacks are placed at the rocker panel for a side pull, as shown in Figure 16-17. All these hook-ups are necessary to distribute the pressure. This will help prevent tearing the thin sheet metal and pulling the spot welds loose as the pulls are made.

Another jack is placed at the front vehicle frame horn to push the side rail to the right (Fig. 16-18). A chain is hooked to the left side rail at the crossmember to exert pressure to the left.

The front inner panel is pulled and aligned (Fig. 16-19), while the strut is pulled forward for the front-end alignment (Fig. 16-20). The vehicle is shown after completion in Figure 16-21. To do this type of repair, good frame equipment must be used by a mechanic with a complete knowledge of frame and panel repair.

Fig. 16-17. *Hook-up for aligning the rocker panel. (Courtesy of Automotive Systems Division, Chief Industries)*

Fig. 16-18. *Frame damage must be repaired before inner panel damage, and inner panels must be corrected before outer panel damage is repaired. (Courtesy of Automotive Systems Division, Chief Industries)*

QUARTER-PANEL SECTIONING

Often, it is quicker and easier to replace a *section* of a damaged quarter panel, if the entire panel has not been damaged. However, if the section is large and contoured, the job must be estimated as if the entire panel is to be replaced. This is done because an entire new panel will have to be purchased, even if only part of it will be used. The amount of damage to be cut away must be determined by the body repair worker for the particular job being repaired.

Figures 16-22 through 16-37 show a section of a quarter panel being replaced. Such quarter-panel sectioning will save a good deal of repair time and help maintain the body panel's original alignment, strength, and appearance in the areas that are not affected.

Patching Quarter Panels

The smallest *replacement* repair normally done to a quarter panel would be to *patch* the panel. Here, an even smaller area of the panel is cut away than in the *sectioning* process. Any repairs smaller than patching would not include installing part of a new quarter panel. Figures 16-38, 16-39, and 16-40 show a typical quarter-panel patch repair.

LIGHTWEIGHT PANELS

Manufacturers are using more lightweight panels made from materials such as aluminum, plastic, galvanized metal, and high-strength steel. These panels must be worked differently from mild steel panels.

Galvanized metal is being used widely in lightweight vehicles. Figure 16-41 shows a molded side panel that is galvanized. It is made in one piece, instead of the three-piece panels used in the past.

High-strength steel (HSS) is being used in many lightweight vehicles. This type of steel is very thin and

Fig. 16-19. *The front sheet metal is pulled forward into alignment. (Courtesy of Automotive Systems Division, Chief Industries)*

Fig. 16-20. *The hook-up for aligning the MacPherson strut. (Courtesy of Automotive Systems Division, Chief Industries)*

Fig. 16-21. *The finished vehicle, with all alignment and metal work completed.*

Fig. 16-22. *The rear portion of this quarter panel will have to be replaced with a new or salvaged quarter panel.*

Fig. 16-24. *Before the damage is cut away, a turnbuckle is used to bring the panel into alignment.*

Fig. 16-23. *A used quarter panel from the salvage yard. A section of this panel can be cut to repair the damage shown in Figure 16-22.*

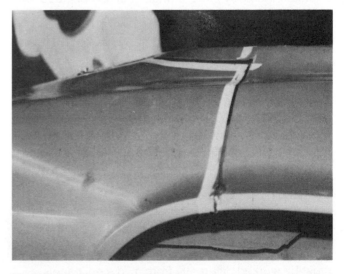

Fig. 16-25. *The damaged section of the panel has been cut along a masking tape marking line.*

light and cannot be heated to more than 1400°F (76°C). To weld high-strength steel, the wire or MIG welder must be used. The *oxy-acetylene torch* cannot be used on high-strength steel.

Plastic and aluminum panels are used on many vehicles. The repair of such panels is discussed in a later unit.

Fig. 16-26. *The damaged section and the replacement piece, side-by-side. The replacement piece is cut slightly larger to leave about a ¾ in. (19.0 mm) overlap for welding.*

Fig. 16-27. *The damaged section has been removed from the car.*

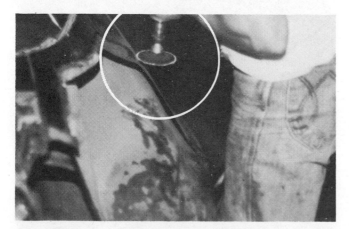

Fig. 16-28. *All paint is sanded off the area of the quarter panel where the replacement piece will be welded. The matching edge of the replacement is sanded clean, as well.*

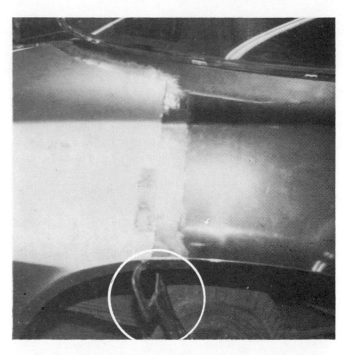

Fig. 16-29. *The replacement piece is clamped into place on the quarter panel.*

Fig. 16-30. *Welding clamps (marked by arrows) hold the parts snugly together for welding.*

Fig. 16-31. *At the luggage compartment, the pieces are brazed together. In this area, brazing is easier than spot-welding.*

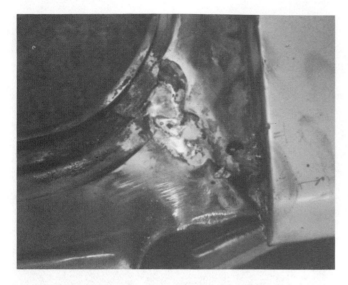

Fig. 16-32. *A closeup view of the brazed area.*

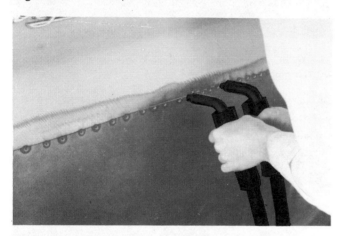

Fig. 16-33. *A resistance spot welder (panel spotter) being used on a quarter panel.*

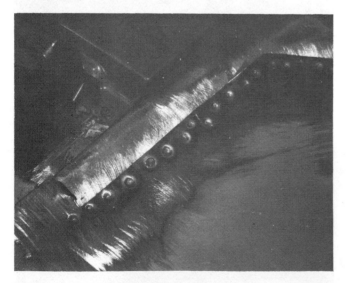

Fig. 16-34. *The replacement piece spot-welded in place. Spot-welding generates a smaller amount of heat and causes less warping of the metal than oxy-acetylene welding.*

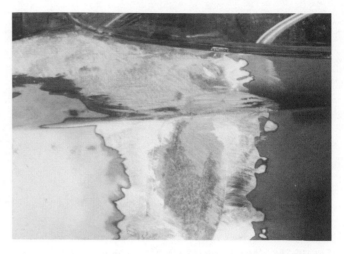

Fig. 16-35. *Plastic filler is used to level the area where the replacement is welded to the quarter panel.*

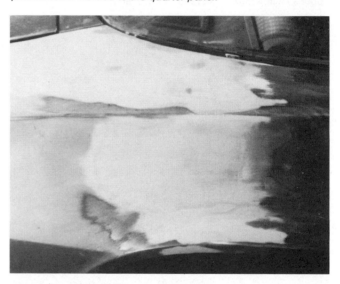

Fig. 16-36. *The filler has been sanded smooth and feather-edged, ready for primer.*

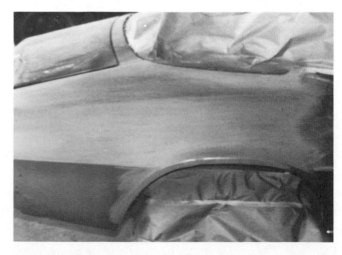

Fig. 16-37. *After priming, the repair is sanded again to prepare for the finishing coats.*

Door Damage

Almost all automobiles involved in a side collision will have *door* damage. Often, the *inner* door panels will be undamaged or will have only minor damage that may be easily straightened.

Replacing a Door Skin. The outer panel of a door is also known in the auto body trade as the door skin, or simply *skin*. This is the outside surface of the door. Figure 16-42 shows a new door skin.

Replacing an outer door panel is one of the most common replacement jobs done in a body shop. If the skin is damaged to a great extent, it is almost always replaced. Door skins are among the easiest panels to replace. When the labor charge to straighten a door skin would amount to 3 or 4 hours, it would probably be less expensive to replace the panel with a new skin.

Generally, door skins are inexpensive. They can be quickly installed, when compared to an entirely new door. A new skin gives the appearance of a new door. Also, the skin can often be installed without removing the inner working parts of the door or window glass. However, the inside trim panel may need to be removed. The outer door handle is usually bolted to the door skin from the inside.

Figure 16-43 shows a damaged door. Since only the outer panel is damaged, a new skin will be installed. This will save the time required to work out the damage. Figures 16-44 through 16-55 show the procedure to follow when replacing a typical door skin.

MAJOR SIDE DAMAGE

The vehicle shown in Figure 16-56 has been badly damaged on the right side. When a vehicle is hit hard on the *side*, major body parts are often severely damaged. When repairing this type of damage, more emphasis is placed on the *inner* panel areas. These are

not normally *replaced* when they are damaged, whereas outer panels normally *are* replaced. The *inner* panels must be properly aligned before the *outer* panels will line up correctly. Thus, it is *very* important that the inner

Fig. 16-39. *The patch has been spot-welded in place on the car. The pliers were used to clamp the patch in position for welding.*

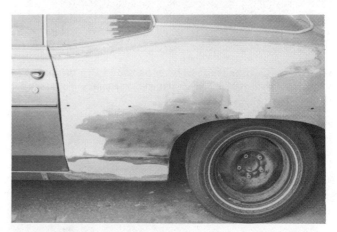

Fig. 16-40. *The patch has been leveled with plastic filler, ready for refinishing.*

Fig. 16-41. *A galvanized side panel that has been produced as one piece.*

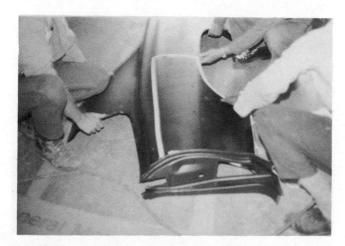

Fig. 16-38. *Marking a section of a new quarter panel, which will be cut for use as a "patch" on a damaged panel.*

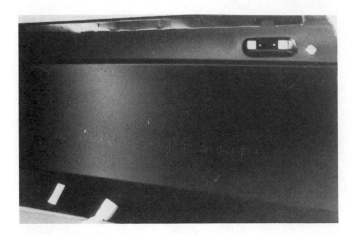

Fig. 16-42. *A new door "skin" (outer panel). Such panels are shipped from the factory already primed, and with holes punched for door lock parts.*

Fig. 16-43. *A door that has been damaged in a collision. The simplest way to repair this damage is to replace it with a new door skin.*

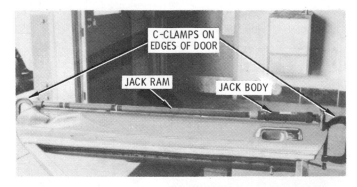

Fig. 16-44. *If the inner structure of the door has been damaged in the collision, it must be repaired before the new skin is attached. Here, a body jack is being used to stretch the door to its original dimensions.*

panels be straightened properly when they are repaired. The fit of the doors and windows will be poor if work on the inner panels and floor is not done correctly.

The ability to "think out" the repair is needed to locate and repair inner body panel damage from a side

Fig. 16-45. *It may be necessary to remove the inside trim of the door before replacing the skin.*

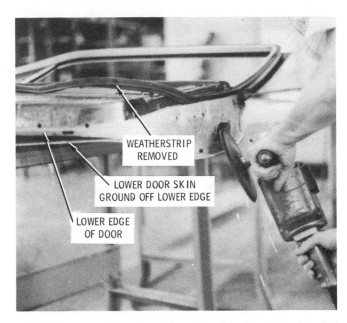

Fig. 16-46. *One method of removing the old skin is to grind away metal all around the edges. The skin is crimped over a flange to hold it in place.*

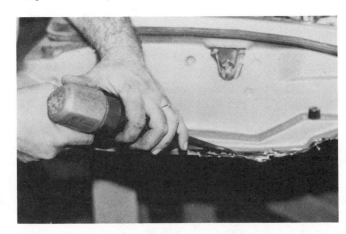

Fig. 16-47. *Another method is to use a power chisel to cut away the door skin along the flange.*

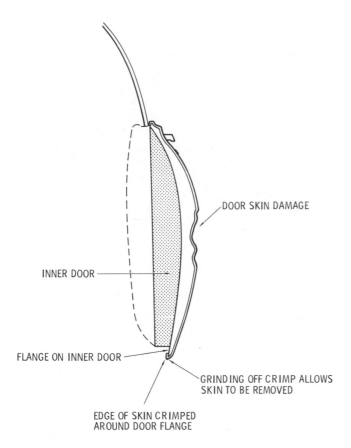

Fig. 16-50. *Using a hammer and a block of wood to bend the edge of the new skin over the door flange. New skins are usually provided with the edges bent at a 90° angle to make this step easier.*

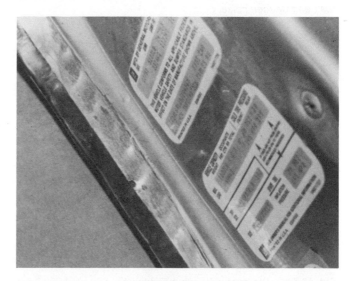

Fig. 16-51. *A closeup view of the new skin crimped over the door flange.*

Fig. 16-48. *In this cutaway view, the way in which the skin is crimped over the flange can be seen.*

Fig. 16-49. *A door with the skin removed, showing the inner structure. A hammer and dolly should be used to straighten any damaged metal before the new skin is installed.*

collision. Figure 16-57 shows some of the damage that will need repair. This photo shows damage to the bumper, headlight assembly, side marker light, and chrome molding.

Fig. 16-52. *The crimped metal has been cleaned and spot-welded to the flange.*

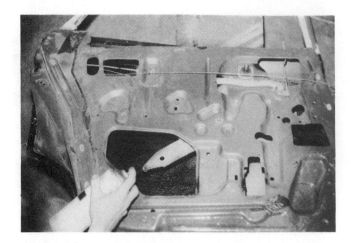

Fig. 16-53. *The back side of the new door skin should be sprayed with an undercoating material to seal the seams, help prevent rust, and deaden noise.*

Fig. 16-54. *The door trim, weatherstripping, and hardware have been replaced. The door is now ready for refinishing.*

Fig. 16-55. *The completed repair. Usually, doors with replacement skins are refinished before being mounted on the car. This allows the edges and the outer face to be finished at the same time, for a neat appearance.*

Fig. 16-56. *Major body panels have been damaged in this side-swipe collision.*

Fig. 16-57. *The front bumper, headlight housing, side marker light, and front fender have been damaged.*

Fig. 16-58. *Damage to this fiberglass header panel can be repaired.*

Fig. 16-59. *The repaired and re-installed header panel.*

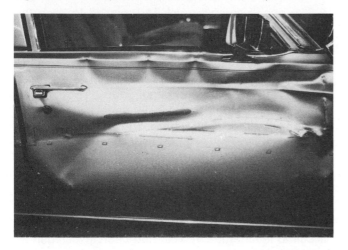

Fig. 16-60. *A new door skin and new molding will have to be installed on this door.*

HOLES FOR DOOR HANDLE

Fig. 16-61. *The door handle will be mounted from behind the new panel with two screws.*

Header Panel Repair

The header panel on this vehicle is made of fiberglass. Repair of fiberglass panels with fiberglass matting, and fiberglass resin is discussed in another unit. Figure 16-58 shows the header panel damage; Figure

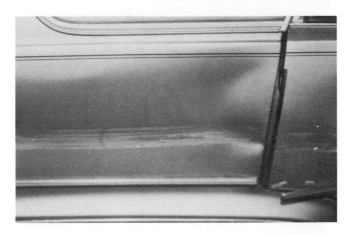

Fig. 16-62. *Quarter-panel damage, which can be repaired.*

Fig. 16-63. *Plastic filler was used to level the damaged panel for refinishing.*

Fig. 16-64. *The rear door and quarter panel have been aligned.*

16-59 shows the panel after being repaired and reinstalled.

The front fender (outer panel), the light assembly, and the chrome molding all need to be replaced.

Fig. 16-65. *The repaired area has been primed and is ready for finish coats.*

Door Damage

Almost all automobiles involved in a side collision will have *door* damage. Often, both the outer and the inner door panels are damaged. Figure 16-60 shows damage to the door *jamb* (the edges of the door and its opening on the car's body). When the *outer* door panel is removed, the door jamb will have to be aligned with a hammer and dolly.

To replace an outer door panel, the *inside* door trim must be removed. After the door skin is attached to the door frame, the screws for the outside door handle must be installed before replacing the inside trim (Fig.

Fig. 16-66. *All repairs have been completed, and the vehicle is ready to be returned to its owner.*

16-61). These screws must be replaced to keep the outside door handle in position.

The rear door panel shown in Figure 16-61 was damaged and had to be replaced. The same procedure is used to install the rear door outer panel as was used to repair and install the front door panel.

Quarter-panel Repair. The quarter panel has extensive damage, as shown in Figure 16-62. The damaged quarter panel is first aligned, then paint is sanded off around the damage. The dented area is filled with plastic, as shown in Figure 16-63. The rear door is then aligned to fit the repaired quarter panel (Fig. 16-64). All the damage has been repaired and is being prepared for refinishing in Figure 16-65. In Figure 16-66, it is difficult to tell that the vehicle had been involved in an accident.

Section VI

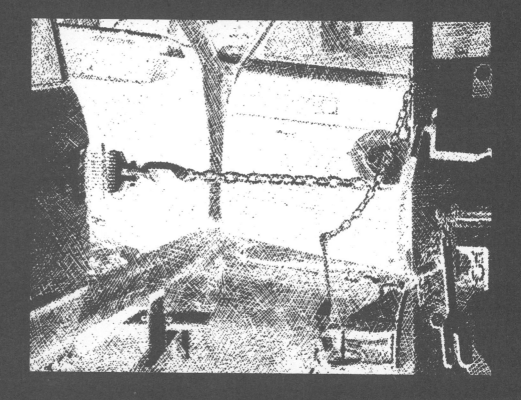

Minor Repairs

Basic Metal Straightening

Metal straightening is probably the most important part of total auto body repair. Metal straightening is also an *art*. A dented or damaged automobile panel cannot be measured as can a table or a chair needing repair. For this reason, a body shop *metal worker* has to form a mental picture of what the panel looked like, how it was shaped, *before* it was damaged. Then, the worker will be able to restore the metal to its original shape more easily.

The basic problems of metal straightening can be described by a comparison with a length of wire. If a length of wire (Fig. 17-1) is bent into a loop (Fig. 17-2), the wire's *elasticity*, or ability to regain its original shape, is lost. When an attempt is made to straighten the wire, the large curve in it cannot be removed completely. Figure 17-3, for example, shows the curve in the wire after an attempt was made to straighten it. *This same problem exists when trying to straighten damaged metal.*

BASIC STRAIGHTENING METHODS

To remove the curves or bends that make up the metal damage, the low spots must be lifted up and the high spots worked down. On a given job, this may be done by using one or more of the *eight basic methods* of straightening metal. These are:

1. Aligning the metal with a *power jack*.
2. Working the metal with a *hammer* and *dolly*.
3. Pulling the metal with one or more *vacuum cups*.
4. Pulling the metal with *pull rods* and *slide hammer*.
5. Pulling the metal with *pull tabs*.

6. *Heat shrinking* the metal to provide a repair without additional stretching.
7. *Kinking* the metal to provide a surface for body filler.
8. Using *pry bars*.

Fig. 17-1. *A length of wire, like a metal panel, is straight and smooth before being bent.*

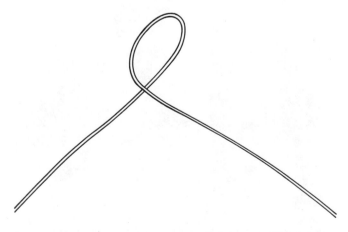

Fig. 17-2. *When the wire is bent into a loop, it is stretched beyond the limits of its elasticity. When pressure is released, it will not return to its original shape.*

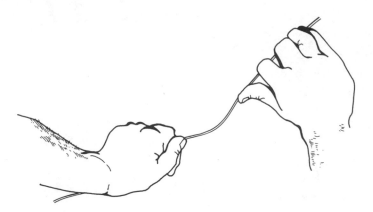

Fig. 17-3. *Even when an attempt is made to force the wire back into its original shape, a "hump" will remain where the metal was stretched.*

All eight of these methods may be used either separately or together on a job. The method used depends on many different factors on each job. These include the *amount* of damage, the *size* of the affected area, the *extent* to which the metal has been stretched, and how *accessible* the damage is from the front and back sides of the panel. After considering the factors involved, a technician must select the best method or combination of methods to use for the damage being repaired on that job.

After metal has been straightened, any small high places remaining on the surface may be filed down. The area may then by ground smooth and prepared for refinishing. If the surface is completely level and shaped

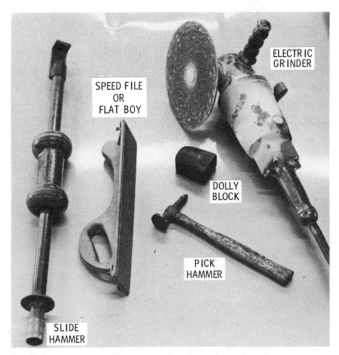

Fig. 17-4. *Some of the tools needed to straighten and smooth stretched sheet metal.*

to the correct contour, the area may be filled with a body filler before refinishing.

A Word About Tools

All *tools*, especially hammers, dollies, and files, must be free of dirt, dents, or marks. Dents or dirt on the face of a hammer or dolly will be transferred to the metal being worked. For the same reason, *undercoating* and mud must be scraped off the panel before straightening it. Use sandpaper to "dress" the faces of hammers and dollies and make them smooth.

The tools a body worker uses are very important, especially during straightening. The right tool is always the best tool for the job being done. Using the right tool is a good safety practice and will help make sure that the job is done *correctly*. The tools used for a typical metal straightening job are shown in Figure 17-4.

Power Jack

Normally, large damaged areas are aligned with a power jack. This is done by either *pushing* a dent out or by *pulling* on the panel using power jack attachments. Figure 17-5 shows several common uses of a power jack.

Large power jacks (panel pullers) can also be used to stretch a panel when repairing collision damage. Figures 17-6 through 17-8 show how this is done. The damaged panel is first clamped on each end with a pinch-weld clamp to hold the jack attachments in place. Pressure is then applied to the jack. As the jack extends, the damaged panel is stretched and straightened. Figure 17-8 shows what the damaged panel in Figure 17-6 looks like after it has been pulled. Note that it is not completely repaired. Additional body work and filling will be required, but the panel is now basically straight.

Hammer and Dolly

Metal damage that is not severe is often repaired with only a hammer and dolly. Also, a hammer and dolly are often used on any remaining high and low spots *after* a power jack or panel puller has been used. Hammer and dolly straightening may be done on small damaged areas that can be reached from both the inside and the outside of the panel.

To straighten damaged metal with a hammer and dolly, the basic procedure is to use a dolly *under* the damage and a hammer on *top* of the damage. The dolly is used to shape and support metal as the hammer works (Fig. 17-9).

A *dolly* may also be used by itself to knock up low spots from under the damage, as shown in Figure 17-10. This has to be done carefully so that the dolly

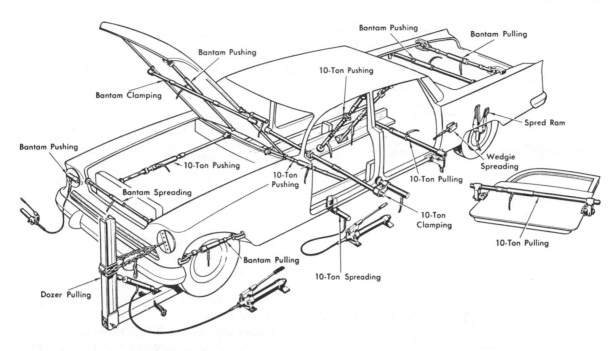

Fig. 17-5. *Combinations of accessories with a body jack for basic body straightening jobs. (Courtesy of Blackhawk Division, Applied Power Industries)*

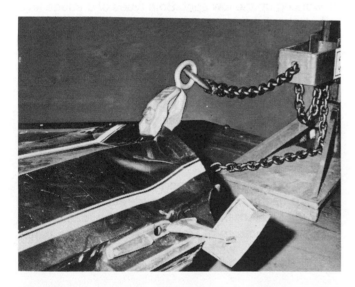

Fig. 17-6. *A pinch-weld clamp fastened to a door flange. Both the door skin and the door structure will be straightened by the same pull. (Courtesy of Grabber Manufacturing Company)*

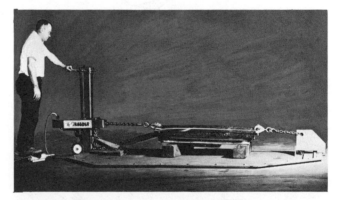

Fig. 17-7. *Making the pull for the door hook-up shown in Figure 17-6. (Courtesy of Grabber Manufacturing Company)*

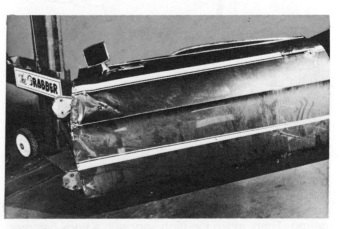

Fig. 17-8. *The door after being straightened. (Courtesy of Grabber Manufacturing Company)*

does not lift the low spots too high. If the spots are lifted too high, a sander or a grinder may cut off the *top* of the high spot, leaving a hole in the metal. It takes a good amount of practice to repair damaged areas without leaving high and low spots. This takes time, patience, and experience in hammer and dolly work.

There are three basic hammer and dolly processes. These include hammering *on* the dolly, hammering *off* the dolly, and *picking*. Picking is done by either the dolly *or* the hammer in very small areas.

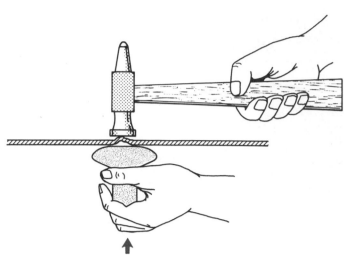

Fig. 17-9. *Using a pick hammer and dolly to work down a small area of stretched metal.*

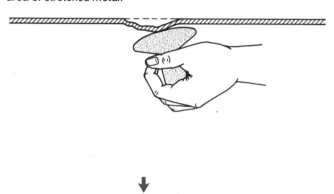

Fig. 17-10. *The dolly can be used alone to work up a dent from the underside, if working room is available.*

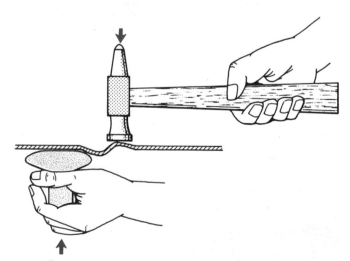

Fig. 17-11. *Hammering off the dolly.*

Hammering on the Dolly. To work down a high spot, first place a dolly *under* the high spot. The dolly should have the contour desired for the panel *after* it is repaired. Then, strike the high spot with a body hammer, as shown in Figure 17-9. The blows should be *light*

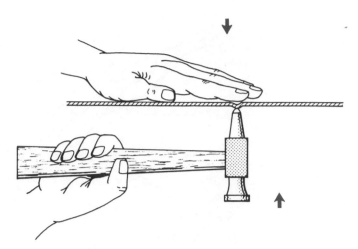

Fig. 17-12. *The point of the picking hammer is used on very small dents or high spots.*

and several should be used to work the metal down, *gradually* moving the hammer and dolly around the area as needed.

Hammering off the Dolly. Hammering *off* the dolly is done to remove a high spot and a bordering low spot at the same time. Figure 17-11 shows how this is done. While the hammer works down the high spot, the dolly is working up the low spot. Both types of damage level off at about the same time. The pressure and "high" metal from the hammer blow is displaced (spread out) from the high spot to the low spot. This causes the low spot to rise.

Picking. When *either* the hammer *or* the dolly is being used alone to work metal, *picking* is being done. Figure 17-12 shows how the picking end of a hammer can be used to level very small high or low spots left in the metal *after* using the hammer and dolly together on an area.

Picking may also be done using only a dolly. A dolly is more useful for picking hard-to-reach low areas of the repair. Often, these areas cannot be reached with a hammer because of limited space under the panel. Figure 17-13 shows how one corner of a dolly may be used to "pick up" low spots from inside the panel.

Vacuum Cups

One or more *vacuum cups* may be used to pull out shallow, low-crown dents *where there is no buckled metal*. Figure 17-14 shows how this is done on a simple job using one vacuum cup. Special plates are available with as many as *three* vacuum cups, allowing very large areas to be pulled (Figs. 17-15 and 17-16).

To use a vacuum cup, the panel being pulled *must* be clean and, preferably, *wet*. If possible, the panel should have paint on it and must not be sanded or "roughed up" before using the vacuum cup. The cup itself will usually grip better if it is also wet.

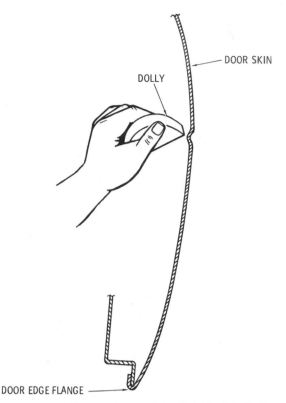

Fig. 17-13. *A dolly may be used for "picking" in tight spots where a hammer will not reach.*

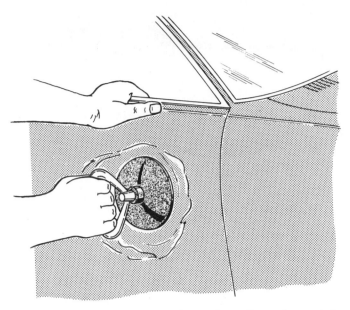

Fig. 17-14. *A suction cup may be used to pull out a large, shallow dent.*

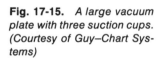

Fig. 17-15. *A large vacuum plate with three suction cups. (Courtesy of Guy–Chart Systems)*

Fig. 17-16. *Using a vacuum plate to pull out a dented area of a car roof.*

To make a pull, first push *in* on the vacuum cup to force out all the air. Then, pull slowly on the vacuum cup to pull out the dent. Although this is a very quick procedure, it is limited to use on low-crown dents. These are dents that have no sharp ridges around the outside edge of the damage.

Pull Rods or Slide Hammers

Sometimes, a dent cannot be worked with a hammer and dolly because it cannot be reached from the back side. Also, the dent may be too deep or have edges that are too sharp to use a vacuum cup. In this case, a *pull rod* or a *slide hammer* can be used to pull out the dent. A major disadvantage of these pulling tools is that *holes* must be drilled in the panel being repaired.

Slide Hammer. To use a slide hammer, first drill a series of holes in the panel along the deepest part of the crease. Then, insert a sheet metal screw, slightly larger than the drilled holes, into the end of the slide hammer (Fig.17-17). Turn the hammer handle *clockwise*, screwing the metal screw into the drilled hole (Fig. 17-18). Then, pull out the dent by pulling on the slide hammer.

A pick hammer may be used to tap around the *outer* edge of the dent. This is done to help release the pressure causing the dent to stay in, so that the slide hammer can easily pull the metal out. The hammer *weight* may be slid back and forth to help pull the dent out, if it is large or deep (Fig.17-19). When the dent is pulled out and the metal is fairly well straightened, the repair area may be ground smooth and filled with body filler.

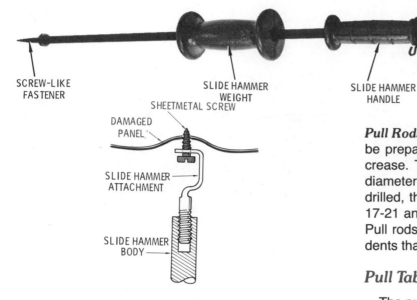

SCREW-LIKE FASTENER

SLIDE HAMMER WEIGHT

SLIDE HAMMER HANDLE

Fig. 17-17. *A slide hammer has a screw or screwlike attachment at one end. It may be threaded into holes drilled in the damaged area. (Courtesy of Guy–Chart Systems)*

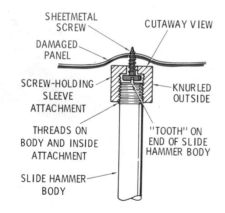

SHEETMETAL SCREW

DAMAGED PANEL

SLIDE HAMMER ATTACHMENT

SLIDE HAMMER BODY

SHEETMETAL SCREW

DAMAGED PANEL

CUTAWAY VIEW

SCREW-HOLDING SLEEVE ATTACHMENT

KNURLED OUTSIDE

THREADS ON BODY AND INSIDE ATTACHMENT

"TOOTH" ON END OF SLIDE HAMMER BODY

SLIDE HAMMER BODY

Fig. 17-18. *Two methods of attaching the screw to the slide hammer.*

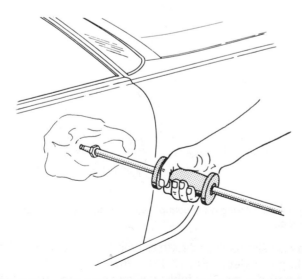

Fig. 17-19. *Using the slide hammer to pull out a large, difficult dent. (Courtesy of Guy–Chart Systems)*

Pull Rods. To use *pull rods* (Fig. 17-20), the area must be prepared by drilling holes along the bottom of the crease. The holes should be slightly larger than the diameter of the pull rods. When the holes have been drilled, the pull rods may be used, either alone (Figs. 17-21 and 17-22) or with a pick hammer (Fig. 17-23). Pull rods are normally used on smaller, more shallow dents than is the slide hammer.

Pull Tabs

The pull tab is a new way of pulling from one side of the boxed-in construction of panels on the vehicle. A spot welder (panel spotter) is used to attach the tabs to the damaged panel for pulling and aligning the metal.

Pull Tab Kit. The pull tab kit consists of several attachments, as shown in Figure 17-24. The kit includes pull

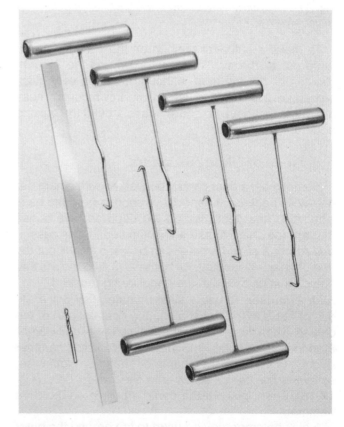

Fig. 17-20. *A pull rod set includes a drill bit, a straightedge, and several pull rods. The bit is used to drill holes for the rods, and the straightedge is used to judge when the pulled area is reasonably level. (Courtesy of Snap-On Tools)*

tabs, a pull plate assembly, a spot pull ground, a welding tip assembly, a hook pull assembly, an accessory stand, and adapter bushings. The panel spot welder in Figure 17-25 is used to weld the pull tabs to a damaged panel.

The pull tab welding tips are installed on the panel spot welder as shown in Figure 17-26. Use a sander to remove paint, or use the ground tip to scratch away the paint for a good ground, as shown in Figure 17-27. After the first tab has been welded to the panel, it can be used as the ground to weld the second tab in place (Fig. 17-27). Weld as many tabs to the panel as needed for pulling the damaged area (Fig. 17-28).

Attach a *pull plate assembly* to the pull tabs. Use your fingers to guide the pull tabs into a parallel position to attach them to the pull plate (Fig. 17-29). A heavy *slide hammer* can be used to pull the damage, as shown in Figure17-30.

A single pull tab can be used on a small damaged area. Attach the pull tab to the center of the damaged area, and use the *pull hook assembly* to pull the area up. Use a *hammer* or *slapper* to bump down the high crowns around the damaged area, as shown in Figure 17-31. Pull tabs can easily be removed by using a twist motion (Fig. 17-31). The pull tabs also can be used with a power jack, such as the one shown in Figure 17-32.

Heat Shrinking

When metal is damaged (dented) by an object, it will usually stretch. Many times, an experienced technician can repair the damage without stretching the metal even more. This is one of the "secrets" of good metal straightening—restoring the damaged area without any further *stretching* of the metal.

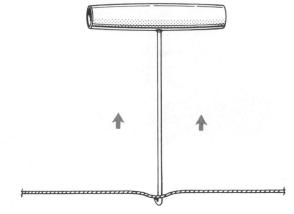

Fig. 17-21.   *Using a single pull rod on a small dent.*

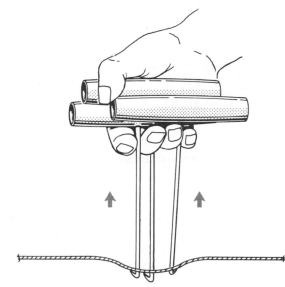

Fig. 17-22.   *For larger dents, several pull rods may be used together. Spacing of the rods determines whether one hand or both hands are used to pull.*

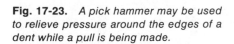

Fig. 17-23.   *A pick hammer may be used to relieve pressure around the edges of a dent while a pull is being made.*

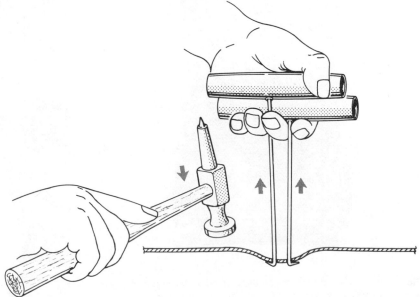

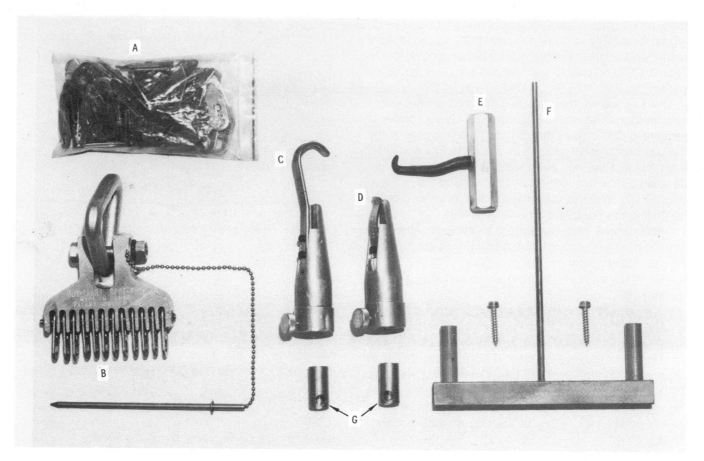

Fig. 17-24. *Components of a pull tab system used with a resistance spot welder. (A) Package of pull tabs. (B) The pull plate assembly. (C) Ground tip assembly for welder. (D) Welding tip assembly for welder. (E) Pull hook. (F) Accessory stand. (G) Adapter bushings. (Courtesy of Guy–Chart Systems)*

Fig. 17-25. *A resistance spot welder used with the pull tab system. (Courtesy of Automotive Equipment Division, Lenco, Inc.)*

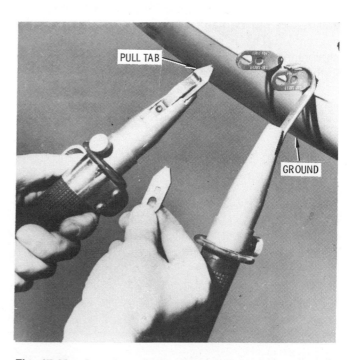

Fig. 17-26. *Pull tabs are spot-welded to the damaged area. (Courtesy of Guy–Chart Systems)*

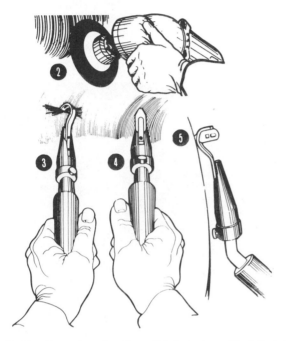

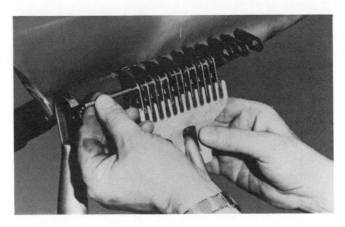

Fig. 17-27. *Steps in using the pull tab system. (1) Setting the welder time control. (2) Sanding the damaged area to bare metal. (3) Scratching the metal for a good ground. (4) Welding a tab in place. (5) Using the first tab as a ground for welding the next tab. (Courtesy of Guy–Chart Systems)*

Fig. 17-29. *A pin is used to attach the tabs to the pull plate assembly. (Courtesy of Guy–Chart Systems)*

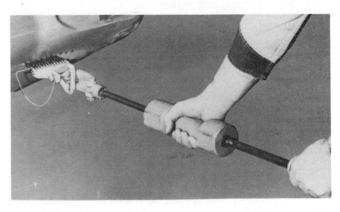

Fig. 17-30. *A heavy slide hammer is attached to the pull plate and used to pull out the damaged area. (Courtesy of Guy–Chart Systems)*

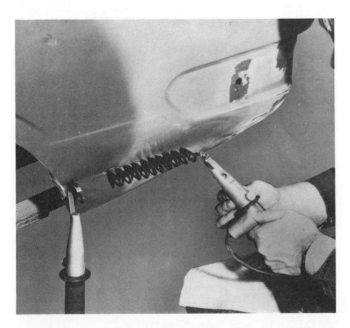

Fig. 17-28. *As many pull tabs as needed are welded to the damaged area. (Courtesy of Guy–Chart Systems)*

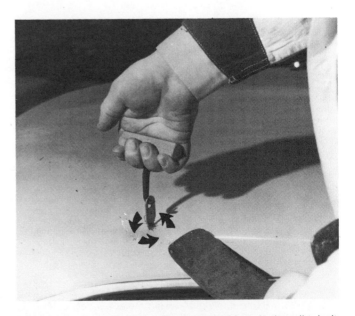

Fig. 17-31. *The pull hook can be used with a single pull tab. It also is used to remove tabs after use. The tabs are removed with a twisting motion, as shown here. (Courtesy of Guy–Chart Systems)*

However, if metal is stretched too far (either in the original accident or while straightening), it must be shrunk. *Heat shrinking* the metal makes it occupy the same area on the panel that it did originally. Shrinking is done, basically, by softening the metal with heat, then applying *force* to flatten the area or *water* to contract ("shrink") the area.

Quenching the hot metal with a wet sponge or rag is one of the better ways to shrink the stretched area back to its original shape (Fig. 17-33). When hot metal is cooled faster than it would normally cool by itself, it will shrink. The faster it is cooled, the more it will shrink.

CAUTION: Quenching should never be done while the metal is red-hot. Wait until the metal has turned dark before applying water.

Fig. 17-32. *A power jack may be used with pull tabs if more force is needed. (Courtesy of Guy–Chart Systems)*

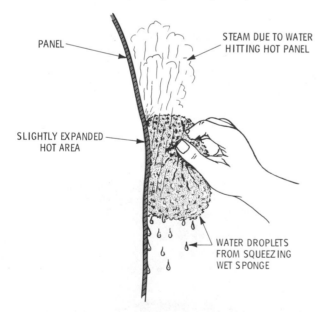

Fig. 17-33. *Rapid cooling of heated metal will help shrink it to its original area. To prevent steam burns, care must be used. The metal should be allowed to cool to the point where it begins to turn dark before water is applied.*

The basic theory and procedure for heat shrinking is discussed in the unit on "Oxy-acetylene Brazing and Heat Shrinking." Figures 17-34 through 17-36 review the basic heat-shrinking process.

Kinking

A metal-working process used *only* to prepare an area for filler is *kinking*. Basically, kinking is a method used to deal with stretched metal *without* actually shrinking the metal itself *or* straightening it. Kinking is not supposed to return the metal to its original contour.

Fig. 17-34. *The stretched area is heated with an oxy-acetylene torch. This softens the metal and allows it to be "worked" easily.*

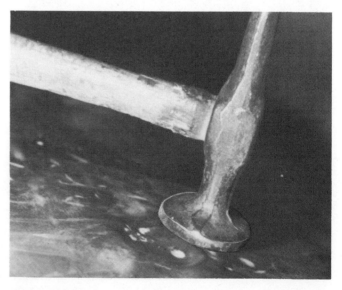

Fig. 17-35. *A hammer can be used to flatten and shape the heated metal.*

During this process, the warped, wavy, stretched area is worked into a series of lowered kinks. A pick hammer is used to do this by tapping the metal with a scratch awl or "picking" metal against the edge of a dolly (Fig. 17-37). Both the awl and the hammer have the sharp point necessary to make a small kink in the metal.

After the stretched area has been kinked several times, it will be slightly lower than the rest of the panel. The kinked area is then filled with body filler and prepared for refinishing.

Pry Bars

Many times, interior trim panels may be removed to provide access to the damage from behind. Then, *pry bars* may be used to pry out the damage. This will avoid the need to drill holes for a slide hammer or pull rods.

When using pry bars, care must be taken so that the metal is not pried out *too* far. This might stretch the metal and will cause more work to complete the repair. Figures 17-38 through 17-41 show a pry bar being used.

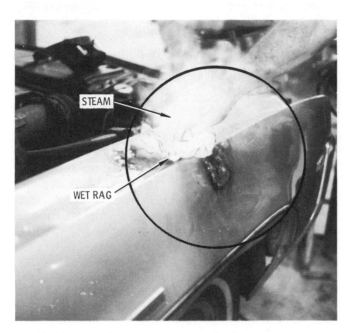

Fig. 17-36. *Quenching (cooling) the heated area with a wet rag to help shrink the metal.*

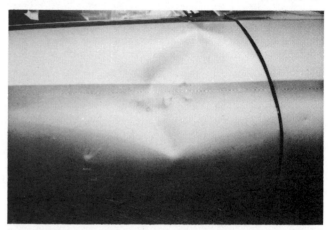

Fig. 17-38. *Door panel damage that is not severe enough to warrant replacing the skin. Such damage may be worked out from behind by using a pry bar.*

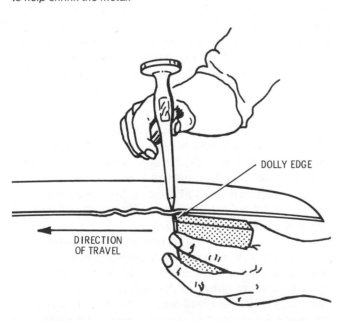

Fig. 17-37. *A picking hammer and the edge of a dolly are used to kink stretched metal.*

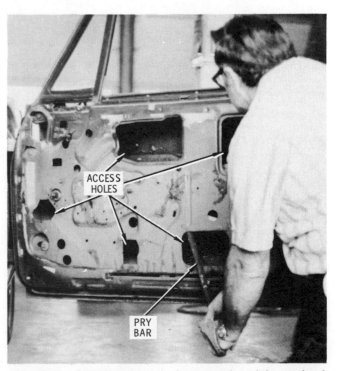

Fig. 17-39. *The inner door trim is removed, and the pry bar is inserted through access holes to put pressure on the dented area.*

Fig. 17-40. *The pry bar may be used at different angles through different access holes to force out the dented area of the door skin.*

Fig. 17-41. *After the pry bar is used, a hammer and dolly may be used to work out smaller areas of damage. Plastic filler is then applied to level the surface.*

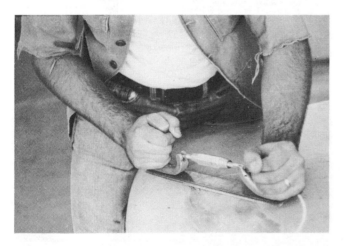

Fig. 17-42. *Filing a repaired area to level and smooth the surface and find high and low spots.*

LEVELING BEFORE REFINISHING

After the metal in a damaged area has been straightened, it must be *leveled* (made flat) and worked very smooth before refinishing. Leveling may be done by one or more of the following processes:

1. Filing.
2. Grinding.
3. Filling.

Filing removes any tiny high spots remaining on the metal itself after the area has been straightened (Fig. 17-42). *Grinding* is used to remove damaged paint, knock off rough high places, and further prepare the area for refinishing (Fig.17-43). If the area is not completely level after filing or grinding, it can then be built up by *filling* (Fig.17-44). Any of the body fillers may be used before refinishing, depending on the job being done.

Generally, the basic repair methods discussed earlier should be used before any filing, grinding, or filling is done. *Filing, grinding, and filling are not substitutes for good sheet metal repair.* Good body work depends on *first* using the basic methods to do as much repair as possible, and *then* finishing very minor damage by filing, grinding, or filling.

Filing

Basically, a metal *body file* is used to level very small high spots. To do this, the file is *carefully* moved back and forth across the repair area (Fig. 17-42). A body file must be used carefully, because if too much metal is cut off, holes may result. A hole would be made if the file completely cut off a high spot. Also, care must be taken so that the metal is not cut too thin. If the metal is made very thin by the file, it may dent easily or flex, causing paint or filler to lose their grip. Like many other tools, a body file has a limited, but very important, job.

Grinding

Sheet metal repairs normally leave heavy marks or scratches on the repair area. These marks are usually too deep to be filled and covered with primer–surfacer before refinishing. Because of this, a disc grinder and grinding disc are used to remove the file marks, work marks, and any damaged paint in the area *before* body fillers are used.

If grinding is done with a *very fine* disc further filling with body fillers may not be necessary. However, this usually is not the case. Instead, most grinding is done to level *and* roughen up the surface, preparing it for body filler. Figures 17-43 and 17-44 show rough grinding discs being used to prepare a repaired surface for body fillers.

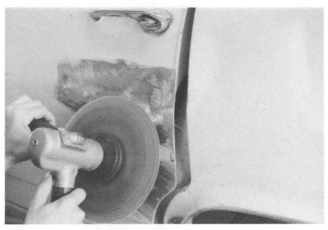

Fig. 17-43. *A grinder is also used to level a repaired area. Care must be taken to avoid grinding through the metal when leveling small high spots.*

Fig. 17-44. *A grinder being used to prepare an area for body filler. (Courtesy of Automotive Trades Division, 3M Company)*

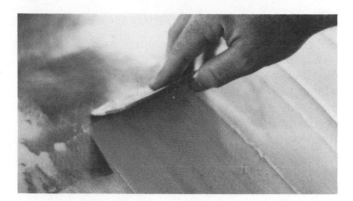

Fig. 17-45. *Using filler to level a repaired area.*

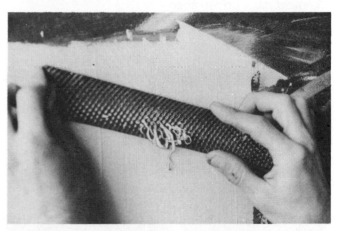

Fig. 17-46. *A Surform tool can be used to grate away excess filler while it is still soft.*

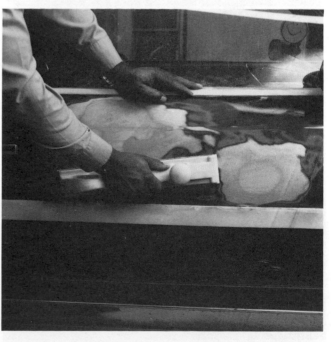

Fig. 17-47. *After the filler thoroughly hardens, it may be worked down with abrasives and tools like the file shown here. (Courtesy of Automotive Trades Division, 3M Company)*

Filling

Generally, *filling* the repair area with body filler is done *after* the area has been filed and then ground with a disc grinder. An area may usually be filled with any of the body fillers: plastic, fiberglass, or lead. The areas needing filling are those that cannot be worked out completely because they are in hard-to-reach places or cannot be worked from the back side.

Plastic filler, the type most often used today, is first mixed and then applied, as in Figure 17-45. As the plastic *begins* to harden, it may be grated with a *Surform* tool (Fig. 17-46). Then, it may be sanded with a sanding tool, such as the file being used in Figure 17-47. Finally, the filled area is *featheredged* with a sanding block and at least #240 sandpaper before being painted with primer–surfacer. Note that plastic *must always be applied less than* 1/4 in. (6.4 mm) thick. Coating of plastic thicker than this will tend to crack.

TYPICAL MINOR REPAIRS

Almost all minor sheet metal repairs may be made with one or more of the basic straightening methods, plus leveling, discussed in this unit. An auto body repair worker with a good knowledge of these methods *and* the ability to use them will be a valuable employee in any body shop. For example, notice the quality of the repair being made in Figures 17-48 through 17-58. Very shallow damage (such as that in Fig. 17-48) requires a good knowledge of leveling and refinishing practices. The repaired panel should not have any waves in it to suggest that it has been repaired. After the repair has been completed, any molding or other parts that were removed must be replaced.

Fig. 17-48. *A dent between the molding and taillight on a quarter panel. This can be a difficult repair, because of the location.*

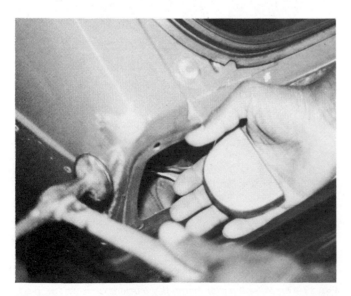

Fig. 17-49. *After the light housing is removed, a hammer and dolly may be used to work out the dent.*

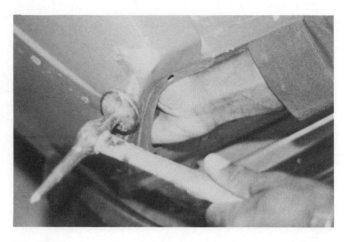

Fig. 17-50. *The dolly is placed inside the panel, and the hammer is used with light, rapid blows to straighten the bent metal.*

Fig. 17-51. *Once the metal is straight, the finish is ground off around the damaged area. A bare metal surface is needed for good adhesion of the plastic filler.*

Fig. 17-52. *A featheredging sander is used to smooth the hardened filler.*

Fig. 17-53. *Hand-sanding with a sanding block is done to give the "finishing touch" to the filler before primer is applied.*

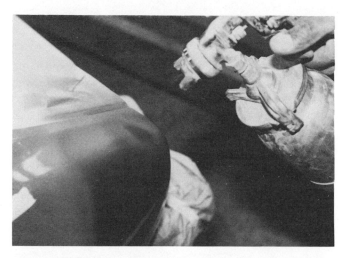

Fig. 17-54. *After cleaning with a solvent, the repair area is sprayed with primer–surfacer.*

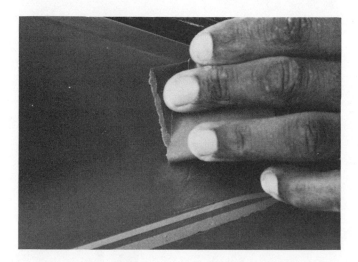

Fig. 17-55. *A very fine (400 grit) sandpaper is used to sand the primer–surfacer after it dries.*

Fig. 17-56. *The lacquer topcoats are sprayed on the repair area.*

Fig. 17-57. *To achieve its full gloss, lacquer must be compounded.*

Fig. 17-58. *After the taillight and other parts have been re-installed, the car is ready for delivery.*

Unit 18

Plastic Panels

The use of plastic exterior panels on automobiles increases each model year. The repair of such panels with a hot-air welding is a skill that body shop workers will find increasingly important.

PLASTIC RESINS

There are two types of resins used in plastics: *thermosetting* resin and *thermoplastic* resin. Plastic made with thermosetting resin *cannot* be welded. These plastics must be shaped when they are molded or during the curing process. Once a thermosetting plastic has been molded, it cannot be reheated for reshaping. Thermosetting plastics can be glued with special adhesives, however. A good example of a plastic containing thermosetting resin is the fiberglass panel shown in Figure 18-1. If heat is applied to fiberglass, it will melt, destroying the resin's structure and, thus, its adhesion to the glass fibers. The fiberglass panel will be ruined.

Thermoplastic resin becomes soft when heated and gets hard when cooled. Therefore, panels made with thermoplastic resin can be heated for reshaping and also can be welded (Fig. 18-2). Welding damaged plastic panels and parts is profitable, quick, and simple. In many cases, repairs are less costly than new parts. Many plastic panels on today's automobiles can be welded. These include bumper covers, fender skirts, radiator overflow tanks, fan shrouds, grilles, filler panels between bumper and body, and instrument panels. Some of these parts are shown in Figure 18-3.

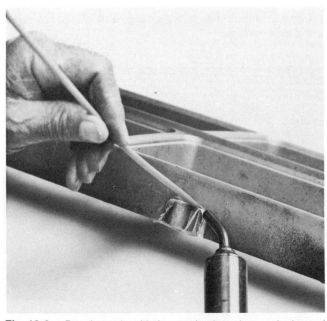

Fig. 18-2. *Panels made with thermoplastic resins can be heated for reshaping and repair. (Courtesy of Seelye, Inc.)*

Fig. 18-1. *A damaged fiberglass (thermosetting resin) panel.*

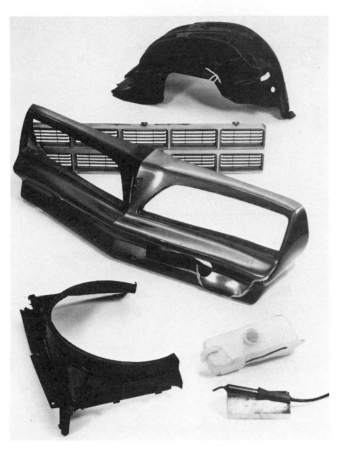

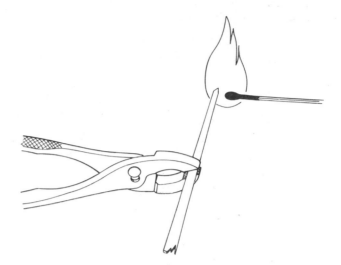

Fig. 18-4. *Lighting a sliver of plastic material to determine its type.*

Fig. 18-3. *Some plastic parts that can be repaired by hot-air welding. (Courtesy of Seelye, Inc.)*

The plastic welder can be used to weld polyurethane (TPUR), polypropylene (PP), polyethylene (PE), polyvinyl chloride (PVC), and acrylonitrile butadiene styrene (ABS). In this unit, the proper use of plastics is discussed, as is the importance of knowing how to repair plastic parts.

IDENTIFYING PLASTICS

The following test is used to determine the type of plastic to be repaired:

1. Remove a sliver of plastic from the back side of a part.
2. Hold the sliver with pliers, and ignite it with a match (Fig. 18-4).
3. Observe the odor of the burning plastic, the flame color, and the color of the smoke.
4. Classify the plastic, using the descriptions below. This information should be memorized for easy identification of plastics.
5. Select the proper color-coded rod for welding, using Table 9. Also make a "rod selection test" as described below.

Polypropylene (PP)

This plastic burns with little visible smoke and continues to burn when the flame is removed. It floats in water. Its odor is a distinguishing characteristic (Fig. 18-5).

Polyethylene (PE)

Polyethylene smells like burning wax. This plastic continues to burn when the flame is removed. It floats in water.

Acrylonitrile Butadiene Styrene (ABS)

ABS plastics burn with a thick, black, sooty smoke, which hangs in the air (Fig. 18-6). The plastic continues to burn when the flame is removed. ABS has its own distinguishing smell.

Polyvinyl Chloride (PVC)

This plastic is self-extinguishing. The material chars and gives off gray smoke. It can be identified by its characteristic odor.

Polyurethane (TPUR)

This is the most flexible of the five basic plastics. It burns with a yellow-orange flame and black smoke. The plastic continues to burn when the flame is removed, but the flame sputters (Fig. 18-7).

Rod Selection Test

To determine whether the proper rod has been selected for the type of plastic being repaired, make the following test.

Table 9

Plastic Welding Guide

Plastic	Polyurethane	Poly-propylene	Polyvinyl-chloride	Polyethylene	ABS
Welding Rod Color Code	Yellow/Clear	Black	Light Grey	Brown	Blue
Welding Gas	Air	Air	Air	Air	Air
Recommended Pressure—psi(kPa)	4 (28)	3 (21)	3 (21)	3 (21)	3 (21)
Welding Temperature—°F (°C)	500 (260)	575 (302)	525 (274)	550 (288)	500 (260)
Forming Temperature—°F (°C)	300 (149)	350 (177)	300 (149)	300 (149)	300 (149)

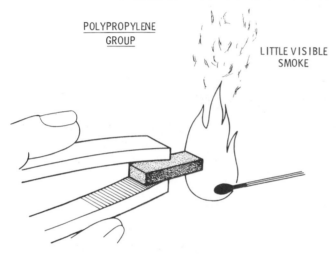

Fig. 18-5. *Polypropylene burns with little visible smoke. (Courtesy of Ditzler Automotive Finishes Division, PPG Industries, Inc.)*

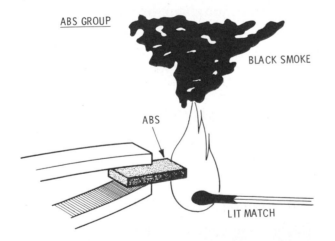

Fig. 18-6. *Acrylonitrile-butadiene-styrene (ABS) burns with a black, sooty smoke. (Courtesy of Ditzler Automotive Finishes Division, PPG Industries, Inc.)*

On a hidden side of plastic material, melt a small sample area, along with the rod selected. This is done by holding the rod against the surface briefly. Pull to test the bond. An incompatible rod will pull away easily, with no adhesion.

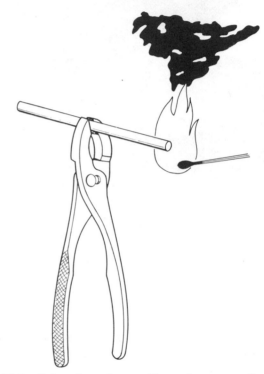

Fig. 18-7. *Polyurethane burns with a yellow-orange flame and produces black smoke.*

ACHIEVING A QUALITY WELD

Welding plastic is very much like welding metal. The repair worker must practice to get the "feel" of the process. The welder should have three types of tips to choose from: the tack welding tip (for aligning a torn place or a split panel), the round welding tip (for general welding and tight corners), and the high-speed welding tip (for automatic feed tip operation and fast one-handed welding). Figure 18-8 shows a tack weld and the use of a high-speed welder.

A good final weld, with either a round or high-speed tip, is easy to achieve with practice. On most plastics, a good weld *cannot* be pulled apart, even when hot. The final weld area can be stronger than the surround-

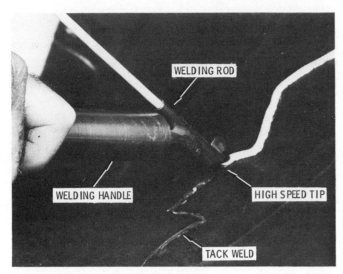

Fig. 18-8. *This high-speed welding tip automatically feeds welding rod as it is used. (Courtesy of Seelye, Inc.)*

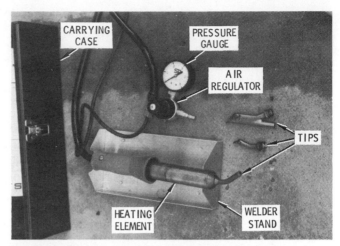

Fig. 18-9. *The hot-air welding unit used for plastics.*

ing parts. For a good plastic weld, observe these basic guidelines:

1. Small beads of "juices" should form along each side of the weld, where the rod meets the base material.
2. The welding rod should hold its basic round shape.
3. Neither the rod nor the base material should char or discolor.
4. Never stretch the rod over the weld. The length of the rod should match that of the weld.
5. Use air only

CAUTION: Never use oxygen or other flammable gases.

6. Keep downward pressure on the rod at all times to achieve a good bond between materials.

Practice both tack welding and welding methods with the proper tips and rod. This should be done before trying to repair a damaged auto body part.

USING THE PLASTIC WELDER

The plastic welder has five parts, as shown in Figure 18-9: welding tips, air regulator and pressure gauges, welder stand, heating element, and carrying case.

Using The Welding Tips

The *tack welding tip* is very important to welding any torn or split plastic panel. The panel is aligned and tack-welded as shown in Figure 18-10. The tack welds keep the two sides in alignment until they can be welded permanently. They also hold the damaged panels to-

Fig. 18-10. *Aligning and tack-welding the edges of the break.*

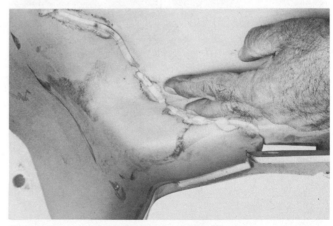

Fig. 18-11. *The back side of a urethane bumper cover, showing the tack welds used to align edges of the tear. (Courtesy of Seelye, Inc.)*

gether during welding and are ideal for long cracks. If necessary, tack welds can be easily broken loose for re-aligning. Tack welding is usually done by holding the edges of the split panel together and pressing the hot tip of the welder against the plastic. This makes them melt together and ensures a uniform solid weld later.

Tack welding should be done along the entire length of the split. Figure 18-11 shows a tack weld on the back side of a split urethane bumper.

Round welding tips are used when damaged automobile parts have hard-to-reach areas, tight sharp corners, or small holes. Select the proper welding rod, and cut the end to a 60° angle with cutting pliers. Hold the rod at right angles to the work and heat the plastic and the end of the rod with the round welding tip. Once the rod and the base material are tacky, press the rod firmly into the joint with the point away from the direction of the weld (Fig. 18-12). Getting a good start is important, since the beginning point is the most difficult part of the weld.

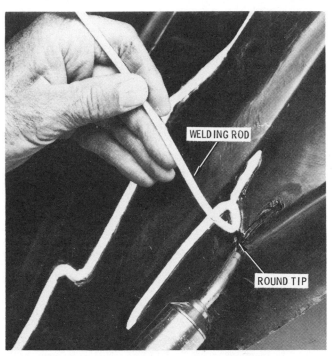

Fig. 18-12. *Welding corner damage on a bumper. (Courtesy of Seelye, Inc.)*

Fig. 18-13. *The broken plastic part should be cleaned thoroughly before being repaired. All grease, road grime, or mud should be removed.*

Welding with the Round Tip

To weld small cracks in plastic, use the following procedure with the round welding tip:

1. Clean any mud, dirt, or road tar from the broken plastic area (Fig. 18-13).
2. Bevel the edges of the broken plastic (Fig. 18-14).
3. Heat both the welding rod and the broken plastic. Use a slight fanning motion, moving with the direction of the weld. Keep an even, firm downward pressure on the rod at right angles to the work. The rod will begin to move forward, as shown in Figure 18-12.
4. Watch the weld. A small bead should form ahead of the rod along the entire weld joint.
5. Hold the rod down briefly at the end of the weld, then cut it with a knife or clippers.

High-speed tip welding is best for auto body plastic repairs where there are long straight cracks in plastic parts. Figure 18-15 shows a long split in an overflow

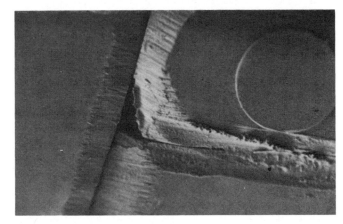

Fig. 18-14. *The edges of the tear or break are beveled to form a "V."*

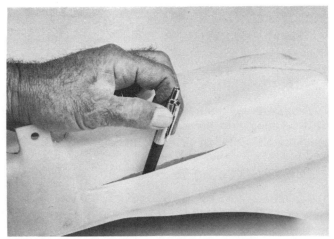

Fig. 18-15. *A long split in a plastic tank. (Courtesy of Seelye, Inc.)*

tank. To repair this damage, cut the welding rod at a 60° angle, and insert it in the tube of the high-speed welding tip. Tack-weld the crack, then start the weld as usual. Hold the welding unit so the welding rod is at a 90° angle to the work. Press the end of the rod into the weld with the curved foot of the high-speed tip (Fig. 18-16). Move the welder forward along the weld. Drop the angle of the welder immediately to 45° as shown in Figure 18-16. Feed the welding rod manually into the feeder tube until the welding bead begins to feed automatically. Firm downward pressure should be exerted.

The high-speed tip is continually melting the rod and must be kept moving. Watch the formation of the weld bead, and adjust the heat or speed as needed. To stop a high-speed weld before the rod is fully used, set the end of the weld with firm pressure. Then, draw the welder off the remaining rod, and cut the weld bead with a knife. *Do not allow the welding rod to remain in the hot feeder tip!* It will melt and clog the opening. Clean the feeder foot with a soft wire brush as soon as welding is finished.

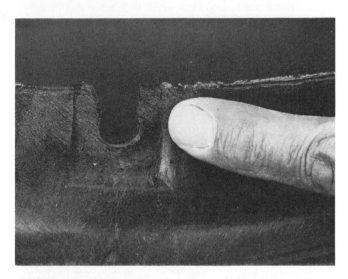

Fig. 18-17. *A broken plastic part, which can be repaired. (Courtesy of Seelye, Inc.)*

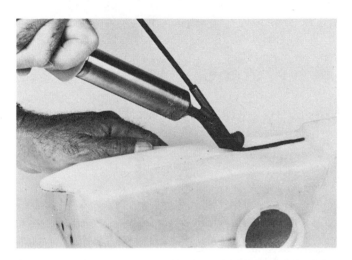

Fig. 18-16. *The high-speed welding tip being used to repair the split shown in Figure 18-17. (Courtesy of Seelye, Inc.)*

Fig. 18-18. *Cutting a piece of scrap plastic to make a patch. (Courtesy of Seelye, Inc.)*

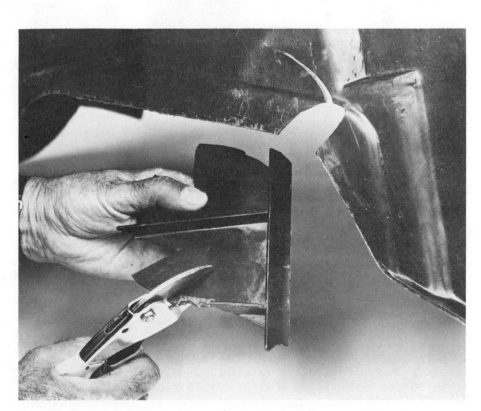

REPAIRING PLASTIC PARTS BY WELDING

A broken plastic part or a torn bolt hole (Fig. 18-17) can be repaired by using the following procedure:

1. Make a replacement piece for a damaged fender out of the same kind of plastic, using plastic cutters (Fig. 18-18).
2. Check for proper fit of the replacement piece by placing it in the broken area (Fig. 18-19). Bevel the edges, and tack-weld the piece in place.
3. Weld the replacement part on the fender skirt. Small cracks and patching may be welded on only one side of the part (Fig. 18-20). Figure 18-21 shows the penetration of a good weld.

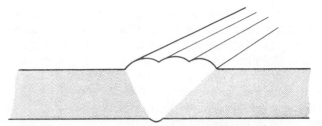

Fig. 18-21. *The penetration achieved with a good weld.*

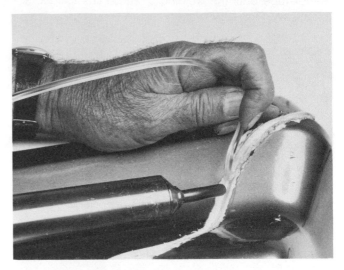

Fig. 18-22. *The front side of a urethane bumper cover being welded. (Courtesy of Seelye, Inc.)*

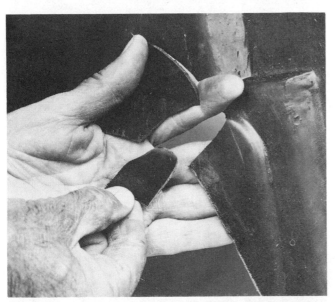

Fig. 18-19. *Checking the fit of the plastic piece to the damaged area. (Courtesy of Seelye, Inc.)*

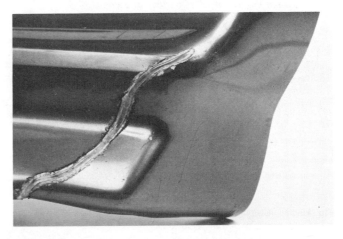

Fig. 18-23. *The completed weld. (Courtesy of Seelye, Inc.)*

REPAIRING BUMPER COVERS

Bumper covers often are torn in an accident. These covers can be repaired by plastic welding. Figure 18-22 shows the front side of a decorative polyurethane bumper cover being welded. To align the tear, short sections of weld were first applied on the reverse side. Figure 18-23 shows the bumper after the welding has been completed.

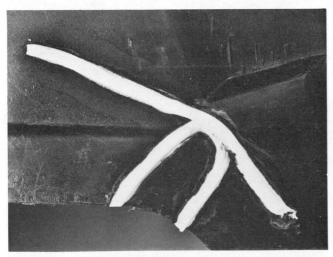

Fig. 18-20. *The plastic piece has been welded in place. Cracks extending from a broken area may be welded on one side only. (Courtesy of Seelye, Inc.)*

REPAIRING A FIBERGLASS PANEL

To repair a damaged fiberglass body part, fiberglass kit materials are used. These are the same materials used to repair damaged sheet metal body parts with fiberglass. However, the *procedure* differs slightly because of differences between the fiberglass and metal.

Damage to a fiberglass body cannot be "worked" with tools before applying fillers, because fiberglass does not stretch or "give" as does metal. Raised areas of damage or repairs on a fiberglass body cannot be tapped down. To solve this problem, the fiberglass matting must be applied from the *inside* to the *outside*. This is done so that the completed repair does not extend above the rest of the panel.

CAUTION: When working with fiberglass, always wear a recommended safety mask to avoid breathing glass particles.

Repairing Holes in Panels

The procedure below is used to repair *holes* in fiberglass panels (Fig. 18-24). This procedure is similar to repairing rust-out holes on a metal body, except that repair on a fiberglass body does not include depressing the damaged area.

Repair work on *holes* in fiberglass panels is done from the *inside* of the panel to the *outside* as follows:

1. Thoroughly clean the outer and inner surfaces around the damaged area with grease and wax remover.
2. Remove any loose fiberglass from the damaged area (Fig. 18-25).
3. Grind or sand off the paint and primer to expose the base fiberglass material 2 to 3 in. (50.8 to 76.2 mm) beyond the damaged area. Grind or sand both the outside and inside surfaces, if possible. Bevel the edges of the hole, as shown in Figure 18-26.
4. Cut two pieces of fiberglass mat material. One piece should be about 2 in. (50.8 mm) larger than the hole on all sides. This piece will be used on the *inside* of the panel. The other piece should be cut to fit just barely *within* the damaged area. The two pieces of matting will fit together so that the repaired area is level with the rest of the panel.
5. Mix the resin with the hardener, following the manufacturer's directions in the kit.
6. Lay a sheet of plastic on the workbench, as shown in Figure 18-27. (Plastic bags such as those used by dry cleaners are handy for this job.)

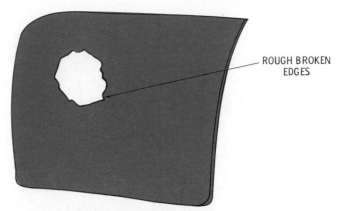

Fig. 18-24. *A fiberglass panel with a hole broken through it.*

ROUGH BROKEN EDGES

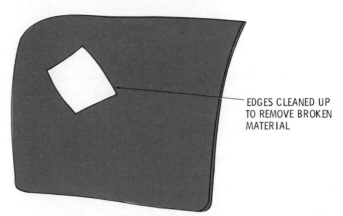

Fig. 18-25. *The first step in fiberglass repair is to clean up the hole, removing all loose and broken pieces.*

EDGES CLEANED UP TO REMOVE BROKEN MATERIAL

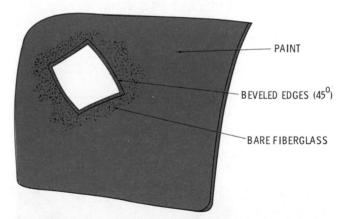

Fig. 18-26. *The edges of the hole are then beveled, and adjoining paint is sanded off, down to the fiberglass surface.*

PAINT

BEVELED EDGES (45°)

BARE FIBERGLASS

7. Lay the two fiberglass mats on the plastic, and pour the mixed resin onto them (Fig. 18-27).
8. Using a spatula, work the resin back and forth on the mats until they are thoroughly saturated (soaked) with the mixture.
9. Lay the *larger* mat on the *inside* of the panel. Work it well into place, squeezing the resin through the mat to help it stick to the panel. Work out any air bubbles, using the spatula.

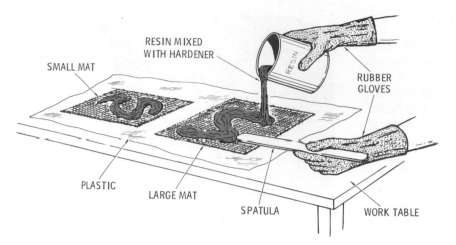

Fig. 18-27. *Cut sections of fiberglass matting are saturated with resin-hardener mixture. Note the rubber gloves being worn by the worker. They prevent skin irritation from the glass fibers. A respirator or particle mask also should be worn.*

10. Place the *smaller* mat on the larger piece, *within* the damaged area. Work the smaller mat into place.
11. Allow the mats and resin/hardener material to cure in place, forming the base of the repair.
12. Apply polyester plastic filler over the hardened area to smooth out the entire surface.
13. Allow time for the filler to harden. Then, sand the area smooth, and featheredge it for painting. The completed repair should be level with the rest of the panel (Fig. 18-28).

Repairing Cracks in Panels

Cracks (Figs. 18-29 and 18-30) may develop in fiberglass panels. When the *back* side of the damaged panel can be reached, the proper procedure after

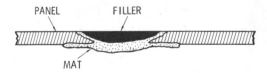

Fig. 18-28. *A cross-section view of a completed fiberglass repair. (Courtesy of Unican Corporation)*

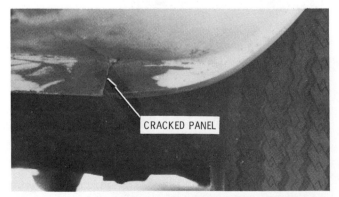

Fig. 18-29. *A stress crack in a fiberglass panel below the front bumper.*

cleaning is to grind or sand the *back* side of the panel for about 8 to 10 in. (20.3 to 25.4 cm) on either side of the crack.

Then, saturate a piece of matting with resin. Roll this piece of matting over the *back* side of the crack. Sometimes, it is wise to use a double layer of matting. This reinforces the area to help prevent further cracking. At this point, however, a crack is still present on the *outside* of the panel.

Bevel the crack's edges, and fill it with resin mixture. After the resin hardens, a coating of polyester plastic filler may be applied to make the final surface of the repair.

When a crack is present but the back side of the panel *cannot* be reached, a different procedure must be used. Figure 18-30 shows a lower body panel with this type of damage. In Figure 18-31, the broken panel has been riveted back in place and the area has been cleaned.

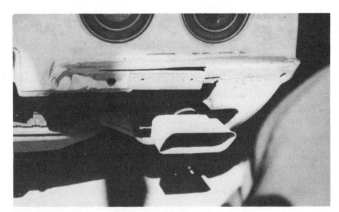

Fig. 18-30. *A damaged lower body panel on a car with a fiberglass body.*

Next, resin/hardener-saturated fiberglass matting is placed on the *outside* of the damaged area, as is being done in Figure 18-32. Figure 18-33 shows the area after the fiberglass repair has been sanded and before it is given a coat of primer–surfacer.

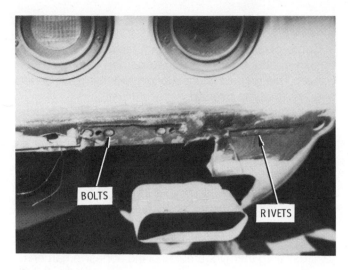

Fig. 18-31. *Reinforcing material has been riveted in place to repair the damage in Figure 18-30.*

On short *minor* cracks or splits resulting from impact, a very fast repair can be made by simply grinding the edges of the crack at about a 20° angle. Then, the cracked area may be filled with a resin/hardener mixture. Allow this mixture to harden, then sand about 1 in. (25.4 mm) beyond the cracked area with coarse sandpaper. Finally, apply and smooth a coat of plastic filler before painting.

Repairing Shattered Panels

Often all of the pieces from a wreck can be salvaged and put back together like a jigsaw puzzle. This forms a basic panel, which may then be repaired. Fiberglass filler is ideally suited for this type of repair. The procedure below should be used.

1. Working from the back side, remove dirt from all the pieces and from the edges of the main structure.
2. Find any piece that mates to the main structure.
3. Clamp the piece into place on the main structure with gripping pliers or clamps.
4. Smear a coating of resin/hardener mixture on both the main structure and the piece, building a resin "bridge" over the crack.
5. Repeat this process with each of the pieces until all of the broken fragments have been glued together. This will form one rough, basic structure. *Overall*, however, it will be properly shaped, as in Figure 18-34.
6. Next, quickly check the assembly for *rigidity*. It will usually need more resin to reinforce the back side of the panel. In any case, most of the broken edges will be visible on the outside surface.

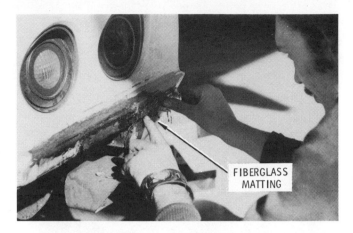

Fig. 18-32. *Resin-saturated fiberglass matting is applied over the reinforcing material.*

Fig. 18-33. *The completed repair, ready for primer.*

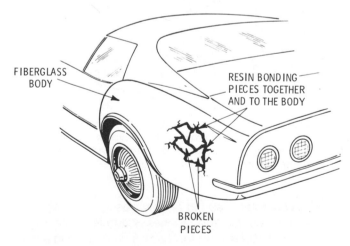

Fig. 18-34. *A reconstructed fiberglass body panel. The repair will not have the same strength as the rest of the panel but will be adequate under most conditions.*

7. With a rough disc, grind the whole outer surface, removing all the high points and corners. This will leave a thin, weak shell, held together with resin (but no fiberglass fibers).

Fig. 18-35. *When a missing contoured section must be rebuilt, a matching section on another car can be used to form a mold core of the proper shape.*

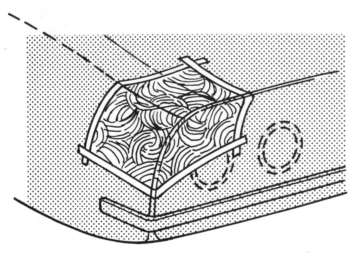

Fig. 18-36. *The surface to be used as a pattern should first be waxed to protect it and allow later removal of the mold core. Strips of masking tape are used to define the area. (Courtesy of Unican Corporation)*

8. A complete rebuild is now possible by using fiberglass matting. Pieces saturated with resin should be laid on the *back* side of the thin shell. This is best done by *shingling* the area (overlapping the pieces). Do not try to work with pieces that are too large. Air bubbles should be carefully removed as the matting is laid in place.
9. Finally, after all the pieces of fiberglass have cured, apply a coating of plastic filler on the outside of the panel. Then, the area may be smoothed and prepared for painting.

Connecting Two Panels

Some plastic companies manufacture a special adhesive product for bonding together two fiberglass panels. This product is used to join two fiberglass panels that are made to overlap.

Generally, fiberglass panels purchased from the manufacturer are made with the *lip* designed to go over or under the adjoining panel. This panel *joint* must be bonded together so that a permanent repair is made. These special fiberglass adhesives, usually pastelike products, are applied to both surfaces of the joint.

The mating surfaces must be rough and clean. If necessary, use rough sandpaper on the joint parts before applying the adhesive. When the two panels are joined, clamp them together until the adhesive hardens.

Making a Fiberglass Core

When a curved section of fiberglass is missing, it would be very difficult to lay a fiberglass mat across the hole and properly reshape the area.

This would be true, for example, on the nose of a fender. In a case such as this, a body repair worker may make one of two choices: a new section can be purchased, or a *mold core* can be made. The following steps are the procedure that would be used to make a *mold core*. A left rear fender section of a Corvette is used as an example (Fig. 18-35).

1. Find an undamaged fender on another car. It will not be harmed during the process. The car may be found at a used car lot, a salvage yard, or anywhere where it may be used for an hour or so.
2. Mark off an area on the fender with a strip of masking tape. Make it slightly *larger* than the damaged area on the body being repaired.
3. Using masking tape and paper, cover the areas outside the tape to protect them from spills.
4. Using paste floor wax, smear the section of the fender being used as a mold. Leave a wet coat of wax all over the surface (Fig. 18-36).
5. The surface is now ready to be used as a mold for making a new section to replace a damaged one on another car.
6. Use a special mold-making veil (a thin layer of mat). Cut from the veil a number of small pieces ranging from 2 × 4 to 4 × 6 in. (5.1 × 10.2 to 10 × 15.2 cm).
7. Mix the resin and hardener according to directions.
8. Lay the small pieces of cut veil on a plastic sheet, and use a spatula to spread the resin/hardener

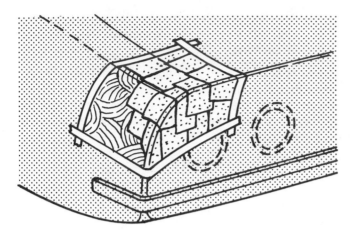

Fig. 18-37. *Strips of very thin fiberglass matting (veil) are used to cover the surface. (Courtesy of Unican Corporation)*

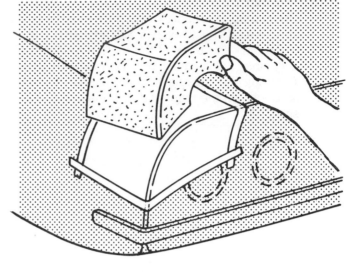

Fig. 18-39. *When the resin has cured, the thin shell (mold core) is carefully removed from the pattern area. (Courtesy of Unican Corporation)*

mixture on them. Pick up the small pieces with the spatula, and lay them on the waxed surface. Use smaller pieces of veil on the edges and around difficult curves. In all cases, use only *one* layer of veil (Fig. 18-37).

9. To force the veil into curves and around corners, use a small, inexpensive paint brush. Wet the paint brush in resin, and push the material into place with the ends of the bristles. Do *not* brush back and forth (Fig. 18-38).

10. Continue laying small pieces of fiberglass veil on the waxed surface until the *entire* surface has been covered with only one layer. The layers should be slightly overlapped and shingled, like the roof shingles on a house (Fig. 18-37).

11. After the surface has been covered, allow the "shell" to harden at least 1 hour.

12. After the shell has thoroughly cured, gently work the piece away from the original panel (Fig. 18-39). This shell will be an excellent reproduction of this section of the panel. (Of course, it will be slightly larger than the original area.)

13. The wax that was protecting the paint finish may be removed and the panel polished.

14. Place the shell under the damaged panel. Align it with the damaged area on the vehicle (Fig. 18-40).

15. Cement the shell into place with fiberglass adhesive. Then allow the shell and panel to cure.

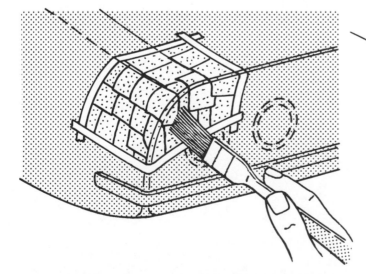

Fig. 18-38. *A paint brush is used to smooth the resin-saturated veil, forcing it down firmly on the surface. This captures the exact contour of the part. (Courtesy of Unican Corporation)*

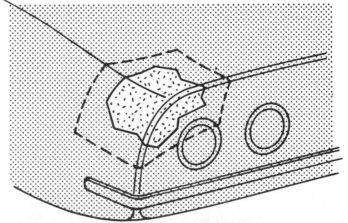

Fig. 18-40. *The mold core is then fastened in place behind the damaged area. It forms a support for the repair and gives it the proper shape. (Courtesy of Unican Corporation)*

16. The remaining steps are the same as for any other fiberglass repair. The surface must be built up to the original thickness with fiberglass mat.

17. Grind back the edge of the original fender to a long taper, being careful not to damage the shell. Then lay the fiberglass mat, soaked in resin/hardener, on the taper and over the entire inner shell.

18. After the fiberglass mat hardens, it may be leveled with a coating of plastic filler, then prepared for painting.

The operation discussed above will not usually take more than 2 hours. The cost of a new section will be saved. So will the time neeeded to get parts from the factory. This will allow the repair to be done faster and at a lower cost.

Aluminum Panel Repair

Damaged aluminum panels can be repaired in many of the same ways as sheet metal. Aluminum panel repair is more common on trucks than on automobiles, but the use of aluminum panels on automobiles is increasing. For aluminum repair, the procedures and the tools are the same as for sheet metal repair. The steps for aluminum repair are:

1. Carefully estimate the damage to the panel (Fig. 19-1). Aluminum is much softer and lighter than steel.
2. Clean the damaged panel with soap and water.
3. Wash the panel with a mild cleanser.
4. Align (rough-out) the panel. Be careful with the *roughing-out* procedure, since aluminum is softer and tears more easily than steel.
5. Align and weld all broken places.
6. Remove paint with a sander using an 80-grit disc and soft backing plate.

ESTIMATING ALUMINUM DAMAGE

Estimating aluminum damage is different from estimating sheet metal damage. The aluminum panel is much softer, and the roughing and bumping must be done very carefully. Also, the aluminum panel stretches much more easily than steel. Welding aluminum is more expensive than welding steel. All these factors need to be considered when making an estimate.

Look the panel over carefully, making a mental estimate. If the repair is too extensive, a new panel may be the best solution. However, if the damage is repairable, then itemize it and compute the charges (Figs. 19-1 and 19-2).

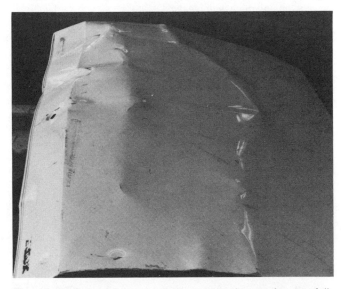

Fig. 19-1. *Damage to an aluminum panel must be carefully estimated.*

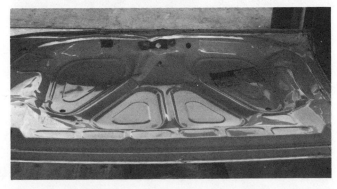

Fig. 19-2. *Be sure to examine both sides of the panel while making the estimate.*

REPAIRING AND ALIGNING PANELS

There are several repair procedures that can be used successfully with aluminum. One is the use of tension plates fastened to the panel with fiberglass plastic. First, the paint is sanded off the damaged area as shown in Figure 19-3. A coat of plastic is placed on both the damaged area and the tension plate (Fig. 19-4). Figure

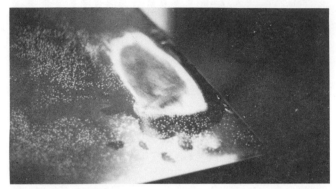

Fig. 19-3. *Paint has been sanded off the panel to allow attaching of a tension plate with plastic.*

Fig. 19-4. *Plastic is spread on both the panel and the plate.*

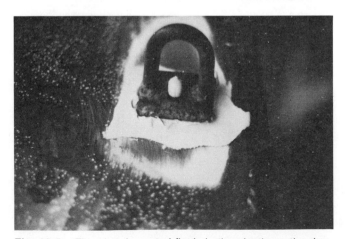

Fig. 19-5. *The plate is seated firmly in the plastic on the damaged area of the panel.*

19-5 shows the tension plate placed in the plastic on the panel. Once the plastic cures, this method of attachment is more than adequate for pulling out a soft damaged area (Fig. 19-6).

Spring hammering the buckled areas with a body spoon or flapper while pressure is applied does no harm to the base metal and releases tension for correct alignment. Spring hammering must be done carefully. Since aluminum is soft, it reacts quickly to spring hammering, prying, and picking.

Another way to repair aluminum panels is to divide them. Use a power chisel, or a chisel and hammer, to divide the inner panel from the outer panel (Fig. 19-7). The panels then can be repaired separately.

Aluminum Repair Examples

Figure 19-8 shows an inner panel being aligned with the hammer and dolly. In Figure 19-9, an awl and hammer are being used to pick up the low spots in the outer panel. Notice the spots of cement that keep the panel from vibrating. Figure 19-10 shows high places being

Fig. 19-6. *A power jack and chain hook are used to pull the tension plate, straightening the damaged area.*

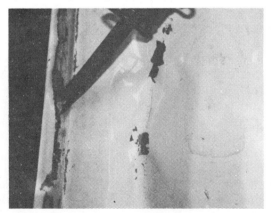

Fig. 19-7. *A power chisel may be used to separate panels for repair.*

bumped down from the outside with the hammer and awl. In Figure 19-11 and 19-12, cement is applied, and the inner and outer panels are put back together after aligning and roughing. Figure 19-13 shows the two panels clamped together for welding, while Figure 19-14 shows a close-up view of a finished weld.

When sanding aluminum, use an orbital sander with a foam pad and 80- or 100-grit sanding disc (Fig. 19-15). The foam backing helps to minimize the heat buildup.

The air sanding machine is best for aluminum finishing because the speed is controlled with the trigger. An electric polishing machine works well, if the speed is no higher than 2500 rpm.

Fig. 19-8. *Using a hammer and dolly to work out dents on an inner panel.*

Fig. 19-9. *An awl and hammer may be used to "pick up" small low spots. The spots of cement keep the panel from vibrating when it is assembled to the inner panel and used on the car.*

Fig. 19-10. *An awl and hammer being used to lower high spots from the outside of the panel.*

Fig. 19-11. *New cement is applied to the old cement spots on the panel before reassembly.*

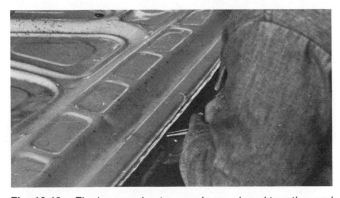

Fig. 19-12. *The inner and outer panels are placed together and the edges aligned.*

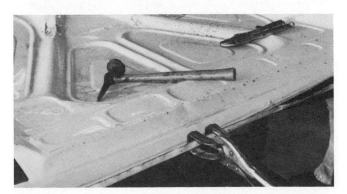

Fig. 19-13. *The edges are clamped to hold them firmly in place for welding.*

Aluminum Finishing

The best method of finishing aluminum after it has been welded and aligned is *picking up* low areas and *pecking down* high places. Hammering on the dolly results in *over-stretch*. Hard hammer blows on soft aluminum cause indentations.

Filing. When the metal file is used, one with rounded edges is best to avoid leaving file marks.

Sanding. When the sanding machine is used, the sanding disc should be no coarser than 80-grit. Use an air sander for speed control. Aluminum heats up quickly, and a sander used at high speed can warp the metal.

Removing Paint. Chemical removers can be used to remove paint from panels. However, some harsh caustic paint strippers should not be used on aluminum. The safe way to remove paint from an aluminum panel is with the air sander and a sandpaper disc.

Filling. Plastic fillers adhere as well to bare aluminum as they do to steel. The area to be filled must be cleaned to remove all oil, wax, or grease.

The grater file (cheese grater) is ideal for smoothing the plastic filler (Fig. 19-16). Care must be taken when filing around the edges. The grater file can gouge into the aluminum, causing deep scratches.

Smooth the plastic with an orbital sander or an air reciprocating sander to take down the high places and featheredge the old paint (Fig. 19-17). A hand-sanding block also can be used to smooth and featheredge the filled area (Fig. 19-18).

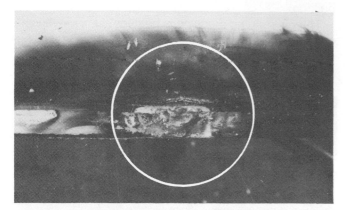

Fig. 19-14. *A weld on the edge of an aluminum panel.*

Fig. 19-15. *Using an orbital sander to remove paint from a panel before filler is applied. (Courtesy of Automotive Trades Division, 3M Company)*

Fig. 19-16. *Plastic filler can be shaped, before it hardens, by grating with a Surform tool.*

Fig. 19-17. *Smoothing plastic with an air-reciprocating sander.*

Fig. 19-18. *File marks are removed by hand-sanding with a sanding block.*

Refinishing. The aluminum panel is finished using the same steps as steel panels:

1. Clean metal with metal conditioner.
2. Use a primer that is recommended for use on aluminum (Fig. 19-19).
3. Sand primer with 400-grit sandpaper, and wipe clean.
4. Use an air hose to remove all sanding dust.
5. Spray topcoat in the same way used for steel panels.

Fig. 19-21. *Using a sander to remove paint from the panel. (Courtesy of Eutectic Corporation)*

WELDING AND REPAIRING AN ALUMINUM DECK LID

When an aluminum panel is damaged, it often will crack or break. Figure 19-20 shows a deck lid that has a tear in the lower part of the high crown area. There is also a small tear in the lock area. The aluminum is sanded with an 8 in. (20.3 cm) disc sander and 80-grit sandpaper (Fig. 19-21); then, in Figure 19-22, the area to be welded has been surrounded with an asbestos compound. This helps contain the heat in the welding area to minimize heat distortion. A wet rag can be used instead of asbestos. Figure 19-23 shows the oxy-acetylene torch being used to weld the tear.

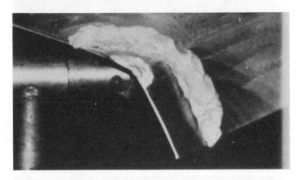

Fig. 19-22. *An asbestos putty dam is built around the area to be welded. It controls the spread of heat to the rest of the panel. (Courtesy of Eutectic Corporation)*

Fig. 19-19. *Priming should be done with a primer made for use on aluminum.*

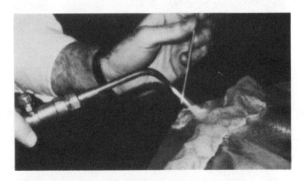

Fig. 19-23. *Welding the aluminum panel with an oxy-acetylene torch. (Courtesy of Eutectic Corporation)*

Fig. 19-20. *An aluminum deck lid with a tear on the high crown. (Courtesy of Eutectic Corporation)*

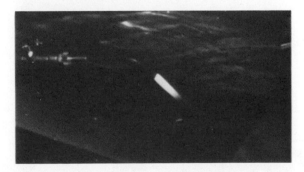

Fig. 19-24. *The correct flame for welding aluminum is a reducing flame. (Courtesy of Eutectic Corporation)*

Heating for Welding

Watch carefully when heating aluminum for welding, since it melts at about 1200°F (649°C). When a slight ashy cast appears on the bare metal (Fig. 19-22), then the aluminum is ready for the filler rod.

NOTE: Goggles with blue lenses are recommended for aluminum welding.

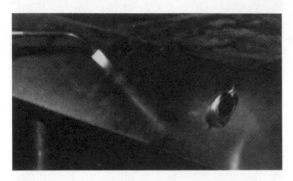

Fig. 19-25. *The aluminum panel also has a tear around the lock opening. It can be repaired by welding. (Courtesy of Eutectic Corporation)*

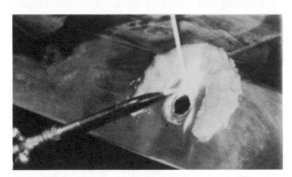

Fig. 19-26. *An asbestos putty heat dam is used to protect the rest of the panel. Aluminum transmits heat more quickly than steel, and melts at a lower temperature. (Courtesy of Eutectic Corporation)*

Use a reducing (carbonizing) flame for aluminum welding. Figure 19-24 shows a reducing flame. Align the broken or torn edges and clamp them if possible. If the edges of the cracked or torn place are not clamped, they will be misaligned (distorted) by the heat. The base metal must be cleaned to remove any oil or grease and abraded (cleaned with a wire brush).

Using the Flame and Rod

The torch and carbonizing flame is held a few inches (several centimeters) away from the aluminum panel. The panel is heated for several inches (several centimeters) around the area to be welded (Fig. 19-25). The correct way to weld a small tear around a lock hole in an aluminum deck lid is shown in Figure 19-26.

After the weld has been completed, the welding flux must be cleaned from the area. Aluminum welding flux (Fig. 19-27) causes corrosion if left on the repaired area. Use a wet sponge or rag to clean off all the flux.

If distortion appears after welding, fill with plastic filler. Plastic adheres well to aluminum.

Fig. 19-27. *Welding rods for aluminum may be plain, or may have a flux coating or a flux core. Plain rods must be heated and dipped in flux before being used. (Courtesy of Eutectic Corporation)*

Unit 20

Body Panel Adjustments

Most of the panels that are bolted to an automobile or small truck body may be *adjusted* to fit their openings or match adjoining panels. These "adjustable" bolt-on panels usually include the front fenders, the hood, the doors, the deck lid, and many small body parts. Each normally has at least two adjustment points. These points are used to position the panel or part forward, backward, inward, or outward so that it is properly aligned. An auto body technician must be able to align and adjust panels or parts to fit properly.

There are two main reasons for having adjustable body parts:*appearance* and *tightness*. If body parts are not properly adjusted, the vehicle's appearance may suffer because of uneven gaps between parts. Paint may be chipped from adjoining parts because of too small a gap if they rub together as the vehicle moves along. On the other hand, body tightness may suffer if the parts are improperly adjusted. Loose panels may cause rattles, wind noises, and water leaks. For all of these reasons, properly adjusting new or repaired body parts is very important.

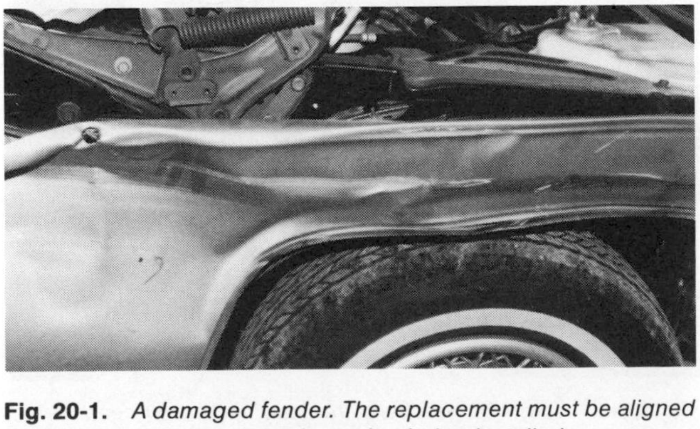

For example, notice the damaged fender in Figure 20-1. This fender will have to be replaced, not repaired. When the new fender is installed, it must be adjusted to fit properly at the front, top, and rear (Fig. 20-2).

Figure 20-3 shows good door alignment after a major repair. Note that the door is reasonably well centered in its opening. Proper door alignment is very important in auto body repair. Although a door must line up with many different panels (fender, quarter panel, roof, and rocker panel), customers often judge body alignment quality by the look and fit of the car's *doors*.

Fig. 20-1. *A damaged fender. The replacement must be aligned at the front, top, and rear edges after being installed.*

Fig. 20-2. *The proper alignment of parts such as this newly installed fender is a sign of quality body work.*

HOW ADJUSTMENTS ARE MADE

Not all auto body and part adjustments are made in the same way. Different methods are used by automobile manufacturers and body repair workers to make the adjustments during auto body construction, assembly, and repair. Generally, these methods include:

1. Slotted holes.
2. Caged plates.
3. Adjustable stops.
4. Shims.
5. Bending.

These methods may be used alone or in combination to provide the adjustment and fit necessary on a given part or panel. *Which* methods to use depend on how the car was *designed* to be adjusted and what type of adjustment needs to be made. When all of the possible adjustments have been made, but the part or panel *still* does not fit correctly, *bending* may be done to align it further.

Slotted Holes

One of the most common methods of providing an adjustment is to use *slotted holes* for the bolts holding the part in place (Fig. 20-4). These allow the part to be

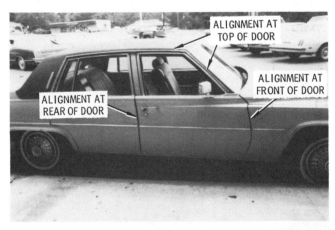

Fig. 20-3. *A properly adjusted door will have approximately equal gaps at the top and at both sides.*

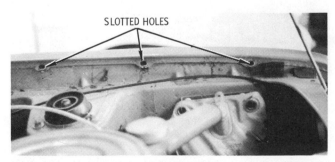

Fig. 20-4. *Slotted holes on many body parts allow some side-to-side or up-and-down adjustment.*

shifted into position before the bolts are tightened. If the part is especially heavy, *two* repair workers may be required: one to hold the part in the correct position and the other to tighten the bolts.

Slotted holes are usually larger than the heads of the bolts going through the holes. For this reason, large *flat washers* must be used under the *heads* of the bolts so that they do not "pull through" the holes. Also, the large washer allows the bolt to grip the metal all around the slotted hole. This helps hold the panel or part and prevent it from slipping out of adjustment (Fig. 20-5).

Caged Plates

Many times, especially on door hinges, slotted holes cannot be provided for adjustments. For example, notice the small area around each hinge bolt in Figure 20-6. Because this area is small, there is little room for slotted holes to be provided on the hinge. Also, slotted holes provide only for up-and-down *or* in-and-out adjustment, not both. If *both* adjustments were provided, the hole would be far too large for even a flat washer to cover *tightly*.

To solve such problems, *caged plates* are designed into the doors or door posts. Caged plates are heavy, thick pieces of metal into which holes are drilled. The holes are *threaded* so that the door bolts or hinge bolts *screw directly into the caged plate itself*. To hold the plate in position, a thin sheet metal *cage* is spot-welded inside the door or door post after the plate is in position. Then, when the bolts are removed or loosened, the plate can move inside the door or door post, but it cannot fall down inside the post (Figs. 20-7 and 20-8).

Caged plates are normally used in doors and door posts so that hinges may be moved around when the bolts are loosened. Extra-large holes in the *door*, for

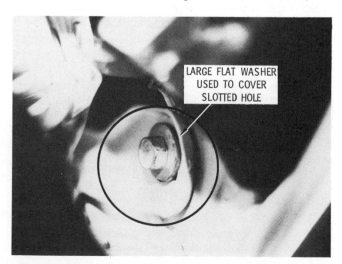

Fig. 20-5. *Large flat washers are used under bolt heads when the bolt goes through a slotted hole.*

example, allow the hinge *and* the caged plate to move around together when the bolts are loose. Then, when the door is adjusted, the bolts are tightened. This squeezes the door's sheet metal *between* the hinge and the caged plate. Since the hinge and caged plate are squeezing the metal, the door cannot move, thereby holding the adjustment. In the same way, when the hinge and plate are squeezing the *door post's* sheet metal, the hinge cannot move on the post. In Figure 20-6, the bolts shown are screwed into caged plates. Of course, the caged plates cannot be seen because they are *inside* the door and door post.

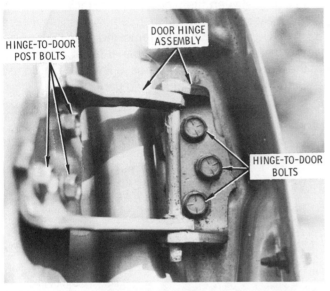

Fig. 20-6. *On this door design, there is little room for slotted holes. Instead, caged plates are used to provide for adjustment.*

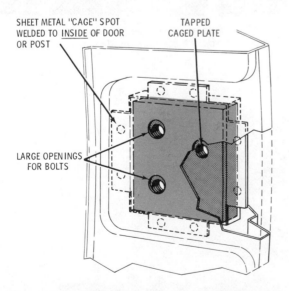

Fig. 20-7. *Caged plates are usually used inside door posts or doors. The sheet metal cage keeps the plates from sliding down inside the door or post when the bolts are removed.*

Adjustable Stops

Many times, the height or position of a panel (usually the hood) is at least partly controlled by *adjustable stops.* They are large bolts (Figs. 20-9 and 20-10) that are threaded toward the bottom. The lower part of the bolt screws into a fixed nut that is clipped to the body or bracket. A second nut on top, the *locknut,* holds the adjustable stop in position after it has been screwed up or down in the fixed nut.

After an adjustable stop is moved up or down, it changes the height of the panel when the panel is closed. For example, *raising* the adjustable stop in Figure 20-9 would cause the left rear corner of the hood to be higher (raised) when the hood is closed. Likewise, lowering the stop will cause the hood to be lower when it is closed (assuming the hood hinge is adjusted down as well).

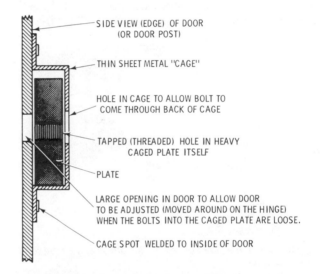

Fig. 20-8. *A cutaway view of a caged plate. In effect, the plate is a large "nut" with threads to accept the hinge bolts.*

Fig. 20-9. *An adjustable stop to regulate the height of the hood. This one is at the left rear corner of the hood.*

Most adjustable stops have a rubber cap on top. This cap helps keep the stop from rattling against the underside of the hood on rough roads. Also, it prevents the stop from chipping the paint on the underside of the hood, which would cause rust. Most cars have at least two adjustable stops, one on each side of the hood at the front.

Shims

Small wedges of metal known as *shims* are often installed between two parts to make body alignment adjustments. These pieces of metal (Fig. 20-11) are made in many different shapes and widths. The purpose of any shim is to change the *distance* between two parts permanently. This is done to move the parts farther apart or (when shims are removed) closer together.

Shims have a *mouth* that allows them to be slipped around bolts holding two parts together (Fig. 20-11).

The mouth of the shim makes removing the bolt unnecessary. This speeds up the job of adjusting body panels when adding or removing shims.

Shims are commonly used to make adjustments at fenders (Fig. 20-12) and deck lids (Fig. 20-13). In Figure 20-12, the upper bolt of the front fender rear bracket was loosened, allowing shims to be replaced between the fender bracket and the cowl. Then, when the fender bolt is tightened with the shims in place, the fender will be moved *out* at the upper rear corner. If the fender is out too far, the bolt may be loosened and one or more shims removed *or* thinner shims installed.

In Figure 20-13, a deck lid is being adjusted by adding shims between the hinge and the deck lid. Adding shims makes the deck lid higher; removing shims makes it lower. Usually, adding and removing shims is a "trial-and-error" procedure until the panel being adjusted is at the correct height. In all cases, shims are positioned *around* the bolt and *between* two parts.

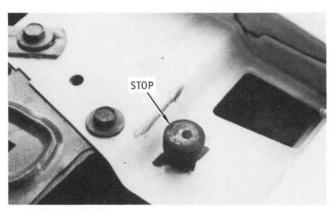

Fig. 20-10. *Another adjustable stop. This one is at the right front corner of the hood.*

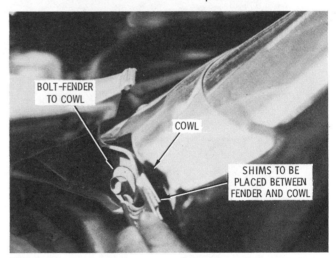

Fig. 20-12. *Shims are often used between the fender bracket and the cowl to adjust the alignment of the fender.*

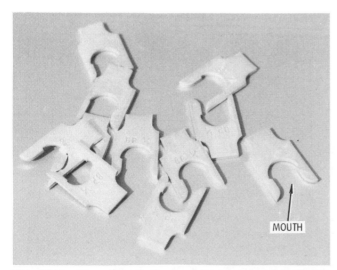

Fig. 20-11. *The open mouth of a shim allows it to be slipped under the head of a bolt, or between pieces that are bolted together.*

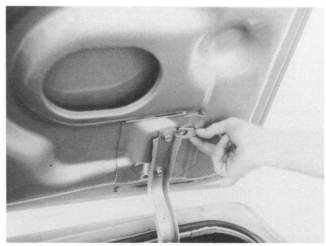

Fig. 20-13. *Adding a shim between the hinge and the deck lid to adjust the lid height.*

Bending

A final method used to align body parts is by *bending* the parts. *Bending should be done only if the parts or panels cannot be aligned by any other method.* That is, if the adjustment cannot be made by using slotted holes, caged plates, adjustable stops, or shims.

Bending is *not necessarily* a bad method of adjusting body panels. All automobile manufacturers use force to bend body panels into alignment during final inspection. Normal body adjustments only allow for a small amount of movement in, out, up, or down. If more serious adjustment is necessary, the panel or part may have to be bent to bring it into alignment.

Whenever a part or panel is to be bent into alignment, the following rules should be kept in mind:

1. Be sure that the panel cannot be adjusted by any other means. Check to be sure that *all* the bolts were loose when the panel was being adjusted; one or two tight bolts may have prevented the panel from moving over its normal adjustment range.
2. Use only large, soft objects for bending. These would include large blocks of *wood* or pry bars heavily padded with *rags*.

3. If heavy *metal* tools are being used to bend a part, *protect* it with heavy pads or blocks of wood. This will ensure that the panel is not damaged when pressure is applied.
4. Try to pry against surfaces that are not normally seen (for example, the edges of parts or the underside of doors). Then, if prying leaves any small marks on the panel, they will not be easily noticed.
5. Use jacks or prying tools to apply pressure to the area *gradually* and *evenly*. Using a hammer to *hit* a panel is more likely to dent the panel than to bend it into alignment.

HOOD ADJUSTMENTS

A vehicle's *hood* is usually the largest adjustable panel on the vehicle. Because the hood is easily noticed, it is very important that it be adjusted correctly. The hood must fit evenly along both fenders, at the cowl, and at the front.

Basically, the hood is held in place by the *hinges*. When the hood is open, usually only the hinges are supporting it (Fig. 20-14). When the hood is closed, of course, it is also held in place by the hood latch assembly (Figs. 20-15 and 20-16). Finally, adjustable stops at the corners help position the hood so that it is level on the front and along the sides. These were shown earlier in Figures 20-9 and 20-10.

Hood Hinges

The *bottom* of each hood hinge is usually attached to the cowl or to the inner fender panel (Fig. 20-17). Normally, either three or four bolts are used to hold the hinge in place on the body. The bolt holes in the hinge

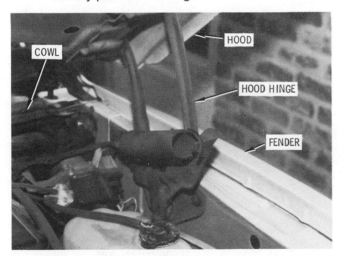

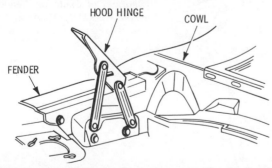

Fig. 20-14. *The hinges are the main support for the hood. Two different types of hinges are shown here. (Line drawing courtesy of Customer Service Division, Ford Motor Company)*

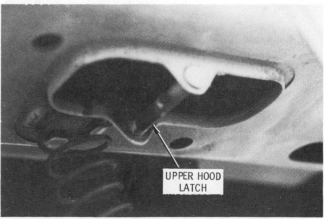

Fig. 20-15. *The striker bar of the upper hood latch supports the front of the hood and holds it closed when it engages the lower latch.*

Fig. 20-16. *The lower hood latch assembly is usually bolted to the radiator core support.*

may be *slotted* so the hinge can be adjusted in place on the inner fender panel or cowl. The hinge may be moved up or down, raising or lowering the hood when it is in the closed position.

The *top* of each hood hinge is bolted to the hood itself with two or more bolts. The upper hinge holes are also slotted, allowing the hood to be moved forward or backward (Fig. 20-17).

When the hood adjustments are made at the hinges, more than one person is usually required. The procedure is to install the hinges on the body, then install the hood on the hinges, *not quite tightening* all the bolts. Then, lower the hood *slowly*, watching to see that it does not bind or chip paint as a result of incorrect fit. With the hood lowered, shift it as required. Finally, *slowly* raise the hood to avoid disturbing the hinge positions. Tighten all the hinge attaching bolts.

Hood Height Adjustment

On most hood designs, at least two and sometimes four *height adjustment bolts* are used to hold the hood level with the panels around it. If one corner is lower than the other three, the adjustable stop under the low corner may be raised to make the hood level all the way around the opening.

Raising or lowering the stops should be done only to *support* the hood once it is lowered. Moving the adjustable stops *must not be a substitute for correct hinge adjustment*, especially at the rear. If the rear hinge is too low and the stop is too high, it will cause the hood to bind when it is closed. This could permanently bend the hood, causing *more* work than was originally needed to align it!

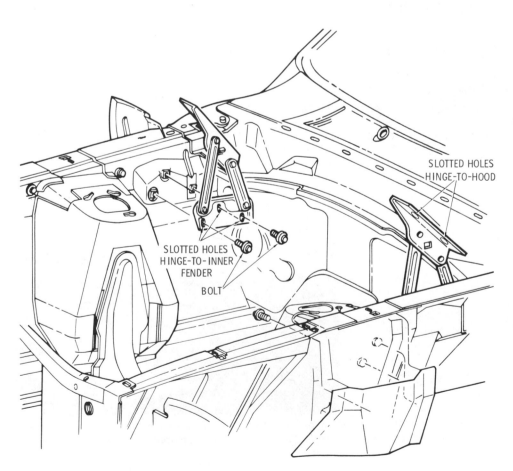

Fig. 20-17. *Slotted holes on the hood hinges allow for adjustment. (Courtesy of Customer Service Division, Ford Motor Company)*

At the front, the adjustable stops control the height of the hood. However, the stops must work *with* the hood latch assembly. Once the hood is level when closed, it must be noted how easily it closes and latches. If the hood must be slammed very hard to close, even though it is level, the latch assembly must be adjusted.

Hood Latch Adjustment

Almost all hoods today are held closed at the front with a *hood latch system*. Hood latch systems have a latch assembly (Fig. 20-16) and a striker bar (Fig. 20-15). The latch assembly is normally bolted to the radiator core support (Fig. 20-18). The latch assembly has a V-shaped opening in which the striker bar fits when the hood is closed. The bar pushes down on the latch, tripping the catch so that it holds the striker bar. When the hood is closed, the latch assembly on the front and the hinges at the rear hold it in place.

There are two basic types of *controls* for the latch assembly. These are the external (outside) hood release and the internal (inside the car) hood release. The latch assembly itself is basically the same, whether controlled from inside or outside the car. All latch assemblies are also "backed up" by a *safety catch* (Fig. 20-18). This catch holds the hood almost completely closed if the regular latch assembly fails.

Repairing and adjusting safety latches on hood latch assemblies is serious business. If a car is turned out of the shop and the latch or safety catch fails, the hood could fly up and cause a serious accident. Whether the hood latch assembly has an internal or external control, it must be carefully adjusted as follows:

Adjustment. Basically, the hood latch has two adjustable parts: the *striker bar screws* on the underside of the hood and the *latch assembly screws* holding the assembly to the radiator core support. To be certain that the hood is latching correctly, slowly lower it and watch the striker bar enter the "V" of the latch assembly. If the striker bar does not enter the "V" squarely *and the hood hinges are properly adjusted*, adjust either the bar *or* the latch assembly sideways until the bar squarely enters the latch.

The *last* hood adjustment to be made is the *height* of the latch assembly. This should be done *after* the hinges, height adjustment stops, and the striker bar and latch assembly have been adjusted. The bolts and slotted holes holding the latch assembly to the radiator core support are used to change the height of the latch assembly.

If the hood will not latch or must be slammed down hard to latch, loosen the bolts and *raise* the latch assembly slightly. Retighten the bolts. Close the hood, and note if it latches correctly.

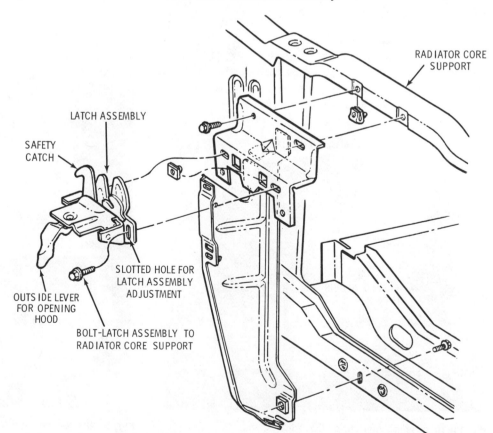

Fig. 20-18. *A hood latch assembly with an external control. (Courtesy of Customer Service Division, Ford Motor Company)*

If the hood does *not* latch tightly, you will be able to lift it slightly even though it is latched. When this is the case, loosen the bolts, and *lower* the latch assembly slightly. Then, close the hood to see if it latches correctly. Make adjustments until the hood closes easily *and* tightly. Finally, check the operation of the *safety catch*. Bend it as needed to "catch" the hood when it is slightly opened.

FRONT FENDER ADJUSTMENTS

The *front* section of most front fenders is attached to the radiator core support or to the grille. Along the sides of the engine compartment, the inner and outer fender panels are normally bolted together (Figs. 20-19 and 20-20). Wherever these bolt locations are used, some type of fender alignment can usually be made.

However, the major fender alignment locations are at the two or more bolts located on the cowl (Figs. 20-21 and 20-22). On the upper cowl area, there is usually a large bolt behind the door, as shown in Figure 20-21. At the lower end of the fender, there is usually a bolt under the car or on the lower part of the cowl, in

front of and below the door (Fig. 20-22). These bolts can be loosened, allowing the fender to be moved in several directions. This is possible because the fender and its brackets have *oversize bolt holes* at these points. Also, *shims* can be removed or added at these locations for added adjustment.

Many times, hood and fender adjustments must be made at the same time. After all the adjustments are made, the gap between the fender and the front door should be no more than ³⁄₁₆ in. (4.8 mm). The gap between the fender and hood should also be no more

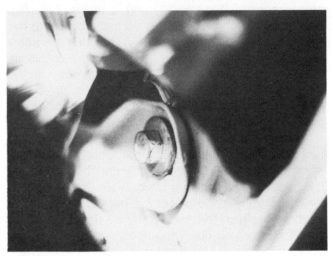

Fig. 20-21. *Bolt location at the rear of a front fender, where it meets the cowl.*

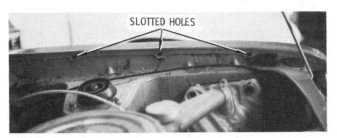

Fig. 20-19. *Slotted holes on the fenders allows them to be adjusted for proper alignment with adjoining panels.*

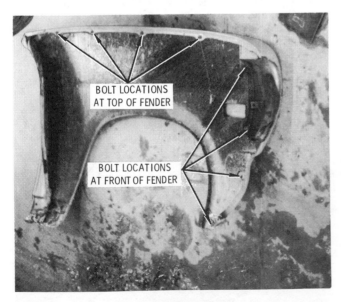

Fig. 20-20. *Typical fender bolt locations.*

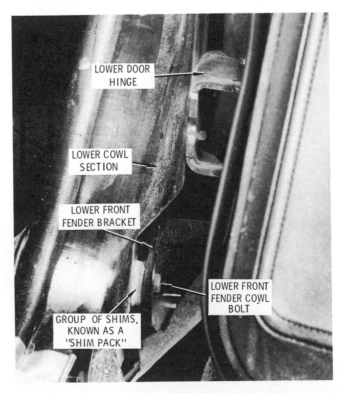

Fig. 20-22. *Bottom rear bolt location on a front fender.*

than ³⁄₁₆ in. (4.8 mm). The gaps should be the same *all around* the edges of the fender to provide uniform alignment and a good appearance.

Adjusting the Radiator Core Support

The radiator core support allows only minor adjustment. The support is fastened at the bottom to holes in the frame of the vehicle. A thick rubber grommet fits into these oversized frame holes. The radiator support bolts are placed through the support and the rubber grommets in the frame. The two fenders are attached to the support.

To adjust fenders forward with the support, loosen the back fender bolts. Place a power jack against the cowl (using a wood cushion), and push the support forward. Retighten the fender bolts.

DOOR ALIGNMENT

Door alignment is one of the most important (and often most difficult) adjustment and alignment jobs in auto body repair. When a door fits the body opening properly, there is an even gap of not more than ³⁄₁₆ in. (4.8 mm) all the way around the door. Such a reasonably uniform gap around the door assembly was shown in Figure 20-3.

The doors are held in place on the body with the door *hinges*. The door *latch assembly* holds the door closed and in position on the body. Both the hinges and the latch assembly on most cars may be adjusted to align and seal the door properly. The hinges fit on the front edge of the door and hold it to either the *door post* or the *cowl*. The latch assembly consists of a latch and striker, similar to the latch and striker bar on the hood but much stronger.

Many door assemblies also have weatherstrip (rubber seals) like the one shown in Figure 20-23. These

seal out water, air, and dust, and help provide a clean, quiet ride. Weatherstrip must fit properly to do these jobs. It must not interfere with good door alignment.

Most doors also have one or more rubber *bumpers* (Fig. 20-23). These help to eliminate metal-to-metal contact and rattles when the door is closed. Bumpers should be replaced if they are missing.

Door Hinges

The hinges actually hold the doors to the vehicle's body assembly. Normally, they are bolted to the front of the door (Fig. 20-24). In some newer designs, however, the hinges are *welded* in place. Front door hinges are attached to the front edge of the door and to the sides of the upper cowl (Fig. 20-25).

Hinge Adjustment

If an automobile has *four* doors, the rear door hinges work in the same way as the front door hinges. The difference is that the rear hinges are attached to the center door post (Fig. 20-26). Both front and rear door hinges are adjusted in the same way, as follows.

1. Remove the striker bolt (Fig. 20-26).
2. Decide which hinge bolts should be loosened to move the door for adjustment.
3. Loosen the bolts only enough to move the door the distance needed for the adjustment.
4. Shift the door to make the adjustment. Tighten the bolts, and close the door, checking for good alignment. Check for binding of the door.

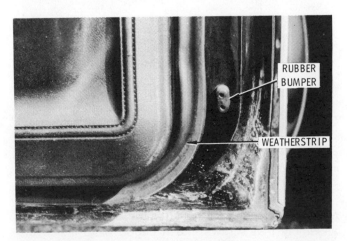

Fig. 20-23. *Doors are usually weatherstripped to keep out dust and water. Rubber bumpers are often used to prevent rattles.*

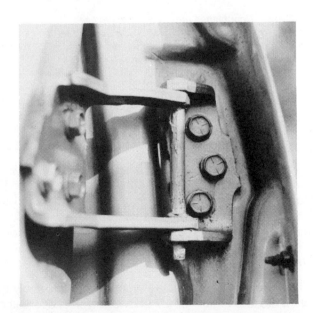

Fig. 20-24. *The door hinge is bolted to the door and to the door opening. Caged plates usually are used in the door to allow adjustment.*

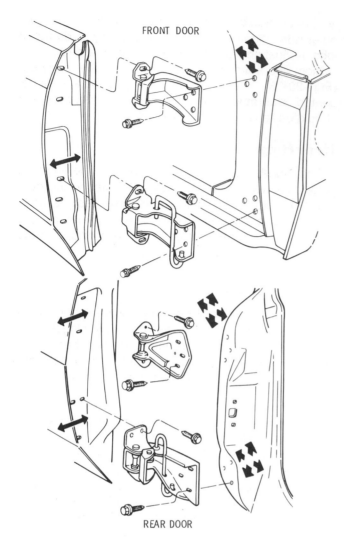

FRONT DOOR

REAR DOOR

Fig. 20-25. *Door hinges are fastened to the cowl (for front doors) or to the door post (for rear doors). In some cars, hinges are welded, rather than bolted, and cannot be adjusted. (Courtesy of Customer Service Division, Ford Motor Company)*

Fig. 20-26. *The striker bolt for the front door latch is located on the door post. The door check allows the door to be held in a partly open position and helps prevent accidental slamming closed of the door.*

5. If the door is still out of adjustment, repeat this procedure until the correct fit is obtained.
6. Re-install the striker bolt. Check for proper closing of the door against the striker, and adjust if needed.

Door Check. One hinge assembly on each door is usually equipped with a *door check*. This is used to hold the door in an open position. A hinge with a door check is adjusted in the same way as any other hinge.

Door Striker and Latch

The door must have some type of latch assembly to hold it closed. Figure 20-27 shows a typical door latch assembly and door handle. The latch holds the door tightly to the *door striker*. To adjust the rear of the door, adjust the striker bolt.

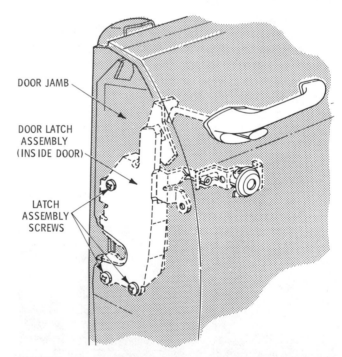

Fig. 20-27. *A typical door latch assembly. The latch assembly itself is not normally adjustable. (Courtesy of Fisher Body Division, General Motors Corporation)*

Striker Bolts. Striker *bolts* are a metal bolt and washer assembly that screws into a caged plate inside the door pillar. Many striker bolts have a Phillips® or Torx® head (Fig. 20-28). To adjust a striker bolt, loosen it with

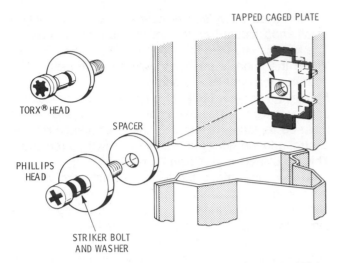

Fig. 20-28. *A typical striker bolt assembly. (Courtesy of Fisher Body Division, General Motors Corporation)*

Fig. 20-30. *A car door handle with a pushbutton latch.*

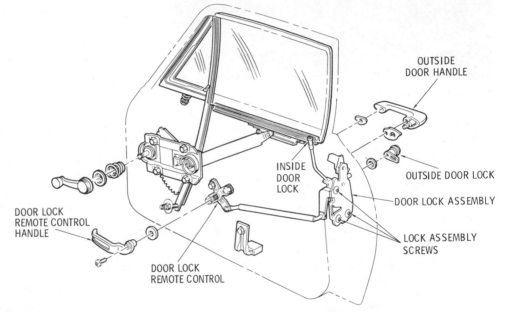

Fig. 20-29. *The basic parts of a door lock assembly and controls. (Courtesy of Fisher Body Division, General Motors Corporation)*

the correct tool. Then, move the bolt up, down, in, or out for adjustment. The caged plate, or course, moves with the bolt until it is tightened again. *Do not cover* a poor door alignment with a striker adjustment.

Door Locks

An important part of a door assembly is the *door lock*. Figure 20-29 shows the basic parts of a door lock assembly. This assembly allows the door to be opened and closed, and when desired, locked. The assembly has three main parts:

1. The door lock (latch) assembly.
2. The outside lock and handle.
3. The inside remote control.

Door Lock Assembly. This assembly is installed *inside* the door itself. It is held in place on the door jamb with several large screws, as shown in Figure 20-29. Both the outside handle and the inside remote control operate the door lock assembly.

Outside Lock and Handle. The outside lock and handle operate the lock assembly from outside the car. There are *push-button* handles (Fig. 20-30) and *pull* handles (Fig. 20-31). When the handle is engaged, the lock assembly releases the striker bolt, allowing the door to be opened.

The lock *cylinder* is operated with a key. The correct key may be turned to lock or unlock the door from the outside. Figure 20-32 shows how the lock cylinder is connected to the door lock assembly.

Inside Remote Control. The inside remote control is normally some type of pull handle. When it is pulled, it causes the door latch to release the striker bolt. This allows the door to be opened.

Fig. 20-31. *A pull-type car door latch.*

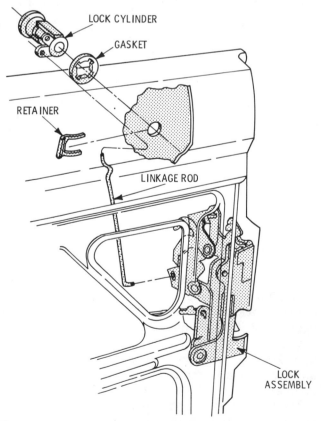

Fig. 20-32. *The door lock assembly is connected to the inner and outer lock controls by a linkage. (Courtesy of Chrysler Corporation)*

The inside *door lock* remote control is normally a small *knob* located on the top of the door trim panel. The knob is attached to a connecting link (Fig. 20-29). When the knob is pushed down, the connecting link operates the door lock assembly.

Replacement Door Lock Assemblies. If a door lock assembly is worn or has been damaged in an accident, it must be replaced. To do this, the door handle remote control and the door trim panel must first be removed. This is outlined in the "Trim Work" unit.

To actually remove the lock assembly, first roll the window glass up. Disconnect the remote control and door lock connecting links. Next, remove the screws that hold the assembly to the inside of the door. Finally, remove the lock assembly by pulling it out through one of the large *access holes* in the inner door panel. To install the new assembly, reverse the procedure.

Door Lock Cylinder Replacement. To replace a lock cylinder, first remove the trim panel. Place a pointed tool or screwdriver behind the lock retainer clip, and pull it sideways, off the cylinder's shoulder (Fig. 20-33). Then, disconnect the cylinder from the door lock assembly or the connecting link, depending on the design.

When the retainer clip has been removed and the cylinder disconnected, it may be removed from the outside of the car. This may require turning the cylinder slightly to remove it from the door. To install a new cylinder, or to install the old cylinder after a door repair, simply reverse the procedure. A few retainers are designed so that they may be removed easily from inside the door jamb. With these designs, it may not be necessary to remove the trim panel.

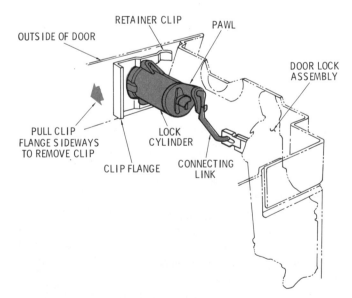

Fig. 20-33. *To remove most outer door lock cylinders, a retainer clip is pulled out to one side. (Courtesy of Fisher Body Division, General Motors Corporation)*

DECK LID ALIGNMENT

The deck (trunk) lid, like the hood, usually has two hinges and a support system to hold it up when it is open. Like the doors, the deck lid has a weatherstrip around the opening. The weatherstrip seals water and dust out of the trunk. The weatherstrip must fit properly, or it can cause the deck lid to be out of alignment. If the weatherstrip is damaged or twisted, it must be re-sealed or replaced.

Most deck lids have three main adjustments for proper alignment:

1. Hinge adjustment.
2. Torsion bar adjustment.
3. Lock adjustment.

A deck lid is properly adjusted when the gap all the way around the lid is no more than 3/16 in. (4.8 mm). Figure 20-34 shows a properly fitted deck lid.

Hinge Adjustment

The front part of the deck lid (near the rear window) can be adjusted forward, backward, up, or down, to fit flush with the other body panels. This is done by ad-justing the deck lid *hinges.* A few deck lids have caged plates inside the lid, but most lid adjustments are made by using the slotted holes in the hinge arms or installing shims between the hinge arms and deck lid (Fig. 20-35).

To adjust a deck lid forward or backward, open the lid, and slightly loosen the bolts holding the lid to the hinge arms. Then, slide the deck lid into a new position, forward or backward, as desired. Carefully close the deck lid, and check its alignment. When the alignment is correct, tighten the bolts.

To move the front part of the deck lid up or down, *shims* may be used. For example, to move the deck lid *down,* remove one or more shims from under the hinge

arms. Note the shim being removed in Figure 20-36. Then, tighten the bolts, and check the new deck lid position. To *raise* the deck lid, *add* one or more shims between the hinge arms and the deck lid.

Torsion Bar Adjustment

Deck lid torsion bars (Fig. 20-37) hold the lid open when it is lifted. The bars are twisted when the hinges close with the deck lid. When the lid is unlocked, the bars can untwist, opening the hinges. This pressure holds the hinges open until the lid is pushed down, twisting the bars and putting them (and the deck lid) under tension again.

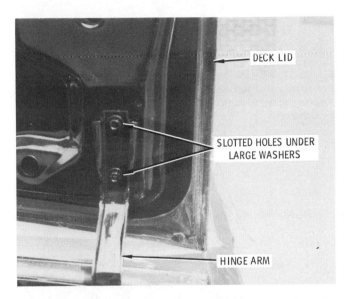

Fig. 20-35. *Deck lid adjustments are usually made where the hinge is attached to the lid. Slotted holes, caged plates, or shims are used to make the adjustments.*

Fig. 20-34. *A properly fitted deck lid, with approximately equal gaps on all edges.*

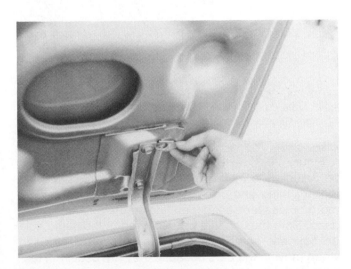

Fig. 20-36. *Adding or removing shims where the deck lid is bolted to the hinge will raise or lower the lid for correct alignment.*

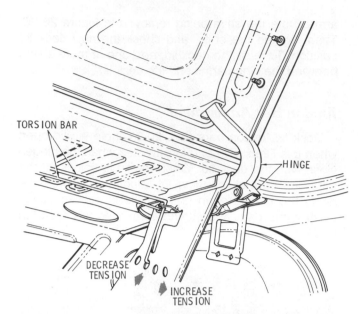

Fig. 20-37. *Torsion bars are often used to hold deck lids open. The tension can be adjusted by moving the end of the bar to different holes. (Courtesy of Customer Service Division, Ford Motor Company)*

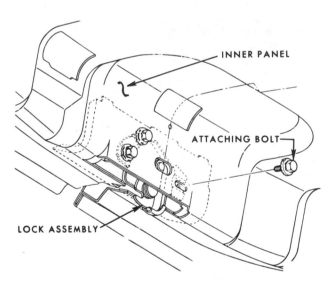

Fig. 20-38. *A typical deck lid lock assembly mounted on the lid itself. Slotted holes allow adjustment. (Courtesy of Fisher Body Division, General Motors Corporation)*

Figure 20-37 also shows how the torsion bars can be adjusted to increase or decrease tension. Moving the adjusting end of each bar in or out gives the bar more or less tension, depending on the anchoring hole used. Both bars should be anchored in the same hole on opposite sides of the trunk. Care must be used when moving the bars because they are usually in tension and can cause injury if they spring loose while being moved.

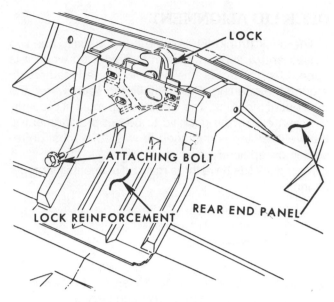

Fig. 20-39. *Another type of deck lid locking assembly. This one is mounted in the lower rear body panel below the deck lid opening. (Courtesy of Fisher Body Division, General Motors Corporation)*

Deck Lid Lock

Deck lid lock systems have two main parts: the lock assembly and the striker plate. The lock assembly is normally attached to the deck lid itself (Fig. 20-38). A lock cylinder, opened with a key, allows the lock to be operated from outside the trunk. In some cars, the lock assembly is attached to the lower rear end panel, below the deck lid. This design is shown in Figure 20-39.

The striker plate, like the lock assembly, may be mounted in either the deck lid itself or the lower body panel. When the *lock assembly* is in the deck lid, the *striker plate* must be in the lower body panel (Fig. 20-40). Of course, if the lock assembly is in the lower body panel, the striker plate must be in the deck lid (Fig. 20-41).

When the deck lid is closed, the striker plate enters the lock assembly. This forces the lock catch to roll shut, automatically holding the striker down.

When the trunk key is used to turn the lock cylinder, the lock assembly releases the striker. The catch rolls loose, releasing the striker as the torsion bars pull the deck lid open.

Lock and Striker Adjustment. Normally, both the deck lid lock assembly and the striker may be adjusted. By adjusting them, the deck lid can be held evenly at the rear edge *and* be closed easily. However, lock and striker adjustments should *not* be used to move the deck lid right or left for alignment. This should be done at the hinges or by bending. Only after the deck lid is properly aligned, side-to-side and front-to-back, should the lock and striker be adjusted.

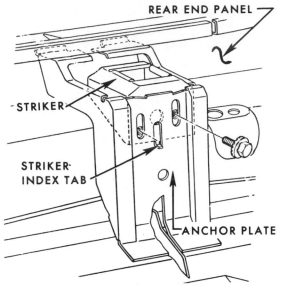

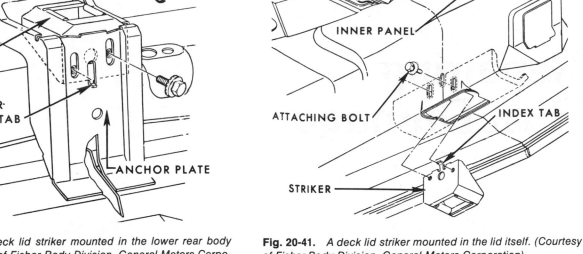

Fig. 20-40. *A deck lid striker mounted in the lower rear body panel. (Courtesy of Fisher Body Division, General Motors Corporation)*

Fig. 20-41. *A deck lid striker mounted in the lid itself. (Courtesy of Fisher Body Division, General Motors Corporation)*

To adjust the lock and striker, slowly close the deck lid, and watch the striker enter the lock. The striker should enter the lock squarely, *without* pulling the deck lid to one side. If adjustment is needed, loosen the bolts holding the lock assembly or the striker. Then, move the lock assembly or the striker right or left as needed. Again, slowly lower the deck lid to see if the striker enters the lock correctly. If it does, tighten the bolts in their slotted holes.

After the side-to-side adjustment is made, the rear edge of the deck lid may be adjusted. This is done moving the striker either up or down, as needed. To do this, open the deck lid and slightly loosen the bolts holding the striker. Move the striker up or down as desired. Tighten the bolts, then close the deck lid. Readjust if necessary. Take care not to change the side-to-side alignment while doing this. Finally, check the entire deck lid for equal spacing and height.

Unit 21

Repairing Rust Damage

Most vehicle bodies will *rust* when moisture and chemicals come in contact with bare metal. Rust is actually a *chemical reaction* known as *oxidation*. In this reaction, *oxygen* in the air, water or chemicals combines with *iron* in the metal to form *iron oxide*. Iron oxide is brown in color and is commonly known as rust (Fig. 21-1). Rust is harmful because it weakens metal by turning it into flaky or powdery iron oxide (rust). If rust is not removed, it will usually "eat through" the metal within a few months, leaving holes (Fig. 21-2).

TYPES OF RUST DAMAGE

Generally, there are *two* main types of rust damage that may appear on an automobile. These are *surface rust* and *rust-out*. Rust-out, where holes are eaten

through the body sheet metal, is also known as *cancer*. Although rust may begin at any point where paint is broken, most automobile rust damage begins along the lower body panels, as in Figure 21-2. This is because the lower body panels are more likely to be damaged by stones, road chemicals, and water thrown up by the wheels. Often, water and chemicals collect *behind* the panel to cause rust-out in several years.

Rust usually begins anywhere that moisture or road chemicals (such as salt) come in contact with bare metal. This may be on either the outside *or* the inside of a panel. This means that rust can begin on the *outside* of the panel and work *inward* or it can begin *inside* the panel and work *outward*. Once rust begins, it will continue "eating away" the metal unless it is stopped.

Surface Rust

Surface rust usually begins wherever paint has been *chipped*, is *flaking off*, or is *cracked*. Moisture and

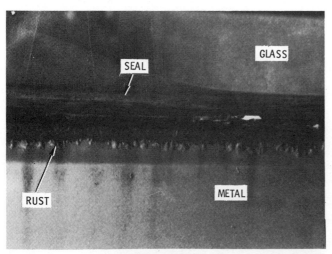

Fig. 21-1. *Common surface rust around a fixed glass seal. If surface rust is not corrected promptly, it can eat through the metal.*

Fig. 21-2. *Lower body panels are the most likely to have rust damage. Here, both surface rust and rust-out are visible.*

334

road chemicals then can reach bare metal, causing surface rust to form. This may happen when panels or trim are not properly aligned, allowing them to rub together and chip the paint.

Surface rust should be repaired as soon as possible. If it is not repaired quickly, it will continue "eating" the metal, eventually causing rust-out. This is what usually happens, for example, when moisture gets under a vinyl top, as shown in Figure 21-3.

Rust-out

Rust-out damage often results when rust is allowed to continue eating away the metal for several months. The metal is damaged, with rust holes completely through it. Although several months is a short time period, it often is long enough for rust-out to happen. Most body panels are fairly thin, and rust can eat through them quickly.

Rust-out from inside-to-outside is the most common type. It is usually caused by moisture and road chemicals getting inside a panel and staying there for some time. Figure 21-2 shows bubbles on the paint near a rusty area. These bubbles indicate rust-out from inside the panel. Moisture is coming through from *behind* the paint, causing a bubble. Areas like this should be carefully inspected for clogged drain holes or leaks at sealers.

To repair any type of rust damage *correctly*, you must *locate and stop the cause of the rust*. Carefully inspecting areas of inside-to-outside rust-out is especially necessary to locate and repair any sealer leaks or clogged drain holes. During all *good* rust repairs, any cancerous rust-out should be removed and the remaining area treated with *metal conditioner*.

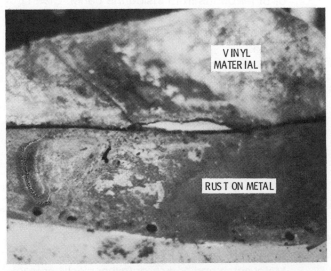

Fig. 21-3. *If moisture gets under a vinyl top, rust will form on the metal surface and can eventually cause rust-out.*

METAL CONDITIONER

An important part of a *lasting* rust repair is to treat the cleaned, bare metal with a good metal conditioner. This product must be used where either surface rust *or* rust-out is being repaired. If metal conditioner is not used, the repair will not last as long; rust will reappear more quickly. Figure 21-4 shows one brand of metal conditioner.

Metal conditioner is an acidlike liquid that attacks the rust itself to help stop it from spreading further. Even though a good deal of rust is ground away during a repair, any remaining rust on edges or in pits will continue to eat away the metal *underneath* the completed repair if metal conditioner is not used. The rust on edges or in pits will eventually come through again because it was not treated.

Using Metal Conditioner

Good brands of metal conditioner have complete instructions printed on the container. Be sure to *follow the instructions carefully and use the product exactly as directed*.

CAUTION: Metal conditioner is a type of acid. Wear rubber gloves and safety goggles when using the product.

Fig. 21-4. *A metal conditioner made by one manufacturer.*

Generally, metal conditioner is mixed with water before being used. Then, it is scrubbed on the area being repaired, using steel wool or old (but clean) rags. Finally, the product *must be completely wiped off the area while it is wet*. Metal conditioner must *not* be allowed to dry on the surface.

RUST-OUT REPAIR

Rust-out is serious body damage. Where rust-out exists, the body's metal has been weakened. Even if only a few bubbles are present, there is likely to be a good deal more rust-out damage than can be seen. Grinding off the paint and metal in the area will likely reveal many more small rust-out holes. To repair rust-out damage *properly*, the panel must be restored so that it is as *strong* as new and *looks* like new.

When repairing rust-out, a body worker must always determine what caused the condition. For example, if the rust-out was caused by uncontrolled *surface* rust, removing the surface rust and repairing the area will eliminate the cause. However, if the rust-out came through from *inside* the panel, the cause will be harder to eliminate.

Many times, clogged *drain holes* will cause rust-out. These holes are designed into auto bodies to let water and road dirt drain out, leaving the backside of the panel clean. If the holes become clogged, then dirt, water, and chemicals can build up behind the panel,

Fig. 21-5. *Typical rust-out damage.*

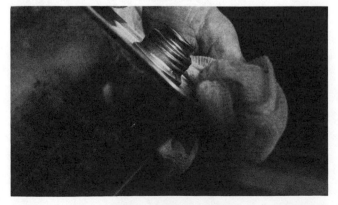

Fig. 21-6. *Using a clean rag saturated with cleaning solvent to remove dirt, tar, grease, and chemicals around the damaged area.*

causing rust to start inside and work out. Clogged drain holes can be worked clear with a knife or other sharp-pointed object.

Even when drain holes are kept open, mud and chemicals may still build up behind panels. Wherever dirt and chemicals become lodged, rust-out can begin on the backside of a panel and later break through the paint. Usually, keeping a car clean in the lower parts of the trunk and many other cracks and "pockets" will *help* prevent rust-out from beginning in these areas.

Rust-out Repair Initial Steps

There are several basic methods by which rust-out may be repaired. Which method to use depends on the location of the damage, how much damage is present, how long the repair must last, and other factors. However, no matter which repair method is used, the *beginning steps* of rust-out repair are always the same. When beginning any rust-out repair, then, follow these steps in order:

1. Thoroughly look over the rust-out damage as in Figure 21-5. Notice the size and location of the holes or paint bubbles.
2. Clean the paint and broken metal around the damage with solvent (Fig. 21-6).
3. Grind off old paint and rust from around the rust-out area (Fig. 21-7).
4. Examine the rust-out holes after grinding, as in Figure 21-8.
5. Using tin snips, cut out any weak metal from around the edges of the rust-out holes (Fig. 21-9). This metal is usually very weak as a result of rust and will cut easily.
6. Using a screwdriver or other tool, clean any dirt or other debris from inside the panel. Clean out the area well, so that there will be nothing to start the rust-out again after the repair has been made.
7. Treat the bare metal in and around the area with metal conditioner. *This is very important if any rust-out repair is to last more than a few months.*
8. Decide on the type of repair to be used and then make the repair.

Basic Types of Repair

There are four basic methods that may be used to repair rust-out damage. Which of these to use depends on how badly the affected area is rusted out.

1. Fiberglass filler.
2. Fiberglass mat and plastic filler.
3. Metal patch and body filler (either plastic or lead).
4. Foam filler.

If the metal is still intact and does not "give" when pressed lightly, the damage is not serious. In this case, and if only *small* holes are present, the area may be filled with fiberglass plastic filler.

Often, a minor rust-out area will have larger holes after the old paint and metal have been ground away. In these cases, the rust-out damage must be repaired by patching with fiberglass mat and plastic filler. If the metal is so weakened that the rust-out area is loose and "gives" when pressed, the damage must be completely cut away before the fiberglass mat is applied.

If the rust-out is extensive and has damaged a major area, the panel must be repaired with a metal patch

and then leveled with body filler. The rust damage must first be cut back to solid metal, leaving a hole as shown in Figure 21-9. Then, the edges of the hole are depressed. A metal patch may then be sized, cut, and placed over the area. Patches of this type are usually brazed in position (Fig. 21-10). The patch and original metal may then be prepared, filled, and refinished.

Fiberglass Patches. Many times, the holes in a rusted-out area are too large to support the repair area and

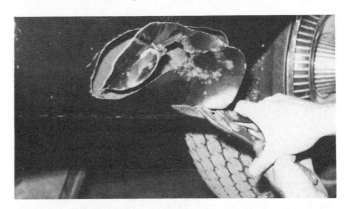

Fig. 21-9. *The panel is cut back to sound metal with tin snips. The cut should be made well outside the rusted area.*

Fig. 21-7. *Grinding away old paint and rust from the area to be repaired.*

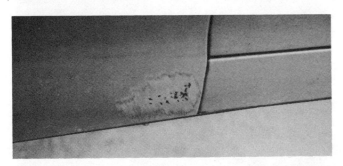

Fig. 21-8. *After grinding, the actual extent of the rust-out will be more visible.*

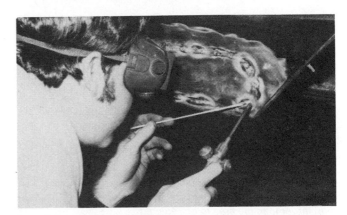

Fig. 21-10. *A metal patch is cut to size and brazed into position.*

Fig. 21-11. *A fiberglass repair kit may be used to repair rust-out. (Courtesy of Oatey Company)*

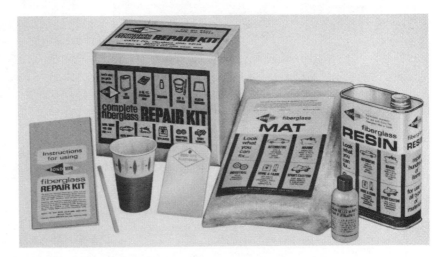
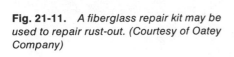

make it as strong as needed. In this situation, or when a stronger *small* repair is needed, a fiberglass patch and plastic filler may be used to make the repair. Properly prepared and applied, fiberglass patch materials will do a good job of repairing rust-out damage. Most fiberglass repair kits include complete directions. These directions must be followed *carefully* if the product is to do a good job. Figure 21-11 shows a complete fiberglass repair kit.

Figure 21-12 shows typical rust-out damage on a lower body panel. The metal has been cleaned, ground, and treated with metal conditioner. The panel has rusted through in several small areas. This rust-out damage is not major, but it does need support for a lasting repair. Figures 21-13 through 21-20 show how the fiberglass mat part of the repair should be done.

The patch in Figure 21-20 should be allowed to *cure* (harden) thoroughly for the time recommended by the manufacturer. The hardened and trimmed repair may

Fig. 21-12. *A rust-out area that will be repaired with fiberglass. The metal has been cleaned, ground, and treated with metal conditioner.*

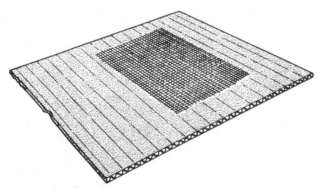

Fig. 21-13. Step 1: *Cut a piece of fiberglass about 1 in. (25.4 mm) larger than the area to be repaired.*

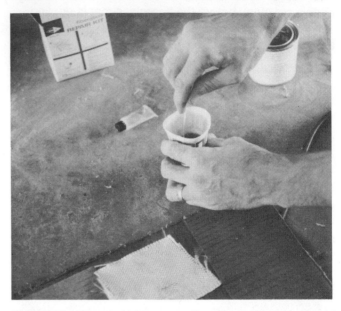

Fig. 21-15. Step 3: *Using a wooden mixing stick, thoroughly blend the hardener and resin. The mixture must be used quickly, before it begins to cure.*

Fig. 21-14. Step 2: *Add several drops of hardener to the fiberglass resin (follow manufacturer's directions).*

Fig. 21-16. Step 4: *Pour the resin mixture onto the fiberglass matting and spread it. A piece of waxed paper or wax-coated cardboard should be used beneath the matting, so that it does not stick to the surface.*

then be covered with plastic filler. Only *plastic* filler is recommended for application on fiberglass. The hardened plastic filler may then be sanded smooth and prepared for refinishing.

Jellied-type Fiberglass. A quick, simple, and permanent way to repair "rust-out" is by using a jellied-type fiberglass. The fiberglass kit contains one quart of jellied-type resin, plastic release paper, fiberglass matting, and spreaders (Fig. 21-21).

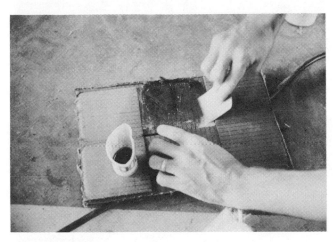

Fig. 21-17. Step 4, continued: *Thoroughly saturate the matting with the resin mixture, working it in well. Cover the entire piece of matting.*

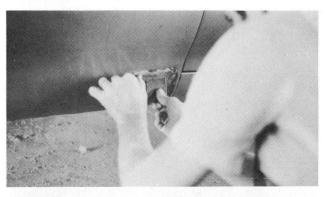

Fig. 21-18. Step 5: *Pick up the saturated matting, and place it over the area to be repaired. It will stick to the surface.*

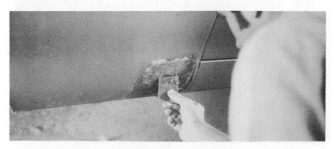

Fig. 21-19. Step 6: *Use a plastic spreader to work out all air bubbles and adhere the matting firmly to the surface. Usually, several layers of resin-saturated matting are applied.*

The large rust hole in Figure 21-22 has damaged the lower fender panel. Such rust-out can be repaired successfully with the jellied-type fiberglass material.

In Figure 21-23, the damaged area is being sanded with a coarse sanding disc. Sanding is extended several inches (centimeters) beyond the damaged area. The area then should be cleaned with lacquer thinner

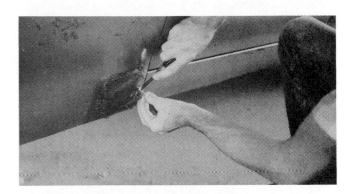

Fig. 21-20. Step 7: *After the resin has cured (hardened), use a razor blade or sharp knife to trim any strings or loose pieces of fiberglass from the edges of the repair area. A plastic filler made for use with fiberglass can be applied to level the surface.*

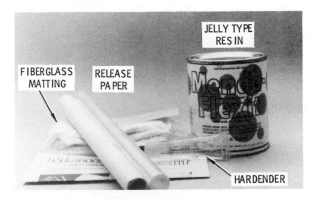

Fig. 21-21. *A jelly-type fiberglass repair kit. (Courtesy of Fibre Glass-Evercoat Company, Inc.)*

Fig. 21-22. *This large rust-out hole in a lower fender can be repaired with fiberglass. (Courtesy of Fibre Glass-Evercoat Company, Inc.)*

and wiped to remove all grease or road tar. In Figure 21-24, the area is ready for the jellied-type fiberglass.

The plastic release paper is measured and cut to approximately the size of the sanded area (Fig. 21-25). Cut the fiberglass matting 1 in. (2.5 cm) smaller than release paper (Fig. 21-26).

Place the cut plastic on a smooth surface and put the jellied compound on it, as shown in Figure 21-27. Usually about 1 tablespoon of compound is used for every 4 in. 2 (square inches) [103 cm² (square centimeters)] of cut fiberglass matting. Add five drops of liquid hardener for every full tablespoon of plastic. Mix

Fig. 21-25. *Clear plastic film is cut to extend well beyond the hole. (Courtesy of Fibre Glass-Evercoat Company, Inc.)*

Fig. 21-23. *Old paint and loose rusted metal are ground away in the area around the hole. (Courtesy of Fibre Glass-Evercoat Company, Inc.)*

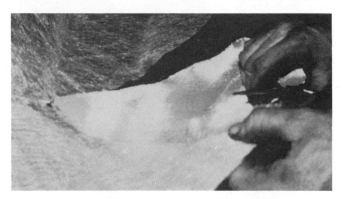

Fig. 21-26. *Fiberglass matting is cut about 1 in. (25.4 mm) larger than the hole to be covered. (Courtesy of Fibre Glass-Evercoat Company, Inc.)*

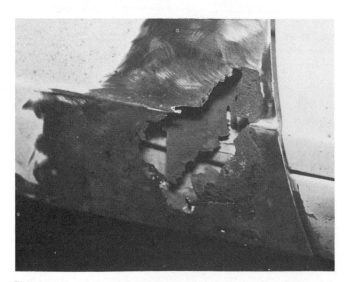

Fig. 21-24. *The area has been ground and cleaned and is now ready for repair work. (Courtesy of Fibre Glass-Evercoat Company, Inc.)*

Fig. 21-27. *Liquid hardener is added to the jellied resin, according to the manufacturer's directions. (Courtesy of Fibre Glass-Evercoat Company, Inc.)*

the plastic and hardener together as shown in Figure 21-28. Lay fiberglass matting over the mixture, and press until the matting is well saturated.

CAUTION: Use rubber gloves and a breathing mask to avoid irritation by fiberglass particles.

Place the prepared fiberglass on the damaged area, with the wet side to the panel. Press until the patch is firmly in place (Fig. 21-29).

Hold the fiberglass patch in place with one hand while using the spreader to press out all air bubbles, as shown in Figure 21-30.

Figure 21-31 shows the patch in place. Wait until the patch has cured (about 10 minutes), then trim away all excess material. The repair then is ready for refinishing.

Sheet Metal Patches. When a large section of a panel has been damaged or weakened by rust-out, a strong and permanent patch is necessary. Sometimes, a *metal* patch is the best choice for strength and lasting contour. Metal patch repairs must be done differently from fiberglass mat repairs because of the larger area being covered and because the repair is being made with metal.

Sheet metal patches are often cut from large, collision-damaged panels. Many body shops save damaged hoods, deck lids, and large fenders for this purpose. Although a cutting torch may be used to cut patches, they may be cut more cleanly by using metal snips (Fig. 21-32). The cut-out area on the part to be

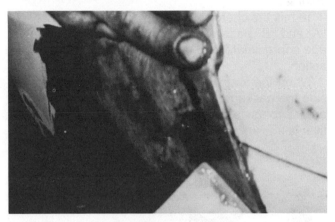

Fig. 21-30. *A plastic spreader is used to work out all the air bubbles and adhere the matting to the surface. (Courtesy of Fibre Glass-Evercoat Company, Inc.)*

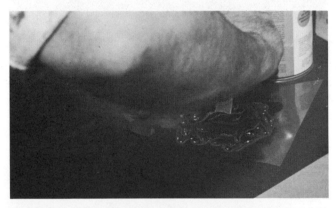

Fig. 21-28. *The resin and hardener are thoroughly blended. (Courtesy of Fibre Glass-Evercoat Company, Inc.)*

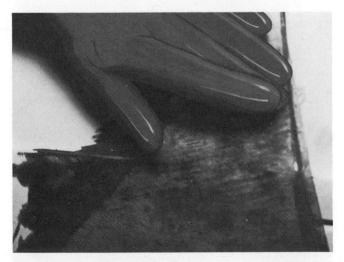

Fig. 21-29. *The fiberglass matting is saturated with resin mixture and placed over the damaged area. Wearing rubber gloves is a good practice when working with fiberglass, to prevent skin irritation. (Courtesy of Fibre Glass-Evercoat Company, Inc.)*

Fig. 21-31. *The patch is allowed to cure, then is trimmed with a knife or sharp razor blade. (Courtesy of Fibre Glass-Evercoat Company, Inc.)*

repaired is sanded with a medium-coarse sandpaper disc (Fig. 21-33).

After a patch has been sized and cut, it may be attached to the damaged area by being *brazed* in position. Brazing will produce the strongest rust-out repair if it is done properly. Sand the brazed area with a disc sander to remove all scale and oxidized metal caused by the heat (Fig. 21-34). Plastic filler then is used to complete the repair before refinishing (Fig. 21-35).

Foam Filler. Foam filler is a chemical packed in two parts ("A" and "B"). When the two parts are mixed together, the material expands to nine times its liquid volume.

To mix the chemical, pull the adhesive strip between "A" and "B" parts of the package. Squeeze the package approximately 25 to 30 times to start the chemical action.

When the foam filler has been thoroughly mixed inside the package, it can be squeezed into the rust-out area through a nozzle. Repairing rust-out with foam filler is shown in Figures 21-36 through 21-44.

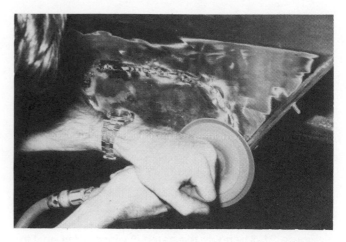

Fig. 21-34. *After the patch is brazed into position, the brazing is sanded to remove metal oxidized by the heat of the torch.*

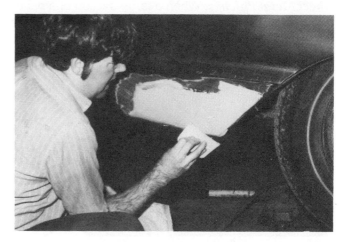

Fig. 21-35. *Plastic filler is applied over the patch to level the surface.*

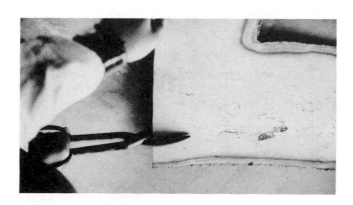

Fig. 21-32. *Using snips to cut a sheet metal patch from a salvage panel. Many shops save large, flat pieces of sheet metal, which have been removed from cars, to be used for such patches.*

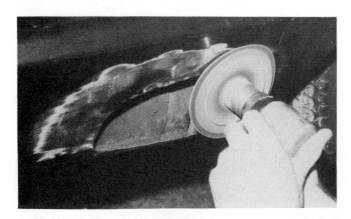

Fig. 21-33. *A disc sander is used to remove paint from around the area to be patched.*

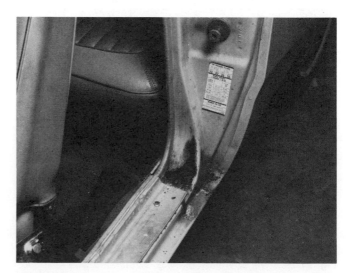

Fig. 21-36. *A rust-out area at the bottom of a door opening. This damage can be repaired with foam filler. (Courtesy of Automotive Trades Division, 3M Company)*

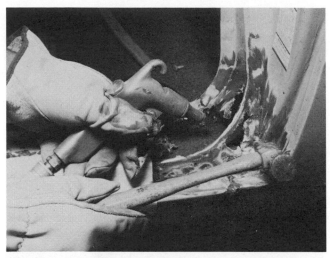

Fig. 21-37. *A sandblaster is used to clean away as much rust as possible. The edges of the hole are trimmed and bent inward to lower the repair area beneath the surface of the door opening. (Courtesy of Automotive Trades Division, 3M Company)*

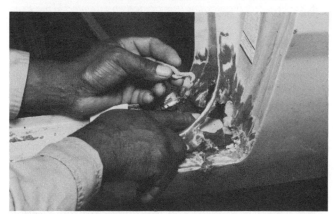

Fig. 21-38. *Caulking compound is used to seal all drains and inner panel holes, so the foam filler will remain in place when it is applied. (Courtesy of Automotive Trades Division, 3M Company)*

Fig. 21-39. *Wide masking tape is used to cover the hole. A small opening is left for the foam package nozzle. (Courtesy of Automotive Trades Division, 3M Company)*

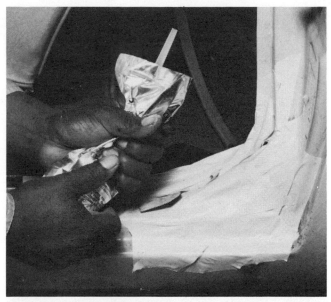

Fig. 21-40. *The foam is mixed as directed by the manufacturer. When the two parts of the product are mixed, a chemical reaction takes place. (Courtesy of Automotive Trades Division, 3M Company)*

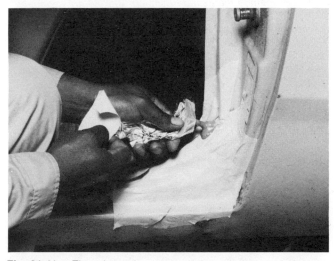

Fig. 21-41. *The mixture is squeezed through the nozzle into the hole being repaired. The liquid will expand greatly into a foam, then harden in place. (Courtesy of Automotive Trades Division, 3M Company)*

Permanent Rust-out Repair

Rust-out is the result of a chemical reaction. It is almost impossible to stop this reaction permanently once it has started, especially on the backside of a panel. Even if the panel is treated with metal conditioner, the rust may continue "working" from the backside until it again rusts through. This usually happens around the *edges* of the first rust-out repair.

For the above reasons, no rust-out repair, *including* the procedure to be outlined below, can be thought of as *absolutely* permanent. Even the best repairs, after many years, may again rust out.

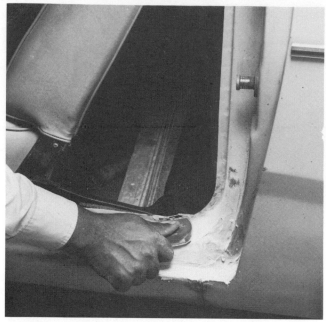

Fig. 21-42. *After the foam cures, the masking tape is stripped away. The foam is then sanded smooth with 36-grit sandpaper. The top surface of the foam should be about ¼ in. (6.4 mm) below the contour of the adjoining metal. (Courtesy of Automotive Trades Division, 3M Company)*

Fig. 21-43. *About 1 hour after the foam has been applied, plastic filler may be used. It is allowed to harden, then it is smoothed with 80-grit sandpaper. Fiberglass-reinforced plastic filler should be avoided for this application. It does not adhere well to the foam. (Courtesy of Automotive Trades Division, 3M Company)*

Every so often, however, a body worker may have a customer who wants the best type of rust-out repair *and is willing to pay the higher price required to have*

Fig. 21-44. *The repaired area is primed and painted in the usual way.*

the job done very carefully. For the customer who wishes to keep a car quite some time, or to restore an older car carefully, the following procedure should be used:

1. If at all possible, *remove the rusted-out panel from the car.* This will allow you to work on the back of the panel (where the rust began), as well as the front.
2. Remove all the dirt, old rust, and undercoating from the backside of the panel. Carefully *clean* the metal all around the rust holes. Note how far out from the holes the rust actually extends on the back of the panel.
3. Using metal snips, carefully cut out *all* of the damaged metal. Cut back from the rust holes as much as needed until only *solid* metal remains around the edge of the cut-out area.
4. From a good, sound piece of scrap metal, carefully cut a patch to fit the size and shape of the hole in the panel exactly. The patch should just fit inside the hole, *not* overlapping or leaving any gaps between the patch and the panel. Take the time necessary to fit this patch correctly.
5. Carefully *braze* the patch in the opening from the *back* of the panel, all the way around. Tack-braze the patch in place first. Then, carefully braze all around it. Braze one area only a short time, and then go across to another edge of the patch. By changing braze positions, there is less chance of overheating and distorting the repair area. When finished, the braze should be *all around* the patch. By brazing the repair on the

backside, the panel will be sealed so that no water or dirt can get through the repair area to the paint and filler on the front side.

6. Turn the panel over, and begin working on the frontside. Using a large disc grinder, grind an area back several inches (centimeters) around the patch, preparing the area for body filler.

7. Fill and level the area with body solder, *not* plastic filler. Keep in mind that this is a high-priced, premium-quality, permanent rust-out repair. While plastic fillers are excellent for virtually all filling jobs, they cannot be considered equal to body solder for the very best repairs.

8. Using body files and leveling tools, level the entire repair area. Finish by block-sanding the entire area with wet #320 or finer paper.

9. Wash the soldered area with cleaning solvent to neutralize the solder flux.

10. Treat the entire area with metal conditioner.

11. Wash the entire area with cleaning solvent.

12. Prime the entire area with *enamel* primer–surfacer. Allow it to dry thoroughly.

13. Turn the panel over, and complete the following steps on the backside. Protect the frontside while doing this by putting old blankets or pads on the work surface.

14. Clean the backside of the *entire* repair area. Clean any *flux* off the brazing repair with a wire brush.

15. Treat the entire backside of the repair area (patch, braze, and original metal) with metal conditioner. Do this only after the back has been thoroughly cleaned.

16. Wash the backside with cleaning solvent. Wipe off the solvent before it dries.

17. Brush or spray rust-proof red primer over the back of the repair. Allow it to dry.

18. Brush or spray *undercoat* over the entire backside. Undercoat must not be applied too thick; a light-to-medium coat is heavy enough. Allow the undercoat to dry.

19. Turn the panel over, and finish preparing the enamel primer–surfacer for refinishing.

20. Apply paint putty to any small nicks or imperfections in the enamel primer–surfacer. Allow the putty to dry.

21. Block-sand the entire panel with #400 wet sandpaper.

22. Refinish the panel as outlined in the paint units.

Unit 22

Auto Body Trim

Basically, any *trim* on a vehicle either beautifies the vehicle, adds strength to an area, or provides comfort. Many pieces of trim are bright moldings on either the outside or the inside of the car. Trim also includes dull (no gloss or shine) metal parts and many parts made of cloth, vinyl, rubber, or plastic. These may be attached to either the exterior or the interior of an auto or truck body (Figs. 22-1 and 22-2).

Repairing and replacing trim is an important part of auto body work. During most body repairs, at least some exterior trim work will be necessary. Interior trim work may be necessary to get at damaged panels from the backside or for repairs to the trim itself. Because trim work largely affects the *appearance* of a repair, it must be done correctly for complete customer satisfaction on even the smallest repairs.

EXTERIOR TRIM

Some of the exterior trim moldings on the automobile are made of bright aluminum or stainless steel. These include side moldings, rocker panel moldings, grilles, and window trim pieces. Most of these parts are replaceable items because it is not practical to repair them; the cost of a new molding is less than the time it would take to repair it.

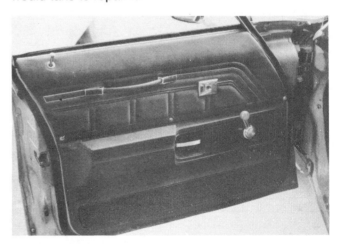

Fig. 22-2. *Most of the interior parts of the vehicle are trim parts.*

Fig. 22-1. *Exterior trim parts of an automobile are made of many materials, such as urethane (bumper covers), plastic (grille), rubber (molding and weatherstripping), and aluminum (molding). Most trim parts are replaced, rather than repaired. (Courtesy of Prostripe Division, Spartan Plastics, Inc.)*

Some exterior trim pieces are simply glued-on rubber or plastic parts. These may have an adhesive backing used to attach the piece to the vehicle. Figure 22-3 shows such a strip of plastic molding being pressed into place. Vinyl top material, a type of plastic, also is cemented in place (Fig. 22-4).

Types of Exterior Trim

Exterior trim moldings and pieces are made from many types of materials. Some of the more common molding and trim materials include:

1. Stamped aluminum.
2. Stamped stainless steel.
3. Plastic.
4. Die-cast, chrome-plated metal.
5. Extruded aluminum.

Stamped Aluminum. Some metal parts are made from aluminum that has been *pressed* (stamped) into shape. The lettering in Figure 22-5 is an example of *stamped aluminum trim.* Usually, stamped aluminum moldings and trim are polished to a bright finish. Sometimes, however, only a raised area, such as lettering, is polished. Then, the lower part of the piece, at the base of the raised section, is left "flat" (unpolished) or is painted flat black. Stamped aluminum trim is rust-resistant, durable, attractive, and inexpensive. Many automobile manufacturers use stamped aluminum trim parts.

Stamped Stainless Steel. The most durable automotive trim is *stamped stainless steel.* This shiny trim may be stamped into shape with contours to fit snugly against the vehicle's body. Stamped stainless steel moldings and parts are polished to a high-gloss finish. Stainless steel moldings are used on many vehicles around the windshield and rear window (backlight). Here, they are known as *reveal moldings.* Many vehicle side moldings are also stamped stainless steel. Figure 22-6 shows a stamped stainless steel drip rail molding. Aluminum moldings are used instead of stainless steel on many newer cars because of its lower cost and weight.

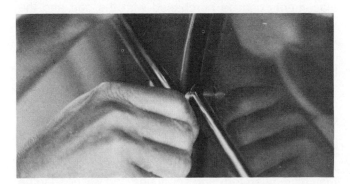

Fig. 22-3. *A glued-on rubber molding being trimmed after application to a panel.*

Plastic. Plastic trim parts are formed in the desired shapes as they cool in the mold used to shape the hot material. Different kinds of plastic parts are being used more and more each year on new cars and trucks. Plastic moldings, grilles, and many types of trim are

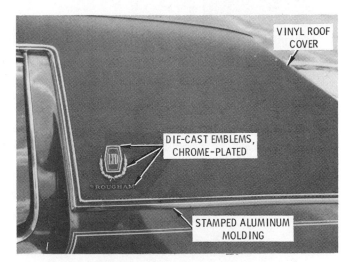

Fig. 22-4. *Vinyl roof covers and moldings and emblems on them are considered trim parts.*

Fig. 22-5. *The letters on this fender are an example of* stamped aluminum *trim.*

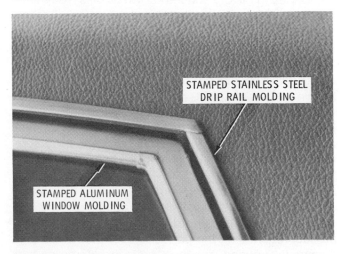

Fig. 22-6. *Most drip rail moldings are stampings of* stainless steel.

Fig. 22-7. *A shiny,* plated plastic *molding is used around the small quarter glass.*

Fig. 22-8. *This nameplate is* die-cast aluminum.

made with either a *painted* color coat or a shiny "plating" made to look like chrome plating. Figure 22-7 shows a "chrome" quarter glass molding made of plastic.

Plastic moldings and trim parts may be cemented to the vehicle's surface or held in place with screws or clips. Plastic trim may be formed to fit almost any contour. Repairing most types of collision damage will include replacing one or more types of plastic parts.

Die-cast, Chrome-plated Metal. Die-cast metal parts are formed in factory shapes known as *dies.* As molten metal injected under pressure into a die cools, it takes the shape of the die. Then, the new metal piece is plated with chromium. Die-cast trim pieces are hard and brittle. Door handles and some small trim parts are usually die-cast pieces. Sometimes, die-cast parts are known as "pot metal."

Aluminum die-cast trim is often used to make lettering strips. Figure 22-8 shows an aluminum nameplate, which has been die-cast to fit the vehicle's body contour. Aluminum die-cast moldings usually cannot be rechromed.

Extruded Aluminum. When metal is forced through an opening so that it takes the shape of that opening, the shaped metal piece is known as an *extrusion.* The process of shaping the pieces is known as *extruding.* Common extruded aluminum parts include grilles and other pieces of trim.

Exterior Trim Fasteners

Exterior trim moldings, grilles, and many other pieces must be attached firmly to the body. These pieces may be fastened to the body by several different types of attachments. On any piece of trim, then, one or more of these methods may be used to hold the trim in place:

1. Glue backing (Fig. 22-3).
2. Attaching screws (Fig. 22-9).
3. Bolt and clip assemblies (Fig. 22-10).
4. Molded studs (Fig. 22-11).
5. Bathtub clips (Fig. 22-12).
6. W-base clips (Fig. 22-13).
7. Welded studs and clips (Fig. 22-14).
8. Retainer inserts (Fig. 22-15).
9. Self-retaining moldings (Fig. 22-16).

Wherever bolts, screws, or studs go *through* a panel, holes will be needed. To prevent water from leaking through the holes, the bolt, screw, or stud must be surrounded with body sealer *before* the molding is installed. When exterior trim pieces are held in place with an attaching screw, sealer should be placed on the screw before it is installed. This helps prevent water leaks around the hole in the panel.

Most pieces of replacement trim are sold in a wrapper that also contains the fasteners (such as clips and screws) that are needed for installation. Be careful when unwrapping a new piece of trim to avoid losing any fasteners packaged with it.

Vinyl Top Coverings

Vinyl top material is made of a special cloth that has been covered with a plastic (vinyl) coating (Fig. 22-17). Most vinyl top material is cemented directly to the steel roof panel (Fig. 22-18). On some higher-priced vinyl top coverings, a *pad* is first cemented to the roof panel, using special cement (Fig. 22-19). Then, the vinyl top covering may be cemented *over* the pad, but not to the pad itself. The vinyl is cemented and fastened along the *edge* of the steel roof panel. Some vinyl top replacements can be purchased with the pad and the vinyl material made together. The vinyl and pad combination is cemented to the top as one unit.

In addition to being cemented, vinyl covering is often held in place by *molding strips.* The edges of the vinyl are concealed beneath the molding strips. When the covering and moldings are properly installed, the edges of the covering will not be visible.

Work on vinyl top coverings often must be done as part of auto body repair. When an automobile has gone through a fence, for example, the original top covering may have been torn and scratched and will need to be replaced. If collision damage has buckled a steel panel

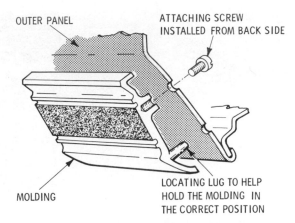

Fig. 22-9. A molding held in place by attaching screws.

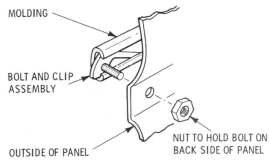

Fig. 22-10. A bolt and clip assembly used to hold molding in place. To remove the molding, the nut must be removed from the back side of the panel.

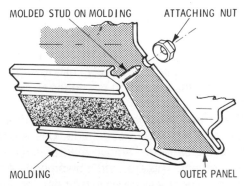

Fig. 22-11. A nut fastened to a molded stud. To remove the molding, the nut must be removed from behind the panel. Whe installing this type of fastener, the nut must not be overtightene since it can cause the stud to break off.

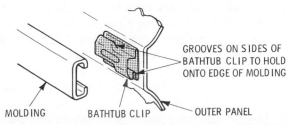

Fig. 22-12. A bathtub clip is used to fasten this molding in place. The molding may be carefully pried away from the clip with a putty knife.

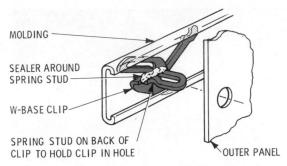

Fig. 22-13. A "W"-base clip has a wedge section that snaps into a hole in the panel. The molding and clip can be pried away from the panel with a putty knife.

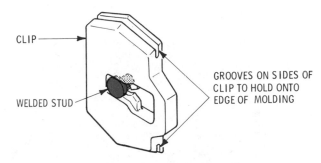

Fig. 22-14. A welded stud and clip fastener. The stud is welded to the panel, and the clip locks to the stud. Molding snaps into grooves in the clip. It can be removed with a putty knife.

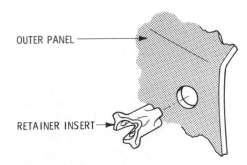

Fig. 22-15. A retainer insert, made of metal or plastic, is often used to fasten nameplates and emblems to panels. The insert snaps into a hole in the panel, and the stud on the emblem is pushed into it. A putty knife can be used for removal.

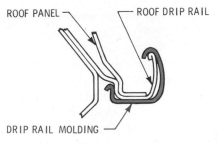

Fig. 22-16. Self-retaining moldings are usually made of stainless steel or aluminum and have tabs formed on their edges. They snap over the part that they are to accent, such as the car's drip rail. On some aluminum moldings, the tabs are bent over the part to hold the molding in place.

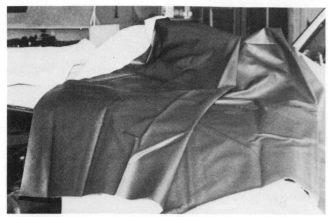

Fig. 22-17. *Vinyl top material is a fabric coated with colored and textured vinyl plastic.*

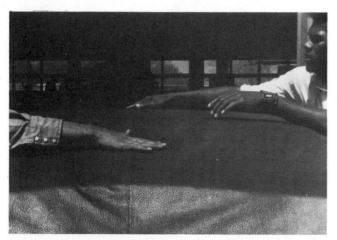

Fig. 22-18. *A vinyl top is cemented to the steel roof panel.*

Fig. 22-19. *Some vinyl tops are installed over a padding that is glued onto the roof panel.*

underneath the covering, the vinyl material must be pulled away so that the buckled panel may be repaired. Then, the vinyl covering must be cemented to the panel again after the repair is completed.

Vinyl Top Replacement. The following steps should be followed when a complete vinyl top covering needs to be replaced:

1. Place all the necessary tools and materials in the work area. These include molding removal

Fig. 22-20. *A molding removal tool makes the job of removing a windshield reveal molding much easier. Moldings must be removed when installing a new vinyl top.*

tools, pliers, putty knife, small paint brush, and pocket knife. Materials include the replacement top and vinyl top cement.

2. Remove the trim moldings around or on the vinyl top. These include the windshield and backlight moldings, drip rail moldings, upper quarter-panel moldings, and any emblems or nameplates attached *through* the vinyl covering to the roof panel. The window moldings should be released with a molding removal tool (Fig. 22-20). The other moldings and emblems usually can be carefully pried off with a putty knife.

3. Clean off any surface cement or caulking material from around the windshield and back glass openings.

4. Slowly pull the old vinyl material from the roof panel. Use pliers or a putty knife to separate the top from the cement at the edges. Then, pull the material back.

5. Clean and smooth the entire roof area where the new top will be cemented. Use a good adhesive cleaner to remove any remaining old vinyl cement. The area *must* be smooth. Any high or low spots will be visible under the installed top.

6. Lay out the replacement top material to make sure it is the correct size for the automobile being repaired.

7. Measure and mark both the roof panel and the underside of the vinyl cover to make sure of a proper fit. Carefully draw a chalk line down the center of both the roof *and* the underside of the vinyl material. *Be sure that the centers are measured correctly* so that the top will fit properly (Fig. 22-21).

8. Lay the new vinyl top on the marked roof panel. Fold the cover material back over itself to the center line of the roof panel (Fig. 22-22).

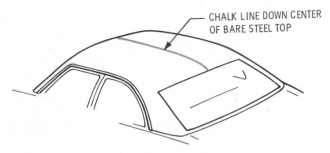

Fig. 22-21. *To fit a replacement top properly, a center line must be chalked on both the roof panel and the underside of the vinyl top material.*

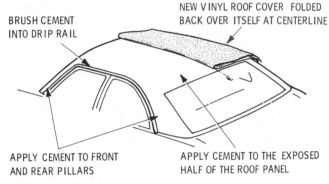

BRUSH CEMENT INTO DRIP RAIL

NEW VINYL ROOF COVER FOLDED BACK OVER ITSELF AT CENTERLINE

APPLY CEMENT TO FRONT AND REAR PILLARS

APPLY CEMENT TO THE EXPOSED HALF OF THE ROOF PANEL

Fig. 22-22. *The material is glued to one side of the roof at a time, working from the center outward.*

9. Apply rubber vinyl cement to *the exposed half of the roof panel*. Apply cement from the center line outward to the drip rail and the other edges (Fig. 22-22).

10. Very carefully pull over the folded half of the covering onto the wet cement. This must be done *while the cement on the roof is still wet*. As the cover is being rolled out onto the wet cement, thoroughly work it down to eliminate any wrinkles or air bubbles (Fig. 22-18).

11. When half of the material is thoroughly fitted and cemented in place, fold the remaining half back over the newly cemented side.

12. Repeat the cementing and application procedure on the other side of the roof panel.

13. Use a dull putty knife to work the material down into and around the edges of the window openings. Trim off any excess material with a sharp knife. Remove the trimmings carefully (Fig. 22-23). Note whether *drive nails* were used originally to hold the edges of the material in place. If so, install new drive nails at the edges of the material where the moldings will cover the nail heads.

14. Replace all the trim and moldings. Clean the vinyl top, windows and moldings as necessary.

Partial Vinyl Top Removal. Many times, a damaged panel is warped or buckled *under* the vinyl roof mate-

Fig. 22-23. *After the top is glued down, it is trimmed with a sharp knife, and the trimmings are removed.*

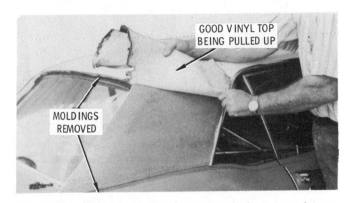

GOOD VINYL TOP BEING PULLED UP

MOLDINGS REMOVED

Fig. 22-24. *To repair damage beneath a vinyl top, complete removal may not be necessary. Only enough of the top is pulled back to allow work on the damaged metal area.*

Fig. 22-25. *New cement is applied to the roof panel after repairs have been completed.*

rial. When this is true, a section of the vinyl material will have to be pulled away *carefully* to allow work on the damaged area. After the metal has been repaired, the vinyl material must be cemented back into place.

To remove part of a vinyl top temporarily, first remove any moldings and trim along the edges of the area to

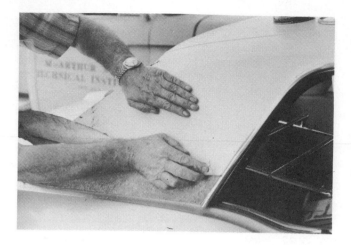

Fig. 22-26. *The vinyl material is carefully stretched and smoothed into position.*

Fig. 22-27. *The completed top repair, with all moldings in place.*

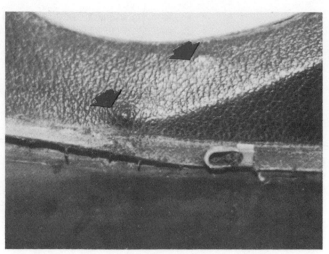

Fig. 22-28. *Lumps appearing beneath the vinyl material are an indication of rust. In this photo, the molding has been removed to allow the top to be peeled back.*

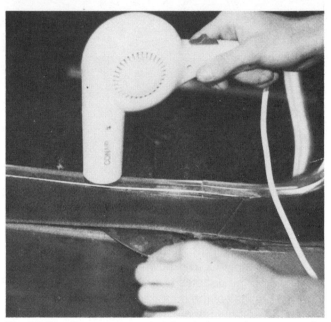

Fig. 22-29. *To ease removal of the vinyl top, a heat gun can be used. The heat softens the vinyl material, making it easier to remove.*

be pulled up. After trim has been removed, very carefully pull the vinyl material upward (Fig. 22-24).

When the metal repair has been completed, the vinyl top covering may be cemented to the roof again. To do this, first brush new vinyl top cement on the roof area (Fig. 22-25). Then, fold the material down over the new cement, and smooth it to press out any air bubbles (Fig. 22-26). Finally, replace the moldings, and clean the repaired area. When the repair is complete, the top will look like new (Fig. 22-27).

Rust Spots Under a Vinyl Top. Many times rust will form on the metal under the vinyl roof top. This is caused by moisture between the metal and the vinyl material. Figures 22-28 through 22-31 show how to remove the vinyl for rust repair.

The rusted area on the roof top is repaired in the same way as any other rust repair. Then, the vinyl material is cemented back in place.

Asbestos Putty. To protect vinyl material, paint, trim, and glass from heat damage resulting from welding, a puttylike asbestos material is available. This material,

shown in Figure 22-32, forms a "heat dam" to protect vinyl, glass, and other trim whenever welding must be done in an area near them. Without the asbestos heat dam, the trim or glass would be damaged by heat.

To use this compound, pack it about ½ in. (12.7 mm) thick along and all around the area to be protected. The compound is designed to stick to any surface and stay put while other work is being done. The asbestos in the compound will keep the heat from burning or discoloring the trim. This may be necessary, for example, if a new quarter panel is being welded near a vinyl roof covering. When the job is finished, the compound may be removed and placed back in the can. It may then be used again later.

Fig. 22-30. *Rust is visible on the metal roof panel, and rust stains may be seen on the underside of the vinyl.*

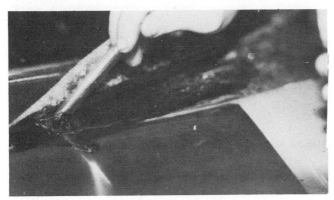

Fig. 22-31. *Using a small brush to spread cement on the roof panel after repairs have been completed.*

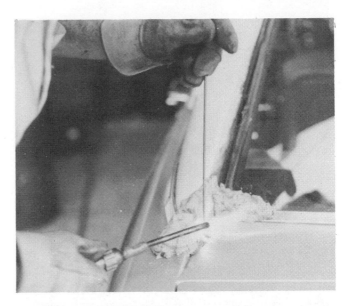

Fig. 22-32. *A heat dam of asbestos putty will prevent damage to nearby trim or glass when welding or brazing.*

Fig. 22-33. *Many different materials are used for trim on the interior of today's automobile. (Courtesy of* Road & Track *Magazine)*

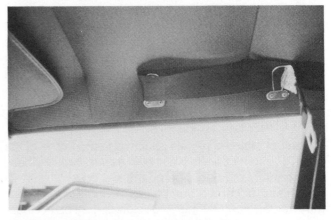

Fig. 22-34. Headliners *may be vinyl or cloth.*

INTERIOR TRIM

The interior trim (Fig. 22-33) includes all the cloth, plastic, vinyl, carpet, and small rubber and metal parts used to make up the complete interior of the vehicle. Also included is the *headliner,* which is the plastic, vinyl, or cloth covering on the inside of the roof panel. Figure 22-34 shows a section of *cloth* headliner. The quarter and door *trim panels* are usually made of either fiberboard or plastic. They are covered with vinyl, plastic, carpeting, or a combination of the three. Figure 22-35 shows a typical door trim panel. A *moisture cover* underneath the trim panel protects it from any water that enters the door at the lower edge of the window (Fig. 22-36).

Floor coverings in an automotive interior may be either fabric, carpet (Fig. 22-37), or rubber mat (Fig. 22-38). These coverings, like headliners, are not normally replaced in an auto body shop. This type of work is usually done in an upholstery shop. However, the floor covering may need to be removed, or moved back out of the way, for auto body repairs. This might be necessary, for example, to work on the metal floor in-side a vehicle. Removing and cleaning floor coverings are simple jobs that are often done in a body shop.

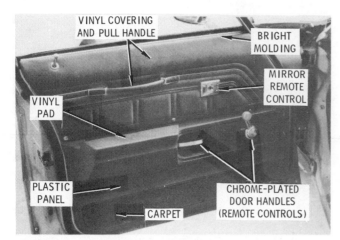

Fig. 22-35.   *A complete door trim panel includes many different parts and materials.*

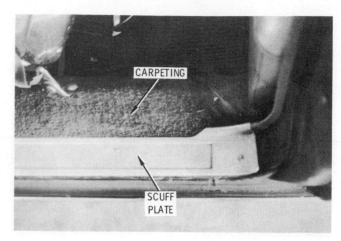

Fig. 22-37.   *Carpeting is trimmed at the door openings by metal scuff plates.*

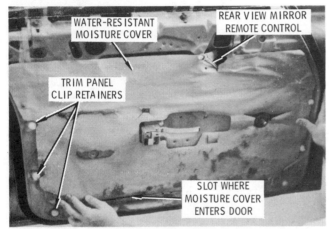

Fig. 22-36.   *A moisture cover ("water dam") is used behind the interior trim panel to direct water away from the trim panel.*

Fig. 22-38.   *Some cars have rubber or vinyl floor coverings.*

Successful auto body shops must pay close attention to the *interior* as well as the exterior, of a car being repaired. A clean, neat interior leaves the customer with a good impression of the shop's work. Careful attention to both the exterior *and* the interior shows that the shop does good work and is concerned about the entire automobile. Exterior repairs and sheet metal work will be more highly thought of if the interior is neat and clean.

Trim Panels

The upholstered panels attached to the inside of the doors or quarter panels are known as *trim panels*. These are normally made of fiberboard and covered with vinyl, plastic, or carpet. Sometimes, an interior trim panel may be damaged during a collision or may be accidentally cut. If work is to be done inside the door or panel, the trim panel must be removed and replaced.

Removing and Replacing Trim Panels. Most interior trim panels are held in place in the same basic manner.

For this reason, the general instructions below may be followed to remove and replace them. (In some cases, special fastening methods or accessories may be used on a given model. In these cases, refer to a body shop manual when removing and replacing.)

1. Unscrew the *door lock knob*. Figure 22-39 shows a trim panel from which the knob has already been removed.
2. Remove the handles from the door lock and window regulator remote controls. These are held in place by screws or horseshoe-shaped clips. Use a screwdriver or an Allen wrench to remove the screws, depending on head design. Use a *clip puller* to remove clips from behind handles (Figs. 22-40 and 22-41).
3. Remove any screws holding the trim panel in place. These may include arm rest retaining screws and any screws along the bottom of the trim panel.

4. Remove any accessories attached to the trim panel. A common example is an outside rear view mirror control (Fig. 22-35). Remove the screws holding the control in place, and pull it out slightly, to free it from the trim panel.

5. Use an upholstery tool (Fig. 22-42) to pry the trim panel clips out of the inner door panel holes. These clips are located along the edges of the trim panel.

6. Remove the trim panel by pulling up and guiding the panel over the door lock shaft. Guide the rear view mirror control and any other accessories through their respective holes.

7. To install a new trim panel or reinstall an old one, reverse the procedure. Be sure that the trim panel clips are properly "started" in their holes before pushing them into the door panel.

Replacing a Plastic Regulator Bracket. Many door glass regulators move up and down with a plastic regulator bracket. Figure 22-43 shows such a plastic bracket. These brackets sometimes break. The following steps are used to replace the plastic bracket:

1. Remove the trim from the door panel (Fig. 22-44).

2. Pull the *trim* panel away from the *door inner* panel. Leave the electrical wires connected (Fig. 22-45).

3. Use a ¼ in. drive socket set to remove the bolts that hold the regulator bracket, as shown in Figures 22-46 and 22-47.

4. Take the broken bracket out through the access opening in the inner door panel (Fig. 22-48). Figure 22-49 shows the broken bracket after removal.

5. Place the new bracket in the door (Fig. 22-50), and replace all the screws, nuts, and bolts.

6. Replace the door panel trim.

Removing Inside Quarter-panel Trim. The inside quarter-panel trim, shown in Figure 22-51, is removed much like the door trim. The rear seat and back cushion should

be removed before attempting to remove the inside quarter-panel trim. Remove the panel as follows:

1. Remove the sill scuff plate.
2. Remove the glass regulator handle (Fig. 22-52).
3. Remove the screws that hold the arm rest, ash tray, moldings, and trim on the panel.

Fig. 22-39. *An interior door trim panel with the window regulator handle and door locking knob removed.*

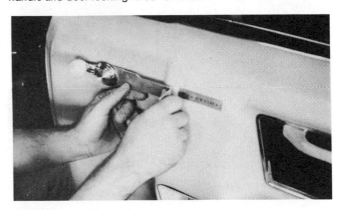

Fig. 22-40. *Using a clip puller to remove a door handle.*

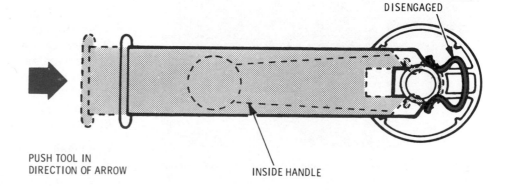

Fig. 22-41. *The ends of the clip puller force the spring clip off the shaft of the window regulator handle.*

Fig. 22-42. *An upholstery tool may be used to pry out clips holding door trim panels to the door structure.*

Fig. 22-43. *A plastic door glass bracket replacement.*

ELECTRIC POWERED PUSHBUTTON

Fig. 22-44. *Remove all trim parts from the door panel, then release the clips holding it to the door.*

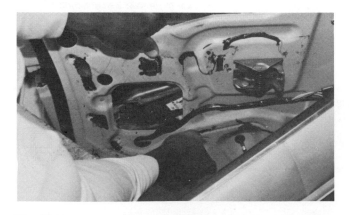

Fig. 22-45. *The trim panel is pulled away from the door, without disconnecting the electric window regulator wiring.*

Fig. 22-46. *Through an access hole, use a socket set to remove the regulator bracket.*

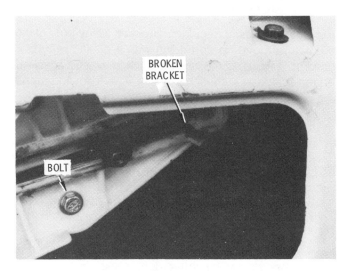

BROKEN BRACKET

BOLT

Fig. 22-47. *Remove the bolt holding the broken bracket.*

4. Remove the lock pillar and all finishing panel trim.
5. Remove the trim panel assembly from the vehicle.

Before installing the panel, check all the retainers that hold it in position. If any are broken or worn out, replace them. Check to see if all retainers are installed securely. Install as follows:

1. Position the trim panel, aligning the trim retainers with the matching holes.
2. Replace the screws in the panel trim.
3. Replace the lock pillar trim finishing panels.
4. Replace the sill scuff plates.
5. Replace all hardware that was removed from the panel.
6. Replace the seat back and cushions.

A moisture cover, also known as a *water dam*, is used behind the door trim panels. It is cemented in place on the metal inner door panel. This cover is im-

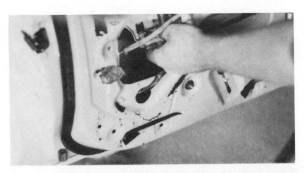

Fig. 22-48. *Pull out the broken bracket through an access hole.*

portant because whenever it rains or the car is washed, water passes *through* the inside of the door. Water enters at the bottom of the glass opening, runs down the inside of the door itself, and finally drains out the bottom of the door through the drain holes. If the moisture cover is not in place, water will stain and damage the door trim panel.

Figure 22-36 shows a properly installed moisture cover. When replacing a moisture cover, be sure to put the bottom edge of the cover into the slot at the bottom of the inner door panel. If any water hits the moisture

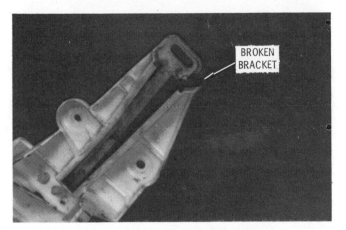

Fig. 22-49. *A closeup view of the broken bracket.*

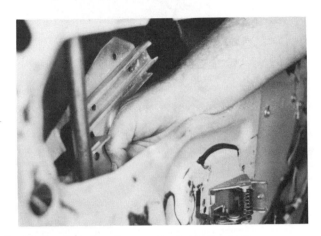

Fig. 22-50. *Installing the new bracket in the door.*

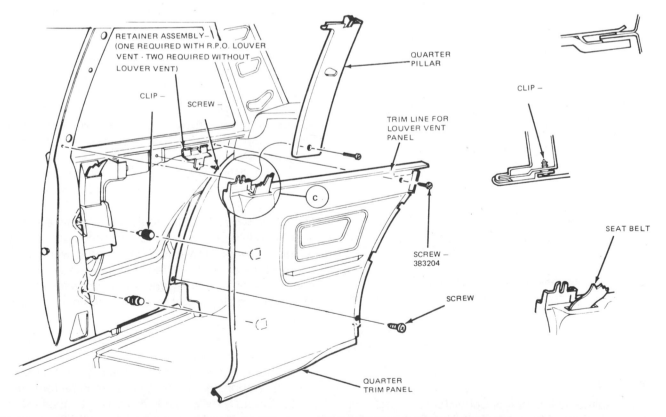

Fig. 22-51. *An interior quarter trim panel. (Courtesy of Customer Service Division, Ford Motor Company)*

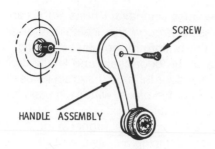

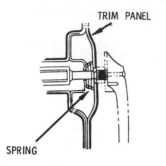

Fig. 22-52. *The inside door handle that regulates glass movement. (Courtesy of Customer Service Division, Ford Motor Company)*

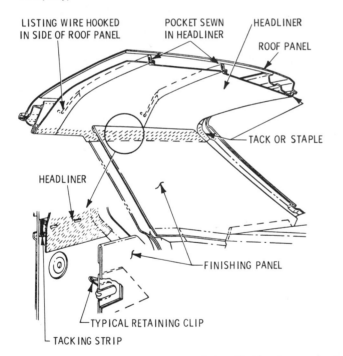

Fig. 22-53. *A typical headliner installation. Listing wires support the headliner. (Courtesy of Fisher Body Division, General Motors Corporation)*

cover, it guides the water down, through the slots. This forces the water to go down inside the door and drain out.

Headliner

The headliner is the interior upholstery trim that covers the underside of the roof panel. Headliners may be

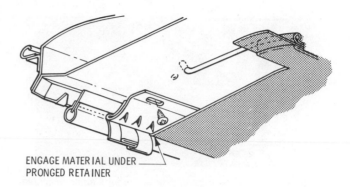

Fig. 22-54. *Toothed holders ("pronged retainers") hold the headlining material in place at the sides.*

made of cloth, vinyl-coated cloth, or, in some cases, plastic. Plastic or plastic foam may be formed as "one piece" headliners. This upholstery helps to beautify the car's interior and to insulate the interior from road noise.

Most conventional headliners are held in position smoothly and tightly with listing wires, toothed holders, and cement. These are concealed between the headliner and the inner roof panel. Like other trim parts, there are many types of fasteners used to hold headliners in place.

Listing Wires. Listing wires (Fig. 22-53) are used to hold most headliners in place at the top. These wires are ¼ in. (6.4 mm) in diameter. They are held in a cloth pocket sewn across the inside of the headliner. The wires run from one side of the roof panel to the other. The *ends* of the listing wires are usually color-coded to fit matching color-coded holes along the side roof header plate.

Toothed Holders. The *outer* edges of headliner material are often held in place along the sides of the roof interior with toothed holders, sometimes known as *pronged retainers*. These are positioned between or around the listing wire holes. The holders are held in place on the roof header with sheet metal screws (Fig. 22-54).

Headliner Work. Usually, replacing a complete headliner is work for an automotive trim shop specializing in upholstery work. However, if you need to work on only a small area *under* the headliner, only the section covering the area to be repaired needs to be taken down. The following steps may be used to remove part of the headliner.

1. Place a protective cover over the seat in the area to be worked upon.
2. Remove the upper trim moldings and hardware surrounding the headliner area to be removed.
3. Carefully remove any drive nails or staples holding the headliner in place (Fig. 22-53).

4. Pull carefully to remove the edge of the headliner from any cement used to hold it in place. Avoid pulling too hard, since this might tear the material instead of pulling it away from the cement.

5. Use a wide-blade upholstery tool to pry up on the pronged retainers holding the headliner between the listing wires. This will release the material.

6. Work along the sides of the roof panel to disengage the listing wires from the roof header. To release the listing wires, simply pull them out of their holes. *Remove only as much of the headliner as is needed to make the repair.*

7. Make the needed sheet metal repair in the area. *Be careful when using any heat or flame* near the partially removed headliner.

8. Position the *sides* of the headliner on the roof panel by placing the listing wires back in the holes. Place each listing wire in the hole from which it was removed.

9. Secure the edges of the headliner under the pronged retainers. This can be done by pulling up on the retainers with a wide-blade upholstery tool and pushing the material into place. When the retainer is released, it will snap back and hold the headliner material.

10. Staple or tack the edges of the headliner, if staples or tacks were used along the edges of the original installation.

11. Use trim cement, as required, to secure the front and rear edges.

12. Install any trim molding removed earlier.

VINYL TOP REFINISHING

A vinyl top can be repainted with vinyl paint to match the original color, or the color can be changed (Fig. 22-55). Figure 22-56 shows refinishing materials for vinyl tops. The steps to follow when refinishing a vinyl top are:

1. Use a stiff brush, soap, and water to remove wax or foreign material, such as bird droppings and tree sap stains.

2. Use masking paper and tape to protect all panels that will *not* be painted (Fig. 22-57).

3. Spray on three coats of vinyl paint reduced according the manufacturer's specifications.

The vinyl paint will dry to touch in approximately 20 minutes. Remove the tape, and allow to dry at least 2 hours. The paint must be completely dry before delivery to the customer.

Fig. 22-56. *Refinishing and repair materials for vinyl tops. (Courtesy of Customer Service Division, Ford Motor Company)*

Fig. 22-55. *Spraying a refinishing material on a vinyl top.*

Fig. 22-57. *This vehicle has been masked and the top has been cleaned in preparation for respraying the vinyl top. (Courtesy of Customer Service Division, Ford Motor Company)*

Fig. 22-58. *The roof vent glass on this car can be removed by slipping it off its hinges.*

Fig. 22-60. *The vent glass has been reinstalled by slipping it over the hinges and fastening the latch.*

Fig. 22-59. *The vent opening after the glass panel has been removed and stored away.*

SUN ROOFS

Many sport-model vehicles, recreational vehicles, and some more expensive model cars have a sun roof. The sun roof has a visual attractiveness that takes the place of the convertible roll-back top. The sun roof is used to allow sunlight and fresh air into the vehicle. When the sun roof is open, inside air is pulled out, clearing cigarette smoke or stale air from the interior.

A sun roof can be purchased and installed in a vehicle that was not equipped with one at the factory. Instructions for cutting the roof panel and fitting the gasket and housing are enclosed with the sun roof assembly. A worker should be thoroughly skilled in auto body and auto upholstery repair before attempting to install a sun roof. Most auto body repair shops can install a new sun roof for a customer. However, this work is done more frequently in customizing shops.

Sun Roof Operation

Many sun roof panels can be removed and stored, then later reinstalled on the vehicle (Figs. 22-58 through 22-60).

Some vehicles have two sliding panels as shown in Figure 22-61. One is a clear glass panel, and one is a sunshade panel. To allow more sunlight to enter the vehicle, the shaded panel is slid back (either electrically or manually) inside the storage housing. The housing is located between the headliner and the roof panel. The shaded panel can be moved forward if less sunlight is needed. Both the clear glass panel and the shaded panel can be slid into the storage housing to admit fresh air to the inside of the vehicle.

To keep the sun roof from leaking, a flexible gasket is installed around the roof opening. When the sun roof panels are closed, they press the gasket to seal out any water or air.

Figure 22-62 shows one type of electrically operated sun roof, which has both a clear glass panel and a shaded panel. Figure 22-63 shows the inside sun roof finishing cover, retainer tabs, attaching screws, and finishing cover clips. Figure 22-64 shows the sun roof housing weatherstrip.

Vent-type Sun Roofs

Some sun roof glass does not slide back and forth. The glass panel in Figure 22-65 can be removed and stored as shown in Figure 22-66. Figure 22-67 is a view from inside the vehicle, showing the sun roof and adjusting handle, which opens the vent glass. Figure 22-68 shows the glass in the open position.

Some sun roof panels move back and forth on a track runner installed between the headlining and the roof panel. An electric motor turns a flexible cable, which moves the panels into the storage area.

Lift-off Panels. Side roof twin lift-off panels (sometimes called "T"-tops) are used mostly on two-door sports-

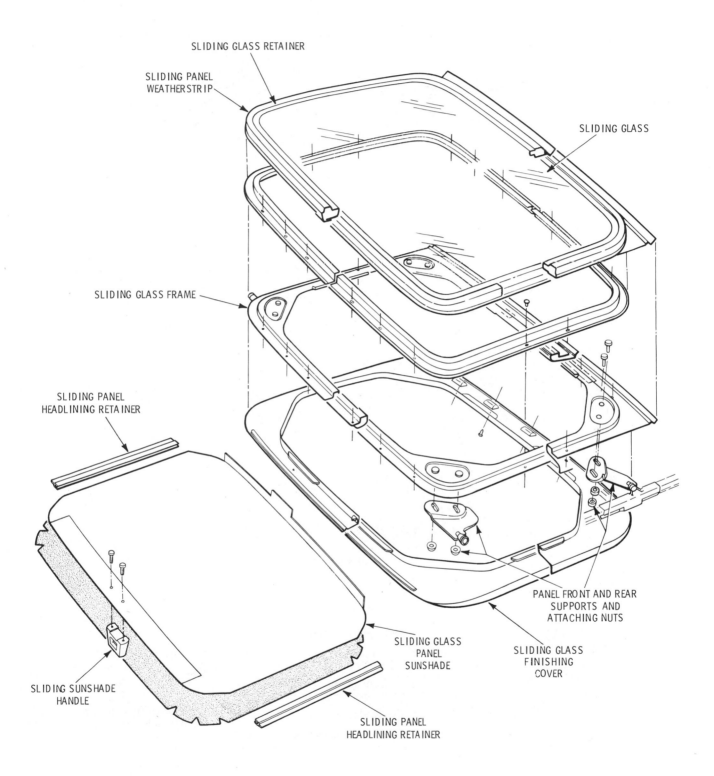

SLIDING GLASS RETAINER

SLIDING PANEL
WEATHERSTRIP

SLIDING GLASS

SLIDING GLASS FRAME

SLIDING PANEL
HEADLINING RETAINER

SLIDING PANEL
HEADLINING RETAINER

SLIDING GLASS
PANEL
SUNSHADE

PANEL FRONT AND REAR
SUPPORTS AND
ATTACHING NUTS

SLIDING GLASS
FINISHING
COVER

SLIDING SUNSHADE
HANDLE

Fig. 22-61. *A sun roof panel assembly. (Courtesy of Fisher Body Division, General Motors Corporation)*

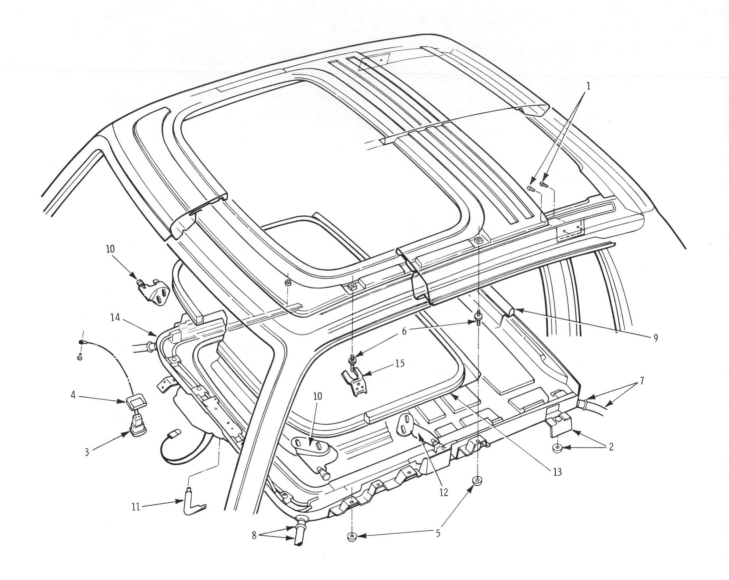

1. Side Roof Rail Support Attaching Screws
2. Side Roof Rail to Housing Support and Attaching Nut
3. Switch
4. Headlining at Switch Retainer
5. Housing to Roof Attaching Nut
6. Roof to Housing Screw
7. Rear Drain Hose and Attaching Clamp
8. Front Drain Hose and Attaching Clamp
9. Housing Weatherstrip
10. Sliding Panel Front Support
11. Manual Crank
12. Sliding Panel Rear Support
13. Sliding Panel
14. Housing
15. Roof Reinforcement to Side Rail Front and Rear Support

Fig. 22-62. *An electrically operated sun roof. (Courtesy of Fisher Body Division, General Motors Corporation)*

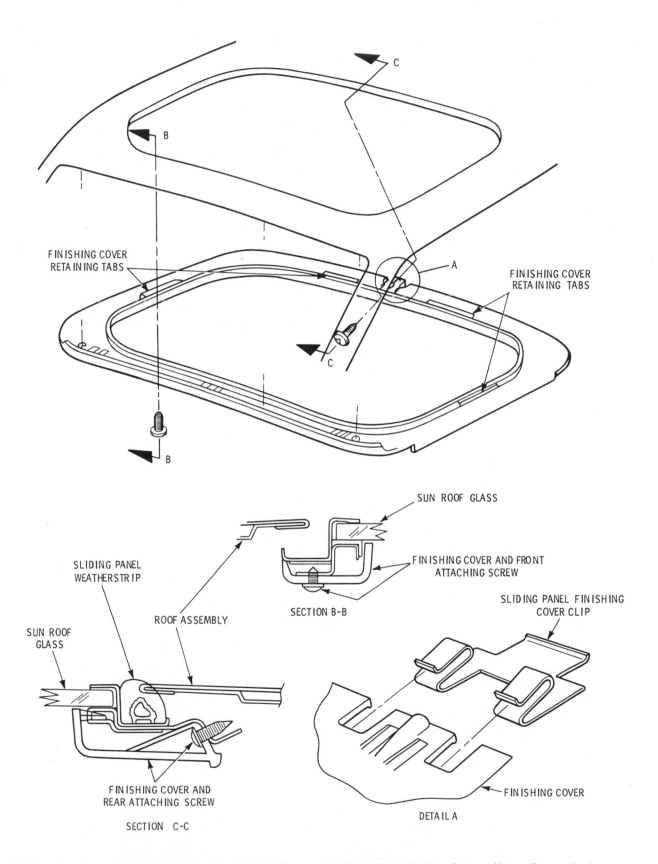

FINISHING COVER
RETAINING TABS

A

FINISHING COVER
RETAINING TABS

C

B

B

C

SUN ROOF GLASS

SLIDING PANEL
WEATHERSTRIP

FINISHING COVER AND FRONT
ATTACHING SCREW

ROOF ASSEMBLY

SECTION B-B

SLIDING PANEL FINISHING
COVER CLIP

SUN ROOF
GLASS

FINISHING COVER AND
REAR ATTACHING SCREW

FINISHING COVER

SECTION C-C

DETAIL A

Fig. 22-63. *The sun roof glass finishing cover assembly. (Courtesy of Fisher Body Division, General Motors Corporation)*

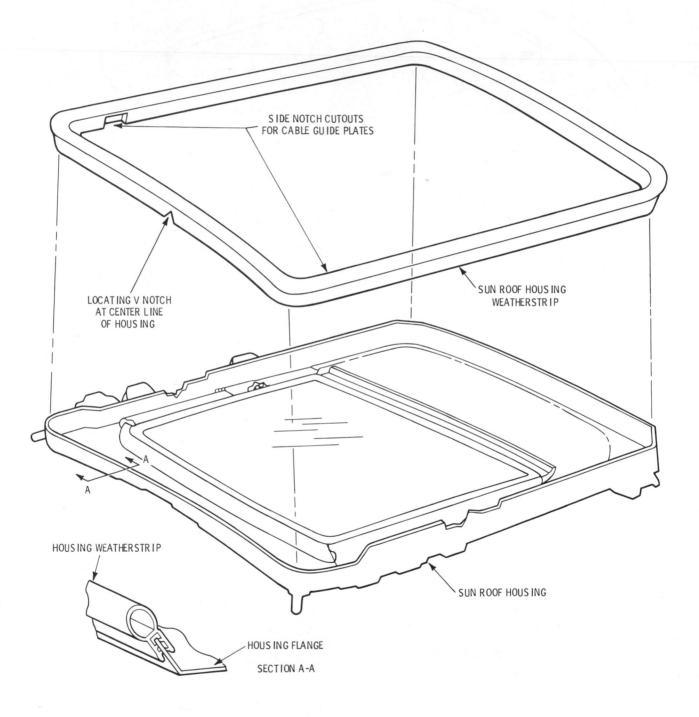

SIDE NOTCH CUTOUTS
FOR CABLE GUIDE PLATES

LOCATING V NOTCH
AT CENTER LINE
OF HOUSING

SUN ROOF HOUSING
WEATHERSTRIP

HOUSING WEATHERSTRIP

SUN ROOF HOUSING

HOUSING FLANGE

SECTION A-A

Fig. 22-64. *The sun roof weatherstrip. (Courtesy of Fisher Body Division, General Motors Corporation)*

Fig. 22-65. *The sun roof in a closed position.*

model vehicles (Fig. 22-69). These tops are manually operated. The glass assemblies are curved to match flush with the roof panel, and are fabricated from tinted tempered glass. The roof weatherstrips are of one-piece construction to fit the roof opening.

The twin lift-off panels can be removed and stored in the rear compartment. Remove the glass by pulling downward on the release handle located at the center of the lift-off panel cover. Place the glass panels in the storage bags to prevent scratching or other damage.

INTERIOR TRIM CLEANING

Cleaning cloth and vinyl interior trim is an important part of auto body work. Most customers expect a thorough repair job and are impressed when a repaired vehicle is returned with "like new" interior trim. Removing any stains and dirt from upholstery adds to customer satisfaction.

Most stains are more easily removed while they are fresh, before they have dried and "set" into the fabric. Clay and mud, however, should be left to dry and may then be brushed off. Removing difficult stains is easier if the *type* of stain is known. The correct cleaning agent then may be used.

When dealing with any stain, use a clean cloth to absorb as much of the liquid as possible. Wipe very lightly with the cleaning agent, working from the outer edges of the stain to the center. Keep turning the cloth so that a *clean* surface is always being used. Depending on the type of stain, use one of the specific procedures outlined below.

Blood

Hot water or soap and water must *not* be used on blood stains. These will set the stain and make removing it all but impossible.

To remove a blood stain, rub it with a clean cloth saturated with *cold water* until no more of the stain will come out. Turn the cloth frequently so that only *clean*

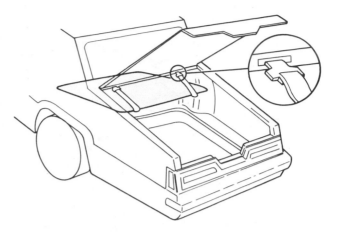

Fig. 22-66. *Storage area for a sun roof glass panel. (Courtesy of Customer Service Division, Ford Motor Company)*

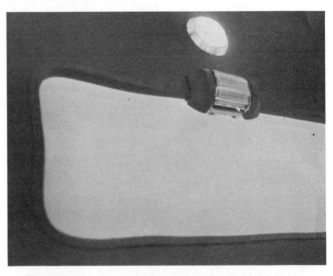

Fig. 22-67. *The sun roof panel from the inside, showing the adjusting handle.*

Fig. 22-68. *The sun roof glass in the raised (vent) position.*

portions are used to rub the stain. If this does not remove all the stain, apply a small amount of household ammonia water to the stain with a cloth or brush. Wait about one minute. Then, continue to rub the stain with a clean cloth dipped in clear, cold water.

If the water and ammonia treatment does not remove the blood, a thick paste of corn starch and cold

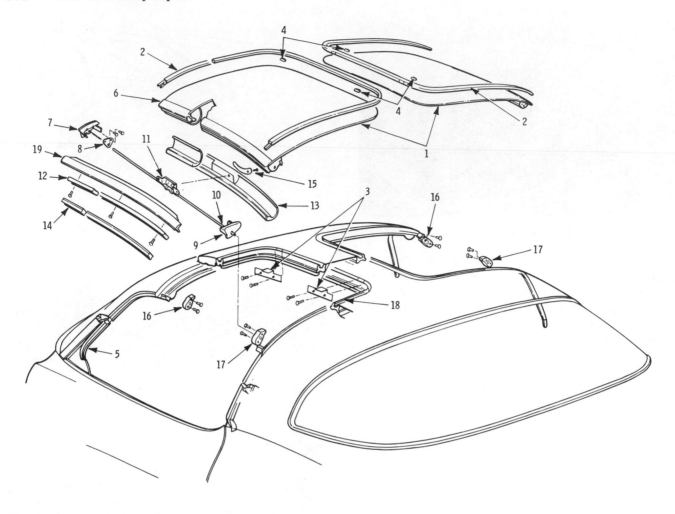

1.	Lift-off Glass	6.	Glass Panel Support	12.	Weatherstrip on Lift-off Panel Retainer	16. Latch Rod Front Guide and Attaching Screws
2.	Twin Lift-off Glass Frame	7.	Front End Plate	13.	Twin Lift-off Panel Cover	17. Latch Rod Rear Guide
3.	Lift-off Glass Frame	8.	Front End Adjusting Plate	14.	Lift-off Panel Weatherstrip	18. Glass Panel Opening Weatherstrip
4.	Frame Grommet	9.	Rear End Plate	15.	Roof Latch Handle and Attaching Screw	19. Drip Molding
5.	Windshield Pillar Weatherstrip Retainer	10.	Rear End Adjusting Plate			
		11.	Latch Assembly			

Fig. 22-69.   *A lift-off panel ("T"-roof) assembly. (Courtesy of Fisher Body Division, General Motors Corporation)*

water may be used. Apply the paste, and allow it to remain until it has dried and absorbed the stain. Then, pick off the dry starch. Brush the surface to remove any starch particles that remain. On very bad stains, several applications of the paste may be necessary.

Candy

Candy stains *not* containing chocolate can usually be removed by rubbing the stain with a cloth soaked in

very hot water. If the stain is not completely removed after the area dries, rub lightly with a cloth wetted in cleaning fluid.

Candy stains due to cream or fruit-filled chocolates can be more easily removed by rubbing with a cloth soaked in lukewarm soapsuds. Then, while the area is wet, scrape it with a dull knife. Follow this treatment by rinsing with a cloth dipped in cold water.

Chocolate stains can be removed by rubbing with a cloth that has been dipped in lukewarm water. After the spot dries, rub it lightly with a cloth dipped in cleaning fluid. Use a clean white blotter to remove excess cleaner and chocolate stain. Do so until stain is no longer transferred to the surface of the blotter.

Chewing Gum

To remove chewing gum, first use an ice cube to harden the gum. Then, scrape off the particles with a dull knife. If the gum cannot be completely removed by this method, moisten it with cleaning fluid and then work it out of the fabric with a dull knife while still moist.

Fruit and Liquor Stains

These stains can usually be removed by treating them with very hot water. Apply hot water to the spot with a clean cloth. Rub the spot vigorously, then allow the fabric to dry.

If this does not remove the stain, rub the stain *lightly* with a clean cloth dipped in cleaning fluid. This is the only further treatment recommended. Soap and water are *not* recommended because they may "set" the stain and cause a permanent discoloration. Using heat to dry the fabric *also* is not recommended.

Grease and Oil

If *grease* is on the material, scrape off as much as possible with a dull knife. Normally, the remaining grease or oil stain may be removed by rubbing it lightly with a clean cloth saturated in cleaning fluid. Be sure to rub toward the *center* of the stained area to avoid spreading the stain. Finally, use a clean white blotter to remove excess cleaner and loosened grease or oil.

Ice Cream

Basically, the procedure recommended for removing ice cream stains is the same as that used to remove fruit stains. However, if the stain is stubborn, rub the spot with a cloth wetted in warm soapsuds *after* the treatment with hot water. Then, rinse the area by rubbing with a clean cloth wetted in cold water. After this dries, lightly rub the area with cleaning fluid on a clean cloth. This will clear up the last of the stain by removing any fatty or oily matter.

Vomit

To remove vomit, sponge the area with a clean cloth dipped in clear, cold water. After most of the stain has been removed, lightly wash the area with mild soap and lukewarm water. Use a clean cloth. If *odor* persists, treat the area with a water and baking soda solution. Use 1 teaspoon baking soda to 1 cup lukewarm water. Then, rub the area with another clean cloth dipped in cold water. If any of the stain remains after this treatment, gently clean with a cloth moistened in cleaning fluid.

Shoe Polish

To remove shoe dressings that contain starch, dextrine, or some water-soluble vehicle, first allow the polish to dry. Then, brush the spot vigorously with a stiff brush. This will probably be all the treatment that is necessary. If further treatment is required, moisten the spot with cold water, and, after it has dried, repeat the brushing.

Paste or wax-type shoe polish stains may require using cleaning fluid. Rub the stain gently with a cloth wetted in cleaning fluid until the polish is removed. Use a clean part of the cloth for each rubbing. Rub the stained area from the outside toward the center. Blot the stained area to remove as much of the cleaner as possible.

Urine

To remove urine stain, first sponge with a clean cloth saturated in lukewarm soapsuds. Then, rinse the area well by rubbing it with a clean cloth dipped in cold water. Saturate another clean cloth with a solution of one part household ammonia to five parts water. Apply this cloth to the stain and allow the solution to remain on the area for 1 minute. Then, rinse the area by rubbing it with a clean, wet cloth.

Lipstick

The composition of different brands of lipsticks varies, making the stains very difficult to remove. For some brands, cleaning fluid may remove the stain. If some stain remains after repeated use of cleaning fluid, it is better to leave the stain than to try other measures.

Unit 23

Automotive Glass Work

Automotive glass and hardware necessary to attach and move it are very important to the safe and comfortable use of a vehicle. The glass and its hardware must be in good condition. Replacing auto body glass is a common body shop job as part of collision repair.

Fig. 23-1. *The largest piece of fixed glass on the automobile is the windshield.*

Fig. 23-2. *Most of the glass in automobile doors is movable glass. Regulators in the door control the up-and-down movement of the glass.*

Sealing glass leaks and replacing and adjusting window regulators are also frequent body shop jobs.

The glass in an auto body may be either *fixed* (such as the windshield glass in Figure 23-1) or *movable* (such as the large side glass in Figure 23-2). Whether movable or fixed, glass that is damaged must be replaced. The replacement procedures differ because fixed and movable glass pieces are fitted to the vehicle's body in different ways.

Fixed glass is designed to stay in one place on the body. The most common pieces of fixed glass are in

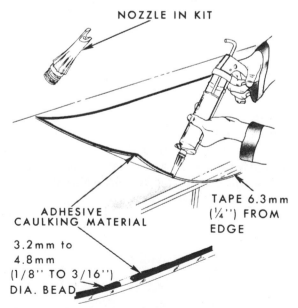

Fig. 23-3. *Adhesive material is often used to hold fixed glass in place. (Courtesy of Fisher Body Division, General Motors Corporation)*

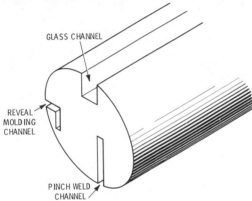

Fig. 23-4. *A rubber channel is sometimes used to hold fixed glass in a window opening. The channel has grooves for the glass, the pinch weld, and the reveal molding.*

Fig. 23-5. *A roll of rubber sealer.*

Fig. 23-6. *Applying rubber sealer to the edges of a new windshield.*

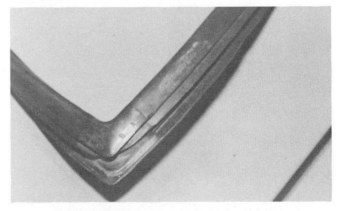

Fig. 23-7. *A rubber channel used to hold fixed glass in place.*

the *windshield* and the *backlight.* Fixed glass parts may be held in position on the body by *adhesive caulking material* (Fig. 23-3) or by *rubber channels* (Fig. 23-4).

Adhesive caulking compound is used on both the windshield and backlight (rear window) of most late-model cars and some small trucks. This sealer is a self-curing rubber adhesive material, and it is fairly sticky and gummy.

Another type of material for installing fixed glass is called *rubber tape sealer.* It usually comes in rolls about 10 ft (3.0 m) long (Fig. 23-5). In Figure 23-6, a roll of rubber sealer is being applied to the edge of a windshield. Some fixed side glass pieces are held in place with rubber tape and sealed with adhesive caulking.

Many auto body repair workers refer to rubber tape seal as butyl rubber, rubber tape, rubber seal, and other names.

On most older cars, a few newer cars, and many trucks, fixed glass is held in place with a *rubber channel* (Fig. 23-7). This channel is molded with grooves on each side. The *inside* groove is the one into which the glass fits. The *outside* groove (Fig. 23-8) fits around

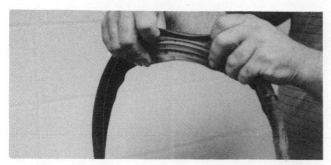

Fig. 23-8. *The groove in a rubber channel that holds the window glass in place.*

DAMAGED MOLDING

Fig. 23-9. *The windshield glass and the side molding have both been damaged and will be replaced.*

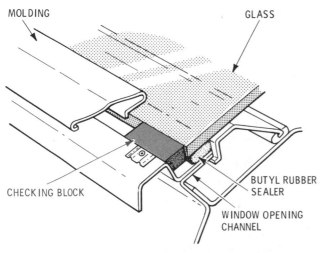

MOLDING

GLASS

CHECKING BLOCK

BUTYL RUBBER SEALER

WINDOW OPENING CHANNEL

Fig. 23-10. *Parts of a windshield installation using rubber tape sealer. Checking blocks are used to position the glass in the opening. (Courtesy of Customer Service Division, Ford Motor Company)*

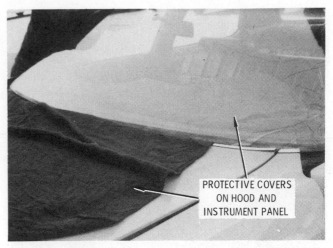

PROTECTIVE COVERS ON HOOD AND INSTRUMENT PANEL

Fig. 23-11. Step 1: *Place protective covers on the hood and the instrument panel.*

Fig. 23-12. Step 2: *Remove the moldings around the windshield, inside and outside the car. If antenna wires are in the glass, disconnect the leads beneath the cowl.*

the opening in the metal body. Thus, the rubber seal has one groove for the body and one for the glass.

When fixed glass pieces or rubber channel are damaged, a body shop may have to make the repair or replacement as part of normal repair work. If the glass pieces are not installed and sealed correctly, serious water and dust leaks may result.

FIXED GLASS

If glass is damaged in a collision, it must be removed and replaced (Fig. 23-9). During most body shop repairs of this type, one basic procedure may be used for all jobs. Although other methods are available, learning this basic procedure will be the easiest way to handle all the *fixed glass/rubber tape* jobs that come

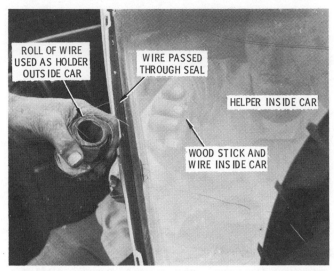

Fig. 23-13. Step 3, Method A: *Cutting of the rubber seal around the old windshield can be done by forcing a wire through the material at one side of the windshield. The inside end of the wire is wrapped around a stick and the outside end around another stick (or the roll of wire itself) to serve as a handle. With a helper working inside, the wire is pulled tight and slid along the windshield edge to cut the rubber seal.*

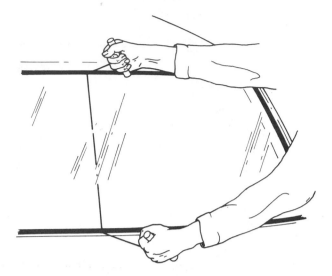

Fig. 23-14. Step 3, Method B: *By pushing the wire through to the inside, then back out again at the opposite end of the windshield, the seal can be cut by one worker from the outside.*

Fig. 23-15. Step 3, Method C: *A special knife may be inserted through the sealing material and pulled around the edges of the windshield to cut the seal.*

into the shop. Figures 23-10 through 23-25 show the correct procedure for replacing a windshield held in place with rubber tape. After the new windshield is in place and caulked, it should be tested for water leaks before moldings are installed.

Small hard rubber *checking blocks* are used on designs using rubber tape. Checking blocks help hold the glass in position inside the opening. Figure 23-10 shows a checking block in position on a window held in place with rubber tape. When replacing a fixed glass held in place with rubber tape *the checking blocks must always be in the correct position before the glass is permanently installed.*

Replacing Fixed Glass—Rubber Channel Seal

If either the glass or the rubber channel seal are damaged in a collision, the glass must be removed to repair the damage. A common procedure uses a putty knife and heavy cord to replace fixed glass held with a rubber channel. Figures 23-26 through 23-31 show the basic procedure for replacing a fixed glass with a rubber channel seal. After the new glass or channel is installed, the installation should be checked for leaks before the moldings are reinstalled.

MOVABLE GLASS

Movable glass pieces include those windows that can be raised or lowered (Fig. 23-32). The rear glass in many station wagons also is movable. Most movable

glass pieces can be moved up or down, except *vent windows*. Vent windows, on cars so equipped, can be moved in or out to allow more or less air inside the vehicle. Figure 23-33 shows a typical vent window assembly.

Movable glass pieces must have some type of *regulator* to move the glass up and down. Regulators are either *manual* or *power-operated*. Figure 23-34 shows a typical *manual regulator*.

The glass in a movable window is attached, usually at the bottom, to the regulator assembly. To do this, some designs use a *channel*, as shown in Figure 23-35. Other designs have the glass itself *bolted* to the regulator by plastic-covered bolts or bushings through holes near the bottom of the glass. This design is shown in Figure 23-36.

The opening all around the inside and the outside edges of a movable glass piece must be trimmed with

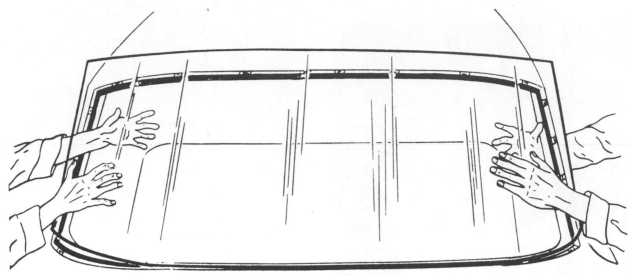

Fig. 23-16. Step 4: *The windshield is removed with the help of a second worker. If the glass is intact and will be reused, it should be rested on a soft surface to prevent damage. (Courtesy of Fisher Body Division, General Motors Corporation)*

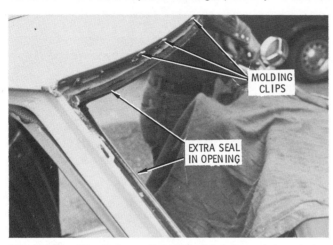

Fig. 23-17. Step 5: *Inspect molding clips around the window opening, and replace or repair them as needed. Check the window opening and make any needed repairs.*

Fig. 23-19. Step 7: *Thoroughly clean the windshield opening, removing old rubber seal and caulking material. Use denatured alcohol for a final cleaning of the opening.*

Fig. 23-18. Step 6: *Temporarily position the glass in the opening. Shift it until a fairly equal gap is visible on all sides, shimming or shaving the checking blocks if necessary. When it is in position, place strips of masking tape on each side as shown. Slit the tape between the glass and the frame. When the window is permanently installed, these pieces of tape will serve as alignment marks.*

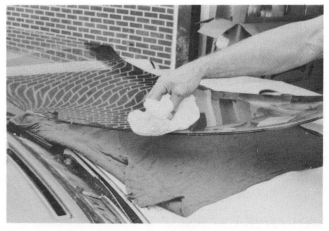

Fig. 23-20. Step 8: *Thoroughly clean the glass. If a used windshield is being installed, use a razor blade to cut away any old seal still adhering to the glass. As a final cleaning step, wipe the glass edges with denatured alcohol.*

Fig. 23-21. Step 9: *Carefully position the rubber sealing tape along the edges of the windshield. Leave the paper backing in place until all edges have been covered. Follow specific directions packaged with the tape.*

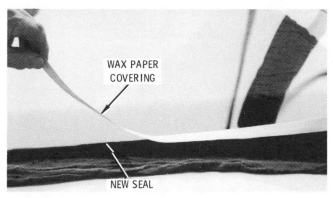

Fig. 23-22. Step 10: *Remove the wax paper backing material from the tape.*

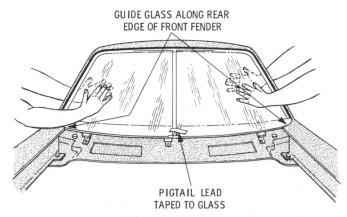

Fig. 23-23. Step 11: *With a helper, lift the windshield and carefully position it in the opening. Use the masking tape marks for correct alignment. Position the glass before allowing the sticky rubber seal to touch the metal around the opening. Once the rubber seal is in contact with the metal, the glass cannot be shifted.*

Fig. 23-24. Step 12: *Using the heel of your hand, carefully pound all around the edges of the windshield to be sure of good adhesion.*

Fig. 23-25. *After installing a new windshield, make a water test to detect leaks. If any are found, apply windshield sealer.*

Fig. 23-26. Step 1: *To replace a broken rear window held in place by a rubber channel, first remove any moldings around the glass.*

some type of soft material. Normally, felt or rubber is used to form this "pad" around the window opening (Fig. 23-37). This padding helps prevent the glass from breaking as a result of hitting the metal around the glass opening. The felt or rubber strips also help seal out water and wind and help prevent rattles by holding the glass tight around the top and sides.

Fig. 23-27. Step 2: *Use a putty knife or heavy fiber stick to pry the rubber channel away from the pinch-weld, all around the opening.*

Fig. 23-28. Step 3: *Once the channel is free of the pinch-weld, remove the window from the opening.*

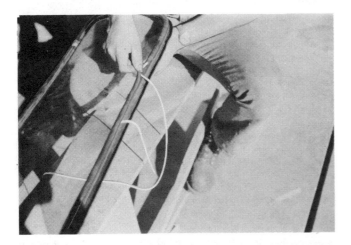

Fig. 23-29. Step 4: *Prepare the new glass for installation. Clean glass edges and the pinch-weld flange around the opening. Slip the rubber channel onto the glass edges, and tuck a heavy cord into the pinch-weld groove, as shown. The cord should be well inside the groove all the way around the window, with the ends hanging out as shown. Lubricating the cord and pinch-weld groove with soap or soapy water may make the installation easier.*

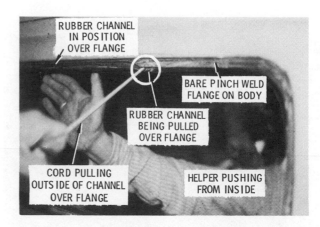

RUBBER CHANNEL IN POSITION OVER FLANGE

BARE PINCH WELD FLANGE ON BODY

RUBBER CHANNEL BEING PULLED OVER FLANGE

CORD PULLING OUTSIDE OF CHANNEL OVER FLANGE

HELPER PUSHING FROM INSIDE

Fig. 23-30. Step 5: *Place the window and rubber channel in the opening, slipping the bottom groove over the pinch-weld flange. The ends of the cord should extend outside the window, as shown in the circle. By pulling on the cord, you will force the rubber channel over the flange.*

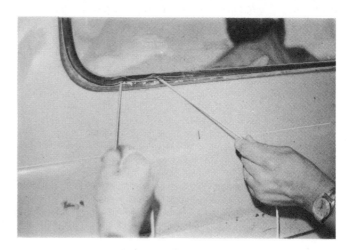

Fig. 23-31. Step 5, continued: *The last few inches (centimeters) of channel being forced over the pinch-weld flange by pulling on the cord.*

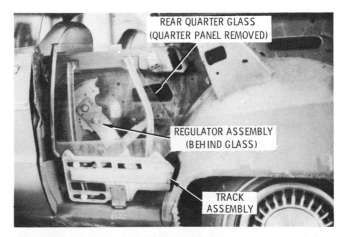

REAR QUARTER GLASS (QUARTER PANEL REMOVED)

REGULATOR ASSEMBLY (BEHIND GLASS)

TRACK ASSEMBLY

Fig. 23-32. *The rear quarter glass and regulator assembly. The quarter panel has been removed for visibility.*

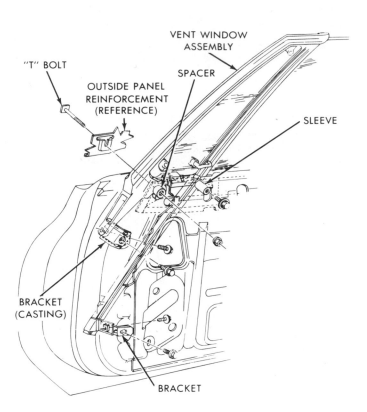

Fig. 23-33. *A typical vent window assembly. (Chrysler Corporation)*

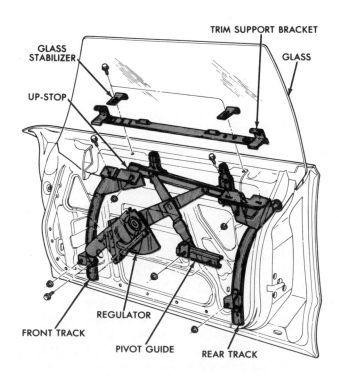

Fig. 23-34. *Parts of a typical manual regulator assembly. (Courtesy of Chrysler Corporation)*

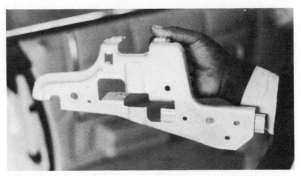

Fig. 23-35. *A plastic bracket used to hold the glass to the regulator.*

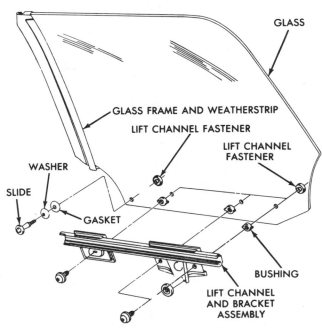

Fig. 23-36. *Some movable glass is held to the regulator track (lift channel) by bolts that pass through the glass itself. (Courtesy of Chrysler Corporation)*

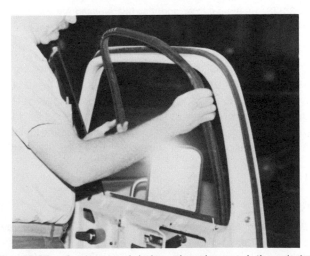

Fig. 23-37. *A glass pad being placed around the window opening.*

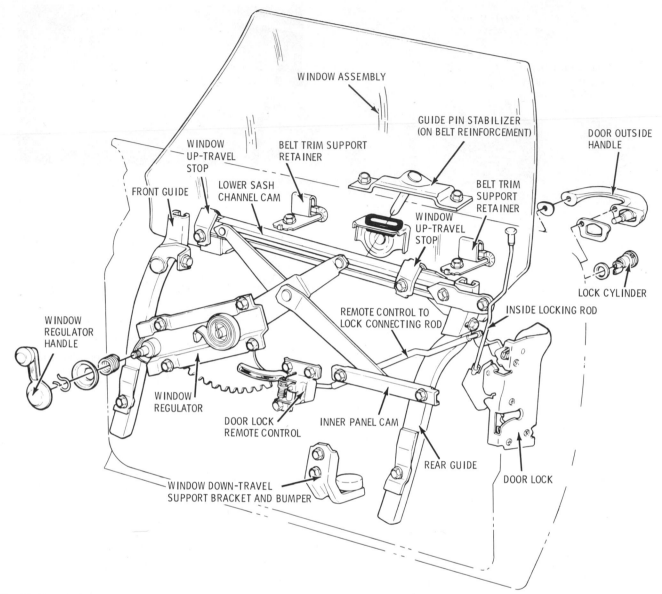

Fig. 23-38. *A typical front door hardware assembly. Most of the hardware forms the regulator assembly. (Courtesy of Fisher Body Division, General Motors Corporation)*

Glass *hardware* includes all the parts needed to hold or move the glass in the body. The largest pieces of glass hardware are regulator assemblies. These are the mechanisms that move the glass up and down. The regulators are normally located between the outer door panel and the inner door, or in the quarter panels. Figure 23-38 shows typical window regulator assembly and door lock parts.

Regulators

All window regulators do basically the same job. They move the glass up or down and hold the glass in position once it is moved. Different automobile manufacturers have slightly different types of regulators, depending on the car and window glass design. Even so, important parts of all regulator designs are the metal guides "tracks" that hold the glass in alignment as it moves up and down.

Manual Door Regulators. Manual regulators are standard equipment on most cars. The mechanism is fairly simple, as in Figure 23-38. Turning the crank (regulator) handle moves the regulator arm, causing it to push up or pull down on the front of the lift channel and glass. On some designs, a *second* arm holds the lift channel in alignment so that the window and glass do not "cock" in the door and become jammed.

Power Door Regulators. Power regulators work much like manual regulators and do the same basic job. The main difference is that power regulators have an elec-

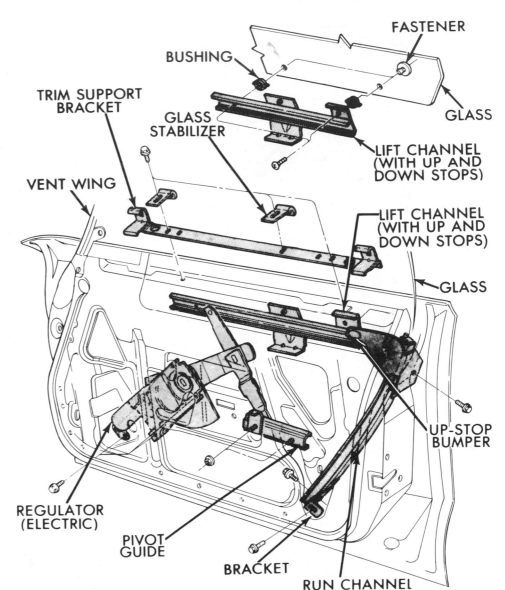

FASTENER

BUSHING

GLASS

TRIM SUPPORT
BRACKET

GLASS
STABILIZER

LIFT CHANNEL
(WITH UP AND
DOWN STOPS)

VENT WING

LIFT CHANNEL
(WITH UP AND
DOWN STOPS)

GLASS

UP-STOP
BUMPER

REGULATOR
(ELECTRIC)

PIVOT
GUIDE

BRACKET

RUN CHANNEL

Fig. 23-39. *A door assembly that includes a power (electric) window regulator assembly. (Courtesy of Chrysler Corporation)*

tric motor to turn the regulator shaft. Figure 23-39 shows a typical power regulator ("power window") installation. ***Quarter Glass Regulators.*** Rear quarter window regulators are generally similar to door glass regulators. However, *some* designs have important differences from door regulator designs. This is because some quarter windows move up and down in a *curved* path rather than *straight* up and down. For example, note that the quarter glass regulator in Figure 23-40 has curved guides and that they are positioned at an angle. This is designed so that the glass will curve as it travels up and down.

Movable Glass Repairs

During ordinary collision work, or as a result or normal wear and tear, repairs to movable glass parts may be needed. The exact procedure for making these repairs will vary from one make or model to another, so it is almost impossible to outline all the details of each repair. However, the *general* procedure for each repair may be discussed. If a shop manual is not available for the specific make and model of car being worked on, then you must carefully reason out the exact procedure to use. Understanding the general procedure will help you to better "think out" the details of each different job.

There are four general repairs that may be needed during automotive glass work on doors and movable glass parts.

1. Replacing regulators.
2. Adjusting regulators.
3. Replacing glass (channel type).
4. Replacing glass (through-bolt type).

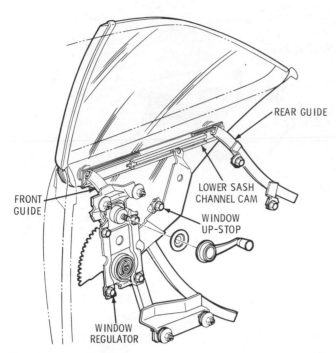

Fig. 23-40. *A typical quarter window regulator assembly. (Courtesy of Fisher Body Division, General Motors Corporation)*

Replacing Regulators. When replacing regulators, it is helpful to remember that the lift channel (track) is *not* a permanent part of the regulator itself. Therefore, installing a new regulator does not necessarily mean that you must remove or replace the lift channel. As a general procedure, follow these steps to replace a regulator assembly:

1. Remove the door or quarter-panel *trim pad*, as discussed in the Trim Work unit.
2. Carefully remove and set aside the *water dam* (moisture cover) behind the trim panel.
3. With the trim panel and water dam removed, study the door assembly *before* removing any screws. For example, notice the regulator attaching screws and parts in Figures 23-34, 23-38, and 23-39. Determine which screws hold the regulator assembly itself and which screws hold the other parts of the door and window mechanism.
4. Raise the window to a point where the lift channel screws can be reached though the door panel *access hole*. On most door assemblies, this will be with the window about three-fourths up.
5. Disconnect the glass, and lift channel assembly from the regulator arms.
6. Grasp the glass on both sides, and raise it up out of the way. It may be necessary to remove the *up-stops* to do this.
7. Use a screwdriver or similar tool to *hold* the glass and lift channel up, out of the way. Usually, the screwdriver can be placed through a hole some-

where near the top of the inner door panel to hold the glass up.
8. Remove the regulator mounting screws.
9. Move the regulator around as needed to disengage the regulator arm rollers from their channels.
10. Remove the regulator through an access hole in the door.

To install the new regulator, reverse the basic procedure outlined above. Be sure to lubricate the roller and lift channels with a good amount of white grease before installing the new regulator. Unless the regulator itself is mounted in slotted holes (many of them are not), no regulator adjustment should be necessary.

Adjusting Regulators. Before adjusting a regulator and the glass attached to it, the door itself *must be correctly fitted in its opening.* Also, the weatherstrip surrounding the door and glass must be properly installed. When working on a car with no center post (a "hardtop"), the front glass should be adjusted *before* the rear glass is adjusted.

Correctly adjusting a regulator may include adjusting regulator *pivot guide tracks,* track *brackets, up-stops,* and (if so equipped) *stabilizer bars.* Again, the exact location, method of attachment, and method of adjustment of these parts will vary from one make and model to the next. However, if you understand the general procedure and the reason why certain adjustments are made, it will be easier to "figure out" and adjust any given regulator.

Before adjusting a regulator, *locate all the screws or bolts used to attach the above parts.* Place the tools needed to loosen the fasteners (screws or bolts) in the work area. However, do not completely loosen or remove the fasteners until necessary. The following steps outline how to adjust the regulator shown in Figure 23-41. (Of course, the trim panel and water dam must be first removed before adjusting the regulator.)

1. Raise the glass until it is 1/8 in. (3.2 mm) from the weatherstrip at the top of the window opening.
2. Loosen the nuts at the *pivot guide.* Adjust the guide up or down until the top of the glass is *parallel to the top weatherstrip.* Tighten the pivot guide nuts.
3. Use the regulator to raise the glass to the "full up" position.
4. Locate the *track* that is nearest the adjoining glass or post edge. In this example, it is the front track. Adjust this track at its *upper* bracket so that the front edge of the glass (or molding attached to the glass) contacts the adjoining glass or post when the glass is in the *full up* position.
5. Lower the window to about one-fourth up.
6. Adjust the stabilizer bracket to position the outer edge of the glass just against the rubber molding at the top outside edge of the door.

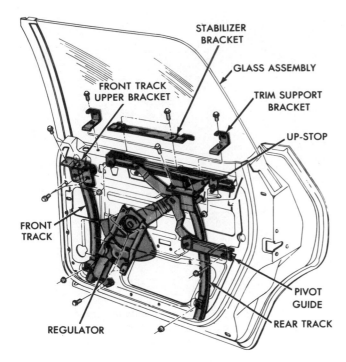

Fig. 23-41. *A typical regulator assembly used with frameless window glass. (Courtesy of Chrysler Corporation)*

7. Raise the window to the *full up* position.
8. Loosen the upper and lower track bracket screws on both tracks.
9. Position the *inside* edge at the *top* of the glass so that it firmly contacts the weatherstrip for a good seal.
10. Tighten all the track bracket screws.
11. With the window still up, adjust both *up-stops* down against the top of the channel and bracket assembly at the bottom edge of the glass. Tighten the up-stop retaining nuts.
12. Operate the regulator through one cycle (glass full up to full down and back) to check the effort required. Watch for interference in the "scissors" action of the window regulator arms. Readjust if necessary.

Replacing Glass (Channel Type). If damaged glass is held in place by a *metal channel*, the glass and channel together must be removed from the inner door panel. Then, a new piece of glass may be installed in the channel. The channel and the new glass then may be reinstalled in the door. Figures 23-42 through 23-47 show the procedure used.

Replacing Glass (Through-bolt Type). Replacing a window glass held with *through-bolts* is easier than replacing a window held in a channel. Glass held with through-bolts (Figs. 23-36 and 23-38) must be carefully handled and installed, however. This is because almost all the sides of the glass are exposed. Since side glass

Fig. 23-42. Step 1: *To replace a window held in a metal channel, first remove the inner trim panel to expose the regulator and lower edge of the glass.*

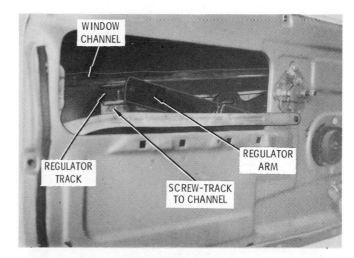

Fig. 23-43. Step 2: *Remove the track-to-channel screws, which hold the regulator track to the window channel.*

Fig. 23-44. Step 3: *Remove the window glass and metal channel assembly from the door. It may be necessary to tilt the window, as shown.*

Fig. 23-45. Step 4: *Remove the broken glass from the window channel. Place the glass and channel in a vise, and soak the old sealer tape with lacquer thinner. When the tape has been softened, use a screwdriver to pry out the glass pieces.*

Fig. 23-47. Step 6: *Fit the channel onto the taped edge of the glass, and use a piece of wood to tap it into place gently. Replace the channel and the glass in the door.*

Fig. 23-46. Step 5: *Clean the metal channel and the glass thoroughly. Place a new piece of sealer tape along the bottom edge of the glass, and fold it over along the sides.*

is *tempered*, a slight chip on one exposed edge could shatter the entire glass. The bushings and bolts must be carefully installed and tighened to avoid placing stress on the glass.

The procedure is similar to that used to replace glass held with a channel. The trim panel is first removed, and the regulator track is separated from the regulator mechanism. Then, the window and track (also known as the *lift channel*) both may be removed from the door or quarter panel. Finally, the track is unbolted from the old glass and bolted to the new glass.

Section VII

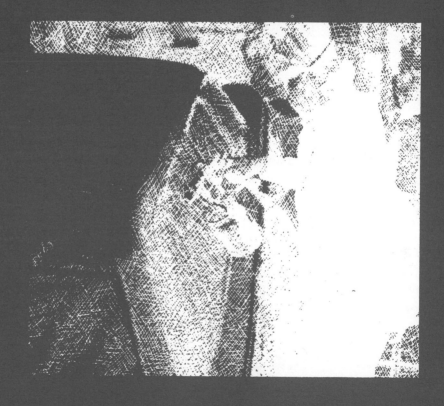

Automotive Painting

Automotive Painting and Equipment

An automobile would not be very attractive if it were not for the topcoat. It would be drab and would rust very shortly after leaving the factory. Obviously, an automobile's finish (topcoat) is a very important factor in making the car attractive and protecting it from rust and corrosion. Because an automobile's topcoat is so important, paint work is a vital part of auto body repair.

Anyone who chooses to make a specialty of automobile refinishing will find that the choice is a good one. Automobile refinishing and paint work has become one of the most important jobs in the auto body repair industry. Thousands of complete repaint jobs are done in body shops each year. An example is the newly repainted automobile drying in the paint booth in Figure 24-1. Equally important is the painting of only *part* of a car, as in Figure 24-2. This is often more difficult because the painter must *match* the new color to the older color already on the car.

A BRIEF HISTORY OF FACTORY FINISHES

In a body repair shop, the types of paints used must be changed to keep up with changes in the paints used at the *factory* by automobile manufacturers. As manufacturer's paint ("factory paint") changes, older types of paint and material may not work well with the new material being used. For this reason, the auto body refinishing business, also known as the "aftermarket," must change with the automobile industry.

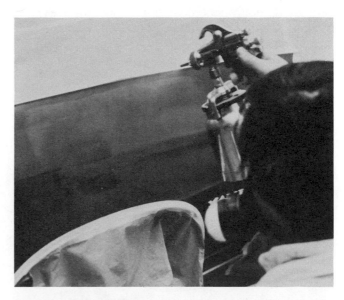

Fig. 24-2. *When repainting only a part of a panel on a car, color matching is a critical skill. (Courtesy of Rinshed–Mason Products Division, Inmont Corporation)*

Fig. 24-1. *A completely repainted vehicle drying inside a paint booth. (Courtesy of Binks Manufacturing Company)*

Early Factory Finishes

The very first automobiles, such as the restored antique car in Figure 24-3, were painted with a *brush*. Lampblack color and varnish were used for the painting process. *Lampblack* is the very fine, black pigment of *carbon*. Originally, lampblack was collected as *soot* from the smoke of burning oil and other materials.

On these early factory jobs, each painter applied several coats of paint with a brush. Each coat was given plenty of *flash-off* time before the next was applied. Flash-off time is the amount of time needed for the thinner to evaporate from the paint. However, the paint does not dry thoroughly in this period of time.

After each coat, the paint had to be sanded to a smooth finish with water and *pumice* (finely ground volcanic rock). After the last coat had thoroughly dried, *wax* was rubbed over and into the finish. This method of painting usually took about 30 days. The process was not very adaptable to mass production, since it was very time-consuming.

Later Factory Finishes

In the 1920s, the DuPont Company developed an entirely new type of finish. It was named *Duco*. This was the first type of modern *lacquer finish*, and it is technically known as *nitrocellulose lacquer*. Duco was applied with a spray gun instead of a brush, greatly speeding up automobile body manufacturing.

Later, in the 1930s, the first enamels were developed. These were known as *alkyd* enamels and were extremely tough, making them good for use on trucks as well as on cars. Alkyd enamels dry with a high shine, so they do not require buffing to a high shine as does lacquer. Alkyd enamels and nitrocellulose lacquers were used well into the 1950s.

Fig. 24-3. *An antique car (1908 REO). The original paint work on this car was done with brushes.*

Current Factory Finishes

During the 1950s, the paint products used on most of today's cars and trucks were developed. These include *acrylic* lacquers and *acrylic* enamels. The first of these to be developed was acrylic *lacquer*. General Motors began painting all their new cars with acrylic lacquer in the late 1950s. They have continued to do so into the 1980s.

Following developmental work in the 1950s, acrylic *enamels* were introduced in 1963. Acrylic enamel gradually replaced the older *alkyd* enamel on production lines. Today, all cars made in the United States are finished in either acrylic lacquer or acrylic enamel. Almost all the paint repair done in a body shop will be done with one of these two products. These paints are discussed in a later unit.

PAINTING EQUIPMENT

No matter what type of paint is being applied, several basic pieces of *painting equipment* are needed. The size and amount of any shop's paint equipment depends largely on the volume of business. A smaller shop, for example, may need only one *paint booth* (Fig. 24-4).

To dry new paint properly, some shops have *heating ovens* to heat the surface, helping it to dry. Behind the paint booth in Figure 24-4, for example, is a large heating oven. Figure 24-5 shows a smaller bank of "heaters" with infrared elements. These would be used for spot-drying both primer–surfacer and topcoat repairs.

Other equipment needed for auto body refinishing will be the *exhaust fans* discussed in an earlier unit. These provide air circulation for good health and safety. Refinishing work also requires many tools and pieces of equipment, including the air compressors and separator–regulators discussed earlier. "Paint work only" tools include the paint spray gun and (in some shops) a paint thickness meter used to measure the thickness of paint film on a vehicle.

Paint Booth

The size of a shop's paint booth (or booths) depends on the amount of refinishing business that the shop does. A large shop may have a large paint booth that can turn out more than one paint job per day. The large paint booth in Figure 24-4 is designed for *spraying* the vehicle in one compartment (toward the front) and then *drying* the vehicle in another compartment (toward the rear). This allows two vehicles to be refinished at the same time.

The paint booth shown in Figures 24-4 and 24-6 provides a *totally enclosed* room in which to paint and dry an automobile or small truck. All the features of this booth make it ideal for fast, top-quality automotive refinishing. Controls for the dryers, ventilation, and other features are mounted *outside* the booth. Having the controls outside allows the dryers and other features to be controlled without having to enter the booth itself.

Lighting. To be able to do good work, an automotive painter must have plenty of *light*. This is necessary so that the painter can see exactly how the paint is going on and how the color is matching. Figure 24-7 shows the fluorescent light fixtures on the side and top of the booth shown in Figures 24-4 and 24-6.

Note that the lights are mounted *outside* the booth so that they shine *inside* the booth. This is done as a safety precaution. Fumes from automotive paint are very flammable and may explode if they are exposed to a spark. For this reason, the best paint booth designs have all the electric wiring and light fixtures *outside* the paint room itself. The front sides of the lights themselves are sealed so that no paint fumes can enter the fixture.

Ventilating and Filtering. While a car is being painted, there must be a constant flow of clean, fresh air in the paint room. This is necessary to remove paint particles and fumes from the air. If air was not "pulled through" as the painter sprayed the paint, it would soon be so thick with paint particles that it would be difficult to see the car being painted.

Deluxe paint booths have filters built into the sides *and* doors of the booth itself. Many shops have filters in only the *door* of the paint room. In either case, the filters are usually a woven mat of hairlike fiberglass (Fig. 24-8). These filters are designed to be replaced easily. How often they are replaced depends on the amount of paint work done in the shop *and* on how dirty the shop's air is normally. However, they must always be replaced regularly.

To pull the air through the filter and paint room, some type of *exhaust fan* is needed. (In many areas, health and safety regulations require that a certain amount of air per minute be circulated through paint booths.) An exhaust fan Figure 24-9, should be "standard equipment" in any body shop. The fan should be large enough to remove paint dust and fumes quickly from the paint booth. Deluxe paint booths have built-in exhaust fans and air supply ducts.

A paint booth or room without an exhaust fan allows paint dust to settle onto the fresh paint and causes the

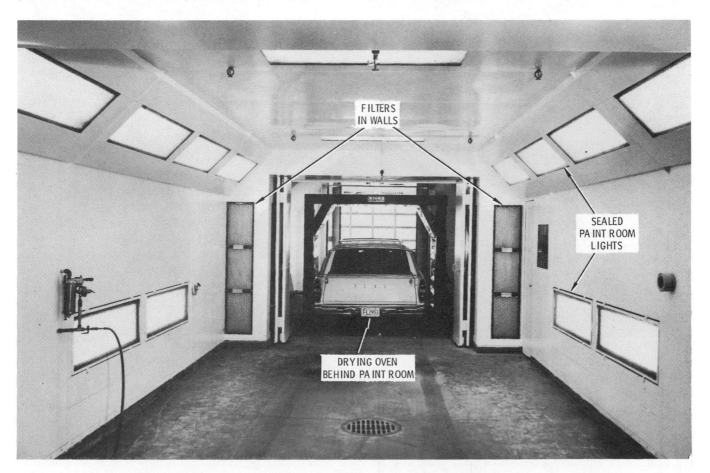

Fig. 24-4. *A typical paint booth and drying oven. (Courtesy of Binks Manufacturing Company)*

Fig. 24-5. *A bank of infrared heaters used to dry paint on panels or spot repairs. (Courtesy of Refinish Division, DuPont Company)*

paint to *dull*. Without an exhaust fan, the shop may also have trouble with paint not drying (evaporating) correctly. Both lacquer and enamel paints need a good supply of fresh air to dry properly, even after the spraying has been done. If the paint room does not have the needed supply of fresh air, the paint may go flat, lack gloss, or be off-color.

Paint-measuring Meter

Many shops have a *paint-measuring meter*, such as the one shown in Figure 24-10. This instrument is used to determine the thickness of the paint on a vehicle. This meter works on electricity and a type of magnetic action. It measures the thickness of the paint and any body filler by "sensing" the magnetic pull of the metal *under* the paint and filler. If the paint and filler are *thick*,

Fig. 24-6. *A paint booth that provides a totally enclosed environment for top-quality finishing work. (Courtesy of Binks Manufacturing Company)*

the magnetic pull will not be as great as if they are thin. The meter then changes this "pull" to read the approximate thickness of the filler or the paint.

The thickness of paint (or paint and filler) is measured in *mils*. A mil equals 1/1000 of an inch (0.025 mm). The paint thickness on most new cars is about 3 mils (0.075 mm). This is the total thickness of the primer and the topcoats (color coats). During auto refinish work, the total thickness should be no more than about 7 mils (0.175 mm) after the new paint has been applied. Paint that is thicker than this may tend to crack.

Fig. 24-7. *All electrical wiring is outside the booth, and lighting is provided through sealed windows (fixtures are at lower left) to provide maximum safety from explosions. (Courtesy of Binks Manufacturing Company)*

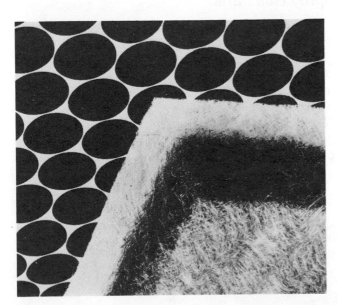

Fig. 24-8. *A fine fiberglass material is used to make the air filters for paint booths. (Courtesy of PPG Industries, Inc.)*

Air Supply System

Important equipment for autmotive refinishing is the shop's *air supply system*. The system includes the air compressor, the air lines, the air separator–regulators, and the air hoses. These pieces of equipment are thoroughly described elsewhere. Their job of providing the shop with a good supply of clean, dry air is very important for quality auto body refinishing. For this reason, *a good auto body painter must know about and properly maintain the air supply system to the paint room*.

Fig. 24-9. *A paint booth exhaust fan, as viewed from the outside of the building. A safety screen would normally be placed in front of the blades. (Courtesy of DeVilbiss Company)*

Fig. 24-10. *A meter for measuring paint thickness. (Courtesy of PPG Industries, Inc.)*

Paint Hoses. The air hose *from* the separator–regulator *to* the spray gun is an important part of the air supply system. *Regular shop air hose must not be used for this job.* Special *paint room* air hoses should be used for best results. The special hose is smoother inside and will not lose pressure over the length of the hose as easily as will regular shop air hose. Figure 24-11 shows paint room air hoses from one manufacturer.

Paint room hoses are available in *two* basic inside diameters: ¼ in. and 5⁄16 in. (6.4 and 7.9 mm). For best results, only 5⁄16 in. (7.9 mm) hose should be used. Regardless of hose diameter, air pressure will be lost between the regulator and the spray gun. How *much* pressure is lost depends on three factors:

1. The *hose diameter.* A smaller hose loses more pressure than a larger hose.
2. The *age* of the hose. An older hose will lose more pressure than a new hose.
3. The *type* of hose connections used. Generally, "quick-change" adapters will lose 1 psi (7 kPa) when compared with threaded, screw-in hose connections.

There are two methods to determine the *actual* air pressure at the gun. The best way is to install an air pressure gauge *at the gun itself* (Fig. 24-12). Then, the air pressure at the gun may be compared with the air pressure at the regulator (Fig. 24-13). By using this method, the exact air pressure drop will be known.

The *second* method to determine the air pressure at the gun is to use Table 10. In this table, the approximate air pressure drop is listed for hoses of different diameters. These figures are for *new* hose. Older hose will likely have an even greater pressure drop than listed in the table. In any case, it is always important for the painter to know the exact air pressure *at the gun* for the hose being used.

Spray Guns

The most important tool in the paint department is the *spray gun*. All good automotive painters have mastered the skill of using a spray gun. This skill can be learned only by practice.

Spray guns are built to do one basic job: to break up the paint material (liquid) into tiny droplets. To do this, a spray gun needs clean, dry compressed air. It uses the compressed air to pull liquid paint up through a tiny hole or holes. When the paint passes through the holes, it is broken up into the small droplets. This process of breaking the liquid up into droplets is known as *atomizing* the paint.

There are two basic types of spray guns: the *pressure pot* gun and the *siphon* gun. Either gun turns the liquid into a spray of droplets by using air pressure.

Pressure Pot Gun. A pressure pot spray gun (Fig. 24-14) works on compressed air and paint supplied from a "pot." Air pressure forces the paint *from* the pot, out *through* a paint hose, and then *into* the spray gun head. After the paint moves through the hose, it is forced out the paint gun nozzle. When it leaves the nozzle, the liquid is mixed with air, causing a fine spray.

Pressure pot spray guns are not widely used in body shops because they weigh more than siphon guns and are harder to move around. They are more often used in industry.

Siphon Gun. A siphon gun (Fig. 24-15) works on a vacuum (suction) system. For this reason, siphon guns are also known as *suction* guns.

In a siphon gun, air rushes through the *air nozzles*, creating a suction in the *vacuum tube*, as shown on Figure 24-15. This suction pulls the paint from the paint cup into the gun. The liquid paint is sucked out the tip by the compressed air leaving the tip. The air "breaks up" the paint just outside the tip of the gun, making a spray of tiny liquid droplets.

Spray Gun Parts

Either type of spray gun (siphon or pressure pot) has many important features. The principal parts of both guns are the same. Figure 24-16 shows the major parts of an auto body paint spray gun. To clean and adjust the spray gun properly, a painter must know the principal parts described below.

Nozzle (Air) Cap. The nozzle cap directs the compressed air into the stream of paint coming out of the gun. This air is blown into the stream of paint, atomiz-

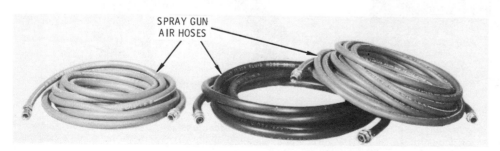

SPRAY GUN
AIR HOSES

Fig. 24-11. *Paint room air hoses. (Courtesy of Binks Manufacturing Company)*

ing the liquid into a spray. The compressed air may be forced through the holes in the nozzle cap horns or through holes around the center of the cap.

Fluid Nozzle. The fluid nozzle is also known as the fluid *tip.* When the fluid nozzle is open, paint can be pulled through it by the air rushing through the nozzle cap holes. When the fluid nozzle is closed, no paint can come out of it. The fluid needle valve is in the center of the nozzle and controls whether the nozzle is open or closed. A painter can change how much the nozzle is open with the trigger or with the *fluid control valve.* The fluid control valve controls the *position* of the fluid *needle* valve.

Fluid Needle Valve. The fluid needle valve controls the flow of paint out of the nozzle. It does this by opening or closing the nozzle. One of the jobs of the *trigger* is to pull back on the fluid needle valve, allowing paint to come out of the nozzle.

How much the trigger can pull back on the needle valve is controlled by the fluid control valve. When the fluid control valve is almost closed, for example, very little paint will come out of the nozzle when the trigger is pulled back. If the fluid control valve is wide open, on the other hand, a large amount of paint will be allowed past the needle valve because the trigger will pull farther back on the needle valve.

Trigger. Spray guns are designed to be adjusted and used *with the trigger all the way open during spraying.* With this feature, a painter does not have to worry about how far back the trigger is pulled. Instead, the proper adjustments (fluid control and pattern control) can be made *before* the paint is applied. Then, the trigger may simply be pulled back all the way and held in that position.

As the trigger is pulled back, it has two "stops." The first is about halfway open. When the trigger is pulled back to this stop, it allows only *air* to pass through the air valve and out the nozzle cap. This is used to blow any "last minute" dust off the vehicle just before the paint is sprayed. When the trigger is pulled open to the second "stop," the fluid needle valve is pulled back. This allows paint to go past the needle valve and out the air nozzle cap.

Air Valve. The air valve, shown open in Figure 24-15, is the main air control valve in the paint gun. When the trigger is pulled back, it opens this valve and allows air to go through the gun's air passages.

Fluid Control Valve. The fluid control valve governs the position of the fluid *needle* valve when the trigger is pulled all the way open. It *presets* the needle valve so that it will be in the position desired when the trigger is pulled all the way back during actual painting.

The fluid control valve is the *bottom* adjustment knob on the back of the spray gun. In Figure 24-17, a painter

is adjusting the fluid control valve. If the job to be done is a small spot repair, the fluid control valve would first be adjusted about halfway open. When a large panel or a complete paint job is to be sprayed, however, the valve may be completely opened for a trial adjustment. In all cases, practice settings should be tested by being sprayed on scrap material before the actual paint work is done.

Pattern Control Valve. The pattern control valve sets the width of the spray pattern. Figure 24-18 shows a pattern control valve (the *upper* knob) being adjusted. A small, round spray pattern is normally used for spot repairs. A large, oblong pattern is used for large panel repairs and for overall paint jobs.

When the pattern control valve is *closed,* the spray pattern is *round,* because the air is coming through the holes around the center of the nozzle cap. As the valve is opened, the spray pattern becomes more oblong (egg-shaped). This is because the air is also coming through the holes in the horns of the nozzle cap. This "blows" the paint up and down as it tries to come straight out.

Safety Equipment

Automotive paint, paint products, and the process of painting can all be very dangerous to good health if common "safety sense" is not used. Paint fumes, for example, can cause headaches and stomachaches. Paint *particles* (small droplets of paint in the air) can cause breathing trouble because they will stick to your

Fig. 24-12. *A gauge installed at the spray gun will give accurate readings of pressure at the gun. (Courtesy of DeVilbiss Company)*

Fig. 24-13. *Checking the drop in air pressure at the end of a paint hose. The workers are comparing readings at the separator–regulator gauge and the gauge on the spray gun.*

Table 10

Approximate Air Pressures at the Gun for Paint Room Hoses of Different Lengths

Hose Diameter	Regulator Pressure—psi (kPa)					Hose Length—ft (m)	
		5 (1.5)	10 (3.0)	15 (4.6)	20 (6.1)	25 (7.6)	50 (15.2)
¼ in. (6.3 mm)	30 (207)	26 (7.9)	24 (7.3)	23 (7.0)	22 (6.7)	21 (6.4)	9 (2.7)
	40 (276)	34 (10.4)	32 (9.8)	31 (9.4)	29 (8.8)	27 (8.2)	16 (6.4)
	50 (345)	43 (13.1)	40 (12.2)	38 (11.6)	36 (11.0)	34 (10.4)	22 (6.7)
	60 (414)	51 (15.5)	48 (14.6)	46 (14.0)	43 (13.1)	41 (12.5)	29 (8.8)
	70 (483)	59 (18.0)	56 (17.1)	53 (16.2)	51 (15.5)	48 (14.6)	36 (11.0)
	80 (552)	68 (20.7)	64 (19.5)	61 (18.6)	58 (17.7)	55 (16.8)	43 (13.1)
	90 (621)	76 (23.2)	71 (21.6)	68 (20.7)	65 (19.8)	61 (18.2)	51 (15.5)
⁵⁄₁₆ in. (7.9 mm)	30 (207)	29 (8.8)	28 (8.5)	28 (8.5)	27 (8.2)	27 (8.2)	23 (7.0)
	40 (276)	38 (11.6)	37 (11.3)	37 (11.3)	37 (11.3)	36 (11.0)	32 (9.8)
	50 (545)	48 (14.6)	47 (14.3)	46 (14.0)	46 (14.0)	45 (13.7)	40 (12.2)
	60 (414)	57 (17.4)	56 (17.1)	55 (16.8)	55 (16.8)	54 (16.5)	49 (14.9)
	70 (483)	66 (20.1)	65 (19.8)	64 (19.5)	63 (19.2)	63 (19.2)	57 (17.4)
	80 (552)	75 (22.9)	74 (22.6)	73 (22.3)	72 (21.9)	71 (21.6)	66 (20.1)
	90 (621)	84 (25.6)	83 (25.3)	82 (25.0)	81 (24.7)	80 (24.4)	74 (22.6)

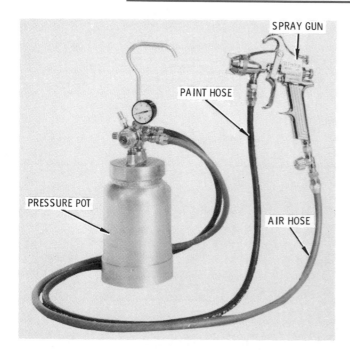

Fig. 24-14. *A pressure pot spray gun. This type of gun is more often used in factory work than in body shops. (Courtesy of Binks Manufacturing Company)*

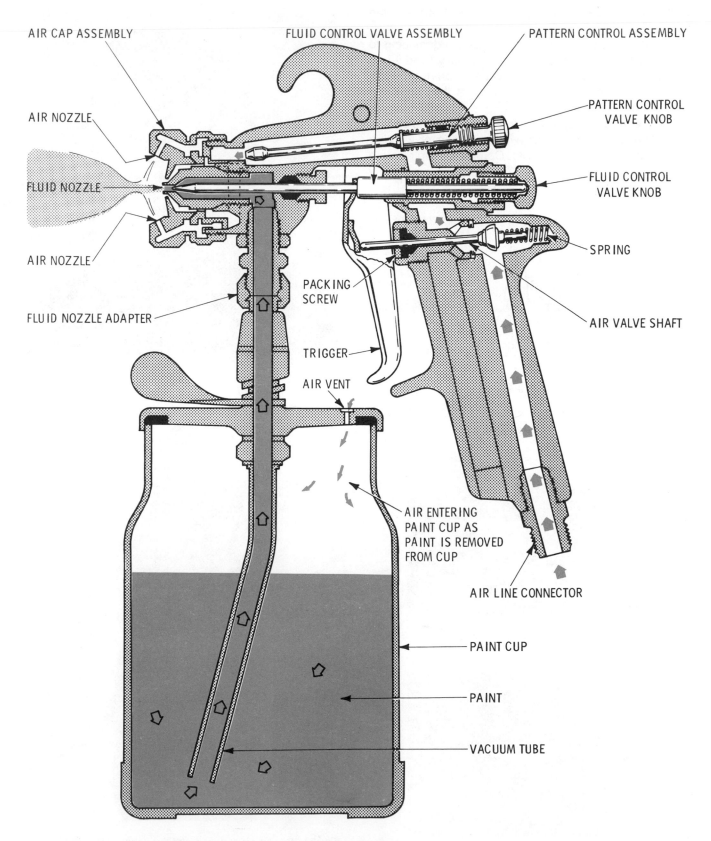

AIR CAP ASSEMBLY

AIR NOZZLE

FLUID NOZZLE

AIR NOZZLE

FLUID NOZZLE ADAPTER

FLUID CONTROL VALVE ASSEMBLY

PATTERN CONTROL ASSEMBLY

PATTERN CONTROL VALVE KNOB

FLUID CONTROL VALVE KNOB

SPRING

AIR VALVE SHAFT

PACKING SCREW

TRIGGER

AIR VENT

AIR ENTERING PAINT CUP AS PAINT IS REMOVED FROM CUP

AIR LINE CONNECTOR

PAINT CUP

PAINT

VACUUM TUBE

Fig. 24-15. *A typical siphon (suction) spray gun and its parts. This type of gun is most often used in body shop work. (Courtesy of DeVilbiss Company)*

body's air passages and partially clog the breathing system.

Paints and paint products also can be damaging to your *eyes*. Several products may actually blind you if splashed into your eyes. All paint and paint products will cause at least *some* eye trouble if they enter the eyes.

For these reasons, proper eye and breathing protection *always must be used when painting or working with paint and paint products*. Common shop painting

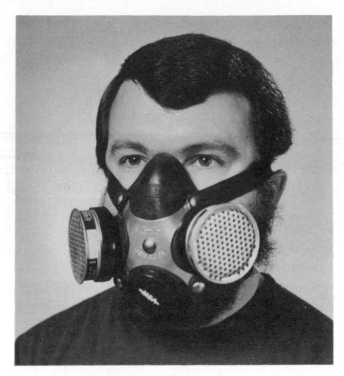

Fig. 24-19. *Typical respirators, which will filter out paint particles and most paint fumes.*

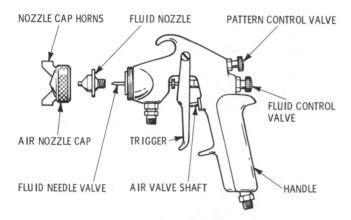

Fig. 24-16. *The major parts of a spray gun.*

NOZZLE CAP HORNS   FLUID NOZZLE   PATTERN CONTROL VALVE

AIR NOZZLE CAP   TRIGGER   FLUID CONTROL VALVE

FLUID NEEDLE VALVE   AIR VALVE SHAFT   HANDLE

Fig. 24-17. *Adjusting the fluid control valve. (Courtesy of Refinish Division, DuPont Company)*

Fig. 24-18. *Adjusting the pattern control valve. (Courtesy of Refinish Division, DuPont Company)*

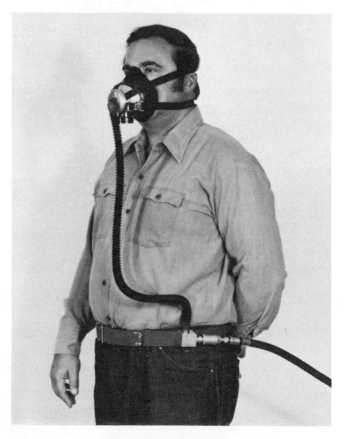

Fig. 24-20. *An air supply respirator uses air from an air compressor, protecting the worker from the effects of breathing paint fumes. (Courtesy of Pulmosan Safety Equipment Corporation)*

safety equipment includes three items:

1. Respirators.
2. Face masks.
3. Safety goggles.

Respirators. A good respirator, with clean filters, is absolutely necessary for safe paint work. This equipment (Fig. 24-19) thoroughly filters *all* the air breathed in through either the nose or mouth. The round filters on the side of the respirator may be easily replaced. These filters take out *both* the paint particles and *most* of the paint fumes, so the filters must be replaced, not cleaned. For the safest breathing, the filters should be replaced after each overall paint job.

Air Supply Respirator. The air supply respirator is one of the safest paint respirators on the market. This respirator provides all the air that the worker breathes while painting.

The air is fed continuously from an air compressor, which provides a constant flow of controlled clean air (Fig. 24-20).

The unit has a face mask and a flexible hose connecting the face mask to the belt valve. The belt valve is connected to the air supply line.

Face Mask. Face masks are used for all repairs where sanding is to be done. The mask that is used for sanding is a *particle mask*. The particle mask keeps dried paint and metal dust from getting into the worker's lungs. Figure 24-21 shows a worker properly dressed for sanding.

CAUTION: Do not use a particle mask for painting with any type of acrylic or urethane finishes.

Safe Charcoal Mask. The masks in Figure 24-22 are used in the paint room for spraying paint. This type of mask removes particles and fumes and is safe to use in the paint room. Some paint masks have a valve for easier breathing. All paint masks should be OSHA (Occupational Safety and Health Act)-approved. These paint masks should be used according to the manufacturer's directions regarding types of paints and painting time for which they remain effective.

CAUTION: Catalyst paint has fumes which are extremely dangerous to breathe. Always use the proper mask.

Safety Goggles. When working with paint or painting chemicals, *safety goggles* must be worn. In Figure 24-23, for example, a painter is filling a spray gun cup with cleaning solvent. This product can cause severe eye damage if it is accidentally splashed in the eyes. Every shop must have safety goggles in *both* the painting and grinding areas.

MASKING

Masking products are used to protect parts of a vehicle that are *not* to be painted. A good masking job will make the overall job easier by reducing the clean-up time needed after the paint has been applied. A good masking job also helps the overall paint job look better. The paint will be exactly on the painted parts and not on other parts of the car, such as rubber weatherstripping, glass, and bright trim. Figure 24-24 shows a car

Fig. 24-21. *The proper safety equipment for working with plastics, and for all sanding operations, includes a face shield (or safety glasses), a particle mask, and gloves. (Courtesy of Automotive Trades Division, 3M Company)*

Fig. 24-22. *Two different types of face masks used in the paint booth. One has a valve in the center, which allows easier breathing. Masks of these types can only be used for a limited time and should be changed at recommended intervals. (Courtesy of Automotive Trades Division, 3M Company)*

that was properly masked for overall painting. The paper on the windshield was removed so that the car could be driven from the paint room.

Fig. 24-23. *Safety goggles should be worn while mixing paint. They protect the eyes from paint chemicals, which can cause irritation or eye damage.*

Fig. 24-24. *A car that has been masked for repainting. The paper over the windshield was removed so that the car could be driven from the paint booth. (Courtesy of Binks Manufacturing Company)*

Masking Tape

The basic material for any masking job is *masking tape*. Most masking tape is ¾ in. (19.0 mm) wide and is sold in rolls (Fig. 24-25). The tape is also sold in thin rolls of ¼ and ½ in. (6.4 and 12.7 mm) widths, and wider rolls of 1 in. (25.4 mm) or more. Special masking tape is also available with *strips* that may be pulled out. This tape is used for making stripes. When the tape is in position, one or more strips may be pulled out. Then, stripes may be painted (Fig. 24-26).

All masking tape should be stored in a cool, dry place, away from heaters or sunlight. This will help keep the tape sticky and flexible.

Masking tape should be carefully removed *before* the paint hardens. To see if the tape may be removed, touch the fresh paint that is *on the masking tape*. If your finger seems to stick to the paint when you pull it away, the paint is "tacky" and the tape may be removed. To do so, pull the tape straight up from the painted surface.

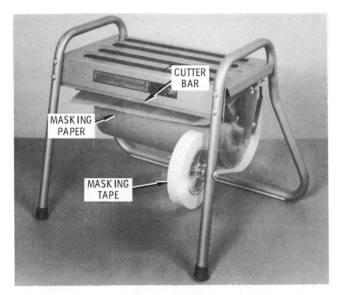

Fig. 24-25. *A typical masking paper and masking tape dispenser. (Courtesy of Automotive Trades Division, 3M Company)*

Fig. 24-26. *A special masking tape that has strips, which can be pulled out for striping a vehicle.*

Masking Paper. To cover large areas that will not be painted, masking *paper* should be used (Fig. 24-27). Like masking tape, masking paper is available in different widths. The most common width is 15 in. (38.1 cm).

Masking paper is better for paint work than newspaper or other papers because it is less likely to allow any paint to *bleed through.* When paint *bleeds,* it soaks through the paper and reaches the glass or trim. Use of masking paper is the best way to prevent paint bleed-through.

Cleanliness. Before applying masking tape to an area or a part, be certain that the surface is *clean* and *dry.* If a car has just been washed, check to be sure that the areas around small parts have thoroughly dried. *Masking tape will not stick to even slightly damp surfaces.*

One sign of a good overall paint job is when the *rubber weatherstrip* around the doors and deck lid has been masked off. The paint job looks much better when there is good, black rubber weatherstripping seen around the door jambs and deck lid opening. However, masking tape will not readily stick to rubber weatherstrip. To help the tape stick, apply *clear lacquer* to the weatherstrip with a rag, as in Figure 24-28. Allow the lacquer to dry on the weatherstrip. Then, the tape will stick to it readily.

Basic Procedure

When masking tape and masking paper are applied, there are two basic "ground rules" to follow. The *first* of these is that masking tape should be applied firmly and stretched tightly as it is put in place (Fig. 24-29). This is important if the paint is not to "creep" under the edges of the tape. Be certain that the tape goes *all the way* to the edge of the trim or piece it is protecting.

The *second* "ground rule" of masking is to *tear* the tape correctly. Figure 24-30 shows how this is done. Use your thumbnail to cut the tape while quickly pulling up on the roll. The key is to cut or tear the tape *without* stretching or mangling it in the process. Correctly tearing the tape will help ensure good, "clean" masking jobs.

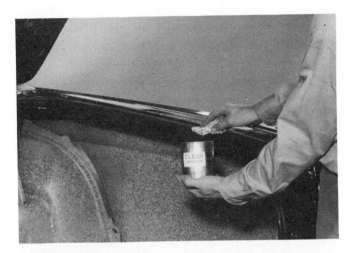

Fig. 24-28. *To help masking tape adhere more tightly to rubber weatherstrip, apply clear lacquer to the rubber, and let it dry. (Courtesy of Automotive Trades Division, 3M Company)*

Fig. 24-27. *This paper and tape dispenser automatically applies tape to two edges of the paper. It can be used for paper up to 18 in. (45.7 cm) in width. (Courtesy of Automotive Trades Division, 3M Company)*

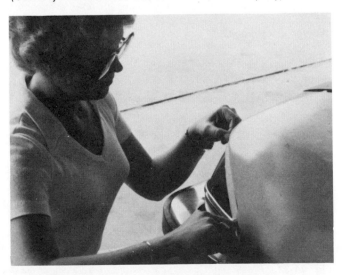

Fig. 24-29. *For a clean, professional masking job, tape should be stretched slightly and pressed down firmly as it is installed.*

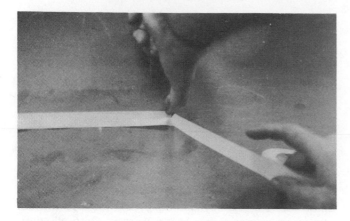

Fig. 24-30. *To cut masking tape correctly, quickly tear upward against your thumbnail.*

Fig. 24-31. *Proper masking of windows includes overlapping the top piece of masking paper. (Courtesy of Automotive Trades Division, 3M Company)*

Fig. 24-32. *Plastic light covers, available in a variety of sizes and shapes, simplify masking the light assembly for painting. (Courtesy of Automotive Equipment Division, Lenco, Inc.)*

Masking Glass. Glass should be masked carefully to prevent any overspray from reaching it. Common 15 in. (38.1 cm) masking paper is wide enough and flexible enough to make masking glass an easy job. In Figure 24-31, two widths of masking paper have been overlapped to cover a windshield.

To install the paper, first use masking tape *alone* to tape along the very top and edges of the window moldings. The tape must be pressed down firmly along the outer edge of the molding. Then, use two pieces of masking paper to cover the windshield. The tape on the *edge* of the paper should overlap the tape placed on the molding. The top piece of masking paper should overlap the bottom piece of paper. This helps to protect the glass from dust seepage. If need be, *fold and tape* any pleats in the paper so that sanding dust cannot collect in them before painting.

Masking Antennas and Wiper Blades. To protect these small parts, first mask the very *base* of the part (where it meets the paint) with regular, ¾ in. (19.0 mm) masking tape. Wiper blades are usually removed before painting, since it is easier to remove the blades and arms from their shafts than it is to mask them. The small wiper shafts may then be taped with regular masking tape.

To mask an antenna, an easy method is to place one width of tape on one side of the antenna and another width on the other side, along the entire length. The two widths are then pinched together along the opposite sides of the antenna.

Masking Lights. Narrower widths of masking paper generally work best around large lights. Using narrow masking paper 3 to 6 in. (7.6 to 15.2 cm) wide on these jobs makes them easier, because the papers are very flexible. The paper can be cut, folded, and worked around before being held down with masking tape.

Light Covers. Stock covers are available for use on most lights before painting. This saves time masking the glass parts. Figure 24-32 shows an assortment of these covers. Figure 24-33 shows how the light covers are used to keep paint off the glass.

Masking Door Jambs. Door jambs must be masked carefully to avoid getting any paint on the car's interior. A 6 in. (15.2 cm) wide masking apron attached with masking tape is usually wide enough to prevent overspray on the car's interior, when used as shown in Figure 24-34. The door jambs are sprayed at "close range," so the entire interior does not need to be covered. Before taping the rubber weatherstripping on the door, a thin coat of clear lacquer should be applied.

Masking Small Trim and Lettering. One sure sign of a first-class painter is the way that he or she tapes small trim and lettering on an automobile. Because these are difficult to mask, they are often *removed* during metal work or paint preparation. However, if the job does not call for a good deal of metal work, it may be more economical to mask these small pieces. By masking the pieces, the possibility of *breaking* them during removal is eliminated.

In Figure 24-35, small lettering is being masked. This

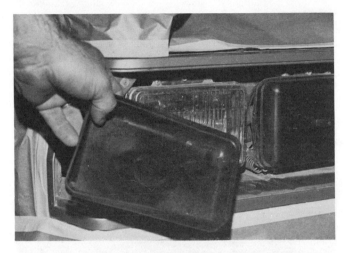

Fig. 24-33. *Light covers being installed. (Courtesy of Automotive Equipment Division, Lenco, Inc.)*

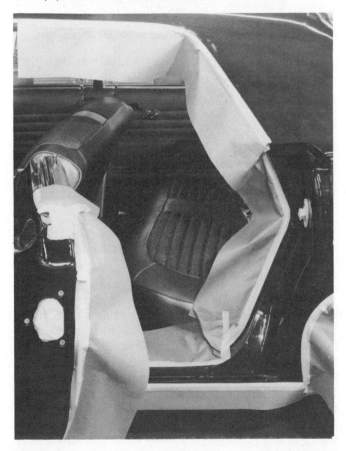

Fig. 24-34. *A door jamb being masked for painting. Note that the door lock assembly and the striker bolt have been masked. (Courtesy of Automotive Trades Division, 3M Company)*

job, of course, can be most easily done with narrow, 1/4 in. (6.4 mm) wide masking tape. This tape is very flexible and can be worked into small cracks. When applying tape to small trim or lettering, care must be taken to press it down tightly on the edges of the trim. Painters often use a pocket knife to work the tape into place on the edges of small trim.

Masking Along Natural Breaks. Whenever only *part* of one panel is to be refinished, the area to be painted should be masked along *natural breaks* (Fig. 24-36). These breaks may be at the top of a fender, at a sharp bend, at the edge of a door, or along moldings. By masking along natural breaks, it is more difficult to tell that only part of the car or part of a panel has been repainted.

In Figure 24-37, note that the very top of the fender panel is *not* to be repainted. The area has been masked off along the sharp natural break at the top of the fender. After the refinish work has been done, it will be difficult to see where the new paint stops because the line between new and old will be along the natural break.

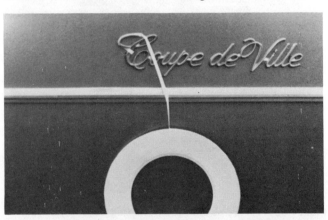

Fig. 24-35. *Narrow masking tape is used to mask small emblems and lettering.*

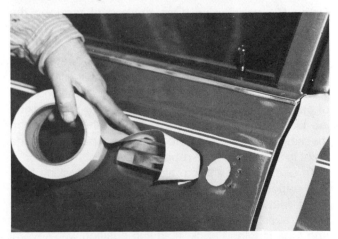

Fig. 24-36. *Masking along natural break lines will help "blend" the new and old paint on a car. (Courtesy of Automotive Trades Division, 3M Company)*

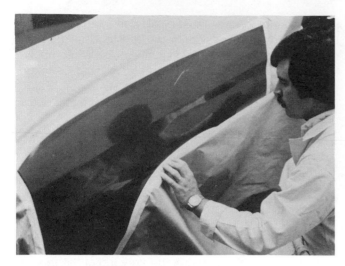

Fig. 24-37. *Using reverse taping along the upper edge of a fender panel. (Courtesy of Rinshed–Mason Products Division, Inmont Corporation)*

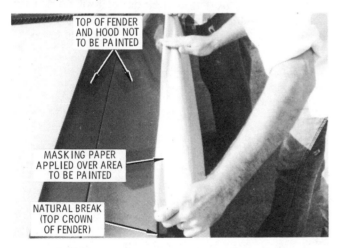

TOP OF FENDER AND HOOD NOT TO BE PAINTED

MASKING PAPER APPLIED OVER AREA TO BE PAINTED

NATURAL BREAK (TOP CROWN OF FENDER)

Fig. 24-38. *In reverse taping, the masking paper is placed over the area to be painted and taped in place along the definition line.*

Using Reverse Taping. One method of reducing the definition line (the line between the old paint and the new paint) is by using the *reverse taping* technique. Reverse taping was used along the upper edge of the fender (the natural break) in Figure 24-37. Another advantage of reverse taping is that it reduces the chances of paint *bleed-through* along the edge of the masking job closest to the new paint. This is the area of the masking that gets saturated with new paint when the paint is sprayed on the repair area.

To use reverse taping, first apply the masking tape and paper *over the area to be painted* (Fig. 24-38). Then, fold the paper (and the tape stuck to the paper) *back*, over the area to be protected. After the paper and tape is folded back, hold it in position with several small pieces of masking tape.

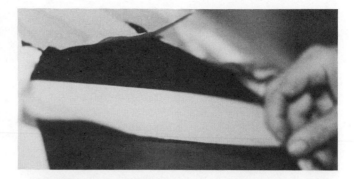

Fig. 24-39. *The tape is pressed down along the top edge.*

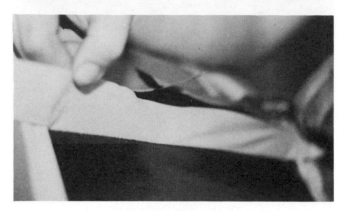

Fig. 24-40. *Pull the tape back about two-thirds of its width.*

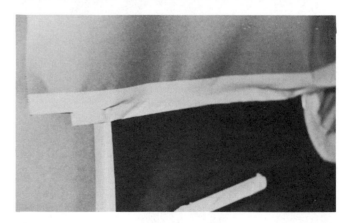

Fig. 24-41. *Place paper and tape on the sticky side of the folded-back tape.*

Using Reverse Taping Through the Middle of a Panel. Sand the area to be painted, then compound to clear the panel of any contamination. Place 2 in. (50.2 mm) tape along the edge to be painted as in Figure 24-39. Pull the tape back about two thirds of its width (Fig. 24-40). Place tape and paper over the sticky side of the folded-back tape. Leave both tape and paper loose (Fig. 24-41). As each coat of the paint is sprayed, pull the tape and paper back slightly, forming a new line to keep the paint from building up in any one coat.

Automotive Paint and Paint Products

There are many different types and brands of automotive paints (Fig. 25-1) and paint products (Fig. 25-2). Several companies market good, complete lines of automobile paint materials. Usually, a body shop will use one company's line of products and get to know that company's local salesperson. Then, this salesperson will be able to help the shop with any new paint products or with problems that come up. Most paint company salespeople will also be able to provide the shop with specific literature and instructions on the company's line of products.

PAINT INGREDIENTS

Although automobile paints may seem very different, they all have common ingredients. Actually, the word "paint" is a broad term. It is used to describe many different finishing materials with many different properties and uses. Such terms as "lacquer," "enamel," "primer," "sealer," or "putty" all apply to some form of *paint*. Because they are all paints, *they all have several ingredients in common*.

In other words, no matter what the product is, *if it is a paint, it contains at least these three basic ingredients*:

1. Pigments.
2. Binders.
3. Vehicles.

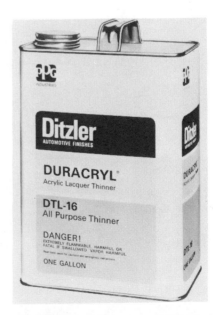

Fig. 25-2. *A typical automotive paint product, lacquer thinner. (Courtesy of Ditzler Automotive Finishes Division, PPG Industries, Inc.)*

Fig. 25-1. *A typical automotive* enamel *paint. (Courtesy of Rinshed–Mason Products Division, Inmont Corporation)*

These ingredients (pigments, binders, vehicles) are found in all paints (Fig. 25-3). Of course, there are different kinds of pigments, binders, and vehicles. Which *kind* of each ingredient and *how much* of each ingredient is used is what makes paints different.

Each of the ingredients has a different "job" to do for the final paint product. If the ingredient does not do its job properly, the paint may fail soon after it is sprayed, or it may cause trouble during spraying. It is a good idea to understand what each ingredient is and what it does for the paint.

Pigments

Pigments are the ingredients that give the paint its *color*. By themselves, pigments are dry and powdery; black pigments look like pure black coal dust, for example. White pigments look like ordinary kitchen flour. Of course, there are many different colors of pigment. The color of a paint depends on what color *pigment* is in it.

Some paints have very, very fine pieces of aluminum *metal* mixed up with the pigments. These small pieces of metal give the paint a "sugary" look, as if it was sprinkled with fine silver chips. These are called *metallic* paints and are discussed in detail later in the unit.

Binders

The second main ingredient of all paints is a binder. The binder is the ingredient that actually *sticks* the pigment to the car's surface. Without a binder, the pigments could be brushed off the car's surface like dust! Therefore, the binder is a very important part of the paint.

By itself, the binder is clear or amber-colored, like very light syrup. Only when the pigment is added to the binder does it have any real color. The binder does not provide any color. Instead, it provides the "stick" to hold the color pigment to the surface.

There are thousands of different paint binders. At the present time, one of the more popular binders being used in paint is a type of plastic known as *acrylic*. From this binder, for example, comes the name acrylic enamel, such as the product shown in Figure 25-1.

Vehicles

The third main ingredient in *wet* paint, ready to spray, is the *vehicle*. The vehicle's job is to allow the paint to be sprayed on the car's surface. Just as a vehicle (car or truck) moves people along a road, the *vehicle* in paint allows the paint to be moved from the spray gun to the car's surface. Without a vehicle, the combination of pigment and binder would be much too thick; it would be like trying to spray syrup.

After the paint has been applied, the vehicle evaporates, leaving only the binder and pigment on the surface. If some vehicle is still present in fresh paint, we say that the paint is "wet," and it is sticky to the touch.

Some vehicle is put into the paint when it is manu-

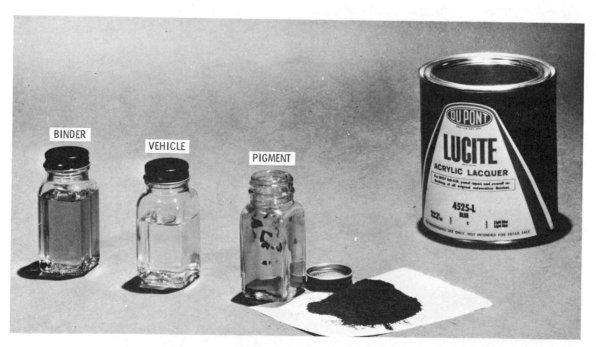

Fig. 25-3. *All automotive paints have three basic ingredients:* pigments *for color,* binders *to hold the pigments to the car's surface, and* vehicles *to make the mixture of binders and pigments more liquid and easier to spray. (Courtesy of Refinish Division, DuPont Company)*

factured. However, *more* vehicle must be put into the paint before it is sprayed. This additional vehicle is known as either a *thinner* (for lacquers) or a *reducer* (for enamel). Figures 25-4 and 25-5 show these products. Both thinners and reducers are vehicles; they have different names because they are slightly different. The different names help keep them separate in the shop's paint department.

Each paint product company offers several different vehicles for both lacquer and enamel paints. There are only two *main* differences between any two vehicles:

1. How fast they *evaporate* (the *evaporation rate*).
2. How much they dissolve and thin the *binder* in the paint.

Because of these differences, it is very important that *only the vehicle recommended by the paint manufacturer be used for a given job.* This is why many shops choose one paint manufacturer's product and use only those products. In any case, there are a few general rules about the different kinds of vehicles that are available.

Thinners. Special paint vehicles known as thinners are to be used with lacquer paint. For this reason, these products are usually known as *lacquer thinners*.

Lacquer thinners from various manufacturers will have different numbers and different names, but they are all basically classified according to *how fast they evaporate.* Which thinner to use depends on the conditions where the painting will be done. Generally, if the shop has a *higher* temperature, the evaporation rate of the thinner should be slower. If the shop is fairly hot [over about 75°F (24°C)], a *slow-dry thinner* should be used.

For average shop temperatures [about 68 to 74°F (20 to 23°C)], a *medium-dry* thinner should be used. Finally, if the shop is cold [67°F (19.5°C) or below], only a *fast-dry* thinner should be used.

To mix lacquer and thinner properly for spraying, first read the manufacturer's directions for the products being used (Fig. 25-6). Then, mix the lacquer and the *correct* thinner for the shop conditions. Usually, one part lacquer is mixed with about 1 to 1 ½ parts thinner. Lacquer and thinner should be thoroughly mixed in a container *outside* the paint gun cup, then strained into the cup (Fig. 25-7).

Reducers. Paint vehicles known as *reducers* are to be used with *enamel* paint. For this reason, these products are usually referred to as *enamel reducers*.

Like thinners, reducers from different paint compa-

Fig. 25-5. *Enamel reducer is the vehicle for enamel paints. (Courtesy of Rinshed–Mason Products Division, Inmont Corporation)*

Fig. 25-4. *Lacquer thinner is the vehicle for lacquer paints. (Courtesy of The Martin–Senour Company)*

Fig. 25-6. *Before using any paint or paint product, carefully read the manufacturer's directions on the container. (Courtesy of Rinshed–Mason Products Division, Inmont Corporation)*

nies will have different names and product numbers. Again, they are all basically classified according to their *evaporation rate*. Slow-dry reducers should be used in a hot shop; fast-dry reducers should be used in a cold shop.

Enamel paints and reducers are mixed in proportions different from lacquers and thinners. While lacquer may be mixed at a ratio of one part lacquer to 1 or 1 ½ parts thinner, enamel is mixed at two to four parts *enamel* to one part *reducer*. The exact amount of thinner varies according to the product used and the shop conditions. For enamels, it is *especially* important that the manufacturer's recommendations be followed.

Fig. 25-7. *Straining a mixture of lacquer and lacquer thinner into a paint gun cup. (Courtesy of Refinish Division, DuPont Company)*

Fig. 25-8. *Usually, automobile paint is thinned to 19–21 seconds viscosity. Use the viscosity cup as shown, and time the paint according to manufacturer's directions.*

Use a viscosity cup (Fig. 25-8), and time the paint according to manufacturer's directions (usually 19 to 21 seconds).

TYPES OF PAINT

Any automobile paint is basically an *enamel* or a *lacquer*. Other words such as "nitrocellulose," "acrylic," "alkyd," or "polyurethane" sometimes may be used to describe an automobile paint. However, these products are still either lacquer or enamel paints. They have been made with different additives or other properties (Figs. 25-9 and 25-10).

The main difference between lacquers and enamels is how the paint film is formed *after* the paint has been sprayed. In other words, how the wet paint "dries" to form a smooth, hard film on the car's surface.

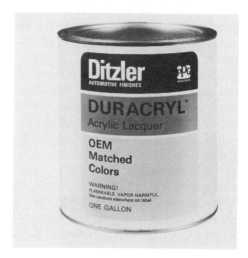

Fig. 25-9. *An automotive acrylic lacquer. (Courtesy of Ditzler Automotive Finishes Division, PPG Industries, Inc.)*

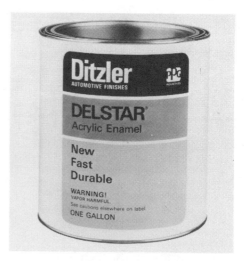

Fig. 25-10. *An automotive acrylic enamel. (Courtesy of Ditzler Automotive Finishes Division, PPG Industries, Inc.)*

In *lacquer* paints, the film is formed *only* by the paint vehicle (thinner) evaporating. Because only the vehicle evaporates, the lacquer film and pigments left on the surface remain *soluble*. That is, if they are touched with thinner, they will again dissolve.

In *enamel* paints, however, not only does the paint vehicle (the reducer) evaporate, but the *binder gradually oxidizes* as the paint dries. This means that part of the binder combines with the oxygen in the air, producing a hard, tough paint film.

Because of their differing properties, lacquers and lacquer products should not be mixed with enamels and enamel products. The mixture would not mix or spray correctly and would cause many paint problems. A good painter must understand the differences between lacquers and enamels *and* the differences between the different *types* of lacquers and enamels.

Lacquers

The first modern automotive paints to be used on new cars were *lacquers*. Since the earliest lacquers were developed in the 1920s, many General Motors automobiles have been painted with lacquer at the factory. At the factory, the lacquer is usually baked at a *very* high temperature, sanded, then baked again. The baking forces the lacquer to "flow out" and achieve full gloss.

To bake lacquer at a high enough temperature to make it flow out, a large amount of thinner and extreme heat is used. The heat used at the factory is applied *before* the body's rubber, glass, and plastic parts are installed. In an auto body shop, it is not possible to bake lacquer at very high temperatures, because the car's glass, rubber, and plastic parts would be damaged.

In a body shop, lacquer paint dries without full gloss. It must be compounded and polished to make it shine. This is known as "rubbing out" the lacquer. If lacquer paint is sprayed and left on the car without "rubbing it out," the finish will look dull, as if the paint is bad.

The main *advantage* of lacquer paint in body shop use is the fact that it dries quickly. For this reason, lacquer paint is not as likely to dry with dirt or dust in it as some enamel. Lacquer can be sprayed in conditions that are not as good as required for alkyd enamel.

Another advantage of acrylic lacquer is that it can be bought locally in small quantities. This helps keep down the cost of repairs and reduces the paint stock kept by the shop. It is ideal for small touch-up jobs on either lacquer or *new car* enamel finishes. A very small brush may be used to touch up the small nicks or chips (Fig. 25-11). On factory-baked acrylic enamel paint, acrylic lacquer may be used for either spot repair (repainting a small area) or for touch-up work.

The main *disadvantage* of lacquer is that it must be compounded to full gloss after it has dried. This requires additional shop time and materials, adding to the cost of making repairs with lacquer paint.

Another disadvantage of lacquer is that it does not hide very small chips, nicks, and sand scratches as well as does enamel. Enamels may "flow out" to partially cover such imperfections, where lacquer would not. Many painters feel that lacquer is more likely to chip than enamel when hit by stones or gravel thrown up by the car's wheels. Newer lacquers, however, are "tougher" than older ones, so this tendency to chip has been reduced.

Another disadvantage of acrylic lacquer is that more coats are needed (compared to enamel) to get the desired finish. The finish must be compounded, which removes some of the color (top)coat. This adds to both labor and material cost. To compound a complete car, for example, up to 5 hours is required *in addition to* the spraying time. This time must be added to the cost of the acrylic lacquer paint used, making the job more expensive.

Enamels

Enamel paints were developed during the 1930s. Since that time, many new cars and almost all new trucks have been painted at the factory with some type of enamel. Enamel paint also is used on most foreign cars. Enamel paint is strong and durable. Properly applied, it will flow out to a high gloss and cover very small imperfections.

In automobile factories, the enamel is baked on at a very high temperature. The temperature used to bake and flow out enamel, however, is not as great as the

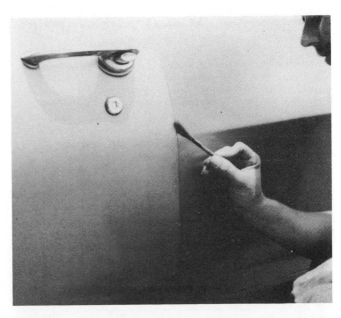

Fig. 25-11. *Using a small touch-up brush to repair a door nick.*

temperature used to bake and flow out lacquer. Even so, the factory baking temperature for enamel is too high to use in a body shop because it might damage glass, plastic, and rubber parts. As is the case with lacquer, the enamel paints used in a body shop cannot be identical to those used at the factory.

The main *advantage* of enamel paint is that it dries to a high gloss and does not need to be compounded. In fact, fresh enamel paint (less than 30 days old) should *not* be compounded or the finish will be damaged.

Since enamels must "flow out" and dry to a glossy finish, *how* the enamel is sprayed becomes very important. Generally, more skill is needed to spray enamel than to spray lacquer. Even so, most enamel finishes will dry with a small amount of *orange peel*. This is a slight texture like the surface of an orange. *Too much* orange peel in either lacquer or enamel is a paint defect. A *small amount*, however, is to be expected in all enamel finishes.

Types of Enamel. There are *three basic types* of enamel paint in use today: alkyd, acrylic, and polyurethane. Each is used on some new cars and trucks, depending on the manufacturer. It is very important that a painter understand the three types of enamels, since all of them are in current use.

Alkyd enamels are widely used for overall refinishing work. Their *advantages* are speed of application, the ability to cover well, and the fact that they can be easily applied over other types of finishes. Preparing a surface for alkyd enamel may be done with sandpaper that is less fine than needed for other types of paint; this makes the job faster. Alkyd enamel is often used to refinish used cars. The speed with which the job may be done and the fact that the finish does not have to

be compounded makes alkyd enamel refinishing popular.

Very small scratches or chips are more easily covered with alkyd enamel than with either lacquer or acrylic enamel. If the paint on a car or truck is in fairly good condition, alkyd enamel may be used *after* the paint has been sanded with at least #240 (preferably #320) wet sandpaper. The old paint should be sealed with enamel sealer before the alkyd enamel is applied.

The main *disadvantage* of alkyd enamel is its slow drying time. This causes problems of dirt and dust getting into the paint before it is dry. If a defect (such as a run) happens while spraying alkyd enamel, the panel either must be washed off and resprayed immediately, or allowed to dry for several hours before correcting the problem.

The most popular enamel in use today is *acrylic* enamel (Fig. 25-12). Almost all new trucks are finished in acrylic enamel. Many new foreign and domestic cars are finished in acrylic enamel at the factory. Under factory conditions, of course, the acrylic enamel is baked on at very high temperatures for a smooth, glossy finish.

The special ingredient in this enamel is the transparent thermoplastic resin known as *acrylic*. This is mixed into the *binder* part of the acrylic paint mixture. There are special paint *products* (such as acrylic enamel reducers, Fig. 25-13), made to be used with acrylic enamel paints. For best results, only products recommended for use with the paint being applied should be mixed with it.

Fig. 25-12. *One brand of acrylic enamel. (Courtesy of The Martin–Senour Company)*

Fig. 25-13. *Acrylic enamel reducer should be used with acrylic enamels. (Courtesy of The Martin–Senour Company)*

The main *advantage* of acrylic enamels is rapid drying. Properly applied, they will dry to a beautiful gloss with almost no orange peel. Most acrylic enamels will dry fairly well in about 30 minutes. This helps eliminate long hours of drying time and the danger of dust and dirt settling on the wet paint. Because of this faster drying time, many more enamel paint jobs can be done in the paint shop.

Acrylic enamel paint may be oven-dried or it may be air-dried in an ordinary refinishing booth.

Although acrylic enamel will normally dry with a high gloss, rubbing compound may be used to make it even smoother. This will also eliminate the slight orange peel present in all enamel refinishing. Compounding can be a real advantage when correcting paint defects since it is much faster than sanding and repainting. For the best results, acrylic enamel should not be compounded until 30 days after it is applied.

Acrylic enamel blends well with original paint, especially original acrylic enamel. For this reason, acrylic enamel may be used for making any spot repairs. This usually will allow a spot repair to be made on a panel without repainting the entire panel.

The main *disadvantage* of acrylic enamel is waiting time. After it has cured about 6 hours, there must be a waiting period of about *1 week* before the recoating. If the job *must* be recoated during this week, *first* spray on two coats of acrylic enamel recoat sealer. Then, allow the sealer to dry for 1 hour before spraying the second acrylic color coat. This quick recoating method

should be avoided whenever possible, since it may reduce the life of the paint job.

The third, and newest, type of enamel paint is *polyurethane* enamel. This is a mixture of alkyd enamel and a clear urethane. The basic pigment is the same as in the older alkyd enamel. The clear urethane portion, however, contains additives that activate the paint chemically and cause its top film to become hard and durable (Fig. 25-14).

Polyurethane enamel has a high gloss, with good toughness, chip resistance, and color retention. Polyurethane enamel topcoats also have the *wet* look of having been freshly painted for several months after they are applied (Fig. 25-15).

A major *advantage* of polyurethane enamel over other enamels is its extremely short drying time. The vehicle being painted can be delivered much sooner than when working with other enamels. Some polyurethane enamels are designed to dry so quickly that they may be sprayed "on location" and will dry dust-free in minutes. Off-road equipment such as construction trucks or bulldozers can be painted without having to be brought into a shop. Because of this, polyurethane enamel is popular for truck fleets, buses, construction equipment, aircraft, and boats.

A *disadvantage* of polyurethane enamel is that it must be mixed differently from other enamels. The painter must learn a new procedure to apply this enamel properly. When purchased, polyurethane enamel comes in two parts—alkyd enamel and clear urethane activator.

Fig. 25-14. *One manufacturer's brand of polyurethane enamel. (Courtesy of Refinish Division, DuPont Company)*

Fig. 25-15. *Polyurethane paints have a "wet look," which lasts for months after application. (Courtesy of Rinshed–Mason Products Division, Inmont Corporation)*

The products must then be mixed according to the manufacturer's directions (often about three parts alkyd to one part urethane). When properly mixed, many polyurethane paints may be sprayed full strength. No reducer is needed. However, a *retarder* may be added to slow the paint's drying time.

Drying Time. Polyurethane dries up to 50 percent faster than enamels without the urethane additive. Polyurethane can be used in the heated paint booth for even faster drying time. This greatly increases shop production. When spraying polyurethane in a regular paint booth, the paint dries to touch in about 10 to 15 minutes. The paint is durable and has excellent resistance to gasoline and chemicals (Fig. 25-16).

Fig. 25-16. *Polyurethane paints are not affected by gasoline spills. (Courtesy of Rinshed–Mason Products Division, Inmont Corporation)*

Fig. 25-17. *Clear urethane comes in a separate container and is mixed with enamel paint. (Courtesy of Rinshed–Mason Products Division, Inmont Corporation)*

Clear Urethane. The clear urethane material comes separate from the enamel color (Fig. 25-17). Mix 1 qt (0.9 L) of urethane with 3 qt (2.8 L) unreduced enamel paint to make 1 gal. (3.8 L) of urethane paint. Mix at the rate of about 8 oz (ounces) [248.8 g (grams)] of urethane to 1 qt (0.94 L) of unreduced paint. Check the paint with a viscosity cup to see if a reducer is needed. The paint mixture should go through the viscosity cup in approximately 19 to 21 seconds (Fig. 25-18).

Spraying Urethane Paint. When spraying urethane paint, pressure should be about 50 psi (345 kPa) at the gun. Spray a light first coat (Fig. 25-19), then two more wet coats.

When a final mist coat is required, remember that polyurethane dries in 10 to 15 minutes. This means the mist coat must be applied soon after the panel has been sprayed with the two wet coats. Usually three panels can be sprayed before returning to the first panel for the mist coat.

CAUTION: **Polyurethane paint contains isocyanate (cyanic acid, an ingredient of plastics and adhesives) and is harmful if breathed.**

Fig. 25-18. *Use the viscosity cup to time paint.*

Fig. 25-19. *The first coat of urethane paint should be a light spray.*

Use a good charcoal mask, as shown in Figure 25-20. Change the filters at recommended intervals. Eye protection also should be worn.

Additives. All enamels and lacquers can be made more flexible and glossy by using an additive with them (Figs. 25-21 and 25-22). Many manufacturers recommend the use of flex agent additive for refinishing vinyl tops.

Additives for enamel paint produce a faster air drying time. This increases shop production. The additive makes paint hard and greatly increases resistance to scratches, chipping, water spotting, gasoline, and chemicals. Paint with such an additive can be sprayed during adverse weather conditions. Read the paint can label and additive labels before spraying, and use both eye and breathing protection.

Lacquer for Vinyl Tops. When a vinyl top gets dull (Fig. 25-23) and needs to be restored, or when a color change is wanted, it can be sprayed with lacquer paint and a flex agent (Fig. 25-24). Pick a color that matches the lower part of the car and the upholstery, and add the flex agent according to the manufacturer's recommendation (usually one part of lacquer to one part of flex agent). Thin the lacquer and spray the vinyl top. Figure 25-25 shows a can of flex agent. Always read label directions before using any paint product.

Another method of restoring or changing color on a vinyl top is to spray it with a vinyl dye. Follow label directions for application.

Flexible Parts. The flex agent can be added to lacquer for painting all flexible (soft) parts, such as urethane bumpers, filler pads, fender extensions, and padded dash boards.

VINYL PAINT AS PROTECTION

Many late-model automobiles use a vinyl paint on the lower body panels. This abrasion-resistant coating protects the lower panels from being chipped by stones and other flying objects.

The vinyl material often used is the same textured vinyl paint that was applied a few years ago to provide a vinyl top on a vehicle. The paint is durable and easy

Fig. 25-21. *An additive for acrylic enamel. (Courtesy of Rinshed–Mason Products Division, Inmont Corporation)*

Fig. 25-22. *An additive for alkyd enamel. (Courtesy of Rinshed–Mason Products Division, Inmont Corporation)*

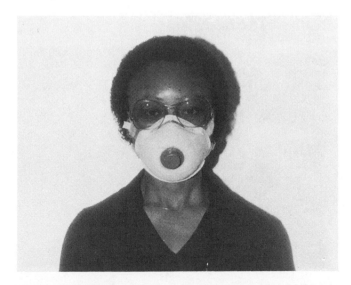

Fig. 25-20. *A mask with a* charcoal *filter is a must when spraying polyurethane paints.*

to apply and can be covered with any color that matches the vehicle (Fig. 25-26). The vinyl paint is sprayed on the lower panels before the color coat is applied. The vinyl paint gives the lower panels a rough look. It is usually applied below the lower chrome molding. This paint need not be a problem if the correct repair procedures are followed.

Parts, tools and material that will be needed are:

1. Vinyl abrasion-resistant coating.
2. Paint pre-cleaner.
3. Narrow masking tape for taping letters and for sharp curves.
4. Paint spray gun (use a large fluid nozzle, air nozzle and needle valve if possible).
5. An approved safety paint mask.

Repairing Vinyl-coated Areas

To repair a vinyl-coated panel, the procedure is much like any other panel repair. The paint is removed with a disc sander and a coarse sanding disc. An alternate method is to use a heat gun and putty knife to remove the paint. The vinyl coating cannot be "spot" repaired, and must be removed completely from each damaged panel.

When a vinyl-coated panel is to be repaired, follow these steps:

1. Remove all the vinyl coating from the panel.
2. Repair the damaged metal.
3. Clean panel with a good cleaning solvent.
4. Scuff-sand with a medium (#150 or #180) grit sandpaper.
5. Remove sanding dust with a lint-free tack cloth and compressed air.

Applying Color

The vinyl paint can be bought in quarts. The specified *dry* film thickness will be 15 to 20 mils (0.381 to 0.508 mm). This will require three or four coats of paint, with *flash off* time allowed between each coat.

The paint should be sprayed without thinning if possible, as the material should be applied thick. It is not unusual to have orange peel with this method of painting. However, since the paint texture is rough, there is no need for concern.

Clean equipment immediately after use with either lacquer cleaning thinner or a recommended pre-cleaner.

If lacquer vinyl paint is used, allow 1 hour of drying time. If acrylic enamel vinyl paint is used, 2 hours of drying time is recommended.

BASE COAT/CLEAR COAT PAINT

Some vehicles are finished in a base coat/clear coat paint. This method of painting is not new. Many vehicles in the 1930s and 1940s were painted with base coat/clear coat paint, and the procedure then was much like the one used today. Ford and Chrysler vehicles, and many General Motors vehicles, are painted at the factory with the base coat/clear coat method. This trend is expected to continue. Figure 25-27 shows a car that has been finished in the base coat/clear coat paint method.

Paint Problems

The base coat/clear coat poses no problem for all-over paint jobs. However, for spot repair and panel repainting, the base coat/clear coat can be a challenge to the refinisher.

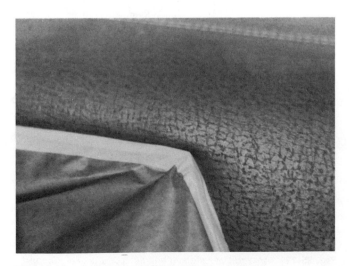

Fig. 25-23. *A vinyl top, which needs repainting.*

Fig. 25-24. *A lacquer paint with a flex agent added is used to refinish a vinyl top.*

This type of finish is repaired in two stages. Extra care should be taken to avoid problems and produce a good color match. Use paint and thinner from a reliable paint manufacturing company, and read the label carefully.

Application of Coatings

The base coat/clear coat is applied much like any *repaint* repair. The clear coat is most important. It can be used with either acrylic lacquer or enamel finishes. When using the base coat/clear coat system, follow these steps.

Metal Preparation. The damage (Fig. 25-28) is sanded and featheredged as shown in Figure 25-29. Treat bare metal with metal conditioner for thorough cleaning. If the sheet metal is aluminum or galvanized, dilute the metal conditioner as instructed on the label.

Undercoating. Apply a good recommended primer–surfacer (Fig. 25-30). Use putty if needed, then sand with #320 dry or #360 wet sandpaper on both the old finish and the primer–surfacer. Compound the primer, old finish, and adjoining panels (Fig. 25-31), then dust and wipe the panel with a tack rag. Seal the entire panel to be painted with a good sealer to ensure adhesion.

Color Coat. Mix lacquer color with recommended lacquer thinner at a rate of four parts of color to five parts of thinner (where the viscosity is 18 to 22 seconds). Air pressure at the gun should be 30 to 35 psi (207 to 241 kPa). Apply a minimum of four medium color coats with the paint gun held 6 to 8 in. (15.2 to 20.3 cm) away

from the panel. Paint that is sprayed with the gun too close or too far away can cause mismatching. Allow flash-off time between coats (usually 15 to 18 minutes). In Figure 25-32, the whole right side of the vehicle was refinished because of scratches in the fender, door, and quarter panel.

After the final color coat, wait approximately 15 minutes before applying the clear coat. While waiting, check the color by pulling up the paper and tape and comparing the new and old finishes (this is the purpose for compounding the adjoining areas). The new paint will be slightly different. The full color match and depth will develop after the clear coat has been applied.

Clear Coat. Thin the material at a rate of 1 ½ to 1, or four parts clear coat to six parts thinner (viscosity 18 to 22 seconds). Air pressure at the gun should be 30 to 35 psi (207 to 241 kPa). Apply two medium wet coats over the color, allowing time for the first coat to flash off. For spot repair, blend beyond the color by reducing air pressure to about 20 psi (138 kPa) to taper the paint. Figure 25-33 shows the right side of a vehicle that was finished with this method.

Fig. 25-26. *Vinyl texture paint is used on the lower panels of some cars to minimize chipping and scuffing of the paint.*

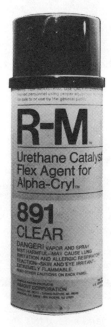

Fig. 25-25. *A flex agent to be added to lacquer paints. (Courtesy of Rinshed–Mason Products Division, Inmont Corporation)*

Fig. 25-27. *This vehicle has damage that will have to be refinished. It was finished at the factory with a base coat/color coat system.*

Compounds and Waxes. Allow the coating to dry overnight or longer before buffing and allow at least 60 days before waxing.

CAUTION: **When spraying any type of paint, use a good organic chemical vapor respirator. Choose one that meets the approved safety standards.**

Fig. 25-28.   *A damaged area on a car with a color coat/clear coat factory finish.*

Fig. 25-31.   *Compounding the primer and adjoining old finish for a good color match.*

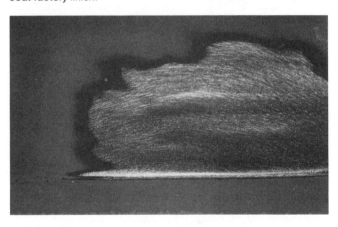

Fig. 25-29.   *The damaged area is sanded and featheredged.*

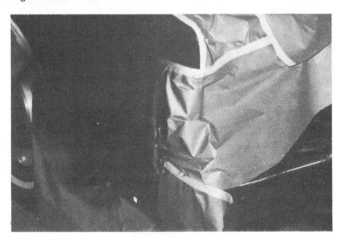

Fig. 25-32.   *Four coats of topcoat paint have been applied.*

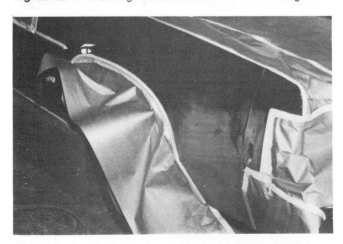

Fig. 25-30.   *Primer has been applied to the prepared surface.*

Fig. 25-33.   *The right-hand side of this vehicle was finished with a color coat/clear coat system. Note the reflection of the fence in the high-gloss finish.*

UNDERCOATS

The normal color finish (topcoat) seen on an automobile will not properly stick to bare metal. This is because properly prepared bare metal is too smooth for the paint to grip it. If the metal was made rough enough for the color to grip, the finish would not be as slick and shiny as is desired.

For the color topcoat to be smooth and shiny *and* properly adhere, some type of *undercoat* must be used. The undercoat must firmly grip the surface to which it is applied (the *substrate*) and must provide a good gripping surface for the topcoat. Some undercoats also are used to fill small imperfections (not *all* undercoats do this).

When an automobile body (or part of it) is painted, paint may be applied to many different types of surfaces. For example, part of a repaired surface may be bare metal, while another part may be plastic filler. The surface that the paint will be applied to is known as the *substrate*.

When all the body work has been done, or when the old paint has been properly prepared, the smooth prepared area is known as the *substrate*. If the substrate is not properly prepared, there will likely be paint trouble during the paint work.

Some type of undercoat is nearly always applied to a substrate before the color coat (topcoat) is applied. One type of undercoat, *sealer*, is applied directly over the substrate *if the substrate is entirely old paint that is not cracked*. It is best to plan on using *some* type of undercoat under *all* topcoats, if this can be done without making the total paint film too thick.

There are four basic types of undercoats: primer, primer–surfacer, putty, and sealer. Although they are all undercoats, each is used for a different purpose. *Primer* is used mainly to provide good adhesion for the topcoat, add to the topcoat's durability, and protect any bare metal from rust. *Primer–surfacer* does everything that a primer does *and* fills small imperfections (such as sand scratches) in the substrate. *Putty* is used to fill any small nicks noticed in either primer or primer–surfacer. Finally, *sealer* is used to seal a substrate that may be a different type of paint from the topcoat to be applied.

Primer

Paint *primer* is normally used on all bare metals during new or replacement panel preparation. This includes galvanized metal, aluminum, and other alloy metals. Good production primers, when properly applied on correctly prepared surfaces, normally do not require sanding. This is because primer is applied in thin coats and contains a small amount of solids (pig-

ment). If any defects appear in the primer, however, it may be sanded with *fine* sandpaper.

Primers may be thought of as the filling in a sandwich (Fig. 25-34). Using a primer, especially on smooth, bare metal, will provide good topcoat adhesion.

Advantages. Good primers spread smoothly and adhere well to bare metal. Good primers help prevent rust and help give the topcoat a full, rich, smooth appearance.

Disadvantages. Primers are not good for use on rough surfaces, because they have poor filling qualities. For this reason, few shops use straight primers during repair work. Instead, primer–surfacers are more often used.

Types of Primers. The two common types of primers, enamel and lacquer, are most often used in shops that use straight primers. While lacquer primer dries more quickly, many painters feel that enamel primer is more durable. Either of these primers may need a light scuffing with #400 paper or steel wool to remove any *nibs* (small particles of dirt) before the topcoat is applied.

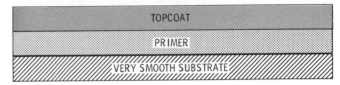

Fig. 25-34. *Primer is the "filling" in a sandwich consisting of substrate, primer, and topcoat.*

Primer–Surfacer

The most popular undercoat products used in body shops are primer–surfacers. These products do the job of a primer *and* fill small imperfections and rough places in the prepared substrate. There are many different types, brands, and colors of primer–surfacers. Figure 25-35 shows a primer–surfacer from one manufacturing company.

Advantages. There are a number of reasons why good primer–surfacers are popular body shop undercoats. They are good for use on slightly rough surfaces, since they will fill well and are easy to sand. The surfacer parts of primer–surfacers provide sanding ease. They do not dry gummy, as primers may, and have a high content of solids.

Both primers and primer–surfacers provide a good surface for topcoat adhesion, but primer–surfacers fill better. They are able to fill small scratches, pinholes, and nicks (Fig. 25-36). However, primer–surfacers *must be sanded* to provide the smoothest possible surface for quality topcoats.

Figure 25-37 shows the qualities of a good primer–surfacer. For example, it must resist settling into its separate parts, since this prevents it from spreading out uniformly. A good primer–surfacer must also have a good *sealing* quality. This gives the topcoat a full, rich appearance and helps prevent it from sinking into the primer–surfacer.

The main *disadvantage* of primer–surfacers is that they do not dry smooth. Instead, they dry to produce a

Fig. 25-35. *Preparing primer–surfacer for spraying. This material is available in either enamel or lacquer forms. (Courtesy of Rinshed–Mason Products Division, Inmont Corporation)*

Fig. 25-36. *A primer–surfacer will fill very small defects in the substrate. (Courtesy of Refinish Division, DuPont Company)*

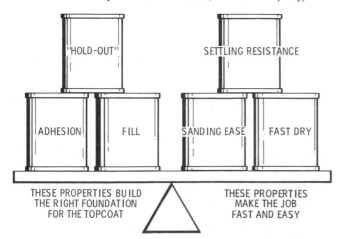

Fig. 25-37. *A good primer–surfacer does many different jobs, so it must have a balance of many different properties. (Courtesy of Refinish Division, DuPont Company)*

thick, slightly rough film. For this reaon, they must be sanded smooth before applying the topcoat on automobiles. However, for commercial work (such as trucks), some enamel primer–surfacers are sold that dry smooth enough to not need sanding. These primer–surfacers are recommended only for commercial work where speed and durability are more important than final gloss.

Types of Primer–Surfacers. There are two basic types of primer–surfacers: *lacquer* and *enamel*. Each type has advantages and disadvantages. For quality paint work, painters and repair technicians must know the differences between the two types and when each should be used. Generally, lacquer primer–surfacers may be used over either type of old paint and *under* either type of topcoat. The same is true of enamel primer–surfacer *with one important exception*: enamel primer–surfacer must *not* be "sandwiched" between an old lacquer topcoat and a new lacquer topcoat. If this is done, the topcoat may lift after it has been applied.

Almost all spot repair work in body shops today is "primed" with *lacquer* primer–surfacer. It has many good qualities. The first of these is *speed*. Lacquer primer–surfacers are fast-drying, making it easy to get repairs done quickly. Properly applied, lacquer primer–surfacers are easy to sand. This makes the job of preparing the surface much quicker and easier. A good lacquer primer–surfacer is probably one of the most frequently-used paint materials in body shops.

Enamel primer–surfacer, on the other hand, is recommended to "prime and surface" large bare metal areas. It also is used for complete refinishing jobs where the old topcoat has been stripped off completely. Enamel primer–surfacer is generally more durable and flexible than lacquer primer–surfacer and offers better rust and corrosion resistance.

The big *disadvantage* of enamel primer–surfacer is that it is much slower drying than lacquer primer–surfacer. Since any primer–surfacer should be sanded to provide a smooth base for the topcoat, there is a much longer waiting period before it can be sanded and the job completed. If *wet sanding* is to be done for the smoothest preparation, enamel primer–surfacer should first be allowed to dry *overnight*. If enamel primer–surfacer is wet-sanded before it is thoroughly dry, moisture may be trapped in it. This could later cause bubbling or blistering in the color topcoat.

Putty

Putty is thick undercoat *filler*. Most often, it is used over primer–surfacers to fill minor imperfections (Fig. 25-38). In fact, putty is like a very thick primer–surfacer in a tube or can. Because putty is very heavy, it cannot be sprayed. Instead, it must be applied with a rubber squeegee, as in Figure 25-39.

Putty is sold under different names, such as the products shown in Figures 25-39 and 25-40. It may be known as spot putty, body putty, or, simply *putty*. Some companies make one putty for use with lacquer paint and another for use with enamel paint. Good quality putties are fast-drying, will sand smoothly, and have good adhesion and color holdout.

Using Putty. To use putty, apply the material with a squeegee over any spots or scratches. (Putty is applied where it is needed, not necessarily over the entire panel.) Allow it to dry, one coat at a time. When one coat is dry, another coat can be applied if needed. Two thin coats of putty work better than one thick coat. If putty is spread too thick in one pass, the drying time is slow and the material may crack.

When putty has been applied and has thoroughly dried (usually about 30 minutes, depending on thickness), it may be wet- or dry-sanded as needed. Color topcoat or sealer may then be applied over any putty repairs.

Sealer

The last group of undercoat products is known as *sealers*. When sealers are used, *they are always used immediately under the topcoat.* They may be used under either lacquer or enamel topcoats. Although they may be used over primers and primer–surfaces, sealers are normally used over old finishes, as in Figure 25-41.

The main reason for using a sealer is to improve adhesion between the old and new finishes. To provide good adhesion, a sealer should *always* be used over an old lacquer finish when the new finish is to be en-amel. Under other conditions, a sealer may be desirable but is not absolutely necessary.

There are three situations where a sealer may be used to "help" the topcoat:

1. To help a light color "hide" a dark color, when the car will be repainted a different color or when the primer–surfacer is darker than the color will be.
2. To help reduce sandscratch swelling, Figure 25-42.
3. To provide uniform, even "holdout." This prevents the new topcoat from "sinking into" the substrate if the substrate is made up of different types of paint, such as primer–surfacer or old topcoat.

Sealers are often misunderstood because they are thought of as "cure-alls" that will take care of any bad conditions on an old topcoat. Actually, this is not entirely true. For example, a sealer will *not* fill cracks or low places in an old topcoat, and many sealers will not adhere well to bare metal. Not all sealers will stop an old topcoat color from "bleeding" into a new topcoat color (as when white is painted over red). Only a few sealers are marketed for this job.

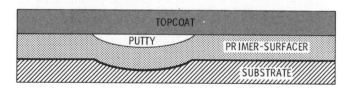

Fig. 25-38. *A typical use of body putty. (Courtesy of Refinish Division, DuPont Company)*

Fig. 25-40. *A typical tube of body putty. (Courtesy of Rinshed–Mason Products Division, Inmont Corporation)*

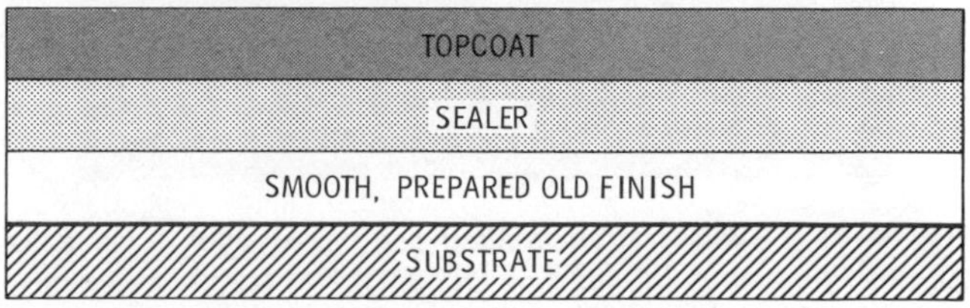

Fig. 25-39. *Putty is applied with a squeegee. It is too thick to be sprayed. (Courtesy of Automotive Trades Division, 3M Company)*

Fig. 25-41. *A sealer is often used to ensure good adhesion between old and new topcoats.*

Therefore, *like any other paint product*, sealers must be used only according to the manufacturer's directions and only on the jobs for which they are intended. One property of virtually all sealers is that they must not remain on the undercoat too long before the topcoat is applied. Usually, paint manufacturers recommend that the topcoat be applied *within 1 hour* after the sealer.

Like other paint products, there are two basic types of sealers: lacquer sealers and enamel sealers. Some are known as *primer–sealers* and may be used over bare metal as both a primer and a sealer. Others are known as *universal sealers* and may be used under any type of topcoat. Because sealer products vary widely from one paint manufacturer to the next, it is best to become familiar with those offered by one manufacturer, then use them for all sealer jobs in the shop.

Using Lacquer Sealer. When a lacquer topcoat will be applied over an old enamel finish, a lacquer sealer *must* be used. If a sealer is not used over the old enamel paint, the new lacquer finish may crack or lift after it has been on the car for several months.

Lacquer sealer is not required for good adhesion when new acrylic lacquer is sprayed over old acrylic lacquer. However, using a lacquer sealer would help prevent sandscratch swelling in the areas where the old acrylic lacquer has been repaired. However, if the old finish is smooth and hard with no sign of cracks or sandscratches, sealer usually would *not* be necessary.

Using Enamel Sealer. When enamel is sprayed over enamel, an *enamel sealer* should be used. The enamel sealer will do two jobs. First, it will help guarantee good adhesion between the two enamels.

Second, and most important, the enamel sealer will help seal and hold any dirt and dust in place. This will help keep any small specks of dust from being blown out of cracks, for example, onto new paint. No matter how much an automobile is cleaned, there is always a chance that some dust may be present in joints or cracks in the body. A sealer will help prevent dirty paint by keeping the dust in place while the new paint is applied.

Enamel paint may be applied over a lacquer finish without using a sealer. However, using an enamel sealer *is* recommended when the enamel will be applied over a large area of lacquer paint, such as an overall repaint or a large panel repair.

Another advantage of enamel sealers (and primer–sealers) is that they may be lightly sanded. Therefore, after enamel sealer has been applied, it may be inspected to see if any dirt or nibs have appeared. If so, they may be lightly scuffed (removed) with #400 dry sandpaper.

TOPCOATS

Whether lacquer or enamel, a vehicle's *topcoat* is the actual paint that provides color and protection for the vehicle. For these reasons, of course, the topcoat is very important in auto body work. Customers usually judge the appearance of the topcoat as a reflection of the entire job, as in Figure 25-43. Therefore, it is very important that a painter know about the different types of topcoats and when each type might be used.

How Topcoats Are Mixed

All topcoat paint *mixes* are either lacquer or enamel. Topcoat *mixes* refer to how the paint is prepared by the paint manufacturer or, as discussed later, by the paint dealer. Depending on how the paint will be used, it may be mixed slightly differently, as follows:

1. The number or color of *pigments* may be slightly changed.

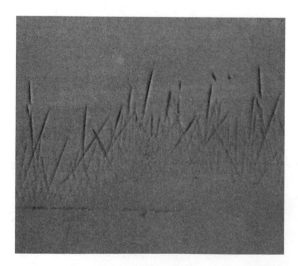

Fig. 25-42. *Sandscratch swelling can occur when a sealer is not used between old and new topcoats. The solvent in the new topcoat softens the edges of sanding scratches in the old finish coat, making them swell. (Courtesy of Refinish Division, DuPont Company)*

Fig. 25-43. *The quality of the topcoat is the first judgment that a customer makes after repair and refinishing work is completed.*

2. The amount and type of *vehicle* may be slightly changed.
3. The amount and type of *binder* may be slightly changed.

There are three basic types of topcoats, only *two* of which are used during auto body repair. When a painter (or the shop) orders paint for a car, it is important to know about the different types of mixes. Normally, the paint store will ask the painter or shop what type of mix is wanted.

New-car Mix. The paint sprayed on a new car *at the factory* is known as *new-car mix.* Because new car paint is baked at very high temperatures, it is mixed differently from paint to be used in a body shop. New-car mix is usually not available to body shops, because even if the shop uses baking equipment, the conditions (spraying and baking) are still not the same as at the factory. For these reasons, painters do not need to know about new-car mix except to understand that it *is* different from the mixes available to a body shop.

Factory-packaged Mix. When a can of color (topcoat) is mixed *at the paint factory* and sold to the painter in a sealed can, it is known as factory-packaged mix, or simply "factory package." When available, factory-packaged mix is the best type to use, especially for spot repairs on late-model cars. Factory-packaged mix is designed to match the color and gloss of baked-on new-car mix exactly. To match the factory's new-car mix, *factory-packaged* mix is carefully designed to work well *under normal body shop conditions*.

Factory-packaged mix always can be easily identified because the label is clearly printed, *at the factory*, with the exact color name and number for that paint (Fig. 25-44). This information usually includes the automobiles on which the color was used, the correct color code for those automobiles, and the paint manufacturer's product number.

Whenever possible, it is a good idea to use factory-packaged color mix. Factory-packaged color can be used for spot repairs, panel repairs, and overall refinishing.

Custom Mix. Factory-packaged mix is not always available in all colors. After a certain number of years, there is not enough demand for older factory-packaged colors, so they are "phased out."

When a color is not available in a factory-packaged mix, it is nearly always available in a *custom mix.* Custom-mix colors are those colors that are mixed to order at the paint supply store. Custom-mix color can always be identified easily because the contents of the can must be written on the label by the paint store that mixed the paint (Fig. 25-45).

For custom-mix colors that match the original color,

paint manufacturing companies must supply paint stores with several basic items:

1. Paint formulas.
2. Paint mixing equipment.
3. Custom-mix base colors.
4. Custom-mix special ingredients.
5. New paint cans.
6. Paint labels.

With the above materials and equipment, the paint store (or the body shop) can accurately mix almost any color ever used on an automobile. Many body shops prefer to have their own mixing equipment, since they can save time and money by mixing their own paints.

Fig. 25-44. *Factory-packaged paint is mixed and sealed at the paint factory.*

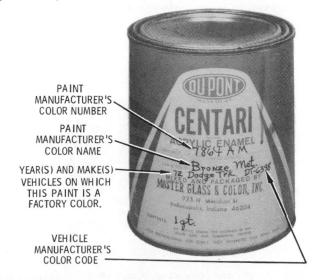

Fig. 25-45. *Custom-mixed paint is mixed to order and packaged at a local paint dealer, for use on a specific job.*

Paint formulas are "recipes" that tell the person mixing the paint how much of each *base color* and *other ingredients* to use to produce the desired color. The base colors and ingredients are put into the mix by *weight* or by volume.

Paint mixing equipment includes all the weighing, measuring, and mixing devices needed to mix a can of color. Some of this equipment is shown in Figure 25-46.

Custom-mix base colors are the basic colors (paints) used to prepare custom-mix paints. Base colors are not normally sold or used for refinishing by themselves. Instead, they are first mixed with other base colors and ingredients to make the needed paint products. Figure

Fig. 25-46. *A typical paint-mixing area. Good equipment is needed to measure accurately and mix the ingredients in a can of custom-mixed color. (Courtesy of Rinshed–Mason Products Division, Inmont Corporation)*

Fig. 25-47. *A base color used for custom-mixed paints. It will be mixed with other colors, as needed. (Courtesy of Acme Automotive Finishes)*

25-47 shows an acrylic enamel base color from one paint company.

Types of Topcoats

When the topcoat of an automobile or truck is clean and polished, it may reflect a bright *solid* color, such as yellow, white, or black. Other topcoats may reflect a bright color *and* very small sparkles that look like "sugar" in the finish. How a topcoat reflects light and color determines what type of topcoat it is. There are *two basic types* of topcoats, depending on how they reflect light. These are known as *solids* and *metallics*.

Solids. Many years ago, all cars were *solid* colors, such as maroon, black, yellow, white, and some blues and greens. When polished, these colors reflect light in only *one direction*, because the solids in the paint are all *pigments*, with no extra ingredients. Many cars today are still painted with solid colors. Solid colors look about the same no matter from what angle you look at them.

Metallics. Many popular colors today have both pigments *and* very small metal flakes mixed into the binder. When the paint is sprayed on a surface, the metal flakes are scattered in the binder along with the pigments. These flakes reflect light at different angles, especially when sunlight hits the paint. When the light is reflected at different angles, it makes the paint look "sugary." These paints are known as *metallic* paints, or metallic topcoats (Figs. 25-44 and 25-45).

Common metallic topcoats are silver and gold. Most green topcoats, many blues, and some reds are also metallics. When a metallic color is mixed, a certain amount of metal flakes (or "dust") must be added to the paint mixture. These flakes quickly settle to the bottom of the can of metallic paint, so *it is very important that metallic paints be stirred and mixed thoroughly before using.* If they are not, many flakes will stay at the bottom of the can. The paint will not match the same color on a car being repaired or refinished.

PAINT VEHICLES

Paint *vehicles*, of course, are one of the three basic ingredients in any paint. All paints are manufactured with *some* vehicle already in the paint when it comes out of the can. However, almost all paint must have *more* vehicle added before it may be sprayed. This is done for two reasons:

1. So that the painter can add the *correct* vehicle for the temperature and humidity conditions where the paint will be sprayed.
2. So that the paint will not have to be sold in such large quantities. If paint was sold with the proper

amount of vehicle already in it, much larger cans would be required.

The *most important* reason for adding vehicle just before spraying is so that the correct vehicle can be used for the existing shop conditions. The temperature and *humidity* (moisture in the air) are very important when choosing a paint vehicle. Different paint vehicles are made and sold for different shop conditions. *Knowing about the different vehicles is very important for successful paint work under all shop conditions.*

What Paint Vehicles Do

The basic job of any vehicle is to thin the paint enough so that the mixture can be sprayed. The paint vehicle *dilutes* the paint (makes it thinner) so that the mixture can be *atomized* as it leaves the gun and travels to the surface being sprayed (Fig. 25-48).

When the mixture reaches the surface being painted, the vehicle must keep the pigments and binder in solution just long enough for the material to flow out and level to a smooth, even surface. On the other hand, it must *not* hold the paint in solution so long that the paint film can sag or run. Finally, the vehicle must evaporate completely over a period of time to leave a tough, smooth, durable film.

Selecting a Vehicle

As a general rule, the shop's *temperature* and *humidity* are the main factors to consider when choosing a paint vehicle. Hot, dry weather will require a vehicle that evaporates *slower* than when the weather is cooler and wet or humid. All paint manufacturers market several different vehicles for use with each of their top-coats. For the best possible results with any manufacturer's automobile paints, *use that same manufacturer's vehicle.* Also, use only the vehicle *recommended by the manufacturer for the temperature and humidity conditions under which the paint and vehicle will be used.* No single factor in choosing automobile paint products is more important for successful automobile painting.

Types of Vehicles

As discussed earlier, there are two basic types of vehicles: *thinners* for lacquer paints and *reducers* for enamel paints. Although they do similar jobs, they are given different names so that they will not be easily confused. If the two products are confused, the paint work will probably turn out poorly. For example, lacquer thinner *will* dilute enamel paint. However, it will *not* properly break up (dissolve) *all* the enamel paint pigments to hold them in the proper balance. If enamel reducer is used in lacquer paint, it usually will curdle the paint.

There is a *third* type of vehicle on the market. Known as "universal" vehicles, or "universal thinners," these products are sold in bulk quantities. They are designed to be able to do *both* vehicle jobs: *thin* lacquers and *reduce* enamels. Universal thinners are normally not used for high-quality paint work.

Thinners. Most lacquer thinners sold today are made for use with acrylic lacquer paints. If nitrocellulose lacquer is being used, be sure to use lacquer thinner that is recommended for nitrocellulose lacquer paint.

Generally, as the shop temperature goes up, a slow-dry thinner should be used. It is a good idea to use a thinner that will dry as slowly as the shop conditions will allow. This ensures as smooth a finish as possible, so that only a minimum amount of compounding will be needed.

Reducers. Many enamel reducers are sold that can be used in *both* alkyd and acrylic enamels. Even so, it is a good idea to check the paint manufacturer's literature to be certain that the correct reducer is being used. Most companies market reducers for different types of enamel painting conditions (Fig. 25-49).

As with lacquer thinners, slower-drying enamel reducers should be used as the shop temperature increases. These allow the enamel to flow out to the smoothest possible finish with a minimum amount of orange peel. It is usually advisable to use the slowest-drying reducer that will work in the existing temperature and humidity conditions.

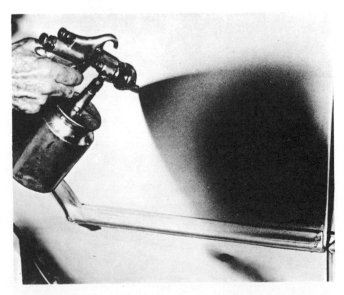

Fig. 25-48. *As the mixture of paint and added vehicle leaves the spray gun, it is broken up into fine droplets (atomized) by air pressure. (Courtesy of Rinshed–Mason Products Division, Inmont Corporation)*

SOLVENTS

Before a damaged area is repaired or prepared for refinishing, the old paint should be cleaned with a *solvent* (Figs. 25-50 and 25-51). Each paint manufacturer usually has its own pre-cleaning solvent product. These products are basically the same and do the same job.

These solvents quickly remove road oil, tar, waxes, silicones, and old films from the existing paint surface.

This is done so that grinding and sanding will not embed these chemicals in the bare metal. If the chemicals were ground into the bare metal, they would later cause paint troubles. The method of using these products is fairly simple. In general, they are "washed" on the surface with a rag, then wiped off, while wet, with a clean, dry rag (Fig. 25-51).

Fig. 25-49. *Enamel reducers are available with different drying speeds. (Courtesy of Rinshed–Mason Products Division, Inmont Corporation)*

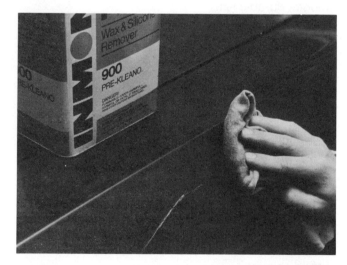

Fig. 25-50. *A typical pre-cleaning solvent. (Courtesy of Rinshed–Mason Products Division, Inmont Corporation)*

Fig. 25-51. *Before an area is prepared for refinishing, a pre-cleaning solvent should be used to remove grease, wax, and oily deposits. (Courtesy of Rinshed–Mason Products Division, Inmont Corporation)*

Preparing the Surface for Paint

To a very large extent, the success and appearance of a topcoat depends on how carefully the surface *under* that topcoat was prepared. The surface under the new paint work, of course, is referred to as the *substrate*. The substrate must be in good condition if the new paint work is to be successful. Properly preparing the substrate is known as *surface preparation*.

Surface preparation includes preparing *all* types of surfaces for new paint. These may include bare steel, aluminum, galvanized metal, and many types of old painted finishes. In any case, surface preparation is an important step. It can be compared to building the foundation of a house. A house is no better than its foundation; a paint job will be no better than the substrate (Fig. 26-1).

PREPARING UNPAINTED SURFACES

Many times, a body shop must do paint work on one or more types of *surfaces*. These are surfaces that have *not* been repaired but *do* need to have paint work done to them. These include replacement panels, aluminum panels, galvanized metal panels, and plastic panels. Each of these panels is different, and making paint correctly "stick" to each of them requires a *different* procedure.

Preparing Replacement Panels

The most commonly prepared metal panels are new *steel* replacement panels. Most car bodies (and the replacement panels made for them) are steel. Figure 26-2 shows a common steel replacement quarter panel.

Most steel replacement panels are painted at the factory with a coat of primer, to help prevent rust before the panel is installed on a vehicle. Normally, this "factory primer" is a good basis for a topcoat. Replacement panels require some preparation before they may be painted with a new color coat.

To prepare a replacement panel for painting, *first* figure out how the panel will be attached to the vehicle. If the panel will be *bolted* to the vehicle, such as a complete door or front fender, then it is usually completely painted off the vehicle, before being installed. On the other hand, if the panel must be *brazed* or *spot-welded* to the body (such as a quarter panel), it should first be attached to the vehicle, *then* painted.

A *second* item to consider is whether all the trim attachment or other holes are already in the panel. If one panel is used for several models of a car or truck,

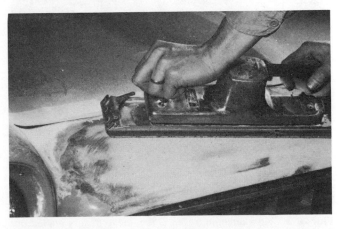

Fig. 26-1. *Preparing the substrate for refinishing. (Courtesy of Automotive Trades Division, 3M Company)*

not all the trim holes necessary for every model are drilled in the panel at the factory. A body shop usually must drill holes in replacement panels for the specific trim on the car or truck being repaired. It is a good idea to drill these holes *before* the panel is painted. The edges of the holes then will be painted along with the rest of the panel.

When a replacement panel has been installed (if necessary) and any needed trim holes drilled, it may then be prepared for final painting. To do this, proceed as follows:

1. Wash the entire panel with pre-cleaning solvent. Wipe the solvent off with a clean rag *before* it dries on the panel.
2. Block-sand the entire panel with wet #320 sandpaper. Pay special attention to any runs or sags in the factory primer.

Fig. 26-2. *A replacement quarter panel. Preparing such panels for painting is one of the most basic jobs in a body shop.*

Fig. 26-3. *An aluminum trailer. Often, these trailers are left unpainted. If they are painted, however, specific procedures must be followed so that the topcoat will properly adhere to the metal.*

3. The block-sanding usually will leave a few bare metal places on the panel. Treat these bare places with metal conditioner.
4. If there are any serious dents on the panel, repair them with body filler.
5. Wash the entire panel, including any body filler repairs, with a mild cleaner. Be sure to wipe the cleaner off the panel before it dries.
6. Apply primer–surfacer to any bare, thin, or repaired areas on the panel. Although *enamel* primer–surfacer would be preferred for this job, many shops use lacquer primer–surfacer successfully.
7. Allow the primer–surfacer to dry thoroughly.
8. Inspect the primer–surfacer for any nicks or small defects. If there are any, fill them with putty.
9. Carefully block-sand the entire panel with wet #400 sandpaper.
10. Wash the panel with final cleaner. Again, be sure to wipe the cleaner off before it dries.
11. If enamel primer–surfacer was used and the topcoat will be *lacquer*, apply the correct *sealer* to the panel surface. When the sealer has dried, scuff off any nibs with dry #400 sandpaper.
12. If the panel has been installed on the car, blow any dust or dirt out of cracks near the panel.
13. Wipe the panel with a tack rag. It is now properly prepared for the color coat.

Preparing Aluminum Panels

Figure 26-3 shows a truck trailer with an *aluminum body*. Aluminum is used on trucks, trailers, vans, and automobile bodies. A technician may have to work on aluminum metal as part of auto body repair. Many times, owners of van and camper bodies may ask a shop to do repair or repaint work on bodies with aluminum panels. A definite procedure *must* be followed if topcoats are to adhere (stick) to aluminum metal properly.

Manufacturers of aluminum and galvanized parts often spray (or dip-coat) their panels with an oily solution after they are manufactured. This is done before the metal is shipped from the plant to the assembly plant or to a body shop. Therefore, parts other than sheet metal usually have some type of oily coating applied to keep them from corroding.

To prepare *unpainted* aluminum panels properly for refinishing, any oily protective film must be removed. This may be done as follows:

1. Wash the panel thoroughly with hot, soapy water. Rinse thoroughly, and allow the panel to dry.
2. Remove any remaining oil or grease deposits by washing with trisodium phosphate or by steam-cleaning.

3. Wash the panel with pre-cleaning solvent. Wipe the solvent off the surface before it dries.
4. Treat any bare metal with metal conditioner. Wipe the metal conditioner off the panel before it dries.
5. Wipe the panel with a tack rag.
6. Apply zinc chromate or other aluminum primer to the panel. Allow it to dry for 30 minutes.
7. Block-sand the aluminum primer with wet #400 sandpaper.
8. Wash the surface with final cleaner. Wipe off the final cleaner before it dries on the surface.
9. If the panel is mounted on a body, blow any dust out of cracks near the panel.
10. Wipe the prepared surface with a tack rag. The surface is now ready for topcoat.

Preparing Galvanized Metal Panels

Figure 26-4 shows a school bus with a *galvanized metal* body. Galvanized metal is often used on automobile body panels and on different buses and commercial bodies.

Often, truck and bus companies have their own shops to repair damaged vehicles. However, more automobile manufacturers are using galvanized panels and pieces. Body shop employees must know how to work with galvanized metal and how to prepare it for painting.
How Galvanized Metal Is Made. Galvanized metal is actually normal sheet metal with a very thin coating of zinc on it. When the sheet metal piece is coated, a thin layer of zinc is "floated" onto the metal. This zinc layer grips the metal tightly and stays in place even when the metal is bent into shape for a body part.
Procedure. Because of the zinc coating, galvanized metal is one of the most difficult surfaces on which to make paint "stick." Galvanized metal must be prepared as outlined below if the topcoat is to adhere to the substrate properly:

1. Wash the panel thoroughly with hot, soapy water. Rinse it completely, and allow it to dry.
2. Thoroughly wash the panel with water and tri-sodium phosphate. Rinse it with clear water, and allow it to dry.
3. Wash the panel with pre-cleaning solvent. Wipe off the solvent before it dries on the panel.
4. Treat the bare galvanized metal with metal conditioner. Wipe off the metal conditioner before it dries.
5. Blow dust out of any cracks with compressed air.
6. Wipe the panel with a tack rag.
7. Thoroughly mix and strain the correct amounts of galvanized primer and activator. Follow the directions on the can carefully. Do *not* substitute other products.

8. Spray a *thin* coat of galvanized primer on the clean metal.
9. Allow the primer to dry for 30 minutes.
10. Fill any imperfections in the primer with putty.
11. Allow the putty and primer to dry overnight.
12. Block-sand the surface with wet #400 sandpaper.
13. Wash the panel with final cleaner. Wipe off the cleaner before it dries.
14. Blow dust out of any cracks around the panel.
15. Wipe the prepared surface with a tack rag. The panel is now ready for the topcoat.

Refinishing Galvanized Panels

In the past few years, manufacturers have begun using galvanized panels on their vehicles. Examples are Ford cowl panels and General Motors lower top extension panels. Often, paint will peel off such galvanized panels. Figure 26-5 shows a panel that has started peeling. The broken paint will not featheredge, so the panel must be stripped (Fig. 26-6). On these panels,

Fig. 26-4. *Schoolbus bodies are usually galvanized sheet metal. Like aluminum, galvanized metal must be finished by using specific procedures to obtain good results.*

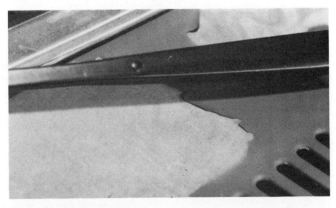

Fig. 26-5. *Paint peeling off a galvanized panel. The flaking paint can be removed with a razor blade in a holder.*

the easiest way to peel off the paint is with a razor blade and holder (Fig. 26-7).

You can use a chemical paint remover, but care must be taken to prevent the paint remover from touching adjoining panels and taking the paint off them, as well. The safer method is to remove the paint with the razor blade.

After the paint has been removed, the panel should be scuff-sanded with 180-grit sandpaper, then treated with a solution of metal conditioner that is recommended for galvanized metal. Compound all adjoining panels to give a better color match.

Next, mask the area with tape and paper. Prime the panel with a good primer that is recommended for galvanized metal (Fig. 26-8).

The secret of a good reliable repair is following the correct procedure and using only material recommended for galvanized metal.

PREPARING PAINTED SURFACES

Most paint work in a body shop is done on metal that already has *some* paint on it. This may be a panel that has been repaired or an old finish that will be covered when new paint is applied to the entire car or panel. Properly preparing (in some cases, removing) the old

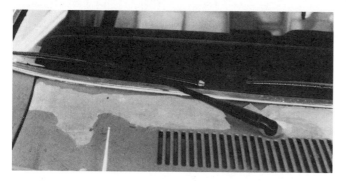

Fig. 26-6. *The paint on this panel will not featheredge to allow blending of the new and old finishes. The old paint must be stripped off.*

Fig. 26-7. *A razor blade scraper is an easy way to peel paint from small areas of galvanized metal before refinishing.*

paint is very important for the life and durability of the new topcoat.

Choosing the Type of Repair

When a car is to be refinished after a collision repair, the painter and body worker must decide how much of the car is to be repainted. Several factors are involved, such as the type of metal repair that was done, the type and condition of the paint already on the car, and the cost of the total job. Once it is decided how much will be repainted, either *definition lines* or *spot repair* must be decided upon.

Definition Lines. Whenever only *part* of a car is to be painted, the painter must decide exactly how much will be covered. The painter determines what area will have new paint, how big an area it will be, and which areas to *mask* off so that they will not be painted. The *edges* of the area to be painted are known as *definition lines* (Fig. 26-9).

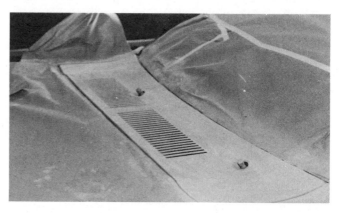

Fig. 26-8. *This panel has had the old paint removed and a recommended primer sprayed on.*

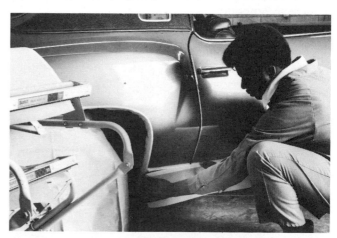

Fig. 26-9. *Definition lines (breaks between panels, sharp bends in metal, moldings) can be used to disguise the line between old and new paint. (Courtesy of Automotive Trades Division, 3M Company)*

Definition lines must be chosen carefully. If masking tape and paper were put right down the center of a door, for example, there would be a definition line down the center of the door after the paint work was done. It would be easy to see the difference between the old and the new paint. Therefore, this would be a *poor* definition line. *Good* definition lines (such as moldings or panel edges) make it very difficult to see the difference between the old and the new paints.

Spot Repairs. When only part of a panel is painted, the new paint is said to be "spotted in." This is known as a *spot repair.* Figures 26-10 and 26-11 show a typical spot repair.

When a spot repair is made, there are no definition lines. That is, there is no one line where the old paint ends and the new paint begins. Instead, the new paint gradually "blends" into the old paint around the spot. Making a good spot repair that blends well is a skilled job. It can be "tricky," even for good painters.

Preparing the Surface

As soon as you know exactly *what* area will be refinished, prepare the surface for the new paint. Generally, this procedure is the same for all types of repairs and painted surfaces. However, based on the *specific* job being done, some procedures may need to be done extra carefully, whereas others may not need to be done. The *general* procedure given here should be followed as closely as possible.

Wash the Car. This should always be the first step before *any* refinish work. Washing the *entire* car (Fig. 26-12), will help remove any dust or dirt that might otherwise be blown into the new paint, even if only part of the car is to be refinished. Washing the car also helps ensure a good color match since the old color can be more accurately seen and matched. With no dirt and dust on the car, masking tape will stick more easily to the parts that will not be painted.

Clean the Area. After the entire car has been washed, work only on the area to be repaired. The first step is to clean it with pre-cleaning solvent. Wipe the solvent off the area *before* it dries (Fig. 26-13).

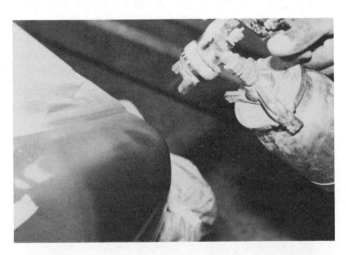

Fig. 26-10. *Spot refinishing requires skill in blending the new and old finishes.*

Fig. 26-11. *A completed spot repair, with no visible difference between the repainted area and the original finish.*

Fig. 26-12. Step 1: *Wash the car before any other preparation is done for body or paint work.*

Fig. 26-13. Step 2: *Use a pre-cleaning solvent to remove grease and wax from the area to be refinished. (Courtesy of Refinish Division, DuPont Company)*

Make Metal Repairs. After the old surface has been cleaned with pre-cleaning solvent, it may be ground off for repairs. If the old paint is ground off *before* it is cleaned, waxes and chemicals in the old paint might be ground into the bare metal. These waxes or chemicals could later cause a serious paint problem known as *fish-eye*.

Metal repairing will usually include grinding the old finish to remove it (Fig. 26-14) and filling the area with body filler (Fig. 26-15). Any number of metal repair methods may be used to make the *substrate* as smooth and level as possible. These repair methods are discussed elsewhere in the book.

Featheredge Any Broken Paint. Even if metal repairs were not made, most areas to be refinished will have small nicks and chips. These are a result of car doors hitting each other in parking lots or small stones being thrown up by the car's wheels and chipping the paint. In all cases, the broken paint must be *featheredged* before primer–surfacer is applied.

A *featheredge* (Fig. 26-16) is a tapered edge of the old paint that smooths down to the bare metal. This is done so that there is not a sharp edge around the paint break. A sharp edge would show as a defect under the new paint and make the repair look poor. For this rea-

son, featheredging broken paint is *very* important. *It must be done thoroughly and carefully all around the damaged area.*

There are two methods used to featheredge old paint: *mechanical* and *chemical*. Which method to use depends on personal preference. *Chemical* featheredging (lacquer only) requires that the shop buy another solvent chemical. Many shops prefer to do mechanical featheredging.

During *mechanical* featheredging, *sandpapers* are used to taper the old paint. Mechanical featheredging, using sandpaper, *must be done with a sanding block.* If the featheredging is done without a sanding block ("fingertip sanding"), the surface will not be cut evenly, and the featheredge will not be as smoothly tapered as it should be (Fig. 26-17).

Sanding a featheredge may also be done with an orbital (power) sander (Fig. 26-18). When this sander is used, #180 sandpaper should be used to *begin* the featheredge. If a sanding block is used, #220 sandpaper would be used to *begin* the featheredge (Fig. 26-19).

To *finish* a featheredge, #360 or #400 *wet* sandpaper should be used. This paper should always be used *by hand, wet,* and *with a sanding block.*

To *chemically* featheredge broken lacquer paint, use a special solvent designed to dissolve the edges of

Fig. 26-16. Step 4: *Featheredge the broken paint to prevent the presence of a sharp line between new and old finishes.*

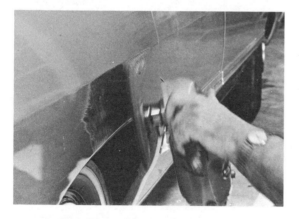

Fig. 26-14. Step 3: *Make any needed metal repairs. Here, a grinder is being used to remove old paint from a panel. (Courtesy of Refinish Division, DuPont Company)*

Fig. 26-15. Step 3, continued: *Plastic body filler is being used here to level the surface of the metal for refinishing. (Courtesy of Refinish Division, DuPont Company)*

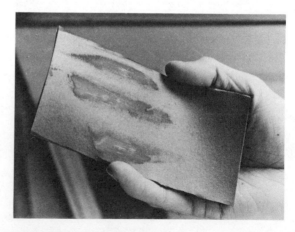

Fig. 26-17. Step 4, continued: *A sanding block should be used for an even featheredge. When finger pressure alone is used, as shown here, the sandpaper will cut unevenly. (Courtesy of Refinish Division, DuPont Company)*

broken paint. Properly used, this product will *not* dissolve the car manufacturer's original undercoat primer (Fig. 26-20). The instructions for using this product are usually printed on the can and should be followed carefully.

Prepare Any Remaining Areas. During a panel repair or an overall refinishing job, there are usually areas that do not need either metal repairs or featheredging. These are areas where the old paint has not been broken. For such areas, it must be decided how the paint already on the surface will be prepared.

Methods by which this old paint may be prepared include *sanding* and *stripping.* Whether the new topcoat is to be *lacquer* or *enamel,* #400 sandpaper should be used.

Stripping the finish involves using a chemical *paint remover* to remove the old paint from the surface completely (Figs. 26-21 and 26-22). If the old finish is badly weathered or scarred, it should be stripped. It would be poor foundation for a lasting new topcoat. Paint remover must be used *according to the directions on the can* and with proper safety precautions. Stripping the

Fig. 26-20.   Step 4, continued: *On lacquers, chemical featheredging can be done with a special solvent. It will partly dissolve the lacquer, without affecting the underlying primer. (Courtesy of Refinish Division, DuPont Company)*

Fig. 26-18.   Step 4, continued: *An orbital sander may be used for mechanical featheredging of the old finish. (Courtesy of Refinish Division, DuPont Company)*

Fig. 26-21.   Step 5: *If the old paint is in poor condition, it may be easier to prepare the surface by* stripping *the old finish. A chemical stripper (paint remover) is applied as shown. (Courtesy of Refinish Division, DuPont Company)*

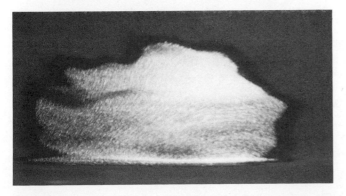

Fig. 26-19.   *An area to be refinished, after featheredging has been done.*

Fig. 26-22.   Step 5, continued: *The stripper will cause the old finish to wrinkle and lift away from the metal. It may then be washed off with a stream of water, or scraped off with a putty knife.* Note: *Because of the strong chemicals involved, safety goggles and rubber gloves should always be worn when stripping paint. (Courtesy of Refinish Division, DuPont Company)*

finish also will soften and remove any plastic filler *under* the finish. Because of this, be prepared to replace any plastic filler in the area if paint remover is used.

Treat Any Bare Metal. An important step to *lasting* paint work is to treat any bare metal with metal conditioner. This product will help to etch the metal for good paint adhesion *and* protect it from further rusting. Read instructions carefully before using metal conditioner. This product must *always* be wiped off the bare metal before it dries (Fig. 26-23).

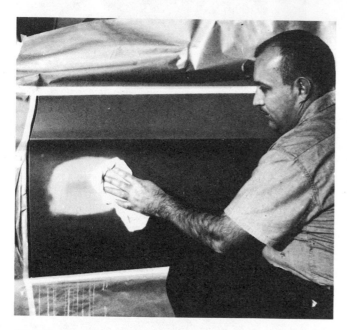

Fig. 26-23. Step 6: *Bare metal should be treated with a metal conditioner to prevent rust from occurring again. The conditioner also helps paint to adhere better. (Courtesy of Refinish Division, DuPont Company)*

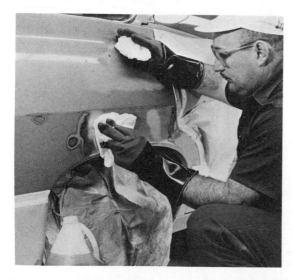

Fig. 26-24. Step 7: *Wash the area to be refinished with a final wash solvent. Wipe the solvent off the surface before it dries. (Courtesy of Refinish Division, DuPont Company)*

Wash the Area. After metal repairs have been made, featheredging completed, and any old paint prepared or stripped, the *entire area* to be refinished should be washed with final wash solvent (Fig. 26-24). This is a very important step. It will help to neutralize any chemicals and remove any sanding dust or other dirt from the surface.

Mask the Area. During almost all refinishing or repair work, there will be at least *some* bare metal that must be primed with primer–surfacer. Before this is done, it is a good idea to take the time to mask off all trim and other areas that are not to be painted (Fig. 26-25). This should be done carefully, so that the masking may be left in place until *after* the new color topcoat is applied. Be certain to mask all around the area to be painted, if the entire vehicle is not being repainted. Choose the *definition lines* carefully if a panel repair is being done (Fig. 26-26). Careful masking will help prevent excessive clean-up time and will do a good job of hiding definition lines.

Apply Primer–Surfacer. After the area has been masked and washed with a final wash, primer–surfacer may then be applied. Whether lacquer or enamel primer–surfacer is used, it is important that the mixing and application instructions on the can be followed. The instructions will include *how much* thinner or reducer to use, *what type* of thinner or reducer to use depending on shop conditions, and the approximate *air pressure* to use at the spray gun.

In general, *lacquer* primer–surfacers are thinned with medium-dry ("mid-temp") thinners. About 1 ½ to 2 parts of thinner should be used with one part of lacquer primer–surfacer (Fig. 26-27). When applying lacquer primer–surfacer to a *spot* repair, adjust the spray gun for a small pattern and use from 25 to 35 psi (172 to 241 kPa) of air pressure at the gun (Fig. 26-28). For large repairs (panel or overall), 35 to 45 psi (241 to 310 kPa) of pressure may be used.

Fig. 26-25. Step 8: *Mask all trim and other areas that are not to be painted. (Courtesy of Refinish Division, DuPont Company)*

Enamel primer–surfacers generally are reduced with either mid-temp or low-temp reducers, depending on the shop conditions. About two parts of enamel primer–surfacer should be mixed with one part of the correct enamel reducer for the best results (Fig. 26-29).

If an *enamel* finish is being repaired, enamel primer–surfacer may be used to fill and prime any bare metal, featheredged areas on the surface. For these "spot-priming" jobs, about 35 to 40 psi (241 to 276 kPa) of air pressure at the gun should be used with a small spray pattern.

When spraying primer–surfacer, allow each coat to *flash off* (evaporate from wet glossy to a dull appearance) before applying the next coat. Do not build up too great a thickness of primer–surfacer by using too many coats. Four to six coats of primer–surfacer are usually all that are required. Be careful to not make any one coat too heavy. It will dry slowly and may crack.

Apply Putty. If any nicks or chips are noted in the surface of the primer–surfacer, *putty* may be applied to fill them (Fig. 26-30). The putty may be applied either

Fig. 26-28. Step 9: *Apply primer–surfacer to the area being refinished. Depending on the product used and the area being covered, technique and air pressure may be varied somewhat.*

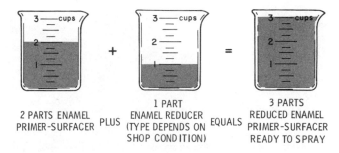

2 PARTS ENAMEL PRIMER-SURFACER PLUS 1 PART ENAMEL REDUCER (TYPE DEPENDS ON SHOP CONDITION) EQUALS 3 PARTS REDUCED ENAMEL PRIMER-SURFACER READY TO SPRAY

Fig. 26-29. *Mixing enamel primer–surfacer.*

Fig. 26-26. Step 8, continued: *On a panel refinishing job, carefully choose difinition lines to make the boundary between old and new paint less noticeable. (Courtesy of Refinish Division, DuPont Company)*

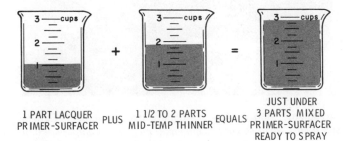

1 PART LACQUER PRIMER-SURFACER PLUS 1 1/2 TO 2 PARTS MID-TEMP THINNER EQUALS JUST UNDER 3 PARTS MIXED PRIMER-SURFACER READY TO SPRAY

Fig. 26-27. *Mixing lacquer primer–surfacer.*

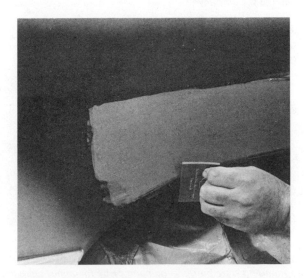

Fig. 26-30. Step 10: *Apply putty to fill minor surface defects. Putty may be applied after the primer–surfacer has been sanded. (Courtesy of Refinish Division, DuPont Company)*

before or after the primer–surfacer is block-sanded. Applying the putty *before* the primer–surfacer is sanded has the advantage of having to sand the area only once. On the other hand, it is easier to see any small defects in the finish *after* the primer–surfacer is sanded. It may be desirable to apply the putty after sanding and then resand the area slightly to level the putty.

Block-sand the Area. The area that will actually receive the new paint must be block-sanded to prepare it for the final color coat. This is done to level the surface properly and make it smooth enough for the new paint to flow out properly. If the block-sanding is not done carefully, it will "show up" under the paint as uneven or rough areas and will make the finish look poor no matter how carefully the topcoat is applied. If any nicks or chips are noticed after block-sanding, fill them with putty and then resand before going on to the next step.

Generally, this is the final sanding preparation on an area to be refinished. This step is best done with wet sandpaper and a sanding block (Fig. 26-31). Which

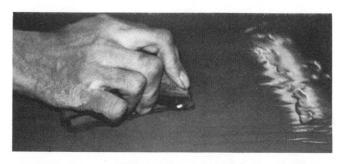

Fig. 26-31. Step 11: *Hand-sand the spot repair area, using a sanding block for even cutting. (Courtesy of Automotive Trades Division, 3M Company)*

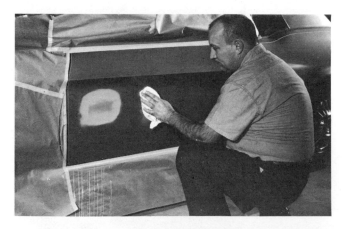

Fig. 26-32. Step 12: *Compound the old finish around a spot repair, to aid in proper blending of the new and old finishes. Compounding may be done by hand or by machine, depending on the size of the spot repair. This step is not done when a complete panel is being refinished. (Courtesy of Refinish Division, DuPont Company)*

sandpaper to use depends on the type of topcoat that will be applied. In all cases, #400 sandpaper will produce the smoothest topcoat finish and is always required before a *lacquer* topcoat is applied. If an *enamel* topcoat will be applied, wet #320 sandpaper may be used to speed up the job. However, the topcoat will not be as smooth as if #400 sandpaper had been used.

It is important to avoid breaking through the old paint or new primer–surfacer during this final block-sanding. If bare metal is exposed, the area will have to be spot-primed and then resanded. Where hand-sanding without a block must be done (such as around corners), be careful to sand the area *evenly*.

Finally, sand *only* the area that actually will be covered with new paint. For a *spot repair*, of course, there are no definition lines to determine where the new paint will stop. Wet-sand only the primer–surfacer area and about 1 in. (25.4 mm) around it for a spot repair. Rubbing compound will be used to prepare the *outer* area around the spot for the new paint.

Compound the Area. To prepare the good paint for "blending in" *around* a spot repair, the area must be compounded. To do this, either hand or "wheel" compounding may be done (Fig. 26-32).

The good paint should be compounded about 10 in. (25.4 cm) around the repair to brighten up and clean the paint thoroughly. This allows the new paint to blend more thoroughly into the old and allows it to more easily grip the old paint. A good compounding *before* painting is necessary if a spot repair is to blend properly into the older paint on the same panel.

Wash the Area. The final step in cleaning is to wash the entire area to be painted with a final wash solution. Any area that was compounded should be carefully washed to remove any compounding *sludge*. Wipe the final wash off the area *before it dries* (Fig. 26-33).

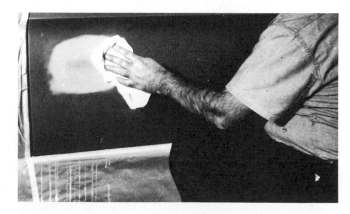

Fig. 26-33. Step 13: *After sanding, wash the repair area again with a final wash solvent. If adjoining paint was compounded, it should be washed with solvent as well. Wipe the solvent off before it dries. (Courtesy of Refinish Division, DuPont Company)*

Dust and Tack. After the final wash, use compressed air to blow any dust off the area (Fig. 26-34). Also, blow any dust out of cracks or moldings in the repair area. If dust remains in these areas, the air pressure of the paint spray gun may blow it out onto the wet paint.

Finally, wipe the entire area with a *tack rag.* A tack rag is a specially treated, sticky cloth that will easily pick up any small specks of dust on the area to be painted. Tack rags are used *without* any kind of reducer or solvent. When a tack rag is dirty, it should be discarded. Tack rags cannot be cleaned and reused (Fig. 26-35).

Sealing and Painting

After the surface has been properly prepared, it is ready for painting. At this point, the new topcoat color may be applied. However, under some conditions, it may be necessary or desirable to apply *sealer* to the area before the topcoat is applied.

Sealer should be applied just after the repair (or refinish) area has been wiped with the tack rag. As usual, follow the directions listed on the can of *sealer.* If these

are not available, the following *general procedure* may be used.

1. Mix the sealer and the correct reducer according to the manufacturer's directions. Some sealers require no vehicle at all. In any case, *strain* the sealer or mixture as it is poured into the paint gun cup.
2. Set the air pressure at 35 to 45 psi (241 to 310 kPa) at the gun.
3. Apply an even, medium coat of sealer to the area (Fig. 26-36).
4. Allow the sealer to dry for at least 15 minutes, but less than 1 hour.
5. Very lightly scuff the area by hand with dry #400 paper to remove any nibs or overspray. Do *not* heavily sand the area; just a very light scuff is all that is required (Fig. 26-37).
6. Wipe the sealed area with a tack rag.
7. Apply the color topcoat.

Fig. 26-36. Step 15: *Spray a single, medium-heavy coat of sealer on the repair area to help adhesion of the new and old paint. (Courtesy of Refinish Division, DuPont Company)*

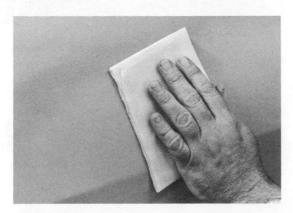

Fig. 26-34. Step 14: *Use compressed air to blow dust off the surface and out of any cracks. (Courtesy of Refinish Division, DuPont Company)*

Fig. 26-35. Step 14, continued: *Wipe the area with a tack rag to pick up any remaining dust particles. (Courtesy of Refinish Division, DuPont Company)*

Fig. 26-37. Step 15, continued: *Lightly scuff the sealer with a 400-grit sandpaper to remove any small nibs or specks. (Courtesy of Refinish Division, DuPont Company)*

Unit 27

Applying Automotive Paint

The actual process of using a spray gun to apply paint is fairly simple. However, because of the many differences in paints, equipment, substrates, and colors, it requires a good deal of *practice* to apply automotive paint properly. A good automobile painter must know about paint and painting equipment *and* must have a good deal of painting practice (Fig. 27-1).

Fig. 27-1. *A good painter must understand both paints and the painting process. (Courtesy of Rinshed–Mason Products Division, Inmont Corporation)*

ORIGINAL PAINT TYPES

An auto body worker must be able to identify the different types of paint that may be on an automobile. Almost all of today's *new* cars, of course, are painted with either acrylic lacquer or acrylic enamel paint (Figs. 27-2 and 27-3). Most new trucks are painted with acrylic enamel, as are most foreign cars.

Fig. 27-2. *Some General Motors vehicles are factory finished with acrylic lacquer.*

Fig. 27-3. *Many domestic autos and most foreign cars are finished at the factory with acrylic enamels. (Courtesy of Prostripe Division, Spartan Plastics, Inc.)*

Lacquers

From a refinishing point of view, *lacquers* are more or less *soluble* (able to be dissolved) no matter how long they have been on the car. This means that the old lacquer finish will dissolve slightly when a new lacquer is sprayed over it. This creates a good bond between the old and new finishes, and is known as *penetration*.

When refinishing a *lacquer* paint job, it is a good idea to use lacquer for the new paint. Often, however, a car that was originally finished in lacquer is refinished in acrylic enamel. This may be done successfully if the old lacquer finish is properly prepared.

Enamels

As enamels dry, they become more *insoluble* and "tougher" than lacquers. They are not easily softened by the reducer in new enamel paint when the new paint is sprayed on the surface. Old *enamel* finishes, therefore, must be carefully sanded before repainting so that they will have *pores* in which the new paint may grip.

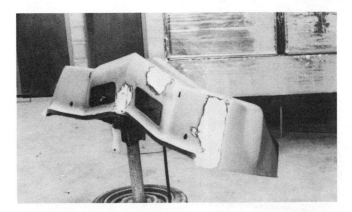

Fig. 27-4. *A repaired urethane bumper cover, ready for flexible paint.*

Fig. 27-5. *Painting the repaired bumper cover.*

Special Paints

Different areas of an automobile or truck may be painted with some type of special paint. A painter must be able to identify and apply these special paints when making routine body repairs (Fig. 27-4). The most important of these, *catalyzed* paints or additives, are used on body parts made of urethane and other plastic parts. Special *trunk* paint is available to refinish trunk interiors, and special *chassis* paint is packaged for use when painting chassis parts.

Catalyzed Paint. Many body panels are now being made with a flexible, rubberlike plastic material. Plastic parts are often used at the front and rear of the automobile where they may partially take the place of a regular bumper. Figure 27-5 shows a painter refinishing a urethane bumper cover.

Special *urethane paint* is available and may be used on urethane body panels. Urethane *additives* also are available, such as the product in Figure 27-6. These products may be mixed with standard lacquers and enamels, *according to directions*, to allow these paints to be used on urethane parts. If the additive is not used, regular enamel or lacquer may crack on the urethane's flexible surface.

The preparation is similar to that used for other topcoats. First, clean the surface with soap and water, then a solvent (mild pre-cleaner).

Next, sand the surface of the vehicle with 150- or 180-grit dry sandpaper on an orbital sander. Prime bare metal with a primer–surfacer. If the metal is aluminum or galvanized, use the recommended primer for these metals.

Fig. 27-6. *An additive used to make paints flexible for application to urethane parts.*

Then, sand the vehicle with 400-grit sandpaper, and seal with a recommended sealer, reduced according to the manufacturer's specifications. Allow the sealer to dry for 30 minutes to 1 hour before applying the topcoat. If the temperature is lower than 70°F (21°C), the drying time should be extended.

CAUTION: Always use a charcoal type mask with new cartridges.

The vapor from the catalyzed paint contains isocyanate, which can be very harmful to your lungs. Isocyanate breaks down the charcoal in filter cartridges, so thay should be replaced frequently.

Urethane must be added to enamel to allow it to dry properly. However, the "pot life" of urethane paint is short. (The paint can jell at high temperatures within 1 hour.) Clean the spray gun immediately after spraying. If paint is left in the gun to harden, all the air passages will be clogged. A complete disassembly of the spray gun then will be necessary to clean it sufficiently to be used again.

Trunk Paint. Special paint for the inside of the luggage compartment (trunk) is known as trunk paint. It is also known as *spatter paint.* In some of these products, small particles of a second paint color are suspended in the base color. These particles do not dissolve because they are a different type of paint than the base paint. When the paint is sprayed onto a surface, the particles spatter to make a speck of a second color in the base color (Fig. 27-7).

Trunk paint can be bought in several basic colors to match the original trunk interior. The trunk may be spot-repaired or completely refinished. All of the normal preparation steps should be followed, except that a paint undercoat does not need to be used unless there are rusted spots (Fig. 27-8).

Chassis Paint. Special tough, black enamel paints are made for chassis parts that need to be replaced or

Fig. 27-7. *Refinishing a trunk interior with spatter paint. Original finish at left, new paint at right. (Courtesy of Ditzler Automotive Finishes Division, PPG Industries, Inc.)*

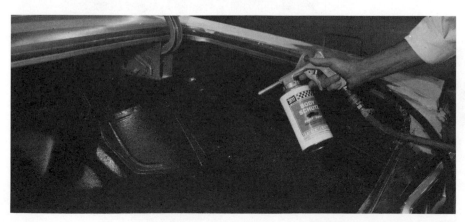

Fig. 27-8. *A sealer is being sprayed into the trunk of a vehicle. (Courtesy of Automotive Trades Division, 3M Company)*

have been repaired. Most chassis paints have an alkyd enamel base. They may be applied to new chassis parts before the parts are installed on the car. Chassis paint should also be used on areas underneath the car where heat, grinding, or hammering have broken the paint film.

MATCHING PAINT TYPES

When a vehicle (or part of it) is to be refinished, it is the painter's job to determine what *kind* of paint is already on the vehicle. If the vehicle is fairly new and has obviously never been repainted, determining the paint *type* will be fairly easy. This is known as matching the original color. If the car has been repainted or spotted in, however, it will be more difficult to determine the type and exact color of the paint.

Matching Undercoat Types

Matching the manufacturer's original *undercoat* will be fairly easy. All American manufacturers basically use the same materials and methods for the original undercoating: enamel primer or enamel primer–sealer. These are used because they have better adhesion and better color holdout. When applied under factory conditions, they may not need as much sanding as would a lacquer primer. The original primer–sealer undercoat dries very hard. For this reason, it may be known as super-hard or *epoxyester* primer–sealer.

Rustproofing the Vehicle Body. Rustproofing a car body at the factory involves dipping the vehicle in a rustproofing solution (Fig. 27-9). This chemical will protect the vehicle from rust for many years.

The original undercoat is applied on some makes by an *electrostatic* process. The metal body is given a *positive* electrical charge, and a big tank of undercoat is given a *negative* electrical charge. Then, when the body is dipped in the liquid, the different electrical charges pull the liquid onto the body, forming a tight bond. Figure 27-10 shows a new car body being dipped in an automatically controlled bath of undercoat. After this dip, the undercoat is baked onto the body and dried in a high-temperature oven.

Matching Lacquer Types

General Motors Corporation is the only major American manufacturer using *lacquer* as the original topcoat on many new automobiles. The lacquer that General Motors uses on its cars (Chevrolet, Pontiac, Oldsmobile, Buick, and Cadillac) is *acrylic* lacquer. To match the original finish on these cars, acrylic lacquer paint should be used.

Some General Motors cars and trucks are finished with acrylic enamel. These vehicle color code letters will be marked on the identification plate.

Some American vehicles are finished with a water-based enamel. This type of paint is identified with the letter "W" on the identification plate.

When the manufacturer uses water-based paint, the repaint procedures are the same as any other factory paint repair.

Cars made by AMC (American Motors Corporation), Chrysler Corporation, and the Ford Motor Company are factory finished with *acrylic* enamel, generally beginning with the 1965 models. Most small and medium-sized American-made trucks are also finished in acrylic enamel, as are many foreign cars.

Some foreign cars are finished in *alkyd* enamel paint. When this is true, a sticker under the hood or on a door post may identify the paint as alkyd enamel. Many large trucks and heavy, off-road equipment may be finished with *polyurethane* enamel.

Matching Repaint Types

If a car has been repainted, it may not have the original, factory-type paint on it. Because of this, a painter

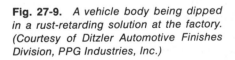

Fig. 27-9. *A vehicle body being dipped in a rust-retarding solution at the factory. (Courtesy of Ditzler Automotive Finishes Division, PPG Industries, Inc.)*

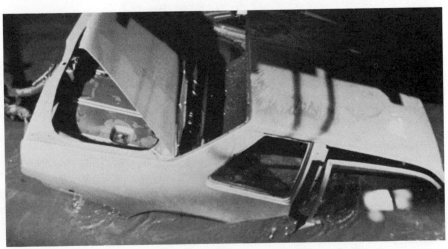

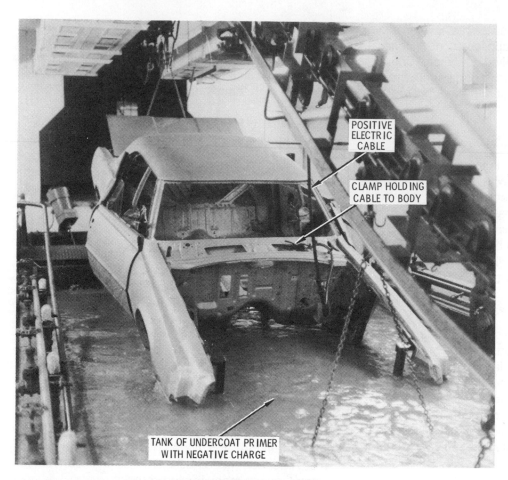

Fig. 27-10. *An electrostatic system used to apply rustproofing primer to an auto body. The primer bath is negatively charged, and the body is positively charged. (Courtesy of Customer Service Division, Ford Motor Company)*

Fig. 27-11. *Testing for paint type by using lacquer thinner on an inconspicuous area of the car.*

must be able to determine what type of topcoat is now on the car. Most experienced painters are able to do this by simply *looking* at the topcoat very carefully.

If there is doubt about what type of paint is on the car, a simple test may be made. To make this test, apply a small amount of lacquer thinner to a rag and rub the paint with the rag. This should be done under a

fender lip or at someplace near the bottom of the body where it will be out of sight (Fig. 27-11).

After rubbing the paint with lacquer thinner, look at both the rag and the paint. If the paint colors the rag, the paint is lacquer. If the lacquer thinner curdles the paint, causing it to lift and bubble, the paint is enamel.

MATCHING COLOR

Matching the color of paint already on a car is one of the most difficult jobs in auto body paint work. This is because there are so many factors that affect a color match. It is affected by paint booth lighting and ventilation, by how well the paint is mixed, by the quality of the materials and equipment used, and, especially, by the *techniques* (spraying methods) used to apply the color.

To match an automobile paint color properly, a painter must know a good deal about paint materials and how to use them. The painter also must understand the equipment and tools used to apply the materials. For this reason, purchasing good-quality materials and equipment is one of the best investments that a body shop can make.

Matching the Original Factory Color

Generally, it is easier to match a factory color than to match an unknown color on the car. As a first step to matching the color, locate the body identification plate, as is being done in Figure 27-12. The plate may be located on the cowl, on a door jamb, or elsewhere. Figure 27-13 shows the identification plate with the paint (color) code circled. This color code then can be used to locate the correct color in a *color chip book*. The book will have a color chip of that code along with the code itself. *If the color chip for that code does not match the car's color, the car has been refinished in a color that was not the original color.*

Matching the Last Color Used

If a vehicle has been refinished, the color code may not be known. In this case, try to find a color chip sample that matches the last color used on the vehicle. Place this chip over a clean polished area on the present paint job. Wet both the chip and a spot on the paint (Fig. 27-14). Putting water on the old paint will give it a gloss so that it will have about the same luster (shine) as the color chip.

While both the chip and the paint are wet, it is easy to determine whether the color on the chip is the same as the color on the vehicle. If the colors look *at all* different, keep experimenting with different color chips until an exact match is found. When an *exact* match is found, the color code for that chip (printed in the chip book) may be used to order paint for the vehicle.

Sometimes, *no* color chip will appear close enough to the paint on the car. In this case, there may have been a special color or a mixture of colors used. In these cases, paint will have to be custom mixed to match the color actually on the car. To do this, remove

a small part that has been painted with the special color. Then, *send this part to the paint store*. They will custom mix an exact color to match the color on the part sent to them. Normally, custom mixes such as these *cannot* be returned to the paint store, so be certain that the customer has paid a deposit on the job to cover the shop's cost for this custom-mix paint.

Getting a Good Color Match

Having the correct color paint in the can is only the *beginning* of a good color match. Even the correct color may not match perfectly the first time it is sprayed. This is because there are several *other* factors that definitely affect a good color match. The following pointers should be kept in mind when trying to get the best possible color match.

Use Top-quality Materials. When buying paint and paint *materials*, always deal with a store that *specializes* in automobile-painting products. For the best results, do not buy from a store that sells the materials only as a sideline. Unknown paints and cheap reducers and thinners often do not give results as good as name-brand, quality products. Good paint materials, purchased from a reliable parts house or supplier, are a wise investment for the best painting results.

Fig. 27-13. *The manufacturer's paint code (circled) is found on the body identification plate.*

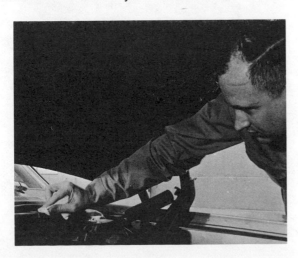

Fig. 27-12. *Locating the vehicle's body identification plate on the cowl, to find paint color code. (Courtesy of Refinish Division, DuPont Company)*

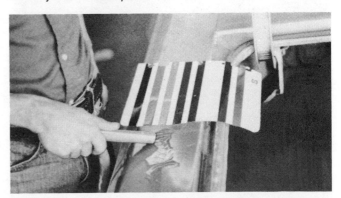

Fig. 27-14. *When the paint on the car is not the original color, a paint chip book must be used for matching. Both the chip and the paint should be wet to obtain an accurate color match.*

Use Top-quality Equipment. Buying paint *equipment* is like buying paint material. The best place to buy equipment is also from a supplier (store) whose main business is selling automobile-painting equipment. They will be interested in selling only equipment that will do a good job. They will have parts and service readily available if repairs are ever needed.

The spray gun itself is probably the most important piece of equipment, since it is used so often and must do so many jobs. Many shops use *three* spray guns (Fig. 27-15). One gun is used for lacquers, one for enamels, and one for the shop's undercoat, which is normally lacquer primer–surfacer. Each spray gun must be cleaned thoroughly after each spraying job.

Use Clean Air. Unbelievable as it may seem, dirt from *compressed air lines* often causes blemishes and trouble during paint work. It is important that good separator–regulators be used to keep the air to the spray gun clean and dry. Equally important is keeping all the *air filters* in the compressed air system clean and draining the separator regularly (Fig. 27-16). The air compressor itself and any drops in the air system should also be drained regularly.

If dirt or moisture in the air lines is suspected during a paint job, turn off the exhaust fan and spray-paint a test panel in the paint room. Carefully look at the test panel for any dirt or moisture in the fresh paint. If dirt or moisture is found, stop painting until the problem is cleared up.

Another method to check for dirt and moisture is to first remove the paint cup and air cap from the spray gun. Then, hold a clean white handkerchief over the gun nozzle, and pull the trigger back *just far enough to release air*, not fluid. This way, any dirt, water, or oil in the air lines will show up on the handkerchief (Fig. 27-17).

Thoroughly Stir the Paint. Mixing the paint *in the can* is very necessary *before* adding any vehicle such as thinner or reducer. To stir and mix the material properly, use a paint paddle made of wood or metal (Fig. 27-18). The end of the paddle is sometimes tapered to a sharp edge, like the edge of a chisel. This makes it easy to break up any material that has settled and stuck to the

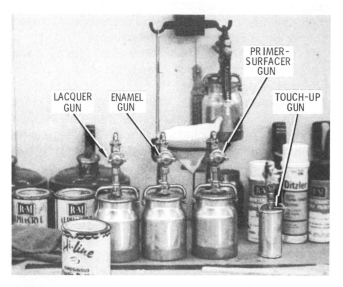

Fig. 27-15. *In many shops, different guns are reserved for each type of paint or paint material.*

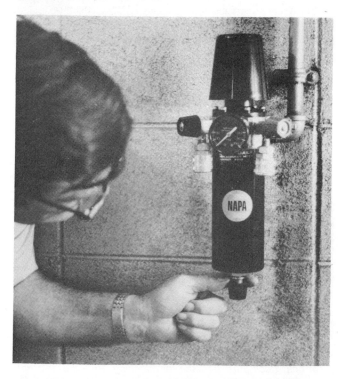

Fig. 27-16. *Draining moisture from the separator–regulator.*

Fig. 27-17. *Using the* handkerchief test *to check for dirt, water, or oil in the air line.*

bottom of the can. Another method of thoroughly mixing the paint, of course, is to use a paint *shaker* (Fig. 27-19).

Paint always must be thoroughly stirred, especially after it has been in storage for a long time. While in storage, paint tends to settle into different parts (Fig. 27-20). If the paint is not stirred, these parts will not be

Fig. 27-18. *Paint must always be thoroughly stirred before thinner or reducer is added. (Courtesy of Refinish Division, DuPont Company)*

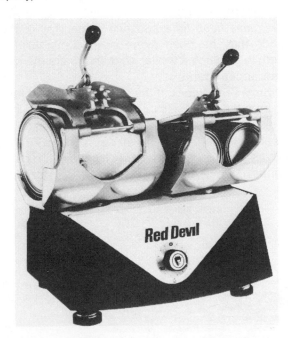

Fig. 27-19. *A paint shaker should be used to mix paint thoroughly in the closed can. (Courtesy of Ditzler Automotive Finishes Division, PPG Industries, Inc.)*

mixed thoroughly. This may cause it to not spray uniformly and will usually cause a poor color match.

After thinner or reducer is added, the mixture must again be thoroughly stirred before being strained into the spray gun cup. One reason for this is that metallic flakes quickly settle to the bottom of the container after thinner or reducer is added. This will nearly always change the topcoat color, causing a color mismatch on the finished job.

Judge the Color in the Correct Light. The *light* in a repair shop can be misleading. If the lights are *incandescent lamps* (ordinary light bulbs), the light will be slightly red when compared to daylight. Matching colors under this type of light is most difficult (Fig. 27-21). Fluorescent lights also give off a reddish color. It is also more difficult to match colors under this light than under natural light. However, fluorescent lights are preferable to incandescent bulbs. Generally *all* artificial lighting makes it difficult to match paint colors.

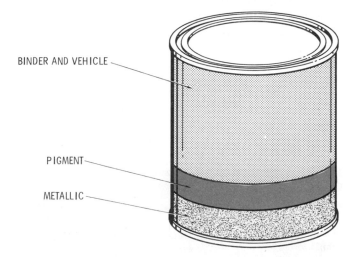

BINDER AND VEHICLE

PIGMENT

METALLIC

Fig. 27-20. *When paint is stored, it tends to separate into its component parts. This is particularly true of metallic paints.*

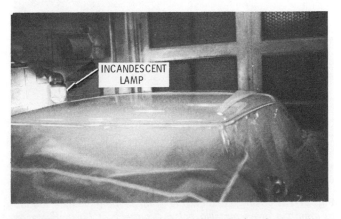

INCANDESCENT LAMP

Fig. 27-21. *Incandescent lighting in the paint booth.*

The *best* light to use when matching paint is in a room with *northern exposure* to as much *natural light* as possible. Natural light is the light of the sun; all other light is artificial light. Under natural light, color matching will be more easily done.

Judge the Color When It Is Dry. Generally, new paint that is sprayed on a panel will darken slightly as it dries. Fresh, wet paint may be slightly lighter than the older, dry color. An experienced painter allows for this difference in color when judging a color match.

MATCHING METALLIC PAINTS

One of the most skilled and difficult jobs for automotive painters is matching *metallic* paints. This is very important because paints with metallic *flakes* added to the pigment are very popular original colors. Because flakes reflect *light* while pigments reflect *color,* how the flakes are arranged has a good deal to do with how well the new paint matches the old paint.

The metal flakes give the paint a sparkling jewellike appearance whenever light is reflected from it. Therefore, metallic paint is not only a color but also a color

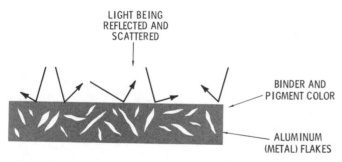

Fig. 27-22. *In a metallic topcoat, small flakes of metal (usually aluminum) reflect light at different angles.*

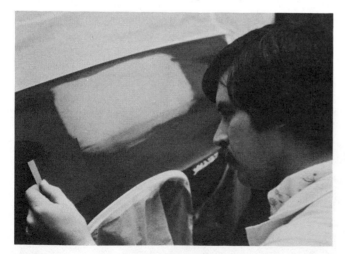

Fig. 27-23. *Using a test card to practice the technique needed to match a given metallic color. (Courtesy of Rinshed–Mason Products Division, Inmont Corporation)*

effect. Figure 27-22 shows how the metallic flakes in the paint reflect light.

There are two main *variables* (items the painter can change) when applying metallic paints. A painter must know what can be changed, and what the change will do to help a new metallic color match the color on the car. These two items are the *spraying technique* and the *vehicle used*.

To match a metallic color properly, it is best to experiment by painting on a *test card*. Then, the card may be compared with the color on the car to be painted (Fig. 27-23). Finally, when the test card and the car's color match, the same technique used to paint the card should be used to paint the car.

Spraying Technique

With exactly the same metallic paint in a spray gun, changing the *spraying technique* will change a color to some extent. This is because metallic colors tend to change with the *wetness* (thickness) of the paint.

Wet Spray Techniques. If the spray gun is held close to the surface being sprayed and lower air pressure is used, more paint will be sprayed on the surface. This is called a *wet spray technique.* It causes the color to be *darker.* This is because the flakes are able to sink down in the wet paint and lay flat, as in Figure 27-24. Because they lay flat and are deeper in the paint, they reflect less light. This makes the paint look darker.

Other wet spray techniques include *opening* the spray gun's *fluid feed valve* more, *reducing* the size of the *spray pattern,* *slowing down* the *spraying stroke,* and allowing *less flash time* between coats. Any of these methods may be used alone or in combination, as needed, to produce a *wetter* coat and make the metallic color appear *darker.*

Dry Spray Techniques. If the spray gun is held farther away from the panel, less paint will reach the surface. This is because a larger area is being sprayed, causing more paint to be lost in the air as *overspray.* This is known as a *dry spray technique.* It causes the color to be *lighter.* This is because metallic flakes stand up in

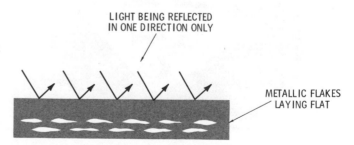

Fig. 27-24. *When a metallic paint is sprayed "wet," the flakes settle to the bottom of the paint film. This makes the color appear darker.*

the "drier" paint, rather than laying flat. Because the flakes stand up closer to the surface of the paint, they reflect more light, and reflect it at different angles. The paint is too "dry" for the flakes to have time to settle down to the bottom of the coat.

Other *dry spray techniques* include *closing* the *fluid valve* slightly, *increasing* the *spray pattern size*, increasing the *speed* of the *spraying stroke*, and *increasing* the *flash time* between coats. Any of these methods may be used alone or in combination, as needed, to produce a drier coat and make the metallic finish appear lighter.

Vehicle Used

Many times, matching metallic colors is made more difficult by not using the correct thinner or reducer for shop conditions. Other times, problems can come from using a vehicle of poor quality. If a poor quality vehicle (reducer) is used, for example, the metallic flakes may not position themselves correctly in the wet paint. If this happens, some flakes will settle down and lay flat, while others will stand up. This causes light and dark spots in the finish and is known as *mottling*.

Using a Slow-drying Vehicle (Reducer). If metallic paint is applied with a slow-drying vehicle (reducer), the effect is the same as when spraying wet and close to the surface; the metallic flakes will settle closer to the bottom of the coat. They will also lay flat on top of each other, as shown in Figure 27-24. This is because the flakes will settle deeper in the finish by the time that the slow-drying vehicle "flashes off." This will produce a darker, stronger color.

Using a Fast-drying Vehicle. If metallic paint is applied with a faster-drying vehicle, the basic effect is the same as when spraying the topcoat dry and farther away from the surface. The metallic flakes will stand up and be "trapped" near the surface because the vehicle will allow the paint to "flash off" before they have settled.

This will produce a lighter, more metallic-looking finish, as in Figure 27-22.

PREVENTING DIRTY PAINT

One of the biggest headaches in automobile refinishing is mysterious dust and dirt that seems to come from nowhere to mar freshly painted vehicles. This dirt usually can be prevented, but some painters do not care enough about their work to take the extra time needed to help prevent dirty paint. The dirt that spoils a nice, fresh paint job may come from the vehicle itself, the painter, the shop, or the paint materials. Discussed below are the basic items to remember when trying to prevent dirty paint.

Clean the Car

Failure to remove dirt from the vehicle's cracks, underbody, and fenders is a main source of dirt. Dirt can fall or be blown off the vehicle and be carried into the fresh paint by air currents (spraying and ventilating) in the booth while spraying is being done. The slight additional time and cost to steam-clean or pressure-clean the underside of a vehicle is good insurance for clean, top-quality paint jobs (Fig. 27-25).

Basic cleaning methods include washing the vehicle *thoroughly* with a water hose (Fig. 27-26). Then, an air gun should be used at 100 psi (690 kPa) to blow any dirt and dust from body seams and moldings. These cleaning jobs should be done before final preparation, so that any dirt that is washed or blown out will not fall on clean, prepared surfaces.

Clean the Shop

Good "housekeeping" will help eliminate dust or dirt on the walls, floor, air hose, or spray gun that could find its way into wet paint. Clean the major shop areas

Fig. 27-25. *The underside of the vehicle should be cleaned with compressed air to remove dust that could be carried into fresh paint by air currents.*

Fig. 27-26. *The underside, wheels, and other body parts should be washed with a stream of water to eliminate dust and dirt particles that could mar the painted finish.*

before paint work is done by washing them down with a water hose or by dusting with *clean* rags. To help keep any stray dust down on the floor, it is a good idea to always *wet down* the floor of the paint booth before spraying (Fig. 27-27).

Oil-saturated sweeping compounds should be used to sweep in and around the paint booth. This will help collect floor dust or keep it settled. In the paint booth's *air exhaust system*, an automatic damper should be installed to prevent any air from blowing back into the booth (and possibly carrying in dirt) after the fan has been turned off. The damper will also keep cold air out in the winter. Finally, be sure that the paint booth is kept free of anything that might be called "junk." These items will add to the dirt hazard in the booth (Fig. 27-28).

Fig. 27-27. *Before painting work begins, the paint booth floor should be washed down to prevent dust from circulating.*

Prepare Car Outside Paint Booth

Always complete body work and most of the paint preparation *outside* the paint booth. Check to be sure that no sanding or body work has been done in the paint booth. If this work *has* been done, the grinding grit and any sanding dust left by that work must be removed.

Prevent Drafts in Paint Booth

Always keep the doors of the paint booth *closed* after the exhaust fan has been turned on. Take enough paint, tools, and materials into the paint booth to complete the job *before* doing *any* actual painting. By doing this, you will be able to avoid opening doors to go in and out for supplies while the new paint job is wet. To leave the booth after painting, use only the small door at the *fan* end of the booth. Leave the large doors to the paint room closed for about 1 hour after the job has been finished.

Use Clean Equipment

Be on the lookout for *dust* that may settle on the air transformer, the hoses, or ledges in the booth. Clean these areas often. Any equipment that might be used during drying, such as traveling ovens or portable heat panels, should be dusted before use and kept covered or stored in a separate compartment at one end of the booth.

Fig. 27-28. *The paint booth should be kept clean and free of any litter or debris that could collect dust. (Courtesy of Econo Booth Industries, Inc.)*

Wear Clean Clothes

If street clothes or untreated coveralls are worn in the paint booth, a big chance is being taken on getting dust in the paint work. For this reason, it is a good idea to wear *starched coveralls*, preferably of *synthetic* (man-made) cloth with antistatic treatment. Gloves, if worn, should be free of lint. If a customer wants to see the car being painted, it is better to buy a paint booth with windows in it than to let people inside the booth with dusty clothes and shoes.

Prepare the Paint Properly

Be careful when choosing containers to mix and prepare the paint. Mixing paint in used paint cans may cause the new paint to be contaminated by old paint skins, dried deposits, or dirt that may be in the can. These are sometimes fine enough to pass through the strainer and show up on the painted car.

For best results, first mix the paint in its own container on a mixing machine. Then mix the paint and vehicle in a separate *clean* can. A large, clean coffee can is good for this job. Be sure to use the right vehicle for the job. (The wrong vehicle may cause rough paint conditions that look like dirty paint.)

After the paint and vehicle are mixed, the mixture should be *strained* to remove any fine dirt or paint scum (Fig. 27-29). Regular paint strainers are sold by paint-manufacturing companies and should be used to strain the mixture into the cup.

Start Painting at Correct End of Booth

When an overall paint job is being done, start painting at the end of the booth *opposite the end where the exhaust fan is located*. Then, move along the car *toward* the exhaust fan. By doing this, the spray mist is pulled by the fan over the panels that have *not* been painted, instead of over the finished work.

Keep Gun's Nozzle Clean

During painting, paint particles will often build up on the spray gun's *nozzle*, forming a kind of fuzz. This build-up should be wiped off frequently with a *clean, lint-free* cloth (Fig. 27-30). If the fuzz is not wiped off, it will continue to build up until parts of it blow off in globs, making a bad blemish on the wet paint surface.

Use Clean Masking Materials

It is best to use only good, clean masking materials. Name-brand masking paper will be fairly clean, as will good masking tape. Masking materials should be stored away from the dust and floor dirt of the shop. Before using any masking tape and paper, wipe off any shop dust that may be on them.

Use Clean Tack Rags

Have on hand a supply of clean, factory-varnished tack rags. When these are available, a painter will not have to use dirty tack rags. When the door jambs and trunk edges are sprayed, any dust blown out of these areas can be removed with a clean tack rag before painting the outside of the car.

Fig. 27-29. *After the vehicle has been mixed in, the paint should be strained into the spray gun cup. The strainer will catch any paint particles or foreign matter. (Courtesy of Binks Manufacturing Company)*

Fig. 27-30. *Any paint buildup should be wiped off the spray gun nozzle with a clean cloth.*

Ground the Vehicle Electrically

During the winter (or when humidity is very low), a vehicle will usually carry a small charge of *static electricity*. This electricity attracts dust like a magnet and makes removing it very difficult. To prevent this problem, run a ground wire from the car body (or frame) to a good ground such as a water pipe, but *not* to the booth itself. This should be done as soon as the car is in the paint booth (Fig. 27-31).

USING A SPRAY GUN

To be successful when using a spray gun, *two basic facts* must be kept in mind. *First*, the gun's paint and air controls must be *properly adjusted*. *Second*, the gun must then be *held and moved* correctly. When these facts are kept in mind, repeated practice will usually build up good painting skills.

Adjusting the Air Pressure

Before adjusting the spray gun itself, adjust the air pressure at the regulator for the paint job to be done. Be certain to use a gauge at the gun to measure the *exact* air pressure *at the gun* (Fig. 27-32). If no gauge is available at the gun, set the air pressure on the regulator gauge slightly higher than needed to allow for a pressure drop in the hose. (The approximate pressure drop may be figured by using Table 10 in Unit 24.) **What Air Pressure to Use.** Usually, the air pressure recommended for the paint being sprayed is listed on the paint can itself. In all cases, any recommendations *on the can* are the air pressures that should be used.

If no recommendations are given, use the following *general recommendations*. With *enamel* paints, for example, many painters use lower pressures and move

in closer to the work. By doing this, less dirt and dust is stirred up, and less paint is lost as overspray. These recommendations, then, are only *general guidelines*. Different pressures may be used if better results are seen under given shop conditions. All pressure adjustments are made at the regulator with the spray gun trigger held all the way back and the gun empty.

- Lacquers, spot repair: 30 to 35 psi (207 to 241 kPa)
- Lacquers, overall refinishing: 40 to 45 psi (276 to 310 kPa)
- Acrylic enamels, spot repair: 45 to 65 psi (310 to 448 kPa)
- Acrylic enamels, overall refinishing: 50 to 70 psi (345 to 483 kPa)
- Alkyd enamels, panel or overall refinishing: 45 to 55 psi (310 to 379 kPa)

Adjusting the Spray Gun

Before a vehicle may be painted, the spray gun itself must be adjusted. There are two basic spray gun adjustments to make: the *fluid control* and the *pattern control*. These must be adjusted *after* the paint is already in the gun and *after* the air pressure to the gun has been adjusted at the regulator.

Fluid Control. The *fluid control valve* adjusts the amount of *fluid* (paint) that is allowed to go through the nozzle. The valve must be adjusted differently for different types of jobs. Figure 27-33 shows the fluid control valve being adjusted. For an approximate setting, first close the

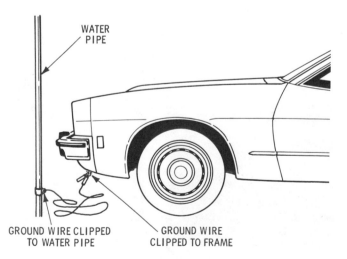

WATER PIPE

GROUND WIRE CLIPPED TO WATER PIPE   GROUND WIRE CLIPPED TO FRAME

Fig. 27-31. *Grounding the car will help prevent dust from being attracted to the new paint by static electricity.*

Fig. 27-32. *Actual air pressure at the gun can be checked by installing a pressure gauge at the gun inlet.*

valve fully. Then, open it about halfway for a small spot repair, or all the way for a panel or overall job.

Pattern Control. The *pattern control valve* adjusts the amount of air that is allowed to go out the air horn holes. This valve, like the fluid control valve, may need to be adjusted slightly for different painting conditions. However, it should first be adjusted like the fluid control valve: about halfway open for spot repairs and all the way open for panel or overall repairs. Figure 27-34 shows the pattern control valve being adjusted.

Making Final Adjustments

Just before beginning a spray job, quickly "shoot" a test spot to check the gun and air pressure adjustments. This should be done on a card or piece of paper, *not* on the job to be painted. First, hold the gun about 6 to 8 in. (15 to 20 cm) from the surface used for testing (Fig. 27-35). Then, quickly pull the trigger all the way back, and release it immediately. This should leave an oval paint pattern, as shown in Figure 27-36.

After spraying the test pattern, look at it carefully. If it is too long or too short, adjust the pattern control valve slightly. If the pattern appears too coarse or too wet (Fig. 27-37), close the fluid valve slightly or increase the air pressure slightly. On the other hand, if

the pattern is too dry and powdery-looking, open the fluid valve or reduce the air pressure slightly. After making adjustments, continue to "shoot" test patterns until the pattern is correct.

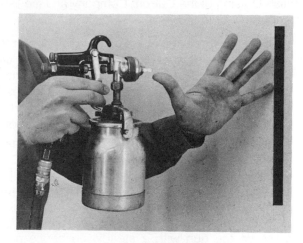

Fig. 27-35. *Estimating the gun-to-surface distance by using spread fingers. (Courtesy of Refinish Division, DuPont Company)*

Fig. 27-36. *A normal test spray pattern. The pattern should be about 5 in. (12.7 cm) long for spot repainting, and about 9 in. (22.9 cm) long for overall panel repainting. (Courtesy of Refinish Division, DuPont Company)*

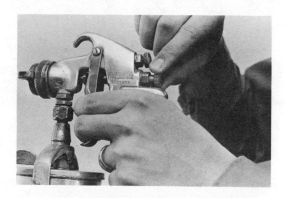

Fig. 27-33. *Adjusting the fluid control valve. (Courtesy of Refinish Division, DuPont Company)*

Fig. 27-34. *Adjusting the pattern control valve. (Courtesy of Refinish Division, DuPont Company)*

Fig. 27-37. *A test spray pattern that is too wet and too coarse. (Courtesy of Refinish Division, DuPont Company)*

Operating the Gun

The following general "rules" for operating a spray gun should be kept in mind while practicing *and* painting. They are based on the recommendations of the Refinish Division of the DuPont Company and are listed here courtesy of that division.

1. Hold the spray gun at the proper distance for the material being sprayed: 6 to 8 in. (15 to 20 cm) for lacquers; 8 to 10 in. (20 to 25 cm) for enamels.
2. Hold the gun *level* so that it is at right angles to most of the car's surfaces, which are vertical (Fig. 27-38). On *flat* surfaces (hoods or roofs), the gun should be pointed straight down, as in Figure 27-39.
3. Move the gun *parallel* to the surface, as in Figure 27-40. Generally, do not *arc* the gun. However, when blending in a spot repair, it *is* necessary to arc the gun (Fig. 27-41).
4. Move the gun with a steady, deliberate pace, about 1 ft/sec (foot per second) [0.3 m/s (meters per second)]. Be careful to *not* stop in one place or the sprayed coat will drip and run.
5. Release the trigger at the end of each stroke or pass *when the spray is off the edge of the panel*. Then, pull back on the trigger as you begin the pass in the opposite direction. In other words, turn off the spray gun at the end of each pass. This helps avoid runs, saves material, and helps reduce overspray.

6. If a panel is being painted off the car, *banding* may help produce a nicer job. Banding is a single coat applied with a small spray pattern to "frame-in" an area to be sprayed. It ensures covering the edges of an area without having to spray a great deal beyond the spray area (Fig. 27-42).
7. Generally, start the *first* pass at the *top* of an upright surface. The spray gun *nozzle* should be level with the *top* of the surface. This means that the upper half of the spray pattern will shoot off into space or will hit the masking around the area.
8. Make the *second* pass in the opposite direction and *one-half* the width of the spray pattern. Hold the nozzle level with the lower edge of the first pass. Thus, one-half of the second pass will overlap the first pass, and the other half will be sprayed on the unpainted area (Fig. 27-43).

Fig. 27-39. *When painting a horizontal surface, the spray gun should point straight down. (Courtesy of Automotive Trades Division, 3M Company)*

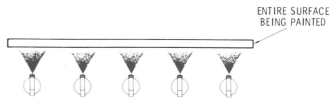

Fig. 27-40. *If the entire surface is being painted, the gun should move parallel to the surface.*

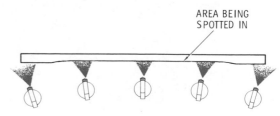

Fig. 27-41. *For spot repairs, the gun may travel in an arc, as shown.*

Fig. 27-38. *When spraying a vertical surface, the spray gun should be held level.*

9. Continue back and forth passes, releasing the trigger at the end of each pass. Lower each pass one-half the width of the pattern.

10. Finally, make the last pass with the lower half of the spray *below* the surface being painted.

Types of Coats

The basic method of spraying, just described, is called a *single coat*. For a double coat, repeat the single coat procedure immediately. When spraying lacquer, double coats should always be used. Generally, two or more *double* coats are required to apply a lacquer topcoat properly, allowing a "flash-off" time of several minutes

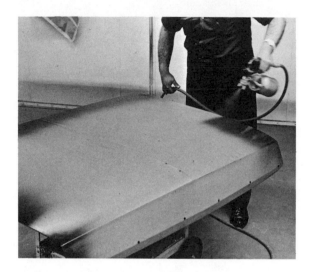

Fig. 27-42. *In* banding, *a first coat is sprayed around the edges of the panel. The panel is then painted normally.*

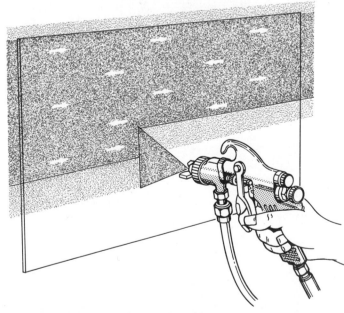

Fig. 27-43. *A single coat is sprayed as shown, so that each pass overlaps the preceding one.*

between each double coat. At least two single coats are normally required to apply enamels. The first coat should be allowed to set up slightly (become tacky) before the second coat is applied.

Coat Thickness. There are three basic coat thicknesses: light, medium, and heavy. The easiest way to control the degree of thickness is the speed with which the gun is moved.

Besides the three basic coats just discussed, there are also *mist coats*. These are normally used as final coats over many types of color coats. Mist coats help to level the final coat and melt in any overspray. A mist coat is made by applying a rich, slow-drying vehicle with just a small amount of paint added for color.

RECOGNIZING SPRAY GUN PROBLEMS

There are five major spray gun problems that may happen while painting. These may be a result of the gun's being dirty or incorrectly adjusted, or the gun's not being handled correctly. Each problem will produce a certain type of defect in the finish. These major problems and the defects they cause are shown in Figures 27-44 through 27-48.

Fig. 27-44. *DEFECT:* Faulty Spray Patterns. *CAUSE: Usually, patterns like these are caused by clogged spray holes. They can be corrected by cleaning the nozzle.*

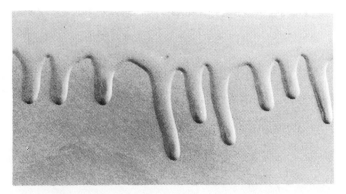

Fig. 27-45. *DEFECT:* Runs and Sags. *CAUSES: Gun held too close to the surface or moved too slowly; fluid control valve too far open; too little air pressure. Arcing the gun can cause this problem in the middle of a panel.*

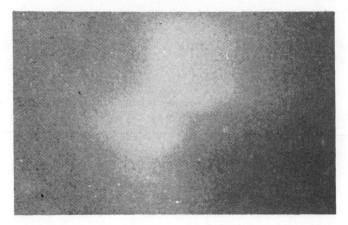

Fig. 27-46. *DEFECT:* Thin Coverage. *CAUSES: Gun held too far away from surface or moved too rapidly; fluid control valve too far closed. (Courtesy of Refinish Division, DuPont Company)*

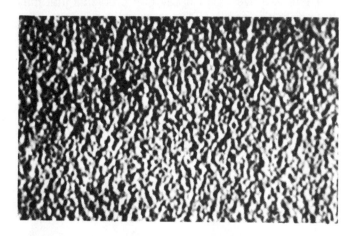

Fig. 27-47. *DEFECT:* Excessive Orange Peel. *CAUSES: Gun held too far away from surface or too much air pressure used. Some orange peel is normal in all finishes. (Courtesy of Refinish Divi-*

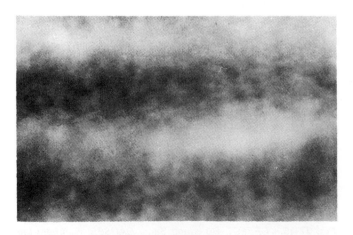

Fig. 27-48. *DEFECT:* Zebra Effect. *CAUSES: Tilting the gun so that one part of the spray reaches the surface before the rest of the pattern. (Courtesy of Refinish Division, DuPont Company)*

CLEANING THE GUN

Immediately after a spray gun is used, it must be *thoroughly* cleaned. This must be done so that paint does not dry inside the gun and clog the gun's passages. If the gun is cleaned just after use, it will be easier to clean than if the paint dries in the passages. Figures 27-49 through 27-56 show how to clean a spray gun.

Fig. 27-49. Step 1: *Unscrew the air nozzle cap about three turns. (Courtesy of Refinish Division, DuPont Company)*

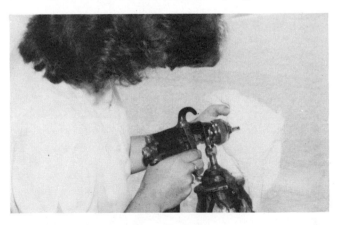

Fig. 27-50. Step 2: *Hold a cloth over the loosened air cap. Pull back all the way on the trigger. This will force most of the paint in the gun back into the paint cup.*

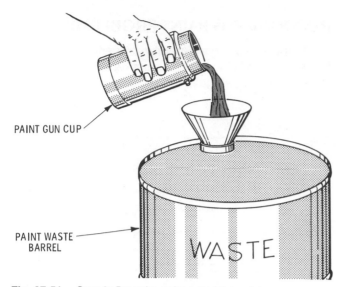

PAINT GUN CUP

PAINT WASTE BARREL

WASTE

Fig. 27-51. Step 3: *Pour the paint out of the paint gun cup.*

GUN AND EQUIPMENT CLEANER

Fig. 27-52. Step 4: *Fill the paint gun cup about 1/3 full of gun and equipment cleaner or thinner.*

Fig. 27-53. Step 5: *Position the gun on top of the cup as shown, and tighten the air nozzle cap. Pull back all the way on the trigger. This will draw solvent up from the cup to spray from the nozzle.*

Fig. 27-54. Step 6: *Remove the nozzle, and clean all gun parts with solvent. Thoroughly clean the paint cup.*

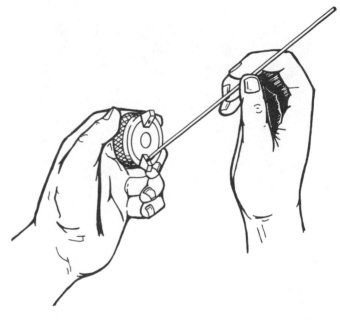

Fig. 27-55. Step 7: *Use a broom straw or toothpick to clean the holes in the nozzle cap. Do not use wire or a metal tool to do this, since metal could damage and enlarge the holes.*

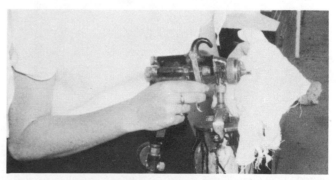

Fig. 27-56. Step 8: *Fill the paint cup about 1/3 full of solvent again, and reassemble the spray gun. Wipe down the outside of the gun with a clean cloth.*

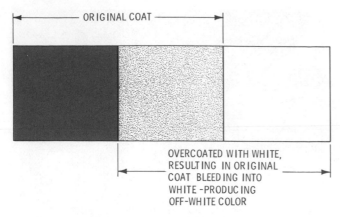

Fig. 27-57. *DEFECT: Bleeding—a different color seeping through a new topcoat. CAUSES: Soluble dyes or pigments in the old finish. Older red finishes are a particular problem. REMEDY: Seal the surface with a primer–surfacer or sealer designed to prevent bleeding. If possible, avoid painting lighter colors over red.*

Fig. 27-58. *DEFECT: Blistering—bubbles in the paint film, sometimes months after the job is done. CAUSES: Moisture or air trapped under the paint film. Improper surface preparation. Using the wrong vehicle. Excessive paint film thickness. Air, water, or oil in the spray gun air line. REMEDY: Sand or strip the blistered area and repaint. (Courtesy of Refinish Division, DuPont Company)*

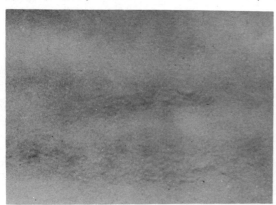

Fig. 27-59. *DEFECT: Blushing—a milky white haze, usually appearing only on lacquers. CAUSES: High shop humidity. Cheap lacquer thinner. REMEDY: Add a retarder to the last color coat, or spray a medium-to-wet coat of retarder on the finish. (Courtesy of Refinish Division, DuPont Company)*

RECOGNIZING PAINT PROBLEMS

Although they have carefully prepared the surface, sometimes even the best painters have paint problems show up on a fresh paint job. These can be caused by

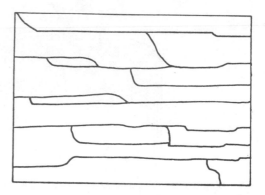

Fig. 27-60. *DEFECT: Cracking or Line Checking—cracks in the surface of the finish. CAUSES: Excessive film thickness. Improper surface preparation. Improper mixing or wrong additives. Not enough flash time between coats. REMEDY: Sand or strip finish and repaint. (Courtesy of Refinish Division, DuPont Company)*

Fig. 27-61. *DEFECT: Crazing—fine cracks ("cobwebs" or "crow's feet") all over the surface. CAUSES: Temperature too low in shop. Original paint under stress, breaking up due to softening action of new finish. REMEDY: Continue applying wet coats of color, using wettest vehicle shop conditions will allow. (Courtesy of Refinish Division, DuPont Company)*

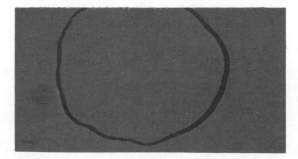

Fig. 27-62. *DEFECT: Featheredge Cracking—splitting to the substrate along the featheredge around a repair. CAUSES: "Piling on" heavy, wet coats. Improper thinning. Force-drying primer–surfacer with compressed air. Poor surface preparation. REMEDY: Sand or strip away defective topcoat and primer–surfacer. Correctly prepare surface and repaint. (Courtesy of Refinish Division, DuPont Company)*

any number of items that may have been overlooked or simply not realized for the job being done. These problems and their probable causes are outlined in Figures 27-57 through 27-71.

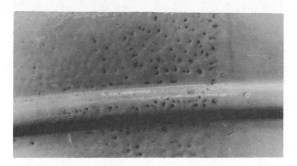

Fig. 27-63. *DEFECT:* Fisheyes—*small, craterlike holes in the finish, appearing soon after the paint is applied. CAUSES: Silicone particles or other dirt-repelling paint, preventing formation of a smooth film. REMEDY: Sand or strip off old finish. Thoroughly clean and prepare substrate, then repaint. Check shop tools, compressed air, cleaning rags, etc., for dirt or oil. In extreme cases, a special additive to help control this condition can be mixed with the paint. (Courtesy of Refinish Division, DuPont Company)*

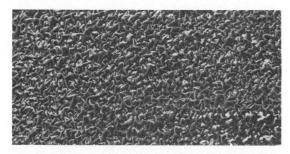

Fig. 27-64. *DEFECT:* Lifting—*distortion or shriveling of the topcoat upon application or as it dries. CAUSES: Solvents in the new paint attacking the old finish. Improper flash time allowed between coats of alkyd enamel. Improper drying time. Applying paint over incompatible sealer or primer. Improper thinning or reducing. Poor surface preparation. REMEDY: Sand or strip off damaged finish and repaint. (Courtesy of Refinish Division, DuPont Company)*

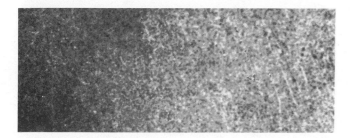

Fig. 27-65. *DEFECT:* Mottling—*metal flakes floating together to give a spotty appearance. CAUSES: Too much thinner or reducer. Insufficient mixing of color and vehicle. Spraying too wet. Using a slow-drying vehicle in cold weather. REMEDY: Allow mottled coat to set up. Apply a "drier" finish coat (or two coats, depending on conditions) over mottled paint. (Courtesy of Refinish Division, DuPont Company)*

Fig. 27-66. *DEFECT:* Peeling, Poor Adhesion, Chipping. *CAUSES: Poor bonding between substrate and topcoat resulting from incomplete mixing of paint and vehicle. Poor surface preparation. Not using the proper sealer. REMEDY: Sand or strip away damaged paint and fair amount of surrounding finish. Prepare surface and repaint. (Courtesy of Refinish Division, DuPont Company)*

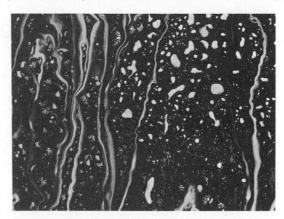

Fig. 27-67. *DEFECT:* Precipitation—*paint film curdles or breaks up. CAUSES: Using the wrong vehicle, or mixing it improperly with the paint. Using old paint. Overheating paint during spraying or storage. REMEDY: Remove curdled paint and refinish the area. Be sure that correct vehicle is used and that it has been mixed properly with good, fresh paint. (Courtesy of Refinish Division, DuPont Company)*

Fig. 27-68. *DEFECT:* Sandscratch Swelling—*raised lines in finish resulting from swelling of scratch edges in old finish. CAUSES: Using too coarse sandpaper to prepare substrate. Failure to use sealer between old and new paint. REMEDY: Sand surface down to smooth finish, then use sealer before repainting. (Courtesy of Refinish Division, DuPont Company)*

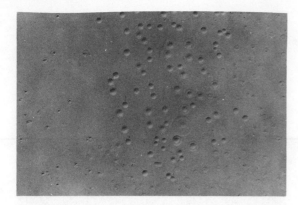

Fig. 27-69. *DEFECT:* Solvent Popping—*blisters appearing on the paint surface soon after refinishing. CAUSES: Poor surface preparation. Using the wrong vehicle. "Force drying" the primer. Allowing too little time between paint coats. REMEDY: Minor blisters may be sanded smooth and the area refinished. Large or numerous blisters call for stripping finish down to bare metal. Prepare substrate and refinish. (Courtesy of Refinish Division, DuPont Company)*

Fig. 27-70. *DEFECT:* Water Spotting—*water stains on finish. CAUSES: Allowing water to contact finish before paint is completely dry. Washing car in hot, bright sunlight. REMEDY: Polish the area after finish has cured at least 30 days. If necessary, compound the finish. In severe cases, sand the area and refinish. (Courtesy of Refinish Division, DuPont Company)*

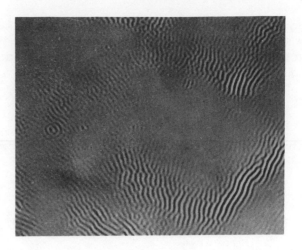

Fig. 27-71. *DEFECT:* Wrinkling—*a defect that appears on enamel as it is sprayed or while it is drying. CAUSES: Baking or force drying enamel too quickly after it is applied. "Piling on" thick, wet finish coats. Warm air drafts in shop. Improper drying techniques. REMEDY: Remove the wrinkled enamel and refinish. (Courtesy of Refinish Division, DuPont Company)*

Unit 28

Paint Rub-out and Restoration

How *good* a vehicle's topcoat looks is very important for customer satisfation. Customers often judge the entire repair job on the appearance of the topcoat. "Spotted areas" that have been refinished and that blend in with the rest of the topcoat are very likely to impress customers with quality work.

Wherever and whenever the topcoat is affected by a technician's work, it provides an opportunity to build a good reputation. A topcoat is usually the most impressive part of the vehicle, since it is the part most often seen and noticed. Notice the body damage in Figure 28-1. In Figure 28-2, the damage has been repaired. In the repair area, note that the refinished *topcoat* is the first part of the job that is seen. Even if the topcoat is *not* affected by the repair work being done, a good cleaning job on it will often impress the customer enough to bring future repair work to the shop.

NEW FINISHES

New automotive topcoats need almost no maintenance and upkeep right away. After *lacquer* paint dries, however, even the best new lacquer paint job will need "rubbing out" with *rubbing compound* (Fig. 28-3). This is because lacquer finishes have an uneven, dull appearance until they are "compounded." Figure 28-4 shows a magnified view of new lacquer paint before it is compounded.

New *enamel* paint jobs, on the other hand, must *not* be compounded because of the way in which they dry. If paint defects in an enamel paint job cause a dull finish, enamel *may* be compounded after it has been on the vehicle for several days. This waiting period allows the enamel to "set up" hard enough so that it will not be damaged by *light* compounding.

Fig. 28-1. *Damage to the quarter panel. After metal repair, the refinishing will be "spotted in."*

Fig. 28-2. *Polishing the completed refinishing work on the car shown in Figure 28-1.*

Both enamel and lacquer paint jobs should be thoroughly washed with *mild* soap and water before being turned out of the shop. It is not necessary or desirable to further treat any new paint right away. *Polish* would not add to the shine at this time, and it might damage enamel paint. *Wax* cannot be used until later on, because the paint must be allowed to "age" about 90 days before it can be waxed.

OLDER FINISHES

After a topcoat has been exposed to weather for several weeks, it will begin to age and will have picked up deposits of road grime. These deposits can be removed by cleaning with a good grease and wax remover. This product should be used any time the topcoat needs to be cleaned of old wax, tar, or stubborn stains. It is the same product used before beginning any body repair on an area. In any case, pre-cleaning solvent (grease and wax remover) must always be used *before* compounding an area, as in Figure 28-5.

After compounding an old finish, a good wax job makes a topcoat easier to keep clean, since dirt will not readily adhere to a waxed surface. Wax is mainly used as a protective coating and is especially useful on old, dull paint jobs *after* they have been compounded. For example, Figure 28-6 shows an old paint job after being restored by compounding and waxing.

If an older paint job is only slightly dulled, the shine may be restored by waxing it with a "cleaner/wax" product. These products contain fine abrasive particles that lightly compound the paint to a smooth finish. Slightly dulled paint, then, can be restored by using these products instead of full hand or machine compounding. Of course, if an old finish is severely dulled, separate compounding and waxing are *both* needed.

Fig. 28-3. *Rubbing compound. (Courtesy of Rinshed–Mason Products Division, Inmont Corporation)*

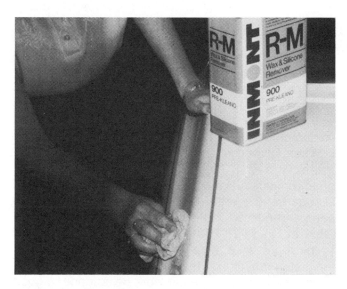

Fig. 28-5. *Pre-cleaning solvent is used to remove road tar, old wax, and grease before compounding.*

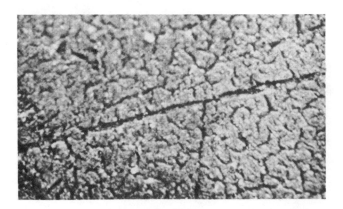

Fig. 28-4. *A magnified view of a lacquer surface before compounding. (Courtesy of Ditzler Automotive Finishes Division, PPG Industries, Inc.)*

Fig. 28-6. *An older paint job that was restored to "like new" appearance by compounding and waxing.*

PAINT REPAIR AND PROTECTION PRODUCTS

There are many different products made to clean and add a shine or gloss to a topcoat. These are known as *polishes* and *compounds*. Other products protect the topcoat from scratches and road grime and make it easier to keep clean. These same products help *preserve* the topcoat so that it will not be broken down by the elements. Such protection products include *waxes* and *cleaner/waxes*. Samples of these products are shown in Figure 28-7.

Grease and Wax Remover

Grease and wax removers, such as the product in Figure 28-8, are also known as *pre-cleaning solvents*. They are mild, solvent-type cleaners. They are designed to clean a surface by breaking up or dissolving any dirt, wax, or silicones on the paint. Good pre-cleaning products will remove wax, grease, oil, tar, silicone polish, road film, and other impurities. They are the same products used to clean an area before any paint or repair work is begun.

Rubbing Compound

Rubbing compounds, also known as *cutting* compounds, contain pumice particles. *Pumice* is very finely ground volcanic rock. There are two basic types of rubbing compound: *hand* and *machine* (Fig. 28-9).

All rubbing compounds actually remove part of the paint. As some of the old "dead" paint is removed, the surface becomes smoother and more even. As this happens, the pumice itself is broken up. It polishes the paint to a finer smoothness as it is broken up into smaller particles.

Rubbing compound is used to polish new *lacquer* finishes after they have cured at least 4 hours and, preferably, overnight. Compound may also be used to smooth defective *enamel* topcoats after they have cured. However, *acrylic* enamel does not cure until at least 30

days after it has been applied, and *alkyd* enamel is not fully cured for *3 or 4 months*. Rubbing compounds must *not* be used on enamel paints until they completely cure.

Hand Compound. Hand compound contains fairly *coarse* pumice grit. This coarse grit does not require heavy rubbing pressure to create friction and "cut" the paint. Hand compound is used mainly on small repair areas and may be applied with a rag or brush. Then, a clean rag is used to work the compound until the finish is as smooth as desired (Fig. 28-10).

Machine Compound. Machine rubbing compound contains *fine* particles of pumice and is designed for use with a power polisher ("wheel"). The coarse particles in *hand* compound would create too much heat and friction if used with a power polisher. Machine compound is normally used for work on an entire vehicle and may be used on both new and old paint. The ma-

Fig. 28-8. *A typical pre-cleaner (grease and wax remover) used to prepare surfaces for compounding. (Courtesy of Rinshed–Mason Products Division, Inmont Corporation)*

Fig. 28-9. *Rubbing compound is made for hand or machine work. (Courtesy of Rinshed–Mason Products Division, Inmont Corporation)*

Fig. 28-7. *Some paint cleaning and protection products.*

chine compound in Figure 28-11 is being used to rub out a new lacquer repair.

Polish

Most *polishes* contain both a cleaner and silicone material. The *cleaner* removes grime and stains from the topcoat and is actually like very fine rubbing compound. The silicone causes the surface to shine, improving the paint's gloss. A common polish product is shown in Figure 28-12.

Polish is used to restore old paint jobs that are not in bad enough condition to need compounding. The vehicle must first be washed with soap and water and cleaned with grease and wax remover. Then, the polish may be applied by either hand or machine.

Wax

Most modern *wax* products contain *silicone* to help shine and protect the topcoat. They should be used *only* after grease and wax remover has been used to clean the vehicle and *only* after a new topcoat has cured for 90 days. Wax is especially useful for shining and protecting old paint that has been restored by polishing or compounding. Figure 28-7 shows a wax product among the other paint products.

Cleaner/Wax

Cleaner/wax products contain both polish *and* wax. Very small abrasive particles and wax are combined in one product designed to smooth *and* wax the vehicle in one operation. These products are ideal for restoring slightly dull older paint jobs. The finish should be cleaned before using cleaner/wax. Applying cleaner/wax is similar to applying regular wax.

COMPOUND APPLICATION

The process of applying rubbing compound, either by "wheel" or by hand, is known as *compounding*. Compounding may be done for either of two reasons. The *first*, and most common, reason is to smooth the rough texture of new lacquer topcoats. Even the best lacquer paints will leave *some* rough texture after they are sprayed. This roughness must be removed to make the paint shiny and bring up its full gloss. Compounding new lacquer paint is also known as "rubbing out."

The *second* reason for compounding is to brighten up (restore) an old finish. Compounding may be used

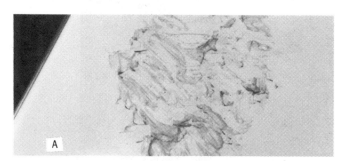

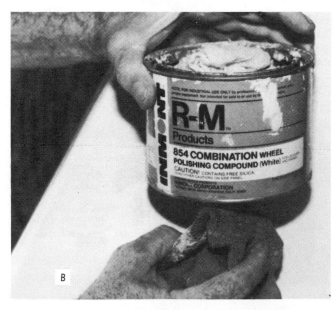

Fig. 28-10. *Compounding a finish is done by (A) placing compound on a small area and (B) using a soft rag to spread and rub it. Rubbing compound actually wears away a portion of the finish.*

Fig. 28-11. *"Wheeling" (machine compounding) a painted surface. (Courtesy of Automotive Trades Division, 3M Company)*

Fig. 28-12. *An automotive polish product.*

in this way to restore an entire paint job or to restore only one panel or one spot on the panel.

For best results, compounding should always be followed by waxing. However, on *new* paint jobs, it is a good idea to wait about 90 days before waxing, even if the paint is lacquer. This is to allow the new paint to *cure* properly.

Hand Compounding

Hand compounding is normally used only for spot repair work. To hand-compound an area, fold a damp, lint-free cloth into a ball. Then, put a small amount of compound on the bottom of the cloth (Fig. 28-13). Apply the compound to the area by rubbing back and forth *in a straight-line motion*. Apply only enough pressure on the rag to actually make the "cut." When the surface has been smoothed enough, wipe off the compound residue with a clean rag.

This is the method used to prepare a panel for a spot repair by removing road grime and old film around the spot. It leaves the original color more visible, so that the new paint will match better and will be better able to grip the old finish.

Machine Compounding

Most body shop compounding is done with a *power polisher*, also known as a "buffer" or a "wheel." These machines (Figs. 28-14 and 28-15) are normally used to compound a large area quickly. Of course, fine-grit *machine* rubbing compound should always be used when machine-compounding. Figure 28-16 shows a worker machine-compounding a spot repair. This is also known as "wheeling off" the area.

Types of Pads. There are two different types of *pads* that may be used for compounding with a power polisher. These pads are known as *compounding* pads and *polishing* pads. Compounding pads are used to work down heavy roughness on new lacquer paints and for general machine compounding. Compounding

Fig. 28-13. *To apply rubbing compound, fold a lint-free cloth into a ball and spread the compound on the surface.*

pads have *short* lamb's wool, as shown in Figure 28-14.

Polishing pads, on the other hand, have *long* lamb's wool, as shown in Figure 28-15. Polishing pads do not cut as fast as do compounding pads, but they do produce a smoother finish. Polishing pads are often used to "fine-polish" a new surface after compounding.

Compounding Heat. Both types of compounding pads create *heat* while they are being used, because they must rub the paint in order to work it down. For this reason, *always keep the machine moving whenever compounding or polishing*. All automotive paint will be easily damaged by heat if the pad is held in one place while the machine is turning.

Typical Compounding Jobs

There are three basic compounding jobs that are done in auto body shop work. These include:

1. Compounding for a spot repair.
2. Compounding new paint.
3. Compounding older paint.

The first of these, compounding for a spot repair, is discussed in the unit *Preparing the Surface for Paint*. *Compounding New Paint.* After new lacquer paint has been sprayed and allowed to dry for at least 4 hours, it

Fig. 28-14. *A power polisher with a short-hair compounding pad.*

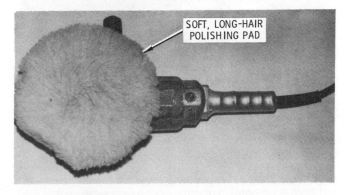

Fig. 28-15. *A power polisher with a soft, long-hair polishing pad.*

must be compounded to full luster. Large areas are difficult to compound all at once because it takes *time* to work on a large area. Some of the compound material may dry and harden on the finish, making it impossible to work. To avoid this problem, finish one small area at a time before moving on to the next section. The largest area compounded at one time should be about 4 ft² (square feet) [1.5 m² (square meters)].

Fig. 28-16. *Compounding a spot repair. (Courtesy of Automotive Trades Division, 3M Company)*

Fig. 28-17. Step 1: *Wet-sand new lacquer with ultra-fine sandpaper. A sanding block should be used so that the sandpaper cuts evenly.*

Fig. 28-18. Step 2: *After sanding, wash the entire panel with water to remove sanding residue. Very small sandscratches will be visible. They will be removed by compounding.*

To compound a new *lacquer* paint job or spot repair, follow the steps outlined in Figures 28-17 through 28-20. Before compounding new *acrylic enamel* paint, allow the paint to cure for several days. Do *not* wet-sand the paint before compounding. Also, it is a good idea to use *milder* compound on enamel paint than is used on lacquer paint.

Compounding Older Paint. It is usually possible to compound an older finish, back to "like-new" gloss when it becomes dull. Compounding will usually bring the luster back to the old finish. However, the finish also should be waxed after compound has been used.

The reason for waxing the restored finish is that the rubbing compound will remove any polish or wax on the surface. Then, the unprotected finish could be easily attacked by the weather and foreign elements such as bird droppings, bug juices, tree acids, and sap.

Restoring old paint by rubbing it out may be done in

Fig. 28-19. Step 3: *Compound is applied in the form of a watery paste and worked in with a polishing machine. The machine should be moved constantly in back-and-forth, up-and-down pattern. The compounding pad must be cleaned frequently to remove paint and compound residue. Compounding is a skilled operation. Before attempting it, have an experienced body worker demonstrate the process.*

Fig. 28-20. *Applying a final glaze material to the finish. The area at right has been treated and polished after compounding. (Courtesy of Automotive Trades Division, 3M Company)*

almost the same way as compounding new paint. To do this, follow the steps below:

1. Thoroughly wash the entire car with soap and water.
2. Clean the finish with wax and grease remover (pre-cleaning solvent). Even after washing and cleaning, marks may remain on the paint (Fig. 28-21).
3. Apply a thin coat of fine, watery compound over a small area (Fig. 28-22).
4. Compound the area with a *polishing* pad, unless the finish is in very poor condition. Hold the polishing machine at a slight angle while moving it back and forth over the area. Allow about 3 in. (7.6 cm) of the pad to touch the surface (Fig. 28-23). Clean the pad as often as required.
5. Look at the paint to see if it has been restored to its natural color and gloss. If not, apply more compound immediately. *Be careful not to compound through the topcoat to the primer!*
6. Continue working around the vehicle from panel to panel, until the entire topcoat has been restored.
7. Again wash the car with soap and water. Clean all the glass and chrome to remove the residue left by compounding.
8. Apply wax or a mild cleaner/wax to provide protection for the newly restored topcoat.

POLISHING

Polish is used to restore slightly dulled paint that is not badly weathered enough to need compounding. Polishing can be done by hand or by machine. In either case, *first* apply the polish to the vehicle by hand (Fig. 28-24). Always use a clean, slightly damp rag to apply polish. Depending on the temperature and humidity, the polish may be applied over the entire vehicle or over a small section. After the polish is applied, allow a few minutes for it to dry to a light-colored haze (Fig. 28-25).

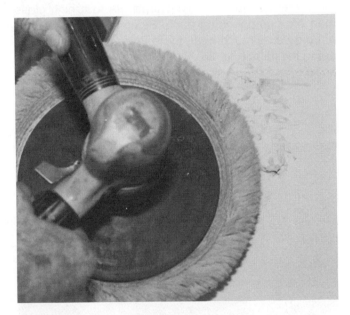

Fig. 28-23. *Machine compounding to remove the marks.*

Fig. 28-21. *Compounding will be needed to remove the marks on this painted panel.*

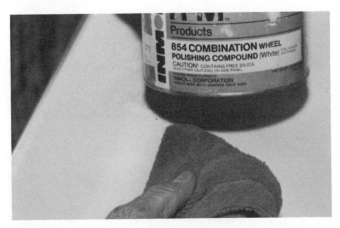

Fig. 28-22. *Applying compound to the panel.*

Fig. 28-24. *A liquid wax product.*

If the vehicle is being polished by hand, wipe off the dried polish with a *clean* soft rag. *Turn* the rag often so that dried polish is not rubbing on the finish at the bottom of the rag. Use only a clean, dry, fluffy rag. Old towels, clean old diapers, and the material known as *cheesecloth* (purchased new) are all good polishing rag materials (Fig. 28-26).

Hand polishing may be difficult and time consuming when an entire vehicle is being done. When a large-sized area must be polished, *machine* polishing is much faster. To machine polish an area, use the "wheel" with a soft polishing pad to remove the dried polish (Fig. 28-25). The polishing pad must be cleaned frequently. It is a good idea to have an experienced person show you how to clean the pad during the polishing procedure.

Polishing pads do not create as much heat as do compounding pads. For this reason, polishing pads are more often used for shining topcoats to a high gloss than are compounding pads. Since polishing pads do not create as much heat, there is less chance of damaging the paint (Fig. 28-20). *Even so, the "wheel" must not be held in one position during polishing.*

WAX AND CLEANER/WAX APPLICATION

After a new topcoat has cured 90 days (or after an old topcoat has been compounded), the finish should be *waxed*. Waxing alone is usually done to make it easier to keep the vehicle *clean* and to provide *protection* for the topcoat. Cleaner/wax is usually applied to complete the restoration of an older paint job. Because cleaner/wax contains very mild abrasive particles, it may be used to restore slightly dulled old paint without having to compound it.

Applying Wax

Wax should be applied over a freshly compounded finish after washing with soap and water to remove the compound residue (Fig. 28-27). Wax is usually sold in *paste* form (Fig. 28-28), although liquid types are available. Either type should be applied with a soft, slightly damp cloth.

Paste wax must be applied only to small areas at a time, usually no more than about 2 ft² (0.4 m²). It is normally wiped off immediately, unless the manufactur-

Fig. 28-25.   *The polish is applied and allowed to dry before buffing. On hot, dry days, only one panel at a time should be polished.*

Fig. 28-27.   *Soap and water is used to remove compounding residue.*

Fig. 28-26.   *A soft rag is used to spread the polish.*

Fig. 28-28.   *Paste wax may be used to polish a vehicle.*

er's instructions say otherwise. This process is then repeated over the entire vehicle. It is important that all excess wax be removed from the vehicle, or it may dull the paint.

Applying Cleaner/Wax

To use cleaner/wax correctly, first wash the dulled finish with soap and water. Then, clean it with a pre-cleaning solvent. This will leave the finish clean enough so that the cleaner/wax will only have to remove any "dead" paint.

Apply cleaner/wax with a soft, slightly damp cloth. Work on an area of about 2 ft² (0.4 m²) at a time. After the product has dried, remove it with a soft, *dry*, clean cloth. The entire procedure is similar to polishing, except that smaller areas should be done at one time.

ACCENT STRIPES

Many newer cars have one or more *accent stripes*. These stripes may be paint or tape and are a color different from the regular topcoat. Accent stripes may be added to older vehicles to make them look more up-to-date. Accent stripes are also known as *pin stripes*.

Stripes may be many different sizes. Some of them seem to be as narrow as a pin, which is why they are called *pin* stripes (Fig. 28-29). Some stripes are fairly wide (Fig. 28-30); others are made up of several stripes as shown in Figure 28-31. Stripes that are not actually paint are made of *tape* with an adhesive backing (Fig. 28-32). These stripes must be applied to *clean* paint or they will not be as durable as painted-on stripes.

Applying Stripes

Whenever body work is done on a late-model automobile, part of the paint work may include replacing stripes that were damaged or removed during the repair. For this reason, painters need to know how to add or replace accent stripes. Also, customers may want stripes added to a repainted car or to "dress up" an older car.

The easiest way to add or replace stripes is to use *striping tape*. This tape comes in many sizes and is available from various companies (Fig. 28-33).

Striping tape is a special masking tape with a number of precut, pull-out sections. These sections may be removed as desired to mask off an area for stripes of different widths. Many stripe combinations can be made

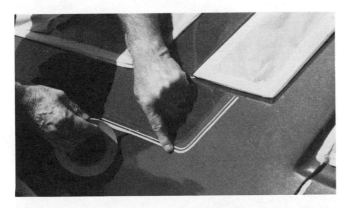

Fig. 28-29. *Applying a thin tape material for accent striping. (Courtesy of Automotive Trades Division, 3M Company)*

Fig. 28-31. *A broad painted stripe surrounded by a narrow "pin" stripe provides an attractive finishing touch on this truck.*

Fig. 28-30. *A wide accent stripe was used on this car.*

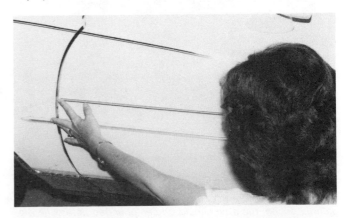

Fig. 28-32. *Applying an adhesive-backed accent stripe.*

by simply pulling out different sections of the tape. Figures 28-34 through 28-44 show the procedure for using striping tape to add or replace stripes.

Fig. 28-33. *Special masking tape used for painting accent stripes on a vehicle. Precut strips of the tape may be pulled out to make stripes.*

Fig. 28-34. Step 1: *Use a pre-cleaner to remove grease and wax from the area where the stripe will be painted or applied. If the paint is dulled, the area should be compounded before the pre-cleaner is used.*

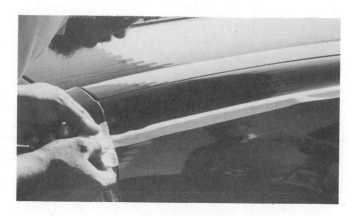

Fig. 28-35. Step 2: *Anchor one end of the special masking tape with a crosswise piece of tape. This will keep the ends of the striping tape from spreading when strips are pulled out.*

Fig. 28-36. Step 3: *Apply the tape to the side of the vehicle, using care to keep the tape straight throughout its length.*

Fig. 28-37. Step 4: *Press the tape firmly into place after it has been positioned. Good contact with the surface is necessary for a cleanly defined stripe.*

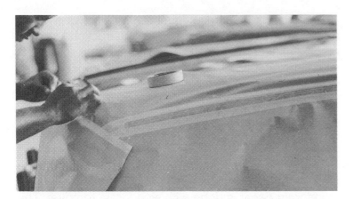

Fig. 28-38. Step 5: *Around the striping tape mask off all the areas that are not to be painted.*

Fig. 28-39. Step 5, continued: *Once masking is completed, the entire surface is covered with masking paper, masking tape, or special striping tape.*

Fig. 28-40. Step 6: *Pull out the precut sections of the tape where stripes will be painted. After the strips are removed, wipe the exposed surface with a tack rag to pick up any dust or paper particles.*

Fig. 28-41. Step 7: *Apply sealer to the area that will be striped. Follow manufacturer's directions for applying the sealer.*

Fig. 28-42. Step 8: *On the first pass, apply a light mist coat of color along the entire length of the area to be striped. When applying enamel for striping, a slightly lower air pressure is used than when finishing an entire panel.*

Fig. 28-43. Step 8, continued: *For the second pass, apply a somewhat heavier mist coat. Usually, two mist coats of color are enough for a well-defined stripe. A common mistake in striping is to use too heavy a paint coat.*

Fig. 28-44. Step 9: *The finished striping job. Enamel should be allowed to dry before removing the masking materials. If masking was properly done, no cleanup or compounding will be necessary.*

DECALS AND ADHESIVE STRIP TAPE

Many sport-model cars and cars with customized paint jobs are finished with decals placed on different parts of the vehicle body. Figure 28-45 shows a decal that has been placed on the hood of a vehicle. Figure 28-46 shows a different hood decal. Sometimes, wide strips are used with a pin stripe as shown in Figure 28-47.

Installing Decals and Stripes

Before installing decals or stripes, the area where they are to be placed must be cleaned. The decal or stripe comes with a removable (usually clear plastic) top sheet. After the decal is pressed in place, the top sheet can be pulled off, revealing the stripe or decal. Figure 28-48 shows a side decal stripe with the top sheet pulled off.

Some decal top sheets must be wet with water to be removed. Read the manufacturer's instructions for correct installation. To install a decal on a panel, follow the steps shown in Figures 28-49 through 28-56.

Figure 28-57 shows several sets of decals used for making stripes or designs on vans, cars, or trucks.

WOODGRAIN INSTALLATION

Removing and replacing woodgrain decals on vehicles should be done very carefully. Removing the old woodgrain decal is done with woodgrain remover. The remover is sprayed on the panel and allowed to penetrate for about 5 minutes. The woodgrain then will peel off easily with a putty knife. Be careful not to scar or punch holes in the panel as the decal is removed. To repair and replace a damaged woodgrain decal, follow the steps shown in Figures 28-58 through 28-69.

Fig. 28-45. *A decorative decal on the hood of a vehicle. (Courtesy of Prostripe Division, Spartan Plastics, Inc.)*

Fig. 28-46. *Different colors, widths, and patterns of decals can be combined to make individualized designs. (Courtesy of Prostripe Division, Spartan Plastics, Inc.)*

Fig. 28-47. *Stripes in decreasing widths were used for this design. If desired, more than one color can be used in such applications. (Courtesy of Prostripe Division, Spartan Plastics, Inc.)*

Fig. 28-48. *A side decal stripe and lettering. (Courtesy of Prostripe Division, Spartan Plastics, Inc.)*

Fig. 28-49. Step 1: *Wash the area where the decal will be applied. Use soap and water. Check the surface for any lumps or rough spots that would show through the decal.*

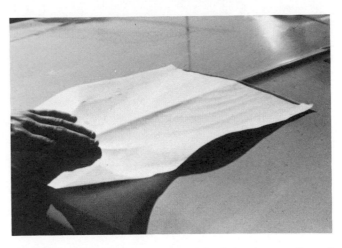

Fig. 28-52. Step 4: *Press the decal firmly in place on the wet panel. The decal can be aligned or adjusted on the wet surface.*

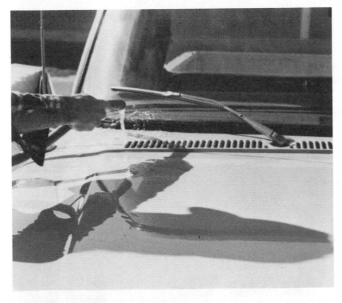

Fig. 28-50. Step 2: *Rinse the surface thoroughly with clear water.*

Fig. 28-53. Step 5: *After the decal is positioned, use a squeegee to remove all air bubbles.*

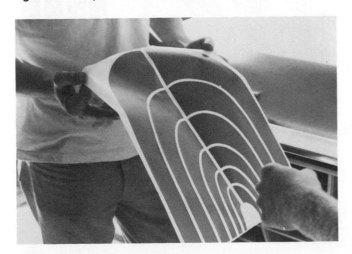

Fig. 28-51. Step 3: *Remove the paper backing from the side of the decal that will be applied to the car's surface.*

Fig. 28-54. Step 6: *Remove the paper or clear plastic from the top surface of the decal.*

Fig. 28-55.   *Follow the same procedure to install other portions of the decal design.*

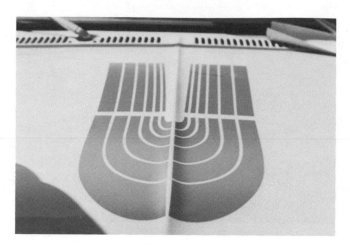

Fig. 28-56.   *The completed decal installation.*

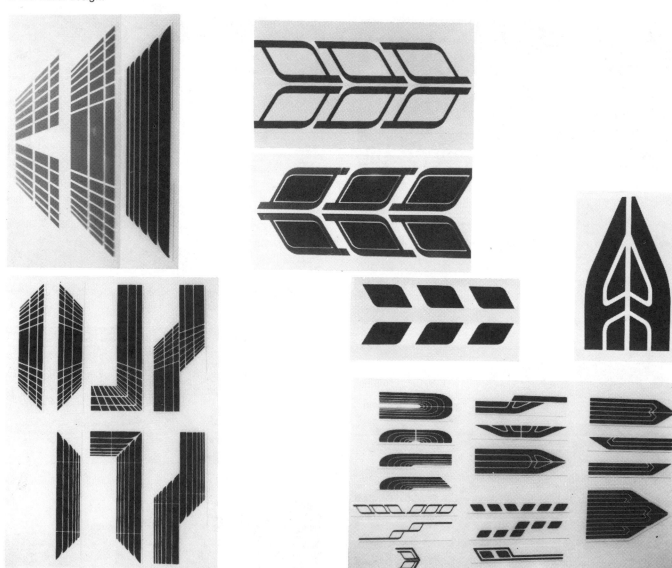

Fig. 28-57.   *A variety of designs and stripes that can be combined to make individualized accents on the car. (Courtesy of Prostripe Division, Spartan Plastics, Inc.)*

Fig. 28-58. *A damaged area on a station wagon woodgrain panel. After the metal damage is repaired, a new woodgrain decal can be applied.*

Fig. 28-59. *After the old decal is removed, the damaged metal is visible.*

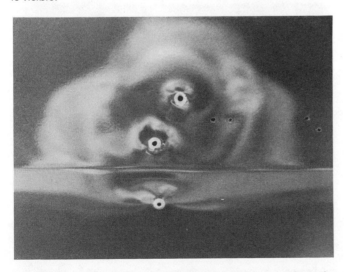

Fig. 28-60. *Holes have been drilled in the dent, so that it can be pulled out.*

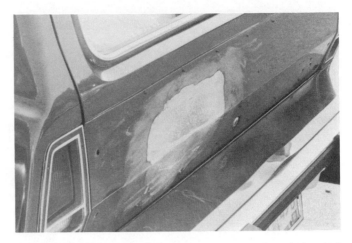

Fig. 28-61. *After the dent is pulled out, the surface is leveled with plastic filler. The filler is featheredged to present a smooth surface.*

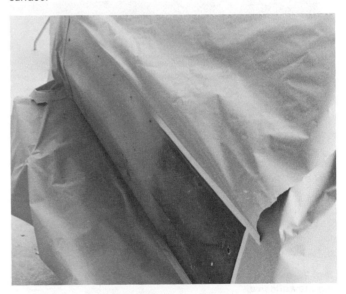

Fig. 28-62. *The surrounding area has been masked, and primer has been applied to the repair.*

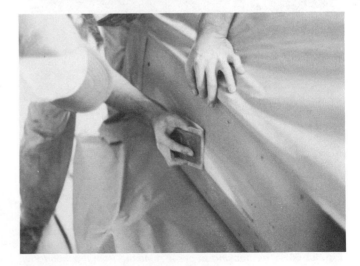

Fig. 28-63. *The primer is sanded smooth.*

Fig. 28-64. *A cleaning solvent is used before the panel is repainted.*

Fig. 28-67. *The woodgrain decal is carefully smoothed in place on the tailgate.*

Fig. 28-65. *The woodgrain decal has a backing paper protecting the adhesive.*

Fig. 28-68. *A squeegee is used to press out all air bubbles trapped beneath the decal.*

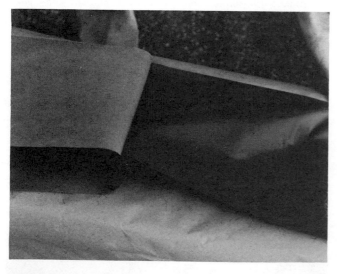

Fig. 28-66. *The backing paper is removed from the woodgrain decal.*

Fig. 28-69. *The finished installation, with all trim and hardware replaced.*

Glossary

abrasive: A substance used to wear away a surface by friction.

absorb: To suck in or swallow up.

accent stripe: Any decorative stripe used on an auto body.

accessible area: An area that can be reached without parts being removed from the vehicle.

acrylic: A type of thermoplastic resin.

adhesion: The ability of one substance to stick to another.

adhesive: A cement or glue that causes two materials to stick together.

adjoining: Lying or positioned next to.

air-dried: Reaching a state of hardness (as in the case of paint) under normal conditions.

air (dust) gun: A small compressed air nozzle used to blow dust and dirt from cracks and the surface of the vehicle.

air compressor: A machine that "squeezes" air into smaller volume so that its expansion can be used as a source of power.

align: To adjust to a line or predetermined relative position.

alkyd: A resin used in some synthetic enamel paints for flexibility, gloss, and adhesion.

alligatoring: A paint defect in which the paint takes on a large "check" pattern.

alloy: A blend of two or more metals.

analysis: The first careful study and observation of a damaged area.

anchor: To hold in place.

angle iron: Automobile frame pieces in which two sides form an angle (usually 90°) to each other.

appraisal: The process of setting a value.

appraisers (adjusters):   Insurance company representatives who estimate damage and authorize payment.

apprentice: A beginner in a trade; one who learns under the supervision of a skilled worker.

arc welding: A process of joining metal that uses heat generated by electric current.

asbestos: A fireproof mineral (silicate of calcium and magnesium) used to prevent spread of heat.

atmosphere: The envelope of gases that surrounds the earth.

atomization: The breaking up of paint in droplets by air pressure as it exits the paint spray gun.

baked-on paint: A factory finish that is heated to a high temperature after it has been sprayed.

banding: Painting all the way around the perimeter of a panel.

bead running: The technique of directing molten metal while welding.

belt line: The horizontal molding or crown along the side of the vehicle.

bench grinder: A rotating electrical tool used to smooth rough edges on metal and to sharpen tools.

bevel: To grind to an angle.

binder: A component of paint that makes pigment adhere to the surface to which it is applied.

bleeding: A paint defect in which the old color seeps through the new topcoat.

blistering: A paint defect consisting of pin holes or bubbles in the paint film.

blushing: A paint defect appearing as a milky white haze or mist.

body solder: An alloy of tin and lead used for filling dents and other body defects.

bonding strip: An aluminum tape used to patch holes in an auto body.

bracket: An attachment used to secure parts to the body or frame.

brazing: A type of welding using brass rods and the oxy-acetylene torch.

bulge: A high crown or area of stretched metal.

carbon black: A nonbleeding black paint pigment used in early automobile finishes; lampblack.

carbonizing flame: The flame produced by the oxy-acetylene torch when a middle or "feather" flame appears between the inner and outer flame cones; also called a "carburizing flame."

carriage bolts: Round-headed bolts with a square shoulder beneath the head.

catalyst: A substance that speeds up a chemical reaction without becoming part of that reaction.

caulking: A sticky, flexible sealer used to fill cracks and seams.

caustic: Able to destroy or burn by chemical action.

channel iron: "U"-shaped metal members used on early automobile frames.

checking: A paint defect that exhibits small parallel cracks.

checking blocks: *See* **glass spacers.**

cheese grater: A coarse, open-toothed file that is used to shape plastic filler.

Celsius: The metric temperature scale.

chisel: A steel cutting tool that is beveled and sharpened on one end.

chrome: Bright metal used for auto trim.

circuit: The path taken by an electric current.

clearcoat: A top coating on a painted surface that is transparent so that the color coat beneath it is visible.

clip pullers: Door handle tools.

color holdout: The ability of a finish to show full-bodied topcoat color.

color effect: The presence of various intensities of color visible at various angles, caused by the use of metallic flakes.

compound: An abrasive paste containing pumice; also the process of using the abrasive to smooth a finish.

compressor: *See* **air compressor.**

concave: Having an inward curve (as in a dent).

cone: The round, inner flame present in the neutral flame of the oxy-acetylene torch.

contaminants: Foreign substances on the surface to be painted (or in the paint) that would adversely affect the finish.

contour: The curve or shape of a panel.

contract: A legal agreement between two or more parties.

conventional frame: An auto body construction type in which the engine and body are bolted to a separate frame.

convex: Having an outward curve (as in a hump).

cowl: The part of the automobile that supports the instrument panels and controls.

crazing: A paint defect, which exhibits fine splits or small cracks.

creeper: A low platform with four rollers used by repair workers to move around easily under a vehicle.

crossmembers: The frame pieces connecting the side rails.

crown: The high curve or line on a body panel.

curdling: A paint defect appearing where paint congeals.

curing: The drying and hardening process of plastic filler, paint, or fiberglass resin.

custom mix: Paint mixed to order by the supplier.

cylinders: Metal tanks used to store oxygen and acetylene gases.

damage-dozer: A portable frame straightener.

dealer: One who is authorized to sell a certain product.

dedicated bench: A frame straightening unit that fits one type of frame.

deductible: An insurance arrangement, under which the customer pays the first portion of the repair cost, and the insurance company pays the remainder.

depression: An inward (concave) dent.

die-cast molding: A type of molding formed in a factory with a die.

distortion: Twisted or misshappen state of a part or assembly.

doghouse: The front-end assembly of a vehicle.

dolly: A small metal block used for removing dents or straightening metal.

droplet: A small drop (as of paint).

electric welder: An arc welder.

electrode: An electric welding rod.

enamel: A synthetic finish that dries by oxidation and by evaporation of its reducers.

estimate: An appraisal of the approximate cost of repair.

etch: To cut or bite into the surface of.

expand: To swell or enlarge.

extension: A device used to make a tool (such as a wrench) reach farther.

exterior trim: All the molding, bright metal, and vinyl on the outside of the vehicle.

external rust-out: Rust that has eaten through a panel from the outside to the inside.

factory package: Paint mixed and sealed in a can by the paint manufacturer.

Fahrenheit: The temperature scale used on a conventional thermometer.

feather flame: The middle flame of the oxy-acetylene torch.

featheredging: Tapering the edges of ground-off or chipped paint or plastic by use of an abrasive such as sandpaper.

fiberglass kit: A repair kit containing the needed resin, hardener, and fiberglass matting.

filler: Any material used to fill (level) a damaged area.

firm commitment: A binding bid on repair work.

fisheye: A paint defect in which small craters appear on freshly painted surfaces.

flash-off time: The period needed for the thinner to evaporate from a coat of paint.

flashback: A dangerous condition that occurs when the oxy-acetylene flame enters the mixing chamber of the torch and begins to burn inside.

flat: Free of gloss.

flat boy: A term used for the speed file that is used to smooth plastic filler after it has been grated.

floor jack: A portable piece of equipment used to lift a vehicle to check underneath for damage.

flow-out: The self-leveling process of newly applied paint.

flux: A cleaning agent used during brazing and welding.

force-dry: To speed up the drying time of the final coat of paint by use of heat or moving air.

frameless glass: Movable glass held in place by bolts through a channel, rather than a surrounding metal frame.

frame straightener: A pneumatic-powered machine used to align and straighten a distorted frame or body.

friction lighter: A striker and flint device used to generate a spark for lighting oxy-acetylene torches.

gap: The distance between two points.

glass spacers: Small rubber blocks that help hold stationary glass in the proper position.

gouged: Pierced or severely distorted by a sharp object.

greenhouse: The passenger section of an automobile.

grille: Parallel bars or similar metal constructions used to protect the radiator of the car.

ground cable: The return cable of an arc welder, used to provide a path for electricity back to the machine.

hardener: A curing agent used in plastics.

hinge: The pivot on which a door turns or moves.

hydraulic: Relating to the exerting of force by oil or other liquids in a closed system of cylinders and tubing.

I-beams: Automobile frame beams with a cross section shaped like an "I."

ice pick: Term for the scratch awl used to punch small holes in thin metal.

imperfections: Small damaged areas on the auto body.

ingredients: The elements making up a mixture.

insurance adjustment: An agreement between the insurance agent, repair shop, and vehicle owner regarding the amount of money to be paid by the insurance company toward the cost of repairs.

insurance report: The insurance company's copy of the repair shop's damage report.

interior trim: All the upholstery and molding on the inside of the vehicle.

internal rust-out: Rust that has eaten through a panel from the inside to the outside.

jamb: The vertical part of a door frame.

kink: To bend sharply; also, the sharp bend itself.

label: A piece of paper attached to a product, bearing printed instructions and other information.

labor: Hours of time spent on the repair work.

lacquer: A paint that dries by evaporation of its thinners and contains resins and plasticizers.

lampblack: *See* **carbon black.**

latch: A catch or fastener used with a striker to hold doors, hoods, and trunk lids closed.

lifting: A shriveling of topcoat paint during application, caused by applying incompatible types of paint one on top of another.

line up: To align to the correct relationship.

lock assembly: The handle release, outside cylinder lock, and inside door lock.

low crowned: Having slight convex curve.

low spots: Small inward (concave) dents.

lug wrench: A hand or power tool used for removing wheel nuts.

luster: Shine or glow exhibited by a painted surface.

market value: The retail selling price of a vehicle.

marred: Scratched or damaged.

masking: Using tape and paper to protect an area that will not be painted.

matting: Fiberglass material consisting of loose or woven strands.

metal conditioner: A cleaning agent used to chemically remove rust.

metal plastic: A blend of resin and ground-up aluminum.

metal-working stalls: Areas in an auto body shop where metal is straightened.

metallic: Small particles of ground-up metal used in combination with paint; also, paint containing such particles.

MIG welder: Welding equipment (metallic inert gas welder or "wire welder") in which the electrode wire is surrounded by an inert gas to prevent oxidation by atmospheric oxygen.

moisture: Dampness.

molecules: The smallest possible division of a substance.

mottling: A paint defect that occurs when metallic flakes float together forming light and dark streaks.

movable glass: Automobile glass that can be raised or lowered.

mud: A term used for plastic filler in the mixed, ready-to-use state.

multiple hook-up: An arrangement in which a frame straightener is connected to make more than one pull at a time on a vehicle.

mushrooming: Spreading out of the tip on a tool.

natural break: A crown, chrome strip, or other definition line on a panel.

negligent: Careless or irresponsible.

net income: Clear profit after all expenses have been paid.

neutral flame: The flame produced by the oxy-acetylene torch when a rounded inner flame is obtained; the so-called "X" flame.

nibs: Small pieces of dirt and foreign matter on a surface.

nitrocellulose: A substance used in lacquer paints and made from cellulose and cotton.

oblong: Longer than wide in shape; elongated.

offset: Bent at an angle.

orange peel: A textured paint finish caused by the failure of droplets to flow together.

orifice: A hole in the welding torch tip.

overspray: An overlap of dry paint particles on an area where they are not wanted.

oxidizing flame: The flame produced by the oxy-acetylene torch when the inner cone is pointed and there is no middle flame.

oxy-acetylene welder: A welding torch that burns oxygen and acetylene gases.

oxy-acetylene welding: A process of fusing metal by means of heat from burning oxygen and acetylene gases.

overlapping: Positioning metal pieces with one edge over another.

psi: Abbreviation for "pounds per square inch" (pressure measurement).

paddle: A flat object used to stir paints.

parallel: Positioned side-by-side and extending in the same direction.

parts worker: A person in a large body shop who orders parts needed for repairs.

penetrating: Extending all the way through a substance.

pigment: The color matter of paint.

pinholes: Tiny holes in paint or other materials.

pitted: Having holes or cavities in the surface.

plastic filler: A material that can be shaped and molded into any desired form to fill flaws in a body.

plasticizers: A material added to a plastic to make it flow evenly.

pneumatic: Referring to operation by means of air pressure.

polisher: A tool used to apply cutting compound, polish, and some waxes to paint finishes.

polyester: A synthetic resin used in plastics.

pop gun: A term for a riveting tool or rivet gun.

portable gasoline welder: An arc welding machine that can be operated on electrical current produced by a gasoline-powered generator.

power jack: A machine used to apply force to align damaged panels and frames.

power train: The moving parts of a vehicle, including the engine, transmission, and differential.

pre-accident condition: The state of a vehicle before being wrecked.

primer: The paint or undercoating applied directly to the bare metal surface.

profit: The difference between expenditures and net income in a business.

puddle: A deposit of molten metal on a surface during welding.

pumice: Finely ground volcanic rock used for polishing.

putty: A material made for filling small holes or sandscratches.

quench: To cool rapidly with water.

quarter panel: The exterior automobile body panel extending from the door to the rear bumper.

rechrome: To plate again with chrome.

reducer: A solvent used to thin or dilute enamel paint so that it can be sprayed.

refinish: To remove or seal the old finish and apply a new topcoat; to repaint.

regulator: The hardware mechanism that allows glass to be moved upward or downward.

reinforced channel: The box-shaped frame parts obtained by welding two pieces of channel iron together.

reimburse: To refund or repay.

resin binder: A thick liquid solution that acts to suspend the pigment particles in paint.

rim: The metal part of the wheel upon which a tire is fitted.

rocker panels: Metal body panels located beneath the doors.

roughing-out: Aligning a panel to its original shape.

rust: A form of corrosion in which oxygen combines with metal, causing it to turn brown in color and deteriorate.

rust-out: Body damage in which rust has eaten all the way through metal.

safety stand: A device that is used to support a vehicle safely after it is jacked up.

salvage: The value of a wrecked vehicle that is beyond repair.

saturate: To fill an absorbent material with liquid.

scuff: To rough up a surface by rubbing lightly with sandpaper.

sealer: A liquid material used to help paint adhere; also, any material used to keep out moisture.

semi-hard: A state in which a material is beginning to harden.

separator–regulator: Equipment that receives air from compressor tank, removes dirt and moisture, and controls the amount of air supplied to the paint spray gun and other air-powered equipment.

serrated: Having a raised grid or saw-tooth pattern.

shank: The shaft of a tool, bolt, or rivet.

sheath flame: The outer flame of the oxy-acetylene torch.

shim: A small metal spacer used behind panels to bring them into alignment.

shop hammer: A ball peen hammer.

shingling: The process of overlapping small strips of thin fiberglass matting to form a strong durable repair patch.

shrinking: Heating and cooling metal to return it to the original shape.

side rails: The side beams of the automobile body frame.

slide hammer: A hammer with a movable weight used to pull out dents by means of a detachable screw; also called a "snatch hammer."

solder: A metal alloy that is melted to join metals together.

soldering: The process of using solder to join metals.

solid color: Any of the basic colors (white, gray, yellow, orange, red, blue, green, black) used on auto bodies.

solvent: A liquid capable of dissolving a material.

spatula: A flexible, knifelike tool used to mix substances.

spreader: A small, flat rubber or plastic tool used to spread filler on panels.

spring hammering: Using a hammer and body spoon to smooth raised metal areas.

spring steel: A strong, flexible type of steel used for bumpers.

squeegee: A small rubber blade used to wipe off sanded areas, to clean surfaces, or to apply putty.

stationary glass: Nonmovable (fixed) glass.

steel tape: A metal tape measure.

stick-on molding: Molding with an adhesive backing.

straight: Without a bend or curve.

straining: The filtering or screening of paint to remove lumps.

stretched metal: Metal that has been pushed out of shape and made larger than normal.

striker: A metal catch or plate used with a latch to hold doors, hoods, and trunk lids closed. Also, the device used to light an oxy-acetylene torch.

stub frame: A unitized body-frame with only front and rear stub sections of side rail and no center side rail portions.

stud: A threaded fastener without a head.

subcontracting: "Farming out" certain types of body repair and other work to other shops.

substrate: The surface to be painted, or base material of a painted area.

supply cable: The arc welder's output cable, used to hold the electrode.

surface: The outside or face of a panel.

surface rust: Rust on the outside of a panel that has not eaten through the metal.

synthetic: Man-made.

tack welding: The process of making a series of short welds spaced along the edges of two pieces of metal, usually to position them for more extensive welding.

tacky: Very sticky.

tar: Highway material that sometimes sticks to a vehicle.

test plate: A cardboard or metal piece used for testing the paint spray gun.

texture: The general surface structure of dried paint.

thinner: A solvent used to dilute lacquer paint so that it can be sprayed.

tinning: The application of a coat of solder to prepare a metal surface to be soldered or brazed.

torque: A twisting or turning force.

torque box construction: A type of automobile frame construction in which the passenger section is wider than the front and rear sections of the frame.

torque boxes: Metal boxes attached to some frames, which twist and turn to absorb road shock and minor collision shocks.

transformer: A machine that cleans contaminated air and provides clean air for air-powered tools.

traveling oven: An oven used to dry paint as it moves along the length of the vehicle.

unitized body-frame: A vehicle in which the body and frame are welded together to form one unit.

universal bench: A frame straightening unit that fits many types of frames.

universal thinner: A thinner that can be used with both lacquer and enamel paint.

upholstery: The fabric-covered inside door panels, seat covers, headliner, and floor covering of a vehicle.

urethane: A tough, flexible plastic material used for some body parts.

vacuum: To clean by means of air suction.

valance: A metal panel located beneath the bumper face bar.

ventilation fan: The fan used to move paint spray dust out of the paint booth.

vinyl: A plastic material coated on fabric for upholstery and other uses.

viscosity: The rate at which paint flows; how thick the paint is.

vise: A piece of equipment with two flat faces used to clamp and hold objects for welding or other work.

vee weld: A process for joining two pieces of metal by positioning beveled edges side by side to form a "V" shape, then fusing the edges together with heat.

waterproof sandpaper: Any sandpaper designed for use with water.

weld: To join two metal pieces together by bringing them to their melting points, often involving use of a welding rod to add metal to the joint.

wetcoat: One smooth, heavy coat of paint.

wrinkling: A paint defect in which the surface resembles a prune skin.

X flame: The neutral flame of the oxy-acetylene torch, present when a rounded inner flame is obtained.

zinc chromate: A paint material that is used for primer to protect steel and aluminum against rust and corrosion.

Index